Cambridge studies in medieval life and thought

Edited by WALTER ULLMANN, LITT.D., F.B.A.
Professor of Medieval History
in the University of Cambridge

Third series, vol. 6

DURHAM PRIORY

1400–1450

CAMBRIDGE STUDIES IN
MEDIEVAL LIFE AND THOUGHT

THIRD SERIES

DURHAM PRIORY

1400–1450

R. B. DOBSON

Reader in History at the
University of York

CAMBRIDGE
AT THE UNIVERSITY PRESS
1973

Published by the Syndics of the Cambridge University Press
Bentley House, 200 Euston Road, London NW1 2DB
American Branch: 32 East 57th Street, New York, N.Y.10022

© Cambridge University Press 1973

Library of Congress Catalogue Card Number: 72-89809

ISBN: 0 521 20140 3

Printed in Great Britain
at the University Printing House, Cambridge
(Brooke Crutchley, University Printer)

M

CONTENTS

Contents

FIGURES

TO NARDA

PREFACE

Although this work is a study in the history of one of medieval England's most famous corporations, my greatest obligations have always been to individuals. First and most obviously, this book owes its very existence to the labours of 123 monks who entered the religious life at Durham between 1390 and 1446, men whose activities form the primary subject of the following pages. What they would have thought of this retrospective and inevitably distorted description of their monastic community I hesitate to think; but they might have derived some consolation from the knowledge that I personally find their lives much more mysterious now than on the day I first began to look at the voluminous records they have left to posterity. In many ways a twentieth-century historian is singularly ill-equipped to understand the personal passions and aspirations of a late medieval monk. I must, in other words, have often failed in my desire to understand rather than to judge the monks of Durham. Nevertheless, to my surprise and against my initial expectations, I have come to respect the aims of the late medieval community of Saint Cuthbert more rather than less during the many days in which I have kept their posthumous company. For myself, and I hope for some readers of this book, their traditional offer of assistance still retains some validity: '*Vestris nostra damus, pro nostris vestra rogamus*'.

One of the greatest pleasures to be enjoyed by students of Durham Priory is the ability to read its records within a few yards of where they were originally written. In addition to my obligation to the Dean and Chapter, I am indebted to the modern custodians of their archives for their generous assistance – to the late Dr James Conway Davies, to Mr J. E. Fagg, Mr Alan Piper and, above all, to Mr Martin Snape, whose familiarity with the medieval muniments in his care must now surpass that of his great nineteenth-century predecessors, the elder James Raine, Joseph Stevenson and William

Greenwell. Of the many other present or past residents of Durham who have helped me in various ways, I should particularly like to thank Professor H. S. Offler, Doctor and Mrs Geoffrey Scammell and Miss Barbara Harbottle. So numerous are the Durham records that this can be in no sense a final and definitive study. I can only wish my many successors in the Prior's Kitchen there the same good fortune as myself in being the recipient of so much generosity at the hands of the modern equivalents of 'Saint Cuthbert's folk'.

Outside Durham my debts are also heavy and almost innumerable. Among those who have given me their help or read parts of this book at one or other of its various stages are Professor L. H. Butler, Mr R. A. Fletcher, Mr J. H. Harvey, Professor S. L. Greenslade, the late Mr K. B. McFarlane, Dr D. M. Smith, Dr R. L. Storey and Dr D. E. R. Watt. I am grateful to them all. To the two greatest English monastic historians of this century I owe of course a very special debt. It was Dr W. A. Pantin who first suggested, more years ago than either of us would care to remember, that I might write a thesis on the history of the late medieval Durham Priory. Both before and after the completion of that thesis, now transformed almost out of recognition, he has been a source of frequent advice and constant encouragement. My obligation to Dom David Knowles must be even more apparent to every reader of this book. For many years his four great volumes on the history of the English religious orders in the middle ages have never been far from my reach. Although our attitudes to medieval monasticism are inevitably sometimes different, he will, I hope, be the first to recognise that I have been fortunate to follow in his wake. I should also like to express my thanks to Professor Walter Ullmann, the editor of this series, for his interest in my work on Durham Priory, and to Mrs Christine Linehan, Miss Diane Speakman and the staff of C.U.P., for their meticulous attention to my typescript. Mrs Vicki Liversidge proved, as so often in the past, an unusually accurate and uncomplaining typist. To the generous assistance offered by Dr Claire Cross I owe more than I can adequately say. Finally, and above all, I should like to thank my wife, Narda, who has read the whole of my text and whose detailed advice and general encouragement have made this volume possible.

September 1972   R.B.D.

ABBREVIATIONS

MUNIMENTS AND MANUSCRIPTS OF THE DEAN AND CHAPTER OF DURHAM
(CITED WITHOUT ANY PREFIX)

(See bibliography for a brief description of these classes of Durham capitular records.)

Archid. Dunelm.	Archidiaconalia Dunelmensia.
Archid. North.	Archidiaconalia Northumbrensia.
Archiepisc.	Archiepiscopalia.
Cart.	Cartuarium.
Ebor.	Eboracensia.
Loc.	Locellus.
Mines Accts.	Accounts of Receivers of Payments from Coal Mines held by the Prior and Chapter of Durham.
Misc. Chrs.	Miscellaneous Charters.
Pap.	Papalia.
Pont.	Pontificalia.
Reg.	Registrum.
Reg. Parv.	Registrum Parvum.
Regal.	Regalia.
Spec.	Specialia.

Account rolls of all Durham cells, manors and obedientiaries are cited by their names alone, and in the following form:

Jarrow, 1416/17	The single account roll of the master of Jarrow for the year 1416–17.
Jarrow, 1416–46	All surviving account rolls of the master of Jarrow between 1416 and 1446.
Sacrist, 1416/17	The single account roll of the sacrist of Durham for the year 1416–17.
Sacrist, 1416–46	All surviving account rolls of the sacrist of Durham between 1416 and 1446.

N.B. References to the account rolls of the Durham bursar also indicate in what section of the roll a particular entry is to be found, e.g. Bursar, 1416/17, Expense Prioris.

OTHER SOURCES

Arch. Ael.	*Archaeologia Aeliana.*
B.M.	British Museum.
C.Cl.R.	*Calendar of Close Rolls.*

Abbreviations

C.F.R.	Calendar of Fine Rolls.
C.P.L.	Calendar of Papal Registers: Papal Letters.
C.P.R.	Calendar of Patent Rolls.
Catalogi Vet.	Catalogi Veteres librorum ecclesiae cathedralis Dunelm., ed. B. Botfield (Surtees Soc. VII, 1838).
Coldingham Corr.	The Correspondence, etc., of Coldingham Priory, ed. J. Raine (Surtees Soc. XII, 1841).
Concilia	D. Wilkins, Concilia Magnae Britanniae et Hiberniae (4 vols.; London, 1737).
D.C.D.	Dean and Chapter of Durham.
D.N.B.	Dictionary of National Biography.
Dur. Acct. Rolls	Extracts from the Account Rolls of the Abbey of Durham, ed. J. T. Fowler (Surtees Soc. XCIX, C, CIII, 1898–1901).
Dur. Coll. Rolls	Some Durham College Rolls, ed. H. E. D. Blakiston (Oxford Historical Soc. XXXII, 1896: Collectanea III, pp. 1–76).
Dur. Obit. Rolls	The Obituary Roll of William Ebchester and John Burnby, ed. J. Raine (Surtees Soc. XXXI, 1856).
Durham Annals	Durham Annals and Documents of the Thirteenth Century, ed. F. Barlow (Surtees Soc. CLV, 1945).
E.H.R.	English Historical Review.
Econ. H.R.	Economic History Review
Emden	A. B. Emden, A Biographical Register of the University of Oxford to A.D. 1500 (3 vols.; Oxford, 1957–9).
Emden (Cambridge)	A. B. Emden, A Biographical Register of the University of Cambridge to 1500 (Cambridge, 1963).
Fasti Dunelm.	Fasti Dunelmenses, ed. D. S. Boutflower (Surtees Soc. CXXXIX, 1926).
Feodarium Dunelm.	Feodarium Prioratus Dunelmensis, ed. W. Greenwell (Surtees Soc. LVIII, 1872).
Finchale Priory	The Charters, etc., of the Priory of Finchale, ed. J. Raine (Surtees Soc. VI, 1837).
Jarrow and Wearmouth	The Inventories and Account Rolls of . . . Jarrow and Monk-Wearmouth, ed. J. Raine (Surtees Soc. XXIX, 1854).
Knowles, Mon. Order	M. D. Knowles, The Monastic Order in England (Cambridge, 1940).
Knowles, Rel. Orders	M. D. Knowles, The Religious Orders in England (3 vols.; Cambridge, 1948–59).
Liber Vitae	Liber Vitae Ecclesiae Dunelmensis, I, ed. A. H. Thompson (Surtees Soc. CXXXVI, 1923).
Lincoln Visitations	Visitations of Religious Houses in the diocese of Lincoln, ed. A. H. Thompson (Lincoln Record Soc. 7, 14, 21, 1914–29).
P.R.O.	Public Record Office.
Pantin, Chapters	Documents illustrating the activities of the General and Provincial Chapters of the English Black Monks, 1215–1540, ed. W. A. Pantin (Camden Third Series, 45, 47, 54, 1931–7).
Raine, North Durham	J. Raine, The History and Antiquities of North Durham (London, 1852).

xii

Abbreviations

Reg. Langley	*The Register of Thomas Langley, Bishop of Durham*, ed. R. L Storey (6 vols.; Surtees Soc., 1956–67).
Reg. Richard of Bury	*Richard d'Aungerville, of Bury, Fragments of his Register, etc.*, ed. G. W. Kitchin (Surtees Soc. CXIX, 1910).
Rites	*The Rites of Durham*, ed. J. T. Fowler (Surtees Soc. CVII, 1903).
Rot. Parl.	*Rotuli Parliamentorum* (London, 1783).
Rot. Scot.	*Rotuli Scotiae* (Record Commission, 1814–19).
Scrip. Tres	*Historiae Dunelmensis Scriptores Tres*, ed. J. Raine (Surtees Soc. IX, 1839).
Surtees, *Durham*	R. Surtees, *The History and Antiquities of the County Palatine of Durham* (4 vols.; London, 1816–40).
Symeon, *Hist. Ecc. Dun.*	*Historia Ecclesiae Dunhelmensis*, ed. T. Arnold in *Symeonis Monachi Opera Omnia* I (Rolls Series, 1882).
Symeon, *Hist. Reg.*	*Historia Regum*, ed. T. Arnold in *Symeonis Monachi Opera Omnia* II (Rolls Series, 1885).
T.R.H.S.	*Transactions of the Royal Historical Society*.
V.C.H.	*Victoria County History*.

INTRODUCTION

Here we have the richest Treasury of antient Evidences that are now extant: perhaps no Church of England can shew the like.[1]

The proud comment of an early eighteenth-century antiquary on the 'Multitudes of Records' preserved by the Dean and Chapter of Durham can still afford to stand. Indeed the very wealth of the medieval muniments extant within the precincts of the monastic cathedral presents the student of Durham Priory with both his greatest opportunities and his greatest problems. Such richness is genuinely embarrassing. Although a comprehensive narrative history of the priory of Durham during the 456 years between its foundation in 1083 and its dissolution on the last day of the year 1539 remains an ultimate objective, it is clear enough that for many years to come this must be an unattainable ideal. The volume of original evidence for the convent's conduct of its internal and external affairs is so large that only a series of detailed analytical studies of the priory at various stages of its evolution could hope to do full justice to the complexities of its changing role in the fabric of medieval church and society. As all its practitioners are well aware, the study of medieval history is often most meaningful, its sources being what they are, when concerned with the development of medieval institutions. This present work attempts to make some virtue out of necessity and to investigate the operations of one of medieval England's greatest institutions at that particular point in time when its organisation had reached its most advanced and elaborate stage.

Although virtually all eras of the history of Durham Priory deserve and would repay close investigation, the early fifteenth century pro-vides an especially significant period for detailed examination. The monk who entered the community of Saint Cuthbert at Durham in or about the year 1400, and who lived most of his monastic life under the thirty-year long priorate of John Wessington (1416–46), was to conduct his life in an atmosphere of genuine *stabilitas*. By the end

[1] J. Gutch, *Collectanea Curiosa* (Oxford, 1781), II, 115.

of the fourteenth century the greatest ages of Durham Priory's spiritual prestige and territorial expansion were undoubtedly over; but so too were the spectacular conflicts which had so often disrupted and distorted the main lines of monastic development on the Durham peninsula. In neither the spiritual, political nor economic spheres did the monks of early fifteenth-century Durham experience the intoxicating victories and humiliating defeats of their predecessors. In the century that followed the episcopate of Antony Bek (1283–1311), by any standards the crucial turning-point in the history of medieval Durham, the character of monastic life within the convent had been transformed almost out of recognition under the impact of such developments as the outbreak of sustained Anglo-Scottish hostility, the economic decline of the north of England, the establishment of an effective *modus vivendi* with the bishop of Durham, and the adoption of the ideal of *le moine universitaire*. It can be argued that it was only after 1380 or so that the monks of Saint Cuthbert came completely to terms with the realities of their new religious and social position.

The stability achieved within the convent during the priorates of John Hemingburgh (1391–1416) and John Wessington did not of course come to a close with the latter's resignation from office in 1446; and there is much evidence to suggest that the Benedictine priory of Durham preserved both its own self-respect and its prestige in local and national affairs relatively unimpaired until a very few years before its final dissolution. Although the last phase of monasticism at Durham, as elsewhere in England, demands more sympathetic attention than it has usually received, it is, however, deliberately excluded from detailed consideration in the following pages. As Professor Knowles's four great volumes on the history of the English religious orders have taught us, no student of monastic history should avoid facing the fundamental question, whether a particular religious house was fulfilling its spiritual as well as social functions; but this is a question more realistically answered for a period when the consciousness of impending doom cannot complicate and prejudice the real issues. Those prepared to survey the history of Durham Priory during the limited period studied in this book have the inestimable advantage of being able to appreciate, so far as the evidence will allow, the opportunities and problems of monastic life as they presented themselves to its inmates. The need to see late medieval monasticism in its own terms has moreover never been more urgent than at the present time. The greatest danger is no longer that English monastic history should be the subject of passionate and often misconceived controversy but rather that it is quietly and increasingly being ignored.[1]

Monastic life at Durham in the first half of the fifteenth century deserves detailed scrutiny for yet another and more practical reason. The range and quantity of original unpublished evidence which survives for these years is of an almost extraordinary plenitude, unparalleled at any other stage of the convent's history. Needless to say, not all the records produced by the monks of early fifteenth-century Durham are still extant; we have it on the evidence of the Durham monks of the 1430s that many of their records '*consumpti sunt, partim per pluviam, partim per ratones et mures*'.[2] Nevertheless, there are good grounds for believing that we can still read the great majority of the written material that the members of the community of Saint Cuthbert themselves thought worthy of preservation. No detailed description of the medieval archives of the Dean and Chapter of Durham can be provided here.[3] However, as the footnotes and bibliography of this book reveal, the way in which a great variety of different categories of document can be made to illuminate the history of the convent is so distinctive a feature of its muniments that they remain unsurpassed even by such other great

---

[1] One may note in this connection the almost complete omission of any discussion of the religious life from such otherwise excellent surveys as F. R. H. Du Boulay, *An Age of Ambition, English Society in the Late Middle Ages* (London, 1970), or the representative remark by the latest historian of the English Reformation: 'If the secular clergy have received too little notice from historians of the Reformation, the regulars have perhaps received too much': A. G. Dickens, *The English Reformation* (London, 1964), p. 51.   [2] Loc. II, no. 14.

[3] The best general survey is still Dr W. A. Pantin's *Report on the Muniments of the Dean and Chapter of Durham*, presented as part of a privately printed report to the Pilgrim Trustees in 1939. Cf. J. Conway Davies, 'The Muniments of the Dean and Chapter of Durham', *Durham University Journal* XLIV (1952), 77–87; 'Ecclesiastical and Palatinate Archives at Prior's Kitchen, Durham', *Journal of the Society of Archivists* I, no. 7 (1958). The medieval muniments of the Dean and Chapter were transferred from the room over the abbey gateway to their new repository in the Prior's Kitchen shortly before a formal opening by the late Lord Macmillan in May 1950. Since that date many new indices, hand-lists and calendars have been produced under the supervision of Dr J. Conway Davies, Mr J. E. Fagg and Mr M. G. Snape.

that only a monastic chronicle can properly provide of the community's attitudes to national, local and indeed domestic events. But even this silence, characteristic of nearly all fifteenth-century English monasteries, is not without its significance. Far from being uninterested in history, it is clear from the records they have left to posterity as well as their literary compositions – most notably Prior Wessington's own compilations – that the monks of fifteenth-century Durham preferred to contemplate and write about the glories of the past rather than the realities of the present. As authors and collectors of evidence, the late medieval prior and chapter stand revealed as essentially conservative figures, more interested in citing the examples of their predecessors than in inaugurating any major changes in the traditional order of Durham life and letters.

The richness of the medieval Durham archives has of course been well known and indeed proverbial since at least the time that Sir Walter Scott envied 'my Surtees' happier lot' and his freedom 'to roam these venerable aisles, With records stored of deeds long since forgot'.[1] But it is no disrespect to the particularly distinguished historiographical tradition at post-Reformation Durham to suggest that it has rarely done full justice to the brightest jewel in its crown, the medieval community of Saint Cuthbert. Somewhat paradoxically, the majority of Durham historians have been comparatively uninterested in the subject – the history of the Benedictine priory – about which the surviving records can tell us most. Until the twentieth century the study of medieval Durham was inevitably pursued in a spirit of intense and often chauvinistic local patriotism. For obvious reasons the long line of Durham county gentlemen and lawyer antiquaries, beginning as early as the 1570s and 1580s with the precocious historical plans of Christopher Watson and William Claxton of Wynyard,[2] concerned themselves little with the internal history of a medieval convent. Concentration upon the history of the knightly families of the county and upon the temporal

[1] *Harold the Dauntless*, Third Canto, I.

[2] Christopher Watson's fragmentary history, dated 1574, survives as B.M. Cotton MS. Vitell. C. IX, fos. 61–125; also see H. S. Offler, *Medieval Historians of Durham* (University of Durham, 1958), p. 3; Surtees, *Durham* I, 5–6; III, 77–8; John Stow, *Survey of London*, ed. C. L. Kingsford (Oxford, 1908), I, lxix–lxx; *Durham Wills and Inventories* (Surtees Soc. XXXVIII, 1860), p. 272; M. McKisack, *Medieval History in the Tudor Age* (Oxford, 1971), pp. 63, 149.

the labours of the late medieval monks of Durham as well perhaps as to the indifference of their post-Dissolution successors that we owe the preservation of such unusual prizes as (to take a famous example) *Locellus* xxv, one of the most important collections of private correspondence to survive from the century of the Pastons, Celys and Plumptons.

An even more remarkable and distinctive feature of the fifteenth-century Durham archives is the survival of so many documents of an ephemeral and apparently – although not to the historian – trivial character. Large numbers of these heterogeneous records were eventually and very crudely catalogued by Joseph Stevenson and Canon Greenwell in the nineteenth century as 'Miscellaneous Charters', a classification which was itself a symptom of despair at the amount of material that had survived to the Victorian period. The preservation of long series of financial records, the annual account rolls produced by Durham obedientiaries and the heads of the nine Durham cells, is perhaps a little more explicable; but here again, and despite occasional breaks in the sequences of Durham *compoti*, no other English monastery has preserved a more comprehensive collection. Equally fortunate is the survival of a very different type of documentary legacy from the past, an astonishingly large proportion of the contents of the conventual library of medieval Durham. Although comparatively few of the surviving manuscripts were written at Durham itself during the first half of the fifteenth century, their inscriptions and annotations as well as contemporary catalogues of the library provide a unique opportunity to examine the reading habits and intellectual tastes of a late medieval religious community. Only in one area does the evidence for early fifteenth-century Durham offer justifiable cause for regret. Soon after 1400 the long but recently erratic tradition of writing contemporary annals reached vanishing point. The student of the community of Saint Cuthbert during the priorates of John Wessington and his successors is denied the possibility of reading the explicit account

Durham, see *Repertorium Magnum*, fos. 19v, 80, and R. B. Dobson, 'The Last English Monks on Scottish Soil: the Severance of Coldingham Priory from the Monastery of Durham 1461–78', *Scottish Historical Review* XLVI (1967), 12–13. It is virtually certain that the Locelli classification dates from the closing years of the fifteenth century when Master Thomas Swalwell, whose distinctive hand is responsible for the original endorsements and pressmarks, was monastic chancellor.

that only a monastic chronicle can properly provide of the community's attitudes to national, local and indeed domestic events. But even this silence, characteristic of nearly all fifteenth-century English monasteries, is not without its significance. Far from being uninterested in history, it is clear from the records they have left to posterity as well as their literary compositions – most notably Prior Wessington's own compilations – that the monks of fifteenth-century Durham preferred to contemplate and write about the glories of the past rather than the realities of the present. As authors and collectors of evidence, the late medieval prior and chapter stand revealed as essentially conservative figures, more interested in citing the examples of their predecessors than in inaugurating any major changes in the traditional order of Durham life and letters.

The richness of the medieval Durham archives has of course been well known and indeed proverbial since at least the time that Sir Walter Scott envied 'my Surtees' happier lot' and his freedom 'to roam these venerable aisles, With records stored of deeds long since forgot'.[1] But it is no disrespect to the particularly distinguished historiographical tradition at post-Reformation Durham to suggest that it has rarely done full justice to the brightest jewel in its crown, the medieval community of Saint Cuthbert. Somewhat paradoxically, the majority of Durham historians have been comparatively uninterested in the subject – the history of the Benedictine priory – about which the surviving records can tell us most. Until the twentieth century the study of medieval Durham was inevitably pursued in a spirit of intense and often chauvinistic local patriotism. For obvious reasons the long line of Durham county gentlemen and lawyer antiquaries, beginning as early as the 1570s and 1580s with the precocious historical plans of Christopher Watson and William Claxton of Wynyard,[2] concerned themselves little with the internal history of a medieval convent. Concentration upon the history of the knightly families of the county and upon the temporal

---

[1] *Harold the Dauntless*, Third Canto, I.

[2] Christopher Watson's fragmentary history, dated 1574, survives as B.M. Cotton MS. Vitell. C. IX, fos. 61–125; also see H. S. Offler, *Medieval Historians of Durham* (University of Durham, 1958), p. 3; Surtees, *Durham* I, 5–6; III, 77–8; John Stow, *Survey of London*, ed. C. L. Kingsford (Oxford, 1908), I, lxix–lxx; *Durham Wills and Inventories* (Surtees Soc. XXXVIII, 1860), p. 272; M. McKisack, *Medieval History in the Tudor Age* (Oxford, 1971), pp. 63, 149.

life as they presented themselves to its inmates. The need to see late medieval monasticism in its own terms has moreover never been more urgent than at the present time. The greatest danger is no longer that English monastic history should be the subject of passionate and often misconceived controversy but rather that it is quietly and increasingly being ignored.[1]

Monastic life at Durham in the first half of the fifteenth century deserves detailed scrutiny for yet another and more practical reason. The range and quantity of original unpublished evidence which survives for these years is of an almost extraordinary plenitude, unparalleled at any other stage of the convent's history. Needless to say, not all the records produced by the monks of early fifteenth-century Durham are still extant; we have it on the evidence of the Durham monks of the 1430s that many of their records '*consumpti sunt, partim per pluviam, partim per ratones et mures*'.[2] Nevertheless, there are good grounds for believing that we can still read the great majority of the written material that the members of the community of Saint Cuthbert themselves thought worthy of preservation. No detailed description of the medieval archives of the Dean and Chapter of Durham can be provided here.[3] However, as the footnotes and bibliography of this book reveal, the way in which a great variety of different categories of document can be made to illuminate the history of the convent is so distinctive a feature of its muniments that they remain unsurpassed even by such other great

---

[1] One may note in this connection the almost complete omission of any discussion of the religious life from such otherwise excellent surveys as F. R. H. Du Boulay, *An Age of Ambition, English Society in the Late Middle Ages* (London, 1970), or the representative remark by the latest historian of the English Reformation: 'If the secular clergy have received too little notice from historians of the Reformation, the regulars have perhaps received too much': A. G. Dickens, *The English Reformation* (London, 1964), p. 51.   [2] Loc. II, no. 14.

[3] The best general survey is still Dr W. A. Pantin's *Report on the Muniments of the Dean and Chapter of Durham*, presented as part of a privately printed report to the Pilgrim Trustees in 1939. Cf. J. Conway Davies, 'The Muniments of the Dean and Chapter of Durham', *Durham University Journal* XLIV (1952), 77–87; 'Ecclesiastical and Palatinate Archives at Prior's Kitchen, Durham', *Journal of the Society of Archivists* I, no. 7 (1958). The medieval muniments of the Dean and Chapter were transferred from the room over the abbey gateway to their new repository in the Prior's Kitchen shortly before a formal opening by the late Lord Macmillan in May 1950. Since that date many new indices, hand-lists and calendars have been produced under the supervision of Dr J. Conway Davies, Mr J. E. Fagg and Mr M. G. Snape.

monastic archives as those of Westminster Abbey, Norwich, Winchester and Christ Church, Canterbury.

The historian of Durham during John Wessington's priorate is especially fortunate in that the years at the middle of the fifteenth century mark the culmination of the long and sophisticated tradition of archive preservation and cataloguing in the medieval convent. At the centre of the impressively miscellaneous Durham archive collection stand the great series of capitular and prior's registers or letter-books. Although the prior and convent of Durham had begun to preserve copies of some of their incoming as well as outgoing correspondence in systematic register form from at least the early years of the fourteenth century, the period after 1400 saw a considerable expansion in the number of items recorded and the care with which the registers were kept up to date.[1] Similarly the even more valuable, because more private and personal, letter-book of Prior Wessington himself (*Registrum Parvum* II) has as its only known predecessor a much less complete and satisfactory volume of letters dispatched under the seals of various fourteenth-century priors of the convent.[2] Hundreds of other documents dating from Wessington's priorate, in either their original, draft or copied forms, owe their present survival to the good fortune that they were listed and arranged by a series of late fifteenth-century chancellors of the monastery at the time of the compilation of the *Repertorium Magnum* in the late 1450s and of the supplementary class of *Locelli* a generation later.[3] It is therefore to

[1] A study of the thirteenth-century Durham formularies, and especially of B.M. Stowe MS. 930, fos. 15–26, led Professor Barlow to the conclusion (confirmed by Mr Snape) that the convent may have already been maintaining an official register during the first priorate (1258–73) of Hugh of Darlington (*Durham Annals*, p. xxxvii). But the first of the extant large Durham registers begins only in 1312 (see Reg. II, fo. 1 for the contemporary heading '*Registrum tempore fratris Johannis de Laton, A.D. 1312*') and includes items from that date until the end of the century. Its two successors, now Registers III and IV, were much more meticulously written and cover the much shorter periods of 1401–44 and 1444–86 respectively. See, on the value of such sources, W. A. Pantin, 'English Monastic Letter-Books', *Historical Essays in honour of James Tait*, ed. J. G. Edwards, V. H. Galbraith and E. F. Jacob (Manchester, 1933), pp. 203, 215–17.

[2] B.M. Cotton MS. Faustina A. VI includes documents from *c.* 1322 to 1406, whereas Reg. Parv. II, III and IV, all still at Durham, date from 1407–45, 1446–81 and 1484–1519.

[3] For the evidence that Richard Billingham, as Durham chancellor between 1459 and 1464, completed the rearrangement of the convent's muniments and was himself responsible for the most comprehensive inventory of records ever produced at

rather than spiritual power of the bishops of Durham was still the hallmark of historical writing during the golden age of the Durham antiquary, the century of the Mickletons, Spearmans, John Smith, Christopher Hunter and George Allan, all of whom projected histories of the palatinate. It was, however, left to a Barnard Castle solicitor and self-styled 'first adventurer', William Hutchinson, and his successor, Robert Surtees of Mainsforth, to bring the eighteenth-century historical tradition at Durham to its impressive climax.[1] Yet here again it seems important to stress that Hutchinson and Surtees were not much interested in the history of the medieval monastery of Saint Cuthbert. Surtees never wrote an account of Durham Cathedral at all, while Hutchinson's references to the convent's records and charters 'inclosed in wooden cases' are couched in terms that leave little doubt that he had made no serious attempt to read them.[2]

The real turning-point in the tradition of historical writing at Durham can be dated quite precisely to 1812, the year in which a twenty-one-year-old schoolmaster from Richmond in Yorkshire arrived in Durham, met Robert Surtees in the North Bailey and paid the first of his many visits to Mainsforth. Despite his many and perhaps over-criticised failings, James Raine, Chapter librarian at Durham from 1821 until his death in 1858, is unquestionably the founding-father of modern historical enquiry at Durham. The crude prejudice, at times remarkably reminiscent of Gibbon, which informed Raine's attempt to damn 'that tale of centuries, invented for interested purposes in a superstitious age – the incorruptibility of St Cuthbert' ought not to be allowed to conceal the fact that in his *Saint Cuthbert* (1828) he was the first historian to approach one of England's greatest myths in a properly critical spirit. Similarly Raine's *Brief Account of Durham Cathedral* (1833), although little read these days, deserves to be remembered as the first of all guides to an English cathedral which was firmly grounded on a study of the existing documentary evidence, a genuine 'Jewel of the first water'.[3]

---

[1] W. Hutchinson, *The History and Antiquities of the County Palatine of Durham* (3 vols.; Newcastle-upon-Tyne, 1785–94); R. Surtees, *The History and Antiquities of the County Palatine of Durham* (4 vols.; London, 1816–40).

[2] Surtees, *Durham* IV, iv; Hutchinson, *Durham* II, 263.

[3] Robert Surtees's congratulatory letter, carefully copied by Raine into his own copy of the *Brief Account* (Newcastle, 1833), now preserved in the Minster Library, York; cf. *Memoir of Robert Surtees*, ed. J. Raine (Surtees Soc. XXIV, 1852), p. 185.

Raine's voracious appetite for the original evidence that the Durham muniments could provide was of course responsible for the greatest single contribution ever made to northern English history, the foundation of the Surtees Society in 1834. Of the thirty-four volumes published by the society in Raine's own life-time, no less than twenty-six (fifteen edited by Raine himself) comprised original material for the history of the church of Durham and its cells. Few of these editions can stand the test of modern scholarship; and the most accurate of Raine's own volumes were those in which he employed the services of James Gordon, a Richmond solicitor, as his transcriber.[1] Nevertheless the editions, however inadequate, published by Raine continue to provide the essential starting-point for all investigations of the history of the medieval monastery at Durham: it is hardly an exaggeration to suggest that the cause of Durham history has never altogether recovered from his death. Many of Raine's most interesting projects, including the publication of the account rolls of the cells of Lytham, Stamford and Durham College, Oxford, the Durham bursars' rolls *in extenso*, and 'the Theological and Historical Works of John Wessington, Prior of Durham from 1416 to 1446', have even now never reached fruition. Since the 1850s, with the notable exceptions of Canon Greenwell's edition of the *Feodarium Prioratus Dunelmensis* (1872), Canon Fowler's over-selective *Extracts from the Account Rolls of Durham Abbey* (1898–1901) and his more successful revised edition of the *Rites of Durham* (1903), the Surtees Society has published relatively few volumes devoted to the medieval muniments of the Dean and Chapter of Durham. Nothing, one imagines, would have surprised the elder James Raine more than that so little has been done to complete his labours in the century and more since he died.

This is not to discount the invaluable work of various twentieth-century scholars in transforming our knowledge of the historical context within which the monks of medieval Durham conducted their affairs. In recent years the attention of historians has been generally diverted from the Benedictine monastery to the see and to its bishops. G. T. Lapsley's interesting but perhaps fundamentally misconceived attempt to show that 'We have, then in Durham a

---

[1] A. Hamilton Thompson, *The Surtees Society, 1834–1934* (Surtees Soc. CL, 1939), pp. 1–49.

tiny feudal England surviving into the Tudor period', led to the publication of the first thorough investigation of the medieval palatinate.[1] More recently still, the publication of scholarly biographies of no less than three of the more distinguished medieval bishops of Durham has provided an object lesson on the theme of administrative as well as constitutional development in the northern English diocese during the medieval period.[2] These studies, together with such important supplementary works as those by Professors Barlow and Offler and the late Sir Edmund Craster,[3] have thrown much light on some basic and previously confused aspects of the monastery's history. But although the biographers of Puiset, Bek and Langley have certainly all done full justice to these bishops' relationships with the religious community which served their cathedral, in no case was that relationship the central preoccupation of their careers. The recent attention paid to the diocesans of medieval Durham may have the salutary effect of reminding us that the monks of Saint Cuthbert were never quite such important figures to their bishops as they often seemed to themselves; but it has revealed even more strikingly that the history of the Benedictine priory of Durham can never be fully understood solely in terms of its place within the northern English see and its connections with the titular abbot. In the fifteenth century, as now, the importance of the cathedral church of Durham often transcends that of the diocese of which it forms the *matrix ecclesia*. As a national institution it demands attention in its own right.

In the last resort, however, the Benedictine monastery of Durham deserves our interest for two different and apparently contradictory reasons. In the first place it enjoyed a distinctiveness and sense of individuality unique among English religious houses. Constituting

---

[1] G. T. Lapsley, *The County Palatine of Durham* (New York, 1900); cf. J. Scammell's 'The Origin and Limitations of the Liberty of Durham', *E.H.R.* LXXXI (1966), 449–73.

[2] G. V. Scammell, *Hugh du Puiset, Bishop of Durham* (Cambridge, 1956); C. M. Fraser, *A History of Antony Bek, Bishop of Durham, 1283–1311* (Oxford, 1957); R. L. Storey, *Thomas Langley and the Bishopric of Durham, 1406–1437* (London, 1961).

[3] F. Barlow, *Durham Jurisdictional Peculiars* (Oxford, 1950); *Durham Episcopal Charters, 1071–1152*, ed. H. S. Offler (Surtees Soc. CLXXIX, 1968); H. H. E. Craster, 'The Red Book of Durham', *E.H.R.* XL (1925), 504–32; 'The Patrimony of Saint Cuthbert', *E.H.R.* LXIX (1954), 177–99.

the largest, richest and most powerful religious community north of York, the monks of Durham fostered an *esprit de corps* and a sense of exclusiveness unsurpassed elsewhere in the country. The geographical peculiarities of their site, the absence of any other large Benedictine monasteries north of the Tees, the long distances that separated them from London, Canterbury and even York, above all the intense consciousness of long traditions dating back into the Anglo-Saxon period, persuaded the early fifteenth-century monks of Durham that their community was *sui generis*. They were not of course completely mistaken. Yet looking back at their manifold activities 500 years later it would seem unwise to over-emphasise the traits which differentiated Durham from the other religious houses of medieval England. It is just because the priory of Durham was not a typical English monastery that it has so much to tell us about the conduct and quality of monastic life. Durham's distinctiveness, in other words, consists more often than not in the extreme form with which it reveals, under unusual pressure, the universal aspirations and pre-occupations of late medieval monasticism. Whereas other religious communities were always aware of their historical traditions, the monks of Durham were often literally obsessed with the past. Whereas most large monasteries of the later middle ages appreciated the value of university education, Durham was the greatest centre of 'university monks' in the country. Whereas other Benedictine houses possessed monastic cells dependent upon them, at Durham more than elsewhere these dependencies came to form an integral part of the overall monastic polity. Whereas other monasteries may have held important franchises and immunities, nowhere were these liberties more zealously and indeed morbidly preserved than at Durham. For all these reasons one can only hope that an examination of monastic life at early fifteenth-century Durham, by definition a study in comparatively successful conservatism, may throw some general light on a period in English and indeed European history characterised by institutional resistance to social and intellectual change.

Chapter 1

THE ENGLISH ZION:
AN INTRODUCTION TO SAINT CUTHBERT
AND HIS CITY

. . . he that hath seene the situation of this Citty, hath seene the map of *Sion*, and may save a Journey to the *Jerusalem*.[1]

In their own eyes and those of their contemporaries the monks of early fifteenth-century Durham needed little justification other than that they were the 'mynistres of Saynt Cuthbert'.[2] The identification of an ecclesiastical corporation with its patron saint is one of the commonplaces of medieval history; but nowhere in England was such an identification made to seem so complete as at Durham, and nowhere did it prove so powerful and enduring. During the priorate of John Wessington, an assault on the persons and possessions of the Durham monks was *ipso facto* an act of aggression against the greatest of the northern saints. The convent's books were, as a matter of course, the '*libri Sancti Cuthberti*' just as its strenuous legal battles were fought on the saint's behalf and in the ever-present hope of his personal and supernatural intervention. The closeness of the relationship between seventh-century saint and fifteenth-century monk needs particular emphasis, for without an awareness of its fundamental importance much of the history of the convent will always remain literally inexplicable. Only the belief that they were fighting Saint Cuthbert's war explains the willingness of prior and chapter to engage in the long, tortuous, unrewarding and eventually unsuccessful campaign to prevent their cell at Coldingham from falling into the acquisitive hands of Scottish clerks and magnates. Similarly it was their determination not to surrender the inalienable rights of their saint which united the Durham community in the 1440s to oppose a determined attempt to sever their dependency at

[1] Robert Hegge, *The Legend of Saint Cuthbert*, ed. G. Smith (Darlington, 1777), p. 22.
[2] Reg. Parv. II, fo. 152; *Coldingham Corr.*, pp. 130, 231.

Lytham in Lancashire from the mother house.[1] Entry into the religious community at Durham meant more than becoming a Benedictine monk: it made that monk one of Saint Cuthbert's legal as well as spiritual heirs.

There is, of course, no doubt that the prior and chapter were fully conscious of the material advantages to be gained by exploiting the wide-spread veneration for Saint Cuthbert in their own legal and financial interests. Benefactors to the fifteenth-century convent were unquestionably encouraged in their charitable purposes by the information – which they almost invariably received – that their generosity to Durham monks had been duly noted and acknow-ledged by Saint Cuthbert himself. Nor were the prior and chapter of Durham reluctant to publicise the news that '*Terras Cuthberti qui non spoliare verentur, Esse queant certi quod morte mala morientur*'.[2] It would, however, be a mistake to engage in excessive cynicism at the calculated opportunism displayed by fifteenth-century monks and priors who found it difficult to avoid taking the name of their patron saint in vain. Saint Cuthbert was after all their most powerful ally in an often unfriendly society; and in their communications with one another as well as with the world outside the monastic walls, the prior and chapter stand revealed as individuals thoroughly com-mitted to the notions of personal service to their saint and the equation of his interests with their own. For Richard Billingham, a Durham monk writing from the Curia to Prior Richard Bell in 1472, his business at Rome was 'the cause off Saynt Cuthbert' and 'Saynt Cuthbertes commyssyon': he endorsed his letter with the names of 'MARIA . JESUS . CUTHBERTUS'.[3] Many similar examples make it clear that in the fifteenth century as in the twelfth the monks of Durham continued to 'anchor their faith in the Blessed Cuthbert'.[4]

In so doing the prior and chapter were also entering into a binding

---

[1] See below, pp. 316–41.

[2] The closing lines of a metrical life of Saint Cuthbert probably composed by the Durham monk, Richard Stockton, towards the close of the fourteenth century: B.M. Cotton MS. Titus A. II, fo. 148; cf. Craster, 'Red Book of Durham', p. 506. This distich was inscribed on the organ screen of the new chapel of Durham College, Oxford, in 1418: H. E. D. Blakiston, *Trinity College* (London, 1898), p. 22; C. Eyre, *The History of Saint Cuthbert* (London, 1858), p. 279.

[3] *Coldingham Corr.*, pp. 223–5.

[4] *Reginaldi Libellus de admirandibus Beati Cuthberti Virtutibus* (Surtees Soc. I, 1835), p. 2.

contract with the 'British Thaumaturge'. As his servants they were subjected to the ceaseless vigilance of a saint who would, they believed, tolerate no diminution of his rights on earth. When in October 1478, the Durham monks abandoned their attempts to regain Coldingham from the Scots, they professed themselves positively incapable of making a permanent renunciation of their inheritance; the limit of their surrender had to be 'that the mater slepe for a tyme to such season as it may pleas God and Seynt Cuthbert that we may have better spede than we can have yit'.[1] Like Saint Anselm at the beginning of the twelfth century, the Durham priors of a much later age undoubtedly hesitated at the thought of appearing before the divine judgement seat with the rights of their office at all impaired because of their own negligence. This was the fear, at times obsessive, which provided the community of Saint Cuthbert with its *esprit de corps* and explains its extraordinary tenacity in the face of all attempts to deprive the convent of any of its liberties or possessions, however insubstantial. It must be emphasised that to the fifteenth-century Durham monk, Saint Cuthbert was an exceptionally watchful not to say jealous saint, at times very far removed from the gentle ascetic of modern preconception and (apparently) the historic fact. For the late medieval chapter, whose predecessors had to some extent recreated him in their own image, this was a saint to be feared as well as loved. Above all he was a saint to whom they owed their gratitude. As their voluminous records reveal in almost overwhelming detail, the fifteenth-century monks of Durham were if anything only too well aware that it was to Cuthbert they owed their wealth, their prestige and their very existence as well as something more tangible still. Although it is less than likely that Saint Cuthbert himself ever set foot on the peninsula near the Wear where they made their home, Durham was in a very direct sense his own city, then as now the greatest visible memorial to his celebrity and prestige. A study of Durham Priory in the early fifteenth century can only properly begin with some consideration, however brief and inadequate, of the historical and geographical context which provided the community of Saint Cuthbert with its *raison d'être*.

[1] Reg. Parv. III, fo. 186; *Scrip. Tres*, p. ccclxvii; Dobson, 'Last English Monks on Scottish Soil', p. 23.

13

THE LEGACY OF SAINT CUTHBERT

The famous story of Saint Cuthbert presents us, as it presented his fifteenth-century servants, with the extreme case of an apparently simple man whose life gave rise to an extraordinarily complex as well as popular series of legends. Living as he did in an age when 'the historian and annalist was ipso facto a hagiographer',[1] the career, personality and fundamental aims of Saint Cuthbert can never be anything but controversial. To his early biographers it was the exemplary rather than historical significance of Saint Cuthbert's life which was of primary importance. The *Vita Sancti Cuthberti*, written by an anonymous monk of Lindisfarne between 699 and 705, and Bede's *Prose Life* of approximately twenty years later were of course composed within living memory of their subject, who had died on 20 March 687. In the circumstances, and given the existence of a powerful oral tradition, it is not a little remarkable that the main factual outlines of Cuthbert's career remain so obscure. The exact dates of his birth (presumably within a year or so of 635 when the newly consecrated Bishop Aidan first established his missionary headquarters on the old Bernician pirate base of *Metcaud* or Lindisfarne), of his periods of residence at Melrose and Ripon, and even of his first arrival at Aidan's monastery remain conjectural. Nevertheless certain themes emerge unmistakably enough. In his personal attempt to solve the classic problem of 'following the contemplative amid the active life',[2] Saint Cuthbert was never able to emancipate himself from the belief that his own salvation depended on the solitary pursuit of perfection in complete isolation. The celebrated accounts of his life as an anchorite in the dramatic setting of Farne Island lay at the very centre of his future appeal: by seeking seclusion during his life he was ensuring the popularity of his cult thereafter. In this connection Saint Cuthbert clearly belongs – the point has now and rightly become obligatory – to the 'Celtic' rather than the Roman religious tradition: his life and death conform to the pattern admired and followed by Irish monks of his own and previous generations. The later medieval legend, derived from the *Libellus de Ortu Sancti Cuthberti* apparently composed at Melrose in the late

---

[1] C. W. Jones, *Saints' Lives and Chronicles in Early England* (Ithaca, 1947), p. 57.

[2] *Two Lives of Saint Cuthbert*, ed. B. Colgrave (Cambridge, 1940), pp. 94–5.

twelfth century, that Saint Cuthbert was of Irish as well as royal birth has some symbolic if not literal truth.[1]

Certainly Cuthbert's own loyalty to the traditions of Saint Aidan and Iona was never in question. In particular the early biographies and Bede's *Ecclesiastical History* leave no doubt of the great influence on Saint Cuthbert of Saint Eata, the abbot of Melrose who first received Cuthbert as a monk there in 651, and himself traditionally one of the twelve boys '*de natione Anglorum*' selected as his first English disciples by Saint Aidan.[2] For the remainder of their joint lives – Eata lived on until 686, the year before Cuthbert's own death – it seems clear that Cuthbert was content to follow the public and political initiatives of his patron and former abbot. In the long and tortuous struggle for ecclesiastical supremacy in Northumbria between Saint Wilfrid and the spiritual heirs of Saint Aidan (a struggle whose least edifying aspects were undoubtedly suppressed by Bede), Eata and Cuthbert were often able to hold their own. To do so they were prepared, unlike Bishop Colman of Lindisfarne, to pay the price of at least outward conformity to the forms of Roman worship after the Synod of Whitby in 664. Because of Bede's inevitable sensitivity on this issue, it will never be known how far Eata's and Cuthbert's surrender was either genuinely voluntary or at all comprehensive: Saint Cuthbert's own notorious reluctance to accept the bishopric thrust upon him in 685 may owe something to his disinclination to accept consecration at the hands of the 'Roman' archbishop of Canterbury, Theodore of Tarsus, as well as to the customary saintly trait of unwillingness to forsake the contemplative for the public life. In any case the ability of Eata and Cuthbert to survive as abbot and prior of Lindisfarne during the fourteen difficult years that followed the Synod of Whitby received its rewards in 678 when the bishopric of Lindisfarne, previously under

[1] M. H. Dodds, 'The Little Book of the Birth of St Cuthbert', *Arch. Ael.*, Fourth Series, VI (1929), 52–94. The evidence of this 'Irish Life' formed an integral part of the fifteenth-century legend of Saint Cuthbert both within and without the monastery of Durham. An inscription on display within the cathedral church proclaimed that Cuthbert was '*nacione Hibernicus, regiis parentibus ortus*' (MS. B. III 30, fo. 15; *Rites*, p. 131); and a verse translation of the *De Ortu* forms the first part of the mid fifteenth-century *Life of St Cuthbert in English Verse* (Surtees Soc. LXXXVII, 1889), pp. 1–28.

[2] Colgrave, *Two Lives*, pp. 94, 174, 180, 206, 240, 324; Bede, *Historia Ecclesiastica*, in *Venerabilis Baedae Opera Historica*, ed. C. Plummer (2 vols.; Oxford, 1896), I, 190, 270; *Miscellanea Biographica* (Surtees Soc. VIII, 1838), pp. 121–5; MS. B. III 30, fo. 15.

threat of complete extinction, was revived in their own persons. On the division of Wilfrid's great Northumbrian diocese, Eata became bishop of Lindisfarne where he was succeeded by Cuthbert on his own removal to Hexham seven years later.[1] Whatever the precise course of a particularly intricate series of intrigues and events, Eata and Cuthbert – against all the probable odds – had successfully preserved the continuity of the see of Lindisfarne. By so doing, and by coming to terms with the Roman religious observances, Eata and Cuthbert had made their own careers ecclesiastically acceptable and indeed exemplary to a succeeding generation whose attitude to the first four bishops of Lindisfarne, Aidan, Finan, Colman and Tuda (all incidentally of Irish origin) was inevitably tinged with suspicion as to their orthodoxy. It seems to follow, with no disrespect to the admirable qualities of the saint, that there is an uncomfortable degree of real truth in the elder James Raine's somewhat malicious suggestion that Cuthbert 'was the first Bishop of Lindisfarne of whom a Patron Saint could fairly be made'.[2]

During the years immediately following Cuthbert's death in 687 the monks of Lindisfarne, for obvious and not necessarily unworthy motives, themselves sponsored the hagiological process by which their late bishop was rapidly transformed into the object of a wide-spread cult. Although impossible to study in any authentic detail, the unusual speed of this transformation probably owed much to the fact that the bishop and monks of Lindisfarne still found themselves extremely vulnerable to aggression or, even worse, to indifference on the part of the magnates and prelates of late seventh-century Northumbria. Bede himself records that 'a great blast of trial', probably not unconnected with Bishop Wilfrid's desire to extirpate what remained of the autonomy and unorthodoxy of his old antagonists, struck Lindisfarne in the months immediately after

---

[1] Bede, *Historia Ecclesiastica*, I, 229, 272; II, 323; Colgrave, *Two Lives*, p. 239; A. W. Wade-Evans, *Nennius's 'History of the Britons'* (Church. Hist. Soc., 1938), p. 8.

[2] Raine, *Saint Cuthbert*, p. 36. As it is, Bede's *Prose Life* is at somewhat suspiciously elaborate pains to point out that Cuthbert actively opposed those monks '*qui priscae suae consuetudini quam regulari mallent obtemperare custodiae*' (Colgrave, *Two Lives*, pp. 210, 284). For the reasons why Bede could not possibly provide an impartial treatment of the 'ecclesiastical revolution' of the seventh century, see especially N. K. Chadwick, 'The Conversion of Northumbria: A Comparison of Sources', *Celt and Saxon, Studies in the Early British Border* (Cambridge, 1963), pp. 138–66.

Saint Cuthbert's death.[1] But during the ensuing decade, Saint Cuthbert was not only remembered but became the centre of a flourishing *cultus*. Even if we dismiss the innumerable stories of miracles (rarely dated at all precisely) at his tomb, it is significant that the Lindisfarne monks disinterred his body only eleven years after its first burial with the express purpose of raising the bones '*supra pavimentum*' so that they might be more easily venerated.[2] The elevation of Cuthbert's relics on 20 March 698 itself implied his canonisation; and it may well be that the famous discovery of an undecayed body, 'more like a sleeping than a dead man', proved a genuine surprise to the monks who opened his sepulchre.[3] Although not unique (Bede himself provides three other instances during the course of his *Ecclesiastical History*), the phenomenon of the incorrupt body was sufficiently rare to establish Cuthbert as the most powerful of Northumbrian saints and to endow his legend with immortality. Within a few weeks of this first Translation of Saint Cuthbert the body of his successor, Bishop Eadberht, was placed in his original tomb, below the coffin where now lay the priceless corsaint itself. Henceforward the miraculously preserved body of Saint Cuthbert was indisputably the greatest relic in northern England.

By a calculation of which the monks of late medieval Durham were inordinately fond, the original discovery of Saint Cuthbert's incorruption was separated from his final Translation to the new Romanesque choir of Durham cathedral in 1104 by no less than 405 years. Throughout this long intervening period of constant vicissitude and frequent catastrophe, it quite probably is true – as later Durham historical tradition assumed – that veneration for the sanctity of Saint Cuthbert was the one consistent theme in an ever-changing world. All allowances made for our inability to emancipate our own interpretations of northern history between the eighth and eleventh centuries from the vision imposed upon that period by the first

[1] Only the appointment in 688 of Bishop Eadberht as Cuthbert's successor seems to have prevented the complete extinction of the religious community at Lindisfarne, many of whose members had already deserted the island: Bede, *Historia Ecclesiastica*, I, 275; Colgrave, *Two Lives*, pp. 286–7.

[2] Colgrave, *Two Lives*, pp. 292–3.

[3] Otherwise it seems somewhat remarkable that Bishop Eadberht should have been in solitary retreat on an island 'remote from the monastery' at the time that Cuthbert's coffin was opened (Colgrave, *Two Lives*, pp. 292–3).

generation of Benedictine monks at Durham, sufficient contemporary and independent evidence remains to prove that Saint Cuthbert's reputation survived amidst the collapse of royal dynasties, episcopal sees and religious houses. That it did so is at least partly a tribute to the powerful literary and propagandist tradition created almost at the very beginning of the saint's posthumous career.[1] More generally, that career illustrates the familiar paradox that the power and impact of a medieval saint depended on his association with a comparatively small geographical area: in England as in France, 'After the apostles the local saints hold the foremost place in the churches'.[2] The growth of Cuthbert's own legend in later Anglo-Saxon and Scandinavian England is the classic example of the radiation of spiritual and eventually political influence from a fixed centre, the body of the saint itself.

The gradual diffusion of this influence can, of course, be observed in many ways, however difficult it is to interpret these in any detail. Cumulatively most impressive is the exceptionally large number of medieval churches dedicated to Saint Cuthbert, particularly and predictably in what are now northern England and southern Scotland. In the early fifteenth century Prior Wessington of Durham was sufficiently struck by this fact to compile a list of 64 churches or chapels dedicated to his monastery's patron saint, certainly an underestimate for at least 83 medieval dedications to the saint (66 in England and 17 in Scotland) can be traced.[3] The majority of these

---

[1] Eadfrith, the eighth bishop of Lindisfarne (698–721), was arguably the single most influential figure in the diffusion of the cult of Saint Cuthbert: not only did he restore the latter's famous oratory on Farne Island but he encouraged and indeed instructed both the anonymous Lindisfarne monk and Bede himself to write their celebrated prose lives of the saint (ibid., pp. 60–1, 142–3, 302–5). Whether Eadfrith deserves his other reputation, based on a tenth-century colophon, as the writer and illuminator of the Lindisfarne Gospels has been discussed most recently by P. Hunter Blair, *The World of Bede* (London, 1970), p. 230.

[2] E. Male, *The Gothic Image, Religious Art in France of the Thirteenth Century* (London, 1961), p. 310.

[3] Misc. Chrs., no. 5673, printed and discussed by A. Hamilton Thompson, 'The MS. List of Churches dedicated to St Cuthbert, attributed to Prior Wessyngton', *Transactions of the Architectural and Archaeological Society of Durham and Northumberland* VII (1935), 151–77. Professor Hamilton Thompson disposed of the popular legend – derived as much from the elder James Raine as from Wessington himself – that these dedications preserved the memory of the places at which the corsaint rested during its wanderings between 875 and its settlement at Chester-le-Street in 883. The fact remains that more English churches were dedicated to Saint Cuthbert

dedications undoubtedly existed before the Norman Conquest; and Saint Cuthbert, in the company of Saint Oswald, holds the distinction of being the first recorded English patron saint of any English parish church.[1] The existence of various holy wells associated with the saint, for example at Doveridge in Derbyshire and Donington in Shropshire, throws further light on the widespread popularity of the Cuthbertine legend if not on the exact chronology of its development. Saint Cuthbert also left his imprint on both the personal and place names of medieval England. Kirkcudbright in Galloway and Cubert in Cornwall as well as (a little less certainly) Cotherstone in Teesdale probably derive their modern names from the saint. Nor is the continued popularity of the previously infrequent Old English Christian name Cuthbert or Cudbert in late Anglo-Saxon England likely to be unconnected with the fame of the corsaint.[2]

But for the precise narrative of the erratic development of Saint Cuthbert into his role as the unquestionably supreme patron of the north, we are inevitably dependent on later Durham historical tradition in all its diversity, and in particular on Symeon of Durham's skilful and significantly entitled *Libellus de exordio atque procursu istius, hoc est Dunelmensis, Ecclesie* and the much earlier but nevertheless often tendentious *Historia de Sancto Cuthberto*. This famous story has been told many times, most scrupulously perhaps by Sir Edmund Craster,[3] and is too complex, too mysterious, and still in the last resort too problematic to be reviewed here in any detail. But as this saga played so considerable a part in influencing the way in

than to any other native English saint, with the possible exception of Thomas Becket: F. Bond, *Dedications and Patron Saints of English Churches* (Oxford, 1914), pp. 17, 201–16; F. Arnold-Foster, *Studies in Church Dedications* (London, 1899), II, 78–91; Eyre, *History of St Cuthbert*, pp. 242–59.

[1] At 'Scytles-cester iuxta Murum', probably Chesters near Chollerford, in 788 (Symeon, *Hist. Reg.*, p. 52); cf. W. Levison, *England and the Continent in the Eighth Century* (Oxford, 1946), p. 265.

[2] For obvious reasons Cuthbert was not a first name much employed by monks of Durham, only four of whom – all of the early sixteenth century – ever held it. Not one of the 139 monks who entered the convent between 1383 and 1446 was so called (*Liber Vitae*, fos. 70, 75r). In the Tudor and Stuart periods Cuthbert enjoyed a great vogue in Durham and Yorkshire, especially within recusant families; but the name never came into really general use until the Tractarian movement of the nineteenth century: see, e.g., *Register of Freemen of the City of York* (Surtees Soc. XCVI, CII, 1897, 1900), passim.

[3] Craster, 'Patrimony of Saint Cuthbert', pp. 177–99.

which late medieval Durham monks looked upon themselves, it seems worth remembering that it fell into four different phases of approximately equal length. The century which separated the death of Cuthbert from the first Viking raid on Lindisfarne in 793 was followed by a much more insecure period of 83 years, which only came to an end in 875 with Bishop Eardwulf's momentous and apparently forced decision to convey the saint's body to a less vulnerable locale. For 112 years (883–995) the corsaint lay at 'Cuncaceastre' or Chester-le-Street where that small town or village enjoyed the unexpected fame of being the site of an episcopal see and a centre of pilgrimage. In 995 Bishop Aldhun transferred the body of Saint Cuthbert to its final resting-place at Durham; but yet another 88 years were to elapse before the foundation there in 1083 of a regular community of Benedictine monks as the most suitable custodians of what was by now the most famous spiritual tradition in the north and perhaps in England.

Of these four periods, the second is unquestionably the most mysterious but at the same time conceivably the most significant in providing Cuthbert with a reputation qualitatively different from that of other Christian saints. Our knowledge of conditions on ninth-century Lindisfarne is pathetically inadequate. But it is probably safe to infer, by analogy from the fate which befell so many other Christian relics during this turbulent period, that the disruption caused by the collapse of central political authority in Northumbria served to enhance rather than diminish the influence of an eternally powerful saint. In the famous words with which he reacted to the news that Lindisfarne 'a place more venerable than all in Britain is given as a prey to pagan peoples', Alcuin of York pointed to the obvious moral: 'What assurance is there for the churches of Britain, if Saint Cuthbert, with so great a number of saints, defends not his own?'.[1] As the symbol of Northumbrian resistance to external aggression, Saint Cuthbert now began to adopt a more directly political role than ever before and to attract around his person a veritable galaxy of northern saints and their relics. Whether or not there is substance in the allegation of the *Historia de Sancto*

---

[1] *Councils and Ecclesiastical Documents*, ed. A. W. Haddan and W. Stubbs (Oxford, 1871), III, 472–3, 492–5; *English Historical Documents* I, *c. 500–1042*, ed. D. Whitelock (London, 1955), pp. 776, 778.

Cuthberto that Cuthbert's own body was moved from Lindisfarne to Norham on the Tweed during the pontificate of Bishop Ecgred (830–45), it is significant that his remains were then associated with those of the eighth-century Northumbrian king Ceolwulf.[1] But of the various relics placed in Cuthbert's coffin by Bishop Eardwulf and his companions when they fled south from the ravages of Halfdan and his Danes in 875, the most famous was of course the head of King Oswald, that '*rex Christianissimus*' who had originally founded 'the mother church of the nation of the Bernicians'. Henceforward the community of Saint Cuthbert, first at Chester-le-Street and then at Durham, was to enjoy the additional bonus of possessing a treasured relic of a royal saint whose cult at times showed signs of rivalling that of Cuthbert himself.[2] The alliance between Northumbrian ascetic and Northumbrian king was indeed a formidable and almost irresistible one: it found appropriate iconographical expression in the depiction of 'saint Cuthbert with Saint Oswolds head in his hand' which seems by the end of the middle ages to have been the single most common subject for sculpture, painting and stained glass in Durham cathedral.[3]

The political, as opposed to purely spiritual, influence of Saint Cuthbert was perhaps most clearly apparent in the case of the famous *coup* which brought the seven years' wanderings of Bishop Eardwulf, Abbot Eadred and their companions to an end in 883.

[1] *Historia de Sancto Cuthberto*, ed. Arnold (Rolls Series, 1882), p. 201; cf. Symeon's own silence on this translation of Saint Cuthbert to Norham in *Hist. Ecc. Dun.*, p. 52, and the comments (which I find convincing) of Craster, 'Patrimony of Saint Cuthbert', pp. 187–8.

[2] Bede, *Historia Ecclesiastica*, I, 151–2; II, 157–8; J. M. Wallace-Hadrill, *Early Germanic Kingship in England and on the Continent* (Oxford, 1971), pp. 83–5. The possession of Saint Oswald's decapitated body, allegedly translated from Bardney by Ethelfleda of Mercia in the first decade of the tenth century was of course to be central to the future prosperity of the monastery of Gloucester. But veneration for Saint Oswald (to whom was dedicated Durham's own oldest parish church) remained intense in northern England throughout the medieval period: for a particularly magnificent tribute to his popularity, see the memorandum prepared by Abbot Marmaduke Huby of Fountains for submission at Cîteaux as late as August 1496: *Letters from the English Abbots to the Chapter at Cîteaux, 1442–1521* (Camden Fourth Series IV, 1967), pp. 189–91.

[3] *Rites*, pp. 48, 114–18; Eyre, *History of St Cuthbert*, pp. 265–77. For the most evocative survival in the modern cathedral see 'Further Corrections to Dr Pevsner's *Durham*', *Trans. of Architectural and Archaeological Soc. of Durham and Northumberland*, New Series, I (1968), 107.

Eadred's remarkable success in persuading the Danish host to follow his saint's instructions and elect the young Guthred as their ruler ended with a mass ceremony on the hill of *Oswigesdune* where the new 'king and all his army swore peace and fealty on the body of St Cuthbert'.[1] The northern saint has probably never made a more historically significant intervention, one which permanently transformed the political geography of Northumbria. As a consequence of Guthred's election, and no doubt because of that king's munificence towards a saint to whom he owed so much, the body and patrimony of Saint Cuthbert now found its geographical centre '*inter aquas*', between Tyne and Tees – a region with which, paradoxically enough, the saint seems to have had very few associations during his life-time. Within a remarkably short period from the settlement of Bishop Eardwulf and his fellows at 'Cuncaceastre', a site chosen for no very obvious reason, 'One way or another the See of Chester-le-Street had come in the early years of the tenth century to own a considerable portion of the present county of Durham'.[2] Nevertheless there were many occasions when the community of Saint Cuthbert, serving their saint in a wooden church, found it more difficult than the later historical tradition at Durham allowed to hold their own against the violent opposition of a pagan Viking aristocracy.[3] It is therefore no surprise to discover the earliest English kings regarding Saint Cuthbert as a natural ally. Although it would be unwise to give much serious credence to the later legends of the protection afforded by the northern saint to King Alfred at the latter's hour of greatest need, before the battle of Edington, Alfred's successors undoubtedly appreciated the benefits to be gained by

---

[1] *Historia de Sancto Cuthberto*, p. 203. Given the complicated tissue of supernatural legends later woven around this event, it is ironical that in 883 Saint Cuthbert was probably participating in a pagan rather than Christian 'coronation' ritual: see J. Cooper, 'Some Aspects of Eleventh-Century Northumbrian History with special reference to the last four Anglo-Saxon Archbishops of York' (Cambridge Univ. Ph.D. thesis, 1968), pp. 207–8, and the interesting but speculative discussion by D. B. Kirby, 'Northumbria in the Reign of Alfred the Great', *Trans. of Architectural and Archaeological Soc. of Durham and Northumberland* XI (1965), 338–40.

[2] Craster, 'Patrimony of Saint Cuthbert', p. 190.

[3] See the revealing story, later bowdlerised by Symeon, of the Viking Onalafbald who entered the cathedral church at Chester-le-Street only to reject the view that the dead Cuthbert could have any power over him and went on to swear by his '*potentes deos Thor et Othan*' that he would be the congregation's worst enemy (*Historia de Sancto Cuthberto*, p. 209: cf. Symeon, *Hist. Ecc. Dun.*, pp. 73–4, 92).

liberality towards Cuthbert and his servants. King Athelstan's visit to Chester-le-Street in 934, accompanied by the conferment of various costly and now famous gifts, was the first recorded pilgrimage by an English sovereign to Saint Cuthbert's shrine; this was followed during the next decade by similar expeditions on the part of his younger brothers, Kings Edmund and Edred.[1] Even more significantly, it was probably at about this time that the congregation of Saint Cuthbert began to lay claim to those immunities and franchises which were later to develop, although by no means inevitably, into the palatine juris-diction of the bishops of Durham.[2] Unfortunately the second half of the tenth century is one of the most mysterious periods in the history of northern England; but one may guess that it was this age of 'evil days', in which the poor sold themselves for food and only the anger of Saint Cuthbert could be invoked in their protection, that gave rise to the fertile concept of his servants and tenants as the *Haliwerfolc*.[3]

Although we know that Cuthbert's last major migration took place against a background of renewed and continuous harassment by Viking raids, no absolutely precise reason can be given for Bishop Aldhun's fateful decision to convey the corsaint to Ripon, a journey from which it never returned to Chester-le-Street. Indeed the immediate significance, as opposed to the long-term consequences, of the advent of Saint Cuthbert and his congregation to Durham in 995 might easily be exaggerated. It may well be that the foundation of the cathedral church of Durham owed less to the miraculous choice of situation made by the saint himself than to the desire of Uhtred, Bishop Aldhun's son-in-law and future Earl of Northumbria, to establish an impregnable stronghold, a second Bamburgh, from which to resist both Danes and Scots. Uhtred, finally murdered at

---

[1] *Historia de Sancto Cuthberto*, pp. 211–12; Symeon, *Hist. Ecc. Dun.*, pp. 75–8; cf. the chronicle printed in Craster, 'Red Book of Durham', pp. 525–6 (where King Edmund is said – impossibly – to have prayed at the shrine of Saint Cuthbert in Durham). Even more significant than Athelstan's visit was the fact that he gave the community at Chester-le-Street a copy of Bede's prose and metrical lives of the saint (the present Corpus Christi College, Cambridge, MS. 183): see *The Relics of Saint Cuthbert* (Oxford, 1956), ed. C. F. Battiscombe, pp. 31–3.

[2] H. H. E. Craster, 'The Peace of St Cuthbert', *Journal of Ecclesiastical History* VII (1957), 93–5.

[3] *Liber Vitae*, fo. 43, translated in *English Historical Documents* I, 563–4; Lapsley, *County Palatine of Durham*, pp. 22–5; cf. *Durham Episcopal Charters, 1071–1152* (Surtees Soc. CLXXIX, 1968), pp. 57, 68, 72, 125–6, 130.

Cnut's court in 1016, appears to have been the current representative of the native Anglian dynasty which had theoretically ruled the area between the Tees and the embryonic Scottish border since the fall of the ancient Northumbrian kingdom.[1] Until, and indeed well beyond, the date of the Norman Conquest, Saint Cuthbert's power and reputation was therefore entangled – in a way which still needs to be analysed in detail – with the political issue of 'Northumbrian Separatism'. Besieged by Scottish kings in 1006 and 1040, and the scene of violent murder in 1069, the stronghold of Durham never played a more significant strategic role in English history than during the course of the eleventh century.

In an anarchic age the prevailing competition for Saint Cuthbert's favours undoubtedly did much to enhance the prestige and wealth of his congregation, as in the case of Cnut's own barefooted pilgrimage from Garmondsway to Durham (probably in 1031) or the favours displayed by Tostig and Copsi, two successive earls of Northumbria.[2] In other ways it may be suspected that the status of Cuthbert's ministers, although not that of the saint himself, suffered by becoming embroiled in the maelstrom of northern factionalism, so vividly and alarmingly recorded in the mistitled tract *De Obsessione Dunelmi*. Aldhun's successors at Durham between 1019 and 1071, the last four Anglo-Saxon bishops of the see, apparently failed to impress themselves upon the turbulent political situation in the north (even the dates of their pontificates are a matter for conjecture) and left behind them a possibly well-deserved reputation for corruption.[3]

[1] H. W. C. Davis, 'Cumberland before the Norman Conquest', *E.H.R.* xx (1905), 61–5; D. Whitelock, 'The Dealings of the Kings of England with Northumbria in the Tenth and Eleventh Centuries', *The Anglo-Saxons, Studies in some Aspects of their History and Culture presented to Bruce Dickins*, ed. P. Clemoes (London, 1959), p. 82; F. M. Stenton, *Anglo-Saxon England* (Oxford, 1947), p. 411; *V.C.H. Durham* II, 133–4; III, 8. Was it a coincidence that Saint Cuthbert moved to Durham within two years of the destruction of Bamburgh by the Vikings? Cf. *The Anglo-Saxon Chronicle*, ed. G. N. Garmondsway (London, 1953), p. 127.

[2] Symeon, *Hist. Ecc. Dun.*, pp. 90, 94–5, 97–8. But for Tostig's summary disregard of Durham's right of sanctuary see B. Colgrave, 'The post-Bedan miracles and translations of St Cuthbert', *The Early Cultures of North-West Europe*, ed. C. Fox and B. Dickins (Cambridge, 1950), p. 312; F. Barlow, *Edward the Confessor* (London, 1970), p. 196, n. 3.

[3] The last bishop, Aethelwine, tried to escape to Cologne with part of the treasures of his church in 1071 (Symeon, *Hist. Ecc. Dun.*, pp. 91–2, 94, 100–1, 105). Cf. J. Cooper, 'The Dates of the Bishops of Durham in the first half of the Eleventh

Moreover this was a period, all allowances made for the natural disinclination of the Benedictine monks of Symeon's generation to give much credit to their predecessors, when the now almost wholly secular character of the congregation of Saint Cuthbert, apparently a group of married and hereditary clergy living in separate houses around Aldhun's stone church, gave increasing cause for scandal to a new generation of church reformers.

Of greater consequence for the eventual future of the see and convent of Durham was the rapid development during the course of the eleventh century of a veritable 'Cuthbertine renaissance', an enthusiasm for the northern saint which was to carry him to the great triumphs of 1083 and 1104. Even before Cuthbert's arrival in Durham, Archbishop Dunstan had informed his famous teacher, Abbo of Fleury, of the incorruption of the saint's body in terms – 'not only unspoiled and whole but even pleasantly warm to the touch!' – which leaves no doubt that he regarded this as the supreme English phenomenon of its kind.[1] The extraordinary exploits of the Durham priest and relic-snatcher, Aelfred son of Westow, whose most dramatic *coup* was his alleged removal of the bones of Bede from Jarrow to Saint Cuthbert's shrine, testifies to the desire on the part of the community there to attract a flourishing pilgrimage traffic.[2] In this they may have succeeded beyond their expectations. Two southern English monks, Eadwine of New Minster and Bishop Aelfwold of Sherborne, are separately reported to have visited Durham in the 1050s, where they gazed upon Cuthbert's incorrupt body.[3] The widespread devotion to Saint Cuthbert, clearly in full

Century', *Durham University Journal* LX (1968), 131–7, whose argument that Bishop Aldhun moved Saint Cuthbert to Durham in 992 does not seem sufficiently strong to warrant a revision of the traditional date of 995.

[1] *Memorials of St Dunstan*, ed. W. Stubbs (Rolls Series, 1874), p. 379; E. S. Duckett, *Saint Dunstan of Canterbury* (London, 1955), p. 205. The prominent part played by Cuthbert, Oswald and the other northern saints in the writings of Aelfric, abbot of Eynsham, is perhaps the best evidence for their popularity in southern England at the beginning of the eleventh century.

[2] In 'The Date of Durham (*Carmen de Situ Dunelmi*)', *Journal of English and Germanic Philology* LXI (1962), 591–4, Professor H. S. Offler finds plausible grounds for dating this 'pious theft' to before rather than after 1050.

[3] *Liber Vitae of New Minster and Hyde Abbey, Winchester*, ed. W. de Gray Birch (Hampshire Record Soc. V, 1892), pp. 96–8; William of Malmesbury, *De Gestis Pontificum* (Rolls Series, 1870), p. 180; Knowles, *Mon. Order*, pp. 165–6; L. G. D. Baker, 'The Desert in the North', *Northern History* V (1970), 3–6.

spate before the Norman Conquest, grew to even greater heights during the first generation of Norman overlordship in England. Symeon's ingenious stories of the supernatural methods by which Saint Cuthbert brought the Conqueror to acknowledge his spiritual power, contain the allegorical truth that even the notoriously ruthless William I was compelled, like the two continental bishops he appointed to the see of Durham after 1071, to come to terms with what was now an irresistible legend. The Benedictine monastery of Durham was to be founded amidst a wave of conscious and indeed almost antiquarian revivalism. When Aldwin, Reinfrid and Aelfwig made their fateful journey from Evesham to the north in 1073, they did so because their knowledge of Bede's historical writings moved them to live in sites made holy by Saint Cuthbert and the Northumbrian saints.[1] According to Symeon, this small band was invited to settle at Jarrow by Bishop Walcher precisely because he too had read Bede's *Ecclesiastical History* and *Life of Saint Cuthbert*; and after Walcher's violent and untimely death in 1080, Bishop William of Saint Calais was similarly stimulated by the reading of '*antiquorum scripta*' to push his predecessor's plans to their radical conclusion by transforming the congregation of Saint Cuthbert into a regular Benedictine monastery. And so, on 28 May 1083, '*ad illum monachicae conversationis ordinem non novum instituit, sed antiquum Deo renovante restituit*',[2] a belief fundamental to the manner in which the Benedictine monks of Durham were thenceforward to regard themselves and their spiritual role. For Prior Wessington and the fifteenth-century convent of Durham nothing that happened after 1083 ever seemed quite as spiritually significant as the mixture of history and legend which had preceded the official birth of their monastery.

Nevertheless the century which followed the foundation of the Benedictine monastery of Durham, and the subsequent highly publicised translation (in 1104) of Saint Cuthbert's shrine to its new position immediately behind the high altar of the new Romanesque choir of his cathedral church, is probably that of the northern saint's

---

[1] '*Didicerat (Aldwinus) ex historia Anglorum quod provincia Northanhymbrorum crebris quondam choris monachorum ac multis constipata fuerit agminibus sanctorum*' (Symeon, *Hist. Ecc. Dun.*, p. 108). Cf. the premature and abortive attempt made during this period (*c.* 1075) by Aldwin and Turgot, later the first two priors of Durham, to settle near the site of Saint Cuthbert's first monastery of Melrose (ibid., pp. 111–12).
[2] Ibid., p. 11.

most magnificent posthumous triumphs. It was certainly the age of his most extraordinary miracles. By the 1170s the monks of Durham had convinced themselves and no doubt many of their contemporaries that Saint Cuthbert was one of the three most formidable English saints, a patron whose intercession before God outmatched Edmund of East Anglia and Etheldreda of Ely; in the last resort this was a saint capable of working wonders before which even Saint Andrew, Saint James of Compostella and Saint Thomas Becket retired in bafflement.[1] Henceforward Cuthbert was never to lose his place as one of the most prominent members of the pantheon of English saints. By the end of the twelfth century liturgical calendars demonstrate not only that the Feast of Saint Cuthbert on 20 March was customarily graded exceptionally highly throughout the whole of England but that there was an increasing tendency to commemorate the festival of his Translation on 4 September: the observance of the latter feast was made compulsory in the north by the ecclesiastical Statutes of Carlisle in 1258–9.[2] No doubt as a result of the enthusiastic publicity propagated by the first generations of Benedictine monks at Durham, all manner of fertile subsidiary myths began to cluster around the fame of Saint Cuthbert. Most dramatic of these was that of the banner of the saint. Although not recorded at the Battle of the Standard in 1138, it was already conspicuous near Saint Cuthbert's shrine by the 1160s; at the end of the middle ages it had become securely established as the most popular – and on the whole the most effective – battle ensign in England.[3]

---

[1] *Reginaldi Libellus*, pp. 38, 251–2; Scammell, *Hugh du Puiset*, pp. 158–9; *The Priory of Hexham* (Surtees Soc. XLIV, XLVI, 1864–5), I, 179–81.

[2] *Councils and Synods* II (1205–1313), ed. F. M. Powicke and C. R. Cheney (Oxford, 1964), pp. 438, 628, 656. See F. Wormald, 'A liturgical Calendar from Guisborough Priory with some Obits', *Yorkshire Archaeological Journal* XXXI (1932), 7, 15, 21, and C. Hohler, 'The Durham Services in honour of St Cuthbert', *The Relics of Saint Cuthbert*, ed. Battiscombe, pp. 155–91.

[3] *Reginaldi Libellus*, p. 83. For the use of Saint Cuthbert's banner in wars against the Scots from the outbreak of Anglo-Scottish hostilities in 1296 until the battle of Flodden, see Feretrar's rolls, 1400/1, 1439/40; Fraser, *Antony Bek*, pp. 129–30, 212; Raine, *St Cuthbert*, pp. 165, 167; *Dur. Acct. Rolls* III, 654, 663; *Reg. Palatinum Dunelmense* (Rolls Series, 1873–8) III, pp. xxvi, lv. More often than not it seems to have been carried on to the battlefield by one or more Durham monks. The *vexillum Sancti Cuthberti* was apparently destroyed (*Rites*, pp. 26–7, 95; *Dur. Acct. Rolls* II, 483) shortly after its use by the Durham contingent to the Pilgrimage of Grace. Some other references are collected by Battiscombe, *Relics of Saint Cuthbert*, pp. 68–72.

The adroit and sometimes ruthless manner in which the twelfth-century Durham monks exploited this and other attributes of their incorrupt saint is central to their remarkable success in holding at bay the claims of other religious houses, the archbishops of York and, above all, their own bishops. Paradoxically enough, the single most important achievement of Hugh du Puiset, possibly the most powerful and certainly the most ambitious of all bishops of Durham, has been alleged to be the negative one of surrender to the community of Saint Cuthbert in 1195.[1] Thanks to the protection of their patron saint, the Benedictines of Durham emerged from the ecclesiastical revolution of the twelfth century with their spiritual ascendancy in northern England enhanced rather than impaired.

By 1200, in other words, the legend of Saint Cuthbert had reached maturity and the basic themes of his relationship with the monks of Durham were clearly articulated for all time. No attempt can be made here to follow the detailed history of this relationship in the later middle ages. Nor is it necessary, so overwhelming is the evidence, to prove that in the fifteenth century Cuthbert continued to be one of England's most popular saints. Rivalled, but not eclipsed, by Thomas Becket, he received the personal devotion of personages as diverse as John Tiptoft, Earl of Worcester, and Abbot Marmaduke Huby of Fountains.[2] However, just because there was no northern Chaucer, it might be as well to emphasise that in the early fifteenth century the shrine of Saint Cuthbert continued to be the object of a flourishing pilgrimage traffic. Pilgrims to the feretory of the saint during John Wessington's priorate included men as distinguished as Thomas Beaufort, Duke of Exeter, as unusual as an itinerant Italian knight, and as unexpected as the future Pope Pius II.[3] As in previous centuries, Saint Cuthbert's shrine was the customary place at which inhabitants of the diocese swore their most solemn oaths or took the cross before they set out on campaign against the infidel.[4]

[1] The conclusion of Scammell, *Hugh du Puiset*, p. 244.

[2] R. J. Mitchell, *John Tiptoft* (London, 1948), pp. 144–5; *Memorials of Fountains* I (Surtees Soc. XLII, 1863), p. 152. For Cuthbert's appearance among the sculptured effigies of Henry VII's Chapel at Westminster Abbey, see *Inventory of the Historical Monuments in London* I (Royal Commission on Historical Monuments, 1924), 65.

[3] Reg. III, fo. 135; Storey, *Thomas Langley*, pp. 151–2; *The Commentaries of Pius II*, ed. L. C. Gabel (Smith College Studies in History XXII, nos. 1–2, 1936–7), pp. 20–1.

[4] Reg. III, fo. 135; Reg. Parv. III, fo. 121; Reg. Parv. IV, fo. 57v; *Scrip. Tres*, pp. cccxlix-cccl, cccxc–cccxci.

In the nature of things the intensity of veneration displayed towards a particular saint and the popularity of a medieval pilgrimage centre are impossible to quantify. The annual receipts of the pyx of Saint Cuthbert as recorded in the account rolls of the Durham feretrar (for whom these formed much his most important source of revenue) were once used by the elder James Raine to suggest that 'St Cuthbert and his cause were fast falling into disrepute, long before the finishing blow was given to them by King Henry the 8th'.[1] Although it may conceivably be of some significance that these receipts declined from an average of more than £30 at the beginning of the fifteenth century to less than £20 by the 1450s, the difficulty with this argument is that the most valuable gifts to Saint Cuthbert's shrine were jewels and plate rather than cash. In 1425, for example, Nicholas Blackburn the elder, a famous merchant and mayor of York, had 'deliuered to Dane John Weshyngton Priour of Durham to dane John of Durham keper of the Schryn' of Seint Cuthbert of Durham x *li*. of gold whilk sall be warede in a memoriall Jowell' to be 'sett up on the fertur of Seint Cuthbert'.[2] The detailed inventories of the Durham feretrar record many more magnificent prizes, notably the mysterious Great Emerald with its five rings and silver chains which was officially valued at the fabulous sum of £3,336 13s. 4d. in November 1401.[3] Most welcome of all were the gifts made by members of the English royal family, for whom a journey to Saint Cuthbert's shrine was an obligatory part of any progress north of the Tees: particularly noteworthy at the end of the middle ages were the visits of Henry VI in 1448, Richard III in 1483 and Margaret Tudor in 1503.[4] Well might the post-Dissolution author of the *Rites of Durham* look back with justified nostalgia to the period when Durham was 'accoumpted to be the

---

[1] Raine, *St Cuthbert*, p. 117. The fact that very few of the Durham feretrar's accounts (an exceptionally complete series from 1378 to 1461) survive for the immediate pre-Reformation period makes Raine's statistics less convincing than he would undoubtedly have wished.

[2] Misc. Chrs., no. 6771; *Dur. Acct. Rolls* III, xix. Cf. the unusually interesting collection of jewellery bequeathed to Saint Cuthbert by Richard Pudsay, esquire, Bishop Langley's marshal, in 1434 (Reg. III, fo. 173; Reg. Parv. II, fo. 81); cf. Misc. Chrs., no. 6022.

[3] Feretrar's Inventory, 1401; *Dur. Acct. Rolls* II, 454; *Rites*, pp. 102, 284.

[4] Bursar and Cellarer's Indenture, 1448; *Rites*, pp. 106, 122, 292; *Dur. Acct. Rolls* II, 414; Leland's *Collectanea*, ed. T. Hearne (London, 1774), IV, 265–300.

richest churche in all this land . . . soe great was the rich Jewells and ornaments, Copes, Vestments and plaite presented to holy St Cuthbert by Kinges, Queenes, Princes and Noblemen as in theis days is almoste beyonde beleife'.[1]

Despite his national reputation, it would however be a mistake to forget that in the fifteenth century, as earlier, Cuthbert owed his unique vogue to being an essentially northern saint. Written in the 'Language of the Northin lede/That can nan other Inglis rede', the mid fifteenth-century metrical life of Saint Cuthbert is an impressive if laborious tribute to the survival of the myth of the 'Cuthbert folk'.[2] And when, in *The Reeve's Tale*, Chaucer was at pains to contrast the conversational habits of northerners and southerners, he could do so most economically by making his two poor but boisterously resourceful young university scholars swear 'by seint Cutberd'.[3] Nor is it a surprise to discover that 'Cuthbert' seems to have been the most popular name for ships built in the north-eastern ports during the later middle ages.[4] The battle of Neville's Cross, fought just outside Durham in October 1346, was rapidly interpreted as a personal triumph for Saint Cuthbert, a precedent all the more compelling because northerners in the fifteenth century lived with the ever-present possibility of similar dangers. As the Durham monks were well aware – it was an argument they sometimes overplayed – devotion to their patron on the part of the magnates and gentry of the north was always their strongest asset. Enjoying a near monopoly of the patronage that only Saint Cuthbert could offer, Prior Wessington and his fellows dispensed that patronage as successfully and no doubt as sincerely as they dispensed their relics to admiring monasteries in the rest of the country.[5] As late as the Pilgrimage of Grace, the affection of the northerners for their saint, '*adeo sunt suo dicati Cuthberto*',[6] was allegedly the single biggest obstacle to the progress of the English Reformation.

[1] *Rites*, p. 106.   [2] *Life of St Cuthbert in English Verse*, ed. Fowler, pp. xiv, 136.

[3] *The Works of Geoffrey Chaucer*, ed. F. N. Robinson (Oxford, 2nd edn, 1957), p. 58.

[4] *C.P.R.*, *1338–40*, p. 378; *1340–43*, pp. 54–5; *V.C.H. Durham* III, 276; C. M. Fraser, 'The Pattern of Trade in the North-East of England, 1265–1350', *Northern History* IV (1969), 52, 54–5.

[5] Reg. II, fo. 132v; *Scrip. Tres*, p. cxxxv. For a (by no means complete) list see *Relics of Saint Cuthbert*, ed. Battiscombe, pp. 76–8.

[6] *Letters and Papers, Henry VIII*, XI, 203; A. G. Dickens, *Lollards and Protestants in the Diocese of York, 1509–1558* (Oxford, 1959), p. 89.

Outward respect for the prestige of the greatest of the northern saints in the later middle ages may then be taken for granted; but there remains the much more difficult question of the precise place of Saint Cuthbert in the imagination and spiritual life of the fifteenth-century Durham monk. In a relatively stable and less credulous age, perhaps the sermon preached to a Durham synod by Robert Rypon, subprior of Durham until his death in 1421–2, strikes the characteristic note. After lamenting the disinclination of diocesan rectors and vicars to attend the annual Whitsuntide procession to the cathedral church of Durham, Rypon was 'forced to believe that the withdrawing of this devotion is the great cause wherefore this district is infested with wars, pestilences and other ills more than it was wont. And little wonder, surely!, for these saints – Oswald and Cuthbert – withdraw from us their wonted suffrage. Thus it is commonly said, *Saint Cuthbert Sleeps*, because he shows forth no miracles, nor lends aid to his people, as formerly he was wont to do. In very truth we are the cause because we do not lend our devotions as we ought.'[1] Rypon's conclusion is perhaps as significant as his premise. In their attempts to prove that Saint Cuthbert did not sleep, the monks of Durham may have been fighting an eventually losing battle, but we have seen that there is little evidence of a dramatic collapse in either public or their own veneration for the saint. Close and detailed familiarity with the legend of Saint Cuthbert is the leading characteristic of the legal, devotional and historical writing of Prior John Wessington himself, of his monastic chancellors, and indeed of all the Durham monks of the early fifteenth century who are known to have wielded a pen. Nor is there any doubt that, as at all times, more individuals read than wrote about Saint Cuthbert. Bede's life of the Saint figures prominently within the *Vitae Sanctorum* sections of the monastic library catalogues of 1391 and later, often in special prestige editions; it was one of the books, together with the *Libellus de Ortu* or Irish life, dispatched from Durham in 1422 for the personal use of Henry Helay, prior of Stamford, a monk not otherwise noted for either his academic or saintly proclivities.[2] Even more

---

[1] B.M., Harleian MS. 4894, fo. 194v; translated by G. R. Owst, *Preaching in Medieval England* (Cambridge, 1936), pp. 216–17.

[2] *Catalogi Vet.*, pp. 29–30, 107, 116. For the most precious of all the convent's copies of Bede's prose life (the late twelfth-century illuminated version now B.M. Additional MS. 39943) and its loan to Archbishop Scrope of York, Bishop Neville

telling testimony to the continuous influence of Bede's prose life of Saint Cuthbert upon late medieval Durham monks is the fact that it was still being copied within the community as late as 1528 by William Tod, one of the last monks and one of the first prebendaries of the cathedral.[1] Similarly the elaborate eulogy of Saint Cuthbert sent by a Durham monk to Prior Thomas Castell in 1502 may strike us as an old-fashioned exercise on an outmoded theme but is certainly a tribute to the intensity of the author's devotion.[2]

For the fifteenth-century monks of Durham Cuthbert was indeed still capable not only of providing spiritual consolation but of working the occasional miracle. Perhaps the most moving memorial to the fifteenth-century community of Saint Cuthbert is a mutilated scrap of paper before whose evidence a historian can do little but be silent. It records the story of a Devonshire man of 'gret madnesse and bodyly dyseasse' who was brought in a state of intense distress to Saint Cuthbert's shrine. 'And in his slepp he was sor wexit and gaff mony gret grones and syghes. Then an kest holi water uppon hym as he was on slepp, and als son as the holy watyr towchide hys clothes, he start upp sodanly as he war wexhid wyth on wykytt spiritt and wold a passyd fro the feretr'. But he was holdyn styll ther' agayn' his wyll, and son aftyr he fell agayn uppon a slepp, and sleppyt ner' ii houres. And when he wakytt he was in hole mynd and his bodyly diseasse was sodanly takyn away fro hym. He sayd and swayr' that in his slepp came to hym an bysshop, the fayrest man that ever he saw, and touchyd hym in the places off his body. And at the last wher' his most soor was, he gropytt hym be the hertt, and wyth that toyk away all his peyne and seknese off body and mynd.'[3] In the presence of such belief, it is not surprising that the Durham monks of the later middle ages were able to keep Saint Cuthbert awake for others as well as for themselves.

of Durham and Bishop Bell of Carlisle in the fifteenth century, see Misc. Chrs., no. 2352; B. Colgrave, 'The History of British Museum Additional MS. 39943', *E.H.R.* LIV (1939), 673–7.

[1] B.M., Harleian MS. 4843, fos. 13v–30, 262; cf. Colgrave, *Two Lives*, pp. 28–9.

[2] Printed from the same MS. in Eyre, *History of St Cuthbert*, pp. 283–7.

[3] Misc. Chrs., no. 7159*. For the last of Cuthbert's medieval miracles, the healing of Richard Poell, one of Henry VII's retainers, in 1503, see *Scrip. Tres*, pp. 152–3.

THE CITY OF DURHAM

The monks of Durham were however indebted to Saint Cuthbert for something even more specific than their wealth and fame. The fifteenth-century prior and chapter were well aware that ever since the body of their saint had come to rest at *Dunelmi locus* or Dunholm in 995, succeeding generations of canons and monks had glorified his person and defended his rights on exactly that 'island with a hill' where they too lived and worshipped. Much more important was their firm belief that Durham, to an extent greater than any other city in Britain, had been created by divine will, chosen as his final terrestrial home by Saint Cuthbert in person. In the face of such a powerful and appealing legend, it seems ungracious to have to make the now familiar point that the site of Durham was not a deserted wilderness when the community of Saint Cuthbert first arrived there at the end of the tenth century. Recent archaeological discoveries on the peninsula itself, the remains of the most northerly villa yet found in the Roman Empire at Old Durham, the controversial promontory fort at Maiden Castle, and perhaps the consecration of a bishop of Whithorn at *Aelfet ee* (usually identified with the later Elvet) as early as 763, all remind us that Saint Cuthbert was not the first to recognise the potentialities of the Durham site as a centre of communications and agriculture.[1] But despite Symeon's clear statement to the contrary, Prior Wessington and his monks clearly liked to believe that their saint had first called human settlement into existence not only on the Durham peninsula but in the surrounding area.[2] The spectacular nature of that peninsula, the rocky hill surrounded by 'the sweet and delectable ryver of Were', has been transfigured but fortunately never completely destroyed by time. A subject of enthusiastic eulogy by an Anglo-Saxon poet apparently writing within a few decades of its conversion to a holy place, Durham's 'celebrity throughout the kingdom of the Britains' has never needed

---

[1] T. Whitworth, 'Deposits beneath the North Bailey, Durham', *Durham University Journal* LXI (1968), 18–31; *V.C.H. Durham* I, 224–5, 348; III, 6–8; *Anglo-Saxon Chronicle*, ed. Garmondsway, p. 51; I. D. Margary, *Roman Roads in Britain* (London, 1967), pp. 433, 441.

[2] '*Nec protunc nec post* (until 995) *erecta erat ecclesia vel capella sive domus in toto loco vel aliquo parte eiusdem ubi nunc est civitas Dunelmensis cum suis suburbanis*' (Loc. II, no. 5); cf. Symeon, *Hist. Ecc. Dun.*, pp. 80–1.

any particular urging.[1] The towers of Durham Cathedral still dominate the surrounding countryside, and from the twelfth century onwards the residents of the city have always lived – as in Hugh Walpole's Polchester – under the metaphoric shadow of the monastic church.

As the *genius loci* at Durham remains more dramatically apparent than in the case of any other English cathedral city, it is still not hard to appreciate that monastic life there owed many of its most distinctive features to the peculiarities of its geographical context. Not that all these peculiarities were unqualified assets. To the earliest generations of Durham monks, as of course to the attendants on the corsaint when they first saw the site in 995, the greatest merits of the local topography were less its aesthetic charms than its military possibilities. 'For no vulnerable side of the place can be assailed by any weapon, nor is there any spot there which can be made to tremble by its enemy.'[2] By the early fifteenth century this argument was somewhat less compelling. After the battle of Neville's Cross Durham was apparently never seriously exposed to the danger of armed attack, and there is some evidence to suggest that the late medieval prior and chapter were by no means unconscious of the disadvantages which living in a monastery where 'the river obstructs the way' entailed. The Durham monks were not only denied easy access to the surrounding countryside by the obstacles of river, castle and city, but lived within a small as well as isolated enclave.[3] In comparison with the precincts enjoyed by most of the other great English monasteries, those at Durham could hardly be said to be spacious: the four acres or so at the disposal of the community of Saint Cuthbert compare unfavourably even with the not unduly extensive tract of twelve acres inhabited by their most powerful rivals in the north, the Benedictines of Saint Mary's

---

[1] *De Situ Dunelmi*, ed. Arnold (Rolls Series, 1882), pp. 221–2. For the supposed topographical resemblance between the site of Durham and that of Jerusalem, see Eyre, *St Cuthbert*, p. 122; R. H. Allan, *Historical and Descriptive View of the City of Durham* (Durham, 1824), p. 5. For the much debated date of the *De Situ*, see above, p. 25 n. 2.

[2] *Dialogi Laurentii Prioris* (Surtees Soc. LXX, 1880), pp. 8–9.

[3] Possibly made a little less complete by the building of the mysterious '*parvus pons*' or Bow Bridge to Elvet in the later middle ages (Repertorium Magnum, fo. 113): see *Dobsons Drie Bobbes*, ed. E. A. Horsman (Durham, 1955), pp. xiii, 77.

Abbey, York. Even by medieval standards, living conditions within the monastic walls of late medieval Durham must often have been almost intolerably overcrowded. The prior and chapter's complaint to Pope Nicholas V in 1454 that they lacked sufficient space within which to exercise their bodies should not be dismissed out of hand.[1] Nor perhaps should their other allegation that the atmosphere within their convent was subject to pollution. Although impressive latrines projected from the western side of their precincts, the drop to the Wear was at least a hundred feet. At times when the river was low and the prevailing wind from the west, the limitations of Durham's sanitary arrangements must – as Canon Fowler once suggested – have been only too apparent.[2]

More generally the quality of monastic life at Durham depended in ways now almost impossible to recapture on the relationship between the religious community and the neighbouring townsmen. Naturally enough the glamour of its bishops and cathedral church has distracted the attention of Durham historians from the study of its city; but in the case of a monastery so uniquely grounded on local interests and loyalties, it is not a little unfortunate that this relationship should remain so obscure. In the early fifteenth century Prior Wessington and his monks may have been legally correct if historically mistaken to remind the recalcitrant Durham burgesses of Elvet and Old Borough that Saint Cuthbert had brought their ancestors into being; but this argument left open the question whether or not the lay inhabitants of the saint's *civitas* were content to accept the subservient position thrust upon them by the bishop and the convent. At Reading, at Saint Mary's, York, and at Bury St Edmunds, to take some obvious analogies, large communities of Black Monks were notoriously enmeshed in an intimate and usually stormy association with the townsmen outside their monastic walls. How, and to what extent, did Durham Priory avoid these dangers? Because of the very inadequate and partial survival of the city's records, a definite answer will probably never be available. Nevertheless, no survey of the monastery of Durham in the early fifteenth century can hope to be complete without some comments, however

[1] Cart. III, fo. 201; *Scrip. Tres*, p. cccxxx.
[2] *V.C.H. Durham* III, 17. For other references to '*aer corruptus*' at Durham, see Loc. XXI, no. 22; *Scrip. Tres*, p. 49.

impressionistic and insecurely based, upon the city which surrounded and sustained it.

According to one important authority, Durham belongs to that group of English towns, like Chester and Carlisle, of whose economic importance at the end of the middle ages 'we can form almost no idea'.[1] Yet there seems little doubt that Durham was then one of the larger urban communities in the country. Surpassed by Newcastle-upon-Tyne (already an important ship-building centre in the 1160s[2]) as early as the twelfth century, Durham nevertheless seems to have retained an economic as well as honorific ascendancy between Tees and Tyne throughout and beyond the medieval period. On the eve of the Industrial Revolution it still held pride of place as the most commercially important as well as historically notable of the dozen leading market towns in the county, the others – all of medieval origin – being listed in 1767 as Darlington, Stockton, Sunderland (the successor of the medieval South or Bishop Wearmouth), Hartlepool, Bishop Auckland, Barnard Castle, Stanhope, Sedgefield, Staindrop, Wolsingham, and South Shields.[3] With its seven (after 1431) parochial churches or chapels, three important hospitals and a wide variety of other public and private buildings, the amenities of the city of Durham were unique in the palatinate. No estimate of its population in the later middle ages can hope to be at all reliable; but the suggestion that in 1377, the year of the first poll tax returns, the town comprised perhaps 2,000 inhabitants out of an estimated total county population of approximately 24,000 may not be too wildly off the mark.[4] A good deal less than half as populous as Newcastle-upon-Tyne, it might be

---

[1] W. G. Hoskins, *Provincial England* (London, 1963), pp. 70–1.

[2] *Reginaldi Libellus*, p. 227; G. W. S. Barrow, 'Northern English Society in the early Middle Ages', *Northern History* IV (1969), 4–5.

[3] *A Particular Description of the Bishoprick or County Palatine of Durham*, ed. P. Sanderson (Durham, 1767), p. 4. The first six towns in this list were all rated as boroughs for the purposes of a subsidy on moveables levied in 1306 (Fraser, *Antony Bek*, p. 81). On the neglected topic of urban development in the north-east, see M. H. Dodds, 'The Bishops' Boroughs', *Arch. Ael.*, Third series, XII (1913), 81–185; A. E. Smailes, *North England* (London, 1960), pp. 109–26; M. Beresford, *New Towns of the Middle Ages* (London, 1967), pp. 430–2.

[4] R. Donaldson, 'Patronage and the Church: a study in the social structure of the secular clergy in the diocese of Durham (1311–1540)' (University of Edinburgh Ph.D. thesis, 1955), pp. 10–19; J. C. Russell, *British Medieval Population* (Albuquerque, 1948), p. 145.

argued that late medieval Durham was in the same order of demographic dimension as Northampton, Nottingham and Stamford, towns of a substantial if not spectacular size.

The intriguing evidence of the Durham chantry returns points to much the same sort of situation at the time of the Reformation. In 1548 it was certified that about 547 'howseling people' resided in the parish of Saint Margaret's, Crossgate, 680 in Saint Oswald's, 712 in Saint Nicholas's, 240 in Saint Mary's in the North Bailey and 420 in Saint Giles's, a total of almost exactly 2,600.[1] The notoriously complicated problems of calculating total population figures from the houselings of the chantry certificates are conceivably exacerbated here by the absence of any independent return from Saint Mary's in the South Bailey. More seriously still, two of the parishes attached to Durham's medieval churches, Saint Oswald's and Saint Giles's, ran for several miles into the surrounding countryside. All the same it is hard to resist the tentative conclusion that at the time of the dissolution of the monastery the population resident within the city of Durham and its suburbs was between 2,000 and 3,000, a figure which was to remain comparatively stable for at least the next century.[2] But the chantry certificates are undoubtedly a more reliable guide to the distribution of the city's population than to its absolute size. Then as now only a relatively small proportion of the town's inhabitants lived on the peninsula itself: the latter was an area dominated and indeed largely occupied by the bishop's castle, the cathedral church and the monastic precincts. Under closer examination still the 'little compact neatly contrived city' of Defoe's description reveals itself as a complex web in which the unique *conjoncture* of Durham's history and topography had produced a chaotic mixture of rival communities and jurisdictions.

In the fifteenth century, as until comparatively recent times, the most densely populated part of the city was the area of 58 acres lying immediately north of the bishop's castle and largely coincident with the parish of Saint Nicholas. Here was the nucleus of the *burgus Dunelmensis* proper, the bishop's borough probably founded by

[1] *Injunctions and Ecclesiastical Proceedings of Richard Barnes* (Surtees Soc. xxii, 1850), pp. lix–lxiii.

[2] *V.C.H. Durham* iii, 46, where however the calculations of Durham's population in the seventeenth and eighteenth centuries are admitted to be 'rather guesswork'. At the time of the 1801 census, the population of the city had risen to 7,530.

Rannulf Flambard early in the twelfth century. Although there is evidence of urban activity at Durham before the establishment of the Benedictine monastery there (including a reference to a '*forum*' as early as 1040), the decisive events in the formation of this borough are likely to have been Bishop Flambard's deliberate destruction of the houses on what is now Palace Green and his building of Framwellgate Bridge in stone.[1] Separated from the 60 or so acres of the Durham peninsula by the formidable defensive walls constructed by Flambard and his successors, the history of the 'bishop's borough' consequently conforms to the classic pattern of a *faubourg* created immediately outside the fortified stronghold it was intended to serve. Much more distinctive was the borough's site around that part of Durham's famous horse-shoe bend where an incised meander of the Wear leaves an interval of only 250 yards, Leland's 'length of an arow shot'.[2] At the very neck of the peninsula and immediately south of the church of Saint Nicholas lay the *Forum Dunelmensis* or market place, the centre of the communal and commercial life of the late medieval borough and an open space – as emerges clearly enough from the famous plan of Durham first published by John Speed in 1611 – considerably larger than at present.

In common with the great majority of English towns, the *burgus Dunelmensis* clearly underwent considerable territorial as well as economic expansion during the twelfth and thirteenth centuries. Murage grants of 1315 and 1337 almost certainly relate to the building of the new northern protective wall, running from the tower on the east side of Framwellgate Bridge around the market square and past Claypath Gate to Elvet Bridge, itself no doubt a reaction to the threat of Scottish raids in the early fourteenth century.[3] But long before this period the cramped situation of the bishop's borough and the importance of Durham as a route centre had already led to ribbon development of the type that gave – and still gives – Durham

---

[1] Symeon, *Hist. Ecc. Dun.*, pp. 91, 140; Scammell, *Hugh du Puiset*, pp. 214–15.

[2] *Itinerary of John Leland*, ed. L. Toulmin Smith (London, 1906–10), I, 73; *Six North Country Diaries* (Surtees Soc. CXVIII, 1910), p. 7; cf. P. M. Benedikz, *Durham Topographical Prints up to 1800* (Durham University Library, Publication no. 6, 1968).

[3] *Rot. Parl.* I, 302; *C.P.R., 1334–38*, p. 387; H. L. Turner, *Town Defences in England and Wales* (London, 1971), pp. 102–3.

its characteristic and much noticed 'crab-like' appearance.[1] Probably from its inception the bishop's borough of Durham had included burgages and pasture rights along both sides of the important street of Framwellgate, the old road to Newcastle-upon-Tyne which ran north from its junction with Milnburngate on the west side of the river. On the opposite, north-eastern side of the city, tenements in Claypath and its eastwards extension of Gilesgate similarly lined the road that led to the coastal ports of Hartlepool and Bishop Wearmouth.[2] In the *Vicus Sancti Egidii* (elevated to separate borough status by Bishop Puiset for the benefit of Kepier Hospital in about 1180), Framwellgate and the other streets of the bishop's borough, the fifteenth-century obedientiaries of Durham Priory seem to have held more urban property than any other landlord;[3] but they had of course no control over the constitutional fortunes of a borough which was almost invariably farmed by its bishop for a fixed annual sum throughout the middle ages and had to wait for incorporation under an alderman until 1565.[4] It was in other, and almost as important, sections of the city that they wielded direct seigniorial authority.

Besides the bishop's boroughs, the urban complex of late medieval Durham comprised two others, Elvet and the *Vetus Burgus* or Old Borough of Crossgate, both part of the prior's fee until the Dissolution. Old Borough – so called, as Prior Wessington realised, to distinguish it from the more recent borough foundation of Elvet[5] – may have been the original Anglo-Saxon trading-centre in the area, already in existence before Bishop Flambard built his 'ald brig' to connect western Durham with the peninsula. Located on the west bank of the Wear and covering a wide stretch of territory between

[1] Hegge, *Legend of St Cuthbert*, ed. Taylor (Sunderland, 1816), p. 2; *A Relation of a Short Survey of 26 Counties, Observed in a seven weeks Journey begun on August 11 1634*, ed. L. G. Wickham Legg (London, 1904), p. 25.

[2] D. M. Meade, 'The Medieval Parish of Saint Giles, Durham', *Trans. of Architectural and Archaeological Soc. of Durham and Northumberland*, New Series, II (1970), 63–9.

[3] For the convent's massive holdings of urban property everywhere in the city, see especially the bursar's rentals and Loc. XXXVII, nos. 87, 113 (a sixteenth-century plan of the market place).

[4] Durham was farmed for £40 as early as the time of Boldon Book in 1183; cf. Scammell, *Hugh du Puiset*, p. 216; *V.C.H. Durham* III, 54–6; Beresford, *New Towns of the Middle Ages*, pp. 430–2.

[5] Cart. IV, fo. 90; *Feodarium Dunelm.*, pp. 191–5.

Elvet to the south and Framwellgate, across the stream of Milnburn, to the north, the Old Borough was to develop on the '*terra ultra pontem Dunelmi*' restored to the monks of Durham by an allegedly contrite Bishop Flambard in 1128. Although its inhabitants never seem to have received a comprehensive charter of privileges from the convent, it probably attained a vague form of borough status shortly thereafter: part of a Durham *burgus* which '*ad monachorum ius pertinebat*' was burnt to the ground in the civil wars of 1144.[1] Throughout the later middle ages the prior and convent maintained effective rule over their tenants of the Old Borough, whose bailiffs they seem to have appointed and whose public affairs they regulated by means of the court they held at the Tollbooth on the north side of Crossgate. But this was one of those many English boroughs which, in Maitland's phrase, never became ripe enough to rot. The account rolls of the obedientiaries of Durham Priory leave no doubt that most of the Old Borough, whose boundaries ran far west to the extensive 400 acres of Beaurepaire or Bearpark Moor, was still agricultural land in the fifteenth century. Only in Allergate, South Street, Milnburngate and Crossgate itself was there much in the way of urban tenements or housing.[2] In most respects the Old Borough retained the characteristics of a rural village until long after the dissolution of the monastery. Pigs and other live-stock wandered its streets in the early sixteenth century, while the great majority of its inhabitants depended on the cultivation of the soil rather than trade or industry for their livelihood. There is little evidence of marked specialisation of labour at any period in the medieval history of the Old Borough. Of the 20 tenants who appeared before the prior's Marshalsea court there at Easter 1392, nearly all were otherwise obscure bakers and ale-brewers.[3] Not surprisingly, the convent's jurisdictional rights over the Old Borough brought them little in the way of profit. Between 1408 and 1410 the fines and amercements of the Durham sacrist's court at Alvertongate or Allergate averaged only 4s. 7d. per annum, a smaller sum than the half-mark the sacrist was obliged to pay one of the monastery's clerks to preside over the

---

[1] Symeon, *Hist. Ecc. Dun.*, pp. 141, 159; *Durham Episcopal Charters, 1071–1152*, pp. 107, 109.

[2] Bursars' rolls, passim, *Vetus Burgus* section; cf. *Halmota Prioratus Dunelmensis, 1296–1384* (Surtees Soc. LXXXII, 1889), pp. 192–5; *Dur. Acct. Rolls* I, 66–7.

[3] *Dur. Acct. Rolls* II, 346–7; *V.C.H. Durham* III, 60.

proceedings there; and even when the Old Borough was put to farm in the early fifteenth century it produced an annual return of less than £3.[1]

Considerably more profitable was the convent's possession of a second and more important borough at Elvet. As we have seen, there is some evidence that the hilly ground near Saint Oswald's church, to the east of the Durham peninsula, had begun to be colonised before the arrival of Saint Cuthbert's body in the vicinity in 995. Not much more than a century later it can be deduced from a famous forged diploma of Bishop William of Saint Calais that Elvet had been allotted to the monks of Durham as part of their share of the patrimony of the saint; more interestingly still, it was then said to include houses of or for forty *mercatores*, the first reference to the deliberate sponsorship of urban activity in the Durham area.[2] But it was the building of a second stone bridge across the Wear, the *Novus Pons* of Elvet, at some undetermined date during the pontificate of Hugh du Puiset (1153–95) which presumably transformed the northern and low-lying part of Elvet into an important route-centre. Perhaps for this reason Bishop Puiset himself usurped all or part of this area as an episcopal borough: only after he had restored the latter at the end of his life did the prior and chapter address their first charter to '*fidelibus burgensibus nostris de novo burgo nostro in Eluetehalch*'. Thenceforward urban settlement in medieval Elvet centred round the two main streets, now called Old and New Elvet, which met at the eastern side of the bridge and were linked 300 yards to the south-east by the cross street of Raton Row.[3] The land lying to the north of Raton Row formed the *novus burgus*, often called New Elvet, as opposed to the more southerly and much more extensive 'barony' of Upper Elvet, administered from the convent's manor house of Elvet Hall. Both borough and barony of Elvet had their separate courts, but the complications caused by rival juris-

[1] Sacrist, 1408–10, 1415–17; Bursar, 1416/17, 1418/19, Varia Recepta.
[2] *Durham Episcopal Charters*, pp. 8, 11–12, where it seems to be implied that at least as many *mercatores* already resided within the bishop's own *civitas*.
[3] *Feodarium Dunelm.*, pp. 198–9; Scammell, *Hugh du Puiset*, pp. 111, 131, 154, 215. The streets of Old and New Elvet, terms originally applied to the barony and borough of Elvet respectively, exchanged their names at the end of the middle ages (Loc. II, no. 5; *V.C.H. Durham* III, 61; and the interesting pre-Dissolution map of the Scaltock Mill area preserved as Misc. Chrs., no. 7100).

dictions in adjacent areas were so great that the distinction often came to be blurred and in the fifteenth century had lost much of its practical consequence.[1]

From the standpoint of the late medieval prior and chapter, much their greatest asset in the area was their possession of the lordship of Elvet Hall. The great value of this manor, the later Hallgarth or Hallyerds farm, to the economy of the convent has often been overlooked. The most important endowment of the Durham hostillar, who supervised the operations of the manor through the agency of a steward, reeve and forester, Elvet Hall not only contributed revenue and agricultural produce to the convent but was used as a place of entertainment for visiting magnates as well as the monks themselves.[2] Although the prior and chapter's tenants in the Elvet area were more populous and prosperous than those of the Old Borough, it would be a mistake to believe that economic and social conditions in either place were those of a predominantly industrial or commercial community. Most of the inhabitants of both borough and barony of fifteenth-century Elvet were husbandmen or small craftsmen, interspersed with a dominant group of clerks and *armigeri* who appear to have regarded Elvet as a desirable residential area. The twenty or so free tenants of the prior who came to an agreement with the convent in September 1442 on the vexed issue of their right to common pasture in Elvet included no merchant among their numbers. Apart from the vicar of Saint Oswald's church and its two chantry priests, it was members of the lesser gentry, like Robert Danby and Thomas Claxton, and clerical dynasties serving the bishop and the convent (the Racketts, Berehalghs and Tangs) who then ranked as the leading burgesses and inhabitants of Elvet.[3]

In many ways the town and suburbs of late medieval Durham therefore stand revealed as a heterogeneous collection of small villages rather than an integrated urban community. Probably just the central area of the bishop's borough deserved to be termed a town in any meaningful sense of the word. Shops, stalls and booths,

[1] Loc. II, no. 14.
[2] Elvethall Manorial Accounts, and Hostillar, passim, especially the inventory of the '*manerium de Elvethall*' in 1454; *Dur. Acct. Rolls* I, 16, 117, 129, 149–50, 162; II, 523; *Dobsons Drie Bobbes*, ed. Horsman, 77. One of the half-timbered out-buildings of the manor survives as the so-called Hallgarth Tithe Barn, now a prison officers' club.   [3] 4.16. Spec., no. 26; Reg. III, fo. 281; cf. fos. 68, 143, 174.

although occasionally mentioned outside the peninsula, were only thickly concentrated on and near the two bridges of Framwellgate and Elvet as well as the streets which led steeply upwards from the Wear to the market place.[1] Few of these, or indeed any of the houses and urban tenements of fifteenth-century Durham, are likely to have been particularly imposing. Possible exceptions were the town houses and inns held by local magnates and ecclesiastics along the North and South Baileys; but many of these had been sub-let by the time of Wessington's priorate and others were undoubtedly in a state of decay. Elsewhere in Durham, as in so many medieval cities, dwellings seem to have been remarkably small. Of five burgages in South Row, Elvet, leased by the convent in 1430, one had a street frontage of 48 feet but the others were all between 18 and 22 feet in width. Even the exceptionally desirable 'Corner Bothe' on the angle of the market place was less than five yards square 'on the ground' when rented by Prior Richard Bell to a Durham mercer, William Cornforth, for ten shillings per annum in May 1465.[2] The other dimensions recorded in this lease suggest that the 'Corner Bothe' was a timber-framed building with overhanging storeys of the type still represented in the modern city by the solitary surviving example of No. 5, Owengate. It is however impossible to recapture the physical appearance of the houses in the late medieval city in any detail. In 1432 the Guild Hall in the market place was alternatively known as the 'stone hall', a usage which seems to suggest what one would expect – that secular buildings made entirely of stone were a rarity in fifteenth-century Durham.[3] Copious references to the construction of new burgages in the convent's account rolls of the period convey a general impression that these involved the labour of carpenters as well as stonemasons and tilers, presumably resulting in structures of stone foundations and ground-floor walls but with timber-framed upper storeys. John Leland is unlikely to have been mistaken when he recorded that 'The building of Duresme toun is meately strong, but it is nother high nor of costely werke'.[4]

---

[1] The evidence of the monastic archives is amply confirmed by that of the fourteenth-century Salvin Deeds, nos. 355–96 (Durham County Record Office).

[2] Loc. xxxvii, no. 74*; *Feodarium Dunelm.*, pp. 74–5; Surtees, *Durham* IV, part ii, 163; *V.C.H. Durham* III, 23–4.

[3] Surtees, *Durham* IV, part ii, 48. Like other English cities, Durham had long been vulnerable to fire (*Reginaldi Libellus*, pp. 82–3).   [4] Leland's *Itinerary* I, 73.

Although an important route-centre and the site of celebrated fairs, notably that at the feast of Saint Cuthbert on 4 September,[1] fifteenth-century Durham shows few signs of having been either a major manufacturing centre or a significant entrepôt for long-distance commerce. As Robert Surtees remarked many years later, 'The Trade of Durham has never been much extended beyond the establishment of many substantial shops for the supply of the City and neighbourhood with the usual articles'.[2] One of the features of the site which originally attracted the community of Saint Cuthbert in 995 was no doubt Durham's immunity from Viking raids by river; but their descendants have always had to pay the price of an unnavigable Wear.[3] It is certainly difficult to find much evidence for the existence in the late medieval city of a powerful merchant patriciate analogous to that which dominated the political as well as economic life of so many English towns of the period. At any one time in the fifteenth century, Durham's population admittedly always included a few merchants, men like John Bernard who held property in Claypath and sold small quantities of wine and iron to the monastic bursar between 1424 and 1432, or the spicer, William Aldyngsheles, who lived in Elvet and whose business activities left some mark on contemporary monastic account rolls.[4] But the same accounts leave absolutely no doubt that for their bulk supplies of cloth, wine, spices, iron and other commodities, the obedientiaries of Durham relied heavily on the great merchants of York, Hull, Hartlepool and Newcastle-upon-Tyne, but on native Durham merchants only to an extremely limited extent. It is perhaps symptomatic of the real balance of economic power in the north of England that one of the few Durham mercers to be recorded in the mid-fifteenth century, John Coken, was arrested because of his debts to a Newcastle merchant.[5] No burgess of Durham in the fifteenth century came remotely near emulating the success of Robert Rodes,

[1] *Scrip. Tres*, pp. ccccxxx–ccccxxxi; *Reginaldi Libellus*, pp. 54, 98; *V.C.H. Durham* III, 56.   [2] Surtees *Durham*, IV, part ii, 25.

[3] For various 'chimerical, impractical schemes to make the River navigable to ye City' in the eighteenth century, see E. Hughes, *North Country Life in the Eighteenth Century: The North-East, 1700–1750* (Oxford, 1952), pp. 13, 262, 302.

[4] Bursar, 1416/17, Expense Prioris; 1424/25, Empcio Vini; 1429/30, 1432, Marescalcia; Misc. Chrs., nos. 1784, 6671; *Dur. Acct. Rolls* II, 369; III, 709.

[5] P.R.O., Palatinate of Durham, Chancery Enrolments, 3/46, memb. 4.

a member of a Newcastle merchant family who became a prominent councillor and eventually chief steward of the prior and chapter; the founder of a perpetual chantry in the cathedral, he lived in some state in the South Bailey, where he received permission in 1449 to occupy the South or Water Gate of the city wall.[1] Remarkably few of the chantries in Durham's cathedral and parish churches were ever founded by merchants. Nor can it be coincidental that a surprisingly high proportion of the property within the city was held by clerks rather than laymen.[2] Fifteenth-century Durham presents us with an interesting example of a moderately large urban community in which the dominance of the town's society by a merchant élite, so common elsewhere, was replaced by that of a 'professional' hierarchy of ecclesiastical administrators and officials who served either bishop or monastery or both.

The peculiarities of its social structure did not of course isolate the city of Durham completely from the economic developments characteristic of fifteenth-century English urban history. As a medium-sized service and market centre rather than the scene of intensive commercial and industrial activity, Durham may have been spared a few of the more extreme manifestations of late medieval 'urban decay'. Nevertheless some symptoms of economic decline, however difficult to quantify, were clearly apparent in the years after 1400. Unless the mortality rate within the monastic walls was altogether exceptional, the inhabitants of Durham certainly suffered severely at the time of the first onslaught of the Black Death in 1349. Perhaps more disastrous in the long term were the renewed outbreaks of the 'great pestilence' which are known to have disrupted the public life of the city in the following century, notably in 1416 and 1438.[3] The remarkably large number of wasted and decayed burgages and tenements recorded in the early fifteenth-century city,

---

[1] Surtees, *Durham* IV, part ii, 44; see below, p. 130.

[2] Misc. Chrs., nos. 1720, 1792, 1795, 1814, 1919, 2016, 2399.

[3] P.R.O., Palatinate of Durham, Chancery Enrolments, 3/35, memb. 10; 3/46, memb. 2; *34th Report of the Deputy Keeper of the P.R.O.* (1873), Appendix p. 227. Like other English landlords, the prior and chapter of Durham sometimes calculated their financial position with reference to the '*pestilentia magna*' of 1349 (Reg. II, fo. 356v; *Scrip. Tres*, p. ccxlviii); and a memorandum prepared on behalf of Prior Wessington in 1446 mentioned the '*graves pestilentie in quibus tenentes mortui sunt*' of the previous thirty years (Loc. XXI, no. 20, vii).

and particularly in its more central areas, testify to the probability of serious economic dislocation caused by a demographic decline. Thus at the end of John Wessington's priorate in 1446, two of the monastic bursar's four tenements in the *burgus Dunelmensis* itself lay completely waste. Within the Durham Baileys, the position was even more serious: 13 tenements there ought to have provided the bursar with a clear annual income of 62*s.* 4*d.*, but of this sum he received only a few shillings because of wastes and decays estimated at no less than £3.[1] Admittedly subsequent financial records of the monastery, and especially the great bursar's inventory of 1464, reveal a real degree of financial recovery later in the fifteenth century; and it would be misleading to state categorically that late medieval Durham was always in the throes of acute economic crisis. However, there are other grounds for believing that the hundred years after the first outbreak of bubonic plague was a period of economic depression for north-eastern towns. The terms, for example, on which the bishops of Durham were ready to farm their own borough of Durham seem to reflect, albeit obliquely, a prevailing atmosphere of stagnation and gradual although not irreversible decline. In 1387 Bishop Fordham was able to lease the *burgus Dunelmensis* and its appurtenances for a farm of £86 13*s.* 4*d.*, a figure which gradually fell to as little as £56 in 1435 before rising again to £60 in 1466.[2] It would of course be extremely dangerous to treat such evidence as an exact index of economic decline in the medieval city as a whole; but it confirms the general impression that during the first half of the fifteenth century conditions there were less prosperous than in the past or indeed in one or two other towns within the county.[3]

The adverse economic circumstances of the period, in combination with the Durham burgesses' failure to develop a powerful manufacturing interest, go far to explain the lack of evidence for industrial organisation in the city. A very large proportion of the inhabitants

---

[1] Bursar, 1445/46, Burgus Dunelmi, Ballium Dunelmi; Granator, 1442/43, Ballium Dunelmi; Hostillar, 1446/47; *Scrip. Tres*, p. cccii; *Feodarium Dunelm.*, pp. 191–9.

[2] Lapsley, *County Palatine*, p. 278; *V.C.H. Durham* II, 254–5; III, 23, 56; Storey, *Thomas Langley*, p. 72.

[3] Especially Darlington, where the bishop's borough was farmed for 100 marks in 1421 (P.R.O., Palatinate of Durham, Chancery Enrolments, 3/37, memb. 13), and which struck Leland as 'the best market town in the bishoprick saving Duresme' (*Itinerary* I, 69).

of Durham must always have been committed to staffing and ser-
vicing the monastery, the castle and – conceivably as demanding of
labour as either – the heterogeneous collection of palatine administrative offices (chancery, exchequer, courts of law) that lay between
the two. Few fortunes were likely to be made from this type of
service, and the citizens of Durham even failed to make much profit
out of the potentially lucrative operations of the bishop's mint near
Palace Green. The latter was often under the control of Italian
moneyers, and in 1473 the bishop commissioned not a Durham but a
York goldsmith to make a new supply of coining dies.[1] The organisation of craft or occupational guilds consequently appears to have
emerged at a later date and at a more rudimentary level than was
common in the case of most substantial medieval English towns.
Only after 1447 do references to craft fraternities at Durham begin
to survive in any number. During the following thirty years there is
proof of some form of corporate organisation on the part of the
Durham shoemakers, fullers, weavers (in 1468 divided into the two
categories of woollen and shalloon weavers), cordwainers and
barbers. This last guild included waxmakers and surgeons amongst
its members; and when the ordinances of the barbers' craft were
compiled or revised in 1468, they were witnessed by 28 brethren
(including one Robert, barber of the priory), a figure which may
give some indication of the size of the Durham craft fraternities.[2]
There is, however, no evidence of any particularly sophisticated
economic regulation or policy by such fraternities, and it is unlikely
that any of them owned a hall or held property in common. The
taking of Scots 'to prentes' was absolutely prohibited in the case
of every craft for which ordinances survive; and the probably typical
regulations of the Durham weavers (1450) and barbers (1468) provided for the election of two wardens at an annual meeting of the
brotherhood.[3] But much the most important general obligation

---

[1] Lapsley, *County Palatine*, pp. 280–1; *V.C.H. Durham* III, 24–5.

[2] Surtees, *Durham* IV, part ii, 21; cf. C. J. Whiting, 'The Durham Trade Gilds',
Trans. of Architectural and Archaeological Soc. of Durham and Northumberland IX (1941),
143–72.

[3] Surtees, ibid., pp. 20–1; *34th Report of the Deputy Keeper of the P.R.O.* (1873),
Appendix, pp. 244, 258; and the somewhat suspect late transcript of the Durham
butchers' ordinances, allegedly sealed on 14 June 1403, printed in F. J. W. Harding,
'The Company of Butchers and Fleshers of Durham', *Trans. of Architectural and
Archaeological Soc. of Durham and Northumberland* XI (1958), 93–100.

imposed upon the members of the crafts, and perhaps one which itself accelerated the growth of occupational guilds in Durham more than any purely economic considerations, was that of processing on Corpus Christi day to 'playe the playe that of old time longed to thaire craft'. Although only part of the prologue of one of these dramatic productions survives, it is clear that Durham, like Newcastle-upon-Tyne and York, was the scene of annual cycles of 'mystery' plays or pageants.[1]

The citizens of fifteenth-century Durham were also fully involved in the late medieval vogue for religious and social fraternities of all types. The churches of St Nicholas and St Giles were the spiritual headquarters of the two parish guilds of those names. However, although Matilda Bowes left gold and silver 'to the fraternity of the gild of St Nicholas in Duresme' in 1421, neither that guild nor its counterpart at St Giles's church was ever well endowed.[2] In line with similar developments elsewhere, notably at York, a much more prominent role in the last century before the Reformation was played by the guild of Corpus Christi. The latter was attached to the church of St Nicholas and sponsored the great Corpus Christi procession to the cathedral, nostalgically remembered by the author of the *Rites of Durham* as the ceremonial highlight of the urban year. It is symptomatic of the balance of social influence in the late medieval city that the Durham Corpus Christi Guild, eventually wealthy enough to afford its own priest, was established or re-organised in 1436 not by the merchants and craftsmen of the town but by the chancellor, receiver-general and other officials of the palatinate.[3] Even richer at their joint dissolution than the Corpus Christi guild was the much older 'fraternity of the gild of Saint Cuthbert' which apparently usually met within the cathedral itself and was financially administered by the Durham sacrist and other obedientiaries. It was in associations such as these, at sermons in the cathedral, and on the occasion of the many formal processions around

---

[1] R. M. Wilson, *The Lost Literature of Medieval England* (2nd edn, London, 1970), p. 218; cf. M. H. Dodds, 'The Northern Stage', *Arch. Ael.*, Third Series, XI (1914), 31–64.

[2] *Wills and Inventories* I (Surtees Soc. II, 1835), p. 64; *Injunctions of Richard Barnes* (Surtees Soc. XXII, 1850), pp. lix–lxiii.

[3] P.R.O., Palatinate of Durham, Chancery Enrolments, 3/36, memb. 11; Storey, *Thomas Langley*, p. 101; *Rites*, pp. 107–8; *V.C.H. Durham* III, 26.

the city, that monks and burgesses of Durham must have felt their fortunes most closely if imponderably intertwined, bound together by acts of public worship and veneration for Saint Cuthbert.

In the last resort it is in fact difficult to resist the conclusion that the relationship between the prior and chapter of late medieval Durham with the secular world immediately outside its gates was a good deal happier than in the case of most 'urban monasteries'. It seems reasonably clear that the Durham monks of John Wessington's priorate maintained a sufficiently respectable standard of behaviour to avoid exposing themselves to the sort of scandal and moral criticism common elsewhere. No monastery has ever been permanently successful in preserving itself from contamination by the world outside its walls. Yet the occasional disputes between the Benedictines of Durham and its citizens evoked no serious riots or other demonstrations of public hostility. The leading role played in the city's affairs by a class of ecclesiastical administrators, with whom the prior and chapter were on hospitable and often intimate terms, always made a direct confrontation between monks and townsmen unlikely. As landlords of so many Durham residents, the community of Saint Cuthbert could not of course be completely immune from the problems that set seigneur and tenant against each other in the later middle ages. Much the most common cause of ill-feeling in the early fifteenth century was a series of complicated disputes over rights to common pasture. Not unnaturally many of the prior's tenants cast covetous eyes on the large tracts of grazing land held by the monks immediately to the south and west of Durham, notably on Elvet and Beaurepaire Moors as well as near Aldin Grange. The most serious of these quarrels was that between the chapter and the burgesses and free tenants of Elvet in the late 1430s: this led to various acts of insubordination (including the breaking of the convent's closes, withdrawal of suit from the prior's mill and oven, and the unauthorised setting up of 'buttes' for their 'disporte') before an apparently amicable compromise was reached in September 1442.[1] But it is significant that the most bitter adversaries of the prior and chapter were not the poorer inhabitants of Durham but several members of the county gentry who lived on the outskirts of the city.

[1] Loc. II, nos. 5, 14; Misc. Chrs., nos. 2608, 7147; Additional Rolls, nos. 17, 42; Reg. III, fos. 175, 281–2.

Most turbulent of these was Thomas Billingham of Crook Hall who waged a veritable campaign of terror on the Durham monks in 1419, assaulting various members of the community on Framwellgate Bridge as well as on the roads leading to the city.[1] The records of the litigation that followed show no indication that Billingham and his colleagues received assistance from the burgesses of Durham itself. If the monks of Durham owed everything to Saint Cuthbert, the lay inhabitants of the city owed nearly everything to the monastery which provided them with employment and reflected glory. Like the residents of a modern university town, the inmates of fifteenth-century Durham may have sometimes looked askance at the impressive corporate monster in their vicinity; but they were wise enough to realise that it brought them less pain than profit.

[1] Loc. XXI, no. 11; Bursar, 1419/20, Expense Necessarie; Reg. III, fo. 68; cf. Storey, *Thomas Langley*, p. 113; see below, p. 194.

Chapter 2

THE MONKS OF DURHAM

What sholde he studie and make hymselven wood,
Upon a book in cloystre alwey to poure,
Or swynken with his handes, and laboure,
As Austyn bit? How shal the world be served?[1]

Between 1390, when John Wessington took the religious habit, and 1446, when he resigned the priorate of Durham, 123 monks were received into the community of Saint Cuthbert. Little can ever be known for certain about the individual characters of these men or their attitudes to each other, their superior, their order and their religion. The few monks like William Partrike, prior of Lytham, and Henry Helay, terrar and then prior of Holy Island, who have left some impression of their personalities to posterity were usually those who were particularly troublesome and unruly inmates of the convent. Although the private desires and aspirations of the individual monk are largely a matter for speculation, it is, however, possible to establish the main outlines of his career. Little as we know about the monks of Durham, we are better informed as to their recruitment, their education, their employment, their ambitions and their interests than those of any comparable group of men in early fifteenth-century England. Such an opportunity should not be left unnoticed by the historian, even if he is compelled to recognise that many of the most important questions will remain forever unanswered. An analysis of the members of a late medieval religious community based on its surviving records is bound to present us with a picture of a monastery as 'a club of celibate landlords under a rule'.[2] Such a picture may well be misleading, like the confidence with which so many medieval writers condemned fifteenth-century regulars for being bailiffs in monastic habits. The reconciliation of the things of this world with those of the next has never been a simple

[1] The Works of Geoffrey Chaucer, ed. F. N. Robinson (Oxford, 2nd edn, 1957), p. 19: Prologue to Canterbury Tales, lines 184-7.
[2] H. B. Workman, The Evolution of the Monastic Ideal (London, 1931), p. 337.

matter, as the monks of Durham were even more aware than their contemporary or later critics.

An important preliminary if not infallible index to the welfare of any corporation or society is its ability to maintain its membership at a high level. It is therefore of some real significance that the total number of Durham monks, including those resident in the nine monastic dependencies, remained extremely stable throughout the fifteenth century. Lists of the professed members of the community formed an obligatory part of visitation certificates and election decrees at Durham as elsewhere; and from such sources it is consequently relatively easy to estimate the size of the monastic population with a considerable degree of accuracy. Not all these lists are complete: it was, for example, unusual for monks living at the cells of Coldingham and Durham College to be included in the visitation records of their mother house. Failure to recognise this fact, and more especially to distinguish between lists of all Durham monks and lists of those resident at Durham, has unfortunately invalidated most attempts to outline population trends at the monastery.[1] The following figures include the prior, if alive, as well as all professed novices, who were usually present at capitular elections even though they had no canonical right to a vote on such occasions.[2]

At the election of Bishop Langley on 17 May 1406, there were 56 monks present in chapter, 1 represented by a proctor and 12 absent without formal excuse, a total of 69. John Wessington's own election as prior on 5 November 1416 was also made by 69 monks, including 5 who had appointed proctors but not 3 apostates. On 27 January 1438 Robert Neville was elected bishop at a chapter meeting where 53 monks were present in person, 11 sent proctors and 9 others were without representation, a total of 73. Sixty-five monks were mentioned in connection with Prior Ebchester's election on 30 June 1446, 69 at the time of John Burnby's election in October 1456 and 70 at the election of Bishop Lawrence Booth in

---

[1] E.g., *Dur. Acct. Rolls* III, ii; D. Knowles and R. N. Hadcock, *Medieval Religious Houses: England and Wales* (London, 1953), p. 64; J. C. Russell, 'The Clerical Population of Medieval England', *Traditio* II (1944), 187, 190.

[2] Thus the novices professed in 1455 (*Liber Vitae*, fo. 75r) had no voice at the election of a prior in October 1456 (*Dur. Obit. Rolls*, p. 92); on this issue see *Letters of Richard Fox*, ed. P. S. and H. M. Allen (Oxford, 1929), pp. 79–80.

September 1457.[1] These figures may be supplemented by the less complete schedules of Durham monks returned before episcopal or archiepiscopal visitations of the house in July 1408 (58 monks), January 1438 (63 monks), and March 1449 (60 monks).[2] After making allowances here for residents at Coldingham and Oxford, it is abundantly clear that the total strength of the Durham community in the first half of the fifteenth century was rarely much below or above 70. The profession of a group of 6 to 8 novices in a particular year might raise the total higher than this figure, but the deaths of older monks in subsequent months soon restored the regular number.

Such numerical stability appears to have been maintained until the Dissolution, for there were 66 monks present at the elections of Priors Bell and Castell in 1464 and 1494 respectively, 74 at that of Hugh Whitehead in 1520, and 66 again in 1539.[3] Far from undergoing severe numerical decline at the end of the middle ages, the community of Saint Cuthbert maintained its membership at a consistently high level and never suffered from a serious problem of recruitment. Admittedly Durham, like the great majority of English monasteries, had accepted a larger number of monks in earlier centuries. The speed and scale with which the group of 23 monks summoned to Durham from Jarrow and Wearmouth by Bishop William of Saint Calais in 1083 expanded their numerical size remains a matter for conjecture, as only in the thirteenth century does some evidence on the subject begin to survive. According to a statute approved by the Durham chapter in 1235, a deliberate attempt was then being made to maintain 70 resident monks at the mother house and no less than 30 others at Coldingham.[4] But by the close of the thirteenth century, the total number of Durham monks had certainly dropped below 100, to 90 at the election of Bishop

[1] Reg. III, fos. 22–3, 213; Loc. XIII, no. 11; Reg. IV, fo. 46; 1.7. Pont., no. 17; *Reg. Langley* II, 117–19; *Dur. Obit. Rolls*, p. 92.

[2] *Reg. Langley* I, 67–8; *Visitations of the Diocese and Province of York* (ed. A. H. Thompson in *Miscellanea* II, Surtees Soc. CXXVII, 1916), pp. 223–6; Reg. IV, fo. 69.

[3] Reg. IV, fo. 159v; Reg. V, fos. 24–5, 184–5; S. L. Greenslade, 'The Last Monks of Durham Cathedral Priory', *Durham University Journal* XLI (1948–9), 112, supplementing and correcting D. Hay, 'The Dissolution of the Monasteries in the Diocese of Durham', *Arch. Ael.*, Fourth Series, XV (1938), 72–3.

[4] Symeon, *Hist. Ecc. Dun.*, p. 122; *Scrip. Tres*, p. xliii.

Robert of Holy Island in 1274 and to 85 at that of Bishop Bek nine years later.[1] During the first half of the fourteenth century there is further evidence of gradual decline. Ninety-four monks received individual absolution from Bishop Bek's sentences of excommunication in 1310, but only 81 were listed at the time of Bishop Bury's visitation in January 1343, and 73 at the election of Bishop Hatfield in 1345.[2] As we have already seen, the size of the community of Saint Cuthbert was never to fall much lower than this last figure during the remainder of its existence. The Black Death did not entail a permanent reduction in the number of Durham's monks; and one of the most remarkable features of the monastery's history in the later middle ages was its ability to maintain a steady complement of 70 religious against all the apparent economic odds.

Of the 70 monks of Durham, approximately 30 were dispersed and settled in the monastery's cells.[3] It need therefore occasion no surprise that when the convent issued letters appointing proctors at the Roman Curia in October 1418, June 1422 and June 1425, the number of brethren – including Prior Wessington himself – then present in the Durham chapter-house was 46, 43 and 42 respectively.[4] Twenty years later 36 monks appealed from Durham in January 1445 against the contumacy of their fellow, William Partrike, and 42 witnessed his reconciliation in April 1446.[5] Both before and after, as well as during, Wessington's priorate the number of monk residents at the mother house stood at this same average figure of 40. A stray list of monks which can be dated on internal evidence to the early 1390s provides the names of 41 monks, while in 1449 there were 39 religious resident at Durham, of whom seven were novices.[6] All claustral monks at Durham received terminal money oblations from the feretrar and commoner; and that each of these two obedientiaries rarely provided much more or much less than £25 per annum to their colleagues during the early fifteenth century is another argument for numerical stability within the convent.[7] It was therefore

[1] *Historians of the Church of York* (Rolls Series, 1879–94), III, 190–9; *Records of Antony Bek* (Surtees Soc. CLXII, 1953), p. 182.

[2] Misc. Chrs., no. 5985; Fraser, *Antony Bek*, p. 175; *Reg. Richard of Bury*, pp. 154–5; Misc. Chrs., no. 2636.

[3] See below, p. 300 n. 1.   [4] Reg. III, fos. 62, 96, 113.

[5] Reg. IV, fos. 16v, 27v.   [6] Misc. Chrs., no. 6862; Reg. IV, fo. 69.

[7] Feretrar, 1397–1446; Commoner, 1416–42; cf. *Dur. Acct. Rolls* II, 457–8.

slightly optimistic or disingenuous of the prior and chapter in 1454 to present themselves to Pope Nicholas V as a resident community of '*quinquaginta vel circa religiosi*'.[1] But after serving its dependencies, the monastery of Durham was still left with a numerical strength comparable to that of Westminster, Gloucester, Norwich or Worcester, and not so much less than the largest English Benedictine houses, St Albans, Bury St Edmunds and Christ Church, Canterbury. In a century when the most famous and sizable Cistercian monastery, Fountains Abbey, could only boast a population of 35 (in 1449), Durham Priory was undoubtedly one of the ten largest religious communities in England.[2]

The maintenance of a steady total of 70 or so monks, of whom only 40 were normally resident at the mother house, was not of course the result of chance but rather the effect of a deliberate recruitment policy. On the one hand, it was undoubtedly believed that the size of one's monastery was a genuine reflection upon its spiritual welfare; on the other, no prior of Durham was expected to raise the number of his monks to a point beyond which the resources of the convent would be unable to sustain them. The inevitable result of this dilemma was that the prior and chapter of fifteenth-century Durham practised a thoroughly conservative admissions policy aimed at replacing one dead colleague by a new one. To do otherwise was to risk immediate censure: one of Prior Wessington's immediate predecessors was criticised at a Black Monk visitation of the convent for tonsuring only 8 novices when 26 monks had recently died. But Wessington himself could be safely praised at the end of his life for clothing 69 monks with the habit during the thirty years of his priorate: by doing so, he had maintained the size of the community at its now traditional level.[3] Given the operation of such a system it follows that a sudden increase in the number of novices at Durham is much more likely to be a sign of heavy mortality among existing monks than of genuine expansion: Prior John Fossor admitted 120 monks to the convent in a period

[1] *Scrip. Tres*, p. cccxxx.
[2] *Letters from English Abbots to the Chapter at Cîteaux, 1442–1521* (Camden Fourth Series IV, 1967), p. 22; *Lincoln Visitations* III, 83–9; *Historia et Cartularium Monasterii Sancti Petri Gloucestriae* (Rolls Series, 1863–7), III, xxxii, xlviii; Knowles and Hadcock, *Medieval Religious Houses*, pp. 61, 66, 72, 75, 80, 81.
[3] Pantin, *Chapters* III, 83; Loc. I, nos. 8, 9; *Dur. Obit. Rolls*, p. 72.

(1341–74) only slightly longer than Wessington's priorate, but one which coincided with the worst ravages of the Black Death.[1] As the normal death-rate in the fifteenth-century convent was considerably less severe (about 24 deaths in every decade), the convent's primary obligation was to recruit a group of six to eight novices every three or four years. This process can fortunately be studied in some detail thanks to the survival of the celebrated Durham *Liber Vitae*. As this 'excellent fine book . . . did lye on the high altar' of the cathedral church, there can be no reasonable doubt that the names of the Durham monks recorded on its 70th and 75th folios form genuine profession lists and are a complete guide to the names of all the monks who entered the religious life in the late fourteenth and early fifteenth centuries. After a group of novices had made their profession to the prior, their names were entered in the *Liber Vitae* (probably by the feretrar who retained the profession slips themselves in an aumbry) and so preserved for this world and the next, even in the event of future apostacy.[2]

Of the 139 monks who became monks of Durham between 1383 and 1446, all but 7 bore the six thoroughly conventional Christian names of either John, William, Thomas, Robert, Richard or Henry.[3] Except in the case of the solitary '*Georgius*' (George Cyther), a second or surname was therefore an essential aid to identification, both in the *Liber Vitae* and in the administrative records of the monastery. In the late thirteenth and early fourteenth centuries the second names of nearly all Durham monks had been toponymics and it seems probable if not certain that at this period such names pro-

---

[1] *Scrip. Tres*, p. 134.

[2] *Liber Vitae*, fos. 70, 75r; *Rites*, p. 16. It is tempting to suppose that the prior himself entered the names of his monks in the *Liber Vitae* but at least four different hands can be detected between 1416 and 1446. Compare *Reg. John Whethamstede* (Rolls Series, 1872–3), II, 72–3, where the abbot of St Albans is said to have been dressed '*in pontificalibus*' when he received the profession of his monks at the high altar.

[3] I.e. John 33%; William, 23%; Thomas, 21%; Robert, 8%; Richard 8%; and Henry, 2%. The comparative percentages for the names of all 855 recorded late medieval Durham monks (see Prof. S. L. Greenslade's index cards deposited at the Prior's Kitchen) are 26, 19, 14, 10, 9 and 3 respectively. These were also the commonest names of Westminster monks, York freemen and members of the English parliamentary commons in the fifteenth century: see E. H. Pearce, *The Monks of Westminster* (Cambridge, 1916), p. 36; *Reg. York Freemen* I, 102–224; J. C. Wedgwood (ed.), *History of Parliament, 1439–1509*, I (London, 1936), xvii.

vided a genuine indication of their place of origin.[1] By the early
fifteenth century this was no longer necessarily the case. The pre-
position 'de' between Christian name and toponymic went completely out of use soon after 1400, while a fifth of the monks received
at Durham between 1383 and 1446 bore family or occupational
names. Although a family name may sometimes have been retained
to avoid confusion between monks of the same village or town
(most obviously Durham itself), this was by no means always so.
There was no Durham monk called Brancepeth in this period, but
John Oll, a native of the barony there, was known by his father's
name throughout his religious life.[2] It is also more than probable
that some names which appear to be indications of provenance were
in reality family names held by descendants of immigrants to the
city and neighbourhood of Durham. Any generalisations based on
inferring places of origin from surnames derived from place-names
would therefore be of doubtful value; but it is not, in any case, surprising that two-thirds of the monastic toponymics relate to villages
in the more densely populated central and eastern parts of Durham
county. Many monks bore surnames deriving from places in Yorkshire (Crayk, Howden, Pocklington, Rypon) or Northumberland
(Corbridge, Hexham, Rothbury, Tynemouth) and a very few may
conceivably have come from areas west of the Pennines (Appleby,
Blackburn, Brogham, Lytham). There were naturally no Scots
among the monks of Durham and probably, on the admittedly
dubious argument from the toponymics, no recruits from midland
and southern England. Nor is there any very obvious correlation
between the monastic surnames and places where the convent is
known to have held property; Canon Pearce's suggestion that the
great majority of Westminster monks were recruited by the abbot
and obedientiaries on their circuits of their estates can hardly be
applied with confidence to Durham, where not one member of the
community can be proved to have entered the monastery in this
way.[3] But one main conclusion, however imperfectly documented,

---

[1] D. Robinson, *Beneficed Clergy in Cleveland and the East Riding, 1306–40* (Borthwick
Papers, No. 37, 1969), p. 15. See, for a late and famous example of this common
practice, '*Johannes a solo nativitatis Whethamstede, a paterna vero origine Bostok*'
(B.M., Cotton MS., Nero D. VII, fo. 27).

[2] Reg. IV, fo. 34.

[3] Pearce, *Monks of Westminster*, p. 38.

seems incontrovertible. Like nearly every large English monastery for which evidence survives, the inmates of Durham Priory were almost all drawn from a rural area within a radius of thirty or forty miles from the convent. The monks of Saint Cuthbert in the fifteenth century may not have felt it necessary as in the past to conspire to exclude recruits 'born beyond the Trent or other fixed limits' precisely because such conspiracy was no longer necessary.[1]

The Durham evidence also throws some fitful light on the important but still largely mysterious problem of the social origins of the late medieval monk. Despite the lack of direct references to paternity, it seems reasonably clear that most of the Durham brethren came from the middle ranks of urban and rural society, and were men whose family status was – to use the contemporary term – that of *valecti*.[2] The argument *ex silentio* makes it improbable that more than a very few Durham monks were, like John Wessington himself, members of a cadet line of a county gentry family. On the other hand, the prior and chapter appear to have enforced the canonical disqualifications of illegitimate birth and servile origin with a good deal of rigour. Any Durham monk defamed of being 'a bondman and nott of fre condicion' still felt it necessary to go to very great pains indeed to clear himself from the allegation.[3] As in other English monasteries, it seems likely that an increasing number of monks were being recruited from burgess stock. One or two Durham monks are known to have been related to merchants,[4] while many others carried names which associate them with the city's clerical and notarial families (Rackett, Rihall, Bonour) and the convent's tenants in Elvet (Bell, Dautre, Ford, Forster, Hatfield). That so many mothers, fathers and sisters of Durham monks accepted places in the monastery's almshouses as well as small gifts of money from the obedientiaries is itself an indication that they were not people of

---

[1] Loc. vii, no. 4*; Fraser, *Antony Bek*, p. 171.

[2] In 1446 John Oll was said to be '*a valectis valencioribus*' of the barony of Brancepeth (*Scrip. Tres*, p. cclxxxii).

[3] Reg. Parv. iii, fo. 8; Reg. iv, fo. 34.

[4] Thomas Nesbitt's uncle was a Hull wine-merchant (Bursar, 1429/30, 1432/33, Empcio Vini); William Gervace was probably related to the Durham spicer, John Gervace (Bursar, 1438–43, Expense Prioris). For the popularity of the monastic life as a career for the younger sons of merchants, see for example the will of the York mayor, Thomas Bracebridge, proved in 1437 (Borthwick Institute, York; Probate Register III, fo. 487).

great substance.[1] The case of John Oll's mother who lived at
Brancepeth until her husband's death, when she moved to Durham
with all her goods may have been quite representative.[2]

Only two Durham monks are known to have been sponsored by
powerful lay patrons during their early days at the convent. In 1441
the Earl of Northumberland wrote to Wessington asking him to
further the interests of Richard Bell, and two years later he asked the
prior to send the young Thomas Holme to Durham College as soon
as possible.[3] The really important patron, and the agent through
whom most boys were induced to enter religion, was undoubtedly
the Durham monk himself; it was he who normally recommended
candidates for the habit to his prior. It follows that in this sense the
monastery of Durham may be regarded as a genuinely self-
perpetuating corporation. Some members of the community can be
proved to have been blood-relatives and this is likely to have been
true of many others. Robert Blacklaw, William Kyblesworth and
John Fishburn, at Durham College in the 1390s, were all kinsmen,
while in April 1441 Wessington referred to the young monk
William Birden as a relative of Richard Barton, prior of Stamford.[4]
Besides their kindred, Durham monks appear to have pressed for the
reception into the community of those young clerks whose main
function had previously been to assist at the celebration of masses.[5]
In the fourteenth century one claustral monk at Durham is known to
have helped to support two secular students at Oxford while other
boys were granted exhibitions from the priory of Finchale.[6] Robert
Blacklaw, warden of Durham College, sent John Fishburn, a youth
of this sort, to Prior Hemingburgh with the request that he should
be admitted to the monastery provided that he had a tuneful voice
and '*voluerit monachari*'.[7] No prior of Durham appears to have
objected to this type of recruitment which had the obvious advantage of ensuring a steady supply of novices for each of whom some
senior monk could vouch.

[1] See, for example, Thomas Lawson's gift of half a mark to his father, recorded in
his account as cellarer (Misc. Chrs., no. 6080).   [2] *Scrip. Tres*, p. cclxxx.
[3] Misc. Chrs., no. 5193; Reg. Parv. II, fos. 171–2.
[4] Loc. xxv, no. 37; Reg. Parv. II, fo. 136.   [5] Loc. xxvII, nos. 15, 16.
[6] W. A. Pantin, 'Letters from Durham Registers, *c.* 1360–1390', in *Oxford Formularies* I (Oxford Historical Society, New Series, IV, 1942), 235–6; *Finchale Priory*,
p. 29.   [7] Loc. xxv, no. 37.

Whatever the influence of the patronage of elder monks, the common gateway into the religious life at Durham was education at the convent's grammar school. This school, usually known as the almonry school, was ruled by a secular master who taught not only 'the poor children of the Aumery' but also the sons of county gentlemen, lodged in the city and sometimes in the prior's apartments.[1] Although the grammar school itself and the stipend of its master was the responsibility of the almoner, the boys themselves were admitted only after examination by a small monastic committee consisting of the prior, sub-prior and three senior monks.[2] The majority of the scholars of the almonry were nominated by individual monks, and the central place of this practice in the scheme of monastic recruitment emerges clearly from a diffinition made before chapter in 1446, '*quod Pueri Elemosinarie admittantur de cetero primo et principaliter de cognatis et propinquis monachorum infra morancium, et hoc habiliores ad monachatum*'.[3] There could be no more explicit confirmation, both of the prevalence of blood-ties in the monastery and of Professor Knowles's suggestion that 'these clerks (of the almonry) probably themselves became monks far more often than he records suggest'.[4] Priors Wessington and Ebchester both recalled in later years their education at the convent's grammar school, but whether they were there as children of alms or were supported by family and patrons it is impossible to determine.[5] The reference in Warden Blacklaw's letter to a good singing voice as a qualification for a Durham monk makes it probable that several of the eight boys of the convent's small but flourishing song-school also became monks of Durham. No doubt 'exquisite skil in musicke' was as

---

[1] That the convent's almonry and grammar school were the same institution emerges clearly from a dispute of *c.* 1450 with the master of a quite distinct Durham school, the grammar school founded by Bishop Langley (Loc. II, no. 4). A. F. Leach's account of Durham schools in *V.C.H. Durham* I, 365–73, is not altogether satisfactory. For the gratitude of Richard Russell, Mayor of York in 1421 and 1430, to the monks of Durham who sustained him in his youth see *Testamenta Eboracensia* II, 55.

[2] Jesus College, Cambridge, MS. 41, fo. 169v (Durham chapter diffinition of 1416). Cf. the very similar arrangement described by S. Evans, 'Ely Almonry Boys and Choristers in the Later Middle Ages', *Studies presented to Sir Hilary Jenkinson*, ed. J. Conway Davies (Oxford, 1957), p. 159.

[3] Loc. XXVII, no. 15, memb. 3.

[4] Knowles, *Rel. Orders* II, 296.   [5] Loc. II, no. 4; Loc. XXI, no. 23.

important a qualification for entry into the pre-Dissolution monastery as it was for the later 'Canonists in the Cathedrall church of
Durham'.[1]

On the assumption that the great majority of Durham monks
entered religious life after education at the convent's almonry school,
it is probable that they made their profession in the late teens or early
twenties. The case of Master John Kyngton who became a monk of
Christ Church, Canterbury, in 1410 shows that it was still possible
for a secular clerk to take the habit towards the end of his career;[2]
but if there had been many such elderly recruits to the fifteenth-
century Durham community, it is legitimate to suppose that they
would have left some trace among the convent's records. By the
same argument it seems certain that although several Durham
monks left the house to enter a stricter religious order, members of
other monasteries were no longer ever transferred to Durham. On
the rare occasions when the age of a Durham monk can be known,
the result is as might be expected. The three successive priors of
Durham, John Hemingburgh, John Wessington and William
Ebchester, were aged twenty-three, almost twenty and twenty-one
respectively when they began to live '*in monachatu*'.[3] The traditional
English Benedictine rule that monks should not enter religion before
their nineteenth birthday allowed for exceptions in special circumstances.[4] Five Durham monks (Richard Bell, Thomas Heppell,
Thomas Nesbitt, William Seton, John Wycliffe) who received
letters of dispensation to holy orders when in their twenty-second
year, can be shown to have made their professions when sixteen,
seventeen, or eighteen.[5] But there is no trace at Durham of the
admission of monks at a younger age, the fifteen or even twelve
encountered at St Albans and Christ Church, Canterbury.[6]

---

[1] *Dobsons Drie Bobbes*, p. 5.

[2] Emden II, 1,076.

[3] Loc. I, nos. 8, 9; *Dur. Obit. Rolls*, pp. vii, 64, 72.

[4] Pantin, *Chapters* I, 99. Cf. W. Lyndwood, *Provinciale, etc.* (Oxford, 1679), p. 200,
for a commentary on the English law that '*Nemo ante 18. annum Monachatum . . .
profiteatur*'.

[5] These ages emerge from a comparison of the date of dispensation with the date of
profession, as recorded in, or inferred from, the *Liber Vitae*: see Reg. III, fo. 62;
Reg. Parv. II, fos. 65–6, 72, 75; *Reg. Langley* I, 170–1.

[6] *Reg. John Whethamstede* (Rolls Series, 1872–73), II, 90; *Ninth Report of Royal Commission on Historical Manuscripts* (1883–4), Part I, Appendix, pp. 127–8.

It is not always clear whether the monks of Durham considered their religious life to have begun on the day of their profession or at the time when they were first clothed with the monastic habit. In practice, the two ceremonies were rarely separated by a long interval at Durham and the Benedictine statutes requiring exactly a year's probationary period were tacitly ignored, as at Christ Church and St Albans where the '*Professio*' usually followed the '*Rasura mona-chorum*' after a few months only.[1] Between 21 May and 4 September 1414, John Barton, the Durham chamberlain, provided six new monks with their clothes under the heading in his account of *Rastura noviciorum*; these same six monks were professed before the high altar as early as 28 June of the same year.[2] To judge from the account rolls of the chamberlain and other obedientiaries, the 'clothing' and ton-suring of the novice was an occasion more celebrated in the cloister than the profession ceremony itself. Monks were apparently always admitted into the religious life at Durham in groups, usually of six or eight, a practice which was common elsewhere and had the advantage of producing a convenient unit for teaching purposes during the noviciate. Accordingly, every three or four years the chamberlain was called upon to issue the new monks with their clothes and vestments. In 1441, for instance, there were eight entrants to the monastery, each of whom received two under-shirts (*stamina*), two pairs of drawers, two head-caps, one pair of gaiters (*tribuli*), two pairs of slippers, two pairs of blankets, one hood, one cowl, one monk's frock, one white and one black tunic as well as an extra cowl '*pro ludis*' and two pairs of boots. These items comprised the stan-dard dress of the claustral monk at Durham and most were made by the convent's tailors from worsted and linen cloth usually bought at York.[3] The young monks already wore this regular costume when they made their professions to the prior. Although *Le Convenit* of 1229 had reserved to future bishops of Durham the right to confirm professions already made to the prior,[4] there is no evidence that either

---

[1] *Chronicle of John Stone, Christ Church, Canterbury, 1415–71*, ed. W. G. Searle (Cambridge Antiquarian Society's Publications XXXIV, 1902), pp. 192–6; *Reg. John Whethamstede* (Rolls Series, 1872–73), II, 59, 72–3, 190–1. For an apparently con-temporary discussion of the length of the probationary period, see D.C.D., MS. B. IV. 26, fos. 181–2.   [2] Chamberlain, 1414; *Liber Vitae*, fo. 70v.

[3] Chamberlain, 1441/42; cf. Bursar, 1416–46, Garderoba.

[4] *Feodarium Dunelm.*, p. 213.

Bishop Langley, Neville or their suffragans ever availed themselves of this somewhat meaningless privilege.

According to the author of the *Rites of Durham*, 'Ther was alwayes vi novices which went daly to schoule within the house for the space of vii yere'. It is, however, unlikely that in the early fifteenth century the noviciate was quite so long. In one of his letters, William Partrike seems to refer to the ending of his period of tutelage in 1420, after he had been 'vi yheere in the Religion'.[1] But if, as is usually supposed, the saying of his first mass marked the emergence of the young monk '*de custodia*', many Durham novices had an even shorter period of training. Of the six monks professed on 28 June 1414, two (William Crayk and John Lumley) became priests within two years, one (John Mody) within three years and the other two within four years.[2] On the other hand, when the Earl of Northumberland asked Wessington to send Thomas Holme to Durham College, Oxford, in 1443, the prior refused on the grounds that 'the said Th. Holme has been in the Religion bot a yhere and a half and yhit nor Dekynd ne Subdekyn and noght so sufficiantly grondit in the obseruance of the Religion as it wer expedient, also he is yongest person of the monastery and other of his fellows that was profest with hym ar als sufficient or moore than he is'.[3] Wessington obviously took a personal interest in the progress of his novices, whose studies appear to have been supervised by a number of senior monks rather than one *Magister Noviciorum* as was usual elsewhere and the practice at Durham itself in the early sixteenth century.[4] The novices' small *studia* or carrells, reconstructed during Wessington's priorate, were situated in the west cloister together with a large book-cupboard whose contents suggest that before the end of their schooling the young monks had progressed beyond the study of grammar and were reading commentaries on the Bible as well as selections and summaries of the writings of the Fathers. There were 23 books '*in communi almariolo noviciorum*' in 1395, not a static col-

---

[1] *Rites*, p. 96; Loc. IX, no. 18. For an identical situation at Westminster Abbey see *A House of Kings*, ed. E. Carpenter (London, 1966), p. 93.

[2] See the references to first masses in Hostillar, 1415/16; Almoner, 1415/16; Sacrist, 1416/17; Bursar, 1418/19, Dona et Exennia.

[3] Reg. Parv. II, fo. 171.

[4] The common reference in the Durham obedientiary accounts is to the novices and their masters; but see *Rites*, p. 96; Knowles, *Rel. Orders* II, 232.

lection because books were often transferred to it from the main
monastic library by the convent's chancellor.[1] Among the '*manuales*'
assigned to the novices in 1423 were Hugh of Saint Victor's *De
Arrha Animae*, Bede's commentary on the Proverbs ('*super Parabolas
Solomonis*'), a *libellus* by St Ephraem Syrus as well as other works by
Saint Augustine and Saint Gregory.[2] It is probable that for most
monks the noviciate was the only period of their career when they
were sufficiently free from administrative responsibility to undertake
an intensive course in the reading of the classic religious texts.
Similarly, the strict rules of Benedictine observance requiring full
attendance at divine offices and regular eating in the refectory were
applied to all Durham novices but were frequently relaxed in the
cases of their elder brethren.[3]

An essential feature of the Durham noviciate was the steady progress of the young monk through holy orders so that within five or
six years from his profession he was fully priested and able to celebrate mass at one of the many altars in the cathedral church.[4] The
priors of Durham did not receive licence to confer minor orders on
their monks until 1456,[5] and until then it was always the bishop of
Durham, or more commonly, his suffragan who ordained the
brethren as acolytes, sub-deacons, deacons and priests. Ordinations
in the diocese were normally held four times a year, at the Ember
Days, and the survival of Langley's episcopal register shows that
there was often a group of Durham monks among the candidates for
orders on these occasions. Wessington himself normally presented
his young monks to the bishop, not too onerous a duty as most
ordinations took place in Durham itself, either at the cathedral or in

---

[1] *Catalogi Vet.*, pp. 81–4. Many of the books listed *c.* 1416 in the *Spendement*
catalogue (ibid., pp. 85–116) are noted to have been held by a 'Novicius'.

[2] Bodleian Library, Oxford, Carte MS. 177, fo. 40v. The list is badly mutilated but
the second folio identification shows that these were all books from the monastic
library (*Catalogi Vet.*, pp. 95, 96, 97, 103). The volumes of Hugh of Saint Victor
and Bede are now Bodleian MS. Laud. Misc. 392, and B.M. Harleian MS. 4688
respectively.

[3] Loc. IX, no. 30; a letter from William Partrike at Durham in which he wrote that
'I come to the kerk to all the horis except matyns als vel (*sic*) as any novys doos'.
The Durham novices did, however, occasior ally eat in the solar (Jesus College,
Cambridge, MS. 41, fo. 170).

[4] For the requirement '*Ut Religiosi frequenter confiteantur, et frequenter celebrent*', see
Lyndwood, *Provinciale, etc.*, p. 155.

[5] *C.P.L.* XI (1455–64), p. 109; cf. *Reg. Richard Fox* (Surtees Soc. CXLVII, 1932), p. xxxiv.

the church of Saint Oswald, and only occasionally in Langley's chapel at Bishop Auckland.[1] Not all the novices who professed on the same day became priests at the same time for the age and ability of the individual monk were factors which might affect his progress through the orders. The ordinations of the eight monks who professed together in 1426 or 1427 reveal the characteristic Durham pattern. Four of these novices received orders as acolytes on 20 December 1427, as sub-deacons on 28 February 1428, as deacons a few months later, and as priests on 18 December 1428. Three others also eventually received priestly orders within the Durham diocese but had to wait, presumably because of their youth, until 1429, 1430 and 1431 respectively. The youngest and most talented of the group, Richard Bell, future bishop of Carlisle, was however ordained in the south of England after he had taken up residence at Durham College.[2] But whether at Durham or Oxford, the monk invariably received a money gift of half a mark from one or other of the obedientiaries to celebrate the saying of his first mass and his entry into the full life of the convent.[3]

The career of a claustral monk of Durham, like that of all monks at all times, was subject to the famous command that 'Idleness is the enemy of the soul; the brethren, therefore, must be occupied at stated hours in manual labour, and again at other hours in sacred reading'.[4] No fifteenth-century Durham monk is known to have observed the first of these two rules at all literally; but there are indications that some, if not all, members of the community may have 'studied upon there books euery one in his carrell all the after none unto evensong tyme'. In the nature of things, the evidence for private study and writing on the part of the monks is both tenuous and circumstantial: this is a topic which deserves separate attention.[5] But when the author of the *Rites of Durham* eulogised the late medieval community for being 'neuer Idle', he omitted to mention

---

[1] The common formula in Langley's episcopal register (where the lists of ordinations between 1406 and 1437 are by no means complete) is '*Frater A.B. monachus ecclesie cathedralis Dunelmensis per priorem legitime presentatus*'; see, e.g., *Reg. Langley* IV, 7, 11, 33, 49, 110.

[2] *Reg. Langley* III, 61, 76, 106; IV, 7, 33, 70; Bursar, 1429/30, Dona et Exennia.

[3] Compare the practice at Westminster Abbey (Pearce, *Monks of Westminster*, p. 22).

[4] *The Rule of St Benedict*, ed. J. McCann (London, 1952), p. 111.

[5] See below, Chapter 10.

that there were more prosaic reasons for this than the 'writing of good and goddly wourkes or studying the holie scriptures'.[1] For if some Durham monks could escape temporarily into the worlds of spiritual devotion and academic learning, few avoided the burdens of administrative duty for long. Well over half of the 40 or so monks resident at Durham held a regular office within the monastery, and no monk appears to have secured permanent exemption from service as an obedientiary or an obedientiary's assistant. The welfare of the convent depended absolutely on the efficiency of its own monastic officers; and it was inevitable if sometimes regrettable that the Durham chapter, like Abbot Samson of Bury St Edmunds many years previously, often 'had more praise for good obedientiaries than for good cloister monks'.[2]

The monastic offices of the priory of Durham in the early fifteenth century were of widely different degrees of responsibility, but are most conveniently divided into two groups according to whether or not they were liable to account and audit at the convent's annual chapter in June. Eleven obedientiaries were required to draw up regular account rolls, namely the bursar, cellarer and granator (the three officials entrusted with the general sustenance of the community) as well as the terrar, sacrist, feretrar, almoner, hostillar, chamberlain, commoner and master of the infirmary. Eight of the principal obedientiaries (the bursar, terrar, cellarer, sacrist, hostillar, almoner, chamberlain and commoner) had fellows or '*socii*' who took complete charge of the goods of their office when the senior official was absent from the monastery.[3] The sub-sacrist and sub-feretrar also performed a series of specified duties within the cathedral church throughout the year. Among the many obedientiaries who did not render annual account, and about whose functions and names much less can consequently be known, were the sub-prior, third prior, chancellor (who was also custodian of the library), refectorer, precentor, succentor, two deans of the order, two prior's chaplains and master of the Galilee Chapel. The Officials of the prior's archidiaconal jurisdiction were also often monks as were the *supervisores operum*, deputed at frequent intervals to finance a specific building operation.

[1] *Rites*, pp. 83, 88.
[2] *Chronicle of Jocelin of Brakelond*, ed. H. E. Butler (London, 1949), p. 40.
[3] Loc. XXI, no. 20 (ii).

Leaving the associate office-holders out of account, there were still some twenty-five positions to be filled from the ranks of the community. Most of these were of major importance to the welfare of the house; and the obedientiary system at Durham can be seen to have been as fully developed as in other large English monasteries.[1] According to the traditional custom of the monastery, the prior could appoint and remove the sacrist, hostillar, almoner and chamberlain only in chapter and with the consent of his monks. The commoner was appointed by the sub-prior and convent without the prior's consent, but all other obedientiaries were selected by the prior alone.[2] As so many officers were needed, Prior Wessington had little range of choice when appointing to the more unpopular obediences; in 1432 he was forced to make the completely unsuitable Thomas Lawson bursar of the convent, apparently because no one of greater ability could be induced to accept the position.[3] Many English monasteries in the later middle ages attempted to solve such problems by concentrating a number of separate obediences in the hands of the abbot or a few all-powerful monks. In 1429, for example, Abbot Whethamstede removed Robert Ware from the offices of kitchener, refectorer and infirmarer to those of cellarer, bursar, sub-cellarer and almoner; and at the same house of St Albans a generation later William Wallingford held so many offices that he was known as the 'general official'.[4] Prior Wessington did not encourage similar developments at Durham where only a very few obediences were ever held by the same monk. The offices of feretrar and third prior were usually combined, as were those of Official (when a monk and not a secular) and chancellor. In January 1438 William Dalton was chancellor, Official and almoner, but there is no other known case of an early fifteenth-century Durham monk holding

---

[1] Several of the more specialised offices encountered elsewhere do not appear as distinct obediences at Durham, where there was, for example, no anniversarian, penitentiary, bartoner, hordarian, curtarian or pittancer. Cf. *Compotus Rolls of the Obedientiaries of St Swithun's Priory, Winchester*, ed. G. W. Kitchin (Hampshire Record Society, 1892), pp. 31–3; R. A. L. Smith, *Canterbury Cathedral Priory* (Cambridge, 1943), pp. 36–40; R. H. Snape, *English Monastic Finances in the later Middle Ages* (Cambridge, 1926), pp. 29–33; Pearce, *The Monks of Westminster*, pp. 193–213.

[2] Loc. XXI, no. 20 (ii).　　　　　　[3] See below, p. 285.

[4] *Annales J. Amundesham* (Rolls Series, 1870–1), I, 42; Cf. *Lincoln Visitations* III, 76–83; Knowles, *Rel. Orders* III, 8, 65, 67.

more than two major offices.[1] The same man was however often simultaneously terrar and hostillar; this particular association survived until the Dissolution and so explains the otherwise puzzling description by the *Rites of Durham* of the terrar as the keeper of the 'geste Haule'.[2]

Any enquiry into the value of the religious life as conducted at Durham and elsewhere in the later middle ages is soon confronted with the central problem as to whether the claims of the *Opus Dei* were reconcilable with the administrative responsibilities obligatory on the majority of the monks. It has usually been supposed that they were not, and that the more able members of English religious communities were forced 'to leave the word of God and serve tables'.[3] On the same general grounds, it has been suggested that more than two-thirds of the early fourteenth-century Durham chapter can have attended the Hours only intermittently.[4] This seems an unduly pessimistic view, although the study of obedientiary accounts and of diffinitions made at annual chapters leaves no doubt as to the reality of the strains and burdens of office.[5] Whether or not a particular obedientiary was free to attend divine services regularly depended to a large extent on his own inclinations and the ability and honesty of his clerks and servants.[6] Presence of monastic officers at matins was the most contested issue. One of the *comperta* of Bishop Neville's 1442 visitation was that sixteen obedientiaries were excused from matins although only one, the terrar, should rightfully have been exempted. The reply made by Wessington and the senior monks to this charge was '*quod tantum sex singulis noctibus, exceptis principalibus, excusantur*'.[7] The six obedientiaries in question appear to have been

[1] Reg. III, fo. 213.

[2] Terrar, 1401–22; Hostillar, 1406–23; cf. *Rites*, p. 99.

[3] A. H. Thompson, *The English Clergy and their Organization in the Later Middle Ages* (Oxford, 1947), p. 175.

[4] J. Scammell, 'The Case of Geoffrey Burdon, Prior of Durham (1313–1321)', *Revue Bénédictine*, LXVIII (1958), 235.

[5] The functions of the Durham obedientiaries corresponded very closely with those of their counterparts in other monasteries and no attempt will be made to describe them in detail here: but see below, pp. 253–5.

[6] Loc. XXI, no. 20 (ii). The Durham chapter diffinitions of 1446 and 1464 (Loc. XXVII, nos. 15, 29) deal at great length with the problems created by untrustworthy monastic servants; but there is, of course, no answer to the crucial question of the number of hours per week involved in the management of a Durham obedience.

[7] 1.9. Pont., no. 3; 1.8. Pont., no. 2.

the bursar, cellarer, hostillar, almoner, sacrist and chamberlain, each of whom paid half a mark every year to their secular deputies or '*vicarii in ecclesia*'. As well as these six major obedientiaries, the two or three doctors of divinity resident in the monastery were excused matins as were the aged and infirm.[1] On the assumption that the monks' defence before Bishop Neville in 1442 was truthful, the eminently respectable number of twenty to twenty-five monks must have been present at the night Office. The Hours from prime to compline were probably less well attended, and only monks with no administrative duties whatsoever can have been able to recite all the Offices.

At Durham as elsewhere any attempt to compile a detailed time-table of the monastic day is fraught with difficulty because of the complicated variations caused by seasonal change and the different grading of feasts. But although no full description of the late medieval Durham horarium survives, it is possible to reconstruct its main out-lines from a comparison of the scattered and sometimes misleading references in the *Rites of Durham* with a short summary written by a Durham monk, Richard Segbroke, in or shortly before 1396.[2] Segbroke's description suggests that the Durham horarium corre-sponded closely to that of Saint Mary's Abbey, York,[3] and has the advantage of providing the times of the main Offices in terms of clock hours. This may be because the first mechanical clock seems to have appeared at Durham Priory in the late fourteenth century (the period of the famous Salisbury cathedral clock); it was in regular use, and frequent need of repair, during Wessington's priorate.[4] Accord-ing to Segbroke, the Durham monk's daily routine invariably com-menced with matins, which began at midnight and probably occupied at least an hour: Prior Wessington's detailed report to Bishop Langley of the disastrous flash of lightning which destroyed the cathedral's central tower on Corpus Christi Day in 1429 reveals that the monks were then still at matins in the choir shortly before the

[1] Loc. IX, no. 5.
[2] B.M. Arundel MS. 507, fos. 90v, 92v; cf. *Rites* (which seems to describe the winter rather than summer Durham horarium), pp. 22, 82, 86–7, 93–4, 98; Knowles, *Rel. Orders* II, 238–9.
[3] *The Ordinal and Customary of the Abbey of Saint Mary, York* (Henry Bradshaw Society, 1936–51), III, pp. v–xi.
[4] Sacrist 1406/7; 1409/10; *Scrip. Tres*, p. cclxxiii; *Dur. Acct. Rolls* II, 384, 403, 410.

first hour after midnight.[1] In summer, and on Feasts of Three but not Twelve Lessons, prime followed at 6.0 a.m. or 6.30 a.m., probably occupying thirty minutes or more. Minor or Chapter mass, the equivalent of the *missa matutinalis* at Saint Mary's, York, or the morrow mass elsewhere, was sung at nine o'clock and may have lasted for about an hour as it was immediately followed by the daily chapter meeting in the chapter-house at ten.[2] This too occupied, at least in theory, approximately an hour and was succeeded by high mass at eleven. Dinner was taken shortly before noon, and the monks were then allowed to rest until the bell sounded at two o'clock for nones. Vespers began at four, to be followed by a further interval before collation or supper between 6.0 and 7.0 p.m. Compline and the *Salve Regina* ended the day, after which the community was supposed to retire, although it was alleged in 1442 '*quod, finito completorio, multi monachi transiunt in gardinum Abathie et alia loca, et ibidem ludunt et vacant insolenciis*'.[3] In the winter months Segbroke noted that the morning Offices were retarded and the evening ones advanced by an hour or sometimes less; even then collation was not taken earlier than six o'clock, a much more likely time than that suggested by the author of the *Rites of Durham* who remembered that supper was always over 'at fyve of the clocke' and that all monks went to bed shortly after the singing of the *Salve* at 6.0 p.m.[4]

Although the Durham calendars show the extent to which the convent observed the feasts and obits of local saints and benefactors,[5] the liturgical customs of the monastery differed in degree rather than kind from those common to the majority of large English Benedictine houses.[6] The generalisation that 'the Mass, though not form-

---

[1] Reg. Parv. II, fo. 39; *Scrip. Tres*, p. ccxvii.

[2] Confirmed by 2.7. Pont., nos. 12, 13 (episcopal citations of 1442).

[3] 1.9. Pont., no. 3.   [4] *Rites*, pp. 86, 268.

[5] No Durham calendar exactly contemporaneous with Wessington's priorate appears to survive but a late thirteenth-century breviary from Coldingham (B.M. Harleian MS. 4664) received fifteenth-century additions at Durham, while B.M. Harleian MS. 1804 incorporates a calendar and list of obits written *c.* 1500. Cf. *English Benedictine Kalendars After A.D. 1100*, ed. F. Wormald (Henry Bradshaw Society, 1939), I, 161–79; *Liber vitae ecclesiae Dunelmensis*, ed. J. Stevenson (Surtees Soc. XIII, 1841), pp. 149–52.

[6] Cf. *The Ordinal and Customary of the Abbey of St. Mary, York*, III, p. ii, where it is suggested that 'Norman liturgical customs as revised by Lanfranc were established at Durham from the beginning'.

ing part of the Choir Office, was intimately connected with it and is the centre around which the whole revolved'[1] seems completely applicable to the religious life of late medieval Durham. As well as the two masses said at the high altar every morning (the minor and major mass) there were daily masses of the Holy Spirit, of Our Lady and *de Cimiterio*.[2] The Mass of Our Lady, sung in the Galilee Chapel, was an especially elaborate rite and the professional *cantor* or choirmaster of the cathedral was required to attend it each day with his eight choristers and sing '*ad eandem missam planum cantum sive organicum*'.[3] The choirmaster's indentures of appointment also obliged him to be present, when requested, at masses and vespers in the choir, where he played the organ and led his boys through the intricacies of 'playnsange, prikenot, faburdon, dischaunte et countre'.[4]

Splendid though the great liturgical set-pieces of the communal *Opus Dei* must have been, by the early fifteenth century they formed only a part of the individual monk's religious commitments. Like the other sixteen late medieval English cathedrals, the monastic church at Durham can be happily compared to 'a great ship with many decks or departments'.[5] The subdivision of the cathedral into a great number of separate religious compartments is indeed the single most striking impression left by a reading of the *Rites of Durham*. Throughout the later middle ages a bewildering variety of altars were being dedicated or re-dedicated, with the result that by the Dissolution there were over twenty, mostly sited in the transepts and the Chapel of the Nine Altars.[6] The celebration of masses at the great majority of these altars was the responsibility of the monks

---

[1] *The Monastic Breviary of Hyde Abbey: Vol. VI, Introduction to the English Monastic Breviaries*, ed. J. B. L. Tolhurst (Henry Bradshaw Society, 1942), p. 141.

[2] Misc. Chrs., no. 2645.   [3] Reg. III, fo. 137v.

[4] The meaning of these terms has been considered by Professor Knowles (*Rel. Orders* III, 17) who makes valuable use of the indentures between the convent and its choirmasters printed by Raine in *Scrip. Tres*, pp. cccxv, ccclxxxvi, cccxcviii, ccccxiii. The earliest indenture of the series (unprinted by Raine) is of 22 December 1430 and uses almost the same vocabulary (Reg. III, fos. 137v–138). Cf. Dom A. Hughes, 'Medieval Polyphony at Durham', *Relics of Saint Cuthbert*, ed. Battiscombe, pp. 192–201; F. L. Harrison, *Music in Medieval Britain* (London, 1958), pp. 187–9, 210.   [5] E. F. Jacob, *The Fifteenth Century* (Oxford, 1961), p. 289.

[6] Two altars were dedicated within the cathedral on 23 November 1414, in honour of Saints Oswald and Aidan, and Saints Nicholas and Katherine, respectively (*English Benedictine Kalendars After A.D. 1100*, I, 163–4); cf. *Rites*, passim; *Scrip. Tres*, p. 136.

themselves, absolutely and inescapably committed to a ceaseless round of intercession for the living and the dead. Nor were the monks immune from the obligation to serve a few perpetual, as well as innumerable temporary, chantry foundations within their cathedral church. The reluctance of the community to contemplate the burial of laymen or secular clerks within their church (even after the interment in the nave of Lord Ralph Neville of Raby in 1367) ensured that Durham Cathedral would never be similar in this respect to York Minster with its grand total of at least 56 perpetual chantries. The secular chantry priest was a comparative rarity in the monastic church, with the major exception of the two chaplains who served Bishop Langley's impressive chantry in the Galilee Chapel after its foundation in 1414. The other five perpetual chantries within the cathedral during Wessington's priorate (those of Bishops Hatfield and Skirlaw, Prior Fossor, Richard of Barnard Castle and Lord Neville) had been founded in the previous fifty years and were all served by monks.[1] It followed that the *tabulacio* or 'intablyng' of the names of the monk-priests who were to succeed each other in the saying of masses at these chantries and at particular altars was a significant part of monastic routine, one of the main responsibilities of the sub-prior, precentor and succentor. The chance survival of a list of the monks who served the Neville and Hatfield chantries between March 1422 and November 1426 is particularly instructive just because so little evidence survives at Durham or elsewhere of this very prominent feature of the late medieval religious life.[2] Masses at each of these two chantries were celebrated by one monk on a monthly rota system. As no less than 35 Durham monks were liable to 'intablyng', it followed that a particular brother would serve the Neville chantry during March 1422 and not again until February 1425, the Hatfield chantry in May 1422 and not again for nearly three years. Among the names appearing on these two lists occur those of the current bursar, cellarer, feretrar, granator, almoner and chancellor of the monastery. It appears that only the prior himself, the sub-prior, the terrar and possibly the sacrist were exempted from the saying of mass at these two chantry chapels.

[1] *V.C.H. Durham* I, 371; *Reg. Langley* II, p. 133; *Scrip. Tres*, pp. 131, 134–5, 138, 145; Commoner, 1416/17, 1430/31.
[2] Misc. Chrs., no. 6080 (on the dorse of a granator's account); cf. *Rites*, p. 98.

The regular celebration of minor and private masses was therefore one of the most universal, if one of the least publicised, activities of the late medieval Durham monk. But there were of course innumerable other additions to the *Opus Dei*. Ceremonial processions by the whole convent were an especially common, if inadequately documented, part of the monastic life at Durham. In particular the great Sunday procession in which all the altars in the church as well as the monastic apartments around the cloister were visited in turn and sprinkled with holy water formed a central ritual in the community's routine. Sermons too were regularly demanded from a large number of Durham monks, although only in the case of the most famous and sophisticated exponents of the oratorical art (like Robert Rypon, sub-prior from 1405 to 1420)[1] were their texts thought worthy of preservation. Rypon's sermons were composed in Latin, the language used for official intercourse within the cloister as well as in the community's correspondence with other religious authorities. But there can be no doubt that throughout Wessington's priorate the monks of Durham conversed informally with each other and their servants in a northern version of the English vernacular. It seems probable that, as at Saint Mary's Abbey, York, some attempt had been made to enforce the speaking of French as an alternative to Latin during the latter part of the fourteenth century; but the days when a monk could be made to feel ashamed because of his failure to handle French idioms had certainly passed by the time Wessington became prior in 1416.[2] It was precisely in the second decade of the fifteenth century that the monastic and prior's registers reveal the complete and remarkably abrupt extinction of French as a language of written as well as verbal communication. Henceforward the monks of Durham might eulogise each other in sophisticated Latin of a thoroughly conventional type but would slander each other, rather more significantly, in the English 'langage'.[3]

Although the well-established routines of religious observance at Durham were preserved throughout the early fifteenth century, the

---

[1] Emden III, 1618; Owst, *Preaching in Medieval England*, pp. 52, 145, 215–17; cf. *Scrip. Tres*, pp. cxxxiv–cxxxv.

[2] *The Ordinal and Customary of the Abbey of St Mary, York*, I, 76; Pantin, *Chapters* II, 47, 85; H. Suggett, 'The Use of French in England in the Later Middle Ages', *T.R.H.S.*, Fourth Series, XXVIII (1946), 61–83.

[3] Misc. Chrs., nos. 1055, 1056.

life of the monks there was by no means completely tranquil and harmonious. Besides occasional evidence of faction and intrigue among the community,[1] there survive references to several distressing scandals. Shortly before 1400 Hugh Shirburn had stabbed his sub-prior in the side with a knife while in the monastic precincts and only received papal absolution after the recovery of his victim.[2] Blood was drawn again in 1407 when Thomas Esshe wounded Richard Stockton with a knife at the end of a bitter quarrel in the cloister. Prior Hemingburgh followed the usual practice in such cases and sent Esshe to Rome to secure absolution. Before he left London however, Esshe met a papal nuncio prepared to absolve him immediately on learning that Stockton was not permanently disabled. The monk returned to Durham where on 2 September 1408 Hemingburgh received him back into the community.[3] John Tynemouth, a monk who made his profession in the early 1390s, was responsible for an even more atrocious crime. After stealing monastic property and apostatising for a period in 1408 he was licensed to go to the Curia for the sake of his soul on 9 January 1412. His turbulent career ended with the murder of a fellow monk, William Warner, in 1420. After Tynemouth had confessed his guilt to the bishop's justices, he was imprisoned in the common gaol at Durham until Wessington successfully petitioned Bishop Langley to surrender him '*ad carceres et custodiam dictorum prioris et conventus*' on 27 September 1420. The custody of a monk who had killed one of his own brethren was a great embarrassment to the prior who may have been somewhat relieved that Tynemouth died within six months.[4] A monk who spent a longer period in prison was John Bonour, disqualified from voting at Wessington's election in November 1416 because of his infamous but unspecified acts of disobedience. Bonour was released a few months later and given a room in the monastic infirmary where he died in 1418–19.[5] Two other monks were barred from the election of 5 November 1416 on the grounds of their

[1] Loc. XXI, no. 20; Loc. XXV, no. 152; *Scrip. Tres*, p. cclxxxiii, where Henry Helay confessed to accusing John Oll of being a bondman, 'of malice and nott of goode hert nor goode will'.

[2] Loc. III, no. 44. [3] Loc. III, no. 19; Reg. II, fo. 207.

[4] Reg. II, fo. 206v; Loc. XXVII, no. 3; Bursar, 1420/21, Elemos. Consueta.

[5] Loc. XIII, no. 11; Infirmarer, 1417/18; Bursar, 1418/19, Elemos. Consueta; *Reg. Langley* II, 119.

apostasy and subsequent excommunication. One of these was John Fishwick who was licensed to visit Rome in 1411, left Durham in 1413 and obtained a papal chaplaincy for himself at the Curia in the following spring.[1] His renunciation of the monastic habit appears to have been completely successful for he exchanged a rectory in the diocese of London for the vicarage of Glynde on 14 June 1423.[2] The second apostate in November 1416 was Adam Durham (alias Ponne), another monk who failed to return to the fold. On 11 April 1407 Prior Hemingburgh had commissioned the warden of Durham College, William Appleby, to recapture Durham; before the end of the year he was traced to Burton in Lindsey, but Hemingburgh's attempts to sue for a royal writ against this recalcitrant monk did not procure his return to Durham.[3] His apostasy was still remembered there 35 years later.

Four monks were accused of apostasy from Durham during Wessington's own priorate, two in the early 1420s and two not long before his resignation. Thomas Pomfret was a Durham College fellow in 1421 and left the religious life approximately four years later without apparently ever reappearing at the mother house.[4] John Marlay absconded in 1422 and took refuge in Hexhamshire where the archbishop of York's steward was instructed to apprehend him.[5] Marlay was probably the monk who escaped from imprisonment in the monastery after being 'founden gylty of the horrible synne of sodomye' and was consequently the subject of a letter of censure to Wessington from the Duke of Bedford in Paris.[6] To avoid 'disclaundre and dishonur of your said convent', Bedford urged Wessington to recapture the offender and to punish both him and any other monks found guilty of the same crime 'so sharpely and in suche wise that god mowe be pleised, youre conscience kept and the worship of youre howse and religion sauved and conserved'. Bedford's letter expressed the orthodox attitude towards monastic apostasy as well as homosexuality; but Wessington and his senior monks had understandable doubts about the advisability of attempting to recover men like Pomfret and Marlay who were both regarded

---

[1] Reg. III, fo. 35v; Almoner, 1413/14; *C.P.L.* VI (1404–15), pp. 184, 400.
[2] *Register of Henry Chichele* (Canterbury and York Society, 1937–47), I, 208–9.
[3] Reg. Parv. II, fo. 4; Reg. II, fo. 349: *Scrip. Tres*, pp. cxcix–cc.
[4] Feretrar, 1420/21; 1.9. Pont., no. 3.
[5] Misc. Chrs., no. 6565; Reg. III, fo. 98v.   [6] See below, p. 174.

as '*incorrigibiles*'. In 1442 Wessington admitted to Bishop Neville that he had taken the advice of his fellows '*ad evitanda maiora mala, quod prior non laboraret pro reduccione eorumdem*'.[1] The prior did not, however, regard cases of apostasy at all lightly and took to heart Bishop Neville's injunction of 4 November requiring him to be more diligent '*pro apostatis modernis et futuris reducendis*'.[2] A few weeks later he wrote to Richard Barton, the prior of Stamford, asking him to make enquiries as to the whereabouts of the 'ancient' apostates, presumably Pomfret and Marlay.[3] Wessington had also heard that John Heworth, a monk who had gone to the Curia in 1435 for spiritual reasons and whose transfer to a stricter religious order in Ireland he had licensed on 16 September 1438, was in fact enjoying a cure of souls near Coventry.[4] Barton was instructed to find Heworth and send him back to Durham under custody unless he could produce a papal exemption, in which case this was to be transcribed and dispatched for Wessington's inspection. A further licence to transfer to another religious order, made in the last weeks of Wessington's priorate, led to a very different result. Against the resistance of many Durham monks who believed that he wished to apostatise, Robert Erghowe secured Wessington's permission to enter the order of Friars Preachers at Bamburgh.[5] Unable to secure admission there, he spent fourteen days only under the rule of the prior of the Dominican house at Berwick and then decided he wished to return to Durham. William Ebchester had meanwhile succeeded Wessington as prior and refused to restore the unfortunate Erghowe to his original community despite the appeals of Bishop Neville and the threat of papal intervention.[6]

One other monk left the religious life at Durham between 1416 and 1446, namely Richard Fowne who received a licence from Wessington on 3 December 1435 to migrate to the Carthusian priory at Hull.[7] More spectacular was the attempt by Richard Bell, the

---

[1] I.8. Pont., no. 2.

[2] Misc. Chrs., no. 2645.   [3] Reg. Parv. II, fo. 169.

[4] Reg. III, fos. 196, 228v; Feretrar, 1435/36, 1438/39; *Scrip. Tres*, pp. cclvi–cclvii.

[5] Loc. II, no. 1; Loc. xxv, no. 33.

[6] Misc. Chrs., no. 7111; Loc. xxv, no. 66; Reg. Parv. III, fos. 2, 38; *Scrip. Tres*, pp. cccxxi–cccxxiii.

[7] Reg. III, fo. 196. This type of transfer '*ad artiorem religionem*' had been envisaged by Saint Benedict: *Rule of St. Benedict*, ed. McCann, p. 138.

future prior of Durham and bishop of Carlisle, to secure the priorate of Holy Trinity, York, in 1441. Despite Wessington's permission, the Earl of Northumberland's sponsorship, and royal appointment as prior of Holy Trinity on 13 February 1441, Bell was unable to overcome the resistance of the York monks who had elected one of themselves, John Grene, as their superior a few months previously. A most complex dispute developed in which Bell appealed for confirmation of his appointment to the abbot of Marmoutier in France whose spiritual jurisdiction over this 'alien priory' was still being recognised as late as 1460.[1] Bell finally abandoned his claims to the priorate of Holy Trinity in late 1443 and was restored to the Durham community on 13 December; eighteen months previously Wessington had defended his good name in a letter to the royal chancellor, John Stafford, who had been informed that Bell had stolen monastic property and was guilty of a *lapsus carnis*.[2] Two Durham monks, Thomas Nesbitt in 1434 and Richard Blackburn in 1440, were accused of adultery with Durham women but each was able to find twelve compurgators among his senior colleagues, prepared to swear to his innocence.[3] Nesbitt became prior of Coldingham, and Blackburn sacrist of the monastery in later life; it would be illegitimate, when no evidence of collusion survives, to use the purgation of these two men as evidence of their guilt.[4] In any case, neither the incontinent nor the apostate monk was an uncommon fifteenth-century phenomenon,[5] and it is hardly surprising that religious life at Durham was not without an occasional scandal. On the other hand Bishop Neville's testimonial on 18 April 1444 that the Durham

---

[1] E. Martène, *Histoire de l'abbaye de Marmoutier* II (Mémoires de la Société Archéologique de Touraine xxv, 1875), 319–21, 330–1; J. Solloway, *The Alien Benedictines of York* (Leeds, 1910), p. 278; R. B. Dobson, 'Richard Bell, Prior of Durham (1464–78) and Bishop of Carlisle (1478–95)', *Trans. of Cumberland and Westmorland Antiquarian and Archaeological Society*, New Series, LXV (1965), 188–91.

[2] Reg. Parv. II, fos. 178–9; Reg. III, fos. 267, 269v.

[3] Reg. III, fos. 173v, 250; *Scrip. Tres*, pp. ccxxxix–ccxli.

[4] 'The facts show, however, that the definitely guilty persons did not find it easy to make up the number of compurgators required': Thompson, *The English Clergy*, p. 180.

[5] There seems to have been an especially large number of apostate monks from Christ Church, Canterbury, in the fifteenth century: *Chronicle of John Stone* (Cambridge Antiquarian Society's Publications, xxxiv, 1902), pp. 186–92. See the very interesting file of 55 requests for secular aid against Benedictine apostates (among whom no Durham monk figures) in P.R.O. Chancery Warrants, C.81, no. 1786.

monks were, as far as he knew, free from the sins of the flesh[1] must obviously be treated with some reservation in the light of the preceding cases. However, the most serious of the crimes appear to date from the period between 1400 and 1425 and it may not be completely fanciful to suppose that the moral temper of the convent improved during the middle years of Wessington's priorate. If so, much of the credit must go to the sub-prior, Stephen Howden, who held his office for the exceptionally long period of over twenty years from 1420.

Near the end of his life, the Durham monk could look forward to release from both administrative office and the rigours of the *Opus Dei*. Although a few monks died in the monastic cells, the great majority returned home when old age or illness threatened and were assigned a private room in the monastic infirmary. The infirmary, situated immediately to the south-west of the cloister, was one of the focal points of religious life at Durham for it was there, and not in the dormitory, that the monks were periodically bled and the senior obedientiaries and doctors of divinity had their private sleeping quarters.[2] Most of the nineteen *camera* in the infirmary were occupied by the sick and aged who had their own fireplaces, but were expected when possible, to eat together in the *Aula Infirmarie*.[3] The buildings were extensively reconstructed and repaired between 1419 and 1430 at a cost of over £400 and the brethren later expressed their gratitude to Wessington for his attention to the needs of their old age.[4] Life in the infirmary was much freer than in the cloister proper, but diffinitions at annual chapters attempted to prevent too great a relaxation of discipline; the monks were warned in 1446 not to introduce unauthorised clerks, servants and boys into their rooms.[5] On his death the Durham monk was buried in the monastic cemetery (the 'Centory Garth') east of the chapter-house, and the sum of ten shillings was distributed to the poor as alms for his soul. The entry of these payments among the '*Elemosina Consueta*' of the bursars' accounts makes it possible to establish the date of death of many Durham monks with some degree of accuracy. The shortest religious

[1] 2.7. Pont., no. 9; Cart. III, fo. 307.
[2] Infirmarer, 1413–50; Jesus College, Cambridge, MS. 41, fo. 170.
[3] Loc. XXVII, nos. 15, 29. The number of rooms is mentioned in Loc. XXVII, no. 1 (b).
[4] Loc. XXVII, no. 1 (a); Reg. IV, fo. 29; *Scrip. Tres*, pp. cclxvii, cclxxiv.
[5] Loc. XXVII, no. 15.

life of any monk who entered the convent between 1383 and 1446 was apparently the six years of Nicholas Bolton who professed in November 1431 and was dead before Whitsuntide 1438.[1] Although ten per cent of the monks during this period wore the habit for more than 50 years, no one surpassed the total of 66 years in the monastic life enjoyed by Prior Hemingburgh who died in 1416 at the advanced age – by any standards – of 89.[2] The average number of years between a monk's profession and his death was approximately 38 at Durham as compared with under 34 at Christ Church, Canterbury, in more or less the same period.[3] On the probably justifiable assumption that the majority of Durham monks entered the cloister not long before their twentieth birthday, most seem to have lived on until their late fifties and had an expectation of life possibly ten years greater than most other sections of the English population.[4]

That the community of Durham lived better fed and less physically distressing lives than most of their contemporaries needs no particular urging. Much more problematic is the state of their spiritual and mental well-being. The remarkably detailed knowledge of the careers of individual monks that the Durham evidence provides leaves a finally ambiguous impression. Like most religious communities at all periods, the monks of early fifteenth-century Durham deserve our understanding much more than either our censure or our praise. If Abbot Kidderminster of Winchcombe was later justified in alleging that late medieval regular observance at Durham 'surpasses all others in the realm',[5] his remark can hardly bring much cheer to the apologists for English monasticism. On the other hand, it must never be forgotten that the quiet exercise of the Christian virtues always presents the historian with an insoluble problem. By their very nature the ideal monastic qualities of stability, obedience and

---

[1] *Liber Vitae*, fo. 70v; Bursar, 1437/38, Elemos. Consueta.

[2] *Dur. Obit. Rolls*, p. 64.

[3] *Ninth Report of Royal Commission on Historical Manuscripts* (1883–4), Part I, Appendix, pp. 127–8. The Durham average of 38 years is calculated from the figures for 104 monks who entered the monastery between 1383 and 1446: as some of the profession lists in the *Liber Vitae* cannot be dated precisely to a particular year, this estimate does not pretend to be absolutely exact.

[4] J. C. Russell, 'Length of Life in England, 1250–1348', *Human Biology* (Johns Hopkins Press), IX (1937), 532; idem, *British Medieval Population*, p. 186; *Population in Europe, 500–1500* (Fontana Economic History of Europe I, London, 1969), p. 31.

[5] Knowles, *Rel. Orders* III, 93.

humility are unlikely to leave much written record to posterity. From this paradox the student of monastic history has no escape and must always beware of arrogating to himself the unwarrantable attributes of divine judgement. Despite such reservations and the evidence for the occasional scandal and much more common petty misdemeanour within the cloister, it remains significant that the monks of Durham were generally successful in conveying an impression of moral respectability to their contemporaries. On the very eve of the Dissolution it was still widely and probably justifiably believed that 'there was never woman in the abbey further than Church, nor did the monks come within the town'.[1]

By a final irony it seems probable that the influences which helped to preserve an acceptable standard of monastic life at late medieval Durham were exactly those for which the monks have so often been censured. The lack of uniformity and the great variety of activities conducted in the fifteenth-century convent were perhaps a source of strength rather than weakness; they provided the individual monk with a vast range of different employment. As we shall see, the magnificent buildings on the peninsula at Durham still testify to the way in which the community's environment was deliberately transformed to create smaller and more meaningful social and administrative units within the great monastic complex.[2] Similarly, the considerable administrative obligations of the Durham monks, like those of teachers in a modern university, hardly deserve their usual fate of casual dismissal out of hand. They too filled an important if ambivalent role in the social life of the monastery. The Black Monks of the later middle ages may have driven a horse and cart through the Rule of Saint Benedict, but it is doubtful whether they had destroyed it in so doing. Given the intense personal tensions inherent in the life of any closed masculine community, the opportunity to take on important administrative responsibility probably had a salutary effect on most Durham monks at most times. The twentieth-century Christian monastery has yet to find an altogether satisfactory alternative.[3]

[1] *Letters and Papers, Henry VIII*, x, 64–5.
[2] See below, pp. 293–6.
[3] D. Knowles, *Christian Monasticism* (London, 1969), pp. 233–44.

Chapter 3

JOHN WESSINGTON AS PRIOR
OF DURHAM (1416–1446)

Sciatque sibi oportere prodesse magis quam praeesse.[1]

It is a familiar conclusion of monastic historians as well as a truism implicit in the Rule of Saint Benedict itself that the character of a religious house depends largely upon the personality of its abbot or prior. In so far as the primary duty of any religious superior is the care of both the bodies and the souls in his community, John Wessington cannot expect to avoid either praise or criticism for the material and spiritual state of Durham cathedral priory between 1416 and 1446. But in practice the absorption of the prior in his extramural responsibilities, his absences from the convent, the peculiarities of his status as head of a cathedral monastery and, above all, the confining effects of custom and routine make Wessington's personal contribution to the life of his monastery by no means easy to assess. Virtually all official business at Durham was conducted in the joint names of the prior and chapter, or of the prior alone, and accordingly little evidence survives of action taken by the monks independently of their superior. The legal personification of the convent by the prior in its dealings with the outside world has the inevitable effect of concealing the extent to which monastic policy was a communal enterprise and makes it dangerously easy to assume that the will of the superior was the source and origin of all decisions. As in the case of most corporations, religious or otherwise, the outsider can find it very difficult to know whether he is in the presence of an autocratic or democratic regime. Despite these reservations as to the precise constitutional role played by the prior within the monastery, his office was of course a fundamental feature of religious life at Durham. Indeed the following study of the activities of John Wessington between 1416 and 1446 is of particular interest precisely because it throws so much more light on the regular functioning of that office

[1] *Rule of St Benedict*, ed. McCann, p. 146.

than on one man's individual initiatives. As we shall see, it was during the early fifteenth century that the prior's office at Durham was re-defined and transformed to make it a more rather than less integral part of the community's life. Not that these developments detract from the other main interest of Wessington's tenure of the priorate. The voluminous records for his rule provide us with an unusual opportunity to analyse in detail the way in which one of the greater English magnates of the north conducted his public life in a period notorious for displays of aristocratic largesse.

'Ye shall hastly procede to th'elitynge and chesing of a new Priour and governour of youre monastery, which mater sittith us right nigh to hert, and touchith us as intierly, as eny may doe, for therin lieth the wele, honour and goode publique of the said monastery.'[1] Bishop William Dudley's advice to the convent of Durham in 1478 was supererogatory. There is no better testimony to the indispensability of the prior of Durham than the remarkable speed with which the later medieval chapter replaced him after his death or resignation. The reasons for this haste were not primarily the dangers of internal dissension, for during vacancies of the priorate the current sub-prior merely accepted ultimate responsibility for the disciplinary authority normally delegated to him. It was of external rather than internal difficulties that the monks thought when they feared damage to their spiritualities and temporalities on these occasions. Without their superior they were largely defenceless against attacks on their liber-ties and landed property, reduced to an anomalous position at com-mon and canon law from which only a duly constituted prior could restore them to their full legal status. The Durham chapter had pointed out as long ago as 1272 that 'without their head they could do nothing at all'; and before a duly elected prior first took up his office he had to swear a solemn oath to 'keep, defend and protect the possessions, rights, privileges, liberties, immunities and customs' of the cathedral church.[2] As the most consequential corporate act of the Durham community, the election of a new prior therefore attracted more attention among the brethren than any other public event in the history of their monastery. Moreover, interest in elec-tions must have been stimulated by their infrequency, for the average

---

[1] Reg. IV, fo. 182; *Scrip. Tres*, p. ccclxi.
[2] Ibid., p. 52; Loc. XXXVII, no. 3.

length of tenure of the priorate of Durham between 1270 and 1539 was 15 years. When Prior John Hemingburgh died on 15 September 1416 he had ruled the convent for twenty-five years. Even his successor, John Wessington, had enjoyed no voice in an election previous to his own.

Elections to the abbacy or priorate of a religious house in the later middle ages were always well documented and none more so than that of John Wessington at Durham in November 1416. Precisely because monastic chapters were usually allowed to choose their own superiors in comparative freedom from external interference, these occasions have a particular fascination as the only consistently 'free' and comparatively democratic elections in late medieval England.[1] As the election process was subject to extremely close scrutiny by diocesan officials, the procedure followed at fifteenth-century Durham can moreover be studied in almost inordinate detail, although not of course the personal pressures and intrigues which lay behind the choice of a particular individual as prior. So stereotyped and formalised had electoral procedure become that a short description of the steps by which Wessington was raised to the priorate in 1416 may serve as a representative example of such elections at Durham and indeed at other Benedictine monasteries of the period.[2] Within a few days of Hemingburgh's death, and probably before his burial in the south transept of the cathedral on 17 September, the chapter met and took the initial step of dispatching a letter to Bishop Langley of Durham requesting his *congé d'élire* as their secular lord.[3] By an unusual coincidence Langley had crossed the channel in the company of Henry V during the previous week, a fact which prompted a group of monks to suggest that licence to elect should be obtained

---

[1] Even a monastery as directly under royal patronage as Westminster Abbey was allowed to choose its abbot from its own chapter between 1222 and the Reformation (*House of Kings*, ed. Carpenter, p. 108).

[2] Locelli XIII and XVI contain voluminous material for a comparative study of fifteenth-century Durham elections; see also *Dur. Obit. Rolls*, pp. 91–102 (for Prior John Burnby's election in 1456); Knowles, *Rel. Orders* II, 248–52; and R. B. Dobson, 'The Election of John Ousthorp as Abbot of Selby', *Yorkshire Archaeological Journal* XLII (1968), 31–8 (for the *decretum eleccionis* as a historical source).

[3] The copy of this letter inserted into Langley's episcopal register (*Reg. Langley* II, 132) is dated 8 September 1416, a week before Hemingburgh's death; the most likely explanation is a scribal omission of the numeral 'x'; cf. Bodleian Library, Oxford, MS. Fairfax 6, fo. vi r; *Rites*, p. 30; Bursar, 1416/17, Garderoba.

from the vicar-general of the diocese. They based their argument on a misconstruction of the words of the canonist, Guido de Bayso, 'the Archdeacon', who had sanctioned the suing of a licence from the viceregent of a temporal ruler during the latter's absence from his domains.[1] As a delegate in spiritual matters only, the vicar-general of Durham had of course no canonical authority to issue a licence to elect, and fortunately the convent finally decided to adhere to precedent and write to Langley. Their messenger, the notary Thomas Ryhale, had reached the bishop at Calais by 6 October, for it was on that day that the bishop issued the stream of mandates, later copied into his episcopal register, which authorised the forthcoming election.

As the election of a prior of Durham required neither royal nor papal approval, it followed that the most dangerous challenge to the autonomy of the convent during vacancies had traditionally proceeded from their titular abbot and bishop. But not since the pontificates of Antony Bek (1283–1311) and Lewis de Beaumont (1317–33) had any bishop of Durham publicly threatened to intrude a prior into the monastery against the will of the majority of its chapter. Similarly, the previous endemic disputes over the administration of the convent on the death or resignation of its prior had been brought to a generally amicable solution by the important concessions of Bishops Richard Kellaw and Richard of Bury in 1311 and 1343.[2] The terms of these compromises made it virtually impossible for any subsequent bishop of Durham to draw material advantage from the exploitation of a vacancy in his cathedral church; he was consequently more inclined to fulfil his canonical function as protector of the monastery during the interregnum. At Calais, on 6 October 1416, Langley accordingly undertook the three-fold duty incumbent on any late medieval bishop of Durham when informed of a vacancy in the priorate. In the first place he appointed his receiver-general, Master John Newton, as custodian of the priory *vacacione durante*. Such an appointment was very largely a matter of form as the keeper's powers were severely restricted by the fourteenth-century episcopal concessions; in the event, the Durham monks of 1416

[1] 2.6. Pont., no. 9; Cart. III, fos. 298–9; Storey, *Thomas Langley*, p. 56; Bursar, 1416/17, Expense Necessarie.

[2] *Reg. Palatinum Dunelmense* (Rolls Series, 1873–8), II, 1,125–7; *Reg. Richard of Bury*, pp. 185–7; cf. *Scrip. Tres*, pp. 85, 118.

continued to issue letters under the convent's common seal and to make up their accounts without reference to Newton.[1] Langley's second and most important responsibility as temporal lord of the monastery was the provision of the formal licence to elect a new prior. As the *congé d'élire* was to be issued under the bishop's great seal, Langley sent a warrant of privy seal to his temporal chancellor at Durham who then published the licence, a handsome document for which the convent had to pay fifty shillings.[2] The third and least formal letter dispatched by Langley from Calais on 6 October was the customary letter of exhortation, under the bishop's signet, to elect a worthy prior. Such letters of advice and encouragement were written by the bishop in his capacity as spiritual superior of the convent but their language never became completely stereotyped and they remain good evidence of his attitude to a vacancy in the priorate. On no occasion after 1322 did the bishop make any attempt to suggest an individual candidate by name; he might even intervene, as in 1478, to protect the convent's right to a canonically free election against the 'restreints and commaundements' of a late prior.[3]

On 18 October, the day after the issue of the *congé d'élire*, the Durham chapter met and fixed on the remarkably but typically early date of 5 November for the election. Messengers were immediately dispatched to summon those Durham monks serving in the cells to attend; William Cuke, for example, had brought the formal citation to Lytham by 21 October and then continued southwards to Oxford and Stamford.[4] Time was so short that the citation certificates were apparently brought back to Durham by the monks themselves as they rode in from their cells: only five monks found it necessary to send letters of proxy, so that some dependencies, including Lytham, must have been completely denuded of monks in early November. Simultaneously there arrived at Durham for the election a small but

---

[1] 1.6. Pont., no. 8; *Reg. Langley* II, 111–12; Reg. III, fo. 45v. For Bishop Skirlaw's appointment of a keeper in the previous vacancy of 1391, see Cart. I, fo. 88; *Scrip. Tres*, p. clxvi.

[2] The original licence to elect is 1.6. Pont., no. 10, copied in Cart. I, fo. 88 and P.R.O., Palatinate of Durham, Chancery Enrolments, 3/35, memb. 11; cf. *Reg. Langley* II, 110–11; Bursar, 1416/17, Expense Necessarie.

[3] Langley's original exhortatory letter is Loc. XXV, no. 167, copied in Cart. III, fo. 297, and *Reg. Langley* II, 109–10. For later examples (all written in the vernacular) see *Scrip. Tres*, pp. cclxxvii, ccclxi, ccclxxx, ccccxx.

[4] Loc. XVI, nos. 5(a), 5(b); Misc. Chrs., no. 6053; Reg. III, fos. 52–3.

distinguished group of legal advisers, prominent among whom were a triumvirate of lawyers from the York curia, Masters Thomas Greenwood, John Selowe and John Staynton, each of whom was paid £2 by the convent for his services.[1] Finally present at the election were 64 monks (not including the 5 who had sent proxies and 3 who were apostate) as well as 8 clerical witnesses.

The course of the election proceedings on 5 and 6 November can be followed in some detail thanks to the *decretum eleccionis* drawn up at the time by Master John Staynton in his capacity as public notary.[2] Early in the morning and before a large crowd of spectators, the monastic community appeared before the high altar and sang a mass of the Holy Spirit, led by the senior dean of the order, John Durham. The chapter bell was then rung and the monks processed to the chapter-house where the noted preacher and sub-prior, Robert Rypon, delivered a sermon on the text '*vas eleccionis est iste*' (Acts ix. 15) to the audience of clerks and laymen. After the singing of the *Veni Creator*, Rypon read a final collect and called for the expulsion from the chapter-house of all seculars except eight named lawyers and witnesses. Once the cloister gates had been firmly locked, Rypon formally called over the names of those monks present, examined the validity of the five letters of proxy and pronounced contumacious all professed monks of Durham who were absent without cause. The chapter then appointed Thomas Rome their spokesman and proctor for the conduct of the election, whose first act was to read a solemn protestation that the votes of all canonically disqualified monks would be regarded as null and void. There is no reference at Durham to the reading of the sixty-fourth chapter of the Rule (*De ordinando abbate*) as was customary at monastic elections; but the convent listened to a public recital of the Fourth Lateran Council's famous decree, *Quia Propter*, which laid down as alternative methods of capitular election the ways of the Holy Spirit, of scrutiny or of compromise.[3] With no recorded break for discussion of which

[1] Bursar, 1416/17, Expense Necessarie. All three men were apparently Oxford law graduates (Emden III, 1,667–8, 1,771, 2,179).

[2] Loc. XIII, no. 11, is the original draft of the instrument, written on a paper roll. This account of the election has been followed in preference to the official *decretum*, condensed and converted into epistolary form, whose original is Loc. XIII, no. 11(a) and which was copied in Reg. III, fos. 46–8 and *Reg. Langley* II, 116–23.

[3] *Corpus Iuris Canonici*, X, i. 6. 42 (ed. Friedberg, II, cols. 88–9).

method to employ, the Durham monks rose to their feet simultaneously and chanted in unison the name of their unanimous choice. There remained seated and silent only one man, John Wessington, the convent's elect.

No doubt this *via Spiritus Sancti* might conceal the reality of intrigue or faction, but obviously if strong party feeling did exist, acclamation would seem the least likely of the three methods to be adopted. As it is, no hint of a possible rival has survived, and Wessington's election can probably be regarded as a popular one, the convent's recognition of outstanding personal ability. However, in adopting the way of the Holy Spirit, the Durham convent of 1416 was breaking with one of its longest traditions, that of election by compromissaries: the elections of priors in 1258, 1273, 1285, 1290, 1313, 1321 and 1391 had all been conducted by way of compromise.[1] Professor Knowles has pointed out that this electoral method seems to have been much the most usual among late medieval English religious houses. For a large group of monks to be, or to appear to be, simultaneously inspired by the Holy Ghost would certainly seem an unlikely occurrence. Nevertheless most of Wessington's successors at Durham until the Dissolution were also elected by acclamation, and there is evidence that the use of the *via Spiritus Sancti* became rather more frequent in English monastic elections generally towards the end of the middle ages.[2] Possibly this was because, as at Durham in 1416, there was an obvious candidate present in the ranks of the community; but it is hard to resist the suspicion that most of these mass acclamations had been carefully rehearsed beforehand and were introduced, ironically enough, to eliminate the dangerous possibilities of informal and spontaneous behaviour on the most important of all formal monastic occasions.

The election over and Wessington known to be suffering from no canonical disability as to character, age or legitimacy of birth, he was led by the monks from the chapter-house to the high altar to the accompaniment of the *Te Deum*. Here Thomas Rome published the result of the election to the large congregation and then, as the

---

[1] *Durham Annals*, pp. 15, 36; *Scrip. Tres*, pp. 72, 73, 95, 102, clxvii.

[2] *Scrip. Tres*, p. cclxxxv; Reg. iv, fo. 160; Reg. v, fos. 24v, 185. See A. H. Thompson, *The Abbey of St Mary of the Meadows, Leicester* (Leicester Archaeological Society, 1949), pp. 54, 56, 74, 85; *House of Kings*, ed. Carpenter, p. 92; cf. Knowles, *Rel. Orders* ii, 248–52.

seniores of the convent prayed in turn, Wessington was conducted to the infirmary chapel and left to his private meditations. Some show of hesitation was normally expected from the elect but as Wessington – like other monastic prelates on similar occasions – had already allowed himself to be presented to the public, it is difficult to believe that the issue remained open. However, when Thomas Rome and the notaries brought the written process of the election to the chapel '*post horam nonam*', Wessington sent them away and asked for further time for deliberation. The convent did not have to wait long: Wessington presumably spent the night in the infirmary chapel and when Thomas Rome came to see him again the next day (6 November) he finally assented to his own election in the traditional formula, for the honour of the Trinity, the Virgin Mary, Saint Cuthbert and All Saints.[1]

A little more than seven weeks had elapsed since the death of Prior Hemingburgh and it was almost as long again before Wessington finally took his predecessor's stall in chapter and choir. Although Bishop Langley's continued absence from the diocese caused several minor complications and delays, the procedure followed was thoroughly conventional and need only be summarised very briefly here. On receiving the report of the election from two Durham monks, Thomas Rome and William Barry, Langley wrote on 26 November from London to his diocesan vicar-general, Master Thomas Lyes, commissioning him to enquire into its canonical validity. Lyes held his formal enquiry in the nave of the cathedral on 14 December and as no complaints were lodged pronounced a favourable verdict forthwith. The bishop's formal assent to Wessington's election as his temporal lord had already been issued under the great seal of the palatinate a week earlier.[2] Langley's official confirmation of the election had to wait until the bishop reached Howden, where he intended spending Christmas, on 22 December. As Wessington alleged that he was too ill to travel, his proctor, William Barry, swore the oath of canonical obedience to Langley on his behalf. Barry then returned to Durham with two letters under

---

[1] In 1456, Prior Burnby consented to his election after an interval of six days (*Dur. Obit. Rolls*, p. 101); cf. Dobson, 'The Election of John Ousthorp', p. 35.

[2] 2.6. Pont., no. 3, copied in Cart. I, fo. 88v, and P.R.O., Palatinate of Durham, Chancery Enrolments, 3/35, memb. 11; Reg. III, fo. 51; *Reg. Langley* II, 123–7; Bursar, 1416/17, Expense Necessarie.

the bishop's seal *ad causas*, one informing Wessington that his election had been confirmed, the other instructing the sub-prior and chapter to obey their new superior. With Barry rode Master Thomas Lyes, chosen by the bishop in the absence of the archdeacon of Durham to induct Wessington into the corporal possession of the priory. Early in the new year, Lyes certified that he had inducted the new prior and installed him in choir and chapter on Christmas Eve. Wessington's register as prior began on Christmas Day 1416, a day marked by more than usually lavish festivities in Durham that year.[1]

The new prior was no more than 45 years old. By comparison with the most famous of his Benedictine contemporaries, John Whethamstede, who became abbot of St Albans when only 27, Wessington's had not been a meteoric rise to the priorate. On the other hand his age at election was much younger than was normal at Durham, where the evidence suggests that the senile rather than the naturally incompetent superior was a more frequent danger to the well-being of the convent.[2] Only 24th in order of monastic seniority in November 1416, John Wessington's election over the heads of so many of his fellows is a tribute to his possession of personal qualities which the surviving records do little to reveal, to his unusual intellectual abilities and interests, and above all to his fruitful journey along the most profitable *cursus honorum* open to a monk of Durham. Born in or very near the year 1371, he was – as the great great nephew of the prominent early fourteenth-century knight, Sir Walter de Wessington – a junior member of what became posthumously one of the most famous of all Durham gentry families.[3]

[1] Loc. XIII, nos. 11(b) and (c); Reg. III, fo. 48; *Reg. Langley* II, 127–32; R. L. Storey, *Diocesan Administration in the Fifteenth Century* (St Anthony's Hall Publications, No. 16; York 1959), p. 17; Reg. Parv. II, fo. 20; Bursar, 1416/17, Dona et Exennia.

[2] The approximate ages at election of the seven priors of Durham between 1341 and 1478 were as follows: John Fossor, 58; Robert Walworth, 51; John Hemingburgh, 64; John Wessington, 45; William Ebchester, 61; John Burnby, 56; Richard Bell, 54 (*Scrip. Tres*, p. 136; *Liber Vitae*, fos. 69v–70v; *Dur. Obit. Rolls*, pp. vii, xi, 64, 72; Reg. Parv. II, fos. 65–6). For Whethamstede's age see *Annales J. Amundesham* (Rolls Series, 1870–1), II, p. xvi; Knowles, *Rel. Orders* II, 193.

[3] Loc. I, nos. 8, 9; *Dur. Obit. Rolls*, pp. 72–3. The decisive evidence for the prior's relationship to the Wessington family is provided in the course of a plea of Novel Disseisin in 1443 (P.R.O., Palatinate of Durham, Chancery Enrolments, 3/43, membs. 9–10; Loc. V, no. 24). The Durham manor of Washington passed by marriage to the Tempest and Mallory families in 1399, during Wessington's own life-time, so it is rather a tenuous proposition that 'Yet great Potomac and little

He had taken the monastic habit at Durham in 1390 and immediately after receiving priest's orders in the northern diocese was dispatched to Durham College, Oxford, where he was already in residence during the academic year 1394–5.[1] Although he never took a university degree, for the next thirteen years Wessington remained a fellow of Durham College, where he served on several occasions as one of the two bursars and was involved in the extensive rebuilding of the period.[2] When he returned permanently to Durham in 1407 there is still no evidence to suggest that Wessington was regarded as a monk of particular distinction. It was his efficient administration of the two offices of monastic sacrist and chancellor during the ensuing years that earned him the respect and gratitude of his colleagues. While sacrist from February 1409 until shortly after his election to the priorate, he not only proved himself a more than usually active and provident obedientiary but supervised the reconstruction of the Durham cloister, unquestionably the most massive building enterprise in the history of the late medieval convent.[3] Even more outstanding were Wessington's achievements as chancellor of the convent, an office which he seems to have taken over from Thomas Rome immediately on his return to Durham in 1407. In this capacity, Wessington presided over the last stages of the

Wear / Are linked in a memory both hold dear' (lines composed by the late Dean Alington of Durham on the occasion of the opening of Washington Old Hall by the United States ambassador on 28 September 1955). The most relevant of the multitude of studies devoted to the intricacies of George Washington's ancestry is T. Pape, *The Washingtons and the Manor of Warton* (Morecambe, 1948). Much of the literature, by no means all of it convincing, is surveyed in J. B. Whitmore, *A Genealogical Guide, Part 4* (Harleian Soc. Publications CIV, 1953), pp. 537–8. As prior, John Wessington used the heraldic arms of the main branch of the Washington family, the celebrated *Argent two bars gules in chief three molets or* (alternative blazons are quite frequent), based on the Lancaster arms and often but not convincingly alleged to be the influence behind the United States' adoption of a national flag with 'stars and stripes'.

[1] Loc. I, nos. 8, 9; *Coldingham Corr.*, p. 118; *Liber Vitae*, fo. 70; Bursar, 1394/95, Dona et Exennia; Durham College, 1394/95.

[2] Durham College, 1394–1407; B.M. Cotton MS., Faustina A. VI, fo. 108. A purely conjectural dating to *c.* 1400 of a list of books dispatched to Oxford by Wessington as monastic chancellor (*Dur. Coll. Rolls*, p. 38) has led to the mistaken view that the future prior returned to Durham 'in or about 1400'.

[3] All eight of Wessington's annual accounts as sacrist have now been discovered. Loc. II, no. 19 contains his accounts as supervisor of the *opus claustri* in 1409–10, 1411–16, 1418–19.

complete re-organisation of the monastic archives that characterised the early years of the fifteenth century; in particular he supervised the compilation of the three most important cartularies ever produced at medieval Durham.[1] Above all it was as chancellor of the convent that Wessington established his reputation as an astute and energetic defender of the monastery's privileges and liberties against external aggression. Between 1409 and 1413 Durham's archidiaconal rights in its jurisdictional peculiars north of the Tyne and south of the Tees were exposed to serious and unexpected assault by a new archdeacon of Northumberland, Master John Rickingale, and a new archbishop of York, Master Henry Bowet. In both cases the fourteenth-century compromises on which rested the monastery's archidiaconal rights within these peculiars were threatened with extinction; in both cases Wessington was eventually successful in preserving – by an exceptionally ingenious use of Durham's own historical and legal muniments – the *status quo*.[2] As sacrist Wessington had successfully preserved the emoluments of his office; and as chancellor he had shown himself equally adept at preserving the legal franchises of his community. In the early fifteenth century these were qualifications for the priorate not to be lightly disregarded.

Shortly after his installation as prior on Christmas Eve 1416 John Wessington moved from the manor of Beaurepaire to the prior's apartments at Durham, which he gradually began to put into a state of better repair.[3] It was a more significant action than might at first appear for it introduced what was to be the major theme of his priorate, the increased participation of the monastic superior in the life of the convent. Critics of English monastic life in the later middle ages have long pointed to the existence of the absentee abbot as a feature incompatible with however liberal an interpretation of the

[1] The references in Almoner 1407/8, Feretrar, 1407/8, Hostillar, 1408/9, 1409/10, when compared with the catalogue of muniments produced in 1421 (Reg. II, fo. 156v; *Catalogi Vet.*, p. 123) make it clear that Wessington was primarily responsible for the present Cart. I, Cart. II and Cart. III, Part II (fos. 1–152), all evidently written by professional scribes.

[2] The materials for these exceptionally intricate causes are too voluminous to be listed in detail here; but see especially Reg. Parv. II, fos. 11–12; 1.1 Archid. North., nos. 1, 5, 6, 8; Cart. I, fos. 144–7; Bursar, 1409–13, Expense Necessarie; 3.2. Archiepisc., no. 3; 2.2. Pap., no. 11.

[3] Bursar, 1416/17, Expense Prioris.

Benedictine Rule. Further study of the evidence may well qualify the current assumption that the superiors of large Black Monk houses spent much, perhaps most, of their lives outside the monastery walls, in the same way that the examination of episcopal registers has modified Gascoigne's strictures on the absenteeism of Lancastrian bishops from their dioceses.[1] Not that a valid and final conclusion on this issue can ever be reached when the reconstruction of the prelate's itinerary is impossible in all but those few houses where accounts survive in quantity, for example at Westminster, at Christ Church, Canterbury, at Worcester under Prior William More, possibly at Norwich and certainly at Durham. As the fourteenth-century Durham evidence, which shows the prior away from the convent for as long as eight months in the year, has been used to confirm the traditional picture of the peregrinating English abbot,[2] Wessington's movements in the first half of the fifteenth century have a more than local interest.

Even at Durham a complete itinerary of the prior is impossible to establish. No medieval Benedictine superior seems to have issued the number of dated charters and letters required to chart his movements precisely. The Durham registers themselves give an impression of almost continuous residence on the part of the prior which is certainly misleading. Much more conclusive is the evidence of the Durham bursar's accounts. Although the category of *Expense Prioris per Maneria*, which furnishes the relevant details in the fourteenth century, was merged by 1400 into the wider accounting section of *Expense Prioris*, the costs of the prior's journeys remained the responsibility of the bursar and his annual account roll provides the only reliable guide to Wessington's movements. Long and expensive journeys outside the north of England were at all times unusual and, as such, subscribed to by various obedientiaries. There was no equivalent at Durham to Prior More's almost annual visit to London in

---

[1] T. Gascoigne, *Loci e Libro Veritatum*, ed. J. E. T. Rogers (Oxford, 1881), pp. 15, 21–3, 39–41. Less severe views are expressed by Thompson, *The English Clergy*, pp. 42–6; Storey, *Diocesan Administration in the Fifteenth Century*, p. 5; Jacob, *The Fifteenth Century*, pp. 271–3.

[2] E.g. the bursar's roll of 1310/11 (*Dur. Acct. Rolls* II, 507), which shows the prior absent for 249 days out of 395. See E. M. Halcrow, 'The Social Position and Influence of the Priors of Durham', *Arch. Ael.*, Fourth Series, XXXIII (1955), 70–86; Knowles, *Rel. Orders* I, 259; II, 253.

the early sixteenth century.[1] Wessington's distant expeditions were regarded as exceptional events: the prior mentioned them, many years later, as among the most financially burdensome of his duties.[2] During his priorate, Wessington apparently went to London only three times: in May 1421 to the extraordinary assembly of the Black Monks convoked by Henry V; in 1427 to arrange the conversion of the rectory of Hemingbrough, in Howdenshire, into a college; and finally in 1437–8 on what appears to have been a less official visit which ended with a pilgrimage to Canterbury.[3] Wessington also attended two successive Provincial Chapters of the Black Monks at Northampton in 1423 and 1426.[4] His visits to the city and county of York may well have been more frequent and he was certainly there seven times during the last half of his priorate;[5] but these were all short business journeys and, on the other hand, there is no evidence that Wessington ever rode north of Newcastle-upon-Tyne. The perambulations of the prior of Durham were normally confined to that part of the diocese of Durham which lay '*infra aquas*'.

It was in this area (between Tyne and Tees) that the bursar's accounts of the fifteenth century reveal a startling contraction both of the length and, more especially, of the range of the prior's itinerary. During the fourteenth century there were few years in which the prior of Durham did not spend at least two or three days in almost all of those nine or ten manors which the convent classified as his '*maneria maiora*'. In 1310–11, for example, Prior William Tanfield visited his manors of Beaurepaire, Pittington, Ketton, Bewley, Muggleswick, Dalton, Merrington, Westoe and Wardley for periods ranging from 129 days at the first to only two days at the last.[6] The prior of Durham's extensive annual tours of his manors *in patria* survived almost intact until the end of the century and as late as 1405 Prior Hemingburgh was still visiting not only Beaurepaire and

---

[1] *Journal of Prior William More*, ed. E. S. Fagan (Worcestershire Historical Society, 1914), pp. 101–4, 300ff., 381ff. See Knowles, *Rel. Orders* III, 111.

[2] Loc. XXI, no. 20 (vi).

[3] Bursar, 1420/21, Expense Prioris; Sacrist, 1420/21; Feretrar, 1421/22; Terrar, 1421/22; Mines Accts., 1427/28; Bursar, 1437/38, Contribuciones. Wessington dined with royal Exchequer officials on his last visit to London.

[4] Pantin, *Chapters* II, 134–80.

[5] Mines Accts., 1428/29; Bursar, 1430/31, 1432, 1432/33, 1437/38, 1438/39, 1439/40, Expense Prioris. [6] *Dur. Acct. Rolls* II, 507.

Pittington but also Westoe, Bewley and Ketton.[1] But during the following ten years, the decade before Wessington's election, the prior's itinerary was heavily and permanently circumscribed as his manors were put out to farm. In 1407, Hemingburgh still held Westoe, Bewley, Fulwell, Pittington, Ketton, Houghall and Beaurepaire '*in manu*'; but by 1409 only four of these manors (Fulwell, Pittington, Ketton and Beaurepaire) remained unleased and in 1416, when Wessington became prior, only two (Pittington and Beaurepaire).[2] Although the farming of the manors did not necessarily involve the surrender of the manor-hall, the convent undoubtedly found it difficult to resist pressure from tenants who wished to rent the buildings together with the manorial demesne. In any case, the ending of direct agricultural exploitation by the monks themselves removed the economic *raison d'être* for the prior's old-style progress through his manors. Accordingly, with few exceptions, Wessington made no attempt to visit the manors in the fashion of his predecessors. Newton Bewley, a rich manor in the extreme south-east of the county, continued, although farmed, to receive visits from the prior of Durham. During the years between 1420 and 1428 Wessington was often there, once for as long as six weeks at a time, and he spent a considerable sum on repairs to the stables, byres and windows. Wessington's short-lived partiality for Bewley is undoubtedly linked with Bishop Langley's visits to one of his favourite residences, the castle of Stockton-on-Tees.[3] Bewley is only five miles from Stockton and Wessington rode over to see the bishop on several occasions.[4]

[1] Bursar, 1404/5, Expense Prioris. A memorandum, written on behalf of Prior Hemingburgh in or about 1409, noted '*quod antiquitus, maneriis novem vel decem in propriis manibus tentis et non ad firmam dimissis, prior cum terrario et capellanis suis quasi per totum annum morabatur*' (Loc. XXVII, no. 38). For a very comparable pattern of itineracy by fourteenth-century abbots of Westminster see B. Harvey, 'The Leasing of the Abbot of Westminster's Demesnes in the Later Middle Ages', *Econ. H.R.*, Second Series, XXII (1969), 18–20.

[2] Bursar, 1407/8, 1409/10, 1416/17, Redditus Assise; Granator, 1416/17. A few of these manors temporarily reverted into the prior's hands at a later date because of circumstances outside his control, e.g. it was noticed of Bewley (Beaulieu) in 1446 that '*Manerium ibidem est in manu Domini propter defectum tenencium*' (Loc. XIII, no. 22; Scrip. Tres, p. ccxcvi). Nevertheless, Prior Hemingburgh's decision to lease the entire demesnes of almost all the Durham manors was undoubtedly the most dramatic event in the history of the convent's estates-policy during the later middle ages. See below, p. 272.   [3] Storey, *Thomas Langley*, pp. 94, 234–41.

[4] Bursar, 1420–8, Expense Prioris, Reparaciones Domorum.

Apart from these weeks at Bewley in the 1420s, a few excursions to Jarrow, and several visits to see Langley at Auckland or Wolsingham and the Nevilles at Brancepeth, Raby or Middleham, Wessington confined his extramural residence to the two manors of Pittington and Beaurepaire, held in his own hands throughout his priorate. Pittington and Beaurepaire (now Bearpark) were the favourite country-seats of all priors of Durham from the mid-thirteenth century to the Dissolution, but in Wessington's time the bursar's accounts suggest that they enjoyed a patronage more exclusive than earlier or later.[1] Both manors lay close to the monastery, Pittington less than four miles to the north-east and Beaurepaire less than three miles to the north-west, and it seems important to emphasise that residence there need not be equated with complete absence from the convent. The post-Dissolution cathedral statutes of 1555 permitted the dean of Durham to spend 40 days a year at his manor of Bearpark provided that he attended chapter meetings and came into Durham each day for high mass or one of the Hours.[2] There was little to prevent the medieval prior from making similar frequent if unrecorded journeys into Durham to preside at choir or chapter. By Wessington's time the prior's quarters at both Pittington and Beaurepaire were spacious, but had become somewhat dilapidated and were in constant need of minor repair. Pittington was the smaller manor-house of the two. Originally built by Prior Hugh of Darlington in the 1260s, it had been in continuous use throughout the fourteenth century. One prior died at Pittington, and in 1394 Prior Hemingburgh and Uthred of Boldon had welcomed Bishop Skirlaw to the manor.[3] Wessington, although he entertained monks there, obviously preferred Beaurepaire as a personal retreat and it was only after his resignation in 1446 that the convent reconstructed Pittington hall at a cost of about £100.[4]

The aptly named Beaurepaire was an altogether larger establish-

---

[1] Prior Hugh Whitehead visited Wardley and Bewley, as well as Pittington and Beaurepaire, in the twenty years before the Dissolution. See *Durham Household Book*, ed. J. Raine (Surtees Soc. XVIII, 1844), p. 339.

[2] *Statutes of the Cathedral Church of Durham* (Surtees Soc. CXLIII, 1929), pp. 114–15.

[3] *Scrip. Tres*, pp. 46, 47, 130, cxli, clxxiii.

[4] Ibid., pp. cccxxiii–cccxxvi. Despite the leasing of the manorial demesne, Pittington hall apparently never fell into disuse before the Dissolution: it was reconstructed by Prior Whitehead (ibid., p. 155) but is now completely destroyed.

ment which combined the advantage of proximity to the monastery with that of comparative privacy. As at Pittington, the domestic buildings dated from the thirteenth century. Originally designed as quarters for Prior Bertram of Middleton after his resignation in 1258, they soon became the most luxurious and most valued residence of the ruling superior. Not easily defended, Beaurepaire was a constant target for the Scots until and including the Neville's Cross campaign and had also been a prize eagerly fought over during the monastic party warfare that preceded, accompanied and followed the pontificate of Antony Bek.[1] Situated on the crest of a hill overlooking the Browney valley, the prior's manor-house was surrounded by the 400 acres of valuable grazing land on Bearpark Moor which Wessington zealously protected against the claims for common pasture made by the inhabitants of the Old Borough of Crossgate.[2] In normal years the moor was shared between the prior's stud-farm of horses and the bursar's reserve stock of cattle and sheep, while the general supervision of the pasture was in the hands of the keeper or forester of Beaurepaire.[3] Around the central manor there were various satellite communities, houses at the 'Stotgate' and the 'Monkherber' (on sites still occupied by modern farms) as well as the important lesser manor of Aldin Grange which was also reserved for the grazing of the bursar's meat stock. The Browney valley is rich in coal deposits and it was from pits in the area around Beaurepaire that the convent received some of its supplies of fuel. Since the early nineteenth century the development of Bearpark Colliery across the valley has been accompanied by the sad and almost total destruction of the manor-house.[4] The long story of continuous neglect and vandalism is still in progress; and from the few remaining blocks of masonry the modern visitor can gain only a forlorn if evocative impression of what was once one of the

---

[1] *Durham Annals*, pp. 11–12, 18–19; *Scrip. Tres*, pp. 43, 46, 82, 96, 136, cxli, ccccxxxiv; Fraser, *Antony Bek*, p. 158.

[2] See 2.6. Spec., no. 51, for Wessington's compilation '*pro separalitate habenda in mora de Beurepayre adversus tenentes de Veteri Burgo*': cf. above, p. 49, and *Reg. Palatinum Dunelmense* (Rolls Series, 1873–8), II, 1, 141–2.

[3] Reg. III, fo. 212; Reg. Parv. II, fo. 97.

[4] The engraving which faces Surtees, *Durham* II, 372, shows the whole of the south side of the chapel and part of the east gable still erect; cf. J. R. Boyle, *Comprehensive Guide to the County of Durham* (London, 1892), p. 441.

greatest country seats in northern England. During Wessington's priorate there were two chapels at Beaurepaire, of which the larger was dedicated to Saint Katherine.[1] An inventory of 1464 also describes a hall with five dining-tables, a buttery, a kitchen, and two other chambers of which the inner one seems to have contained the prior's bed. But Beaurepaire's greatest attraction, one it still enjoys today, was undoubtedly its seclusion; there was only one village in the immediate vicinity, that of Witton Gilbert to the north-west, where the monks maintained a hospital which Wessington occasionally visited.[2]

It is important to stress that Wessington's periods of residence at Beaurepaire, frequent as they were, did not usually entail his complete withdrawal from the company of his monks. For it was at this manor, and only rarely at Pittington or elsewhere, that each member of the Durham community regularly enjoyed his period of relaxation at the prior's games or *ludi*. At Durham, as at other English religious houses, the practice of adapting a nearby manor as a monastic rest-house seems to have developed in the aftermath of Innocent III's decretal *Cum ad Monasterium*, which was taken to sanction the meat-eating of monks invited to the abbot's table.[3] By the late fourteenth century, *ludi* at the prior's manors had become a regular feature of monastic life at Durham and they continued to enjoy great popularity there until the Dissolution.[4] Wessington appears to have done little to change the system that he inherited from Prior Hemingburgh. In his priorate, as earlier and later, there were normally four *ludi* each year, held at the feasts of the Purification, Easter, Saint John the Baptist and All Saints. An ordinary *ludus* or

[1] For the chapel of Saint Katherine, see Bursar, 1441/42, Reparaciones Maneriorum; *Durham Annals*, p. 25. The chapel of Saint John at Beaurepaire (Bursar, 1416/17, Reparaciones Domorum) may survive as the ruins now at Saint John's Green, a mile to the north of the old manor-hall.

[2] *Feodarium Dunelm.*, pp. 186–91; *Dur. Acct. Rolls* III, 639–40; Bursar, 1418/19, Expense Prioris; Reg. Parv. II, fo. 79.

[3] See the statute of Prior Thomas Melsonby (1235) '*De solacio Fratribus faciendo in esu carnium*' (*Scrip. Tres*, p. xliv).

[4] During periods of financial difficulty at Durham, the *ludi* were sometimes temporarily suspended, as in September 1408 (Reg. Parv. II, fo. 8; *Finchale Priory*, pp. 30–1). But the implication in Knowles, *Rel. Orders* II, 246, that 'the superior's connexion with the routine vanished' does not apply at Durham where the monks continued to enjoy the amenities of the *ludi* in addition to those of another and more permanent rest-house, the priory of Finchale.

period of relaxation lasted for two weeks or more at a time, so that Wessington appears to have devoted at least two months of the year to the entertainment of his monks at Beaurepaire.[1] One of the prior's chaplains, the steward of his household, was responsible for supplying the monks with provisions while at Beaurepaire, and received sums of money for this purpose from other obedientiaries as well as deliveries of grain and meat from neighbouring manors.[2] There is no direct evidence as to the number of monks who attended each *ludus* and no information about the type of entertainment provided there: Raine's suggestion that the monks witnessed miracle plays and mysteries seems hardly likely.[3] Fish was eaten on Wednesdays, Fridays and Saturdays, but nevertheless large quantities of meat were consumed during the course of the *ludus*. At one gathering in the autumn of 1391 the company was able to dispose of the carcases of five oxen or cattle, twenty-two sheep and seven pigs during fourteen days.[4] It would seem that the monks received at Beaurepaire by Prior Wessington formed a comparatively large rather than intimate gathering. Nevertheless, it must have been in the informal atmosphere of the *ludus* and not at the cathedral church that the prior came into closest personal contact with the junior members of his community. Most other large Benedictine monasteries had their manor-houses for monastic relaxation;[5] but the personal intercourse between superior and monk which characterised the Durham *ludi* was much more unusual.

Apart from the period of the *ludi*, Wessington spent some weeks at Beaurepaire every year in the more select company of his chaplains and one or two of the senior obedientiaries. Because this manor, like Pittington, lay so close to Durham, the fifteenth-century bursars rarely found it necessary to be specific in their account rolls as to the exact dates of the prior's residence there. Quite apart from his attendance at the *ludi* however, Wessington was said to have been at Beaurepaire for fifteen days in 1432–3, for sixteen weeks and three

---

[1] Bursar, 1413–38, Expense Necessarie, Expense Prioris.
[2] Sacrist, 1401–46; Hostillar, 1416–30; Pittington, 1427/8.
[3] *Durham Household Book* (Surtees Soc. XVIII, 1844), p. 339.
[4] Misc. Chrs., no. 210, one of the only surviving accounts (the others are ibid. nos. 211–14) of expenses at a *ludus*. All five account rolls date from the 1390s.
[5] E.g. Christ Church, Canterbury, had Caldecote, Westminster had Hendon and La Neyte, Selby had Stainer Grange; and see Knowles, *Rel. Orders* II, 246.

days in 1433–4, and for five weeks and two days in 1434–5.[1] Such figures cast a more optimistic light on the problem of the absentee prior at Durham than might have been expected. In only one year, 1433–4, can Wessington be proved to have spent more than half the year away from his cathedral church. The more general impression that the prior was absent from Durham for four months or less each year seems to be confirmed by the provision made for his wine supply at the annual chapter in 1446.[2] Seven 'doles' of red wine were placed at the prior's disposal for the year, but only one of these was to be consumed outside his quarters in the monastery.[3] Absenteeism among the fourteenth-century priors of Durham might be serious enough to necessitate the transmission of important commands by letter rather than by word of mouth.[4] But in the early fifteenth century there is nothing to suggest that Wessington's absences were either so long or so distant as to impair the effectiveness of his control over his monks.

As it was only in the years immediately after 1400 that the practice of perambulation through the manors *'quasi per totum annum'* was abandoned, Wessington was therefore the first of the late medieval priors of Durham to return, albeit for economic reasons, to a more personal connection with his cathedral church. Nowhere is this change in his position more obvious than in the enhanced importance of the prior's lodgings, the *camera prioris*, at this time. Although the history of the prior's apartments at Durham can be traced back to the twelfth century[5], the buildings themselves received greater attention under Wessington than perhaps ever before. During the thirty years of his priorate, he spent £419 10s. 3½d. on the repair and reconstruction of accommodation which was said to be *'valde ruinosa'* in 1416.[6] No record of comparably heavy expenditure on

---

[1] Bursar, 1432/33, 1433/34, 1434/35, Expense Prioris.

[2] In the first of his articles presented to the Black Monks in 1421, Henry V asked prelates not to remain *'in suis maneriis ultra tres menses'* (Pantin, *Chapters* II, 110–11).

[3] Loc. XXVII, no. 15, memb. 3.

[4] Misc. Chrs., no. 6063. On another occasion, Prior John Fossor admitted that monastic accounts had been rendered at Beaurepaire, and not Durham (2.8. Pont., no. 5).

[5] The surviving crypt of the prior's chapel can be dated on architectural evidence to the first third of the thirteenth century: it must already have been connected to the cloister by a series of rooms built at an earlier date.

[6] Loc. XXI, no. 20 (vii); *Scrip. Tres*, p. cclxxiv.

the *camera prioris* survives from an earlier period: between 1341 and 1374 Prior John Fossor is reported to have spent only £40 on his hall at Durham out of a total expenditure of over £2,000.[1] Even more convincing proof that Wessington intended his quarters at Durham for use as well as display is provided by the large sums devoted to vestments, ecclesiastical ornaments, plate and jewellery for his rooms and chapel. The total monastic bill for all such '*ornamenta et jocalia*' came to £513 16s. 2d. during Wessington's period as prior, of which almost a half was consumed in furnishing and decorating the prior's quarters.[2]

Continual rebuilding and refurbishing of the abbot's lodgings is a constant theme in the architectural history of the late medieval English monastery and Wessington's activities at Durham have many parallels elsewhere. However, this was a sphere in which Wessington's expenses were not, as has been suggested, 'smaller than those of an Eastry, a Chillenden or a Whethamstede'.[3] Only at Westminster sixty years earlier, under Abbot Litlington, is there record of much more costly domestic building than Wessington could hope to rival.[4] Of the total sum spent on the fabric of the *camera prioris* at Durham between 1416 and 1446, about £90 (an average of £3 per annum)[5] was assigned to routine maintenance work on the buildings: the remaining £300 was devoted to major structural alterations. Although few accounts of the work survive, it is certain that the extension of the prior's quarters between 1424 and 1436[6] was the most considerable building operation of the middle years of Wessington's priorate. The more prosperous of the obedientiaries and heads of cells were laid under the obligation of

[1] *Scrip. Tres*, pp. 131–2.

[2] Loc. xxvii, no. 1 (a); *Scrip. Tres*, p. cclxxvi.

[3] Knowles, *Rel. Orders* ii, 192–3. Henry of Eastry is recorded as having spent less than £300 on his apartments at Canterbury (ibid. i, 323). The comparative figure for John Whethamstede (about £230) can be calculated from *Annales J. Amundesham* (Rolls Series, 1870–1), ii, 255–77. For Thomas Chillenden's repairs to his quarters, see *Literae Cantuarienses* (Rolls Series, 1887–9), iii, 115.

[4] The abbot's 'Novum Edificium' of the 1370s alone cost £450: J. Armitage Robinson, *The Abbot's House at Westminster* (Notes and Documents relating to Westminster Abbey, no. 4; Cambridge, 1911), pp. 15–20.

[5] Bursar, 1416–46, Reparaciones Domorum; Loc. xxvii, no. 1 (a).

[6] The prior's apartments were being rebuilt throughout these twelve years, and not merely between 1429 and 1432, the dates given in J. Harvey, *English Mediaeval Architects: A Biographical Dictionary down to 1500* (London, 1954), p. 29.

providing small annual pensions for the *camera prioris* during the mid-1420s; but the work was primarily financed from the profits of the monastery's coal-pits, assigned to the prior's needs and administered by his chaplain.[1] At the height of building activity, between 1429 and 1432, almost £50 per annum was being spent on the wages of twenty *operarii*, including three masons working throughout the year. Although one of the latter was John Bell, responsible for the reconstruction of the central cathedral tower in the 1430s, there was no master mason as such; Wessington and Thomas Nesbitt, his chaplain, directly supervised what were essentially piece-meal extensions to the prior's lodgings and their accounts are consequently lacking in precise architectural information. Nevertheless, it is clear that apart from the provision of a baptismal font for the prior's chapel as well as tracery and glass for various windows and new carved wooden ceilings, a completely new set of rooms was added to the north of the existing apartments between the hall and what is now King James's Room.[2] The '*novae camerae*' were completed by 1434 when a new doorway (presumably the still surviving 'Usher's Door') was built to lead into the prior's quarters. Although subject to much internal modification since 1436 there has been no substantial extension to these buildings, now the deanery of Durham.

Some impression of Wessington's success in rebuilding and re-furnishing his apartments at Durham may be gained by a comparison of the detailed inventory made soon after his resignation with the altogether slighter surveys of thirty years earlier.[3] In 1446, eight rooms were enumerated (the chapel, wine cellar, buttery, upper chamber, lower chamber, '*camera sub volta*', hall, and wardrobe) in what is certainly an incomplete list. Incidental references in the account rolls show that Wessington also enjoyed the use of a

---

[1] Feretrar, 1424/28; Finchale, 1425/26; Lytham, 1424–26; Mines Accts., 1427–37 (a complete series of annual accounts).

[2] Mines Accts., 1431/32, 1433/34 (for the carving of 'le sylyng de le parlour et camere domini prioris' and the making of a 'baywyndowe'); *Scrip. Tres*, p. cclxxvi. Cf. G. W. Kitchin, *The Story of the Deanery, Durham, 1070–1912* (Durham, 1912), pp. 56–7, which is often seriously misleading and has been followed too closely in *V.C.H. Durham* III, 132–5, and N. Pevsner, *The Buildings of England, County Durham* (London, 1953), pp. 115–16.

[3] The Durham inventory of 1446, now Loc. XIII, no. 22, was printed by Raine in *Scrip. Tres*, pp. cclxxxv–cccviii. Earlier inventories are found at the foot of the bursar's rolls for 1416/17 and 1418/19.

series of smaller rooms (study, solar, parlour, napery)[1] which are difficult to distinguish from one another and impossible to reconstruct from an examination of the modern deanery. The use of different names for the same room has led to much confusion in the study of the architectural history of the prior's quarters and it is very likely, for instance, that the '*scaccarium prioris*' of Wessington's day was later known as the bursar's 'checker'.[2] However, the position of the four large rooms which constituted the nucleus of the apartments is not in doubt. To the extreme south-east lay the prior's chapel, dedicated to Saint Nicholas, in which Wessington said mass with the assistance of his chaplain, issued his written *acta* and received the homage of his tenants by knight service as well as the oaths of loyalty of his own, his bishop's and the king's officials.[3] The prior's hall, situated near the east walk of the cloister, was the room where he entertained not only important guests but, in rotation, his own monks as well. Between hall and chapel were the prior's upper and lower chambers connected by a stone newel staircase in a projecting turret. Both rooms were primarily state bedrooms, decorated with red hangings in 1446 and containing Wessington's prize fabrics. Even more valuable was Wessington's collection of plate, which was stored in the buttery and included a square salt cellar with a silver-gilt cover on which his arms were engraved. The prior's favourite pieces of furniture and plate often accompanied him on his visits to his manors, carried on his long cart ordinarily kept in the stable at Durham. The final impression left by the 1446 survey is one of considerable splendour and of a style of living not easily matched anywhere else in fifteenth-century England. So successfully had Wessington remodelled the *camera prioris* that there were no major additions, either to fabric or furnishings, in the eighteen years that followed his resignation.[4]

The inventory of 1446 inevitably suggests that Wessington's

---

[1] Mines Accts., 1429/30, 1431/32; Bursar, 1418/19, 1443/44, Reparaciones Domorum.
[2] See Bursar, 1428/29, Reparaciones Domorum; *Rites*, pp. 99, 280.
[3] D.C.D., MS. C. IV. 25, fo. 126v; 3.8 Spec., no. 21; Loc. I, no. 37; Loc. XXVIII, no. 3; Misc. Chrs., no. 6040; Reg. III, fos. 57v, 136, 268v.
[4] The 1464 Durham inventory is partly printed in *Feodarium Dunelm.*, 98–211, and *Dur. Acct. Rolls* III, 639–40. Cf. the inventory of the abbot of Peterborough's lodgings in 1460 (translated by A. R. Myers, *English Historical Documents* IV, London, 1969, pp. 1146–50) for a close, but less luxurious, analogy.

apartments at Durham were a centre for extravagant display rather than private seclusion. Such privacy and tranquillity as the prior did enjoy would seem to have been secured at Beaurepaire and Pittington rather than in his chambers at Durham. The reason for Wessington's heavy expenditure on the *camera prioris* was less the desire for personal magnificence than an attempt to provide liberal hospitality for seculars and his own monks. As the prior of Durham ceased to perambulate his manors, his obligation to provide such hospitality at home presumably increased: the word '*hospicium*' came into common use as a functional description of his apartments. Of even greater significance than liberality towards strangers was the entertainment of monks themselves at the prior's table: the Durham chapter diffinitions of 1446 recognised that meals in the prior's hospice had become a traditional part of the monastic routine and, far from respecting the prior's independence in his own precincts, were especially concerned (as no earlier diffinitions had been) with the dangers of illicit and nocturnal drinking there.[1] Indeed the monastic chapter of 1446 treated the *camera prioris* as an integral part of the house, suggesting that some of the criticism levelled at the superior's private household by both contemporaries and historians may be misconceived. It has been quite correctly alleged of many English monasteries in the later middle ages that 'the abbot or prior's house became the centre of the life of a reduced convent'.[2] Although so extreme a statement would certainly misrepresent conditions at Durham in the time of Wessington, it is important to stress that the prior's rebuilt and remodelled apartments were for the use of his monks as well as himself.

It is, therefore, as a public rather than a private figure that Wessington is revealed in the Durham records: as prior, he followed a pattern of behaviour which was difficult to reverse whatever his personal inclinations. His everyday dress, for instance, immediately separated him from his monks. The prior's special clothing allowance of £5 per annum enabled him to wear expensive, if sober, cloaks, tunics and cowls; these were cut for him by a professional tailor and, although naturally black in colour, were distinguished

---

[1] Loc. xxvii, no. 15.
[2] R. Gilyard-Beer, *Abbeys: An Introduction to the Religious Houses of England and Wales* (H.M.S.O.; London, 1958), p. 48.

by copious linings and trimmings of fur.[1] Wessington's stud of horses can have had few rivals in the north of England for even the Earl of Salisbury was anxious to buy or borrow a courser from him; but the prior himself rode on palfreys ('*equi ambulantes*'), two of which were kept at his disposal in the Durham stables.[2] However, it is most frequently as a consumer that Wessington stands revealed in contemporary obedientiary rolls. The bulk of Wessington's food was provided by the cellarer and cooked in what is still known (misleadingly) as the Prior's Kitchen, a deservedly famous building of the late 1360s which acted as the central kitchen for the whole convent. The prior's demands for more exotic food and drink were separately accounted for by his chaplains. Malmsey and other sweet Mediterranean wines were often bought in London. Oysters and salmon were sent down to Durham from Northumberland while a bewildering array of 'spices' (pepper, figs, raisins, rice, dates, saffron, sandalwood, currants, cloves, anise, ginger, cinnamon, mace) found their way to the prior's table. All monks had the opportunity to enjoy some of these luxuries at the *ludi*, but the most expensive of all, like cloves and mace which sold in London at three shillings a pound, seem to have been restricted to the use of the prior in his hospice.[3]

Nevertheless, it would be unwise to suggest that this heavy consumption of choice foods during Wessington's priorate was either at all unusual or a reflection of his personal tastes. As fifteenth-century chapter diffinitions amply demonstrate, the presence of authorised or unauthorised guests at the prior's table was a heavy charge on the monastic revenues. Wessington, like his predecessors, kept a literally 'open house', as is proved by the hospitality he offered Richard Bekyngham, a royal chancery clerk who arrived unexpectedly in August 1436 as a most truculent and unwelcome visitor in search of a benefice.[4] This example is hardly typical, for

---

[1] Robert Sartryn was Wessington's tailor from 1418 to 1428. See Bursar, 1416–46, Expense Prioris, and Mines Accts., 1427–37, for details of expenditure on the prior's clothes. Like other Durham monks, Wessington also received a basic clothing allowance from the chamberlain.

[2] Loc. xxv, no. 121; *Wills and Inventories*, Part I, ed. J. Raine (Surtees Soc. II, 1835), pp. 69–70; *Scrip. Tres*, p. cclxxxix.

[3] Bursar, 1416–46, Empcio Vini, Expense Prioris; Mines Accts., 1427–37.

[4] Reg. Parv. II, fo. 95.

most guests of the convent had no official business with the prior but were attracted to Durham by the reputation of Saint Cuthbert's shrine or the monastery's convenient situation near the main road north to Scotland. The most famous visitor to Durham in Wessington's time was Aeneas Sylvius, later Pope Pius II, who had decided to return by land from the court of James I in early 1436 after being violently sea-sick on the outward journey. Lack of reference to him in the Durham sources confirms that he preserved his disguise as merchant beyond the Border zone, while his confusion between the shrines of Saint Cuthbert and the Venerable Bede betrays the cursory nature of his visit.[1] Other visitors demanded more of the prior's attention and the convent's resources.

A major responsibility of the prior of Durham undoubtedly did therefore consist in acting as an often unwilling host to visitors of all descriptions. Even at the lowest level, the number of envoys, heralds, minstrels, mummers and players who appeared at the monastery is somewhat startling. In a quite representative year, 1433–4, gifts were made to players of the king, and also of the Earls of Suffolk, Stafford, Warwick and Huntingdon as well as to two more independent 'variety acts', Lokwood and his fellows and a minstrel called 'Modyr Hakett'.[2] Wessington seems to have found these amusements somewhat tedious, for when criticised on the subject in the 1442 visitation he expressed his willingness to be relieved of the obligation to receive travelling minstrels; as he quite fairly pointed out, he had merely followed the example of his predecessors in watching such entertainments. Moreover, Wessington never admitted to his presence that common companion of fourteenth-century Durham priors, the professional fool ('*ioculator*').[3] More

[1] *Aeneas Sylvius Piccolomini, Pii Secundi Pont. Max. Commentarii* (Frankfurt, 1614), p. 5; *The Commentaries of Pius II*, trans. F. A. Gragg, ed. L. C. Gabel (Smith College Studies in History, XXII, nos. 1–2, 1936–7), 20–1. Cf. J. Wilson, 'The Passage of the Border by Aeneas Sylvius in the winter of 1435–6', *Transactions of the Cumberland and Westmorland Antiquarian and Archaeological Society*, New Series, XXIII (1923), 17–28.

[2] Bursar, 1433/34, Dona et Exennia. Cf. E. K. Chambers, *The Mediaeval Stage* (Oxford, 1903), II, 240–4; M. H. Dodds, 'Northern Minstrels and Folk Drama', *Arch. Ael.*, Fourth Series, I (1925), 121–46.

[3] 1.8. Pont., no. 2. The prior's fool fails to reappear at Durham after Wessington's resignation and seems to be an essentially fourteenth-century phenomenon there. Cf. Knowles, *Rel. Orders* II, 325; III, 67, 118, 285.

frequent visitors than the minstrels were messengers from near and far, carrying presents from local magnates or bringing news of the French wars; most of these received small money payments in their turn, costing the prior an average of almost £5 a year. To this must be added the price of food for the messengers and fodder for their horses, producing a total high enough to alarm many Durham monks who, in the 1440s, asked the prior to cut his money gifts to these casual visitors by half. The convent had heard that many English lords, richer than themselves, forced minstrels and messengers to be content with provisions alone and no money whatsoever.[1]

A much heavier financial liability was the round of feasts and banquets to which Wessington was committed by the nature of his office. These were a regular feature of life at Durham in the fifteenth century although they have naturally left little trace in the records. However, the marginalia sometimes added by the cellarer to his weekly accounts in the 1420s and 1430s make it possible to distinguish between three different occasions for a prior's banquet: the visit to Durham of a distinguished guest with his retinue; the presence on business of a group of episcopal agents; and, most common of all, the annual celebration of a feast-day. Thus between May 1430 and May 1431, there were entertained to dinner the bishop of Durham (on two separate occasions), the bishop of Carlisle, the prior of Tyne-mouth, the abbot of Whitby, Sir Robert Umfraville and a succession of local gentlemen and officials. In the same year, the sessions of Bishop Langley's justices at Durham (August and December), the meeting of his synod (October) and his auditors (November), all provided the justification for a feast in the monastery. Other cellarer's accounts confirm that virtually every week of the Durham year had its feasts of sorts, ranging from the small occasions which cost him little to the greatest celebration of all at Christmas when his average weekly expenditure soared from its normal £6 to £17 or £18.[2] The setting for these meals often alternated from refectory to monastic solar to prior's hall, but characteristic of them all was the presence of some, and occasionally most, of the monastic population. In this sphere, as in others, the prior's entertainment of strangers can

---

[1] Bursar, 1416–46, Dona et Exennia; Loc. XXVII, no. 15, memb. 4.
[2] The Christmas fare in 1430 included 2 boars, 7 cattle, 26 sheep, 44 legs of pork and 4 loads of fish.

hardly be separated from his entertainment of his own monks. Wessington did not, of course, attend all the dinners given in the convent, but he was normally expected to preside at the principal feasts of the year and if unable to do so, delegated his position to the sub-prior or (although this was less to the convent's liking) to the suffragan bishop of Durham, perhaps his most frequent guest at table.[1] The chance survival of a solitary list of seating arrangements for one of Wessington's larger feasts allows us to reconstruct one of these occasions.[2] There were no less than twenty-six guests at this banquet as well as many Durham monks, carefully segregated, except for the sub-prior, on a separate table. The guests of honour were the suffragan and the abbots of Newminster and Blanchland; there were only four laymen present, William Hoton, the prior's steward, and the sheriff, steward and receiver-general of the bishop of Durham. Most prominent were a group of eight university graduates in the persons of the deans of the four collegiate churches of the diocese and the rectors of the richest local benefices. All of these men served under Bishop Langley in one capacity or another; and it is appropriate enough to find Wessington in the convivial company, not of north country lords and knights, but of the ecclesiastical establishment to which he himself belonged.

It may be possible to justify this annual round of Durham feasting on the grounds that the convent's welfare benefited greatly from regular social intercourse with the most influential seculars of the county. The same could not be said of the visits of the greater English magnates and their retinues, visits which the prior saw as a heavy burden on the monastic finances and which had little to recommend them in the form of any material compensation received in exchange. The desire to avoid unnecessary expense came uppermost in Wessington's approach to these occasions of large-scale hospitality and it is typical of him that he should have tried to persuade his new bishop, Robert Neville, to be installed at Christmas (1440), largely on the grounds that this would obviate the need for two different feasts.[3] However, Durham's geographical position

---

[1] Loc. XXVII, no. 15, memb. 4.

[2] Misc. Chrs., no. 1090, a scrap of paper also used to draft two letters relating to Coldingham in August 1441.

[3] Reg. Parv. II, fo. 125; Wessington's advice was discounted and Neville installed in April 1441 (Reg. III, fos. 267–8). See below, p. 228.

made it impossible for the prior to escape from his role of involuntary host. Not only did English armies and embassies visit the monastery on their way to and from the Border, but Durham itself was an obvious choice for both the assembling of troops and the discussion of peace terms in the early fifteenth century.[1] In 1444, when attempting to excuse the monastery from the payment of royal subsidies, Wessington claimed that the visits of magnates engaged on Scottish affairs had cost the monastery over £400 since 1416, at least £100 more than the convent's expenses on major litigation during the same period.[2] Henry VI himself did not visit Durham until 1448, but his lieutenants and wardens of the Marches were regular callers on the prior. The periods of open Anglo-Scottish warfare during Wessington's priorate had an immediately adverse effect on Durham's finances. The expeditions of the Duke of Exeter, the archbishop of York and their colleagues in 1417–18 were said to have cost the bursar almost £150 in hospitality. The Duke of Norfolk's turbulent year as warden of the East March (March 1437 to March 1438) was marked by five visits to the monastery, on one occasion for five days with a retinue of 300 men. Negotiations for peace might be almost as expensive as preparations for war as far as Durham monks were concerned. Wessington calculated that the return of James I to Scotland in the spring of 1424 (formally ratified in the Durham chapter-house where there were discussions between the English and Scottish lords for over a fortnight) cost the convent £100; even the relatively straightforward prorogation of the existing truce at Durham in May 1444 left the convent £20 out of pocket. Such figures need not always be accepted at their face value and sometimes cannot be substantiated by the evidence of surviving account rolls at Durham. Cardinal Beaufort's two visits to the monastery on the way to and from King James I in early 1429, for instance, were referred to by the bursar only in terms

[1] There were arrays at Durham in 1400, 1418, 1435 and 1436 as well as important peace negotiations in 1424, 1444 and 1449. See *Scrip. Tres*, pp. clxxxv–clxxxvii; *Reg. Langley* II, 162–3; Storey, *Thomas Langley*, pp. 159–60; E. W. M. Balfour-Melville, *James I, King of Scots, 1406–37* (London, 1936), pp. 101–5; A. I. Dunlop, *The Life and Times of James Kennedy, Bishop of St Andrews* (Edinburgh, 1950), p. 105.

[2] Wessington's compilation '*ad excusanda priorem et monasterium super solucione subsidii*' survives in three versions (Loc. II, no. 11; Loc. XXI, no. 20 (vii); Loc. XXI, no. 30).

of 26s. 8d. spent on new linen and 13s. 4d. given to his cooks.[1] But although it would be idle to pretend that the visits of the great lords to Durham were financially insupportable, they cannot fail to have been both expensive and unsettling, above all to the prior himself.[2]

Nevertheless it might be unjust to Wessington's conduct of his priorate to assume that these social obligations, heavy although they undoubtedly were, prevented him from the proper exercise of his role as paterfamilias. Compared to the time consumed by public hospitality, periods devoted to private recreation would seem, by contemporary standards, to have been slight. Unlike many fifteenth-century prelates, Wessington did not keep a pack of hounds and can only be found at the hunt on one recorded occasion, in 1418–19 when he was in Langley's company in the bishop's forest at Weardale.[3] Only in the literary sphere did the prior continue to display unusual interest and talents; but Wessington's later works were, with few exceptions, devoted to the defence of the monastery's rights and liberties, while his letter-book suggests neither an interest in correspondence for its own sake nor any serious leanings towards the contemporary fashion for '*florida verborum venustas*'. That there was much delegation of the prior's office is certain. In his absence, the sub-prior, or in the absence of both prior and sub-prior, the third prior, naturally performed Wessington's duties in choir and chapter-house. Even when in residence, the prior of Durham's responsibility for the detailed conduct of the *Opus Dei* was inevitably remote and indirect: attendance and discipline at the Hours were essentially matters for sub-prior, third prior and the deans of order. On the other hand the monastic registers fully confirm Wessington's assertion in 1442 that he often met and consulted his brethren both in chapter and on less formal occasions.[4] The prior's more important prerogatives – the power to allow Durham monks leave of absence for more than two nights, the appointment to the major obediences and to all but two of the headships of the cells, the control of spiritual

[1] Bursar, 1428/29, Garderoba, Dona et Exennia.
[2] A military expedition which called at a smaller monastery certainly had a much more adverse effect on its finances. See J. R. H. Moorman, 'Edward I at Lanercost Priory, 1306–7', *E.H.R.* LXVII (1952), 161–74.
[3] Bursar, 1418/19, Expense Prioris.
[4] 1.8. Pont., no. 2; Loc. XXVII, no. 17.

and temporal patronage, and above all his freedom to move monks from mother house to cell and back again – were always reserved to him.[1] Moreover Wessington's term of office coincided with what was probably a permanent improvement in the prior of Durham's record of attendance at religious services in the cathedral. His own guarded remark, 'that religious observances these days are performed as well or better than in times past', can be applied to himself without hesitation. Whereas Prior Fossor had admitted in 1354 that it was never his custom to appear in the cathedral at all except '*in choro*', Wessington was in the habit of entering the church at frequent intervals to see that his monks were celebrating their masses.[2] The great monastic processions, so common a feature of the liturgical year at Durham, invariably centred round the figure of the prior with (after 1379) his staff and mitre. More generally, the records of the early fifteenth century gave an impression, like the *Rites of Durham* many years later, of a prior in constant contact with his monks at their hours of devotion. The lengthy *comperta* drawn up at the time of Bishop Robert Neville's episcopal visitation in 1442, as well as the chapter's own diffinitions of 1446, criticise the prior's exercise of his office in various ways, but never on the grounds of serious negligence. It was 'the troubles and almost unbearable burdens of old age' rather than a lack of a natural capacity for leadership which brought about Wessington's resignation in June 1446.

The resignation of a prior, although a common enough event at Durham in the thirteenth century, was less so in the later middle ages. Of the last twelve superiors of Durham, seven died in office while two, Richard Bell and Hugh Whitehead, resigned to become respectively bishop of Carlisle and first dean of the post-Dissolution chapter. Only Robert Walworth in 1391, John Wessington in 1446 and William Ebchester in 1456 voluntarily accepted the status of a *quondam* prior and were content to spend the remainder of their lives in quiet if luxurious retirement. By 1446 Wessington himself had reached the advanced age of 75 and for at least the preceding six

---

[1] Loc. xxvii, no. 38; Loc. xxi, no. 20 (i); Reg. Parv. ii, passim; Reg. Parv. iv, fos. 4–5.

[2] Loc. xxvii, no. 17; B. Harbottle, 'Bishop Hatfield's Visitation of Durham Priory in 1354', *Arch. Ael.*, Fourth Series, xxxvi (1958), 92.

years had been plagued by serious and prolonged ill-health. 'Wexit with greyt sekenesse', as he had informed several of his correspondents, Wessington's illness was sufficiently alarming to make it necessary for one of his chaplains to quell the rumour that he was on the point of death.[1] It is unlikely to be a coincidence that this period of continuous sickness coincided with a certain decline in the unity and self-confidence of the monastery, reflected most obviously in the *comperta* of the 1442 visitation. The handling of the three great *causes célèbres* of the early 1440s – the Lytham case, the Scots' renewed assault on Coldingham, and the major financial crisis in the bursar's office – all seem to reveal unusual indecision and an absence of determined and energetic direction from above. But there is no evidence that the Durham brethren conspired to oust Wessington from the priorate. A prior's resignation, the last public act of his office, was a decision for himself alone. Following the usual procedure in these cases, Wessington petitioned his bishop for release from his obligations, a request to which Robert Neville had given his assent at Howden by 13 May. Three weeks later, on Wednesday 8 June 1446, Wessington formally resigned his office in the prior's chapel of Saint Nicholas and by the end of the month (on 30 June) William Ebchester had succeeded him as the new prior of Durham. So ended those twenty-nine years and six months in which he had laboured 'not without tedium' for the care of his flock.[2] In the entire history of the Benedictine priory of Durham, only one prior, John Fossor with 33 years of rule to his credit, is known to have enjoyed or endured a longer priorate.

Like the retired religious superiors of all substantial English monasteries, ex-priors of Durham received a special *provisio*, of which the essential elements were separate living quarters, a food allowance for themselves and a few attendants, and some form of money pension. Wessington's own provision, authorised by a grateful chapter on 11 June 1446, was closely modelled on that assigned to Prior Robert Walworth 55 years earlier. In addition to a suite of

[1] In April 1446 Wessington himself was of the opinion that he would 'more likely within feue days to passe out of this worlde then till abide'; on his illnesses, see Reg. Parv. II, fos. 95, 131, 170, 183; Reg. III, fos. 146v, 190; Misc. Chrs., no. 1087; Loc. IX, nos. 8, 33.
[2] Reg. IV, fo. 48; Cart. III, fos. 297–9; Bursar, 1446/47, Expense Necessarie; *Scrip. Tres*, pp. cclxxvii–cclxxviii; *Dur. Obit. Rolls*, p. viii.

rooms called 'Coldingham' in the monastic infirmary, he and his servants were given the right to occupy the principal *camera* and chapel as well as the Douglas Tower at Finchale priory, perhaps the most splendid set of residential apartments at the convent's disposal. The *quondam*'s wine, the stipends of his five attendants (a monk chaplain, an esquire, a clerk, a valet and a boy) and his other miscellaneous expenses were to be paid out of an annual pension of £40 assigned to his regular use.[1] However comfortable, the provision made for Wessington in 1446 hardly bears comparison with the more splendid treatment of their late superiors made by some other great monastic communities. Richard Harwden and Edmund Kirton, abbots of Westminster contemporary to Wessington, were pensioned at 200 marks a year; and when John Whethamstede resigned in 1441 he had a large enough income to retire to his native village, acquire landed property and rebuild the manor-house there.[2] In the thirteenth century the *quondam*'s provision had been on a similar scale at Durham; but the unfortunate examples of Bertram of Middleton in 1258 and Hugh of Darlington in 1273, who retained to their personal use manors necessary for the sustenance of the convent, must have led to the sad conclusion that the more valuable the provision the more likelihood of an unscrupulous resignation. There followed a transitional period in the fourteenth century when the *quondams* of 1313, 1321 and 1394 (Walworth's second provision) were given the income of a small cell, Jarrow or Wearmouth.[3] This arrangement had its obvious disadvantages, and that adopted in Wessington's case in 1446 was undoubtedly the best practical solution to the embarrassing problem of the status of a retired prior in his own monastery. To judge from the disappearance of his name in the extant records, the old prior faded quietly from the scene. Apart from mention of a minor dispute between Wessington and another elderly and particularly turbulent monk, Henry Helay, about the occupation of a room in the infirmary, the rest is silence. It was

---

[1] Reg. IV, fo. 29; *Scrip. Tres*, pp. cclxvi–cclxviii; Bursar, 1446/47, 1449/50, Pensiones; *Finchale Priory*, pp. ix–xxi, cclxxix, cccvi.

[2] Pearce, *The Monks of Westminster*, pp. 127, 130; Knowles, *Rel. Orders* II, 196. For *provisiones* more comparable with that of Wessington see Thompson, *Abbey of St Mary of the Meadows, Leicester*, pp. 52–3; *Priory of Hexham* I (Surtees Soc. XLIV, 1864), pp. xlix–l, xcviii–xcix, cxxi.

[3] *Durham Annals*, pp. 11–13, 27–32; *Scrip. Tres*, pp. 43–4, 49, 95, 102, clxxiv–clxxv.

almost five years after his resignation that Wessington, 'exhausted by severe illness', took the last sacraments and died: this was on Friday 9 April 1451, at the ninth hour, allegedly 'that very day and hour on which Christ delivered up his precious soul for us on the Cross'.[1] He was almost eighty.

[1] Loc. XXVII, no. 15, memb. 4; *Dur. Obit. Rolls*, pp. 72–3.

Chapter 4

THE PRIOR'S HOUSEHOLD
AND COUNSELLORS

Do all things with counsel, and thy deeds shall not bring thee repentance.[1]

The separation of abbot and convent has been described as 'the first and most important division' in the medieval English monastery, a division whose seeds can be detected in the Rule of St Benedict himself.[2] The church of Durham during Wessington's priorate obviously presents no exception to this general rule, but it would be unfortunate if the effects of this inevitable cleavage between the shepherd and his flock were to be exaggerated. At Durham, as elsewhere, a rudimentary household and an informal group of counsellors had begun to serve the prior long before the end of the twelfth century. Yet there never developed in the northern monastery that sharp separation between the two rival establishments of prelate and convent so characteristic of many other late medieval Benedictine houses.[3] Wessington's household officials and counsellors contributed to the general interests of the community and were not merely the appurtenances of a solitary splendour. A prime concern of Wessington's servants was the well-being of the convent as a whole: and when, for example, Durham obedientiaries used the term *scaccarium prioris*, they were referring to the bursary or central financial organ of the house. A close relationship between the superior and his monks was of course characteristic of all English cathedral monasteries. But there were several of the latter, like Christ Church, Canterbury, and Worcester, where the prior did in fact develop a very separate establishment.[4] At Durham, however, the prior's household and

[1] Ecclus. XXXII. 24.
[2] J. R. H. Moorman, *Church Life in England in the Thirteenth Century* (Cambridge, 1945), p. 273.
[3] Of the many possible examples, the abbeys of Peterborough and Westminster present perhaps the extreme cases of such dualism (*Lincoln Visitations* III, 273; *House of Kings*, ed. Carpenter, pp. 47–50).
[4] Smith, *Canterbury Cathedral Priory*, pp. 23–32; *Journal of Prior William More* (Worcestershire Historical Society, 1914), pp. 357–75.

counsellors, although forming a distinguishable element in the monastic system, operated in very close association with the convent's other consultative and administrative institutions.

The failure of the priors of Durham to evolve a more autonomous household was due to their lack of financial independence. Wessington was not one of those many monastic prelates '*qui habent bona et possessiones a conventu discreta*',[1] and had no regular private income whatsoever. The prior's household owed its subsistence to the bursar's office, either directly in the form of cash payments from the bursar himself, or indirectly in the case of provisions furnished by the cellarer and granator.[2] Similarly, it was the bursar who accounted for the fees and stipends paid to the prior's counsellors and servants. Wessington's financial dependence on the central bursary had a double effect on his relations with his convent. In so far as the prior's bills had to be met out of the bursar's revenues, he was liable to more detailed criticism than seems to have been usual in most monasteries: the Durham chapter felt comparatively free to comment upon his expenditure and to suggest economies.[3] In this, as in other spheres, the thirteenth-century conflicts between Durham priors and their chapters – less severe in any case than at monasteries like Westminster Abbey – had led to the imposition of a series of fairly effective constitutional checks against the former's abuse of his abbatial power. On the other hand, the prior of Durham was no Venetian doge. Just because he had few independent sources of income, he was more concerned than most prelates to direct and supervise the monastery's central financial department. The prior alone appointed the bursar and terrar, the two obedientiaries on whose efficiency the economic welfare of the convent directly depended. The account rolls of these two officers reveal how continuously all priors of Durham intervened at every level of their activity. However, although the main responsibility of the bursar and terrar lay towards their prior, their accounts were also inspected by sub-prior and convent. The dual allegiance of the two monks marks one of the many points at which the prior's establishment merged into the wider field of monastic administration. In this chapter, however, attention will

[1] Pantin, *Chapters* II, 110.
[2] See below, pp. 257–64.
[3] Jesus College, Cambridge, MS. 41, fo. 169v; Loc. XXVII, no. 15.

be reserved for those agents of the prior in a less equivocal position, men whom he appointed and whose primary loyalties were to him alone. Such agents, all with a vested interest in the prosperity of the convent, played a crucial role as the personal intermediaries through whom the monastic life at Durham was integrated into northern society as a whole. They fall into two obviously disparate groups, those who acted as the prior's permanent household officials and those, not normally resident within the monastery, who were retained to give him counsel and expert service when called upon to do so.

The central figures of the prior's household at Durham were the two monks chosen by him to act as his chaplains. In using the services of two chaplains rather than one, Wessington was following the practice adopted by the superiors of all large English religious houses. As early as 1206, the abbot of Saint Mary's, York, had been instructed by a papal legate to limit the number of his chaplains to two; and it was in the company of his two monk chaplains that Abbot John Whethamstede of St Albans went to the Council of Pavia in 1423.[1] The reason for this duplication was less – as has sometimes been suggested – the fear that a single chaplain might be corrupted than the prior's need for two very different services. In the words of a Durham document of the very early fifteenth century, 'from time out of mind the prior had two chaplains, both sleeping in rooms near his own, one to say divine services and the other to supervise his hospice'.[2] During Wessington's priorate no attempt was made to change this long Durham tradition, although the bursar's rolls indicate that there were some years (1418–19 and 1432) in which three chaplains held office simultaneously. But usually there were two chaplains only, each receiving 6s. 8d. annually 'for their cowl'. The records of these payments in the bursar's accounts make it possible to identify eighteen of Wessington's chaplains although there were certainly several more whose names are unrecorded. Perhaps one in five of all Durham monks served as prior's chaplain at some time during their careers. The chaplains were chosen freely by the prior, not imposed on him by his chapter, and held office

---

[1] C. R. Cheney, 'The Papal Legate and English Monasteries in 1206', *E.H.R.* XLVI (1931), 443–52; *Annales J. Amundesham* (Rolls Series, 1870–1), I, 4; Knowles, *Rel. Orders* I, 274.   [2] Loc. XXVII, no. 38.

for varying periods, which might be as long as eleven years (e.g. Thomas Nesbitt, 1425–36) but was usually four or five.[1] The statutes of the Black Monk Chapters requiring prelates to change their chaplains yearly were tacitly ignored at Durham.[2]

Of all the members of Wessington's household, the closest in attendance upon the prior was his domestic chaplain, with whom he prayed and said mass in his private chapel. This chaplain witnessed Wessington's business transactions and accompanied him on all his journeys, for example to the Benedictine Chapter at Northampton in July 1426 where he acted as an official door-keeper.[3] No doubt the most important function of the domestic chaplain – inevitably unrecorded – was to celebrate masses in the prior's chapel. More generally he acted as the prior's personal assistant, the equivalent of a modern secretary, keeping his letter-book and making copies or memoranda of his correspondence. Although Wessington used the services of professional scribes to do much of the written work, his private chaplain was directly responsible for the preservation of the prior's small register, in whose pages he might insert his own name when taking up office.[4] It is probably safe to assume that, just as the chancellor had the custody of the official seal of the prior and chapter of Durham, so the private chaplain held Wessington's own formal seal as prior.[5] Whether Wessington ever allowed his second and more personal seal, an octagonal signet, to pass out of his possession is a more open question.[6] The private chaplain also kept what might be described as the prior's privy purse and made small payments to visiting heralds and minstrels on his master's orders. It is hardly surprising that Wessington's usual choice for this office was a young monk, often just returned from a few years at Durham College, Oxford. Here was a personal and intimate relationship, as the con-

[1] Bursar, 1416–46, Garderoba, Expense Prioris.

[2] Pantin, *Chapters* II, 193.　　　　　　　　[3] Ibid., p. 158.

[4] See Reg. Parv. II, fos. 104 ('*Registrum de tempore Ricardi Parke, Capellani*'), 172.

[5] Wessington's oval or (to use the contemporary description) 'oblong' seal is described in C. H. Hunter Blair, *Catalogue of the Seals in the Treasury of the Dean and Chapter of Durham* II, p. 556 (no. 3444) and is obviously modelled on that of his predecessor, Prior Hemingburgh (ibid., p. 555). In 1446, the cost of making seals for the new prior amounted to 26s. 8d. (Bursar, 1446/47).

[6] Examples of Wessington's signet seal survive on Loc. XXVIII, no. 26 and 1.14. Spec., no. 30. The former is a particularly fine specimen, showing an eagle with raised wings. For a third example, see 4.13 Spec., no. 63.

vent recognised when they allowed the chaplain material compensation if the prior died in office.[1]

Much more prominent among the Durham records is the prior's second chaplain, sometimes called his steward, or to avoid confusion with the prior's lay steward, the *seneschallus hospicii domini prioris*.[2] 'His offis', it was remembered in the late sixteenth century, 'was to Receave at ye Bowcers handes all such sumes of money as was dewe for ye bowcer to paie vnto ye Lo: priors vse for ye mantenance of hime selfe & expencis of his whole howshold, and for all his other necessaries'.[3] Although the fifteenth-century evidence is not sufficiently detailed to confirm that all money received by the prior's household from the bursar passed through the hands of this chaplain, most of it certainly did so. This officer was undoubtedly the prior's main financial agent, the counterpart of the abbot's receiver at Westminster Abbey, Peterborough and elsewhere. The monk-steward's sphere of operations ranged from the provisioning of the prior's household at Durham to the financing of the Beaurepaire *ludi*. He did not, like the other Durham obedientiaries, draw up one annual account roll for his office but rather presented a whole series of small, separate bills to the bursar in the course of the year. The bursar entered the totals of these '*doggeta*' and '*papira*' in his yearly account but had no interest in the survival of the original drafts; consequently, none of the latter remain for the period of Wessington's rule and it is impossible to trace the prior's movements and expenditure in more detail than that provided by the bursar's rolls.[4] There is no evidence that the *seneschallus hospicii* received, by virtue of his office, any income independent of the sums he derived from the Durham bursar; but he was occasionally entrusted with small extra sources of revenue (e.g. the profits from the convent's coal-pits and sales of timber) for which he was obliged to make a regular annual account. Apart from his financial duties, the prior's monk-steward was responsible for the maintenance of his master's apartments, both

[1] Jesus College, Cambridge, MS. 41, fo. 169v.
[2] Cf. the analogous distinction between the *capellanus* and *seneschallus hospicii prioris* at Ely: *Ely Chapter Ordinances and Visitation Records, 1241–1515*, ed. S. J. A. Evans (Camden Third Series, LXIV, 1940), p. 25.
[3] *Rites*, p. 101, where there is no separate reference to the second or private chaplain.
[4] Bursar, 1416–46, Expense Prioris. Thus Henry Helay, prior's steward in 1420–1, was given over £10 by the bursar for Wessington's expenses '*ut patet per papirum*'.

at Beaurepaire and, more especially, at Durham, where he held the keys to the store-rooms and controlled a large and often unruly staff of household servants.[1] Administrative expertise was consequently the essential qualification for such an office; and it is noticeable that this chaplain, more often than his colleague, normally progressed to the most responsible of monastic obediences. Indeed the position of prior's steward had prestige and influence in its own right; it was, for example, held by John Oll in the late 1430s when that monk was well over forty and had already served several years as commoner and bursar. Wessington chose the stewards of his household with a careful eye to their ability. The last of a long line of prominent monks who held this office under him was the most successful of all. Richard Bell, Wessington's steward between 1443 and 1446, was almoner in 1447, warden of Durham College in 1450, terrar and hostillar in 1454, prior of Finchale in 1457, prior of Durham in 1464 and bishop of Carlisle in 1478.[2]

As well as his two chaplains, the prior of Durham was 'attended vpon both with gentlemen and yeomen of ye best in ye countrie as ye honorable service of his house Deserved no less'. This comment by the author of the *Rites of Durham* can fairly apply to the period of Wessington's priorate even if some later historians of the monastery have exaggerated both the size and the magnificence of the prior's permanent retinue.[3] Of the fifty or sixty servants receiving stipends from the Durham bursar early in the fifteenth century, less than a third lived and travelled with the prior while the others were members of Wessington's staff only in the sense that they worked in the interests of the central bursary. The prior's household itself was a relatively small body. In 1446 the convent asked their superior to restrict the number of attendants and servants in his hospice to 14: 4 esquires with a *famulus* to keep their horses, 4 valets as well as the clerk of the prior's chapel, and 4 grooms to care for the buttery, hall, *camera* and stable.[4] Although the imposition of such restrictions was

---

[1] Misc. Chrs., nos. 5649–5651; Loc. xxvii, nos. 15, 29. By the sixteenth century at least, the prior's chaplain had his own 'Checker' in the *camera prioris* (*Rites*, p. 101).

[2] Bursar, 1443–47, Expense Prioris; Dobson, 'Richard Bell, Prior of Durham and Bishop of Carlisle', pp. 182–221.

[3] *Rites*, p. 90; *Dur. Acct. Rolls* iii, pp. iii–vii.

[4] Loc. xxvii, no. 15, memb. 3.

exceptional and intended as a purely temporary economy, it is clear that the Durham monks were not prepared to accept the diversion of large sums to feed, pay and clothe an enormous prior's household. Nor was there any social or legal distinction between the prior's own servants and those of the bursar or any other obedientiary: some, like John Shalden in 1409–10, might be employed by more than one monastic officer in the same year.[1]

Members of the prior's household, in common with all dependants of the monastery, were however subject to an overriding and extremely rigid classification in terms of status. The Durham records provide an unusual opportunity for observing how faithfully the convent implemented late medieval statutes, ordinances and conventions designed to maintain a highly stratified social order. In the middle and lower ranks of society at least, there was apparently little chance of fundamental 'class betterment'. Whether clerks or laymen, all agents of the prior were categorised as either *generosi*, *valecti* or *gromi* and it was almost unknown for a servant to pass from one of these three grades to another.[2] The quality of a man's livery was an accurate index of his position in this rigid hierarchy. During the first half of the fifteenth century the bursar bought woollen cloth from York drapers at standardised prices: he usually paid 50s. 0d. a cloth for the livery of the *generosi*, 43s. 4d. for the valets and 36s. 8d. for the grooms.[3] Although the *generosi* were also provided with white furs each year, the colour of the livery (as opposed to the quality of the cloth) was identical for all three ranks. As the convent rarely dyed its own cloth, the prior's choice of colour was dependent on the stocks held by the York merchants and he was unable to insist on complete uniformity from year to year; but a green or occasionally a blue mixture ('medlid' or 'melly') was brought in bulk when available and combined with a smaller quantity of striped material ('ray') to produce the finished garments. The prior's lay steward might enjoy a more striking livery of red and green, but other members of the prior's household seem to have worn exactly the

---

[1] Sacrist 1409/10; Bursar 1409/10, Expense Minute.

[2] These three Durham grades corresponded to the esquires, yeomen and grooms encountered elsewhere, 'the well-known three estates of a medieval nobleman's household' (Thompson, *The English Clergy*, p. 168) and of late medieval sumptuary legislation (*Statutes of the Realm* I, 380).

[3] Bursar, 1416–46, Garderoba.

same colours as the rest of the monastic staff. Nor did Wessington's attendants receive higher rates of pay than their counterparts outside the *camera prioris*: all were technically in receipt of *stipendia* rather than the *pensiones* delivered to the prior's counsellors, and were paid by the bursar at the terms of Whitsunday and Martinmas. In addition to their food, clothing and other perquisites, the *generosi* normally received a stipend of 20s. a year. The valets were usually paid either 10s. or 13s. 4d.; the minimum stipend for a groom was 3s. 4d., although most servants of this lowest grade received twice that amount.[1] In addition the records of Durham visitations and chapter ordinances reveal the presence of a multitude of boys, providing a chaotic supply of unskilled labour and receiving neither regular wages nor livery. A few of these boys seem to have worked in the prior's apartments, as did one or two women who went there to wash his clothes and linen.

The prior's constant companions, sometimes described as his *domicelli*, comprised a small group of about six or seven esquires or *generosi*. Very few of these men have made much impression on the records of either the cathedral church or the palatinate of Durham. Only occasionally did one of Wessington's esquires appear as a witness to proceedings in the prior's chapel or as a messenger to some north-country lord. These *domicelli* served the prior for many years and usually for life, ate at his table and could look forward to a retirement pension (in the form of a corrody at one of the convent's hospitals) and perhaps eventual burial in the monastic cemetery. The position of prior's esquire was, in short, a career in itself; for, as one prior pointed out in 1495, 'it is one custom of owr place to discharge none old officer ne seruand of hys office ne service with owte resonable cause require it'.[2] It is important to stress that the prior's esquires were not members of prominent knightly families and were never styled as *armigeri*; they seem to have been recruited from the ranks of the more substantial peasantry like the Durham monks to whom they were often related. Richard Hemingburgh, still receiving a stipend as one of Wessington's *generosi* as late as 1443, is known to have been a kinsman of his namesake, Prior John Hemingburgh, who had died in 1416. Similarly, John Killerby, prior's esquire in

[1] Bursar, 1416–46, Pensiones et Stipendia.
[2] Sacrist, 1438/39, 1441/42; Reg. Parv. II, fo. 123; IV, fo. 35v.

1417, was a distant relative of Wessington himself.[1] Most of the prior's esquires were functionaries with a specific duty to perform in the running of his household. Thus the most prominent member of the group was the prior's own chamberlain who co-operated with the monk-chaplains in the administration of the *camera prioris*, where he lived and slept except when sent by Wessington to conduct business at York or elsewhere. John Holme, Wessington's chamberlain from 1418 to 1444 and usually described as *generosus et litteratus*, was the most frequent of all witnesses to the prior's official *acta* and influential enough to persuade the Earl of Northumberland to write a letter of recommendation on his behalf. Holme also acted as the prior's travelling personal representative and it was in this capacity that he attended the installation of Archbishop Kemp at York when Wessington was unable to make the journey.[2] Among the other *generosi* employed by the prior were a butler and a marshal. The names of these two officers were rarely mentioned in the Durham records, but it is clear that the former's duty was to buy wine at Newcastle-upon-Tyne and so replenish the supplies of drink stored in the cellars of the prior's apartments.[3] At various times, Wessington also used the services of a palfreyman, carter, ostler and barber, all men of valet status; and finally, the porter of the abbey (who held an office much in demand among the elderly retainers of north-country lords) seems to have enjoyed a close relationship with the prior's household.[4]

Although the evidence of the bursar's account rolls has suggested that Wessington's permanent establishment consisted of a small group of professional servants, the prior's retinue also included, at any one time, a larger and more ephemeral collection of individuals who received neither regular stipends nor livery. It is clear, for instance, that the prior regularly satisfied his pressing need for clerks to transcribe and witness documents by having recourse to the scores of priests and chaplains serving chapels and chantries in the cathedral and other Durham churches. John Binchester, chaplain of Saint Helen's chantry above the monastic gatehouse, was so frequently

[1] Reg. Parv. II, fo. 29; Misc. Chrs., no. 6013; Loc. XXI, no. 23.

[2] Loc. XXV, nos. 54, 165; Terrar, 1427/28.

[3] Loc. XXVII, no. 15, memb. 2.

[4] Reg. III, fos. 57v, 136, 174v; Bursar, 1416/17, Stipendia; Bursar, 1408/09, Soulsilver; Loc. XXV, nos. 110, 132, 147; Misc. Chrs., no. 1091.

in Wessington's presence that he could be regarded, in fact if not in theory, as a member of his household.[1] Another example of the same process is the indenture made in 1434 by the rector of Saint Mary the Less, South Bailey, in which he undertook to answer any call placed on his services by the prior and chapter.[2] Wessington never had any difficulty in assembling a dozen or more Durham clerks to witness his official *acta* and judicial appeals. No doubt the prior was also surrounded by a similar floating entourage of laymen; but the conventional picture of the prior's household as an educational establishment for the sons of local nobility finds little confirmation among the fifteenth-century evidence at Durham. Besides the small group of careerist esquires who spent their life in his service, Wessington was usually attended by boys of yeoman rather than knightly status.[3] The household of the fifteenth-century prior of Durham cannot be regarded as particularly magnificent by the most lavish medieval standards, or even by those of other prelates with larger revenues at their personal disposal;[4] but it was large enough to maintain the state befitting a prior of Durham and to cater for the distinguished visitors who came to pay their respects, receive his entertainment and give him counsel. It is to this last and large group – the prior's advisers rather than his servants – that we must now turn.

As we have seen, the late medieval prior of Durham could not be a complete autocrat. He tended to appreciate, more perhaps than most prominent abbots and priors of the fifteenth century, the need for regular and judicious counsel. His principal counsellors were of course his fellow monks and it is characteristic of Wessington's own conservative approach to his office that he should quote the third

---

[1] Among Binchester's many appearances in the early fifteenth-century registers, see Reg. II, fo. 207; Reg. III, fos. 59, 63, 96v, 132; Reg. Parv. II, fo. 10.

[2] Reg. Parv. II, fo. 81; *Scrip. Tres*, pp. ccxxxvii–ccxxxviii.

[3] E.g. the son of Thomas Birkhall of Berwick whom the Earl of Northumberland desired the prior to 'forder be goode menys' to Durham College, Oxford (Loc. xxv, no. 163).

[4] Cf. the household of 43 men, including musicians and actors, kept by Abbot Walter de Wenlok of Westminster in the thirteenth century (E. H. Pearce, *Walter de Wenlock, Abbot of Westminster* (London, 1920), pp. 99–104); and the even larger household said to have been maintained by the priors of Norwich (H. W. Saunders, *An Introduction to the Obedientiary and Manor Rolls of Norwich Cathedral Priory* (Norwich, 1930), pp. 86–7). See Moorman, *Church Life in England in the Thirteenth Century*, pp. 275–6.

chapter of the Rule to justify a change in monastic policy.[1] Towards the end of his priorate Wessington claimed that he had always observed the maxim '*quod in negociis maioribus requirit vota singulorum*',[2] an assertion which it is as impossible to prove as disprove. What is certain is that Wessington regularly took the advice of his senior monks and would allow his course of action to be swayed by their opinions.[3] As Durham, unlike many of the major Benedictine houses of the thirteenth century, lacked a formally constituted council of seniors, it is difficult to be more precise; but in 1438 the decision to divide the office of bursar was apparently supported by a special committee of fifteen monks chosen for their administrative experience. Obviously the prior enjoyed considerable discretion in the choice of those monks from whom he received counsel, a discretion restricted by the need to respect the spheres of authority of the major obedientiaries. In particular, the terrar, chancellor and the sub-prior were Wessington's indispensable contacts with the fields of estate-management, legal protocol and monastic discipline; these three officers are accordingly those most often recorded as being in his presence. This triumvirate, and the other trained and experienced administrators with whom they shared the monastic life, helped Wessington to frame the main lines of the convent's policy. But the monastery did not exist in isolation, and for the application of this policy Wessington employed the services of a large number of secular counsellors whose character and functions must now be described. These *iurisperiti* – to give them their most accurate title – fall naturally into the two groups of lay and ecclesiastical counsellors. Both were essential to the welfare of the monastery and both were appointed by the prior alone; but they in no sense rivalled the power of the senior monks who were the real arbiters, with their prior, of the convent's destinies.

The most important and influential of all the prior of Durham's

---

[1] Loc. XXI, no. 20 (ii): alluding to St Benedict's commands '*De adhibendis ad consilium fratribus*'.

[2] Loc. XXVII, no. 17; 1.8. Pont., no. 2.

[3] Loc. XXI, no. 20 (iv). Although the prior was free to issue ordinances on his own authority (Reg. Parv. II, fo. 56), it appears that virtually all domestic legislation at Durham was proposed by a group of monk diffinitors and approved in full or annual chapter. See the contemporary heading, '*Peticiones diffinitorum constitutorum per dominum priorem et capitulum Dunelmensem in Annali Capitulo, A.D. 1464*', to Loc. XXVII, no. 29.

secular counsellors was his steward, an officer who stood at the head of the lay servants of the monastery. The influence wielded by the 'high steward' on the management of late medieval monasteries has still received less attention than it deserves. The often frenzied competition for the office on the part of acquisitive magnate and gentry families in the fifteenth and early sixteenth centuries in itself raises the probability that a monastic stewardship was something more than a well-paid sinecure. Indeed a close survey of the lay steward's role in many religious houses leaves no doubt that he often systematically exploited his influence over monastic estate-management, and particularly over short-term leases of conventual land, in the interests of himself, his friends and his retainers. In many ways it might even be suggested that the late medieval monastic steward was the counterpart of the early medieval continental *advocatus* or *ministerialis*: such men were always likely to sacrifice the loyalty they owed to their local religious corporation on the altar of their own family fortunes.

Many stewards, moreover, shed no tears at the final destruction of the monasteries to which they had sworn their oaths. The dispersal of monastic lands in the 1540s reveals the presence of large numbers of country gentry, like Sir Leonard Beckwith in the case of Selby Abbey, only too eager to buy up property after the Dissolution which they had administered as stewards before that event. Needless to say, it was the smaller and medium-sized monasteries of England which succumbed most readily and completely to exploitation on the part of their lay stewards. The influence of the Stanleys at Lytham and the Homes at Coldingham, or the somewhat sinister activities of Sir Humphrey Neville, steward or bailiff of Hexham Priory in 1461 at the time he 'seems to have been a captain of freebooters', all demonstrate the way in which a lay steward might obtain a financial stranglehold over the monastic community he was supposed to serve.[1] In the larger and therefore more self-reliant religious houses, these pressures still existed but were naturally more easy to resist. At Durham itself the lay steward remained the servant rather than the master of his lord despite his great importance as the prior's most valued link with the non-religious world. When

---

[1] *The Priory of Hexham* I (Surtees Soc. XLIV, 1864), pp. ci, cxii–cxiii; cf. G. Baskerville, *English Monks and the Suppression of the Monasteries* (London, 1937), pp. 58–63; R. B. Dobson, *Selby Abbey and Town* (Leeds, 1969), p. 30.

William Hoton of Hardwick died in the autumn of 1446, Prior Ebchester wrote that this 'deede is to me and my brether . . . , savying the displesaunce of Gode, the most hevynesse and losse of oon that ever befell to us or to the Monastery of Durham'; but this grief did not prevent him, the day after Hoton's death, from immediately taking steps to secure the appointment of a successor.[1]

The functions of the prior's steward at Durham in this period are described in the letters of appointment made out to William Hoton in February 1437.[2] He was to assist in the administration of all demesnes, manors and leased tenements pertaining to the *scaccarium prioris*, and in this capacity was closely associated with both terrar and bursar. Conversely, he had no authority with respect to those estates held independently by the other obedientiaries, whose accounts rarely recognise his existence. Hence the choice of steward was the prior's alone and in no sense was he legally or constitutionally responsible to the chapter as a whole, which on only one occasion (in 1464)[3] is known to have criticised his methods. In theory, the steward could be dismissed if he failed to perform his duties satisfactorily; but although Bishop Langley's injunctions of 1408 had forbidden the granting of offices for life, it seems clear that fifteenth-century stewards were replaced only on their death or at their own wish.[4] The letters of Hoton's appointment in 1437 stressed his duties as president of the prior's manorial courts, of which only the halmote or leet courts were still thriving in the later middle ages. As there were three halmote tourns each year, this would seem to have been the most arduous of the steward's official responsibilities. During the fourteenth century the steward had often been much less assiduous in his attendance at these courts than his two co-presidents, the terrar and the bursar.[5] In Wessington's priorate, however, the halmote court rolls and books show the steward presiding fairly frequently, and leave no doubt that he exercised very real power over the crucial issue of the terms on which monastic land was leased to tenants in the county of Durham. The danger that this might lead to un-

---

[1] Reg. Parv. III, fo. 4, printed by Raine, *Saint Cuthbert*, p. 157.

[2] Misc. Chrs., no. 2363; Reg. Parv. II, fo. 94.

[3] Loc. XXVII, no. 29.

[4] *Coldingham Corr.*, pp. 109–10, 114; Loc. XXV, nos. 47, 133.

[5] *Halmota Prioratus Dunelmensis, 1296–1384* (Surtees Soc. LXXXII, 1889), pp. 148, 157, 162, 176.

authorised leasing of the prior's estates by the steward was explicitly recognised in William Bulmer of Witton's terms of appointment in 1496.[1] Like the superiors of other large English monasteries, the very last priors of Durham took the cautious and ingenious step of employing two stewards, a *seneschallus capitalis* whose position was largely honorary, and a *seneschallus curiae* who was a man of much more humble origin.[2]

In this and other ways, the priors of Durham were therefore successful in curtailing the power of their stewards. Even in the sphere of estate management, it has been noticed that the Durham *seneschallus* 'rarely acted alone'.[3] We have seen that at the end of the fifteenth century William Bulmer was expressly forbidden to lease monastic property without direct warrant from the prior. Wessington's stewards show few signs of independent action and their office had become primarily a consultative one. The steward's counsel was highly valued; although he wore the livery of his prior, the relationship between the two men was less that of servant and master than of 'trusty frenndship'.[4] Wessington raised his steward's annual stipend from five marks to £5 in 1437, a sum which was to be maintained until the Dissolution. As the steward also received five marks per annum from the Durham terrar, he was the most highly paid of all the convent's regular servants.[5] Wessington's stewards seem to have earned their salaries; they witnessed his official business in the *camera prioris*, attended ceremonies of homage made to the prior by his feudal tenants, advised on the complications of land transfer and conducted inquisitions of *diem clausit extremum*.[6] Other duties performed by the prior's steward had less to do with the management of estates: he acted as a courier and messenger to the local nobility and might buy cloth, spices and wine for the prior on

---

[1] *Scrip. Tres*, p. ccclxxxv. Cf. Halmote Court Rolls, 1420, 1423, 1427, 1428; Halmote Court Books, I (1400–39), fo. 105v and passim.

[2] *Valor Ecclesiasticus*, v (1825), 302. The last chief steward of the monastery was Thomas Neville, son of the fourth Earl of Westmorland .

[3] E. M. Halcrow, 'Obedientiaries and Counsellors in Monastic Administration at Durham', *Arch. Ael.*, Fourth Series, xxxv (1957), 13, an article largely based on the fourteenth-century Durham halmote court rolls.

[4] Reg. Parv. III, fo. 4.

[5] Bursar, 1416–46, Stipendia; Terrar, 1401/02, 1419/20, 1421/22; *Dur. Acct. Rolls* III, 703.

[6] 3.6. Spec., no. 21; 3.8. Spec., no. 24; Reg. III, fos. 136, 152, 224, 230, 244, 251, 261.

a visit to London. Thus the ideal steward was a well-known member of the Durham gentry, free to devote much of his time to the prior's service and living within easy riding distance of the monastery where he kept a permanent stable.[1]

Both of Wessington's stewards fell into this category. Neither Thomas Langton, steward from the beginning of his priorate to 1436, nor William Hoton, who held the office from 1437 to 1446, were members of the knightly class. But both were invariably styled esquires and both were experienced administrators in the palatinate of Durham.[2] There were further similarities; Thomas Langton of Winyard and William Hoton of Hardwick Hall both lived in the same area of the county, Stockton Ward, and neither had a male heir. Perhaps for this reason they were prepared to spend freely, not least on their funeral monuments, both of which survive to evoke the considerable state of the lay stewards of the age. Five miles south-east of Hoton's memorial brass at Sedgefield church lie the sumptuous, if mutilated, alabaster effigies (in Saint Cuthbert's, Redmarshall) of Thomas and Sybil Langton. As his body is attired in fashionable plate mail, it is no surprise to discover that Langton had a considerable collection of armour and plate which he deposited in the monastery for safe-keeping and later bequeathed, at least in part, to the priors of Durham.[3] Hoton used his resources to endow a chantry chapel at his parish church of Sedgefield.[4] Both men were clearly prosperous and it is probable, if impossible to prove, that much of their wealth was derived from their positions as stewards. Langton deposited 200 marks in cash with the convent before he died; and Hoton loaned the prior considerable sums of money to pay, for

---

[1] Loc. xxv, nos. 7, 156, 158; Reg. III, fos. 64v, 264v; Raine, *Saint Cuthbert*, pp. 157–8; Bursar, 1430, Reparaciones Domorum.

[2] *33rd Report of the Deputy Keeper of the P.R.O.* (1872), Appendix, p. 81; *34th* ibid. (1873), Appendix, pp. 164–71, 233. There are other references to the two men in *V.C.H. Durham* III, 252, 331; Surtees, *Durham* III, 27, 71; Storey, *Thomas Langley*, pp. 66–7, 187.

[3] Misc. Chrs., nos. 6003–6005; Loc. xxv, no. 40. Cf. *Scrip. Tres*, pp. cclxxxvii–cclxxxviii; C. H. Hunter Blair, 'Monumental Effigies in the County of Durham', *Arch. Ael.*, Fourth Series, VI (1929), 32–3.

[4] Reg. III, fos. 243–4. William Hoton was buried in Sedgefield church, where his memorial brass gives the date of his death as 16 September 1445. In fact, Hoton was witnessing proceedings in the Durham chapter-house as late as 6 September 1446 and it was later in the same month that he died (Reg. Parv. III, fo. 4; *Scrip. Tres*, p. cclxxxiv).

instance, towards the inception of Durham monks at Oxford. Indeed throughout Hoton's tenancy of the stewardship, the monastery was in his debt for at least £60 and he was prepared to offer generous terms for repayment.[1]

A final similarity between Langton and Hoton, and perhaps the most significant, is their connection with the Neville family. Thomas Langton was an esquire of the first Earl of Westmorland.[2] Hoton served his grandson, the second Earl, and was strongly recommended to Wessington by the senior branch of the Neville family. Elizabeth, Countess of Westmorland, revealed that Hoton was already the steward of a landlord even more distinguished than the prior of Durham: 'and for so muche as he (Hoton) is my said worshipfull lord's Steward, he shall cause more goode acord and peis betwen his tenandis and youres at all tymes'.[3] Her argument was a sound one, for the Nevilles, unlike so many other Durham landowners, were never involved in litigation with the convent. The Countess's brothers-in-law, Sir John and Sir Thomas Neville, were equally insistent in a letter sent to Wessington from Carlisle at the same time (May 1436); they lauded William Hoton's qualifications as a man and as a servant of the Nevilles, 'consideryng right wurshipfull Sir that your Stewardes affore tyme has alwaye be toward our saide lord and his auncesters'.[4] The appointment of the prior's steward at Durham can therefore be regarded as yet one more example of the late medieval magnate's desire to provide positions for his clientage. When Hoton died in September 1446, it was to Sir Thomas Neville that Prior Ebchester wrote, soliciting his help in persuading Robert Rodes, 'my Lordes servaunt and youres . . . to be our Stewarde like as William Hoton was'.[5]

The first half of the revealing career of Robert Rodes, prior's steward from 1446 until 1460, coincided with the later years of Wessington's priorate. Between 1433 and 1446 Rodes was the most prominent member of Wessington's council of expert lay lawyers,

[1] Misc. Chrs., nos. 5649–5650, 6001, 7138; Reg. III, fo. 205; Reg. Parv. II, fos. 100, 123–4, 193–4.
[2] Reg. Parv. II, fo. 9. Langton would also appear to have acted as servant and chamberlain of Henry Percy, second Earl of Northumberland, in 1418–19 (Reg. III, fo. 64v; Loc. xxv, nos. 156, 158).
[3] Loc. xxv, no. 133; cf. *Scrip. Tres*, p. cclxxxii.
[4] Loc. xxv, no. 47.   [5] Reg. Parv. III, fo. 4.

the group from which the steward seems to have been invariably chosen. Described as '*in legibus eruditus*' in 1431 and '*jurisperitus*' by 1444, Rodes offers an excellent example of the demand for skilled lawyers not only by the prior but by other lords of north-eastern England. Not a man of knightly stock, nor even a prominent merchant, Rodes came to be the most distinguished citizen of his native Newcastle, where the coat of arms of this '*promotor ecclesiarum*' figures on the remarkable western tower and spire which he added to the parish church of Saint Nicholas.[1] As early as August 1444, two years before Rodes replaced Hoton as steward, the Durham prior and chapter had issued letters of fraternity to him, an unusual honour for one who was never ranked higher than an esquire.[2] Rodes was a man of wide-ranging interests, who combined the administration of estates with the leasing of coal-mines and the owning of missals.[3] Although he seems to have maintained a residence in Newcastle, he made many journeys to London and also had a house in the South Bailey at Durham where he founded a chantry chapel in the cathedral before his death.[4] An escheator of Northumberland as early as 1434, Rodes served on over a dozen judicial commissions in that county before his death in 1474; he was one of Newcastle's parliamentary representatives almost continuously from 1427 to 1442, and when appointed controller of the customs there in 1441 it was Wessington who received his oath of office at Durham on behalf of the government.[5] During the 1430s and 1440s Rodes was the monastery's main link with official circles at Westminster; he was the convent's proctor at the 1442 parliament, helped to settle disputes touching the prior's duties as collector of clerical tenths, and was the intermediary through whom messages and money passed between Wessington and his London agents.[6]

[1] H. L. Honeyman and T. Wake, 'The Cathedral Church of St Nicholas, Newcastle upon Tyne', *Arch. Ael.*, Fourth Series, IX (1932), 122.

[2] Reg. III, fo. 306; *Liber Vitae*, fo. 68r.

[3] Reg. IV, fos. 21, 128. See the description of the magnificent cross which this '*Sancti Cuthberti constans et fidelis amicus*' gave to the Durham feretrar on 10 January 1447 (*Dur. Acct. Rolls* II, 440).

[4] *Durham Household Book* (Surtees Soc. XVIII, 1844), pp. 99, 125, 197.

[5] Reg. III, fos. 271–2. Cf. J. C. Wedgwood, *History of Parliament, 1439–1509*, I (1936), 720; C. H. Hunter Blair, 'Members of Parliament for Newcastle upon Tyne, 1377–1558', *Arch. Ael.*, Fourth Series, XIV (1937), 44–5.

[6] Loc. XXV, nos. 31, 136; Reg. Parv. II, fos. 114, 121.

But his greatest services were in the field of estate management where he acted as an arbiter, a perambulator of disputed lands, and an adviser on the more complex issues concerning the transfer and amortization of real property. Like Langton and Hoton, his two predecessors as steward, Rodes was wealthy in his own right: he was able to take out a lease of the convent's manor of Wardley for forty years and is known to have loaned the monastery considerable sums from 1441 onwards.[1]

The presence of Rodes on Wessington's council is not an isolated phenomenon: among his colleagues was a Newcastle citizen of a slightly older generation, Robert Whelpington, parliamentary representative for Newcastle between 1413 and 1422 and mayor in the 1430s;[2] Whelpington was one of the prior's counsellors from 1427 to 1444. Like Rodes and the others in this group he received an annual pension of £1. The prior undoubtedly valued the services of these advisers for he increased their number from four to eight in the year after his election; towards the end of his priorate Wessington normally had nine such *generosi* in his pay.[3] They were almost always substantial landowners from the county of Durham or the North Riding of Yorkshire, whose common characteristic was a legal training: most were busy professional lawyers in the royal and palatinate courts. Although described as members of the prior's *concilium*, they never met in a body and thereby differed from the inner council of legal experts (usually clerks) who accompanied the prior of Christ Church, Canterbury 'on his frequent travels'.[4] Serving for periods that ranged from ten to twenty years, Wessington's legal counsellors were called upon individually as the need arose; they might attend an act of homage, serve as witnesses, impose a settlement of debt, or (one of their most common functions) take out writs against recalcitrant tenants.[5] For some, like Guy Fairfax, their position was something of a sinecure, but from others, like Robert Lampton, Wessington might demand attendance at a number of inquests and pleas. The service of these local gentry-lawyers was indispensable to the convent in that most of the serious land disputes in the county were increasingly settled out of court by the

[1] Reg. I, fo. vi; Reg. III, fos. 141–2, 222–9, 264; Misc. Chrs., no. 5649.
[2] J. S. Roskell, *The Commons in the Parliament of 1422* (Manchester, 1954), pp. 235–6.
[3] Bursar, 1416–46, Pensiones.   [4] Smith, *Canterbury Cathedral Priory*, p. 73.
[5] Bursar, 1418/19, 1419/20, 1421/22, Expense Necessarie; Reg. III, fos. 64v, 136.

fifteenth century; the prior's three major suits of trespass between 1416 and 1446, against the Gower family, Sir William Bowes and Sir William Elmeden, all eventually went to arbitration. In these cases, and in many others, the convent's urgent need for arbiters and umpires who wished the monastery well was met from the ranks of its counsellors. When in August 1431 Wessington appointed a panel to settle his claims against Elmeden, four of his representatives were county *armigeri* and the others were Guy Fairfax, William Vincent, Robert Danby, John Stafford and Robert Lampton.[1] All five were described as '*in legibus eruditus*' and all were then members of the prior's council receiving their annual pension from the Durham bursar.

In addition to this group of legal counsellors, the prior of Durham employed the services of a handful of men who much resembled them in social status and legal expertise but had somewhat more specific functions to fulfil. Most prominent was the prior's sergeant, a serjeant-at-law in his own right, who received a yearly pension of £2 and represented Wessington at the Westminster law courts. Wessington employed four sergeants in his thirty-year priorate, James Strangways until 1426, Thomas Fulthorpe from 1427 until 1438, John Portington from 1439 to 1442 and Robert Danby, who continued to serve Prior Ebchester after 1446.[2] These men were extremely successful common lawyers, as well known at Westminster as in the palatinate courts: all of them were eventually raised to the bench of Common Pleas, ceasing to represent the prior of Durham after their promotion.[3] Their relationship with Wessington was not completely formal: Fulthorpe described himself as 'your own mane' in a letter to the prior, and it was from Danby that Wessington first heard the unpleasant news that the prior of his cell at Stamford had impleaded a local rector on his own initiative.[4] The prior also found it necessary to retain an attorney at the royal

[1] Reg. III, fo. 141. See *Plumpton Correspondence*, ed. T. Stapleton (Camden Society, Old Series IV, 1839) for the common use of arbitration in land disputes (e.g. pp. 16, l, lxxx) and for the Yorkshire activities of many of the prior of Durham's counsellors, including Guy Fairfax and Robert Danby.

[2] Bursar, 1416–46, Pensiones.

[3] E. Foss, *The Judges of England*, IV, *1377–1485* (London, 1851), 318–19, 354, 361–2, 426–8. For James Strangways as Bishop Langley's chief justice, see Storey, *Thomas Langley*, p. 63.

[4] Misc. Chrs., no. 7191; Reg. Parv. II, fo. 181. Portington's services to the convent were rewarded by letters of confraternity in August 1444 (Reg. III, fo. 306).

exchequer for an annual fee of 13s. 4d. Wessington's correspondence with Thomas Blythe, his 'attornay in the Checker' after 1438, shows that the latter's duties were almost exclusively concerned with the prior's payments of clerical tenths as collector in the diocese of Durham.[1] Apart from these permanent representatives at the royal courts and exchequer, the prior relied on *ad hoc* letters of attorney when he had a case to put before other departments of the government: here his common practice was to appoint a panel of four, usually two monks and two lay counsellors. Wessington also employed a general attorney at Durham, who acted on his behalf in the episcopal courts and held a second office as clerk of the prior's exchequer, i.e. the Durham bursary.[2] As the interests of the convent and its cells were so widely dispersed throughout an England dominated by the influence of local lords, Wessington frequently had recourse to the services of other *generosi* who were rarely seen at Durham. An example is afforded by the Yorkshire family of Babthorpe who became, *de facto* if not *de jure*, hereditary stewards of the prior's liberty of Hemingbrough. The Babthorpes inundated Wessington with a stream of demands for benefices and secular scholarships at Oxford, and there is no doubt that they, like the prior's other lawyers, were rewarded for their services more handsomely than their somewhat slender fees might suggest.[3] Only laymen who were already influential were chosen by the prior as his stewards and legal experts, but in his service they undoubtedly saw their influence increased. As one might perhaps expect, the very considerable 'bureaucratic' needs of the great ecclesiastical corporations of late medieval England made them powerful agencies for the stability rather than redistribution of wealth and social status.

The same generalisation applies in the case of Durham's clerical advisers and representatives, those whom the bursar described as *generosi clerici* when they received pensions from him. Such counsellors formed a large and heterogeneous group, of which the nucleus was a relatively small number of permanent officials retained by the

---

[1] Bursar, 1438–46, Pensiones; Loc. xxv, nos. 25, 30, 31.

[2] Reg. iii, fo. 172v; Bursar, 1416–46, Pensiones.

[3] The steward of Hemingbrough's official fee was only £2 per annum (Chamberlain, 1440/41). The Babthorpe family is discussed at some length in J. Raine (ed.), *The History and Antiquities of the Parish of Hemingbrough* (Yorkshire Archaeological Society, 1888).

prior on the basis of an oath of loyalty and an annual pension. They resembled the lay counsellors both in social standing and in legal training, although legal training of a different sort. Nearly all of the prior's most trusted clerical advisers were Oxford graduates in canon or civil law or both. The prior insisted on such qualifications in his choice of men whose essential duty was the defence of the monastery's rights and privileges in ecclesiastical courts. But although lay and clerical counsellors acted, with few exceptions, in completely different spheres, there were further resemblances between the two categories. Just as William Hoton combined the stewardship of the prior's estates with those of the Earl of Westmorland, so Wessington's advocates, proctors and ecclesiastical agents had other, and usually more important, positions than those for which they were retained by him. For none of the prior's counsellors was Wessington an only master and even Master William Doncaster, certainly the most hard-working of the group, was also employed by the two archdeacons and bishop of the diocese.[1] The incidental personal rewards to be obtained in the service of the prior of Durham were far greater for a clerk than a layman. Doncaster's career again provides an example: of the seven benefices he held either successively or simultaneously between 1418 and his death in 1439, five were in the gift of the prior and chapter.[2] The vicarage of Saint Oswald's, Durham, or the rectory of Meldon is a fairer comment on Wessington's appreciation of his services than Doncaster's annual pension of £3 13s. 4d. It was characteristic of nearly all the convent's clerical counsellors that they should already be holders of prebends or rich rectories and vicarages; it was equally characteristic that, at some stage of their careers, they should benefit from the prior's own ecclesiastical patronage.

Such men formed part of that class of diocesan ministers (already fully in evidence at Durham and elsewhere in the thirteenth century) sometimes likened to the present governmental civil service.[3] They

---

[1] Storey, *Thomas Langley*, pp. 167–8.

[2] I.e. the vicarages of Bedlington, Aycliffe and Saint Oswald's, a prebend at Howden and the rectory of Meldon; cf. Emden I, 585; Bursar, 1416–36, Pensiones. For an earlier and particularly explicit example of the retainer of a clerical *pensionarius* by written indenture see *Scrip. Tres*, pp. clxxvi–clxxvii.

[3] Storey, *Diocesan Administration in the Fifteenth Century* (St Anthony's Hall Publications, no. 16, 1959), p. 21. Cf. *Scrip. Tres*, p. 104, and J. L. Grassi, 'Royal Clerks from the Archdiocese of York in the Fourteenth Century', *Northern History* v (1970), 12–33.

were a more numerous group than the prior's lay counsellors, visited the monastery more often, and exerted a far more continuous influence. Except for the steward, the laymen employed by the prior acted more often as agents than advisers and played a very minor part in the framing of estates policy. The ecclesiastical lawyers, on the other hand, not only appeared in court on behalf of the convent but also acted as technical consultants who might well dictate the prior's approach to a particular problem. Despite the formal restrictions of their letters of appointment and proxy, they were allowed considerable discretion in practice: it is obvious that both prior and monks were extremely reluctant to face the great occasions of monastic life, such as elections and visitations, without their guidance.[1] At such times there came into being a full prior's council consisting of two or more such clerical lawyers together with a select number of senior monks and members of Wessington's household staff. Such councils were relatively rare and it must be emphasised that for the clerk, as for the laymen, '*retencio essendi de consilio prioris et capituli*' did not imply attendance at a regular, far less a standing, council meeting at Durham. The services or presence of individual counsellors was requested as desired and the lists of witnesses to Wessington's official documents show that Master William Doncaster was the only ecclesiastical lawyer frequently at the prior's side.[2] In contemporary Durham parlance the 'grett councell' consisted of experienced obedientiaries, the steward and several household officials and only rarely of the ecclesiastical lawyers '*de consilio prioris*'. The latter, unless they held a specific office under the prior, are not always easy to identify. Copies of a few indentures of retainer survive from the first decade of the fifteenth century but their value is limited for they often disguise what was in reality a simple money pension designed to conciliate a powerful adversary like the archdeacon of Durham.[3] However, an examination of the prior of Durham's correspondence suggests that the problem of defining his retained counsellors is partly academic; he did not hesitate to use the services of any skilled ecclesiastical lawyer who happened to be in the right place at the right time.

[1] Reg. III, fos. 27v, 51, 215; Reg. IV, fos. 29–31; Reg. Parv. II, fo. 7.
[2] 1.7. Pont., no. 2; Misc. Chrs., no. 6815; Reg. III, fos. 63, 64, 96v, 113, 132.
[3] Reg. III, fos. 9v, 12, 20v, 26v, 30, 34, 35, 39; *Scrip. Tres*, pp. cxc–cxci.

It was, however, from the ecclesiastical officials of the archdiocese of York that early fifteenth-century priors of Durham drew over two-thirds of their ecclesiastical counsellors. The wealth of legal talent to be found among Archbishop Bowet's and Kemp's vicars-general, Officials, sequestrators, advocates and proctors had no rival in the north of England and their advice was valued accordingly. Wessington did not confine their services to the management and protection of the priory's spiritualities in the diocese of York, although this was their central responsibility. The wheel had turned full circle since the turbulent years of the thirteenth and early fourteenth centuries, and the once bitter adversaries of the monastic privileges had now become the prior's most trusted advisers. Thus the vacancy in the see of Durham between 1437 and 1438 passed with no serious incident largely because the commissaries appointed by Archbishop Kemp were York officials already well known and liked by the convent.[1] The harmonious relationship between this York establishment and the monastic community can sometimes be traced back to a common Oxford education. Master John Marshall left a large piece of plate to Durham College in 1455, while Master John Selowe acted as a notary there before he moved permanently to York.[2]

Although the Durham registers show that Wessington was in contact with almost all the church lawyers and administrators at York, his special representatives were a small group known to be '*de consilio prioris Dunelmensis*' by their colleagues. This was a self-perpetuating body, for when the prior needed the services of a new *iurisperitus* he wrote to one of his existing York counsellors, who then sent a possible candidate up to Durham with a letter of recommendation; in this way Master John Marshall introduced Master John Paynell to the prior's service in 1439.[3] Wessington's counsellors at York were retained by means of an annual pension or a benefice in the prior's gift; the prior would then have first option on their services, so that even the Dean and Chapter of York could be obliged to secure the prior's permission if they wished to employ one of his *iurisperiti* on a case of their own.[4] The most important of these men

[1] See below, pp. 219–21.
[2] Borthwick Institute, York, Reg. Bowet II, fo. 15v; Emden II, 1228; III, 1668.
[3] Loc. xxv, no. 45; Misc. Chrs., no. 6649. [4] Loc. xxv, no. 48.

were the permanent advocate and proctor retained in the York consistory court at a normal annual fee of 26*s*. 8*d*. and 6*s*. 8*d*. respectively.[1] The proctor also received another 6*s*. 8*d*. per annum from Durham College, Oxford, whose extensive church property in the diocese of York demanded frequent protection at law; but perhaps his heaviest duties arose from litigation concerning Lytham, the only Durham cell under the ordinary jurisdiction of the archbishop.[2] The advocate, on the other hand, acted as a more general consultant to the prior and was often promoted to the position of keeper of Wessington's spiritualities in the liberty of Howdenshire. This officer had his own agents, of whom the Official and registrar were most conspicuous, both appointed by the prior and receiving fees of £1 and one mark respectively.[3] The keeper of the spiritualities received £2 and enjoyed a large measure of control over the liberty, for neither the prior nor his monk delegates visited Howdenshire at all frequently.

Master John Selowe may serve as a typical example of Wessington's counsellors at York, a man whose career illustrates the type of service required by the prior. After an Oxford education in canon and civil law and when already a canon of Hereford, he became an advocate in the York curia before November 1414. He was present at Wessington's election as prior in 1416 and was one of the three proctors appointed to present the result to Bishop Langley. For the next twenty years he represented the prior and chapter regularly at all Convocations and synods at York.[4] From 1416 to 1426 he received his pension as Wessington's advocate at the York consistory and in December 1416 was made Official of the Howdenshire liberty, the first important appointment made by the new prior. Twelve years later, in 1428, he became the keeper of the prior's spiritualities in Howdenshire and held this position until his death in early 1439. Although successively the archbishop's registrar, vicar-general and precentor of York, Selowe is found as a Durham commissary audit-

---

[1] Bursar, 1416–46, Pensiones. A detailed study of the ecclesiastical courts at York is still to be published, but see for a later period C. I. A. Ritchie, *The Ecclesiastical Courts of York* (Arbroath, 1956), and R. A. Marchant, *The Church under the Law: Justice, Administration and Discipline in the Diocese of York 1560–1640* (Cambridge, 1969).

[2] Borthwick Institute, York, CP. F (Cause Papers: Fifteenth Century), no. 167, describes a case in which Master William Driffield acted as proctor for Richard Haswell, prior of Lytham. [3] Bursar, 1416–46, Pensiones.

[4] Reg. III, fos. 51, 54, 57, 59, 70, 94–5, 135v, 212v; cf. Emden III, 1667–8.

ing accounts, visiting the monastery's Yorkshire churches, witnessing the resignation of their incumbents, and assigning houses to servants at the new collegiate church of Hemingbrough. In addition he prepared legal briefs for the prior and presented his arguments in the ecclesiastical courts at York. All these duties were done to Wessington's satisfaction, who wrote to him as a friend, thanking him for his invaluable services.[1]

The prior had considerably less need for the services of counsellors like Selowe at Durham, where relatively few of Bishop Langley's (and later Robert Neville's) diocesan officials were specifically retained by Wessington. Their responsibility towards the bishop may have advised against too close a business association with the prior, but the most obvious reason for Wessington's failure to use their assistance is that at Durham, unlike York, he and his monks were able to intervene directly. Thus the bishop's consistory court, held in the Galilee Chapel of the cathedral, could hardly have been closer at hand; although Wessington kept a proctor there (Thomas Tang from 1419 to 1439), he was a much less important figure than his counterpart at York for the simple reason that either the prior or the monastic chancellor would attend the consistory personally when the convent's causes were at issue.[2] Such a system seems to have worked quite satisfactorily, for the chapter was rarely disappointed at the judgements made by the bishop's Official on the suits it brought before him. In the administrative as well as judicial sphere, Wessington secured full co-operation from the episcopal ministers, for whose sanctions he would appeal in the case of an obdurate spiritual offender.[3] The prior's relations with these men showed few signs of friction, and his disputes with the archdeacon of Durham and Northumberland, rarely resident in the diocese, did not affect the prevailing harmony. Both Master John Lounde and Master Robert Beaumont, respectively Bishop Neville's vicar-general and temporal chancellor, received letters of fraternity from the monastery in the 1440s.[4]

[1] Reg. III, fos. 49, 52, 128, 129, 135v, 136v, 143, 198, 226; Reg. Parv. II, fos. 38, 58.
[2] Bursar, 1418–39, Pensiones; 3.2. Pap., no. 14; Loc. III, nos. 21, 27; Reg. IV, fo. 24; Misc. Chrs., no. 3367.
[3] Reg. III, fos. 98v–99v; Storey, *Thomas Langley*, pp. 172–3.
[4] Reg. III, fos. 285–6; Reg. IV, fo. 17v.

Neither Lounde nor Beaumont was a regular counsellor of the prior, far less an agent, and Master William Doncaster remains the only obvious example of an episcopal administrator deeply involved in the affairs of the monastery. Doncaster's continued prominence in Wessington's entourage is explained by the fact that he was a servant of the prior before he became a servant of the bishop; his career is thus as unorthodox as it is interesting, an object lesson in successful clerical careerism. A Bachelor of Civil Law, he first appeared at Durham as legal adviser to the convent in 1413 and received the substantial fee of 73s. 4d. from 1414 until 1436.[1] Very rapidly he became Wessington's automatic choice as proctor to Convocations and synods and was frequently chosen to notarise the prior's compilations of evidence in defence of Durham liberties. But his most important function was as keeper of the prior's archidiaconal liberties: Wessington's Allertonshire jurisdiction was committed to him in 1420 and he administered this until his death together with the prior's spiritualities in the archdeaconry of Northumberland.[2] In September 1431 Doncaster was appointed Wessington's Official throughout the diocese, a position usually reserved to the monastic chancellor; in this capacity he presided at sessions of the prior's spiritual court, the '*capitula generalia*' normally held every three weeks in the church of Saint Oswald's, Durham.[3] As he was then vicar of Saint Oswald's, the arrangement was obviously convenient and Doncaster was only replaced as prior's Official (by the monk William Dalton) on his collation to the deanery of Auckland in June 1435.[4] By this time he had become one of the most prominent ecclesiastics in the diocese, Official not only of the prior but of the two archdeacons and finally the bishop. A man of substance, he leased burgages in the city of Durham, re-endowed a chantry in the collegiate church of Auckland and, as early as 1427–8, loaned the priory over £10 towards the inception expenses of William

[1] Bursar, 1414–36, Pensiones. He occurs as advocate in the Durham consistory court in 1419 (*Scrip. Tres*, p. ccix) and Official of the archdeacon of Northumberland in 1416 (Misc. Chrs., no. 6053).

[2] 1.7. Pont., no. 2; Reg. III, fos. 76v, 136v, 167, 195; Bursar, 1420–36, Perq. Jurisd. et Synod.

[3] Reg. Parv. II, fo. 50. Cf. '*Capitula Generalia Prioris Dunelm.*', the act-book of the prior's quasi-archidiaconal court from 1435 to 1456.

[4] Reg. III, fo. 195; Emden I, 585.

Ebchester at Oxford.[1] Despite his wealth and his employment by greater lords than the prior of Durham (in 1424 he was sent to Melrose to receive the oath of James I on his return to Scotland),[2] Doncaster remained loyal to his first patrons. Wessington continued to regard Doncaster as primarily his own man and in 1435 pressed for the ultimate reward for his 22 years good and faithful service to the monastery, a prebend at Howden.[3] Four years later his death drew from the aged dowager, Joan Beaufort, Countess of Westmorland, the comment, 'wherof we wold be right sori but as we fully trust yat he is accept to ye everlastyng mercy of god'.[4] Prior Wessington deserved consolation for he had just lost the services of his oldest and most assiduous counsellor.

Although other notaries employed by the prior failed to emulate the unusually successful career of William Doncaster, their more humble duties were indispensable to the well-being of the monastery. The demand for the services of public notaries among the larger English monasteries was always considerable,[5] but especially so at early fifteenth-century Durham because of Wessington's personal need for official copies of charter and chronicle evidence which he discovered among the monastic records and used for purposes of litigation. In a period of two years (1445 and 1446), the notary John Berehalgh was called upon to produce ten public instruments which ratified a series of appeals, proxies, oaths and compurgations and included a detailed inventory of the possessions of the priory which took two months to complete.[6] The chapter sometimes used the services of notaries from York, or others who were clerks in episcopal service, such as Robert Bertram, the registrar of Bishop Neville's consistory court.[7] But it relied more especially on a small group of local notaries, residents of Durham and, more especially, of the

[1] Mines Accts., 1427/28; Reg. Parv. II, fo. 86. Doncaster also presented several books, including an autograph '*Tabula tocius Juris Canonici*' to the monastic library: *Catalogi Vet.*, pp. 48–9; T. Rud, *Codicum Manuscriptorum Ecclesiae Cathedralis Dunelmensis Catalogus* (Durham, 1825), pp. 176, 254.

[2] Balfour-Melville, *James I, King of Scots*, p. 105. Cf. 2.5. Regal., no. 2.

[3] Reg. Parv. II, fo. 89; Reg. III, fos. 195–6.

[4] Loc. XXV, no. 127.

[5] See, e.g., *Reg. John Whethamstede* (Rolls Series, 1872–3), II, *passim*.

[6] Reg. III, fo. 309; Reg. IV, fos. 18, 23, 25v, 27, 28, 31; Reg. Parv. II, fo. 182; Reg. Parv. III, fo. 3; *Scrip. Tres*, pp. cclxxxi, cccviii.

[7] Reg. III, fos. 251, 263v, 268, 284, 290. Cf. Emden I, 193.

convent's borough of Elvet, who staffed the upper ranks of the monastery's secretariat. Men like Thomas Ryhale or John Berehalgh were members of Durham families who specialised in clerical work and catered for the administrative needs of the convent. Whether or not they held formal office under the prior (like John Berehalgh who received an annual fee of twenty shillings as registrar of the prior's Official after 1441), these notaries were professionals who were expected to remain both unmarried and outside priest's orders.[1] Usually described as *magistri*, they formed a small, close-knit community in the cathedral city. The Tang family, which provided Wessington with a notary and proctor in the Durham consistory, was an active clerical dynasty from the thirteenth to the sixteenth century.[2] Most conspicuous during Wessington's priorate were a group of six men bearing the name of Berehalgh or Berall: William, the bishop's sequestrator-general in the archdeaconry of Northumberland; Robert, registrar of the Durham consistory; John, registrar of the prior's Official; Ademar, ordained sub-deacon in the diocese of Salisbury; and finally, Walter and Americ, '*litterati*', who witnessed some of the prior's acts.[3] The will of Thomas Ryhale, who served successive priors of Durham as a notary from the 1390s until his death in 1427, reflects both the bonds between the members of this clerical group and their loyalty to the convent. Ryhale bequeathed most of his moveable property to other notaries in Durham and appointed Robert and William Berehalgh and his kinsman Thomas Ryhale as his executors; he devised his three burgages, held in various parts of the city, to the sacrist, bursar and hostillar of the monastery, inside whose walls he was to be buried.[4] It would be unwise to discount the influence that he, and the other Durham notaries, exercised on a prior who would have been helpless without their services.

In conclusion it may be instructive to compare this description of the secular 'bureaucracy' of a great fifteenth-century monastery with the classic account of Prior Henry of Eastry's council at Christ Church, Canterbury, a century earlier. According to R. A. L. Smith,

1 Bursar, 1441–50, Pensiones et Stipendia; *Reg. Langley* I, 166–9; III, 193–4.
2 3.2. Pap., no. 14; Reg. III, fo. 167. Cf. Emden III, 1884–5.
3 *Reg. Langley* I, xvii, 48; IV, 29–30; Reg. III, fos. 174, 198, 257, 283; Reg. IV, fos. 18, 23, 25v, 31; Misc. Chrs., nos. 2637, 2639.
4 *Wills and Inventories* I (Surtees Soc. II, 1835), p. 76.

the latter 'normally consisted of four different elements': a small group of permanent officials, including one or two monks as well as the abbot's steward; a larger group of local landowners and gentry; a number of trained civil and ecclesiastical lawyers; and finally one or two distinguished judges.[1] All four categories can be readily detected among the Durham counsellors of the early fifteenth century, and there is no doubt that the similarities between the two systems are more significant than their differences. However, it is clear that the prior's council at Durham was a much less formal body than its counterpart at Canterbury and that many of its members were rarely in personal attendance upon the prior. The Durham evidence therefore adds its considerable weight to the general impression that throughout much of England estate and corporation management could be a less formalised and sophisticated art in the early fifteenth century than it had been in the thirteenth. If so, the reasons are not far to seek. Adverse economic pressures in the later middle ages made it difficult for the large corporate landlords to do anything but accommodate themselves to fluctuating market forces as quickly – and therefore as informally – as they could. In all the multitude of memoranda on financial matters that survive for fifteenth-century Durham, nothing is more striking than the lack of any overall and coherent monastic estates policy. It was precisely for this reason that Prior Wessington and his monks were usually able to administer their sources of income without recourse to specialised land agents other than the prior's steward.

It would consequently seem that the senior monks of the Durham chapter, although not forming a regularly constituted committee, exerted greater general influence on monastic planning than had their predecessors, at Durham as well as Canterbury, in the thirteenth century. But the suggestion that the 'presence of trained and experienced administrators within the monastic community made it possible for the abbot and prior to rely less on paid experts than did the secular magnate' may push this argument too far.[2] Contemporary disapproval of the administrative responsibilities of late medieval monks must not be allowed to persuade us that members of religious communities were always, or perhaps usually, efficient adminis-

[1] Smith, *Canterbury Cathedral Priory*, p. 70; Knowles, *Rel. Orders* I, 271–2.
[2] Halcrow, 'Obedientiaries and Counsellors in Monastic Administration', p. 20.

trators. In the increasingly professionalised business and legal world of the fifteenth century, the 'amateur' status of the monk in public life often became more rather than less obvious. Prior Thomas Castell spoke for many monks other than himself when he expressed his fears on being called to high office in 1494, 'being yonge in yeres, noght haveing the use or gret practises of temporall Besynes'.[1] In the world outside the monastic walls, and especially in the dreaded field of litigation, the monks of Durham were in urgent and often desperate need of lay and ecclesiastical advisers and lawyers. For them, as for monks everywhere in England, there was no feasible alternative to the employment of such *iurisperiti*, however much their contemporaries might criticise the money spent by religious houses 'upon worthi gentil men leerned in lawe for mentenaunces of her riytis'.[2] For this practice, moreover, there was the even more important defence, voiced by Bishop Reginald Pecock himself, that it led to the 'nurisching of frendschip and of love' between the monastery and the most influential men in England. Like most bureaucracies at most times, that of early fifteenth-century Durham priory was as significant for the personal opportunities it offered to its officials as for the services they rendered to a common cause. In this sense the counsellors employed by the prior and chapter were an important feature of the elaborate structure of mutual aid and patronage which, as we will now see, bound monastery and the secular world inextricably together.

[1] Reg. Parv. IV, fo. 30.
[2] *The Repressor of over much blaming of the clergy, by Reginald Pecock* (Rolls Series, 1860), II, 370–1.

Chapter 5

MONASTIC PATRONAGE

Patronage is the outward and visible sign of an inward and spiritual grace, and that is Power.[1]

John Wessington's tenure of the priorate of Durham coincides with a period of English history now notorious for the influence of private patronage and protection. Not even a large and apparently self-sufficient Benedictine monastery could insulate itself from the contemporary search for 'good lords' nor prevent the exploitation of its offices and benefices in the interests of their clientele. In a century when the Durham chapter could no longer hope to be as powerful or as prosperous as it had once been, the importance of its patronage would appear to have increased rather than the reverse. Such patronage had never been negligible: and it is unfortunate that only from the fifteenth century does unofficial correspondence survive, at Durham as elsewhere, to fully illuminate the pressures behind the appointment of a steward and the presentation of a rector. Popes and kings had long interested themselves in the richer benefices of the monastery's gift and it would be unwise to stress unduly the novelty of the situation which confronted Prior Wessington in 1416, a situation in which the greatest misfortune that could befall a young clerk was to lack 'cosynage'.[2] Nevertheless, it is clear that an insatiable demand for spiritual and temporal offices at the convent's disposal created more embarrassment for Wessington than his predecessors. After 1400, and particularly after Henry V's death in 1422, the hunger for places showed no signs of abating and was subject to less discipline than in the past. It was literally impossible for the prior to satisfy all his petitioners or to reconcile their claims with his responsibility to provide adequately for his own counsellors and dependants. One of Wessington's more delicate duties was to refuse the magnates' requests for patronage without antagonising them –

[1] Letter of Disraeli to E. H. Stanley, 10 August 1858 (W. F. Monypenny and G. E. Buckle, *The Life of Benjamin Disraeli* [London, 1910–20], IV, 174).

[2] See Loc. XXV, no. 42.

to master the art of writing what were well known at Durham as the '*littera excusatoria*'.[1] The prior and chapter were indeed engaged in a long and never-ending defensive campaign to prevent the encroachment of the fifteenth-century affinity and connection on their freedom of choice. Only a detailed analysis of the range of benefices and offices at the convent's disposal can explain the intensity with which this campaign was fought.

Much the most valuable patronage in the hands of the prior of Durham consisted of the advowsons of numerous churches in the north of England. At the time of Wessington's election in 1416, 17 rectories, 28 vicarages, and the prebends and vicarages of the collegiate church of Howden lay in the presentation of the prior and chapter.[2] Of monasteries in the northern province only the abbey of Saint Mary's, York, with 40 churches in the diocese of York alone, approached this number.[3] The bishop of Durham held 34 advowsons in his own diocese, the prior and convent held 20 and no other patron held more than 5.[4] It is consequently not difficult to account for the stream of requests for benefices directed towards Wessington by kings and bishops, magnates and merchants. These requests find open expression in a group of 175 private letters collected as Locellus xxv in the muniments of the dean and chapter of Durham: more than half of these letters make demands on the convent's spiritual patronage.[5] Although very few of these letters are dated by more than the day of the month, almost all can be assigned to a particular year after comparison with the presentations and '*littera excusatoria*' recorded in the Durham registers. The earliest item in the collection seems to be a letter from Henry Bowet, then archdeacon of Lincoln, in 1394, and the latest a letter from Henry VIII in 1514;[6] but the bulk of the correspondence dates from the years of Wessington's priorate.

[1] Reg. III, fos. 50v, 63, 64, 114v, 119, 195–6, 310v.

[2] These figures are based on the presentations made by the prior and chapter as recorded in Reg. II and Reg. III. They include the rectory of Appleby, in the diocese of Lincoln, to which the prior of Lytham presented on the nomination of his superior at Durham (Loc. xxv, no. 34).

[3] *V.C.H. County of York* III, 110; *Valor Ecclesiasticus* v (1825), 4–11.

[4] R. N. Hadcock, 'A Map of Mediaeval Northumberland and Durham', *Arch. Ael.*, Fourth Series, XVI (1939), 159–207.

[5] Other letters from lords requesting benefices in the monastery's gift have strayed to the group of 'Miscellaneous Charters', e.g., nos. 1061, 1078, 1083, 6649.

[6] Loc. xxv, nos. 49, 100.

Although all presentations to rectories and vicarages issued at Durham were made in the name of prior and chapter, the letters of Locellus xxv are normally addressed to the prior alone and assume that his is the decisive control over ecclesiastical patronage. The names of several of the correspondents and of the clerks on whose behalf they wrote for vacant benefices have already been subjected to statistical treatment;[1] but as the convent was more likely to preserve letters from the king and magnates than from the lower ranks of society, it would be unwise to assume that the contents of Locellus xxv give a complete picture of the interaction between monastic patronage and external sponsorship. In particular, the bishop of Durham's own continuous demand for the convent's patronage seems seriously under-represented in the surviving correspondence – no doubt because he often communicated his desires by word of mouth. However these letters undoubtedly do reveal the special attraction of the monastery's richer benefices in Yorkshire, and especially of its prebends in the collegiate churches of Howden and (after 1427) Hemingbrough, to great lords and prelates wanting to provide for their clerks and relatives.

North of the Tees the churches in the gift of the prior and chapter were more conspicuous for their number than their wealth. In Scotland Prior Wessington still maintained a claim to nine vicarages in what had once been the monastery's Lothian franchise and he was at various times able to present to six of these.[2] The bishops of St Andrews, especially during and after the Great Schism, were invariably hostile to this anomalous survival from an earlier and less nationally conscious period; but despite the attempts of Henry Wardlaw and James Kennedy (who dropped his case on receipt of £150 from the prior of Coldingham) to deprive the convent of its spiritual patronage in Scotland, it survived in an attenuated form until a few years before the final expulsion of Durham monks from

[1] R. Donaldson, 'Sponsors, Patrons and Presentations to Benefices in the gift of the Priors of Durham during the later Middle Ages', *Arch. Ael.*, Fourth Series, xxxviii (1960), 169–77.

[2] See Figure 1. The vicarages of Berwick, Edrom, Ednam, Earlston, Fishwick, Stichill, Old Cambus, Lamberton and Swinton were the subject of a Durham appeal to Rome in 1444 (Reg. iii, fo. 304); but the fifteenth-century monastic registers only record presentations to the first six of these (Reg. iii, fos. 67, 71, 97v, 100v, 101, 152v).

Fig. 1. Durham Priory's churches in Northumberland and Coldinghamshire:
(M) – monastic church; (R) – rectory; (V) – vicarage

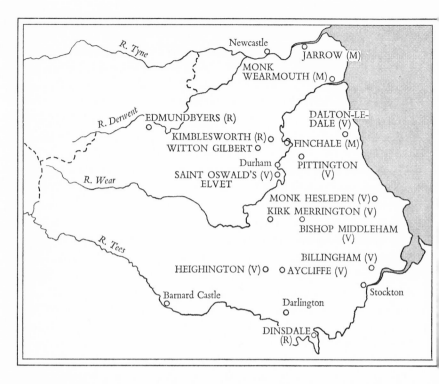

Fig. 2. Durham Priory's churches in County Durham: (M) – monastic church; (R) – rectory; (V) – vicarage

Beaufort's clerks and Thomas Radcliffe a suffragan bishop employed by Bishops Thomas Langley and Robert Neville.[1]

South of the Tees the range of ecclesiastical patronage at Wessington's disposal was much more varied and rewarding than in the diocese of Durham. Apart from the prebends of Howden and Hemingbrough, so outstanding that they deserve separate treatment, the prior and convent regularly presented to seven rectories and six vicarages in the York diocese as well as to five rectories and one vicarage in that of Lincoln. Here the trend towards appropriation had appeared later, met with greater resistance and was less successful

[1] Reg. III, fos. 66, 76, 111v, 294; Loc. xxv, no. 83; Durham Bishopric Records, Receiver-General's Records, Ch. C. no. 189811 (for the year 1438–39). Cf. *Reg. Langley* III, 13; IV, 162–3; Emden I, 585; II, 673.

1423[1]) scarcely affected the extent of the patronage at Wessington's disposal. In this context the distinction between a rectory and a vicarage also had little meaning, for the convent had appropriated all its richer benefices before the end of the thirteenth century.[2] Of the five rectories remaining to the prior and convent (Meldon, Dinsdale, Edmundbyers, Kimblesworth, and Saint Mary le Bow) not one was valued at more than ten marks per annum either in 1291 or 1535.[3] More attractive to the fifteenth-century clerk and his sponsor were the vicarages of Aycliffe, Bedlington, Billingham, Heighington, Norham, Pittington and Saint Oswald's, Durham, each with a net value of between £10 and £16 in 1535.[4] By comparison with the churches in the gift of the bishop of Durham,[5] all these benefices seem poor enough and usually attracted only local candidates prepared to accept residence in their parishes.[6] But there was never any shortage of such candidates – nor of lords who desired the promotion of their chaplains to the convent's churches in the diocese. In the mid-fifteenth century, for example, the Earls of Westmorland and Northumberland were successful in having their nominees presented to the vicarages of Bywell St Peter and Bedlington respectively.[7] Benefice-hunger was so acute that even the 'little vicarage' of Dalton (valued at only £6 in 1535) was the subject of a letter of sponsorship to the prior by some of his more substantial tenants.[8] Moreover, the incumbents of several of the convent's churches between Tees and Tweed were, despite the relative poverty of their benefices, by no means undistinguished. Of the four vicars of Aycliffe between 1419 and 1446, William Doncaster was Prior Wessington's most attentive clerical counsellor, William Paxton an executor of Sir Ralph Eure, John Fayt an Oxford graduate who had been one of Cardinal

---

[1] Reg. Parv. II, fos. 21, 90; Reg. III, fo. 205; Surtees, *Durham* II, 362–4, 370.

[2] R. Donaldson, 'Patronage and the Church' (Ph.D. thesis, Edinburgh), 199–209.

[3] *Taxatio Ecclesiastica . . . P. Nicholai IV* (Record Commission, 1802), pp. 314–17; *Valor Ecclesiasticus* v (1825), 312–30.

[4] *Valor Ecclesiasticus* v (1825), 319–30. The vicarage of Saint Oswald's was omitted from this valuation but the Durham hostillar's rolls show that its incumbent received a portion of £16 per annum in the fifteenth century.

[5] Storey, *Thomas Langley*, pp. 178–9.

[6] Of the seventeen rectors and vicars in the diocese of Durham reported absent from their benefices in the vacancy of 1437–38, not one held a church in the monastery's patronage: Borthwick Institute, York, Reg. J. Kemp, fos. 490v–491.

[7] Misc. Chrs., no. 1083; Loc. xxv, no. 85.   [8] Loc. xxv, no. 24.

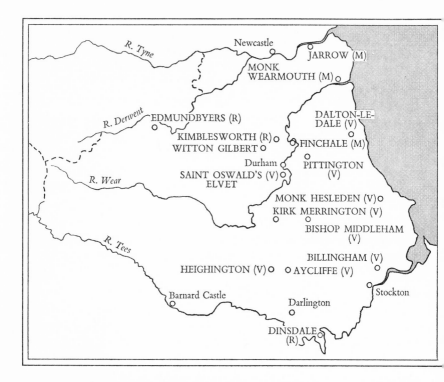

Fig. 2. Durham Priory's churches in County Durham: (M) – monastic church; (R) – rectory; (V) – vicarage

Beaufort's clerks and Thomas Radcliffe a suffragan bishop employed by Bishops Thomas Langley and Robert Neville.[1]

South of the Tees the range of ecclesiastical patronage at Wessington's disposal was much more varied and rewarding than in the diocese of Durham. Apart from the prebends of Howden and Hemingbrough, so outstanding that they deserve separate treatment, the prior and convent regularly presented to seven rectories and six vicarages in the York diocese as well as to five rectories and one vicarage in that of Lincoln. Here the trend towards appropriation had appeared later, met with greater resistance and was less successful

[1] Reg. III, fos. 66, 76, 111v, 294; Loc. xxv, no. 83; Durham Bishopric Records, Receiver-General's Records, Ch. C. no. 189811 (for the year 1438–39). Cf. *Reg. Langley* III, 13; IV, 162–3; Emden I, 585; II, 673.

Fig. 1. Durham Priory's churches in Northumberland and Coldinghamshire: (M) – monastic church; (R) – rectory; (V) – vicarage

Coldingham in 1462.[1] Only one of these vicarages, the parish church of Holy Trinity, Berwick-upon-Tweed, had been valued at more than £20 at the end of the thirteenth century;[2] and of these churches Berwick alone was eventually detached from the diocese of St Andrews. Prior Wessington presented Englishmen to this church and Scots to all the others north of the Tweed; he had no personal knowledge of his presentees and was dependent on the advice offered by the prior of Coldingham. Durham's possession of these advowsons was so insecure by the early fifteenth century that it was only with great difficulty that Wessington could attempt to exercise the freedom of presentation that was nominally his. In 1432 his presentation to the vicarage of Stichill '*non erat executa*' and that of John Loury to Edrom in 1443 was disregarded by Bishop Kennedy who intruded his own candidate and forced Wessington to appeal to Rome.[3] Loury resigned his claims in early 1447 and was compensated by the grant of letters of confraternity from the monastery at Durham.[4]

In the diocese of Durham there were no such difficulties and the prior and chapter's rights of presentation to five rectories and fifteen vicarages were unquestioned. The distribution and arrangement of the convent's spiritualities in the see changed remarkably little in the later middle ages. The extensive appropriation of churches in the twelfth and thirteenth centuries had been succeeded by a period of almost complete stability.[5] The Durham monks were therefore able to appeal to Bishop Neville for licence to amortize lands on the specific grounds that the monastery had not made any new appropriations for 160 years.[6] Such changes as there were (the conversion of the rectory of Muggleswick into a chapelry normally held by the rector of the neighbouring parish of Edmundbyers; the separation of Witton Gilbert from the parish of Saint Oswald's, Durham, in

---

[1] 1.3. Pap., no. 27; Misc. Chrs., no. 1082; Reg. IV, fos. 23, 25. Cf. Raine, *North Durham*, Appendix, pp. 91–2; Dunlop, *The Life and Times of James Kennedy*, pp. 80, 121. For the later history of this patronage, after its alienation from Durham, see *C.P.L.* XIII (1471–84), p. 192; *C.P.L.* XIV (1484–92), pp. 45–50; Dobson, 'Last English Monks on Scottish Soil', p. 7.

[2] *Coldingham Corr.*, pp. cix–cx.   [3] Reg. III, fo. 304.

[4] Reg. IV, fo. 27; *Coldingham Corr.*, p. 158.

[5] See the confirmation '*de ecclesiis quas habemus in proprios usos*' by Bishops Beaumont and Bury; *Reg. Richard of Bury*, pp. 180–5. For the earlier period, see Barlow, *Durham Jurisdictional Peculiars*, pp. 16–43, and Scammell, *Hugh du Puiset*, pp. 97–8. See also Figures 1 and 2, pp. 147, 150.   [6] Loc. XXI, nos. 29, 47.

than in Northumberland and Durham.[1] Consequently there was more room for manoeuvre and the actual number and status of this group of churches held by the monastery changed considerably in the later middle ages. The acquisition of the advowsons of Bossall, Fishlake, Ruddington and Frampton from John, Lord Neville of Raby, in the 1380s (these churches were then appropriated to the use of Durham College) added four vicarages to the convent's patronage.[2] Shortly afterwards, and certainly as part of the same transaction, the prior and chapter alienated to the Nevilles their rights of presentation to the rectories of Walkington and Welton, despite the fact that these two churches belonged to their Howdenshire franchise.[3] Prior Wessington himself eagerly accepted the offer made by Ralph, Lord Cromwell in 1444 to exchange Durham's patronage of Kirkby on Bain for lands in Leicestershire worth six marks per annum; although the transfer never materialised, it is clear that the Durham convent had no objections in principle to the surrender of a distant advowson.[4] This was hardly surprising in the case of those churches granted to the convent in the twelfth century which were now too poor to merit either appropriation or even the imposition of a small money pension. The monastery's two rectories in the city of York (All Saints, Pavement, and Saint Peter the Little) fell into this category as did Saint Mary Bynwerk, destitute of an incumbent for so long that in 1430 Wessington urged its union to Durham's other Stamford church, Saint Mary by the Bridge.[5]

In general, however, the convent's benefices south of the Tees

---

[1] See Figure 3 on p. 155, and also Barlow, *Durham Jurisdictional Peculiars*, p. 88. Before 1380, the prior and convent had appropriated only four churches in the York diocese, i.e. Northallerton, Eastrington, Giggleswick (to the use of Finchale) and Lytham (to the use of the Durham cell there). In the mid-fourteenth century they obtained licences to appropriate the rectories of Appleby, Blyborough and Hemingbrough but were unable to put these into effect: Loc. III, no. 8; *C.P.R., 1381–85*, pp. 10–11; *Dur. Coll. Rolls*, p. 30.

[2] *C.P.R., 1381–85*, pp. 239, 371–2; *C.P.R., 1385–89*, pp. 233, 243.

[3] See *Calendarium Inquisitionum Post Mortem* (Record Commission, 1806–28), IV, 206.

[4] Loc. XXV, no. 136; Reg. Parv. II, fos. 191–2. Kirkby on Bain is only four miles from Tattershall, where Lord Cromwell was at this time rebuilding his castle: see *The Building Accounts of Tattershall Castle, 1434–72*, ed. W. D. Simpson (Lincoln Record Society LV, 1960), p. 51.

[5] Reg. III, fo. 134. For the poverty of almost all York city churches in the later middle ages, see *V.C.H. The City of York*, pp. 370, 400.

were more valuable and accordingly in much greater demand than those in the diocese of Durham. Most attractive of all was the rectory of Brantingham in Howdenshire, valued at £66 13s. 4d. in 1291; both John Stafford, the royal chancellor, and Robert Neville, bishop of Durham, wrote to Wessington on behalf of clerks whom they wished to be presented to this church.[1] The last four rectors of Brantingham (between 1395 and 1458, when the church was appropriated to Durham College)[2] were all non-resident pluralists and included a treasurer of England, Lawrence Allerthorpe, as well as Bishop Neville's temporal chancellor and receiver-general, Master Robert Beaumont.[3] Most of the Yorkshire sponsors who applied to Wessington were, however, local men interested in less spectacularly wealthy benefices than Brantingham. William Pygot, abbot of Selby, Thomas Kar, who wrote from York describing himself as 'your awen draper', and Robert Babthorpe, steward of Hemingbrough, were figures from very different social worlds; but common to all three was the desire to promote the ecclesiastical careers of their friends, relatives and servants.[4]

The most highly-prized of all the patronage at Wessington's disposal derived from Durham's two collegiate churches of Howden and Hemingbrough in the East Riding of Yorkshire. The late medieval fabric of these spacious and architecturally impressive churches has survived remarkably intact; it still bears witness to the period when Howden and Hemingbrough were the greatest outposts of Durham's power and influence in one of the richest areas of northern England. The prebends of Howden and (after 1427) Hemingbrough were both the most desirable and the most contentious benefices in the chapter's gift. No other monastery in northern England, possibly no other monastery in the entire kingdom, had such attractive prizes at its disposal; and their control of Howden and Hemingbrough was in itself sufficient to give the monks of Durham a very special status in the eyes of contemporary lords and prelates. It was of course the possibility of enjoying a Howden or Hemingbrough prebend in plurality and *in absentia* that interested

---

[1] Reg. Parv. II, fo. 112; Loc. xxv, nos. 68, 75. Cf. *Taxatio Ecclesiastica . . . P. Nicholai IV* (Record Commission, 1802), p. 302.

[2] 3.5 Regal., no. 4. Cf. *C.P.R.*, *1452–61*, p. 425.

[3] Reg. III, fos. 20, 93, 302. Cf. *Fasti Dunelm.*, pp. 2–3, 11, 58, 125–6.

[4] Loc. xxv, nos. 15, 27, 28, 29, 74.

and often obsessed the careerist ecclesiastic. And it was for this reason that the actions of the prior and chapter as well as the life expectancy of the prebendaries themselves were watched so carefully and suspiciously by the English magnates. Above all, Howden and Hemingbrough attracted the attention of the royal as well as the local clerk, of the English government as well as the northern earl. The names of the men who held these prebends form a roll-call of many of the most influential members of the English 'civil service' in the later middle ages.

Howden was the oldest and most famous of Durham's two collegiate churches; its association with prominent members of the royal administration dates from at least the 1170s when Master Roger of Howden, almost certainly the chronicler of that name, succeeded his father in the parsonage.[1] An extraordinarily wealthy church which must have been worth at least £200 per annum in the early thirteenth century, Howden was eventually converted into a collegiate church of five prebends in 1265–8.[2] The original Durham plan had been to appropriate the church for the sake of sustaining sixteen more monks at the mother house. It is a significant comment on the fortunes of monasticism in late thirteenth-century England that Prior Hugh of Darlington changed his mind and established a collegiate church in the hope that he would 'acquire friends by presenting clerks to the new prebends'. A generation later, in his struggle with Antony Bek, Prior Hoton was practising the familiar art of winning the favour of royal clerks '*per prebendas de Hofden*'.[3] As a collegiate church, Howden certainly caused the convent less embarrassment than in the days when John Mansel and that notorious pluralist, Bogo de Clare, were attracted by its undivided wealth;[4] but even in the later middle ages it is possible to suppose that their control of the Howden prebends made the Durham monks as many enemies as friends. In 1388, at the end of a period when the practice

[1] Scammell, *Hugh du Puiset*, pp. 146–7.

[2] W. Brown, 'The Institution of the Prebendal Church at Howden', *Yorkshire Archaeological Journal*, XXII (1913), 166–74. At the end of the thirteenth century the Howden prebends were valued at an aggregate sum of £163 6s. 8d. and the church of Eastrington (separated from Howden in 1265) at £60 (*Taxatio Ecclesiastica . . . P. Nicholai IV*, p. 302). See (on the events of 1265–8) *Scrip. Tres*, p. 47.

[3] *Scrip. Tres*, pp. 47, 76; cf. Fraser, *Antony Bek*, p. 129.

[4] *Durham Annals*, pp. 159–61, 226–7.

of papal reservation had further restricted the convent's rights of presentation at Howden,[1] Prior Robert Walworth seriously contemplated the surrender of all his advowsons there (except for the prebend and vicarage of Skipwith) to Henry Percy, Earl of Northumberland, in exchange for the church of Spofforth which would then be appropriated to the use of the monastery.[2] This ambitious scheme was finally abandoned in 1398 after ten years in which the prior and convent presented to four Howden prebends on the nomination of the Earl of Northumberland.[3]

Between 1416 and 1446 Prior Wessington and his chapter enjoyed at least a theoretical freedom of presentation to the six prebends (that of Skipwith had been added in the fourteenth century) and the six vicarages of Howden. The resident vicars-choral lived in a hostel or bedern built by Bishop Skirlaw and in accordance with a series of statutes issued in 1405 and revised by Wessington in 1418.[4] There was much competition for the position of vicar-choral at Howden and the six places were normally filled by local Yorkshire clerks. The six canonries and prebends, on the other hand, were shared among more distinguished ecclesiastics: clerks of the royal household and government, the chaplains of the great magnate families and the professional diocesan administrators of either Durham or York. Only members of this last group were occasionally resident at Howden.[5] Not particularly valuable by fifteenth-century standards (Wessington estimated the clear value of Saltmarsh at less than £5 in 1435),[6] the Howden prebends were in great demand as a source of supplementary income for the able and ambitious. In Wessington's own lifetime, the Howden prebendaries included four future

---

[1] *C.P.L.* III (1342–62), pp. 51–2, 156, 206, 230, 470, 604; *Calendar of Papal Petitions* (1342–1419), pp. 64, 166, 168, 484–5.

[2] 1.2. Ebor., nos. 7, 11, 12; Loc. XXVIII, no. 21; Cart. III, Part ii, fos. 16–17; *C.P.L.* IV (1362–1404), p. 334.

[3] Loc. XXVIII, no. 21.

[4] Cart. III, Part ii, fo. 24; Reg. I, fos. 92–4.

[5] Even when one of the six canons was appointed rector of the Howden choir, the terms of his appointment made specific provision for his absence from the church (Reg. III, fo. 119; Reg. Parv. II, fo. 35). Because the six prebendaries were so rarely in residence, Wessington sometimes found it advisable to choose one of the vicars-choral to rule the choir (Reg. III, fo. 52v).

[6] Reg. III, fo. 196; Reg. Parv. II, fo. 89. A hundred years later no Howden prebend was valued at less than £9 or more than £13 6s. 8d. net: *Valor Ecclesiasticus* V (1825), 136–8.

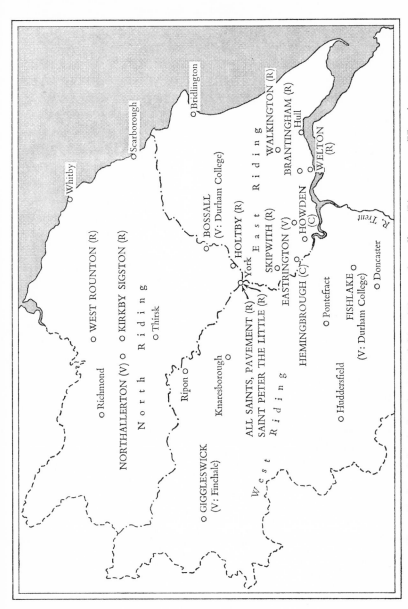

Fig. 3. Durham Priory's churches in Yorkshire: (C) – secular college; (R) – rectory; (V) – vicarage

bishops (William Strickland, John Catterick, Marmaduke Lumley and Robert Neville)[1] as well as two barons of the exchequer (Nicholas Dixon and William Fallan)[2] and a host of other royal and episcopal administrators. The correspondence preserved in Locellus xxv expresses not only the conflicting and largely irreconcilable pressures to which the advowsons of the Howden prebends subjected the Durham monks but also the eagerness of the magnates to forestall their rivals.

These problems obviously have a bearing on Prior Wessington's decision to convert the neighbouring rectory of Hemingbrough into a second collegiate church; this decision (taken in 1426) can be partly interpreted as an attempt to satisfy the craving of contemporary clerks and their sponsors for benefices by adding yet more prebends to those of Howden. The story of the foundation of the collegiate church at Hemingbrough is a complicated one, but it deserves attention for perhaps no other episode in the history of the fifteenth-century convent throws more light on the external forces which impeded the Durham monks' free control over their own spiritual patronage. Moreover, the establishment of the collegiate church at Hemingbrough was one of Wessington's most considerable achievements, commemorated by the carvings of his rebus – a washing tub or tun – on the outside of the tower there.[3] His success is all the more remarkable by comparison with the failure of his predecessors to draw more than a five marks annual pension from a rectory 'whose fruits and income would suffice to sustain many men'.[4] Since the institution of prebends at Howden in 1265, Hemingbrough had been by far the most valuable benefice in the gift of Durham, said to be worth over £100 when held by Bogo de Clare in 1291.[5] But although fourteenth-century priors had tried repeatedly to secure Hemingbrough's appropriation to the monastery, and had at various

---

[1] Borthwick Institute, York, Reg. Sede Vacante (*c.* 1300–1556), fo. 358v; Reg. Bowet II, fo. 18v. Also see Reg. III, fos. 30, 45v, 103; *Fasti Dunelm.*, pp. 24, 81, 92, 125.

[2] Reg. III, fos. 197v, 298; Loc. xxv, no. 53*. Cf. Foss, *The Judges of England* IV, pp. 306–8.

[3] Raine, *History and Antiquities of Hemingbrough*, p. 18.

[4] These are Wessington's own words in a letter of 15 May 1426 to Archbishop Kemp (Reg. Parv. II, fo. 34; *Scrip. Tres*, p. ccxiv).

[5] *Durham Annals*, p. 213; *Taxatio Ecclesiastica . . . P. Nicholai IV*, p. 302.

times obtained the support of Edward III, Archbishop Zouche and the Lords Percy and Neville, all their manoeuvres were frustrated by the lack of papal sanction. Gregory XI's disapproval of the projected appropriation in 1372 on the grounds, among others, that the Durham monks 'spend more on their food and clothing than befits men of religion' has not been neglected by modern critics of the monastery.[1] Undoubtedly it was difficult to alter the status of the church of Hemingbrough at a time when it was often subject to papal reservation and provision; but it is unnecessary to accept Wessington's own somewhat tendentious statement that the rectory was normally held by cardinals.[2] In fact, the last four rectors of Hemingbrough, from 1348 to 1426, were all Englishmen and included two vicars-general and a future bishop, Master John Rickingale.[3]

It was the elevation of Rickingale to the bishopric of Chichester in the spring of 1426 that gave Wessington the opportunity to rush through the conversion of the rectory into a collegiate church. The times were propitious for in the previous year John Kemp, an archbishop well disposed towards the Durham prior and his monks, had succeeded the less amenable Henry Bowet at York. The inevitable queue of clerks eager to fill Rickingale's place as rector of Hemingbrough caused Wessington much anxiety but he was able to overcome this obstacle by explaining that under the new regime there would be more vacancies for benefice-hungry clerks than before. In these circumstances, the outright appropriation of Hemingbrough to the use of the convent would have been as impossible to achieve as in the previous century and therefore the erection of a collegiate church can hardly be regarded as a sign that the monastery had 'few misgivings about the state of its finances'.[4] There were four major candidates for the rectory in 1426, all of them formidable, and Wessington was both skilful and fortunate in gaining their acquiescence to the conversion. The young Robert Neville, future bishop

---

[1] *C.P.L.* IV (1362–1404), 117–18; cited by Snape, *English Monastic Finances*, p. 148; and R. A. R. Hartridge, *A History of Vicarages in the Middle Ages* (Cambridge, 1930), p. 106. Cf. *C.P.R.*, *1354–58*, p. 443; *C.P.R.*, *1374–77*, pp. 112, 191; *C.P.R.*, *1381–85*, pp. 10–11: *Historical Papers and Letters from the Northern Registers* (Rolls Series, 1873), pp. 390–4. [2] Reg. Parv. II, fo. 34.
[3] Borthwick Institute, York, Reg. Bowet I, fo. 271v; *Fasti Dunelm.*, pp. 107, 118; Emden III, 1977–8. [4] Storey, *Thomas Langley*, p. 194.

of Durham, was so strongly pressed on Wessington by his mother and uncle, Joan and Henry Beaufort, that the convent took fright and presented him to Hemingbrough (as rector) in the autumn of 1425 on the false rumour that Rickingale had already vacated the church; but Neville was never admitted to the rectory, and no irreparable damage resulted for he, and Cardinal Beaufort, were already engaged in the negotiations which finally removed him to the higher sphere of the bishopric of Salisbury in 1427.[1] Marmaduke Lumley, another aristocratic younger son who eventually graduated to a bishopric after several years as a 'chopchurch', was the clerk favoured by Queen Katherine who initially hoped he would secure the rectory but was eventually satisfied by the promise of the first prebendal stall in the new collegiate church.[2] The most powerful sponsor of all was the Duke of Bedford who showed signs of desiring permanent control over the advowson. In August 1425 he wrote from Rouen to Wessington asking that Rickingale, his confessor, should be replaced on his resignation by his clerk and secretary, Thomas Bradshaw.[3] The prior pacified Bedford and Bradshaw by promising the latter a prebend at Howden and another at Hemingbrough.[4] The fourth candidate, Master Thomas Chapman, was never seriously considered by Wessington despite his provision to Hemingbrough by Martin V in April 1426.[5] One of the prior's aims was to break the papal claim to reserve the benefice and he was careful not to seek papal confirmation of its new collegiate status. Consequently the operation was comparatively rapid. In May 1426 Wessington informally notified Archbishop Kemp of his intentions; and the official proposal to convert the church was dispatched from Durham on 10 November.[6] In the previous month Wessington had been to London where he obtained the necessary royal licence, couched in terms which obviously reflect the prior's own researches into the abortive attempts to appropriate Hemingbrough in the

---

[1] Reg. III, fo. 114v; Loc. xxv, nos. 103, 124. Cf. Emden II, 1350.

[2] Loc. xxv, nos. 103, 104. Cf. R. L. Storey, 'Marmaduke Lumley, Bishop of Carlisle, 1430–50', *Transactions of the Cumberland and Westmorland Antiquarian and Archaeological Society* LV (1955), 116.

[3] Loc. xxv, no. 117.   [4] Loc. xxv, no. 116.

[5] Reg. III, fo. 120v. Thomas Chapman, here described as '*secretarius*' of Richard Flemyng, Bishop of Lincoln, was at the Curia during the period of the conversion of Hemingbrough into a collegiate church (Emden I, 389).

[6] Reg. Parv. II, fo. 34; Reg. III, fo. 121.

fourteenth century.[1] On 11 January 1427 the cathedral chapter of York consented to the conversion, and on the first day of March Kemp ordained the new collegiate church in a document which was counter-sealed by the Durham prior and monks fifteen days later.[2] In late April presentations were made of the provost, three prebendaries and six vicars of the new foundation; and during the next two months these men were admitted and instituted by the archbishop and inducted into their stalls by Richard Cliff, himself a vicar there and appointed by Wessington as his keeper of spiritualities at Hemingbrough.[3]

Whatever advantages the prior and chapter of Durham hoped to secure by the erection of a collegiate church, there is no doubt that the enterprise left them considerably out of pocket. The royal letters patent of October 1426 alone cost £80 and it was later calculated that the total expenditure on the conversion was over £170, not all of which could be raised from the profits of the vacancy of the church in 1426–7.[4] Wessington hoped to compensate himself by imposing an indemnity pension of four marks per annum on the new provost (in addition to the traditional Hemingbrough pension of five marks to the Durham chamberlain), but he and his successors were rarely able to enforce its payment.[5] Equally misguided was the prior's belief, expressed in the foundation statutes of the college, that after the payment of his own stipend and those of his fellows, the provost would be left with a financial surplus for transmission to Durham. Examination of the eighteen articles of the 1427 ordination shows that the collegiate church, as planned by Wessington, was in fact too ambitious an undertaking for the revenues available. Like the Earl of Westmorland at Staindrop a few years earlier,[6] Wessington seriously underestimated both the running expenses of a collegiate establishment and the contemporary decline of rent incomes. Although the

[1] 1.5. Regal., no. 2; Reg. III, fos. 123v–124v; *C.P.R., 1422–29*, p. 382.

[2] 1.3. Archiepisc., no. 6; Reg. III, fos. 121–3. This, and many other documents from the Durham muniments relating to Hemingbrough, are printed (often inaccurately dated) in the appendix to Raine, *History and Antiquities of Hemingbrough*.

[3] Reg. III, fos. 120v, 125–6.

[4] *C.P.R., 1422–29*, p. 382; *Scrip. Tres*, p. cclxxvi.

[5] See *Scrip. Tres*, p. ccciii.

[6] The Nevilles were compelled to appropriate two more churches to their college at Staindrop in the generation that followed its foundation in 1408 (*V.C.H. Durham* II, 129).

provost of Hemingbrough, who accounted yearly to the prior for all rectorial income and expenditure, rarely received more than a £100 or so a year,[1] he was committed to the payment of stipends which alone exceeded this amount. The provost himself received £40 per annum; each of the three prebendaries was paid ten marks (twice that sum if he resided at Hemingbrough for as much as three months in the year); the senior vicar-choral received fourteen marks per annum, the five other vicars only ten marks; and finally there were four clerk-deacons, each paid £2 per year. Later in the century Archbishop Lawrence Booth found it necessary to issue a new ordination for the collegiate church at Hemingbrough intro-ducing much lower stipends than those established in 1427. At the time of the Dissolution the three prebendaries were reduced to a meagre income of only four marks a year.[2]

Wessington's fundamental error in 1426-7 was his attempt to reconcile, with limited resources at his disposal, the demand by sponsors for prebends for their favourite clerks and his own desire to secure a collegiate church which would be the centre of a genuine corporate and religious life. This last motive, which he shared with his contemporaries, Bishops Langley and Neville,[3] was undoubtedly a genuine one, as is seen by the prior's willingness to double the stipend of any prebendary who resided at Hemingbrough for thirteen weeks in the year. For the non-resident, a Hemingbrough prebend was neither as valuable nor as attractive as one at Howden, a point underlined in a disappointed letter from the Duke of Bedford;[4] but this did not prevent future applicants to the prior widening the scope of their requests and asking for future vacancies at either college. However, it was the institution of a resident provost, an officer unknown at Howden, at the head of the new collegiate church which caused Wessington most anxiety. He was exceptionally unlucky in that his first provost died within sixteen months and his second resigned after seven, while the tenure of the third, John Withyr, proved to be an unmitigated disaster.[5] Withyr, who refused to account to the prior and paid no attention to any of Wessington's

[1] Misc. Chrs., no. 6645 (accounts of the provost of Hemingbrough from 1440 to 1455).   [2] Reg. IV, fo. 190; *Valor Ecclesiasticus* V (1825), 139.

[3] Storey, *Thomas Langley*, pp. 188-90; Reg. III, fos. 244-6.

[4] Loc. xxv, no. 116.   [5] Reg. III, fos. 128, 129.

increasingly hostile letters, survived as provost from 1429 to 1440. The '*materia prepositi de Hemyngburgh*' became, to judge by the contents of his letter-book, Wessington's major preoccupation in the late 1430s, a problem on which he exercised the talents of his most able counsellors, Masters William Doncaster, Thomas Appleby, John Selowe and Robert Ormeshead.[1] Brought to judgement before both the consistory and the chancery court at York, Withyr's deprivation was finally approved at Rome after an awkward period during which Wessington feared that the provost's appeal to the Curia might stand.[2] Even Withyr's successor, Master Thomas Candel, provost from 1440 to 1458, was hardly the ideal spiritual leader of the college for whom the prior must have hoped; he was at one time threatened with deprivation by the archbishop for personal misdemeanours.[3] Apart from the shortcomings of the provosts themselves, Wessington was hard put to it to maintain the residential nature of their office although this was the essence of his original foundation. Only by appealing to Archbishop Kemp did the prior prevent Chancellor John Stafford forcing Richard Bekyngham, one of his chancery clerks, into the provostship; Bekyngham had every intention of changing the 1427 statutes, as he told Wessington in a stormy interview at Durham in August 1436, in the interests of his own non-residence.[4] The vested interests wishing to treat the provostship of Hemingbrough as yet another, and richer, prebend for the careerist ecclesiastic could not be restrained indefinitely. When Archbishop Booth revised the statutes of the college on 20 March 1480, he modified the original clause which had demanded the provost's residence at Hemingbrough.[5]

Although Wessington's original hopes for the collegiate church of Hemingbrough were seriously prejudiced by the fifteenth-century patronage nexus, the foundation was by no means a complete failure. The college continued to fulfil its spiritual functions, including the commemoration of Henry VI and the Dukes of Bedford

[1] Loc. xxv, no. 10; Reg. III, fos. 136, 226, 248, 253; Reg. Parv. II, fos. 47, 52, 70, 94–5, 114, 121, 137; Terrar, 1433/34.
[2] Reg. Parv. II, fo. 113.   [3] Loc. XXI, no. 47.
[4] Loc. xxv, nos. 76, 77; Reg. Parv. II, fo. 95.
[5] Reg. III, fo. 121 (marginal addition). Archbishop Booth's '*reformacio nova*' of Hemingbrough's foundation statutes is printed in Raine, *History and Antiquities of Hemingbrough*, pp. 378–80.

and Gloucester, until its dissolution in the next century. In October 1435, at the height of his litigation with Withyr, Wessington was able to sanction a set of statutes organising the life of vicars and clerks in the Hemingbrough bedern. Although no provision was made for a head warden of the hostel, the statutes otherwise followed the general lines of the 1418 '*statuta vicariorum*' at Howden.[1] The life of a vicar-choral at Hemingbrough, with his stipend of ten marks per annum, was not without its attractions for the sons of local yeomen. Despite the proximity of Howden, the letter of Richard Cliff to Wessington in 1432 reveals the rapid growth of *esprit de corps* among members of the new foundation: 'And if it like your gudnes to presente (to the fifth vicarage of Hemingbrough) a nobill mane of parsone and connyng, ther is thar a tenandes son of yours and a thirsty mans son of ye pariche, the qwilk is of parson a nobill mane to be in any college in Inglande, and of lefyng a gude mane, calide of thame that he is conversande wit all, als we here say, and of connyng sufficiante in redynge and sigynge (*sic*) of plane songe and to syng a tribull til farburdun.'[2]

The final impression left by Prior Wessington's own exercise of his major spiritual patronage, granted the current 'bland assumption that the Church's benefices exist for the benefit of influential people and their relatives',[3] does no particular damage to his reputation. Deluged as he was by requests for vacancies from the English magnates and bishops, the prior was perhaps more fortunate than his predecessors in being comparatively free from papal and royal pressure. The practice of papal provision to the richer benefices in the monastery's gift continued on those occasions when the incumbent died at Rome or was elevated to a bishopric,[4] but no longer gave cause for alarm; either the prior and chapter would disregard the provision (as at Hemingbrough in 1426) or accept it in the case of a clerk like Master John Bonour in 1430, whom they already

---

[1] Reg. III, fos. 193–5.

[2] Loc. xxv, no. 18. The 'nobill mane' in question appears to have been William Watkynson, presented to the vicarage by prior and chapter on 27 November 1432 (Reg. III, fo. 148).

[3] W. A. Pantin, *The English Church in the Fourteenth Century* (Cambridge, 1955), p. 40.

[4] See Loc. xxi, no. 35. In general, however, there seems little doubt that the statutes of Provisors (1390) and Praemunire (1393) had reduced the previous stream of papal provisions to the convent's benefices to a trickle.

intended to present.[1] The death of Henry V in 1422 removed the most powerful and intransigent of all petitioners for benefices, and twenty years were to elapse before his son first wrote to Durham desiring a prebend for one of his chaplains, Master Richard Chester.[2] With his other noble correspondents Wessington managed to secure a series of working agreements by which, for instance, the claims of the Earl of Westmorland were given priority over those of Thomas, Lord Clifford.[3] But the more extreme view that the priors of Durham deliberately played off one lord against the other and ended by presenting their own candidate,[4] finds little confirmation among the fifteenth-century evidence. By finding places for barons of the exchequer, royal clerks and ecclesiastical administrators Wessington was, in any case, likely to win his monastery new and influential friends. It was normal practice at Durham to give preferential treatment to the first supplicant for a vacant benefice. Only when confronted with a particularly powerful and irascible magnate did the Durham monks feel justified in ignoring Abbot Samson of Bury St Edmunds' eminently sensible precept: 'he who comes first to the mill ought to have first grind'.[5]

Although Wessington certainly allowed the exploitation of his spiritual patronage for non-religious ends, he did so less blatantly than many other monastic prelates of the century such as the notorious Abbot Wallingford of St Albans.[6] The prior seems to have remained on the right side of that indistinct line which divided the promise of future benevolence and service from outright simony, an offence with which Prior John Fossor had been charged by Pope Clement VI when he presented to a Howden prebend in the previous century.[7] Nor did Wessington normally indulge in the common fifteenth-century habit of making formal grants to a secular lord of the right to nominate any clerk of his choosing, whom the prior and

---

[1] Reg. III, fo. 134v. Bonour was provided by Martin V to the first prebend of Hemingbrough on the elevation of Marmaduke Lumley to the bishopric of Carlisle.

[2] Loc. xxv, nos. 88, 97. [3] Reg. Parv. II, fo. 129.

[4] Donaldson, 'Sponsors, Patrons and Presentations to Benefices in the gift of the Priors of Durham', p. 174. [5] *Chronicle of Jocelin of Brakelond*, ed. Butler, p. 56.

[6] *Reg. John Whethamstede* (Rolls Series, 1872–73), II, xxv–xxxiii; M. D. Knowles, 'The Case of St. Albans in 1490', *Journal of Ecclesiastical History* III (1952), 153.

[7] *C.P.L.* III (1342–62), 51–2, 230; *Reg. Richard of Bury*, pp. 188–93. The Constitutions of Ottobon (1268) had long since forbidden all '*pactiones factas cum Praesentatis aut praesentandis*'; see Lyndwood, *Provinciale . . . etc.*, Part II, p. 135.

convent would then automatically present on the next vacancy of a particular church.[1] The one instance of this practice recorded in the Durham registers during the first half of the fifteenth century occurred in October 1439 when the nomination of the next rector of Appleby in Leicestershire was conferred on the chancellor and university of Oxford in the interests of a 'graduete manne'.[2] Wessington was reluctant even to make informal commitments for future vacancies; as he pointed out to the Duke of Bedford and Earl of Northumberland in two interesting letters of 1418 and 1419, his predecessor John Hemingburgh had brought the monastery into disrepute by making promises which he could not later fulfil.[3] Before the end of his priorate Wessington was forced to abandon these high principles and found it necessary to conciliate frustrated sponsors by offering to present their clerks when a suitable benefice fell vacant.[4] Yet at all times the prior retained a large measure of control over his patronage. He wished to know both the names and status of the clerks pressed on him by the magnates and was also quite capable of refusing to sanction a 'permutation' involving one of his churches if he doubted the advisability of the exchange.[5] Not all his successors were so conscientious. Prior Richard Bell was apparently in the habit of sending letters of presentation to the more powerful lords with a blank space in which they could insert the name of any clerk they chose.[6]

In addition to those benefices subject to regular presentation by the prior and chapter, Wessington held a wide variety of minor spiritual patronage allowing him to appoint chaplains to chantries and dependent chapelries. In these cases not only was episcopal con-

---

[1] For a contemporary example involving the rectory of Middleton in Teesdale, the abbot and convent of Saint Mary's, York (the lawful patrons) and Richard Beauchamp, Earl of Warwick (the sponsor), see *Reg. Langley* IV, 99.

[2] Reg. Parv. II, fos. 117, 190; Reg. III, fo. 241. For a later nomination to Appleby by the university of Oxford, see *Epistolae Academicae Oxon.*, Part II, ed. H. Anstey (Oxford Historical Society XXXVI, 1898), p. 371. It seems that Wessington and his successors normally reserved the rectory of Appleby for Oxford graduates, possibly in response to the provisions of the Convocation of York in September 1421 (*Reg. Langley* III, 2–5).   [3] Reg. III, fos. 63–4.

[4] Reg. Parv. II, fos. 93, 112; Reg. III, fo. 310v.

[5] Reg. Parv. II, fo. 128. Even in the case of the Howden and Hemingbrough prebends there seem to be few examples of the fraudulent exchanges noticed at the collegiate churches in the diocese of Durham by Thompson, *The English Clergy*, pp. 107–8.   [6] Loc. IX, no. 16.

sent often unnecessary but the collation itself was normally in the hands of the prior alone. Whereas the sub-prior and chapter nominated priests to serve only two chantries (both dedicated to Our Lady, in the churches of Pittington and Saint Margaret, Durham),[1] Wessington nominated to at least a dozen, as well as to several chapels which, like that of Saint Hilda at South Shields, carried parochial functions with them. It is impossible to produce a complete list because the monastic and prior's registers at Durham record very few of these appointments. Except for one or two chantry chapels, notably Saint Helen's above the abbey gatehouse and Saint Katherine's, Beaurepaire, which the priors used to sustain members of their clerical secretariat,[2] it would appear that the chaplains concerned came from the lowest and the most obscure section of the ecclesiastical hierarchy.

In sharp contrast to the strenuous competition for the prebends, rectories and even vicarages in the convent's gift, there was a considerable shortage of unbeneficed priests in the diocese prepared to make their living by serving the chantries at the prior's disposal.[3] In the extreme north of England the scarcity of secular priests was so severe that four Durham monks at Holy Island administered sacraments to the parishioners without licence, an offence for which they received papal absolution in 1422.[4] New chantries continued to be founded in the county at a time when the older foundations were often destitute of a priest or, more frequently, combined with one another under a single chaplain. Reginald Wardowe, collated to Saint Mary's chantry, Pittington, in 1420 was instructed to perform his duties there for four days in the week and to spend the other three serving the chantry of Saint Katherine in the same church.[5] The two chapels of Saint James and Saint Andrew, at opposite ends of Elvet Bridge, were invariably conferred on one clerk, while the revenues

---

[1] Reg. Parv. II, fos. 21–2; Reg. III, fos. 70, 133.

[2] E.g., John Binchester, a chaplain frequently in Wessington's presence, was collated to St Helen's in 1409 (Reg. III, fo. 132v; Reg. Parv. II, fo. 10); and Thomas Ryhale, a Durham notary, was collated to the Beaurepaire chantry in 1407 (Reg. III, fo. 26).

[3] On this point, the monastic records confirm the evidence of the contemporary bishop's register. See Storey, *Thomas Langley*, pp. 181–2.

[4] Loc. III, no. 46.

[5] Reg. III, fo. 70. Twenty-two years later, in 1442, the collation to these chantries in Pittington church devolved to Bishop Neville because they had remained vacant for over two years; see 1.9. Pont., an unnumbered slip of paper.

of Saint Helen's above the abbey gatehouse were augmented by the income from the now deserted chapels of Saint Leonard and Saint Bartholomew.[1] Even chantries in the collegiate churches, where vacancies were less likely to be tolerated and which seem to have been more attractive propositions for the clerical proletariat, were the victims of the same process. In the early 1420s Wessington and Bishop Langley came to an agreement by which a chantry priest in the bishop's manor of Darlington was also to serve the prior's chantry of Saint Mary in the parish church there.[2] The presumption is that only by this combination of revenues from two different sources could a suitable priest be induced to serve the chantries. In the case of the hermitages under the control of the prior of Durham, there are more obvious signs of decay; Wessington made one appointment to a vacant hermitage at Middleton Pounteys bridge in 1426, after which mention of this anchorage disappears completely from the convent's records.[3]

Of more consequence than the right to collate to such chantries and hermitages was the secular patronage at the prior's disposal. This included, most notably, the appointment of the major lay officials of the convent. In particular, the prior's choices of his chief steward, his keeper of Beaurepaire Moor and his abbey porter were closely watched by north-country magnates, many of whom had candidates for these offices.[4] Their response to the selection of a man not to their taste tended to be considerably less polite than when they were disappointed over a benefice; in March 1438 the Earl of Salisbury rebuked Wessington sharply for not giving his servant, William Cowhird, the office of forester of Beaurepaire.[5] But if the prior usually found it advisable to accept the recommendations of local lords on these appointments, so did most monastic superiors in the

---

[1] Reg. III, fos. 26, 34v, 40v, 132v. The problem of the 'impoverished chantry' is discussed in K. L. Wood-Legh, *Perpetual Chantries in Britain* (Cambridge, 1965), pp. 93–129.

[2] Reg. III, fos. 97v, 112; cf. *Reg. Langley* II, 186.

[3] Reg. III, fo. 115v; Reg. Parv. II, fo. 35. Although the county of Durham 'was unusually rich in hermitages', evidence for their survival into the late fifteenth century is very slight: see *V.C.H. Durham* II, 130–1; R. M. Clay, *The Hermits and Anchorites of England* (London, 1914), pp. 214–15.

[4] Loc. xxv, nos. 18, 47, 132, 133, 148; Misc. Chrs., no. 1091 (all letters from lords who wished to nominate their own men to these three offices).

[5] Loc. xxv, no. 120.

later middle ages.[1] On the other hand, Durham avoided, as other religious houses did not, the worst abuses associated with the granting and selling of corrodies. In the previous century Edward III had often sent his retired servants north to Durham to be sustained there by the prior and chapter until they died;[2] but this practice had ceased by the time of Wessington, who was also praised, like his contemporary, Abbot Whethamstede,[3] for his refusal to sell corrodies harmful to the financial welfare of his convent.[4] At Durham the conferment of a daily supply of food and drink, together with an annual livery and money pension, was generally restricted to full-time servants of the monastery. Cooks and victuallers who had spent many years in the convent's employment were often guaranteed security in their old age by the formal grant of corrodies of valet status.[5] *Generosi*, including the prior's esquires and the monastic song master, received bread and ale of a higher quality as well as the promise of sustenance for life when they first entered into their offices.[6] A rare instance of a corrodian who was apparently not a servant of the monastery is Thomas Fery; in April 1423 he and his wife Joan obtained a handsome life allowance of provisions and money (£7 per annum), probably in return for amortizing their lands to the convent.[7]

The monks of Durham also used the term corrody for a place in one of the almshouses or hospitals administered by their almoner. But it was the prior and not this obedientiary who usually admitted applicants to these establishments; memoranda of appointments were consequently most frequently recorded in the prior's register. Thus Wessington was in direct control of what was clearly the most important and most expensive of the ways in which the monastery distributed charity to the poor and deserving. The convent maintained two hospitals, both described by Wessington in his letters of appointment as '*hospitalis noster*', one at Witton Gilbert and the other, dedicated to Saint Mary Magdalen, near Gilesgate on the out-

[1] Knowles, *Rel. Orders* II, 285. See *Reg. John Whethamstede* (Rolls Series, 1872–3), II, 113–14, 199–200, 263–7.
[2] *C.Cl.R.*, *1330–33*, pp. 136, 142; *1337–39*, p. 387; *1339–41*, p. 471.
[3] *Annales J. Amundesham* (Rolls Series, 1870–1), II, 268.
[4] Loc. XXVII, no. I (a).   [5] Reg. II, fo. 225; Reg. III, fo. 71.
[6] Reg. III, fos. 30v, 43, 137–8; *Scrip. Tres*, pp. cccxv–cccxvii.
[7] Reg. III, fo. 100v; cf. *Feodarium Dunelm.*, p. 67.

skirts of the city of Durham.[1] Each house was small and had a complement of only five brothers or sisters; even so, not all of these were regular inmates and the majority of the letters of admission issued by Wessington included a clause allowing non-residence.[2] The hospital of Saint Mary Magdalen was used to support the relatives of Durham monks and among those who received liveries there were the sister of the sub-prior, Robert Rypon, as well as John Holme, Wessington's chamberlain.[3] At Witton Gilbert, near the prior's manor-house of Beaurepaire, the members of the hospital included John and Joan Wessington and others who had served the superior in his years as sacrist.[4]

Much larger institutions were the two almshouses in the Durham Bailey, the '*infirmaria extra portam*' (to be distinguished from the monastic infirmary inside the precinct) and the *Domus Dei*, or *Maison Dieu*, a little further to the north. As at the Dissolution, so in the early fifteenth century, the almoner's rolls show that there were twenty-eight brothers and sisters of the lay infirmary and fifteen of the *Domus Dei*.[5] Some attempt was made to maintain an even balance of the sexes and married couples were a conspicuous feature of both houses. Although Wessington reserved the right to expel any inmate who married after admission to the almshouses, in practice he was prepared to sanction the marriage of widows and widowers with one another.[6] In both infirmary and *Domus Dei*, as in the two hospitals, licences to live elsewhere were common and the number of out-brethren exceeded that of those who resided within the walls.[7] It is clear from an examination of the names of those provided with corrodies of this type that Wessington used at least a third of the places at his disposal to provide what amounted to a small retirement pension to ex-servants of the monastery. Bishops and magnates occasionally wrote to Wessington for a vacancy in his almonry, '*domus sive firmaria*', on behalf of an old retainer of their own; and there is an isolated reference of 1420 to the purchase of a corrody

---

[1] *V.C.H. Durham* II, 114, 119–20.

[2] In the early years of Wessington's priorate, two of the five brothers and sisters at the hospital of Witton Gilbert lived out (Almoner, 1415/16, 1418/19).

[3] Almoner, 1395/96, 1398/99; Reg. Parv. II, fos. 123, 174.

[4] Reg. Parv. II, fo. 79.

[5] Almoner, 1412/13, 1415/16. Cf. *Valor Ecclesiasticus* v (1825), 303.

[6] Reg. Parv. II, fo. 180.   [7] Almoner, 1428/29.

'*apud Magdalen*' for cash.[1] However, most of the men and women admitted by Wessington to his hospitals and almshouses were genuinely old (the average length of tenure before death was less than five years) and at a period when the demand for charity exceeded the supply, the prior fulfilled his traditional obligation of care for the aged and diseased. It would be impossible to maintain that the alms of the Durham monks ameliorated the lot of more than a handful of the poor unfortunates from the city and county. But in view of their financial difficulties in the fifteenth century, it is hardly surprising that the Durham monks did no more. Few monasteries of comparable size did as much.

The almoner of Durham catered for the very young as well as for the very old; and among the responsibilities of the prior was his selection of 'certain poor children called the children of the Almery', who 'went dayly to the Farmary school'.[2] The almonry school at Durham continued to flourish from its beginnings, perhaps before the middle of the fourteenth century, until the Dissolution when the monastery was maintaining thirty poor scholars.[3] It is impossible to estimate the number of these *pueri Elemosinarie* at the time of Wessington's priorate because, as they received their meat and drink from the leftovers of the monastic table, the almoner's accounts made only incidental reference to their existence. According to the chapter diffinitions of 1446, admissions to the almonry school were to be made 'chiefly and principally from the acquaintances of monks resident at Durham'; but the chapter nevertheless acknowledged the prior's right to accept boys nominated by lords and magnates.[4] In February 1448 Prior William Ebchester wrote to Sir Robert Ogle informing him that he would 'with good hertt tendre your entennt in resauying of that childe to our almose and scoole for whilke yhe haue writen'.[5] The almonry school at Durham occupied various rooms in and near the lay infirmary outside the monastic gatehouse and was conducted by a master who taught grammar for a yearly stipend of forty shillings.[6] It is to be distinguished from the smaller song-school consisting of only eight boys when re-organised by

[1] Loc. xxv, nos. 51, 79, 149; *Dur. Acct. Rolls* I, 269.
[2] *Rites*, p. 91. See above, p. 60.
[3] *Valor Ecclesiasticus* v (1825), p. 303; *V.C.H. Durham* I, 368–70.
[4] Loc. xxvii, no. 15, memb. 3.   [5] Reg. Parv. III, fo. 28v.
[6] Almoner, 1412–24.

Wessington in 1430. Before that year professional choirmasters had been employed only intermittently at Durham at small stipends of 6*s*. 8*d*. a year.[1] However, in the indenture made on 22 December 1430 with John Stele (the first of a long line of similar appointments) not only were the duties of the *cantor* carefully specified but the prior reserved the right to assign boys to him for instruction in the techniques of 'playnsange, prikenot, faburdon and dischaunts'.[2] Wessington also appointed masters to the convent's two Yorkshire grammar schools at Howden and Northallerton,[3] but little is known of the numbers and the background of the boys who received education there.

The re-endowment of Durham College, Oxford, by Bishop Hatfield in the late fourteenth century added significantly to the educational patronage in the control of the prior of Durham. The statutes of 1381 provided for the maintenance at the college of eight secular scholars 'who are to concentrate their studies on grammar and philosophy', four from the city or diocese of Durham, two from Howdenshire and two from Allertonshire.[4] The intention was presumably to give a free university education to the most promising students from the convent's three charity grammar schools. At Canterbury College, Oxford, three of the five seculars were nominated by the archbishop,[5] but at Durham College these appointments were in the hands of the prior, who was required to admit boys after examination by a committee of four or five senior monks, themselves chosen by the superior. A letter sent to John Burnby, warden of the college, in March 1445 reveals that Wessington observed these statutes scrupulously. William Robinson of Morpeth had been elected to a scholarship after sponsorship by a Newcastle merchant, Roger Thornton, and examination by five Durham monks; when

[1] Almoner, 1419–22.

[2] The right to choose the eight boys might, however, be delegated by the prior to another monk: Reg. III, fos. 137–8. For later appointments of Durham 'cantores' see *Scrip. Tres*, pp. cccxv–cccxvii, ccclxxxvi–ccclxxxvii, cccxcviii–cccc, ccccxiii–ccccxiv. See above, p. 71.

[3] See the documents from the Durham muniments printed by A. F. Leach, *Early Yorkshire Schools* II (Yorkshire Archaeological Society, Record Series, XXXIII, 1903), 60–2, 84–7.   [4] *Concilia* II, 615; *Scrip. Tres*, p. 141.

[5] *Canterbury College, Oxford*, ed. W. A. Pantin, III (Oxford Historical Society, New Series VIII, 1950), 179; *Register Henry Chichele*, ed. E. F. Jacob, IV (Canterbury and York Society XLVII, 1947), 145–6.

Burnby attempted to refuse him admission, he was rebuked sharply by Wessington who reminded him that he had no authority to receive or reject a secular student except at the prior's own command.[1] Wessington's powers of discretion were, however, severely circumscribed in practice by the need to admit the candidates of powerful lay patrons. Lord Fitzhugh asked for one of the four Durham scholarships for a clerk of Barnard Castle, three miles distant from his manor at Cotherstone.[2] The Earl of Westmorland combined with his brother, Sir Thomas Neville, to request a place at Oxford for Thomas Marley; Marley's letters of admission were issued a few weeks later.[3] Indeed there is no example of a refusal of this type of petition. In the case of the seculars admitted to Durham College from the two Yorkshire liberties, the influence of the local patron was supreme. In the 1430s and 1440s, Sir James Portington and Ralph Babthorpe, stewards and justices of the peace for Howden and Howdenshire, seem to have regularly nominated two students as vacancies occurred at Oxford; Sir William Strangways and Robert Danby did the same in the Allertonshire franchise.[4] The principle was exactly that involved in requests for the convent's benefices, although on a somewhat smaller scale. Even at this humble level, Wessington's patronage as prior of Durham did not escape the attention of lords anxious to provide for their relatives and dependents.

No study of late medieval patronage which depends on the information provided by written evidence alone can hope to be entirely adequate. A full appreciation of Wessington's attitude to the benefices, offices and other positions at his disposal would require a more detailed knowledge than is possible of his personal relationships with north-country lords and their clients. On the other hand, the fifteenth-century records leave no doubt as to the value placed on the prior's patronage by his neighbours as well as himself. In the north-east of England only the bishop of Durham surpassed the prior in the variety of places he could offer to the ambitious and the acquisitive. But even more significant than the extent of the prior and chapter's patronage is the manner in which it was utilised in the

---

[1] Reg. Parv. II, fo. 193.

[2] Ibid., fo. 118.   [3] Loc. xxv, no. 128; Reg. Parv. II, fo. 192.

[4] Reg. Parv. II, fos. 145, 194. Original letters from Locellus xxv asking for secular scholarships at Oxford are printed by Halcrow, 'Social Position and Influence of the Priors of Durham', *Arch. Ael.*, Fourth Series, XXXIII (1955), 70–86.

interests of secular lords rather than the monastery. It has been seen that the monks did not succumb completely before these strong external pressures, but it would be idle to pretend that they could ever present to a valuable benefice or appoint to a valuable office without considering the effects of their choice on their relations with the great lords. As the Durham chapter noted in 1446, it was always essential to respond with great care to 'the demands and requests of the lords and magnates whom we cannot offend *(quos offendere non possumus)*'.[1]

It might well be concluded that its control of benefices and places brought the priory of Durham more annoyance than profit. This, at least, was the view put forward for public consumption by the monks themselves. According to Prior Bell, in a characteristic *cri de coeur* of March 1476, 'I and my brether are so ofte tymes cald uppon in sich things by diverse lords of right high astate that we may noght have our liberty to dispose sich smal benefices as ar in our gifte to our frends, like as our will and intent wer forto do, as God knawith and me repentith'.[2] There certainly is no doubt that the Durham prior and chapter were at least partially the victims of an elaborate and insidious spoils system. But it is easy to forget that even the most lavish dispensers of patronage are never entirely free agents: the most powerful, and the most skilful, English prime ministers of the nineteenth century were conscious that it was dangerous to meet any request for honours with a point-blank refusal.[3] Nor was the game, as Prior Bell was particularly aware, without its compensations. The fact that Thomas Cromwell was a recipient of an annuity from the convent during the 1530s could hardly have postponed the dissolution of the monastery; but it may well help to explain the leniency with which the Durham monks were apparently treated by Cromwell's notorious commissioners. More generally, the late medieval priors of Durham, so often petitioners themselves, must often have enjoyed being the recipients of petitions. The extent of the convent's patronage carried with it the risk of offending the great lords; but at least it ensured, what otherwise was all too possible, that the Durham monks could never be ignored by the territorial aristocracy of England.

[1] Loc. xxvii, no. 15, memb. 3.   [2] Reg. Parv. iii, fo. 168v.
[3] R. Blake, *Disraeli* (London, 1966), p. 448.

Chapter 6

THE PRIOR AND THE LAY LORDS

A man of peace! Give us a man of peace![1]

As the superior of the most celebrated English monastery north of York the prior of Durham was a public figure as well as a spiritual leader. Lords, both spiritual and temporal, requested from him not only benefices, offices and scholarships but also his own services. Prior Wessington had himself no particular desire to play a prominent role in either national or local politics and lacked both the ambition and unscrupulousness which secured the bishopric of Carlisle for one of his successors, Richard Bell.[2] No prior was more sensitive than Wessington to any attempt at depriving the cathedral church of Durham of its traditional privileges and liberties; but his attitude to matters which did not directly concern the welfare of the monastery was cautious and diffident in the extreme. The reasons Wessington gave for his refusal to serve on the English commission negotiating an extension of the truce with the Scots in 1444 are characteristic of his usual prudence. 'And if I wer of connyng and hele to labour and ony poynt where movyd and haldyn agayns the Scottes entent, thei wald pute itt in parte to me, and malyne agens the hoys of Coldyngham, and our lyffolod oppon the marches.'[3] Some priors of Durham were less nervous and not only served on royal commissions of truce but took an active interest in local and especially Anglo-Scottish affairs. Wessington's determination to retain his neutrality ('I have keppid me one euyn person wythoutyn parcialte')[4] during the contest between the two branches of the Neville family in 1440 is, however, more representative of the prevailing mood at Durham throughout the later middle ages. Such impartiality was not without its attractions amid the turbulence and faction of early fifteenth-century England: on various occasions Wessington – like his pre-

---

[1] *Chronicle of Jocelin of Brakelond*, ed. Butler, p. 126.
[2] R. B. Dobson, 'Richard Bell, Prior of Durham (1464–78) and Bishop of Carlisle (1478–95)', pp. 182–221.
[3] Reg. Parv. II, fo. 183.   [4] Ibid., II, fo. 113.

decessors and successors – found himself acting, usually reluctantly, as an important agent of the central government and as peace-maker among the northern nobility and gentry. The monastery and prior of Durham could be relied upon as instruments of stability in an all too unstable political world.

THE KING'S GOVERNMENT AND CLERICAL TAXATION

To the kings of England the priory of Durham was well known as 'oon of the grettest and moost notable churches of oure patrounage within this oure Roy^{me}';[1] but to the monks of Durham in the early fifteenth century the king himself was a remote, if powerful, figure. The pilgrimage of Henry VI to the shrine of Saint Cuthbert in September 1448 was the first visit to Durham by a reigning English sovereign since that July day in 1405 when his grandfather had watched the execution there of several leaders of the Scrope rebellion.[2] Of all the Lancastrians only the Duke of Bedford had anything approaching a personal relationship with the Durham community. As warden of the East March while still an adolescent, Bedford had been entertained at Beaurepaire by Prior Hemingburgh and presented with letters of confraternity.[3] Until the end of his life Bedford continued to show interest in the welfare of the monastery and once wrote to Wessington from Paris to express his shocked surprise that 'oon of the monkes of youre convent was not longe ago proved and founden gylty of the horrible synne of sodomye'.[4] For his part, Wessington followed the progress of the French wars from afar and handsomely rewarded the many messengers bringing letters from abroad '*cum rumoribus de regno Francie*'.[5]

Not himself one of the twenty-four Black Monk superiors regularly summoned as spiritual lords in the fifteenth century, Prior Wessington attended no parliaments, with the possible exception of the assembly of May 1421 which coincided with the extraordinary General Chapter of the English Benedictines at Westminster.[6] The

---

[1] Loc. xxv, no. 96.
[2] *Rites*, pp. 122–3; *C.P.R.*, *1405–8*, pp. 68–73 (letters patent dated at Durham); J. H. Ramsay, *Lancaster and York*, I, 92.   [3] Bursar, 1404/5, Expense Prioris.
[4] Loc. xxv, no. 115.   [5] Bursar, 1438/39, Dona et Exennia.
[6] See below, p. 241. When Prior Thomas Castell was summoned to parliament in 1503, it was noted that this had been done in error. (Cart. III, fo. 301.)

clergy of the Durham diocese were sometimes called to Lancastrian parliaments by means of writs which required the representation of the Durham chapter by one proctor as well as the personal appearance of the two archdeacons and the prior himself.[1] Both Priors Wessington and Hemingburgh disregarded these instructions and usually combined with their chapter to send one or more joint proctors to the parliament in question.[2] It was equally uncommon for Wessington to send his monks to plead in person at Westminster. The prior could normally rely on the services of his secular agents and counsellors, as well as on the knowledge that the usual channel of communication between the central government and himself was the bishop of Durham. The prior made many appeals to king and council for their intervention on behalf of the monastery's liberties and possessions, and he seems to have been rarely disappointed. In 1438 Henry VI took the priory of Coldingham into his special protection; and a few years later the same monarch authorised the convent's refusal to make confirmations under their common seal of annuities granted by Bishop Neville.[3]

In return for royal protection, the prior of Durham, like other monastic prelates in the later middle ages, was expected to contribute to the needs of the central government. To meet the costs of his military preparations in 1415, Henry V demanded a loan of one hundred marks from the prior and chapter on the security of a gold tabernacle as well as ten times that amount from Bishop Langley.[4] However, the fifteenth-century convent never had sufficient capital at its disposal to become an important royal creditor and, as it was, these hundred marks had to be borrowed from Thomas Langton, the prior's steward.[5] More frequent was the king's use of the Durham treasury as a repository of cash, plate, jewels and muniments, including documents relating to the inheritance of Henry, Lord Scrope of Masham, executed for treason in 1415.[6] Only a few weeks

---

[1] E.g. to the parliaments of January 1410 and February 1445 (Loc. xx, nos. 11b, 18; *Reg. Langley* I, 110–11).

[2] Reg. III, fos. 68, 274; cf. Reg. II, fos. 309, 335.

[3] Misc. Chrs., no. 1348; Reg. III, fo. 303; Reg. Parv. II, fo. 187. See *Scrip. Tres*, p. ccclxxv, where these '*Literae regis de confirmacionibus inconsuetis non fiendis*' are printed out of chronological sequence.

[4] *C.P.R.*, *1413–16*, p. 350. Cf. *C.Cl.R.*, *1422–29*, p. 133.

[5] Mines Accts., 1417.   [6] Loc. xxv, no. 99.

after Wessington's election, Bishop Langley wrote to Henry V on the subject of some of the king's possessions 'under the warde of two monkes of the Churche, and the last Priour that ded is, and of a man clepet Mydeltone'; Langley informed the king that he had sent a messenger to Wessington, 'the Priour that now is, that out of the said Churche ne Priory be not remuet ne delyveret no kist ne othir instrument that may contene gold, syluer, or juell, chartre, muniment, or othir evydences that ther has been left to kepe, til the forsaid Prior and I may speke to gedir'.[1] Another duty frequently undertaken by Wessington on behalf of the royal government was the admission to their offices of various royal functionaries in the county of Northumberland. The latter might include the sheriff and escheator as well as the controller of the customs at Newcastle-upon-Tyne. Such officers were spared the long journey to the Exchequer at Westminster and visited Wessington at Durham where, in his private chapel, he led them through the now stereotyped phrases of their oaths before handing them their royal letters of appointment.[2]

But by far the most important and the most onerous of the prior's responsibilities towards the central government was his payment and collection of contributions towards all clerical subsidies granted by the Convocation of York. The clerical tenth and half-tenth were the effective instruments by which the monks of Durham were compelled to give concrete support to the royal revenues. Throughout Wessington's priorate, the spiritualities and temporalities of the convent were assessed for the purpose of these subsidies on the basis of the '*Nova Taxatio*' of 1318.[3] Although their possessions in Northumberland and Lancashire were now exempt from taxation, the

---

[1] H. Ellis, *Original Letters illustrative of English History*, Second Series, I (1827), 51–2. Langley's letter, dated from Pontefract on a Thursday morning, was probably written in January 1417 (see Storey, *Thomas Langley*, p. 232) and may allude to the gold tabernacle already mentioned.

[2] 3.5. Regal., no. 6; Misc. Chrs., no. 6040; Reg. II, fos. 30v, 216; Reg. III, fos. 271–2; Reg. Parv. II, fos. 53, 67; *Scrip. Tres*, pp. ccxx–ccxxi. The swearing in of local royal officials was a task often entrusted to monastic prelates; see, for example, *Literae Cantuarienses* (Rolls Series, 1887–89), III, 234; *Historia et Cartularium Monasterii Sancti Petri Gloucestriae* (Rolls Series, 1863–7), III, 288–90.

[3] The monks of Durham had gained considerably from the reduction in their valuation between 1291 and 1318. The prior's assessment for spiritualities dropped from under £700 to under £400, for temporalities from £620 to £133 6s. 8d. (*Taxatio ecclesiastica . . . P. Nicholai IV*, pp. 318, 330).

monks of Durham were still required to make a total payment estimated at £76 15s. 8½d. every time a whole tenth was conceded by Convocation.[1] Of this sum, slightly over £30 was the responsibility of the superiors of five Durham cells (Durham College, Oxford, paid £14 6s. 8d.; Finchale, £5 17s. 11d.; Stamford, £5 13s. 4d.; Jarrow, £2 16s. 0d.; Monk Wearmouth, £1 6s. 8d.) and the remainder was contributed by various obedientiaries at the mother house.

Although the rates of assessment for the royal tenth had never been accurate indices of the actual value of particular obediences in terms of net annual income,[2] the Durham account rolls show that royal taxation could be a serious liability in individual cases. Whenever Convocation granted a full tenth, the chamberlain was due to pay £6 2s. 8½d. from total receipts of less than £100 per annum.[3] Even the Durham bursar, charged at £35 9s. 11d. for a whole tenth, was sensitive to the incidence of royal taxation; in 1416–17 he delivered to the collector over £52, considerably more than his large wine bill for that year.[4] Between 1399 and 1450 the northern province was subjected to a total of twenty and three-quarters royal tenths (either in single units or fractions).[5] It can therefore be calculated that the Durham monks paid approximately £1,500 in royal taxation during the course of the half-century, an annual average of £30, of which about two-fifths was levied from five cells and the rest from the central monastery: £18 a year (the substantial accuracy of the figure is confirmed by the entries in extant obedientiary accounts) cannot have been a crushing burden on a religious house whose total annual receipts were then reckoned at over £2,000.[6] Yet at a period when other Benedictine houses in the province of York, notably

---

[1] This and the following figures were calculated by a Durham monk early in the fifteenth century (B.M., Stowe MS. 930, fo. 69). The actual sums paid by Durham's cells and obedientiaries, as recorded in their account rolls, were often less, but never much less, than the figures listed in this manuscript. For a late fifteenth-century estimate of clerical taxation within the diocese of Durham, see Reg. Parv. IV, fo. 42.

[2] R. Graham, 'The Taxation of Pope Nicholas IV', *E.H.R.* XXIII (1908), 444, 450.

[3] Chamberlain, 1440/41.   [4] Bursar, 1416/17, Contribuciones.

[5] Loc. XVIII, nos. 47, 62, 73, 87, 96. The incomplete details provided by *Records of the Northern Convocation*, ed. G. W. Kitchin (Surtees Soc. CXIII, 1907), pp. 124–76, may be supplemented from the *Calendar of Fine Rolls* or Ramsay, *Lancaster and York*, I, 152, 310, 314; II, 260. The cells of Stamford and Durham College held spiritualities and temporalities in the diocese of Lincoln which were taxed more frequently than those in the province of York.

[6] *Scrip. Tres*, p. ccli. See below, pp. 250, 253.

Selby and Monk Bretton,[1] were often exempted from royal taxation, it is not surprising that Durham should have wished to join their ranks. In 1444 Wessington appealed to the government for complete exemption from the payment of royal subsidies and prepared memoranda in which he tried to justify his case.[2]

Wessington's ambitious claim for exemption was based on three main arguments: the decline in the monastery's rent income from Northumberland, the expenses entailed by the entertainment of magnates and their retinues at the convent, and the prior's own past labours as collector of the royal tenths in the diocese of Durham. The last of these grievances was the significant one, for what Wessington was attempting to do in 1444 was not only to excuse the monastery from payment of royal subsidies but to excuse himself and his successors from the burden of their collection. He wished to terminate what was, without question, the most laborious and troublesome of all the duties performed by priors of Durham in the interests of the English government. Technically the prior was appointed collector of royal tenths in the diocese of Durham by the bishop and not the king. In the province of York, like that of Canterbury,[3] set procedural forms were followed once Convocation had conceded a grant. On receipt of the royal writ instructing him to appoint a collector or collectors, the bishop of Durham would invariably nominate the prior and return a certificate to that effect to the treasurer and barons of the Exchequer.[4] Copies of the accounts of Priors Hemingburgh and Wessington as collectors survive in considerable numbers both at Durham (in Locellus XVIII) and among the royal Exchequer records,[5] making it possible to reconstruct their methods of operation. On receiving the episcopal mandate to collect, the prior appointed one or two special sub-collectors from among the ranks of his more experienced obedientiaries. The prior, or the sub-collector, then commissioned a clerk to travel through the

---

[1] *Reg. Langley* I, 96, 134. Both Selby and Monk Bretton were fully exempt in 1431–2 (*Reg. Langley* IV, 2, 114).   [2] Loc. II, no. 11; Loc. XXI, no. 30.

[3] Jacob, *The Fifteenth Century*, p. 420.

[4] *Reg. Langley* I, 96–7, 133–5, 138; II, 26, 42, 143, 161, 183; III, 126–7; IV, 2–3, 113–15.

[5] For the original accounts, schedules of exemptions, etc., of the prior of Durham between 1404 and 1445, see P.R.O., Exchequer K.R., Subsidy Rolls, Clerical Series (E.179), nos. 62/11–62/40. These accounts leave no doubt as to the effectiveness of Wessington's work as collector.

diocese raising money from all benefices in the diocese liable to the subsidy. During the 1430s and 1440s Wessington regularly employed the same man, William Bentlay, an inhabitant of Elvet, in this capacity.[1] As all or most benefices in the archdeaconry of Northumberland were exempt, the collection itself was not normally a lengthy process. The royal tenth collected by Wessington in his first year as prior may serve as an example. The York Convocation conceded the grant on 12 January 1417 and, after receiving the necessary royal writ, Bishop Langley appointed Wessington collector on 19 February; by the end of the year (7 December) the prior owed the Exchequer less than £5 on this account.[2]

During the early fifteenth century the prior was held responsible for approximately £210 every time a full tenth was levied in the northern province, as well as for an additional and variable sum (never more than £30) sometimes charged on benefices, prebends and portions assessed at less than ten marks in value. But it was unusual for even half of this money to reach Westminster as there were many allowances on the account, particularly to the bishop of Durham who, by this means, recovered loans he had made to the royal government. As collector the prior himself received allowances of £2 10s. or £5 for his expenses and labour, sums which Wessington later complained were grossly inadequate but which certainly bear comparison with the commission of 8d. in the £ granted to collectors in the northern province at the end of the century.[3] Frequent assignments were made on the tenths collected by the prior, for which tallies had to be presented at the Exchequer with the final account.[4] Particularly large payments were made towards the defence of the northern border; in 1409 Prior Hemingburgh was ordered to deliver £80 to the Earl of Westmorland as warden of the West March; and in 1418 Lord John Neville received £33 6s. 8d. from the proceeds of the subsidy in the Durham diocese to be spent upon the repair of the walls and three gates of Carlisle.[5] The effective-

---

[1] Reg. Parv. II, fos. 52, 183–4, 194; Reg. III, fo. 281.   [2] Misc. Chrs., no. 7127.

[3] *Register of Richard Fox, Bishop of Durham* (Surtees Soc. CXLVII, 1932), pp. 34–5.

[4] Loc. xxv, nos. 25, 31.

[5] Misc. Chrs., no. 5096; P.R.O., Exchequer of Receipt, Receipt Roll no. 683 (Easter, 6 Henry V), memb. 6. See Storey, *Thomas Langley*, p. 146, for contributions of £100 and £60 from the same source to Sir John Bertram, keeper of Roxburgh Castle, in 1419 –20. Cf., for a later example, Receipt Roll no. 885 (Easter, 4 Edward IV), memb. 3.

ness with which the prior performed his duties as collector depended on the coercive powers at his disposal. As a final resort he could employ, in his own right as collector, the powerful weapon of sequestration: in May 1441 Wessington sequestered the fruits of the wealthiest of all Durham benefices, Gainford parish church, when the rector there failed to answer for a half-tenth conceded by the previous Convocation.[1]

Wessington's financial relationship with the treasurer and barons of the Exchequer was not, however, altogether harmonious despite his retention of a permanent attorney to represent his interests before them. On his last visit to London in 1437, the prior attempted to settle his accounts; in his own words, 'wheen I was at Londyn att Michaelmesse was thre yheere, as yhe knawe well, I hadd Sir Nichol Dixson and othere 4 barons, Levesham and othere notabill persons of the Escheker, wyth meat dyner in my lordes place ... and att thatt tyme hadd commonyng with theym for allowance of certeyn taylles lyvered to me for the dyme de anno xv. And so me beand thare full aseth and accompt was made apon the same dyme'.[2] Wessington's distress was therefore all the greater when in December 1440 he was informed that the sheriff of Yorkshire had received a writ of *levari facias* from the Exchequer and seized grain from the church of Bossall, appropriated to Durham College. The prior was being held to account for a sum of £15 said to be owing from his collection of the clerical subsidy '*de anno xiv*', the Exchequer year that ended at Michaelmas 1436. Faced with the threat of distraint, Wessington paid up these arrears but only with a strong sense of injustice. According to his explanation of the debt, the culprit was Henry Helay, sub-collector in 1436, who had omitted to see that the proper allowance for hospitals and portioners was entered on the subsidy account before its despatch to the Exchequer. Helay, who had moved to Holy Island as prior in May 1437, was rebuked for his negligence by Wessington in a letter urging him to ride to London, or send a reliable deputy, and settle the affair 'as you love your own honour and my peace'. In the end, Wessington's full payment of the £15 in January 1441 apparently closed the incident without Helay's intervention. This unfortunate episode was however recalled by

[1] Reg. Parv. II, fos. 138–9.
[2] Ibid. II, fos. 133–4.

Wessington three years later and seems to have been the immediate cause of the prior's decision to seek exemption for himself and the monastery of the payment and collection of royal subsidies.[1]

Wessington's case was not altogether unreasonable even though the collection of clerical tenths had been an onerous obligation laid upon monastic superiors throughout England from the earliest days of the subsidy.[2] It was by no means uncommon for a large religious house to secure official exemption from all compulsory duties in connection with the clerical subsidies: St Albans had received letters patent to that effect from Richard II.[3] As Wessington stated in a message for delivery to Lord Treasurer Cromwell, 'the priours of Durham has been colletoirs, soole and noon othere, of the kinges dymes wythin the diocese of Durham moore than this 50 or 60 yheere, to us ryght grett laboure and notabill losse, whar in York-shire and other places, abays and house of Religion takes thare course aboute'.[4] Wessington's remarks bear on the major difficulty that, except for the prior of Durham, there was no religious superior north of the Tees of sufficient standing to be an acceptable collector. The choice, sometimes made in the fourteenth century, of the arch-deacon of Durham had little to recommend it now that this ecclesiastic was rarely resident in the diocese; moreover, the prior had at his disposal the convent's treasury, perhaps the safest place for the deposit of money in the north of England.

It is all the more surprising that Wessington's campaign for exemption from both payment and collection of royal subsidies should have led, even if only after his resignation, to a real although very temporary success. In the summer of 1446 Henry VI borrowed £100 from the convent in return for a general pardon,[5] and the monks

---

[1] Loc. xxv, no. 30; Reg. Parv. II, fos. 131–4. Distraint on the convent's Yorkshire property seems to have been the normal means by which the Exchequer put pressure on the prior of Durham (Reg. Parv. II, fo. 14; Loc. XVIII, no. 68).

[2] *C.Cl.R., 1330–33*, p. 375; *1337–39*, pp. 65, 81; *1341–43*, p. 335. Cf. *Registrum Palatinum Dunelmense* (Rolls Series, 1873–78), III, 294; W. E. Lunt, 'The Collectors of Clerical Subsidies', *The English Government at Work, 1327–1336*, II, ed. W. A. Morris and J. R. Strayer (Mediaeval Academy of America, 1947), p. 235.

[3] *C.P.R., 1377–81*, p. 532. Cf. Abbot Whethamstede's disinclination to collect royal tenths in Hertfordshire and Buckinghamshire in 1425 (*Annales J. Amundesham* [Rolls Series, 1870–1], I, 198).   [4] Reg. Parv. II, fo. 132.

[5] Bursar, 1446/47, Dona et Exennia, where the words '*pro mutuacione centum librarum ad excusandum nos penes eundem Regem*' presumably refer to the general pardon issued on 29 July 1446 (3.5. Regal., no. 2).

seem to have taken the opportunity of the king's visit to Durham two years later to press home their case. Among their records survives a supplication for exemption from royal tenths 'and of the gaderyng of all suche dismes' initialled by Henry VI himself.[1] Less than two months later, on 19 November 1448, royal letters patent formally excused the prior and chapter, together with the Durham cells, from the payment of all tenths, subsidies, aids and contributions granted by future Convocations and from the collection thereof.[2] Yet the convent's victory in their struggle for freedom from royal taxation was short-lived for Henry VI's letters patent were soon revoked by the authority of a later parliament.[3] When the Convocation of York next granted a clerical subsidy (a half-tenth payable before February 1454), Bishop Neville chose Prior Ebchester of Durham as collector in the usual way.[4] Edward IV raised contributions from the northern clergy much more frequently than Henry VI, and from the former's reign until the Dissolution the Durham obedientiaries and heads of cells regularly paid clerical subsidies and the prior was the normal choice as collector.[5] When the later Durham monk Thomas Swalwell, himself a sub-collector in 1506, unearthed a copy of the 1448 supplication, he was unaware that letters patent conceding exemption had been issued and endorsed the document with the note, 'But this petition was not granted'.[6] Wessington's arguments had been unable to prevail against the king's demands for money and for capable collectors of clerical subsidies. In the 1440s and 1450s when the personal power of the English monarchy was at its lowest ebb, the Durham community may have believed that they could free themselves from the most irksome of their duties to the crown. After the accession of Edward IV in 1461 and under the Yorkists and early Tudors, the

---

[1] Misc. Chrs., no. 5388.

[2] The original letters patent survive as 3.5. Regal., no. 3 (for copies, see Loc. III, no. 23; Misc. Chrs., no. 7040; *C.P.R., 1446–52*, p. 244), and were based on the convent's supplication (Loc. III, no. 37; Loc. XVIII, no. 71; Loc. XIX, no. 1; *Scrip. Tres*, pp. cccxix–cccxxi).

[3] Repertorium Magnum, marginal addition to the entry 3.5. Regal., no. 3.

[4] Loc. XIX, no. 51; cf. *C.F.R., 1452–61*, pp. 40–1.

[5] Loc. XVIII, no. 9; Bursar, 1464/65, Contribuciones; *Finchale Priory*, pp. ccxcvii, cccii; *Jarrow and Wearmouth*, pp. 118, 121; *Register of Richard Fox*, pp. 36, 60–1; *Registers of Tunstall and Pilkington* (Surtees Soc. CLXI, 1952), pp. 15–16.

[6] Loc. XVIII, nos. 20, 71.

Durham chapter could be under no such misapprehension. The king was indeed the monks' 'most souerent dred leige lord' and had no intention of relinquishing the most valuable of the services they could render.

THE NORTHERN MAGNATES AND GENTRY

Besides his services as an agent of the central government, the prior had many obligations towards the local aristocracy and gentry of the county palatine of Durham. The view that he 'was a great county magnate, ranking with the Nevilles of Raby and Brancepeth, the Percys of Alnwick, and the rest of the northern nobles'[1] gives a misleading impression of the prior's position in the fifteenth century. But although Wessington regarded himself as pre-eminently a spiritual leader, his office carried with it certain undefined responsibilities towards the other tenants of the bishop. Such responsibilities do not appear to have been particularly onerous in theory, but in practice Wessington found it both necessary and useful to win the friendship of his more powerful neighbours. A constant interchange of small gifts testifies to the mutual respect normally displayed in these relationships. Two Durham knights complimented Wessington on 'the gret affection and lave that ye have to the gentilmen of this cuntre'.[2] The northern nobility trusted the prior and convent sufficiently to make them guardians and trustees of their valuables, both money and armour.[3] There still survive among the Durham muniments many family title-deeds deposited in the monastic treasury during the fifteenth century.[4] Alternatively, the monastic chancellor might be asked to insert a copy of a particularly important document in his register.[5] Not himself very prominent in local political life, the prior could be relied upon to help in the restoration of peace

---

[1] Canon Fowler in *Dur. Acct. Rolls* III, iii.

[2] Loc. xxv, no. 7.

[3] Reg. II, fo. 271; Reg. III, fo. 205; Misc. Chrs., nos. 6001, 6003, 6004, 6005. The largest sum of money known to have been deposited in the convent for safekeeping during Wessington's priorate is two hundred gold marks, much less than the £2,000 and more held by the abbot of St Benet's Hulme from the estate of Sir John Fastolf in 1459 (*The Paston Letters*, ed. J. Gairdner [Westminster, 1900], 1,468).

[4] Notably those of the Claxton family, many of whose deeds are now dispersed among the present category of Miscellaneous Charters; see Surtees, *Durham* I, 17.

[5] Reg. III, fos. 264v–265.

and tranquillity after the all too common 'grave discords between the magnates of the country'.[1] Two disputes in particular, those involving the Neville and Heron families, absorbed much of Wessington's attention during the middle years of his priorate and drew him into secular affairs. Both controversies merit detailed attention, not only because of the prior of Durham's important role as peace-maker but also because they provide almost classic instances of the dangers of factionalism and civil war in northern England during the generation before the outbreak of the Wars of the Roses.

'*Ibidem et multi et magni sunt*' was Henry VI's accurate description of the position of the Nevilles in the diocese of Durham in 1437.[2] Wessington obviously had much to gain from friendship with this, the most formidable of aristocratic families in the north after 1405. Although the prior seems to have welcomed the restoration of Henry Percy, second Earl of Northumberland, in 1416, and remained on good terms with that most assiduous petitioner for benefices,[3] it was to the house of Neville rather than that of Percy that he looked for help and protection. The connection between the monastery of Durham and the Nevilles of Raby had been particularly close during the late fourteenth century, in the generation which had followed the battle of Neville's Cross in 1346 where monk and baron had been united under the banner of Saint Cuthbert. One of the heroes of that victory, Ralph, fourth Baron Neville, had been the first lay-man to be buried in the cathedral (1367), where he was followed by his son John, Lord Neville, in 1388. Very soon after Wessington's election their bodies, and those of their wives, were removed to the Neville chantry served daily by members of the monastic community according to a fixed rota.[4] The prior was presumably acting

[1] This was the reason Wessington himself gave for his inability to attend the Black Monk Chapter of June 1432; Reg. III, fo. 146v; Reg. Parv. II, fo. 62v; Pantin, *Chapters* III, 220.

[2] *Correspondence of Thomas Bekynton* (Rolls Series, 1872), I, 91–3.

[3] In March 1416 Henry Percy wrote to Prior Hemingburgh thanking him for his prayers and informing him that he had recently performed homage for his lands in full parliament (Loc. xxv, no. 146; cf. *Rot. Parl.* IV, 71–2). His later letters to Wessington are equally friendly (Loc. xxv, nos. 155, 156, 157). For the convent's interest in the fortunes of the Percy family at this time see C. M. Fraser, 'Some Durham documents relating to the Hilary parliament of 1404', in *Bulletin of the Institute of Historical Research* XXXIV (1961), 192–9.

[4] *Scrip. Tres*, pp. 134–5, ccvi; *Rites*, p. 244.

here at the instance of their immediate successor, Ralph, sixth Baron Neville of Raby from 1388 to 1425 and first Earl of Westmorland after 1397. Ralph Neville was eventually buried in his new collegiate church of Staindrop, which consequently still holds what is perhaps the finest sepulchral monument in Durham county. In his will of October 1424, however, he expressed his wish to be buried either at Staindrop or in the cathedral church of Durham, a certain sign that he regarded the monks with no disfavour.[1] Admittedly the full emergence of the Nevilles into national politics during the lifetime of the first Earl of Westmorland weakened rather than strengthened their ties with the monastery; no later member of the family was as generous to the convent as the fifth Baron who in the 1370s gave over £500 towards the cost of Saint Cuthbert's shrine and the Neville reredos.[2] Westmorland contented himself with the occasional visit to the monastery, presents to its prior and the sending of news to Wessington about the progress of Henry V's French campaigns.[3] Prior Hemingburgh had attended the funeral of the Earl's first wife, Margaret Stafford, and had earlier celebrated the marriage of his son John with Elizabeth Holland at Brancepeth in 1394.[4] Wessington continued this tradition and spent £11 in 1417 on a journey to Raby, where he acted as god-father to the latest addition to the earl's numerous progeny.[5]

This uncomplicated and harmonious connection between the monastery of Durham and the Neville family was seriously affected by the death of the first Earl of Westmorland in October 1425. His grandson and heir, Ralph Neville, was nineteen at the time and could do little to prevent the widowed Joan Beaufort from putting into operation that 'grand manoeuvre' and 'elaborate system of fines and conveyances to trustees' by which the bulk of her husband's estates outside the county of Durham were to pass to her own children at the expense of those by his first marriage.[6] Until her death in 1440

[1] *Wills and Inventories*, Part I (Surtees Soc. II, 1835), p. 69.
[2] *Scrip. Tres*, pp. 135–6.
[3] Bursar, 1408/09, 1418/19, 1419/20, 1421/22, Expense Prioris, Dona et Exennia.
[4] Misc. Chrs., no. 6637; *Scrip. Tres*, p. clxxv; *Dur. Acct. Rolls* III, 600.
[5] Mines Accts., 1417.
[6] See Jacob, *The Fifteenth Century*, pp. 319–23, and K. B. McFarlane, 'The Wars of the Roses', *Proceedings of British Academy* L (1965), 106, for the general significance of these transactions.

Joan held in dower by far the largest share of the Neville inheritance, including much of the Durham property (Raby and Staindrop) as well as lordships in Yorkshire (Middleham and Sheriff Hutton).[1] The angry reaction of the elder branch of the Neville family to their dispossession was obviously justified and provoked a contest which dominated northern politics during the 1430s. Whether or not the dispute helped to bring about the Wars of the Roses, as has often been suggested,[2] it created a definite two-party grouping in the north during Wessington's priorate. The dowager Countess of Westmorland was supported most obviously by her brother, Cardinal Beaufort, and her eldest son, Richard Neville, Earl of Salisbury. Bishop Langley, in this affair as in the conduct of English foreign policy, was ranged with the Beaufort group, and never appointed the second Earl of Westmorland to any of his judicial commissions. Ralph Neville, this second Earl of Westmorland, was himself staunchly supported by his two brothers, Thomas and John, and could also rely for material support on his marriage with Elizabeth Percy, the widow of Sir John Clifford. In his enforced absence from Raby and Brancepeth he appears to have spent much time at the Clifford manor of Hart in south-east Durham where he was in close touch with many of the gentlemen of the county.[3] One of these was Sir William Eure, a keeper of the second Earl's Durham lands during his minority, who led the attack on Bishop Langley's palatine franchises in 1433.[4] The possibility that Eure's audacious suit against the bishop was secretly favoured, if not promoted, by the elder branch of the Neville family cannot be ignored.[5]

During the course of this often bitter conflict, Wessington attempted to remain on good terms with both parties. He baptised the son of Ralph Neville in 1427–8, and he or his successor sent a present of

---

[1] *Calendar of Inquisitions Post Mortem of the Palatinate of Durham, 44th Report of the Deputy Keeper of the P.R.O.* (1884), Appendix, p. 525; *Calendar Inquisitionum Post Mortem* (Record Commission, 1806–28), IV, p. 206.

[2] Cf. Storey, *Thomas Langley*, p. 108; C. W. Oman, *Warwick the Kingmaker* (London, 1891), pp. 24–6.   [3] Loc. xxv, nos. 47, 133.

[4] P.R.O., Palatinate of Durham, Chancery Enrolments, 3/38, memb. 15 d. For Eure's cultivation of his connection with the Nevilles, see Roskell, *The Commons in the Parliament of 1422*, pp. 178–9.

[5] Henry Percy was among the opponents of Bishop Langley's liberties in 1433 and may have been aligned with his brother-in-law, Ralph Neville, against the Beaufort party: Storey, *Thomas Langley*, p. 120.

a silver cup (worth five marks and containing five marks) to the christening of his daughter in 1446–7.[1] Ralph's two brothers, Sir John and Sir Thomas Neville, were entertained in the monastery and proved successful in securing the appointment of their nominees to positions as steward and porter of the convent.[2] Nevertheless, it was Joan Beaufort and her children, closely related as they were to the Lancastrian royal dynasty, who acted as the most influential of all aristocratic patrons known to the Durham monks in Wessington's priorate. This 'formidable dowager' showed much interest in the convent's benefices and often adopted a somewhat dictatorial tone to the prior, as she did to her son Robert after his elevation to the bishopric of Durham in 1438.[3] But as a desirable friend of the monastery, Wessington won her favour by gifts of spices and letters of sorority issued on Saint Cuthbert's Day 1430.[4] Her last two years of life were spent at the bishop of Durham's manor of Howden, where she interfered in the organisation of the convent's collegiate church and where she died on 13 November 1440.[5]

Joan Beaufort's eldest son, Richard Neville, Earl of Salisbury, was the one English magnate with whom Prior Wessington's relations can be said to have been unusually close. Their friendship dated from the period when, in his own words, the Earl was 'yhitt a yong housband' (he assumed the title of Earl of Salisbury in 1429 when he was not quite thirty) and was sent north on an embassy to arrange a truce with the Scots. On 3 June 1429 he wrote from Middleham asking for the loan of Wessington's 'chariott and chariotour' to transport his harness to the East March; Wessington complied with Salisbury's wishes and the Earl visited him at Durham a few days later.[6] At the same time Richard Neville wished to buy or borrow the prior's courser 'as me stondes in right grete nede of horses at this time', and his letter closed with an autograph postscript urging Wessington to 'tender thys materes as I may do oght that may lyk you'. This was the first of a series of letters from Salisbury to his

---

[1] Mines Accts., 1427/28; Bursar, 1446/47, Dona et Exennia.

[2] Cellarer, *c.* 1430, 1446; Loc. xxv, nos. 47, 132. In 1446–7 (Bursar, Dona et Exennia) Sir Thomas Neville was paid five marks to maintain and protect the prior's tenants.

[3] Loc. xxv, nos. 123–7.

[4] Loc. xxv, no. 137; Bursar, 1418/19, Expense Prioris; Reg. iii, fo. 138v.

[5] I.2. Ebor., no. 3; Cart. iii, part ii, fos. 39–40; *Scrip. Tres*, pp. cclviii–cclx.

[6] Loc. xxv, no. 121; Cellarer, 1429. Cf. Bursar, 1429/30, Expense Necessarie.

'Reverent fader in gode and my Right tristy frende', thanking Wessington for his kindness at Durham and informing him, for instance, of the siege of Chambrais and Henry VI's coronation in Paris.[1] When in England, Salisbury was the most influential magnate in the north. Warden of both Marches at various stages of his career, he headed Langley's commissions of peace for Durham after 1427, was keeper of the temporalities in the vacancy of the see between 1437 and 1438 (as Bedford had been thirty years earlier) and then became chief lay counsellor of his brother Robert, the new bishop.[2] Throughout this period the monastic obedientiary accounts reveal the frequent arrival of Salisbury's heralds and messengers with news and presents and, like his brother, he wrote to the Scottish court in the interests of the priory of Coldingham.[3] The Earl received letters of confraternity from Durham as early as April 1431; and during the following year Wessington travelled to Middleham to christen his son, George Neville, later archbishop of York.[4] The convent's links with the Earl of Salisbury, and with his brothers, Lords Fauconberge, Latimer and Abergavenny, were to continue long after Wessington's resignation and help to explain the convent's just discernible sympathies in the early stages of the Wars of the Roses.[5]

But for Wessington, as for Prior Bell, one of his successors, the secret of political life lay 'in cherishyng and kepyng in of the love of my lordes Westmerland & Nevyll'.[6] During the 1430s this objective was impossible to achieve in full because of the feud between the two branches of the Neville family. The second Earl of Westmorland's attempt to recover his inheritance from Joan Beaufort and her

---

[1] Loc. xxv, nos. 119–22; Misc. Chrs., nos. 1077, 1085. Several of Salisbury's letters are printed in *Wills and Inventories* I, pp. 69–71, and one in Halcrow, 'Social Position and Influence of the Priors of Durham', pp. 78–9.

[2] P.R.O., Palatinate of Durham, Chancery Enrolments, 3/36, memb. 7; 3/38, memb. 16; 3/42, memb. 1. For a convincing recent assessment of Salisbury's political importance, see R. L. Storey, *The End of the House of Lancaster* (London, 1966), pp. 109–23.

[3] Reg. III, fo. 277; Bursar, 1432, 1435/36, 1437/38, 1438/39, Dona et Exennia.

[4] Bursar, 1432/33, Expense Necessarie, '*Et in diversis expensis factis per dominum priorem equitandum usque Middilham pro quodam infante Comitis Sar' ibidem de sacro fonte levando, xlvi s. x d.*' George Neville was born in 1432 (Emden II, 1347).

[5] In 1461 (admittedly after the battle of Towton) Prior Burnby wrote to Edward IV about 'the quene, late callid quene Margarett' who had 'borrowed of your said oratours cccc marc, agaynst thaire good will': *The Priory of Hexham* I (Surtees Soc. XLIV, 1864), p. cii.   [6] *Scrip. Tres*, p. ccclix.

children already threatened violence in 1430 when the first of a long series of bonds to keep the peace was imposed on him and his rivals by the royal council.[1] In 1434 Wessington was involved most unwillingly in the dispute through no fault of his own. His embarrassment began when an old clerk and familiar of the first Earl of Westmorland informed his grandson, the second Earl, that a box of written evidences relating to the Neville inheritance had been deposited at Durham in 1400. The second Earl of Westmorland, eager to use this collection against his rivals, sent several of his retainers to Durham to claim it from the prior. Wessington, previously ignorant of their existence, became nervous and refused to deliver the documents to the second Earl without further consideration; meanwhile he informed Joan Beaufort of this unexpected find among the convent's muniments. Earl Ralph Neville's reaction was to take out a writ of *praecipe* from the bishop's chancery in August 1434, thus initiating a plea against Wessington before the Durham justices. After failing to appear at three successive sessions the prior faced the threat of distraint on his chattels in early 1435.[2] Meanwhile Wessington was under very heavy pressure from the Beaufort group to hand over the evidences to them; on 7 August Cardinal Beaufort himself wrote to Wessington warning him to avoid peril and danger to his soul by delivering the contested documents to his sister and nephews.[3] The following month, Bishop Langley threatened Wessington with ecclesiastical censure if he continued to refuse delivery to Countess Joan and the Earl of Salisbury.[4] The prior was thus in the unenviable position of facing prosecution in the bishop's temporal court for not delivering the box of evidences to the Earl of Westmorland; while the bishop himself was prepared, for the only recorded time in his episcopate, to take proceedings against Wessington unless it was handed to the younger branch of the Neville family.

The important document in the collection deposited at Durham was the will and testament made by the first Earl on 8 August 1400. As this date preceded by four years Ralph Neville's settlement of his north Yorkshire estates on himself and his second wife and their

---

[1] *C.Cl.R.*, *1429–35*, pp. 67, 125, 346–7; *1435–41*, pp. 56–7, 178–9, 276.
[2] 1.2. Ebor., no. 15 (a long summary of the '*Casus de Testamenti Comitis de Westmorland*'); Misc. Chrs., nos. 6639, 7154.
[3] Loc. xxv, no. 78.   [4] Reg. III, fo. 192; *Reg. Langley* IV, 132–3.

heirs male,[1] it is clear that its contents must have favoured his heirs by his first wife, completely ignored in his final will of October 1424.[2] The earlier will may have been technically invalidated by the later, but the second Earl of Westmorland understandably wished to win sympathy for his cause by exposing it to public view. Thus he wrote twice to Wessington during 1434 suggesting that the first will should be opened and read either at Durham or Bishop Auckland in the presence of the Earl of Salisbury, Langley and the prior, as well as of the Earl of Northumberland and others of his own council. This solution was unacceptable to the Beaufort faction who wished to suppress the will of 1400 completely, an aim in which they were probably successful as no copy survives. Joan Beaufort and her eldest son claimed possession of the early will as executors of the final one of 1424; but as this last will (after considerable altercation)[3] had now received probate, their case was believed questionable. In his perplexity Wessington decided to send the prior of Holy Island, Master William Ebchester, to London in October 1434. Ebchester appeared before Cardinal Beaufort and his sister's legal counsellors in the capital, and was also commissioned to take the case before the royal council where Wessington hoped for help from William Alnwick, bishop of Norwich.[4] No record survives of the results of Ebchester's London mission except that he returned with the advice that the will should not be surrendered to anyone without the written consent of both parties. Not long afterwards Wessington instructed his chancellor, William Dalton, to hand over the contested box of documents (apparently still unopened) to the attorneys of Joan Beaufort and the Earl of Salisbury.[5] In the last resort the prior found himself unable to face the continued displeasure of his bishop and his most influential lay patrons. Once again, the second Earl of Westmorland had been deprived of what he considered his lawful property by the questionable methods of his rivals.

This curious episode only served to increase the ill-feeling between the two branches of the Neville family. Despite the royal council's strenuous attempts to prevent open warfare, the inevitable outbreak

---

[1] *C.P.R., 1401–05*, p. 470.

[2] *Wills and Inventories*, Part I (Surtees Soc. II, 1835), pp. 68–74.

[3] *Rot. Parl.* IV, 469–70; *C.Cl.R., 1429–35*, p. 322; *Select Cases before the King's Council, 1243–1482*, ed. I. S. Leadam and J. F. Baldwin (Selden Society XXXV, 1918), pp. cix–cx, 101–2.

[4] Reg. III, fo. 172v; Reg. Parv. II, fo. 80.   [5] I.2. Ebor., no. 15.

occurred in 1438 when mention was made of 'grete rowtes and compaignies upon ye felde' to the 'slaughter and distruccion of oure peuple'.[1] Although the leaders of both parties were summoned before the council, this body could not be considered impartial at a period when Salisbury had become one of its most regular members. The dispute had to be solved, if at all, at a more local level; accordingly, during this critical period Wessington emerged as an unofficial peace-maker who rode twice to Raby and once to Middleham to arrange a concord between the Earls of Westmorland and Salisbury.[2] That the prior's services during this period of private war were highly appreciated by both parties emerges from a letter written by Wessington to Salisbury from Beaurepaire on 17 January 1440.[3] Wessington refused the Earl's invitation to stand as one of his arbiters on the grounds that he had already been asked to serve in this capacity by his rival, the Earl of Westmorland (who obviously bore him no permanent ill-will for surrendering his grandfather's will to Joan Beaufort), and had declined to do so. The prior wished to maintain his neutrality, but lent his blessing and good will to the complicated negotiations which led to at least a temporary settlement of the family dissensions. The death of Joan Beaufort in 1440 made a solution easier to achieve, and in August 1443 the Earl of Salisbury relinquished his claims to the Neville lands in Durham county in return for his succession to most of the inheritance elsewhere in England.[4] Westmorland, however, remained justifiably aggrieved and suspicious of Salisbury's intentions; he had already secured his Durham estates from further aggression by persuading Wessington 'to putt of record in youre chancery' a conveyance of all his lands to four trustees, headed by his brother, Sir Thomas Neville.[5] Almost twenty years were to elapse before the Earl of Westmorland at last secured his revenge and in early 1461 entrusted Sir Thomas Neville with the task of harrying those estates in north Yorkshire which he had lost long ago to that same Earl of Salisbury whose head now adorned the walls of York.[6]

---

[1] *Excerpta Historica*, ed. Samuel Bentley (London, 1831), pp. 1–3; *C.Cl.R.*, *1435–41*, p. 199. See *C.P.R.*, *1429–36*, pp. 595–6, 601.
[2] Bursar, 1438/39, Expense Necessarie.   [3] Reg. Parv. II, fos. 113–14.
[4] *C.Cl.R.*, *1441–47*, pp. 150–1, 195–9; *Complete Peerage of England*, XII (1959), 549.
[5] 4.5. Ebor., no. 19; Reg. III, fos. 264–5.
[6] Oman, *Warwick the Kingmaker*, p. 103.

Although no other family could hope to rival the ascendancy of the Nevilles in Durham and the Percies in Northumberland, the landed knights and gentlemen in these two counties lacked neither influence nor independence. As elsewhere in England, the effective leaders of political opinion in the palatinate were a group of closely related local landowners, proud of their ancestry and capable of showing much *esprit de corps* in the face of any threat to their traditional rights from king or bishop. The number of Durham knightly families conspicuously active in public life was not large, and almost all must have been personally known to the prior and chapter. The monastic cellarer's rolls reveal a constant succession of visits to the cathedral by neighbouring knights and esquires, especially those (like the Eures and Elmedens) who devoted much of their time to local government and administration.[1]

Many of the county landowners still held a large proportion of their estates from the prior of Durham by military service; but the resulting relationship was somewhat anomalous in fifteenth-century circumstances. Wessington had no intention of allowing his rights as feudal lord to go by default; and he supervised the making of a new edition of the Durham feodary originally compiled in the time of Prior Melsonby (1234–44).[2] But the prior's income from the feudal incidents of wardship, marriage and relief had virtually disappeared during the last years of the fourteenth century. In 1430 it was calculated by the Durham chancellor that of the forty-seven tenants who held of the prior by military service, twenty-seven owed suit at the prior's free court every fortnight and the others three times a year.[3] But the names of these tenants suggest that this was an unrealistic assessment; and there is no doubt that attendance at meetings of the prior's free court was generally extremely poor.[4] Nor was Prior Wessington able to enforce his right to receive homage from all his tenants by military service. Those who did come before him in his chapel at Durham to promise to 'be cume your man fro thys day forth, on lyf and on lymb . . . as God helpe me and All Sayntes'

---

[1] It was, for example, in Durham Cathedral that Bishop Langley took from 5 Durham knights, 51 esquires and 18 others an oath not to maintain evil-doers in the county (23 September 1434): *Reg. Langley* IV, 142–3; Surtees, *Durham* I, p. cxxxii.

[2] Feodarium Melsanby, printed in *Feodarium Dunelm.*, pp. 1–92.

[3] Ibid., pp. 81–3.   [4] Bursar, 1416–46, Perquisitiones Libere Curiae.

were hardly ever members of knightly families.[1] Any attempt by the prior to impose homage against the will of the tenant was likely to cause much ill-feeling,[2] and his feudal rights brought him little but a few small financial emoluments.

There is little evidence of outright anti-clericalism in early fifteenth-century Durham; and on those numerous occasions when monk and gentleman came into conflict, the quarrel invariably arose from a dispute over landed property and its obligations. By fifteenth-century standards, however, it seems unlikely that the monks of Durham were involved in an excessive amount of litigation with local landowning gentry. At various times in Wessington's priorate they were at odds with the Gower family, with Sir William Bowes, and with Sir William Elmeden; but none of these disputes led to a serious breach of the peace. It was characteristic of contemporary practice that all three cases were eventually settled out of court before arbiters appointed by the two parties and consisting of local knights and lawyers.[3] Particularly troublesome was Wessington's litigation with Sir William Elmeden of Trillesden, one of the most influential of the bishop's tenants.[4] The manor of Trillesden (now Tursdale) lay three miles south of Durham and was almost completely surrounded by the prior's demesnes at Shincliffe, Hett and Fery. Between 1430 and 1446 a long succession of disputes occurred on the subject of Elmeden's supposed rights of common pasture and his attempts to divert the stream which supplied the prior's water-mill at Hett. Elmeden was an aggressive and unscrupulous litigant who did not stop at forging three charters which purported to be grants and confirmations made by Bishops Hugh du Puiset, Philip of Poitiers and Prior Absalon. Not surprisingly, Wessington had little difficulty in exposing the fraud and prepared a collection of evidences to justify his case. After several years of expensive law-suits, the prior was completely successful and Elmeden was forced to surrender his manor of Trillesden, if only temporarily, to Bishop Neville.[5]

---

[1] Notes of homages performed were made in the large conventual register (Reg. III, fos. 57, 59, 70, 209v; *Scrip. Tres*, p. cclii). The form of the oaths of homage and fealty in use at Durham is recorded in Reg. III, fo. 57v.   [2] Cart. IV, fos. 142–3.

[3] Reg. III, fos. 140v–141, 231, 288; Reg. Parv. II, fos. 46, 71, 72.

[4] Roskell, *The Commons in the Parliament of 1422*, pp. 175–6.

[5] The dispute initially arose from Elmeden's seizure from the prior of 300 acres of pasture on Quarrington Moor: P.R.O., Palatinate of Durham, Chancery Roll of

More serious was Wessington's collision with the Claxton and the
Hilton families, both of whom showed themselves ready to contemplate violence against the monks of Durham. Thomas Claxton
was the holder of valuable estates dispersed throughout the county and
a relative of Sir William Claxton, sheriff of Durham in the early
years of Wessington's priorate. Soon after his election, the prior
took out a writ of *novel disseisin* against Thomas in connection with
some tenements held by him in Castle Eden.[1] Claxton was so incensed
at Wessington's action that in the summer of 1419 he adopted a
policy of systematic terrorisation towards the Durham monks, using
as his principal agent another of the prior's discontented tenants,
Thomas Billingham. On Sunday 25 June the monastic terrar,
William Barry, and his servants set out on a business journey, but
were attacked by Billingham and his associates as they crossed
Framwellgate Bridge at Durham; Billingham's men were fully
armed and drew their weapons on the terrar, who was forced back
to the monastery. For the next two months, until 24 August 1419,
the convent seems to have been in a state of unofficial siege. Billingham and his company lay continuously in wait and threatened to
kill or wound any monk or monastic servant who left the precincts
without adequate protection. During a nocturnal scuffle at the north
gate of Durham Castle, one of Wessington's *famuli*, John Dale,
received a severe knock on the head from a stick while one of his
companions almost lost his life as the result of a sword-wound in the
neck.[2] Claxton and Billingham pursued their vendetta to a climax
when on 23 August they ambushed William Drax, the prior of
Coldingham, near Chester-le-Street as he was travelling towards the
monastery. In the affray that followed, one of Drax's servants was so
badly wounded in the left arm that it seemed doubtful whether he
would survive. On the following day Wessington appealed for help
to Langley's vicars-general who cited Claxton and Billingham to
appear before them.[3] Shortly afterwards the two offenders were
brought to justice at Newcastle-upon-Tyne;[4] and in November 1421

Bishop Neville (3/43), membs. 9, 10; Loc. v, no. 24; Loc. XXI, no. 9; Hostillar,
1443/44; Misc. Chrs., nos. 6417 (with map), 7138; 4.13. Spec., no. 64.
[1] Bursar, 1416/17, Expense Necessarie.   [2] Loc. XXI, no. 11.
[3] Reg. III, fo. 68; *Coldingham Corr.*, pp. 92–3.
[4] Bursar, 1419/20, Expense Necessarie.

the dispute between Wessington and Claxton concerning the Castle Eden tenements was settled in the prior's favour by four arbiters.[1]

Equally alarming was the ill-treatment suffered in 1439 by the master of the cell of Monk Wearmouth at the hands of the Hilton family. The barons of Hilton were, with the lords of Lumley, among the most powerful of the bishop of Durham's tenants-in-chief, a fact recognised by Wessington in July 1419 when he received William, Baron Hilton, and his wife Dionisia into the fraternity of the monastery.[2] There was already a long history of ill-feeling and bickering between this family and the monastery of Durham, arising from the situation of Hilton Castle in the parish of Monk Wearmouth. As early as 1157 the lords of Hilton had secured from the prior of Durham licence to have their own chapel, by means of an agreement which was intended to safeguard the rights of the mother church but proved to be the occasion for constant friction in later centuries. This old antagonism was revived when in 1435 William, Baron Hilton died and was succeeded by his fifty-year-old son Robert, an apparently lawless individual who in 1411 had been responsible for a murder in the town of Sunderland.[3] During the late 1430s the new Baron Hilton consistently disregarded the terms of the ancient compromise made by his ancestors with the prior of Durham. Despite frequent protests, he refused to deliver his wife's corpse to the master of Wearmouth for burial in the parish church. He withdrew from the same church his 'tendis, oblacions, obvencions and other dewtes', disseized the prior of his property in Hilton itself, and failed to present his priest for admission by Wessington to the Hilton chapel. The most vexed issue was that of the master of Wearmouth's right to tithes: this was challenged by Robert and his brother Alexander who sent their servants to break open the doors of the Wearmouth cell and remove corn from the barn.

The quarrel came to a head on Saturday, 28 March 1439, when the two monks then at Wearmouth were threatened and assaulted first by the servants and then by the son of Robert, Baron Hilton. The latter arrived at the church in the midst of the uproar, whereupon he 'swar a gret hooth that ther was nott so pryue a chambre ne holl

---

[1] 3.8. Spec., no. 21; Misc. Chrs., no. 5214.

[2] Reg. III, fo. 67.

[3] The case is cited by Jacob, *The Fifteenth Century*, pp. 127–8.

within that place then he sulde pull oote John Booth monke and bynde his feete undre a horse baly and so sennd hym to Dorham'. He then turned on Booth's colleague, the master of the cell, William Lyham, 'and askid hym in stoor maner whoo was thi sire' and pulled down his hood. Not surprisingly, the two monks abandoned the cell and returned with their grievances to Durham, where Wessington proceeded to implead the Hilton family before the bishop.[1] The dispute was settled to the extent of Robert, Baron Hilton, consenting to send his new chaplain to Durham for admission by Wessington on 29 June 1439.[2] But the convent's relations with the Hiltons remained troubled, and an even more serious quarrel occurred in the late 1450s when Robert Stainton, chaplain of Hilton, appealed to Rome and involved the monastery in much expensive litigation. It was at this time that the then master of Wearmouth, John Bradbury, wrote an extraordinary letter to Prior Burnby recommending the ambush and highway robbery of one of Stainton's servants carrying papal bulls from Hilton Castle to Wilton in Cleveland.[3] There is no more striking example of the danger that the monks of Durham might themselves be infected by the contemporary disregard for the due processes of law.

The county of Durham may have been disturbed by periodic outbursts of lawlessness, but Northumberland was in a state of constant unrest. Although their geographical isolation usually protected the convent's dependencies on Holy Island and Farne from direct assault, the same was not true of the monastic estates and tenements on the mainland. The last years of the fourteenth century had seen a particularly sharp decline in the monks' income from their Northumberland possessions because of the Anglo-Scottish wars.[4] During Wessington's priorate the Scot remained a dreaded enemy, destroying monastic property and holding tenants and servants to ransom.[5]

---

[1] The prior's *querela* are printed, in their three versions, in *Jarrow and Wearmouth*, pp. 241–3. The date of the episode emerges from the fact that Lyham was moved from Wearmouth to Farne in June 1439 (Reg. Parv. II, fo. 103).

[2] Reg. Parv. II, fo. 104.

[3] Loc. xxv, no. 38; the theft of these bulls presumably never took place, as they included a papal citation attached to the door of Durham Cathedral on 15 July 1461 (*Jarrow and Wearmouth*, pp. 245–6).

[4] 4.6. Ebor., no. 2.

[5] In 1436–7, Richard Kellawe, Master of Farne, accounted for 8s. paid to ransom a *famulus* from the Scots (Farne, 1436/37).

But the prior had cause to fear the unruliness of the English inhabitants of the county as well as the Scottish invader. In 1446 Prior Ebchester complained of cattle rustling in Redesdale, and fifteen years earlier the master of Farne had suffered from the theft of many of his possessions, including gold and silver ornaments as well as fish-nets.[1] In the late 1420s Wessington was compelled to take out writs against several Northumberland knights who refused to pay their debts to the prior, and litigation on this matter was still continuing in 1432–3.[2]

One specific and extreme case of disorder in the Border county is of special interest as the occasion for the prior of Durham's personal intervention as the leading peace-maker among the gentlemen of Northumberland. On the morning of 20 January 1428, William Heron of Ford left Norham with an armed company and in an attack later that day on the Manners's village of Etal was himself killed. Such was the culminating event of a bitter feud between the powerful families of Heron and Manners, a conflict which, according to James Raine, 'abounds with incident, characterising, at the same time, the pugnacious state of the borders, the total absence of every thing in the shape of legal redress, and the omnipotence of the church'.[3] Modern knowledge of the Heron case is largely derived from the file of documents used by Wessington as umpire in the dispute and then deposited by him among the convent's muniments, where they still survive.[4] Both William Heron of Ford and John Manners, lord of Etal, who was accused of his murder, were prominent members of influential Northumbrian kindreds. Each party to this long-standing feud counted on support from his friends among the knights and esquires of the north. The result of William Heron's murder in 1428 was therefore to divide Northumbrian landed society into two opposed factions, led by the two most powerful knights in the county. Sir Robert Umfraville asserted the rights of

[1] Reg. Parv. III, fo. 12; Reg. Parv. II, fos. 55–6, 64.
[2] Bursar, 1428/29, 1429/30, 1432/33, Expense Necessarie.
[3] Raine, *North Durham*, p. 209.
[4] This bundle of evidence survived intact until the early nineteenth century as Locellus V, no. 28, but the individual documents are now dispersed through the Locellus. The Heron case has been briefly described in *A History of Northumberland* (Newcastle-upon-Tyne, 1893–1940), XI, 380–1, and more recently by Storey, *Thomas Langley*, pp. 142–3.

Heron's widow, Isabel; and Sir Robert Ogle was the principal supporter of Manners and his kindred. It was no doubt the impossibility of securing an impartial settlement from the inhabitants of Northumberland that made it necessary to have recourse to the prior of Durham. The dispute itself may have been by no means untypical of conditions in the northern county, but Wessington's own prominence in the settlement of a blood-feud between laymen is obviously exceptional.[1]

Although William Heron of Ford was killed on 20 January 1428 and a royal commission to enquire into the suspicious circumstances of his death was appointed on 8 February,[2] Wessington does not seem to have been connected with the case until 1429. In the spring of that year the prior went to Newcastle in order to begin negotiations with both parties. He was apparently persuaded to intervene by Bishop Langley and Cardinal Beaufort (then on a visit to James I at Coldingham), both of whom expressed a desire for 'gude rest and pece to be had in the Cuntre'.[3] Wessington's attempts at conciliation were aided by the fact of his good relations with Isabel Heron's patron, Sir Robert Umfraville. Umfraville had received letters of confraternity from Durham in July 1419, and later deposited all the deeds relating to his newly founded chantry chapel at Farnacres in Wessington's care.[4] It was from his manor of Farnacres that Umfraville wrote, on 3 April 1429, to the prior informing him that if John Manners was prepared to pay 400 marks as compensation for Heron's murder, the dispute could be satisfactorily settled. Umfraville added that if Manners was prepared to help him redeem the Heron lands from royal custody, he would speak to the widow and friends of the deceased and try to persuade them to lower their monetary demands.[5] Umfraville requested a speedy reply, so Wessington immediately sent a copy of his letter to John Manners at Etal. Manners did not reject the offer out of hand but wrote that a sum of 400 marks was too great a burden for him to bear without the support of his lords and friends; after consulting these he would come to Durham to talk with Wessington on 15 April.[6]

[1] Loc. XXI, no. 20.   [2] *C.P.R.*, *1422–29*, p. 467.
[3] Bursar, 1428/29, Expense Necessarie; Loc. v, no. 47.
[4] Reg. III, fos. 67v, 231–3; Surtees, *Durham* II, 243–4.
[5] Loc. v, no. 47.   [6] Ibid., no. 49.

At Durham on 23 April 1429 the four arbiters chosen by the Heron party put forward their terms for the settlement of the conflict. John Manners and his friends were to submit themselves humbly and in person before the Heron kindred and to promise to pay all the debts (over £600) owed by William Heron at the time of his death. Manners was to ordain a perpetual chantry at Ford with an annual revenue of twelve marks so that prayers could be said there for the souls of William Heron and his servant, Robert Atkinson, who had been killed at his side in the assault on Etal. Atkinson's mother was to be compensated financially by an annual pension of 40s., while John Manners and all others implicated in the homicides were required to leave the north of England for seven years.[1] Although the Heron party described these terms as 'this lytill and esy tretye', they were considerably more severe than those eventually expressed in the final settlement. There is no proof that John Manners formally bound himself to accept the indenture of 23 April 1429, and it is more likely that he, rather than Isabel Heron,[2] refused to accept these proposals. It was henceforward Wessington's aim to moderate the severity of the Heron demands and to achieve a settlement which would be acceptable to both parties.

Negotiations were resumed in the summer and autumn of 1429 when Wessington's connection with the case became even closer. The two parties each delivered bonds of £1,000 'into the meen hand' of the Earl of Northumberland; their redemption was conditional on acceptance of the award to be made by six newly appointed arbiters or, in the event of disagreement, by two of three nominated umpires. All three umpires were monastic prelates;[3] but John Thweng, prior of Guisborough in Yorkshire, was not particularly well qualified to intervene in a Northumbrian dispute, and the negotiations were conducted by Wessington and his other colleague, Thomas Barton, prior of Tynemouth. As umpires, Wessington and Barton were expected to procure a settlement before Michaelmas 1430. Manners continued to deny his personal responsibility for William Heron's death, neither he nor his son 'beand nerhand hym be asper length and more' at the time. As for Isabel

---

[1] Loc. v, no. 51.
[2] As suggested by Storey, *Thomas Langley*, p. 143.
[3] Loc. v, no. 46.

Heron's demand that he should pay her husband's debts and the expenses of her recent law-suits (estimated at £137 5s. 3d.), John Manners replied with a counter-claim for £300 which she had forced him to spend in litigation. All that Manners was prepared to concede was a sum of £80 to be spent on prayers for the souls of Heron and his servant.[1] He expected in return a guarantee that neither he nor his kindred would be victimised by members of the Heron party.

During the next few months it was Wessington rather than Prior Thomas Barton who took the leading role in arranging a compromise.[2] On 27 September 1430 the two priors met at the church of Saint Nicholas, Newcastle-upon-Tyne, where they drafted their award. They agreed that 'John Maners nowther slewe nor willyng was to the slayng of the said William Heron', but stipulated that he was, nevertheless, to pay 200 marks to the Heron party in order to recover the 'good lordship' of Umfraville and the friendship of the widow and her relations. In addition, Manners was to provide for 1,300 requiem masses during the coming year.[3] The following day Priors Wessington and Barton produced their final decree in the prior's quarters at Tynemouth. The 'sum of peace' was raised from 200 to 250 marks, payable in seven yearly instalments, while the number of masses imposed on Manners was reduced to 500. A tripartite indenture was drawn up, so that copies might be retained by John Manners, by the Umfraville–Heron party, and by the umpires.[4] Arrangements were also made for a formal reconciliation of the adversaries at Newcastle, to be held before Midsummer 1431 on a day chosen by Priors Wessington and Barton. Although both parties accepted the award, John Manners approached the Newcastle meeting with much foreboding. He feared that 'the wordes or dedes of humbless' demanded from him might be incompatible with his sense of honour and he asked for stronger sureties from the Heron group. Manners wished to be told how many of his relatives he might bring to the meeting and was significantly concerned that he might be held responsible there for 'an unreule word or dede by the ferrest of his kynn'.[5]

---

[1] Loc. v, no. 44.
[2] Bursar, 1430/31, Expense Necessarie.   [3] Loc. v, no. 52.
[4] Loc. v, nos. 45, 52; John Manners's copy of this indenture was carefully preserved and was to be seen at Haddon in the seventeenth century: W. Dugdale, *The Baronage of England* (London, 1675–6), II, 296.   [5] Loc. v, no. 48.

Despite John Manners's reservations, the ceremony of reconciliation eventually took place at Newcastle-upon-Tyne on 24 May 1431. Many of the northern magnates and gentry attended the meeting, which passed without serious disorder. The bishop of Durham and the Earl of Northumberland were certainly present, while Wessington's original programme for the day's events made provision too for the attendance of the Earl of Salisbury 'and other high persons'. The Herons and Manners were at Newcastle in full strength, as were Sir Robert Ogle and Sir Robert Umfraville together with many Northumbrian knights and esquires. The proceedings began with an oath on the gospels taken by John Manners in the church of Saint Nicholas; he swore that he was innocent of Heron's murder and asked for the friendship of his old enemies 'sa that gude love and charite may ever bide amang us'. After the Herons had received him into their peace, John Manners announced his intention of providing requiem masses for the dead man. The umpires then imposed bonds on both parties to respect the terms of the settlement, and ordered Manners to pay the first instalments of his 250 marks compensation to Isabel Heron and Sir Robert Umfraville. Finally John Manners and Heron's widow formally renounced all personal actions against each other.[1]

So ended Wessington's work as an umpire in a particularly bitter Border feud. A compromise solution to the dispute had not been easy to achieve and the prior may be credited with a major success in an unusual role. The moral and legal rights of the case are not now ascertainable, and perhaps never were; but the settlement of 1430-1 was satisfactory in that it preserved peace and prevented the very real danger of further bloodshed. Although the murder of William Heron of Ford came before both royal and episcopal justices,[2] the whole case reflects the inability of the established law courts to reach an acceptable and impartial verdict. Nor is this surprising when it is realised that both John Manners and his patron, Sir Robert Ogle, held judicial office in the late 1420s, whereas the Heron party appear to have been systematically excluded from commissions of peace and gaol delivery.[3] The Heron case suggests that family alliances,

---

[1] Loc. v, nos. 45v, 53.   [2] Ibid., no. 54; Storey, *Thomas Langley*, p. 143.
[3] Ogle became life justice, steward, sheriff and escheator of Norham and Elandshire (Reg. III, fos. 206, 252v; Roskell, *The Commons in the Parliament of 1422*, p. 152).

accompanied by that sharp sense of kinship to which the Durham documents bear witness, were the decisive force in local politics. The economic position of the Northumbrian gentry was an additional cause for complaint. Contemporary surveys of Etal and Ford show that both lordships suffered considerable financial loss during the mid-fifteenth century.[1] But this was a problem outside Wessington's competence. As an umpire concerned with settling the dispute that arose from William Heron's death, he had shown himself an impartially 'honest broker' among a turbulent and feud-ridden society.

It would be unwise therefore to exaggerate the political influence wielded by the prior and chapter of Durham in the later middle ages. Real power in the north of England was concentrated within the hands of a relatively few territorial families and the bishop of Durham, the natural ally of the monks. Not surprisingly, the great ecclesiastical corporation of Durham generally lent its support to the forces of established authority. Like Prior Bell in 1477, the Durham monks were always perturbed at signs that 'mony of the gentilmen er guydit full menely, and foloweth yonge counsell'.[2] It would seem from the evidence of its court rolls and books that the monastery suffered little from peasant disturbances and riots; but the partial collapse of central authority throughout late Lancastrian England is clearly evident at Durham too. The view that 'by 1440 application to the central courts was entirely useless' and 'the local judicial machinery commanded little or no respect'[3] can be seen to be very relevant to the convent's own experience. Although this situation provided the prior of Durham with an opportunity to play a quasi-judicial role, it was a role he would have preferred to forgo. He looked forward to the far distant day when 'peace and good rule might be had in the country' once again.[4]

---

[1] *A History of Northumberland* XI, 450.
[2] *Scrip. Tres*, p. ccclix.
[3] Storey, *End of House of Lancaster*, p. 121.
[4] Reg. Parv. III, fo. 175*.

Chapter 7

THE LORDS SPIRITUAL

Our singular trust restith in your gracieux lordship, as reason is[1]

The prevailing impression made by the late medieval monks of Durham upon the minds of contemporaries and posterity alike was that of zealous and painstaking defenders of the traditional rights, liberties and possessions of the cathedral church of Durham. In their prayers, their writings and their litigation they were at continuous pains to demonstrate the uniqueness of their own position, the distinctiveness of their convent's history and the large measure of immunity from external interference which was – so they believed – their inalienable right. The prior and chapter looked backwards to a veritable if legendary golden age during which the community of Saint Cuthbert led by the bishops of Lindisfarne had conducted its affairs in harmony and independence. How attractive, in fifteenth-century conditions, to learn from Bede of a halcyon period when the bishops themselves had been monks and only entered Northumbrian monasteries as benevolent and beneficent guests. Such idyllic conditions, as the late medieval chapter was well aware, had been shattered beyond repair, first by the invasions of the Northmen and, secondly, by the post-Conquest separation of the bishop and titular abbot from his monks. Of the thirty bishops of Durham between the 'reformation' of 1083 and the Dissolution, very few had any native connection with the diocese, and only three (Robert Stichill, Robert of Holy Island and Richard Kellaw) were monks of Saint Cuthbert. Not unnaturally, the monks of Durham came to see themselves rather than their bishop as the true champions of their saint, determined to preserve in a later age what vestiges still remained of a once extensive and unchallengeable freedom. Nevertheless, a study of the Durham records can leave one in no doubt that by the fifteenth century the gap between ideal and practice was very wide and that the convent's special traditions and liberties were no longer of such

[1] *Scrip. Tres*, p. ccclx.

primary significance as the monks themselves liked to believe. The monastery of Durham, to state the obvious, had become an integral part of the fabric of the English and Western church, and its position within that system differed in detail rather than in principle from that of any other cathedral monastery. Paradoxically their role as servants of a cathedral church made the brethren of Durham more vulnerable to intervention on the part of spiritual lords than exempt houses such as St Albans or the Cistercian abbeys. Like the monks of Christ Church, Canterbury, of Winchester and of Norwich, those of Durham were involved in close, complex and often strained relations with their ecclesiastical superiors.

Much the most immediate and therefore most powerful of these superiors was of course the bishop of Durham himself. To their 'right reverend father in God' the monks of Durham were bound in a curiously intense love–hate relationship, not – it might be seriously suggested – without genuine Freudian elements. It had, after all and little though the prior and chapter liked to emphasise the fact, been an episcopal act of will in 1083 which brought the Benedictine priory to birth: as the example of Ripon serves to remind us, it had been by no means inevitable that the holy place of Durham should be served by monks rather than canons. More significantly still, the long and eventful series of disputes between the episcopal father and his monastic sons proved to be the single most influential factor in forming the mental attitudes of the fifteenth-century community. It was from their detailed and one-sided familiarity with the early history of these conflicts that the Durham monks learned to adopt their characteristically ambivalent policy towards their bishops. Genuinely grateful for his favours and proud of his prestige, they remained suspicious of his intentions towards themselves. In particular the early fifteenth-century community of Saint Cuthbert were determined never to jeopardise through their own negligence the privileges gained by the labours and ordeals of their predecessors. As a matter of historical fact the constitutional position of the prior and chapter was the direct result of the stormy confrontations of the twelfth and thirteenth centuries. The chapter's right to elect their prior, that prior's right to appoint obedientiaries and masters of cells, the procedure adopted at episcopal visitations, the monks' freedom to recruit new members to their community without episcopal intervention – these liberties, and many more, had been the con-vent's spoils of war, prizes to be triumphantly and jealously preserved for all time.

Not every victory in this long campaign had gone to the monks of Durham; and, as in the case of all intense family struggles, it may indeed be meaningless to speak of victories at all. Even in the calmer conditions of the fifteenth century, the prior and chapter were never either absolutely content with what they had achieved or confident that they could maintain the *status quo*. It was for this reason and to erect some safeguard between themselves and the potentially over-powering attentions of their titular abbot that the monks of Durham had from a very early date deliberately put themselves under the protection of the papacy and other ecclesiastical lords.[1] The moral to be drawn from the greatest of all contests between monks and bishop of Durham, fought during the pontificate of Antony Bek, was that such struggles could not be waged in isolation. Relations between convent and bishop in the early fifteenth century have therefore to be placed within the context of the chapter's close dependence upon alternative sources of church authority – the papal Curia and the archiepiscopal court of York as well as the national organisation of the English Benedictines meeting in Provincial Chapters at Northampton every three years.

THE COURTS OF ROME AND YORK

The relationship between Durham Priory and the papal Curia in the fifteenth century illustrates in perfect if microcosmic form that 'growing disproportion between the growth of papal administration and the effectiveness of papal leadership'[2] which is so notorious a feature of the late medieval Christian Church. It would be difficult to prove that a ruling by any fifteenth-century pope seriously affected the quality of the religious life at Durham in any respect whatsoever. Perhaps such a pronounced absence of initiative made it all the easier for the monks to give the papacy their unquestioning, because unthinking, devotion. Certainly their genuine loyalty to the

[1] *Scrip. Tres*, pp. 21, 31, 37, 40.
[2] R. W. Southern, *Western Society and the Church in the Middle Ages* (London, 1970), p. 168.

ecclesia Romana was never in doubt throughout this period, whatever their misgivings about the manner in which papal justice was dispensed. In 1454 it was reported that the abbot of Bury St Edmund's had publicly declared before the assembled prelates of the Benedictine Order assembled in Northampton 'that our monastery of Durham raised more money for the Roman church by means of indulgences in the Jubilee year (1450) than any three other monasteries in the English kingdom put together'.[1] The Durham monks could no doubt afford to be so generous on the papacy's behalf just because of the extremely light financial burden imposed upon them by papal taxation. The prior and chapter's contribution to the national levy of Peter's Pence was the almost derisory annual sum of 7s., still being paid to the 'bishop of Rome' by the monastic bursar on the very eve of the Dissolution. Somewhat more onerous, and particularly frequent at the height of the Conciliar period, were the monastery's contributions to subsidies granted by Convocation at York 'for the unity of the church' or to relieve the papacy at times of severe emergency. Even on these occasions, it can hardly be alleged that the financial needs of the Curia were a serious drain on the resources of the prior and chapter: the papal subsidy levied from the Durham bursar in 1446–7 at the quite common rate of 3d. in the pound involved him in expenditure of little more than £5.[2] In the fifteenth century the papal collectors who occasionally visited the convent during their travels through the country were no longer dreaded guests: they were indeed often welcomed as dispensers of papal favours, like the famous humanist Piero del Monte who gave Prior Wessington the desirable privilege of the portable altar when staying at Durham in August 1437.[3] Unlike some of the greater monastic prelates of England, notably the abbot of Westminster, the prior of Durham escaped the need to pay handsomely for papal confirmation of his election. For the community of Saint Cuthbert the papacy had the advantage of being an institution to which relatively little was owed but from which much could be asked.

The central theme in Durham Priory's official relationship with

[1] *Coldingham Corr.*, p. 181; cf. Reg. IV, fo. 95.

[2] Bursar, 1406–36, 1446/47, Contribuciones; Misc. Chrs., no. 5840; *Dur. Acct. Rolls* III, 706.

[3] Loc. XXI, no. 40; Reg. III, fo. 256; cf. R. Weiss, *Humanism in England during the Fifteenth Century* (3rd edn, Oxford, 1967), pp. 24–8.

the late medieval papacy was therefore its assiduous petitioning for graces and favours of all types. To the monks of Durham, as to the fifteenth-century English church in general, the pope's authority was in practice appreciated as 'mainly an authority to dispense'.[1] The great majority of the original bulls and '*papalia*', once given pride of place among the convent's muniments, have fallen victim to the iconoclasm of protestant reformers or the light fingers of collectors of curiosities; but the large numbers of copies entered into the monastic cartularies leave no doubt of the value that the prior and chapter set upon papal confirmations and privileges. In particular, there can be no doubt that the overall effect of these concessions was to enhance the dignity and authority of the prior himself, not surprisingly perhaps when one remembers that Durham's representatives at the Curia received their instructions from the latter rather than the chapter. Most honorific of all these privileges had been the conferment of the coveted episcopal insignia – ring, sandals and pastoral staff as well as mitre – upon Prior Robert Walworth and his successors by Pope Urban VI in July 1379. It is remarkable that the priors of Durham had waited so long for the grant of the *pontificalia*, enjoyed by other Benedictine prelates from a much earlier date, as soon as 1256 in the case of the abbot of Selby for example. As it was, Prior Walworth's right to the insignia was soon challenged by Archbishop Neville of York; and Prior Wessington found it advisable to have Urban's grant confirmed by Martin V in 1419. Thereafter he and his successors wore the 'pontificalls' on all possible ceremonial occasions.[2]

Of more practical import to the life of the Durham community were various other papal bulls which added to the judicial prerogatives of their prior. Thus Prior Wessington waged a long and successful campaign to secure for himself and his successors the right to absolve individual members of his community from sentences of excommunication and censure. More important still, in February 1440 Eugenius IV conferred on the priors of Durham the widely sought privilege of being able to relieve their subjects from the

---

[1] A remark by K. B. McFarlane, cited in D. Hay, 'The Church of England in the Later Middle Ages', *History* LIII (1968), 39.

[2] *Scrip. Tres*, pp. 136, cxlvii–cxlviii, cliv–clvi, ccxi–ccxii; Leland, *Collectanea* (1774), IV, 276.

observance of those statutes and precepts 'which are not substantive to their Rule'.[1] Similarly the prior's frequently exercised prerogative of allowing his monks to proceed to priest's orders in their twenty-second year was firmly grounded upon an indult obtained from Pope John XXIII in the summer of 1414.[2] In these and other ways, the Durham prior's legal authority over his flock was undoubtedly strengthened during the course of the fifteenth century, a process which reached its climax in 1456 when Prior Ebchester and his successors were given authority to confer minor orders on their monks and bless the vessels of the liturgy.[3] A logical although extreme extension of the earlier grant of the *pontificalia*, this privilege was the last important papal augmentation of the prior's powers before the Dissolution.

Other papal privileges conferred on the Durham monks of the fifteenth century reflect the corporate obsessions not only of their own community but of the English monastic world in general. Thus their increasingly urgent petitions to be allowed to choose confessors from whom they could receive plenary remission of their sins at the hour of death eventually persuaded Eugenius IV to produce a bull to that effect in March 1437.[4] The convent's motives in seeking this consolatory privilege 'of inestimable price' were naturally more edifying than those which led them to even longer and more tortuous negotiations at the Curia to secure papal relaxation of legislation against the eating of meat. Since Benedict XII's *Summi Magistri* of 1336, the consumption of meat by large numbers of Benedictine monks throughout most of the year had been sanctioned by the papacy; but in the early fifteenth century the Durham chapter, like many others, sought to secure release from the obligation to abstain from meat in the fortnight before Lent. The letters of Prior Wessington and Ebchester to their representatives at the Curia in the 1440s and early 1450s harp insistently and monotonously on the need for a bull '*super esu carnium in Septuagesima*'. Their persistence was

---

[1] Vatican Archives, Reg. Lat. 370, fos. 32v–33; Cart. I, fos. 41v–42; Cart. III, fos. 191v, 195v; *C.P.L.* IX (1431–47), 77; *Scrip. Tres*, pp. lxxxii–lxxxiii, ccx, ccliv–cclv.

[2] Loc. III, no. 21; *C.P.L.* VI (1404–15), 469; *Scrip. Tres*, pp. ccxxv–ccxxvi. For another example of this very common privilege see *House of Kings*, ed. Carpenter, p. 90.

[3] *Scrip. Tres*, p. cccxxxvi.

[4] Cart. I, fo. 41v; Cart. III, fo. 196; *Scrip. Tres*, p. cclxiv; Reg. Parv. II, fo. 114; Reg. Parv. III, fo. 48.

finally rewarded on 21 April 1455 when Calixtus III formally dispensed the monks of Durham and its cells to eat meat outside their refectory on certain days between Septuagesima and Quinquagesima Sundays, as well as on Christmas Eve when that feast fell on a Sunday.[1]

Late medieval monks have often been ridiculed – admittedly by historians who have not themselves experienced the rigours of monastic life – for the way in which they exploited their connections with the papacy in the interests of their material comfort. This may be to miss the important point that, as in more recent times, a papal privilege – like a royal charter – could be valued as much for the prestige it conferred as for its contents. The monks of Saint Cuthbert were at continuous pains to discover what papal graces had been secured by other English Benedictine houses, and it was naturally a matter of overwhelming urgency to themselves to prove that they could be similarly favoured by the head of Christendom. In their quest for papal privileges they were following in the footsteps of the greatest English Benedictine pace-setter of the early fifteenth century, Abbot John Whethamstede of St Albans, whose first action after leaving the Council of Pavia-Siena had been to secure a private audience with Pope Martin V in order to gain concessions on the subject of meat-eating.[2] Even more significant is the fact that the Durham chapter thought it both necessary and urgent to secure papal licence for what were often very slight variations in their religious observances. Far from being an institution to ignore, the papal Curia had to be assiduously courted with all the skill at the prior's command.

Much the most pressing reason for the determination of the monks of Durham to remain in close contact with the papal court was, however, the need to protect their house from legal appeals to Rome by their many adversaries. The prior of Durham had no alternative but to meet these challenges by taking action in the Curia himself; he accordingly expended an inordinate amount of energy and capital on the annulment of sentences and decrees, most of which ought clearly never to have been made in the first place. A detailed

---

[1] Loc. XXI, no. 22; Reg. Parv. II, fos. 114, 121, 137; *Coldingham Corr.*, pp. 172, 174, 181; *Scrip. Tres*, pp. cci, cccxxx.

[2] Reg. III, fos. 203–4; *Annales J. Amundesham* I, 147–54.

study of the complicated litigation conducted at Rome during Wessington's priorate leaves no doubt that it was at this level that the operation of papal administration in the fifteenth century proved most inefficient and inequitable, showing few signs of any redeeming features. Durham's cases before the supreme court of Christendom were subject to almost interminable delay as well as to erratic and often unreasonable judgements. Papal lawyers and scribes were usually invincibly ignorant of English conditions, so that on one occasion Prior Wessington was acutely embarrassed by receiving a favourable sentence which was nevertheless rendered technically invalid because the church of Hemingbrough had been placed in the diocese of Durham rather than that of York.[1] An inadequate knowledge of European geography is no doubt understandable in fifteenth-century conditions, but much less excusable is the way in which different departments of the Curia often came more or less simultaneously to contradictory judgements on the same issue. To the extent that the right hand was often clearly unaware of what the left hand was doing, the judicial processes of the papal court are almost impossible to defend. It might be suggested that the gravest weakness of the late medieval papacy was not, as is often alleged, that it had become an administrative machine but rather that this machine so often sowed discord instead of harmony among its clients.

Among the many possible examples provided by the Durham records, the *locus classicus* is undoubtedly the convent's eventually fruitless defence of its possession of the cell of Coldingham, a perennial issue before the Curia in the mid-fifteenth century and an object lesson in 'the importable costs that we have made in plee at the court of Rome'.[2] The even more scandalous Lytham case was the direct result of misguided action on the part of the papal Curia, for it was William Partrike's possession of a papal bull of capacity which persuaded him to renounce his obedience to his mother house.[3] Partrike's act of rebellion was only the extreme example of the most mischievous of all the effects of papal intervention in English monastic affairs – the exemption of individual religious

[1] Reg. Parv. II, fo. 121.
[2] Reg. Parv. III, fos. 159–60; see below, pp. 316–27, and (for a full discussion of this issue), Dobson, 'Last English Monks on Scottish Soil', pp. 1–25.
[3] See below, pp. 327–41.

from the authority of their superior. Even the community of Saint Cuthbert's remarkable *esprit de corps* was subject to erosion of this type. At Durham as elsewhere the gravest abuses caused by the appeals of individual monks to the Roman Curia receded after the close of the Conciliar epoch; but in the 1470s two Durham monks (Richard Billingham and Thomas Yonge) were still able to secure dispensations to serve benefices outside the convent's walls. As late as 1496 Abbot Marmaduke Huby of Fountains found it necessary to deplore the fact that papal bulls of capacity were still serving as a pretext by which monks could wander at large in town and country to the great scandal of the religious orders. The words of a four-teenth-century Durham monk remained applicable: '*non est gracia sed ira Dei, tales habere gracias*'.[1]

The real problem posed by this evidence of haphazard injustice on the part of the papal court in its relations with English monasteries is whether the fault lay primarily in the corruption of the Curial officials or rather in the inadequacy of monastic representation at Rome. On this last and intriguing issue the letter-books of the Durham priors throw perhaps a more revealing light than any other English source. The biggest single difficulty was inevitably that of communications. Despite the fact that in ideal conditions the journey between England and Rome only took seven or eight weeks, the Durham records make it clear that the prior was usually quite content to receive letters which had taken twice as long to reach him from the Curia. Storms in the English Channel, the whereabouts of a particular cardinal or papal official, the ever-present possibility of robbery, kidnapping and even death *en route* – all these factors made the safe arrival of a message or messenger a matter for congratulation rather than secure expectation.[2] Even more hazardous was the dispatch of money to the papal court. Although the monks of Durham often availed themselves of the services of Italian factors in London

---

[1] *Scrip. Tres*, p. 117; *Letters from the English Abbots to the Chapter at Cîteaux, 1442–1521* (Camden Fourth Series IV, 1967), pp. 188–9; *C.P.L.* XIII (1471–84), 326, 634; 3.2. Pap., nos. 11, 15. Cf. Knowles, *Rel. Orders* II, 170–4; F. R. H. Du Boulay, 'The Fifteenth Century', *The English Church and the Papacy in the Middle Ages*, ed. C. H. Lawrence (London, 1965), pp. 227–8.

[2] For the archbishop of Cologne's 'dampnable ded' in imprisoning and then holding to ransom the Durham monk Richard Billingham in 1468, see Misc. Chrs., no. 1060; Reg. Parv. III, fo. 140v. Cf. G. B. Parks, *The English Traveller to Italy* I (Rome, 1954), 497.

who made out drafts payable by the Alberti of Florence and other bankers, they were constantly bombarded by complaints from their agents at Rome that the cash they needed to further Durham interests in the Curia had not arrived.[1]

Given such difficulties, it might appear at first sight that the most effective manner of presenting the convent's cases at Rome would be by means of members of the Durham chapter itself. In the thirteenth and early fourteenth centuries this had indeed been a usual practice and one Durham prior, Richard of Hoton, the implacable enemy of Bishop Bek, had actually died at the Curia (then at Poitiers) in January 1308.[2] But from the period of the Avignon papacy onwards it had become less and less likely that a Durham monk could hold his own in an increasingly departmentalised and sophisticated Curia. There was the additional, and very real, danger that the monk concerned might be tempted never to return to Durham. So serious was this possibility that although six Durham monks received licence to make a pilgrimage to the apostolic see between 1400 and 1450, they could only do so on the explicit condition that the journey was '*pro salute anime, non animo apostatandi*'. Prior Wessington was clearly extremely reluctant to use individual members of his community as professional agents at Rome: on the only occasion he envisaged sending a monk (John Pencher in September 1444) to prosecute monastic business at the Curia, the journey does not appear to have taken place.[3] His successors, as well as other monastic prelates, were sometimes less cautious in this respect. But the sad story of Richard Billingham's three abortive missions to the Curia between 1465 and 1472 and his final apostacy does much to confirm the view that an English monk across the channel might well prove to be a corruptible innocent abroad.[4]

---

[1] Misc. Chrs., no. 6758; Reg. IV, fo. 152; *Coldingham Corr.*, pp. 218, 226, 230.

[2] Fraser, *Antony Bek*, pp. 44, 157, 214; *Durham Annals*, pp. 8–9, 46–8, 205; *Scrip. Tres*, pp. 37, 40, 55, 78, 84–5, 99, 113–16; R. Brentano, *York Metropolitan Jurisdiction and Papal Judges Delegate, 1279–1296* (University of California Publications in History LVIII, 1959), p. 155.

[3] Reg. III, fos. 308–9; Reg. Parv. II, fo. 188. A generation earlier Thomas Rome had been a delegate to the Council of Pisa (Hostillar, Almoner, 1408/09), the only Durham monk to attend one of the fifteenth-century Councils.

[4] Dobson, 'Last English Monks on Scottish Soil', pp. 12–22; cf. U. Balzani, 'Un Ambasciata Inglese a Roma, 1487', *Archivio della Società di Storia Patria* III (1880), 187, 208.

It was therefore *faute de mieux* rather than with any great enthusiasm that the priors of Durham entrusted their business at the Curia to the class of resident professional agents there. Prior Wessington kept himself fully informed of the names of all the current or potential proctors at Rome; and there were few members of the small but famous galaxy of English representatives there (from William Swan to Andrew Holes) who did not act on one occasion or another in his convent's interests. From the closing years of the fourteenth century the prior of Durham was however rarely content with temporary *ad hoc* arrangements and preferred to retain the services of a permanent resident proctor at the Curia. Masters Robert Appleton, John Catterick, William Swan, Robert Sutton (at an annual fee of £2), Andrew Holes (at £2 13s. 4d.), William Gray and John Lax successively served the priory in this capacity during the first half of the fifteenth century.[1] Such men were often remote figures, representing many English bishops and monasteries simultaneously at the Curia; they were sometimes as little known in person to the Durham monks as the Italian papal chaplains and auditors on whom their fortunes rested. Although 'men experienced in Roman chicanery', these English proctors at the Curia often failed to inspire confidence for they were always liable to succumb in person to the occupational diseases of their position – excessive litigiousness, improvidence and neglect of their duties. Their letters to Prior Wessington and his successors make it abundantly clear that they consistently misled their English employers by over-optimistic estimates of Durham's prospects at the Curia – for the obvious reason that they had a vested interest in legal delay.

Prior Wessington was alert enough to these dangers to use as his more informal messengers to the Curia a wide variety of less distinguished and more occasional proctors, as well as diocesan officials making a journey to Rome on national or church business. The five letters written by the prior to Master William Freeman, an Oxford graduate in canon law, between January 1440 and April 1441, provide the best surviving example of the crucial role some-

---

[1] Bursar, 1438–66, Pensiones; Loc. xxv, no. 36; Reg. iii, fo. 113, 231; Reg. Parv. ii, fos. 112–13, 121, 137; Reg. iv, fo. 70. Several of these proctors figured in the successful campaign to secure the canonisation of Saint Osmund of Salisbury in 1457: A. R. Malden, *The Canonization of St Osmund* (Wilts. Record Soc., 1901), pp. xvii, xxii, 141.

times played by an intermediary in pressing for action on the part of the convent's regular proctor at the Curia.[1] Shortly afterwards a system of representation which had brought Durham Priory excellent results in the late 1430s deteriorated under the pressure of the Lytham and Coldingham causes and never fully recovered. Adequate representation at the Curia was not easy for Durham or other English monasteries to secure when the demand for skilled proctors greatly exceeded the supply, and amid an atmosphere in which it seems to have been very rare for an Italian cardinal to 'shaw favour to Englysshe men'.[2] By the end of Wessington's priorate the problem became particularly serious for the number of resident English proctors at Rome then declined sharply.[3] In a letter of 1447 or 1448 the dissident Durham monk William Partrike proposed to exploit this situation: 'I lat yow wyt that the prior has nor had no proctor at the court of rome this thre yer' for maister Wyllyam Freston was mayd proctor and he bydys all at the harchys at London, and so was is procreci revokyt sen Wytsonday bot the prior trists mykyl in maister Willyam Gray and in maister Ion' Lax bot thai yyt ar' no proctors.'[4] For the rest of its history the community at Durham was represented erratically and ineffectively at the Curia and came – significantly enough – to have less and less reason for gratitude to the popes who presided over this cumbersomely formidable machinery. As long ago as the 1280s Prior Claxton of Durham had sadly conceded that '*cause in curia Romana quasi immortales existant*';[5] but there is no doubt that the chastening experience of being ensnared in the mesh of the Camera's net was becoming more rather than less frustrating as the fifteenth century progressed.

At the York curia, like that of Rome, there were benefits to be gained and enemies to be defeated. As one of the greatest monasteries in the northern province, the chapter of Durham was

---

[1] Reg. Parv. II, fos. 112–13, 114, 121, 137; *Coldingham Corr.*, p. 110.

[2] Misc. Chrs., no. 1065; cf. the examples cited by Du Boulay, 'The Fifteenth Century', pp. 235–6.

[3] Cf. E. F. Jacob, 'On the Promotion of English University Clerks during the later Middle Ages', *Journal of Ecclesiastical History* I (1950), 179. ..

[4] Loc. IX, no. 30. For Lax's later inadequacy as a proctor see Dobson, 'Last English Monks on Scottish Soil', p. 11.

[5] Brentano, *York Metropolitan Jurisdiction*, pp. 163, 216.

regularly represented – sometimes by its own monks, usually by secular clerks – at all meetings of the Convocation of York and was bound by its acts and decisions.[1] But it was the convent's possession of extensive and prestigious spiritualities in the diocese of York that brought archbishop and monks most closely and sometimes uncomfortably into contact. Durham's peculiars south of the Tees, when combined with the traditional disinclination of the church of Durham to recognise its subjection to York, were an inevitable source of friction throughout the fifteenth century. But no late medieval prior or metropolitan would have been able, even if he had wished, to revert to the nakedly aggressive tactics employed in the days of Archbishops Wickwane and Romeyn. The convent's carefully cultivated good relations with the clerks who administered the exercise of archiepiscopal power at York paid the dividend of ensuring that for most of the time such crucial matters as presentations to the priory's benefices in Yorkshire fell into a quiet and monotonous routine. Even at the highest level the personal factor could never be neglected, for in much of the business and litigation conducted by the Durham monks at York the good-will of the archbishop himself tended to be all-important. Such at least is the conclusion that emerges from a comparison between the two successive metropolitans in the first half of the fifteenth century, Henry Bowet (1407–23) and John Kemp (1425–52). We have it on Prior Wessington's own authority that Bowet 'was highly indignant with the monks of Durham for many years' because of his humiliation at their hands in 1406: on 17 May of that year, and under pressures from the young John of Lancaster and Henry IV, 47 Durham monks had voted for Thomas Langley's election as bishop of Durham and only one for Bowet himself.[2] When translated to Richard Scrope's vacant diocese of York in the autumn of the next year, Bowet took his revenge by questioning the convent's rights to its Yorkshire churches and spiritual franchises. Although this direct onslaught on the prior and chapter's liberties was satisfactorily parried by 1412, Bowet's attitude to the Durham monks remained somewhat distant

---

[1] Reg. III, fos. 59, 70, 94, 98, 106, 115v, 281. Prior Wessington can be proved to have attended only two Convocations between 1416 and 1446 (Bursar, 1432, Expense Necessarie; Loc. xxv, no. 30).

[2] Additional Rolls, no. 11, and Loc. VI, no. 2 throw intriguing light on the manoeuvres after Archbishop Scrope's execution; Storey, *Thomas Langley*, pp. 165–6.

until his death in 1423.[1] Prior Wessington's relationship with Archbishop Kemp was much more happy. The latter sent presents to Durham, borrowed books from the monastic library there, protected Durham's new collegiate church of Hemingbrough and explicitly expressed his unfaltering support towards Saint Cuthbert's church.[2]

With so benevolently disposed an archbishop of York it followed that the church of Durham's spiritual possessions in the archdiocese were immune from the dangers of a really radical challenge. Nevertheless the rapidity with which an ancient *casus belli* could be brought to life again is one of the most remarkable features of fifteenth-century jurisdictional conflict. Thus the curious if short-lived revival in the 1420s of the issue of the Durham chapter's 'obedience' to the archbishop of York is unimportant in itself but deserves attention for the way in which it demonstrates the intense sensitivity of both archiepiscopal lawyers and monks of Saint Cuthbert to their respective rights. Shortly after Bowet's death a letter of presentation was issued at Durham on 11 December 1423 asking the Dean and Chapter of York, as keepers of the spiritualities in the vacancy, to admit John Regill to the rectory of West Rounton, an Allertonshire church in the patronage of the convent. Although the form of the presentation followed the regular pattern, when Regill came before Thomas Haxey, canon of York, the latter refused to accept it on the grounds that the letter failed to include the word '*obediencia*' in its greeting.[3] So was revived an antiquated controversy dating from 1280 when, as the Durham monks reminded themselves, Archbishop Wickwane's refusal to accept a presentation 'quia *obedientiam* non scripserunt' was the first stage in his more general assault on their liberties.[4] In 1423, it was unlikely that Haxey's scruples were the result of anything more serious than his ignorance of the monastery's exemption from the use of a once objectionable word. Unfortunately Regill, whose institution to

[1] Loc. xxv, nos. 50, 51; see above, p. 91, and 3.2. Archiepisc., nos. 1, 3; Cart. I. fos. 22–7.

[2] Loc. xxv, no. 54; Misc. Chrs., no. 7192; Reg. Parv. II, fos. 34, 92–3; Reg. III, fos. 205, 272; Bursar, 1427/28, Dona et Exennia; Bursar, 1439/40, Dona Prioris.

[3] Reg. III, fos. 101v–104v.

[4] In 1280 too, West Rounton was the church involved: see *Scrip. Tres*, pp. 58–9; Barlow, *Durham Jurisdictional Peculiars*, pp. 112–13; Brentano, *York Metropolitan Jurisdiction*, pp. 115–16.

West Rounton was part of an exchange of benefices, failed to refer the matter back to Durham. Instead, he rapidly forged new letters of presentation into which he inserted the word 'obedience', transferred the monastic common seal from the original presentation to the one he had just fabricated and consequently had no difficulty in securing admission from Haxey on 15 December. This prejudice to one of the convent's most cherished privileges became known at Durham when their next presentation to the Dean and Chapter of York was rejected in its turn a few weeks later. As this second presentee was no less a personage than the archdeacon of Northumberland, Marmaduke Lumley, intent on exchanging the church of Charing, Kent, for a Howden prebend, Wessington could afford no delay. When Lumley's proctor came before the prior in his chapel on 20 January 1424 to inform him of Haxey's refusal to admit his master, Wessington 'somewhat angrily' produced the monastic registers to prove that neither he nor his predecessors had ever included 'obedience' in their letters of presentation to York. Armed with two hastily composed public instruments, Master William Doncaster was sent directly to York where on 26 January he exposed Regill's forgery and asked the Dean and Chapter to respect Durham's traditional formula of presentation. Accordingly, Lumley was admitted to the prebend of Saltmarsh, Howden, and in the following month Regill was presented to West Rounton once again and in the conventional manner.[1]

Although the Dean and Chapter of York raised no further difficulties for the remainder of the vacancy, a final settlement had to await the succession of Archbishop Kemp. Wessington took the opportunity of supplementing the instruments of January 1424 with a more polished and learned compilation which he sent to the new archbishop for his personal examination, Kemp was convinced by the results of Wessington's labours among the Durham archives and in 1428 formally excused the prior and chapter from using the word '*obediencia*' in their letters of presentation addressed to him.[2] The prior and convent were clearly in the right on this issue, but the whole episode reflects both Wessington's determination not to surrender the privileges of Durham and his preoccupation with a

---

[1] Borthwick Institute, York, Reg. *Sede Vacante*, fo. 358v; Reg. III, fo. 103.
[2] Additional Roll, no. 11; Reg. III, fo. 127v; Reg. Parv. II, fo. 36.

past where his church and that of York had been in almost permanent conflict. Twenty years later, in 1447–8, when the controversy over '*obediencia*' was revived yet again and Wessington's compilation pressed into further service, the monks of Durham were still expressing their indignation at the way in which Henry I had violated the northern diocese by conferring the peculiar of Hexhamshire on the archbishop more than 300 years before.[1] By the fifteenth century the prior rather than the bishop of Durham had inherited the traditional role of defender of the liberties of Saint Cuthbert's church against the metropolitan.

In the later middle ages however, as at all times, the ultimate test of the attitude of the church of York to its northern neighbour was the policy it adopted during a vacancy in the see of Durham. To the general rule that such occasions have always elicited a quite extraordinary stream of comment and commotion, the two Durham vacancies which followed the deaths of Bishops Walter Skirlaw (on 24 March 1406) and Thomas Langley (on 20 November 1437) are certainly no exception. Against all the probable odds the famous settlement of 2 November 1286 which conceded the right of archbishops of York to exercise '*jurisdiccionem diocesanam . . . in ecclesia, civitate et diocesi Dunelmensibus, sede Dunelmensi vacante*' in return for the implied freedom of the diocese from metropolitan visitation *sede plena* proved (for the medieval period only) a viable and lasting compromise.[2] On the one hand, the only serious attempt at metropolitan visitation *sede plena* in the later middle ages – by Archbishop Alexander Neville in 1376 – was almost immediately subjected to royal inhibition;[3] on the other, the prior and chapter of Durham usually if reluctantly conceded the archiepiscopal right to spiritual jurisdiction in their diocese when they were without a bishop.

Much more problematic and indeed almost incapable of legal resolution was the situation in a double vacancy, a problem posed by Skirlaw's death in 1406 – during a two-year interlude in the succession of the archbishops of York. On the occasion of the only

---

[1] Additional Roll, no. 11. For the prior's serious disputes on the '*obediencia*' and other issues with the archbishop of York in the 1470s, see Reg. Parv. III, fos. 125v-6, 128, 131, 133-4, 173v, 175.

[2] 4.2. Archiep., no. 3; *Reg. John le Romeyn* I (Surtees Soc. CXXIII, 1913), 358-9; *Scrip. Tres*, pp. xciv-xcvi; Brentano, *York Metropolitan Jurisdiction*, pp. 144-5.

[3] *C.Cl.R.*, *1374-77*, p. 427; *1377-81*, p. 111; *Scrip. Tres*, pp. cxliii-cxliv.

previous double vacancy in the northern sees since the compromise of 1286, that of 1316, the chapters of Durham and York came to a preliminary compromise but seem to have been unable to reach a definitive agreement.[1] Ninety years later the vigorous stance taken by the Durham monks was completely successful in holding the claims of the Dean and Chapter of York at bay. In 1406 the convent satisfactorily delegated two of its own members, the sub-prior, Robert Rypon, and John Barton, as keepers of the Durham spiritualities; the York Dean and Chapter's protestation that they were the lawful custodians led merely to an appeal to Rome and apparently ineffective arbitration before the bishop of Exeter.[2] At the time of the next double vacancy in 1507, almost exactly a century later, Prior Castell was sufficiently confident to follow up this precedent by publicly committing the administration of the diocesan spiritualities to his fellow monks on the grounds that such '*jurisdiccio spiritualis*' pertained to the Durham prior and chapter '*de jure ac consuetudine*'. He was undoubtedly optimistic if not disingenuous. According to the opinion of Elizabethan lawyers required to pronounce on the precedents of 1507, 1560 and 1576, the York Dean and Chapter had the best right to exercise spiritual jurisdiction in the diocese of Durham when both sees were vacant; and at a period when, as we will see, the rights of the archbishop *sede vacante Dunelmensi* were generally admitted by the Durham monks, their refusal to admit the Dean and Chapter of York in 1316, 1406 and 1507 would indeed seem difficult to justify at law.[3]

The Durham vacancy of 1437–8 was happily free of all such complications, for at the time Archbishop Kemp of York was not only alive but kindly disposed to the Durham chapter. Prior Wessington was nevertheless undoubtedly nervous for he went to the considerable pains of compiling a series of notes on the procedure adopted by the priory in the case of six previous vacancies of the see of Durham, those of 1274, 1283, 1311, 1316–18, 1333 and 1381.[4] His attentive reading of Graystanes's chronicle and other

---

[1] *Historians of the Church of York* (Rolls Series, 1879–94), III, 237–40.

[2] Misc. Chrs., no. 5723 (the register kept by Rypon and Barton as keepers of the spiritualities); Reg. III, fos. 21, 25v; Loc. XXI, no. 50.

[3] Reg. v, fo. 88; *Scrip. Tres*, p. cccciv; Misc. Chrs., no. 7099.

[4] Reg. III, fo. 211, printed by R. Brentano as 'The *Jurisdictio Spiritualis*: an example of fifteenth-century English historiography', *Speculum* XXXII (1957), 330–2.

Durham records left him, of course, with no alternative but to accept the unpalatable fact that the archiepiscopal right to exercise spiritual jurisdiction within the diocese implied a visitation of his own monastery. But the precedents of 1333 and 1381 could be used to show that such a visitation was subject to the famous papal privilege of *Debent Superioribus,* by which a Benedictine monk had to be among the assessors.[1] By a more subtle argument these precedents proved that the archbishop was to use his authority in the vacancy as a diocesan and not *iure metropolitico.* This last distinction was of more than academic interest to Wessington in 1437, for a diocesan – unlike a metropolitan – visitation would be subject to various agreements with past bishops of Durham, all of them favourable to the convent. In the event Archbishop Kemp allayed any doubts the monks of Durham may have entertained by appointing as custodian of the Durham spiritualities during the vacancy his registrar, Master John Marshall. Marshall was one of the most prominent of the prior's own legal agents at the York curia, a church lawyer who went on to receive a Howden prebend in 1439 and the keepership of the convent's Howdenshire spiritualities in 1444.[2] Marshall conscientiously performed his duties as Kemp's delegate until his replacement by the new bishop of Durham, Robert Neville, in May 1438. The most impressive testimony to his labours is the elaborate but undoubtedly largely formal visitation of the archdeaconries of Durham and Northumberland he conducted between 20 January and 19 February.[3]

For the prior and chapter themselves the most perturbing episode during the vacancy was of course Marshall's visitation of their own cathedral monastery on 17 and 18 January 1438. But here again Marshall was clearly more interested in fulfilling his legal functions than in making a searching investigation into the conduct of religious life on the Durham peninsula. By choosing as his monastic assessor

---

[1] Secured by Bishop Bek from Pope Boniface VIII in 1302 and later incorporated into the *Corpus Iuris Canonici* as Extra. Comm. i. 7. 1 (ed. Friedberg, cols. 1243–4).

[2] Borthwick Institute, York, Reg. Kemp. fos. 489, 497; P.R.O., Exchequer K.R. Subsidy Rolls, Clerical Series (E.179), 62/33; Reg. III, fos. 238, 304v.

[3] 2.7. Pont., no. 11; Reg. Kemp, fos. 45, 491–2. The records of Marshall's visitation of the diocese of Durham were printed from Kemp's register by Professor A. Hamilton Thompson in *Miscellanea II* (Surtees Soc. CXXVII, 1916), pp. 221–38, but his introduction to these documents (ibid., pp. 145–7) contains a surprisingly large number of dating and other errors.

the convent's chancellor, William Dalton, the archbishop's commissary satisfactorily observed the terms of *Debent*; and although he went through the motions of interviewing each Durham monk in turn, neither his articles of enquiry nor any written *detecta* or injunctions survive. The only untoward incident was caused by Prior Wessington himself, who could only be persuaded to swear an oath of obedience to Archbishop Kemp after lodging an objection that his earlier oath to the bishop of Durham had automatically implied his obedience to that bishop's successors. This episode should be associated with the convent's disinclination to use the word '*obediencia*' in their letters of presentation to the archbishop, and is one more indication of Wessington's reluctance to recognise Kemp's authority as deriving from anything but his purely temporary custodianship of the diocesan spiritualities.

It is therefore absolutely clear that the archbishop of York's custodianship of the church and diocese of Durham in 1437–8, like that of the archbishop of Canterbury in vacant sees of the southern province, was aimed much more at the vindication of his jurisdictional rights than the reform of religion as such. On the other hand it is equally evident that Professor Hamilton Thompson was mistaken when he wrote that on Durham vacancies 'the archbishops of the fourteenth and fifteenth centuries . . . were usually content to let sleeping dogs lie'.[1] This particular dog has never slept for long, and from 1286 until the Reformation archbishops of York always expected to administer the Durham spiritualities during vacancies. Very reluctantly the monks of Durham conceded their right to do so, a grudging concession which was to be shattered by Henry VIII's refoundation of the Durham chapter as a secular body. In the later stormy history of the contested vacancy jurisdiction at Durham the Dean and Chapter were even more successful than their medieval predecessors, thanks to the support of royal inhibitions and such judgements as that of the King's Bench (which found against the archbishop) in 1672. The controversy has flared up again in more recent times, in 1890, 1920 and – perhaps most notably – after the resignation of Bishop Hensley Henson in 1939. On this

[1] A. Hamilton Thompson, 'Archbishop Savage's Visitation of the Diocese of Durham *sede vacante*, 1501', *Arch. Ael.*, Third Series, XVIII (1921), 44, and (for a more considered view) *The English Clergy*, pp. 2–3.

last vacancy, and under pressure from Archbishop Lang of Canterbury, Dean Alington and his chapter were appointed guardians of the Durham spiritualities 'without prejudice to the general issue'. That issue, then 656 years old, is deservedly notorious as the occasion for the most protracted litigation in English and indeed world history. *Autres temps, autres moeurs.* Few modern historians are likely to treat this famous dispute with the seriousness it was once thought to deserve, and even the most recent and sympathetic student of its complex origins finds them reminiscent of the world of Kafka's *Das Schloss*.[1] But it is not, after all, entirely inappropriate to find the late medieval monks of Durham helping to break a world record for the cause that always lay closest to their hearts – the defence of the liberties of Saint Cuthbert against aggression from outside his diocese.

THE BISHOP OF DURHAM

If the benevolence of the papal Curia and the archbishop of York was desirable, that of the bishop of Durham was essential to the late medieval convent. On the whole, and with minor exceptions, it was always forthcoming. At a period when the careers of the Durham diocesans were primarily identified with national rather than with local interests, they were generally content enough to accept the monastic argument that to be a 'goode and tendre lorde' to the priory of Durham would help bring them God's 'everlasting rewarde'.[2] The spectacular conflicts between monks and bishops which had bedevilled the earlier history of the community undoubtedly remained a vivid memory in the fifteenth century; but although grounds for ill-feeling inevitably continued to recur, Lewis de Beaumont (1317–33) is the last bishop of Durham who can be said to have been on notoriously bad terms with his chapter. Even Beaumont's capacity for interference had been circumscribed by a series of concessions from earlier bishops which protected the convent from excessive intervention by its titular abbot. Until the Dissolution, *Le Convenit* (an agreement made with Richard Poore in 1229) remained the monastery's basic charter of liberties.[3] As we

[1] Brentano, *York Metropolitan Jurisdiction*, pp. 145–7, 164; and see *Regs. of Tunstall and Pilkington* (Surtees Soc. CLXI, 1952), pp. xiii, xxxii; *Reports of Sir Peyton Ventris* (London, 1696), I, 234; *The Guinness Book of Records* (London, 1967 edn), p. 203.
[2] Reg. IV, fo. 182v.   [3] I.4. Pont., no. 4, printed in *Feodarium Dunelm.*, pp. 212–17.

have seen, Antony Bek's ability to exploit a vacancy in the priorate, whether genuine or forced, was denied his successors by Bishop Kellaw's generous surrender of episcopal rights in 1311, the year after Bek's death.[1] The priory of Durham consequently gained an earlier and more complete emancipation from its bishop than perhaps any other English cathedral monastery. In sharp contrast to contemporary practice at Christ Church, Canterbury, for example, the prior of Durham was able to admit novices, appoint obedientiaries, control the movement of his monks from cell to cell and even sanction their 'migration' to a stricter religious order without the need for episcopal consent. The bishop's disciplinary authority over the convent was only fully exercised during very infrequent visitations. Otherwise the bishop's good-will was required not for the sake of internal reform but to aid the monks '*in exterioribus agendis*'. Here the influence of one of the three or four greatest prelates in the country, later said by Cardinal Wolsey to be almost as wealthy as the bishop of Winchester, could not fail to be of supreme importance to the monks of his cathedral.

These constant themes emerge readily enough from a comparison between the otherwise two very dissimilar men who held the bishopric of Durham for the half-century between 1406 and 1457. Despite his important role in royal administration and his many absences from the diocese, Bishop Langley was in constant and friendly contact with Prior Wessington and his monks. He could be relied upon to use his secular powers against a recalcitrant spiritual offender, to help the priory recover its debts, to advise on the financial straits of the cells of Jarrow and Wearmouth, and to express his sympathy on the damage by lightning of his cathedral tower. Well might Wessington write to him, even before his resignation of the Great Seal of England, thanking him for the excellent counsel which he never failed to provide on request.[2] The relationship was not, however, altogether one-sided. Wessington's monks acted as penitentiaries in the diocese, and the prior himself visited Bishop Auckland on many occasions as well as acting as the bishop's com-

---

[1] *Reg. Palatinum Dunelmense* (Rolls Series, 1873–8), II, 1,125–7; *Reg. Richard of Bury*, pp. 24–6, 185–7. See above, p. 84.

[2] Reg. Parv. II, fos. 29, 39; Reg. III, fos. 62, 203; Bursar 1418–31, Expense Necessarie, Expense Prioris, Empcio Vini; cf. *Reg. Langley* III, 101–2.

missary and judge in extraordinary spiritual cases.[1] Wessington's familiarity with the contents of the monastic archives allowed him to furnish Langley with invaluable evidence for the defence of the latter's own privileges. In particular the prior played a central role in 'the great crisis of Langley's pontificate', the assault made by a powerful group of Durham knights on the bishop's palatinate franchise in 1433. At the height of this conflict Wessington received a letter from Sir William Elmeden and Sir William Eure, the leader of the local opposition to Langley, in which he was asked to conciliate and was thanked 'all ways for the hertly mocions that ye haue meuid for us to our wirshipfull lord of Durham'. But when the struggle reached its climax and criticism of the conduct of palatinate administration was transformed into a more general attack on what Langley himself described as 'the fraunchises of Goddes Kirk and Sent Cuthbert of Duresme', the prior immediately lent his weight to the cause of established authority. A memorandum prepared by Wessington on the historical origins of the liberties of the see of Durham helped to secure for his bishop a favourable judgement from the Crown's legal advisers in the parliament of 1433. Langley had cause to be grateful to Wessington for 'your good affeccion the whiche alwey ye haue to me'.[2]

Langley's successor as bishop of Durham was Robert Neville (1438–57), a lord of a very different and less admirable type. Neville is the only clear example in the later middle ages of a clerk who secured the bishopric of Durham because of his aristocratic origins rather than for administrative or diplomatic work on behalf of the royal government. More precisely still, he was the only holder of the northern see between 1333 and 1476 who did not serve, at some time of his life, as Keeper of the Privy Seal. The fifth son of the first Earl of Westmorland by his seoond marriage with Joan Beaufort, Robert Neville was recommended to Pope Eugenius IV by Henry VI in 1437 on the specific grounds of 'his birth and kynsmen ye which been of right greet and notable estat'.[3] He may have had

[1] Storey, *Thomas Langley*, pp. 184–5, 199–201; 1.3. Pap., no. 5; Misc. Chrs., no. 2613; *Reg. Langley* II, 5, 48, 97, 149, 157, 178; III, 30, 75, 147, 183.

[2] Loc. XXV, nos. 7, 58; Reg. Parv. II, fo. 112; Reg. III, fos. 164–7; B.M. Cotton MS., Vitellius A. IX, fos. 77–81; Craster, 'Red Book of Durham', pp. 520–1; Storey, *Thomas Langley*, pp. 116–34.

[3] Loc. XXV, no. 96.

few other qualities to recommend him. His family's formidable influence had already secured for him one of the convent's Howden prebends at the age of twelve and the bishopric of Salisbury (in 1427) at twenty-three. Although he spent some time at Oxford University in his youth, learning seems to have left comparatively little mark upon him: in 1435 he found it necessary to apologise to Prior Wessington for a letter written '*manu propria quam rudi et inculta*'.[1] In the absence of any episcopal register it is hardly feasible to compare Neville's exercise of his diocesan functions at Durham with that of his predecessor. But the most obvious and intriguing aspect of his episcopate was undoubtedly his exploitation of the patronage at his disposal to provide for members of his own family. To take the most blatant example, the £100 annuity by which the bishop retained his famous eldest brother, the Earl of Salisbury, for life has no parallel among the financial records of Bishop Langley's pontificate.[2] The new bishop's determination to promote the interests of the Neville kindred and their dependants was not without its adverse effects on the monks of Durham. Robert Neville was a frequent petitioner for benefices in the convent's gift, asked the monks to let him farm some of their Northumberland tithes, and compelled them – against their will – to confirm the grant of offices and lands in perpetuity.[3] But despite the fact that Neville undoubtedly adopted a more aggressive attitude towards the convent than his immediate predecessors, it is even more significant that the conventions of the relationship between bishop and monks were by now so firmly established that there was little likelihood of open conflict.

For the monks of Durham, as for all cathedral chapters, the replacement of a deceased or translated bishop by a new one was of particular moment as the occasion of the three most elaborate public ceremonies in their lives – the bishop's election, his enthronement in the cathedral, and his primary visitation. Quite apart from the personal considerations in play, the exceptionally well-documented episodes of Neville's election (27 January 1438), enthronement (11 April 1441), and visitation of the monastery

[1] Loc. xxv, no. 67; cf. Reg. III, fo. 45v; Emden II, 1350.
[2] Durham Bishopric Records, Receiver-General's Roll, Ch. C. no. 189811; cf. *34th Report of the Deputy Keeper of the P.R.O.* (1873), Appendix I, pp. 169, 175; Surtees, *Durham* I, lvii–lviii; Lapsley, *County Palatine of Durham*, p. 147.
[3] Loc. xxv, nos. 59, 68, 69, 71; Reg. III, fo. 303.

(9 July 1442) deserve detailed attention as classic examples of the procedures adopted and the problems encountered on those great occasions when bishop and monks were inescapably compelled into close confrontation. They illustrate to perfection that most fascinating of all features of the late medieval English Church – the way in which strong personal emotions were contained, but only just, within some of the most elaborate and formal legal machinery ever devised.

Bishop Neville's election need not, however, detain us for long. Sponsored by the Beaufort connection within England, and by Henry VI to Pope Eugenius IV, he was the only candidate for the bishopric. The monks of 1438 were therefore denied the very limited freedom of choice enjoyed by the chapter of Durham in 1406 and that of York in 1405 and 1423. As nearly always in the fifteenth century, 'the act of election was simply an act of consent to the king's choice'.[1] Nevertheless, the prior and chapter cannot have known definitely that Neville had secured his papal bull of translation before late February 1438. On the morning of 27 January, 53 Durham monks had already processed from choir to chapter-house where, after the reading of the royal *congé d'élire* and a detailed examination of certificates and proxies, William Ebchester preached a preliminary sermon which was followed by the *Veni Creator*.[2] Wessington then directed the monastic chancellor, William Dalton, to call for the removal from the chapter-house of all seculars except a group of 9 specially selected witnesses who included 5 graduates and 2 public notaries. After the reading by Dalton of the Fourth Lateran Council's decree, *Quia Propter*, Wessington and his monks decided after some discussion to proceed *per viam compromissi*. Despite the use of scrutiny in 1406, this was the customary procedure employed at Durham in episcopal elections; but it was less usual for the chapter to select, as they did on this occasion, only one compromissary, the prior himself.[3] Such was clearly the safest method of ensuring that the royal candidate met with not the slightest show of opposition. After what must have been a meaningless consultation with the senior members of the chapter, Wessington read out from a paper schedule the name of Robert Neville. Singing

[1] Thompson, *The English Clergy*, p. 17. [2] 1.7. Pont., no. 5; Reg. III, fos. 213–21.
[3] Thirteen compromissaries elected Graystanes in 1333 and 13 (to whom 6 were later added) elected John Fordham in 1381 (*Scrip. Tres*, pp. 120, 143).

the *Te Deum*, the prior then led his monks through the cloister to the high altar of the cathedral where he publicly announced the postulation to the waiting crowd. On the following day (28 January) 32 monks assembled in chapter to appoint William Ebchester and John Mody as their proctors to secure the assent of Neville to his election and then to obtain royal approval. Wessington did not formally recognise his new bishop until 15 May 1438, by which date Neville had received his bull of translation, undergone consecration at the hands of Archbishop Kemp and obtained the restoration of the temporalities from the Crown.[1]

Although the spiritualities of his new see were also released to Neville in May 1438, he was not enthroned at Durham until 11 April 1441, after an unusually long interval.[2] During these three years the bishop exercised genuine control over his diocese; but it was at least arguable whether he had full powers to intervene officially in the affairs of his cathedral church.[3] There is, for instance, no record that the prior and chapter made any oath of canonical obedience to Robert Neville until after his enthronement and installation. Meanwhile the prior personally carried much of the responsibility for the administration of the spiritualities of the bishopric during the transitional period. He acted as Neville's vicar-general for at least part of the time, thus following the example of many of his predecessors who had filled the office either singly or in association with a secular clerk.[4] Two years after his election, Neville still displayed no particular eagerness to undergo the ceremony of enthronement. In July 1440 Wessington wrote to him urging that he should come to be installed (the word used by the

[1] Misc. Chrs., nos. 2638, 2639; Reg. III, fo. 221; Reg. Parv. II, fo. 115; Reg. Kemp, fo. 45; *C.P.R., 1436–41*, p. 154.
[2] At Durham enthronement was rarely separated from consecration by more than a few months (*Scrip. Tres*, pp. 92, 128, 137). Bishop Langley had been consecrated on 8 August 1406 and was enthroned on 4 September 1407 (Storey, *Thomas Langley*, pp. 104, 166).
[3] See the 'admirable exposition of the things which a bishop ought not to do before he has been enthroned' made by Archbishop Arundel of Canterbury and printed in I. J. Churchill, *Canterbury Administration* (London, 1933), I, 278.
[4] Loc. xxv, nos. 64, 67, 70; Reg. Hatfield, fo. 126v; I.2. Archid. Dunelm., no. 57; *Scrip. Tres*, pp. cxi–cxii. It was by no means unusual for priors of English cathedral monasteries to act as vicars-general for their bishops: see, e.g., Churchill, *Canterbury Administration* II, 5–6; C. R. Cheney, 'Norwich Cathedral Priory in the Fourteenth Century', *Bulletin of the John Rylands Library* XX (1936), 95.

prior for what was a composite process including enthronement and induction) at Durham the following Christmas. The prior pointed to the illustrious precedents provided by Bishops Bek, Hatfield and others who had been installed at this time, and stressed that Neville would save money by combining his enthronement with the major feast of the year.[1] It is possible that the bishop took umbrage at Wessington's expression of his very definite ideas; and certainly the installation did not take place until the spring of 1441.

More irritating to the new bishop must have been the squabble which arose between the archdeacon of York and the prior as to who should enthrone him at Durham. By no means a new dispute, this issue had been raised as long ago as the thirteenth century when the archdeacons of York had attempted to emulate the example of their Canterbury counterparts who enthroned bishops of the province on a mandate from the metropolitan. Antony Bek's re-action to this problem in December 1285 had been characteristically abrupt for he cut short the argument by inviting his brother, the bishop of Saint David's, to perform the ceremony.[2] But in 1441 Wessington had little to fear from an appeal to precedent; there is no evidence that archdeacons of York ever enforced their claim to enthrone a bishop of Durham, while the priors of the monastery certainly had done so.[3] Wessington heard that the archdeacon of York proposed to challenge his own right to install the bishop as early as 6 January 1439. He immediately informed Neville that when a similar claim had been made in 1407, Bishop Langley had con-sulted Prior Hemingburgh, examined the evidence produced by the monks and been so convinced by it that he formally stated that he would be installed by the prior and no one else. Neville failed to follow his predecessor's example and on 5 February 1439 Wessington wrote to one of his counsellors at the York curia, Master John Marshall, proposing a meeting between the two parties to the dispute. The prior confessed that he was particularly anxious not to

[1] Reg. Parv. II, fos. 124–5; *Scrip. Tres*, pp. cclxi–cclxii.

[2] Churchill, *Canterbury Administration*, I, 276–8; *Durham Annals*, p. 64; *Scrip. Tres*, pp. 69–70; Fraser, *Antony Bek*, pp. 42–3; cf. *Reg. William Greenfield* v (Surtees Soc. CLIII, 1940), p. 105.

[3] Richard Bury had been installed by Prior William Cowton in the presence of the king of England, his wife and mother, the king of Scotland, two archbishops, five bishops and seven earls (*Scrip. Tres*, p. 128).

antagonise the archdeacon of York because of his reverence for Archbishop Kemp whose nephew, Thomas, held the archdeaconry from December 1436 to November 1442. But Thomas Kemp pursued his claim to conduct the enthronement ceremony and Wessington was compelled to make a formal appeal to Rome on 5 September 1439.[1] The prior could rely not only on his prescriptive right but on those famous if fraudulent Durham charters which equated his position with that of the dean of York.[2] Moreover, Wessington had heard that twenty years previously Bishop William Heyworth had been installed at Lichfield by the dean, and at Coventry by the prior. It was not clear to him whether the prior of Coventry had acted in his own right or on commission from the archdeacon of Canterbury, but in November and December of 1439 he wrote to York and to Bishop Neville asking for an enquiry into installation practice at Winchester, Rochester, Bath, Coventry, Norwich, Worcester and Ely, all monastic cathedrals in the southern province.[3] The results of this survey would undoubtedly have favoured the case of the archdeacon of York and Wessington appears to have dropped this dangerous argument from analogy. The climax to the dispute came on 10 April 1441, the day before the ceremony, when Wessington had a turbulent interview in his chapel with Master Robert Dobbes and John Sendale, sent to Durham by Thomas Kemp in the hope that they might brow-beat the prior into a surrender of his right to install.[4] Wessington showed commendable firmness and preserved for himself and his successors this valued privilege. Despite later revivals of the issue, as in 1457 on Neville's succession by Lawrence Booth,[5] the dean of Durham still enthrones the bishop of Durham although now (as was not the case in 1441) on the mandate of the metropolitan.[6]

[1] Reg. Parv. II, fo. 100; Reg. III, fos. 251v–2.

[2] In the later middle ages the dean of York enthroned the northern archbishop as the prior of Christ Church enthroned the archbishop of Canterbury. See E. C. Ratcliff, 'On the Rite of the Inthronization of Bishops and Archbishops', *Theology* XLV (1942), 80.

[3] Reg. Parv. II, fos. 111–12. Cf. Bursar, 1440/41, Expense Necessarie.

[4] Reg. III, fo. 268v–9.

[5] P.R.O. Palatinate of Durham, Chancery Enrolments, 3/206, file 2(a).

[6] This was explicitly stated by the dean of Durham in his declaration of enthronement during the ceremony of 25 July 1956 which followed the translation of Maurice Harland to Durham from Lincoln.

So on 11 April 1441 Wessington himself conducted what was probably the most magnificent ceremony that ever fell to the lot of a prior of Durham. There were present at the enthronement Neville's suffragan bishop, Thomas Radcliffe of Dromore, seven monastic prelates, the Earl of Salisbury and his brothers Latimer and Abergavenny together with many other north-country lords, knights and esquires. Although Wessington had feared a month previously that he would be too ill to preside over the lengthy proceedings, the official record shows that the prior performed his duties competently enough. The traditional forms were followed exactly: Neville was met by Wessington and his monks in the cathedral cemetery and then led to the high altar where he and the prior prayed in turn. Both men then washed their feet in the sacrist's 'checker' and crossed to the revestry where they were robed in their pontificals. Wessington accompanied Neville to the bishop's throne where he sat while the prior solemnly inducted him into possession of his episcopal dignity and led the *Te Deum* which followed. The monastic procession moved to the choir, where Neville was installed, and then to the chapter-house where Wessington showed his bishop to his special seat. Here, after more prayers and the *Veni Creator*, Neville made his oath to preserve the rights and privileges of the church of Durham and Wessington followed by swearing obedience to his lord. Once each Durham monk present, in order of his seniority, had humbly kissed the bishop, the company returned to the high altar where Neville conducted his first mass in the cathedral. Besides being an elaborate religious rite, the enthronement of the bishop had a more than symbolic importance for Wessington and his monks. In an age when capitular election was itself little more than a formality, the convent was anxious to receive from the new bishop that oath of loyalty to his church (carefully written out in preparation for the enthronement) which provided some protection against future arbitrary action on his part.[1]

After the splendours of the enthronement ceremony, there followed fifteen months later the most serious and nervously anticipated occasion of the monastic life, the bishop of Durham's primary visitation of his cathedral church. The results of the episcopal visitation of 9 July 1442, occurring as it does less than four years

[1] Reg. III, fos. 221v, 267–8.

before the prior's resignation, cannot fail to be of significance as a commentary on Wessington's exercise of his office. More generally, this visitation is of especial interest as the last recorded occasion on which the monastery of Durham is known to have been subjected to systematic and critical external inspection before the Dissolution. The monastery had last been visited by a bishop in July 1408, no less than thirty-four years earlier.[1] Even by late medieval standards, the monks of Durham had been fortunate to enjoy so long an immunity from episcopal visitation. In theory, as the prior himself acknowledged in a formal protest made on the day before Neville's 1442 visitation, the bishop was entitled to visit the convent once a year, and twice if necessary; this agreement had been reached as long ago as 1229 in *Le Convenit*, itself apparently influenced by Honorius III's judgement in the case of Saint Mary's, York, in 1226.[2] In practice, the community of Durham, like that of the few other cathedral monasteries where visitation records also survive in number,[3] was rarely visited by its bishop more than once in each decade. There is evidence of only nine episcopal visitations of Durham in the 105 years before 1442. Richard of Bury visited in 1337 and 1343, Thomas Hatfield in 1347, 1354 and 1371, John Fordham in 1383, Walter Skirlaw in 1391 and 1397 (of which record was made in his now missing register), and Langley in 1408.[4] Documents relating to most of these visitations were preserved among the convent's muniments and were carefully consulted by Wessington in the early summer of 1442 as he prepared to face the arrival of Neville and his assessors.[5]

---

[1] Langley apparently projected a second visitation of his cathedral church in early 1420 but this never materialised (Reg. III, fo. 69).

[2] 1.8. Pont., no. 16. Cf. *Feodarium Dunelm.*, p. 214; C. R. Cheney, *Episcopal Visitation of Monasteries in the Thirteenth Century* (Manchester, 1931), p. 122.

[3] *Ely Chapter Ordinances and Visitation Records*, ed. Evans, pp. xvi–xvii.

[4] 2.7. Pont., nos. 1, 2; 1.8. Pont., no. 9; 1.9. Pont., no. 4; Misc. Chrs., no. 6068; *Reg. Richard of Bury*, pp. 263–4; Cart. I, fo. 116.

[5] The late medieval Durham visitation records, largely surviving among the *Pontificalia* and in Locellus XXVII, were surprisingly neglected by James Raine and other nineteenth-century Durham historians. Of all the fifteenth-century visitations, that of 1442 is easily the best documented and in this respect compares favourably with those studied by J. Scammell, 'Some Aspects of Medieval English Monastic Government: The case of Geoffrey Burdon, Prior of Durham (1313–1321)', *Revue Bénédictine* LXVIII (1958), 226–50; and B. Harbottle, 'Bishop Hatfield's Visitation of Durham Priory in 1354', *Arch. Ael.*, Fourth Series, XXXVI (1958), 81–100.

The procedure adopted by Bishop Neville in his primary visitation of the monastery adhered closely to the traditional Durham pattern and demands no special attention. Wessington prepared, as was his habit, for a revival of past disputes but Neville infringed none of the convent's cherished privileges. The bishop tacitly accepted that clause of *Le Convenit* which excused the monks from the payment of a procuration fee because their visitor could live in his castle of Durham during the period of his examination.[1] The bishop, according to the terms of the papal privilege, *Debent*, was accompanied on his visitation by only two of his clerks, a notary and a Durham monk, William Ebchester, the future prior and an eminently acceptable assessor in Wessington's eyes.[2] A more debatable question was whether those Durham monks serving in cells outside the diocese of Durham were nevertheless subject to the bishop's visitation of the central house. The priories of Stamford and Lytham were undoubtedly liable to ordinary visitation by the bishop of Lincoln and the archdeacon of Richmond respectively; and there had been occasions in the past when the prior of Durham refused to summon the monks from these dependencies on the grounds that they should not be liable to a double correction. No definite ruling was apparently ever made on this subject, and in 1442 Wessington certified that he had personally cited only those monks who ought to be present, with the additional reservation that no cell (inside or outside the diocese) could be left completely deserted. In practice, Bishop Neville was able to examine some members of all the monastic cells except Durham College, Oxford.[3]

In the five weeks interval between his reception of Neville's notice of visitation (2 June 1442) and the visitation day itself (9 July) Wessington made elaborate preparations.[4] Two of the prior's legal representatives at York, Masters Robert Ormeshead and William Bispham, were called to Durham to give their help. Wessington

---

[1] 1.8. Pont., no. 16. In 1408 Bishop Langley had taken procurations in respect of the convent's appropriated churches but there is no trace of such payments in 1442.

[2] Bishop Skirlaw had given offence in the 1390s by attempting to introduce Benedictine monks from other houses, and Langley too had used the services of a monk from Saint Mary's York, in 1408: see Loc. xxvii, no. 11; *Reg. Richard of Bury*, pp. 263–4.

[3] Cart. iii, fos. 341–2; university students seem to have been usually exempted from a visitation at their mother house (*Lincoln Visitations* iii, 270).

[4] 2.7. Pont., nos. 12, 13; Bursar, 1441/42, Expense Necessarie.

drew up a variety of tuitorial appeals to York and Rome, searched the convent's records for possible precedents and compiled a brief but extremely practical guide to traditional Durham visitation practice.[1] It was therefore ironical that when a conflict did occur it was at a totally unexpected stage of the proceedings. When, on the morning of 9 July 1442, Bishop Neville and his attendants were met by the prior and chapter in what is now Palace Green, he was much taken aback to find that they were dressed only in their ordinary frocks and cowls and not '*albis et capis, modo processionali, induti*'. Wessington alleged that, according to Durham custom, bishops were only met in albs and copes when they came to be installed, to be buried or had returned from abroad. After great debate, the prior withdrew for a private conversation with the bishop's spiritual chancellor and vicar-general, Master John Norton. It was agreed between the two men that the monks need not change their dress on this occasion; but Wessington promised that if it could be shown to him that albs and copes were worn at visitations of any six of the more notable cathedral churches in England, whether secular or monastic, then the community of Durham would do likewise in the future. The dean and canons of Lincoln had certainly been dressed in silken choir-copes ('*capis cericis de choro*') at William Gray's 1432 visitation and it is likely that Wessington's promise was ill-advised.[2] But the prior was naturally anxious to cause his bishop no offence before the real work of visitation began. Once again, the loss of Bishop Neville's register renders it impossible to follow the actual proceedings in complete detail; but it can be deduced from the resulting *comperta* that the visitation was not only extremely thorough but also based on a set of interrogative articles addressed to each monk in turn. The exhaustive series of questions asked by Bishop Langley in 1408 formed an obvious precedent.[3]

There does survive at Durham, moreover, a most revealing list of forty-six '*articuli de et super detectis in visitacione ... extracti et indentati*'.[4] According to the standard terminology now employed in the discussion of medieval visitations, these articles may be described as *comperta*, a balanced summary and selection of the

---

[1] I.8. Pont., nos. 13–16; I.9. Pont., no. 4; Loc. XXVII, no. 23; Reg. III, fos. 282–4.
[2] Loc. XXVII, no. 28; *Lincoln Visitations* I, 128–9.   [3] *Reg. Langley* I, pp. 71–6.
[4] I.9. Pont., no. 3.

detecta revealed by individual Durham monks. Monastic visitation records are notoriously difficult to interpret and, as always, much depended on 'what had happened at the house after the bishop's mandate for visitation arrived'.[1] On the other hand, in many fourteenth-century visitations the community's sense of *esprit de corps* had not prevented individual monks from making bitter personal criticisms of their colleagues and superior.[2] Although the failings revealed by the Durham *comperta* of 1442 are relatively colourless and undramatic, it would be as well to take them at their face value rather than to suggest the operations of a conspiracy of silence, for which there is no proof whatsoever. A striking feature of the 1442 findings is the comparative absence of any sign of serious divisions or personal feuding within the house. No Durham monk was detected of a serious spiritual offence except for three apostates, all of whom had in fact disappeared at least fifteen years before. The prior, sub-prior, chamberlain and deans of order as well as the almoner were accused of negligence or partiality in the exercise of their offices; but only two monks, neither resident at Durham, namely the priors of Holy Island and Lytham, were charged with *proprietas*. Many of the *comperta* deal with themes monotonously encountered in late medieval visitation records and little need be said about such perennial complaints. The supply of victuals was alleged to be insufficient and of poor quality, dogs befouled the cathedral choir, there were too many private drinking parties especially after compline, secular songs disturbed the claustral silence, and no doctor was provided to care for the sick. The Durham *comperta* of 1442 have, in short, no scandalous revelations to offer the historian, and suggest that religious life there was conducted in a more respectable manner than, to take three notorious examples, at contemporary Bardney, Eynsham or Peterborough.[3] The most obvious feature of the forty-six articles is their preoccupation with financial shortcomings in the administration of the convent. Although the order of the criticisms made follows no logical principle, the first of the articles questioned Wessington's

---

[1] Jacob, *The Fifteenth Century*, p. 301; cf. Knowles, *Rel. Orders* I, 83–4; *Lincoln Visitations* I, pp. ix–xiii; II, pp. li–lxii.

[2] 2.8. Pont., no. 12; Loc. XXVII, no. 35.

[3] *Lincoln Visitations* I, 1–4, 54–63, 100–3; II, 24–34, 90–1; III, 269–302. Cf. Knowles, *Rel. Orders* II, 210.

decision to divide the office of bursar between three obedientiaries: this was the burning issue in internal monastic politics at the time.[1] Other complaints were made of extravagant expenditure by the prior and obedientiaries; and it was petitioned that the monastery's building programme should be suspended until repairs had been carried out on existing property.[2]

This list of *comperta*, in indenture form, was sent by Bishop Neville to the monastery on 17 September 1442, over two months after his visitation. The bishop felt himself bound by that sentence in *Le Convenit* which allowed the prior and convent to take part in the '*correctiones compertorum*' and to advise on the ways in which reform might be made.[3] Consequently Neville commissioned a panel of seven monks to consider the indenture together with his monk-assessor at the visitation, William Ebchester.[4] Besides Ebchester and Wessington himself, the other members of the committee were the sub-prior, hostillar, cellarer, and bursar as well as William Dalton, ex-chancellor, and Robert Westmorland, then chancellor of the monastery. Bishop Neville only allowed these senior monks nine days within which to reply, but during this time they produced a detailed set of recommendations combined with remarks on the truth or otherwise of the *comperta* presented for their inspection. This was the '*Deliberacio, Avisamentum et Consilium*' which commented on each of the forty-six *comperta* in turn and of which an indented copy was preserved at Durham. There also survives a draft of Wessington's personal replies to those articles which seemed to him directed specifically against the prior's exercise of his office.[5] Wessington was concerned to show that in the case of thirteen of the *comperta* he was not himself to blame: '*defectus non est in priore*'. The other members of the committee seem to have accepted Wessington's arguments, for they assimilated these into their more general report to the bishop.

---

[1] See below, p. 289.

[2] Similar financial distress, partly caused by an over-ambitious building programme, was discovered at Westminster Abbey two years later: V. H. Galbraith, 'A Visitation of Westminster in 1444', *E.H.R.* xxxvii (1922), 83–8.

[3] Reg. iii, fos. 283–4.

[4] 2.7. Pont., no. 8. Bishop Hatfield appointed ten Durham monks to help him reform the monastery after his visitation: Harbottle, 'Bishop Hatfield's Visitation of Durham Priory in 1354', p. 85.

[5] 1.8. Pont., no. 2; Loc. xxvii, no. 17.

The replies returned by Wessington and the other senior monks are often more revealing than the *comperta* themselves. In general the prior and his colleagues showed themselves prepared to co-operate with the bishop. Although they denied the accuracy of some of the accusations, they conceded their general validity and put forward constructive proposals for future reform. Wessington had been censured for failing to treat his brethren benevolently and preventing them from speaking freely on common business at chapter meetings. He denied this absolutely and cleared himself from such criticism by appealing to the opinion of his fellows. As for the complaint that he had not made a public statement of the financial position of the monastery, Wessington reminded Neville that all obedientiaries had their accounts audited yearly at the convent's *capitulum generale*. Nor do the other replies suggest that the prior's rule was either arbitrary or negligent. A more obvious fault was insufficient firmness in controlling his obedientiaries. Thus Wessington declared that he had frequently, both in private and public, corrected the chamberlain, Thomas Nesbitt: yet this officer had apparently taken little notice and was extremely unpopular among his brethren in 1442 for his failure to distribute the goods of his office. The responsibility for the maintenance of discipline in choir and cloister belonged properly to the sub-prior rather than the prior, and it was the former, not Wessington, who was most frequently requested to perform his duties more efficiently.

At Auckland on 4 November 1442 Bishop Neville finally issued his injunctions on the late visitation.[1] As was usual at Durham, if not elsewhere, these were addressed in the first place to the prior alone with the command that he should publish them to the convent in chapter. Neville's injunctions were largely based on the recommendations made by Wessington and the select monastic committee, but both the language and the arrangement of the items were changed considerably. The result testifies to the conscientiousness of Neville or his clerks, for an attempt was made to produce statutes of general application. Yet the bishop was specific where necessary: the case of Thomas Nesbitt was mentioned by name and Wessington was ordered to see to his correction before Christmas. A few subjects make their appearance for the first time: old and infirm

---

[1] Misc. Chrs., no. 2645, a slightly mutilated paper copy of the injunctions.

monastic retainers were to be given houses in the almonry; and the bishop, as a contribution towards improving the quality of monastic food, ordered all cooks to take a special oath before the convent each year. Wessington himself was warned not to sell or give timber from his woods without careful consideration and the consent of the chapter. The bishop's injunctions ended with the familiar command that no monk should be victimised for anything he had said under private interrogation during the visitation.[1] Neville had found it unnecessary to remove or require the removal from office of any obedientiary. On the other hand his visitation did leave behind it some quite serious and unresolved problems, particularly on financial matters. Wessington evidently felt that his conduct of the priorate had been unjustly criticised and required his chancellor, Robert Westmorland, to produce an elaborate survey of his expenditure as prior on building and other 'good works'. Ironically enough, this detailed statement of Wessington's contribution towards the welfare of his monks, to which he attached a list of his written compilations, was therefore originally prepared for presentation to the bishop in self-defence and justification; but at the time of Wessington's resignation four years later it was re-drafted in such a way as to suggest only the convent's unsolicited gratitude for their prior's labours.[2]

In the last resort the episcopal visitation of 1442 is of most significance as the best evidence we have that the quality of monastic life at mid fifteenth-century Durham was of an eminently respectable and indeed commendable level. Robert Neville's own final comment on his findings was a formal declaration that he had found the Durham monks sober and chaste, leading lives free from serious moral blemish.[3] A comparison, dangerous though this is, of the *comperta* and injunctions produced in 1442 with those surviving from earlier visitations leaves the impression that conditions at the monastery had positively improved towards the end of the middle

---

[1] Cf. Cheney, *Episcopal Visitation of Monasteries*, pp. 85–6.

[2] In the earliest version of this statement, totals of repairs and building expenses are recorded for the first 26 years of Wessington's priorate, i.e. only to Christmas 1442 (Loc. xxvii, no. 1a). Later copies and drafts which complete the details to 1446 survive as Loc. xxvii, no. 1b; Misc. Chrs., nos. 7111, 7131, 5727 (c) and (b), the last printed in *Scrip. Tres*, pp. cclxxi–cclxxvi.

[3] 2.7. Pont., no. 9; Cart. iii, fo. 307.

ages. On the other hand, the 1442 visitation proceedings make it clear that even at this moment of his greatest authority the bishop's capacity to control the internal affairs of the priory was in practice extremely limited. It was no doubt partly because the late medieval bishops of Durham were so well aware of this fact that they seem to have visited the convent so infrequently during the last century of its existence. Neville himself, after abandoning a plan to conduct a second visitation of the monastery in the spring of 1446, seems to have visited the convent again in March 1449; but no detailed *comperta* or injunctions appear to survive from this or indeed any other later medieval episcopal visitation.[1] Only to a very limited and painless degree did the monks allow their bishop to be their judge and castigator of their errors. No longer seeing him as their spiritual pastor in any but the most formal and general sense, they valued their 'special relationship' with the bishop of Durham because of the power and influence he could wield as a great magnate. 'For my lord in tyme of neide or cause of compleyntt I have none othir comfort or of refuge and counsell bod onely in your good lordship.'[2] The Durham priors' frequent appeals to their bishops in terms of the familiar late medieval cliché of 'good lordship' suggest what was indeed the case – that in practice as opposed to theory the connection between bishop and convent had become almost completely secularised. The wheel had undoubtedly turned full circle since the summer months of 1083 when Bishop William of Saint Calais had brought twenty-three monks from Jarrow and Wearmouth to found the priory of Durham under his personal protection.

THE ENGLISH BENEDICTINES

By far the largest and wealthiest English monastery north of York, the cathedral church of Saint Cuthbert dominated the diocese of Durham at the cost of other manifestations of the religious life in the northern see as well as its own geographical isolation from fellow Benedictine houses. There could be little opportunity for the monks of Durham to enjoy either the varied intercourse with other

[1] 2.7. Pont., nos. 7, 10; 1.8. Pont., no. 12; Loc. XVI, no. 6(a); Loc. XXVII, no. 18; Misc. Chrs., nos. 5179, 5187.
[2] *Register of Richard Fox* (Surtees Soc. CXLVII, 1932), p. xxxii.

monasteries reflected in, for example, the Worcester *Liber Albus*, or the more formal ties which bound the Black Monks of Winchcombe and Coventry into close association.[1] Apart from Durham and its cells, there were nine other houses of religious in the diocese of Durham; but all were comparatively small, four were nunneries, and only one was served by Black Monks. Prior Wessington and his obedientiaries occasionally entertained and sometimes had business dealings with the abbots of Newminster and Blanchland, but there is little evidence of any closer relationship. Only with Tynemouth, a dependency of St Albans, was there a more intimate connection. Their stormy quarrels of the twelfth century were now forgotten in a common hostility towards the encroachments of the citizens of Newcastle-upon-Tyne on their respective fishing rights at the mouth of the Tyne. The two priors now saw each other as good neighbours and often interchanged gifts and even visits. In 1419 Wessington made the long journey over the Tyne ferry to attend the funeral of Prior John Macrell of Tynemouth, and in later years he entertained at Durham various members of that community. During the early fifteenth century at least, Durham's association with Tynemouth seems to have been unquestionably closer than with any other religious house.[2]

At the national level, however, Durham monks came into regular contact with other members of their Order through the medium of the Provincial Chapters of the Black Monks, held at Northampton every three years. The priors of Durham were not only legally bound to observe and implement the statutes produced by the Provincial Chapters but generally showed themselves eager to participate in this Benedictine organisation. The prominent role played by Durham monks at the chapters has been fully revealed by Dr Pantin's important and detailed researches, and is perhaps in itself a sign of their reaction from the convent's geographical isolation. As in the sphere of university education, the church of Durham made a much larger contribution than many other houses which were equally wealthy and much less remote. During the

---

[1] *The Liber Albus of the Priory of Worcester* (Worcestershire Historical Society, 1919), pp. xxix–xxxi; G. Haigh, *The History of Winchcombe Abbey* (London, n.d.), p. 154.

[2] Bursar, 1418/19, Expense Prioris; Misc. Chrs., no. 7156; Cellarer, 1430, 1446; Loc. v, no. 45.

period between the Fourth Lateran Council of 1215 and Benedict XII's constitutions of 1336 there had been a separate chapter for the province of York and it was therefore hardly surprising that the prior of Durham should then have been a frequent President of a body which often met in his own monastery.[1] But after 1336 Durham monks still continued to be active and loyal members of the now unified chapter. As the records of the chapters in this later period are very incomplete, it is less clear how often the priors of Durham continued to attend chapters themselves and serve as Presidents. Although Robert Walworth was one of the three Presidents in 1387, most Durham priors in the later middle ages were obviously content to send capable official proctors to Northampton every three years. All the more interesting, therefore, is Wessington's personal appearance at two Provincial Chapters, those of 1423 and 1426, in the last of which years he was there as sole President. One of the beneficiaries of Wessington's activity at Northampton in these years is the modern historian, who is indebted to him for the fullest accounts that survive of the *acta* of a late medieval Provincial Chapter.[2] It is particularly intriguing to discover Durham monks playing a prominent role in the Benedictine reform movement of the 1420s, by all accounts the last serious attempt ever made by the medieval English Black Monks to put their houses in a degree of order by means of national legislation.

It is unlikely that Wessington had ever attended a Black Monk chapter at Northampton before his appearance there in 1423. During the last years of his life Prior Hemingburgh regularly made out letters of proxy to Thomas Rome, the warden of Durham College, Oxford.[3] In June 1417 Wessington followed his predecessor's example and sent Thomas Rome to Northampton on his behalf.[4] As yet there was no sign that the new prior was contemplating a personal visit to Northampton; but it may be significant that in 1420 he dispatched not only Rome but also his chancellor, John

---

[1] Pantin, *Chapters* I, 295–6.

[2] The acts of the assemblies of 1423 and 1426 are preserved in D.C.D., MSS. B. IV. 26 and B. IV. 25, into which volumes they were apparently copied directly from the official roll of the Chapter proceedings (Pantin, *Chapters* II, 152). The *acts* of 1423 and 1426 have been printed most recently and accurately by Pantin, *Chapters* II, 134–80.   [3] Reg. Parv. II, fo. 15; Bursar, 1414/15, Expense Necessarie.

[4] Reg. III, fo. 53.

Fishburn, to the chapter, and that the latter brought back with him to Durham a few notes of the proceedings.[1] Whatever his future intentions in 1420, Wessington can hardly have anticipated that within a year he would find himself in the company of perhaps the largest and most distinguished assembly of Benedictines known to the history of the English Order. The extraordinary meeting of the Black Monks convoked at Westminster in May 1421 by King Henry V was remarkable for many reasons, not least for the rapidity with which it was summoned.[2] As in the case of other Benedictine superiors, Wessington's personal attendance was desired; and he was asked to bring with him the heads of his dependent houses and two or three theologians. In fact, Wessington was accompanied by only four other Durham monks when he entered the Westminster chapter-house in May.[3] Even so, the expenses of Wessington's journey to London (well over £20) were still remembered at Durham twenty years later, and indeed the cost of an abbatial progress cannot have been the least of the reasons for the poor attendance by prelates at ordinary Provincial Chapters. It is impossible to know how active was the part played by Wessington in the lengthy debates at Westminster which followed the statement of the king's articles of reform; but it may be noted that, although there were no less than sixty prelates at the meeting, the prior of Durham was one of the select committee of six elected to represent the monks at the outset of the proceedings.[4] Another member of the committee, Abbot John Whethamstede of St Albans, was to bring this unusual episode in the history of the English Black Monks to a close by drawing up an alternative set of seven articles, more acceptable to monastic opinion. Enough is known of Wessington's own attitude to such matters as the 'esus carnium' and private chambers in the monastery to make it almost certain that he too must have associated himself with the general criticism of the rigours of the original royal articles.

The Provincial Chapter which assembled at Northampton in July 1423 was a smaller as well as a more conventional body than

---

[1] Reg. III, fo. 71; Bursar, 1420/21, Expense Necessarie. Cf. Pantin, *Chapters* II, 95–8.

[2] Reg. Parv. II, fo. 89v; Pantin, *Chapters* II, 106; and see Knowles, *Rel. Orders* II, 182–4.

[3] Loc. XXI, no. 20 (vi); Bursar, 1420/21, Expense Prioris; Sacrist, 1420/21; Feretrar, 1421/22. [4] Pantin, *Chapters* II, 107.

that which had met at Westminster two years earlier. John Whet-hamstede was absent in Italy and only fifteen monastic prelates attended the chapter. Prominent among these was Wessington himself, accompanied by two Durham monks, Thomas Rome and William Ebchester, both of whom were given official duties to perform during the course of the assembly. The chapter lasted for the three days of 5, 6 and 7 July, meeting in both morning and afternoon. Much of the business was purely formal, but towards the end of the first day Wessington was appointed a diffinitor and in this capacity helped to produce four reforming articles, largely directed against extravagance on the part of abbots and priors.[1] On the final morning of the chapter Wessington was nominated as one of the twelve diffinitors for the next meeting three years later; and a little later he received the supreme honour of election as President for 1426. For obvious reasons the choice of future President rarely fell on prelates *in absentia*. On his return to Durham in 1423 Wes-sington brought back with him a detailed account of the proceedings of the Provincial Chapter so that he might be able to observe the established forms when he came to preside three years later.

It was therefore only to be expected that the records of the Provincial Chapter of 1426 should bear a close resemblance to those of 1423: the extent of Wessington's personal influence lies concealed under the traditional formulas of the official *acta*. Never-theless, the Northampton Chapter of 1426 marks the climax of Wessington's activity as an English Benedictine, especially as his two co-Presidents did not appear and left sole authority to their junior colleague. When the chapter began, as usual, on the first Monday of July, Wessington had with him a train of Durham monks worthy of the occasion. John Fishburn, the Durham chancellor, was the President's scribe during the course of the meeting and hence responsible for the production of the official record of the assembly. Thomas Nesbitt, the prior's monk chaplain, and two young fellows of Durham College, Oxford, Thomas Forster and John Birtley, were appointed door-keepers by Wessington early on the Monday morning. William Dalton and John Mody, both notable 'university monks', led the initial religious service, while William Ebchester, warden of Durham College, was present in his own right, preaching

[1] Pantin, *Chapters* II, 145, 154–5.

in Latin and helping to elect the future Presidents.[1] Such a company of attendant monks was not unusual and symbolised the President's formal authority during the three days of the chapter. Nor was this authority purely formal, for although most of the President's functions were delegated to committees, it was he who nominated the diffinitors, electors and auditors, he who received petitions from inside and outside the Order, and he who decided what documents should be included in the chapter's register of acts. At a Provincial Chapter attended by only seven prelates other than Wessington himself, it is no doubt legitimate to link the name of the President with the measures enacted there.

Wessington's presidency of 1426 obviously coincided with an attempt to consolidate and strengthen the machinery of the Black Monk Chapters, no doubt in reaction to the royal criticism of 1421 and in indirect response to the Conciliar Movement. Of the thirteen diffinitions approved by Wessington on the third and last day of the chapter, several were directed against laxity in monastic dress and discipline. The most significant and original of the thirteen articles, however, were those designed to enhance the powers of the national Benedictine organisation. The third diffinition, for example, encouraged the personal appearance of prelates by exempting those who attended from the payment of a third of their monastery's financial contribution.[2] The fourth article proposed that henceforward one President should come from the east, the second from the west and the third from the north of England. A more radical suggestion was a scheme for co-operative study, by monks nominated by the Presidents, of the major problems of the '*esus carnium*' and the '*recepcio pecuniarum*', followed by a united monastic appeal to Rome for a general dispensation. The sixth article made provision for a permanent register of chapter acts, the twelfth for a common Benedictine chest, and the thirteenth for the transmission of central diffinitions to individual monasteries by means of their proctors to Northampton. Not all of these measures were innovations,[3] but in the context of 1426 they provide clear evidence of the diffinitors' determination to regularise and increase the

[1] Ibid., pp. 157–9, 168, 173, 179.
[2] Ibid., p. 176 (cf. p. 218); Bursar, 1424/25, 1427/28, Contribuciones.
[3] Pantin, *Chapters* I, 131.

authority of the Provincial Chapter. This attitude Wessington presumably shared and it is noticeable that, as President, he criticised the irregular meat-eating of 'university monks' at Canterbury College, Oxford. Christ Church Priory, and so presumably its dependencies, had been legally exempted from control by the Benedictine Chapters since 1379, but Wessington was apparently determined that the external monk-lodgers at Canterbury College should not evade the rules common to all other English Benedictines.[1]

All in all, the enactments of the Provincial Chapter of 1426, even more than the longer and more general recodification of the Benedictine statutes in 1444,[2] reflect hopes of central direction and a new initiative from the Presidents of the Order. These hopes were to remain largely unfulfilled. The failure of the English Black Monk Chapters to develop into an active agency of radical reform is perhaps partly due to Wessington's own desertion of the cause. Like most Benedictine prelates who appeared once or twice at the Provincial Chapters, he was later content to retire from the national scene and confine himself to the welfare of his own monastery. Wessington never returned to Northampton after 1426 despite his continued tenure of the presidency: he was still President in January 1435, so must have been re-elected at the chapters of 1429 and 1432. But by this time Wessington had reverted to the traditional practice of sending to represent him at Provincial Chapters his most eminent university graduate, William Ebchester in 1429, 1432, 1435, 1438 and 1441, to be followed in 1444 by John Burnby who served Prior Ebchester in the same capacity in 1447 and 1450.[3] Ebchester and Burnby, like later Durham proctors to the Provincial Chapters who became priors of Durham (Richard Bell, Robert Ebchester, Thomas Castell and Hugh Whitehead), helped to make each chapter primarily an assembly of able young graduates rather than of elderly prelates.

One of the reasons for Wessington's abandonment of central Benedictine politics after 1426 may have been his conviction that

---

[1] Pantin, *Chapters* II, 173. Cf. Pantin, 'The General and Provincial Chapters of the English Black Monks, 1215–1540', *T.R.H.S.*, Fourth Series, X (1927), 223.

[2] Pantin, *Chapters* II, 183–220.

[3] Reg. Parv. II, fos. 76, 186; Reg. III, fos. 223, 305, supplementing the table of proctors in Pantin, *Chapters* III, 212–15.

excellent leadership would henceforward be provided by his younger and more brilliant colleague, John Whethamstede, abbot of St Albans from 1427 to 1440 and 1451 to 1465. Although the reasons for Whethamstede's high reputation inside and outside his Order have often puzzled modern historians,[1] there is no doubt that the Durham prior shared in the widespread admiration for the abbot's ability. Wessington must have left Oxford University before Whethamstede's arrival there, but it is known that he attended the funeral of the latter's uncle at Tynemouth and that the two had met at Westminster in 1421.[2] Relations between the two prelates remained cordial thereafter, as is revealed by their intercourse in 1426. In that year Whethamstede, who had lately returned from the Council of Pavia-Siena, visited the dependencies of St Albans and arrived at Tynemouth in June. Here he showed a pleasing respect for northern traditions by rebuking the monks for making the Feast of the Deposition of Saint Cuthbert an excuse for a holiday; henceforth they were ordered to observe this festival as carefully as St Albans herself observed the martyrdom of Saint Thomas Becket.[3] After his visitation, Whethamstede began taking oaths of homage from the local tenants but was called away to the Northampton Chapter 'sooner than he had planned' by the prior of Durham.[4] The two prelates presumably travelled south together, and at the chapter Wessington attempted to avoid the responsibility of sole presidency by associating Whethamstede with him. Although the abbot refused outright to countenance this irregular proposal, the incident is revealing for its comment on Wessington's attitude towards the abbot of St Albans.[5] However, Whethamstede was elected a future President in 1426, and so from at least 1429 until 1435 was the prior's colleague in office. There is no doubt as to which of the two men really directed the Benedictine organisation during these years. An extraordinary visitor of Abingdon and Saint

[1] See Knowles, *Rel. Orders* II, 184, 193–7.
[2] For the verses written by Whethamstede in memory of John Macrell of Tyne-mouth, see *Annales J. Amundesham* (Rolls Series, 1870–71), I, 220–1.
[3] Ibid., p. 214.
[4] Jesus College, Oxford, MS. 77, fos. 65–6; cf. *History of Northumberland* VIII (Newcastle-upon-Tyne, 1907), 102.
[5] Pantin, *Chapters* II, 159–60. Wessington's intention was that Whethamstede should act as President on a commission from the absent prior of Worcester.

Augustine's, Canterbury, and the only President in attendance at the 1429 Chapter, Whethamstede appointed the Oxford *prior studentium*, assigned contributions to the new Divinity Schools, and arranged for the English Benedictines' representation at Rome and Basle.[1] During this period, St Albans became the standard model in matters of monastic dress, discipline and privileges, a model studiously emulated by the monks of Durham.

In the last resort, both Wessington and Whethamstede failed to make of the Benedictine Chapter and Presidency an agency of more than occasional co-operation. Combination for the common good appears to have been in practice largely restricted to action in the university. It is significant that by far the largest part of the Provincial Chapters' income from monastic contributions was devoted to the upkeep of Gloucester College, Oxford, and the expenses of the *prior studentium* there.[2] The Durham monks, with their own college at Oxford and their refusal to accept the jurisdiction of the *prior studentium*, would appear to have had little to gain from such expenditure. It is therefore a tribute to their loyalty to the English Benedictine organisation that they contributed so regularly to the triennial levy. Unlike some large monasteries, notably Westminster, Durham rarely fell into arrears in the payment of her financial contributions to the Provincial Chapter. It must be admitted that these impositions did not place an undue strain on the convent's resources for Durham had been fortunate in her assessment for contributions. The Benedictine valuation, although not identical with that of the royal exchequer, was obviously related to it, and the priory of Durham had therefore profited by the large reduction in the royal assessment between 1291 and the *Nova Taxatio* of 1318.[3] The Provincial Chapter's register of taxation valued Durham at only £435 per annum; in practice, at the usual rate charged throughout Wessington's priorate (a penny in the mark), the convent was asked to pay £8 3s. 1½d. every three years. Of the twenty wealthiest

---

[1] Pantin, *Chapters* II, 174, 182–3; III, 102–5.

[2] Ibid., III, 160–94.

[3] See above, p. 176. The origins of the Benedictine *Registrum Taxacionis* (which survives in four Durham manuscripts) are obscure; this valuation was probably one of the products of the reforms of 1336 and was certainly established by 1360 (Pantin, *Chapters* II, 167–8; III, 141; see Pantin, 'The General and Provincial Chapters of the English Black Monks, 1215–1540', p. 236).

Benedictine houses, only the priory of Worcester paid less.[1] At Durham the bursar was responsible for the raising of the entire contribution whereas at many other houses this duty was divided among several obedientiaries. The bursar's rolls also reveal that the priors of Durham usually paid their contribution in one lump sum at the end of the triennium and it seems likely that the money was often taken south to Northampton by the official proctor.[2]

One of the most important functions of the Provincial Chapter was the appointment of visitors for the next three years. Prior Wessington, with his chapter, like all other Benedictine prelates, was subject to regular visitation by members of his Order and he was himself twice elected as a visitor. For the purposes of the Benedictine visitation machinery the dioceses of Durham and York were treated as a single unit. As there were only five independent Black Monk houses in the York province and one of these, Monk Bretton Priory, was apparently too small to provide a visitor, the work of visitation was undertaken in turn by four prelates. Thus the prior of Durham visited in 1413, the abbot of Saint Mary's, York, in 1417, the abbot of Whitby in 1420, the abbot of Selby in 1423; a second cycle began in 1426 when the prior of Durham was visitor again, and there then followed visitations by the prelates of York (1429), Whitby (1432), Selby (1435), Durham (1438), York (1441), Whitby (1444), Selby (1447) and Durham (1450).[3] It was the normal practice for the Durham visitor to call at the four Yorkshire houses on the way south to the Provincial Chapter. For example, in 1426 Wessington proposed to travel via Whitby (3 June), York (6 June), Selby (8 June) and Monk Bretton (11 June) in order to arrive at Northampton in good time to preside at the Chapter.[4]

Durham itself was subject to ten ordinary Benedictine triennial

---

[1] B.M., Additional MS. 6162, fos. 34v–35v; Pantin, *Chapters* III, 141, 157–9.

[2] Bursar, 1424/25, 1427/28, 1432/33, 1437/38, 1440/41, 1443/44, Contribuciones. The Durham bursar's rolls can be used to supplement and correct the table of contributions constructed by Dr Pantin (*Chapters* III, 258). Thus the rate of taxation in the late 1430s was 1*d.* and not 3*d.* in the mark.

[3] Cellarer, 1429; Reg. III, fos. 188–9; Pantin, *Chapters* III, 238–43. The years given above are those of actual visitation, a few weeks before the Provincial Chapter *succeeding* that in which the visitors had been formally elected. The visitor's own monastery did not itself escape visitation, generally by a prelate from the province of Canterbury (*Chapters* II, 148, 169).

[4] Reg. III, fos. 32v–33; Pantin, *Chapters* III, 240–1.

visitations during Wessington's priorate. These occasions have left little trace in the monastic records except for a few formal citations and certificates and an occasional reference to the entertainment of the visitors by the convent.[1] It is true that at the end of the fourteenth century two monks from Saint Mary's, York, had found the religious life of the Durham monastery in urgent need of reform. But in July 1426 the abbot of Bardney reported that on his personal visitation of Durham, 'he had found no *comperta* or *detecta* whatsoever, all the monks living of one accord in peace and charity'.[2] Although it would be over cynical to discount this verdict entirely, it seems probable that the Benedictine visitation in fifteenth-century England was often an occasion for social intercourse rather than an instrument of effective discipline. After one visitation Abbot William Pygot of Selby thanked Wessington for the '*hilaritas magnifica*' he had enjoyed at Durham.[3] Even if the system of triennial visitations may have acted as a salutary check on monastic life in some religious houses, there is no evidence that it seriously disturbed or altered domestic arrangements at Durham.

Regularity of routine may be a symptom of strength rather than weakness in any organisation; but the historian is unable to make any accurate assessment of a system whose records consist largely of letters of proxy, citations, and other formal documents. Perhaps it may be said of the Benedictine Provincial Chapter in the early fifteenth century that it encouraged a corporate sense among many English monks out of proportion to its effectiveness as a force directed towards specific aims. The constitutions of Benedict XII had been successful in drawing approximately 150 English Black Monks to Northampton every three years; but it was apparently with an emotional ideal rather than a programme for action that they returned to their houses. Such an ideal is well expressed in a moving letter written to Wessington on 12 May 1444 by the elderly abbot of Glastonbury, Nicholas Frome, who compared the last judgement to a *capitulum generale* in which Christ would be principal President and the Holy Fathers would act as diffinitors.[4]

[1] E.g. Cellarer, 1429, 1431.
[2] Reg. Parv. II, fo. 33; Pantin, *Chapters* II, 166; III, 82–4.
[3] Loc. xxv, no. 74.
[4] Reg. Parv. II, fo. 186; *Scrip. Tres*, pp. ccccxlv–ccccxlvi.

Both the melancholic content and the allegoric style of Frome's letter are highly reminiscent of the contemporary obituary rolls which provide us with a final and evocative example of intercourse between the church of Durham and other English monasteries. The object of the obituary roll or 'mortuary brief' was to procure for the soul of a dead monk the prayers of members of other religious communities.[1] The fifteenth-century Durham records are particularly rich in references to a flourishing traffic in these '*supplicaciones suffragiorum*'. The precentor was responsible for the production of an appropriate 'lamentation' and illuminated heading, while the roll itself was carried from monastery to monastery by a professional *breviator*, usually paid a regular stipend of four shillings per annum.[2] Some of the Durham obituary rolls undoubtedly circulated very widely indeed and one *breviator* is known to have visited no less than 639 houses in the mid-1460s.[3] Brief-bearers from other monasteries regularly visited Durham, and the popularity of the system naturally rested on mutual good-will and a sense of monastic companionship in the face of the hereafter. Raine's assertion that the obituary rolls 'had degenerated into little more than a form, complied with in a careless way' is certainly too severe. For members of religious orders the obituary roll was no doubt the equivalent of the chantry foundations made so enthusiastically by their secular contemporaries. At the very least the priors and monks of Durham were eager to be assured of temporary remembrance in the prayers of brethren other than their own.

[1] See N. R. Ker, 'Mortuary Briefs', Worcestershire Historical Society, *Miscellany I* (1960), 53–9; and, for a particularly famous and late example, probably decorated by Holbein, W. H. St John Hope, 'The Obituary Roll of John Islip, Abbot of Westminster', *Vetusta Monumenta* VII, part iv (Soc. of Antiquaries, 1906).

[2] Almoner, 1419/20, 1423/24; Reg. III, fos. 51, 58v, 60; Loc. I, nos. 14–17. Cf. the similar systems employed at the priories of Worcester and Christ Church, Canterbury: *Compotus Rolls of the priory of Worcester*, ed. S. G. Hamilton (Worcestershire Historical Society, 1910), p. 49; C. E. Woodruff, 'Notes on the inner life and domestic economy of the priory of Christ Church in the fifteenth century', *Archaeologia Cantiana* LIII (1940), 14–15.

[3] See D.C.D., MS. B. IV. 48, the celebrated Durham obituary roll printed by Raine in *Dur. Obit. Rolls*, pp. 1–44.

Chapter 8

THE MONASTIC ECONOMY

'Wherever you see a big cathedral', Ernest said, 'it's grain country.'[1]

The late medieval monastery of Durham presents us with the familiar historical problem of an extremely wealthy religious corporation whose financial situation was nevertheless always a cause for concern and often for alarm. Shortly before the Dissolution, Durham's annual gross income was estimated at over £1,572, a figure surpassed by only fourteen English religious houses. The church of Saint Cuthbert was then the richest cathedral priory in the kingdom except for Christ Church, Canterbury, and Saint Swithun's, Winchester.[2] A century earlier the yearly revenues of the mother house at Durham, quite apart from those enjoyed by her monks in the nine dependencies, were in the order of £2,000. North of the Tees such an income could only be matched by that of the bishop of Durham himself. The opulence of the monks of Durham, already legendary at the date when the author of the *Rites of Durham* set down his nostalgic reminiscences, was proverbial in their own time: in the early fourteenth century the pope was informed that it was their wealth which had driven the prior and chapter so mad that they would obey neither bishop nor archdeacon. In the north of England at least, critics of the disproportionate affluence enjoyed by the monastic 'possessioners, that mowen lyve,/Thanked be God, in wele and habundaunce' did not have far to look: it is hardly surprising that in 1410 a group of Lollard knights allegedly proposed the secularisation of the wealth of the convent as well as the bishop of Durham.[3]

For the monks of Durham themselves the realities of their financial position seemed very different. The fifteenth century

[1] A. E. Hotchner, *Papa Hemingway* (London, 1968), p. 114.
[2] A. Savine, *English Monasteries on the Eve of the Dissolution* (Oxford Studies in Social and Legal History, I, 1909), pp. 270–88; Knowles, *Rel. Orders* III, 473.
[3] *Scrip. Tres*, pp. 103–4; Chaucer, *Summoner's Tale*, 1722–3 (*Works of Geoffrey Chaucer*, ed. Robinson, p. 94); *The St Albans Chronicle, 1406–20*, ed. V. H. Galbraith (Oxford, 1937), p. 53.

opened with the gloomy plea (put forward in 1405) that 'the goods, rents and income of the said monastery have been so notoriously wasted and diminished that they no longer suffice to pay the usual debts and support the convent in all its necessities'. Over sixty years and many such lamentations later, the prior of Durham was still predicting 'that our monastery is likly within processe of tyme to be cast so ferr in dett that withoute the more speciall grace of Almighty God, supportacion also of you and other good frends of the said (papal) Courte, it shall noyt in many yeres here aftir be broght to as goode state as it was within thies few yeres'.[1] As in the case of individual fortunes or those of modern governments, it is never an easy matter to resolve the contradiction between apparent wealth and a sense of financial desperation on the part of the wealthy. Whether the Durham monks of the fifteenth century were as severely hampered by financial stringency as they themselves believed is an exceptionally difficult question. The following attempt to provide an answer is put forward with a considerable degree of diffidence and at the cost of much over-simplification. The survival of so many monastic obedientiary account rolls and indentures, supplemented by a vast range of material ranging from manorial rolls and halmote books to mines and stock accounts, reveals the complexities and intricacies of the Durham financial system in exceptional detail. Until a considerable proportion of these records appear in print, any attempt to produce a balanced picture of the monastic economy at late medieval Durham is bound to be premature. The intricacies of accounting and other financial procedures at the priory have rarely been completely comprehended by modern commentators. Even more sadly, the few extracts from the convent's accounts and inventories already published have often confused rather than clarified the main issues of Durham's financial organisation.[2]

---

[1] 4.6. Ebor., no. 2; Reg. Parv. III, fos. 139–40.

[2] As Professor Knowles has already remarked (*Rel. Orders* II, 315), the three volumes of printed selections from Durham's obedientiary rolls transcribed (often inaccurately) by Canon Fowler seventy years ago (*Dur. Acct. Rolls*) 'are of little use for economic or statistical purposes'. Much confusion, for instance, has been caused by Fowler's failure to distinguish between the bursar's gross receipts (which include previous arrears) and net receipts. Thus Professor Knowles himself was naturally led to compare the bursar's receipts as recorded in his 1292/3 and 1308/9

The reader of this chapter is faced with an even greater problem. The financial operations of the monastery of Durham in the early fifteenth century can only be made intelligible when placed within the context of the general economic histoɪy of northern England at the same period. As yet, that history remains completely unwritten. Although recent years have seen the appearance of a number of interesting and valuable studies of various aspects of the north-eastern economy during the two preceding centuries,[1] the fifteenth-century diocese of Durham is still a literal *terra incognita*. Although lip-service is often paid to the distinctiveness of the north-east and to the fact that in terms of human geography the Tees may be a more important boundary than the Tweed,[2] the regional economy of this area in the later middle ages remains profoundly mysterious. A close study of the priory records themselves does much to challenge some of the more familiar but unsubstantiated preconceptions on this subject, most notably the view that the county of Durham was primarily an area characterised by pastoral and mining activity. The countryside revealed to us by the priory accounts is one in which the plough was still very much the king. Nor, despite the undoubted economic problems of the early fifteenth century, is one completely convinced by that 'picture of universal desolation and decay', of northern primitivism and barbarity, so beloved by many writers.[3] To anticipate the tentative conclusions of this difficult

account rolls with those for a later period, despite the fact that the former were gross and the latter net totals. The effect has been a wildly misleading exaggeration of the decline of monastic revenues in the fourteenth century, worth mentioning because it has passed into general currency: see Knowles, *Rel. Orders* II, 317; E. Miller, *War in the North* (University of Hull Publications, 1960), p. 8; M. McKisack, *The Fourteenth Century* (Oxford, 1959), p. 329; *Cambridge Economic History of Europe* I (2nd edn, 1966), 704.

[1] E.g., E. M. Halcrow, 'The Decline of Demesne Farming on the Estates of Durham Cathedral Priory', *Econ. H.R.*, Second Series, VII (1955), 345–56, summarising part of her 'The Administration and Agrarian Policy of the Manors of Durham Cathedral Priory' (B. Litt., Oxford University, 1949); C. M. Fraser, 'The Pattern of Trade in the North-East of England, 1265–1350', *Northern History* IV (1969), 44–66; J. B. Blake, 'The Medieval Coal Trade of North East England: some Fourteenth-Century Evidence', *ibid.* II (1967), 1–26.

[2] A. E. Smailes, *North England* (London, 1960), p. 5.

[3] *V.C.H. Durham* II, 226–7. Frederick Bradshaw's discussion of the late medieval social and economic history of County Durham in this volume (pp. 209–29) is not without its merits, but relies too heavily on an over-impressionistic treatment of the convent's halmote records to be of real value.

enquiry immediately, the prevailing impression left by the sources we have is of severe adversity successfully faced and eventually surmounted by convent and tenant, landlord and villager, alike. In September 1446, after a particularly melancholy period in the monastery's fortunes, Prior Ebchester wrote to one of his monks at Lytham that the state of the priory '*non mediocriter est collapsus*'.[1] The severity of this 'collapse', caused as much by administrative as economic difficulties, led to the most radical financial re-organisation ever made at Durham – the division of the central office of bursar between three obedientiaries from 1438 to 1445. But it would be a mistake to think that this was a permanent crisis. Nothing is more remarkable than the resilience with which Durham Priory, like so many English religious houses, refused to accept economic defeat and retained so large a proportion of its wealth to the very end.

The essential preliminary to any attempt at the elucidation of the complex workings of the late medieval Durham financial system is the crucial distinction between the central receiving office administered by the bursar and the independent departments administered by individual obedientiaries. As the bursar's office, alternatively known as the *scaccarium prioris*, was the agency directly or indirectly responsible for the general provisioning and sustenance of the Durham monks as well as their prior, its operations were of immediate concern to every member of the community. The other accounting obedientiaries spent their revenues in the exercise of their much more specialised offices and had in any case much smaller incomes at their disposal. During Wessington's priorate it was estimated that whereas the net annual receipts of the bursar totalled £1,500, the combined annual income of the seven other major obedientiaries amounted to only £553 6s. 8d. In detail their respective receipts were valued as follows: the hostillar at £170; the almoner and chamberlain at £100 each; the sacrist and commoner at £66 13s. 4d. (100 marks) each; the feretrar at £30; and the terrar at only £20. Despite Professor Knowles's understandable fears that these figures 'seem too symmetrical to be trustworthy', comparison with the original account rolls of the period leaves little doubt as to their substantial accuracy as approximate estimates of the net annual

[1] Reg. Parv. III, fo. 2.

income of each obedientiary.[1] The only serious discrepancies occur in the cases of the sacrist and commoner, the first of whom usually received at least £80 and the second £90 rather than the £66 13s. 4d. with which they are both credited in the estimate.[2] The receipts of the master of the infirmary were omitted altogether from the monastic valuation, no doubt because of their insignificance: food and drink for monks living in the infirmary were provided by the bursar and cellarer, and its master's income averaged only £6 per annum during Wessington's priorate.[3] The cellarer and granator were similarly omitted from these calculations for the very different reason that, as will be seen, they enjoyed no independent income but were supplied directly from the bursar's office. Also neglected in this rough estimate of the convent's receipts were those minor and irregular sources of income administered by monks specially appointed by the prior, who often used these revenues as a reserve fund to meet extraordinary expenditure on building or litigation. Three such separate funds can be regularly distinguished during Wessington's priorate: profits from the sale of coal dug from pits retained in the prior's possession: issues from woods, parks and forests: and annual contributions from Durham's cells and obedi-ences.[4] But the total net income from all three sources rarely seems to have exceeded £100 per annum; and neither here nor elsewhere is there much likelihood that the convent enjoyed large sources of income completely unmentioned in the surviving records.

Although overshadowed by the great sums at the disposal of the bursar, the revenues handled by the other accounting obedientiaries comprised over a quarter of the total monastic income and can hardly be completely ignored even in a brief survey of the convent's financial situation. Needless to say, each office had its own account-ing problems as well as responsibilities. The control of individual obedientiaries over their sources of revenue was in theory very con-siderable indeed. In practice, however, the discretion enjoyed by any office-holder was severely limited by the fixed nature of most of his income and expenditure, and by the obligation to produce accounts

---

[1] Reg. II, fo. 357, printed in *Scrip. Tres*, p. ccli; Knowles, *Rel. Orders* II, 316.
[2] However, only four commoner's accounts (two badly damaged) survive before 1453, and this is the obedientiary about whose finances least can be known.
[3] Infirmarer, 1416–46.
[4] Mines Accts; Loc. XXVII, no. 15, memb. 3; see below, pp. 307–9.

for audit at the convent's annual chapter in June. The format as well as the contents of the surviving monastic account rolls changed so little during decades and even centuries that they are themselves the best tribute to the extraordinary conservatism and rigidity of Durham's accounting organisation. Such rigidity, moreover, although it has often been maligned, had the great practical advantage of insulating the convent from the personal mismanagement of a particular monk and preventing an extraordinarily complicated system from falling into complete incoherence. Each officer accounted annually in the conventional and stereotyped Durham form, by which the so-called remainder (if any), previous arrears, and current receipts were set off against the so-called surplus (if any) and current expenses, with allowances made at the foot of the roll for arrears, wastes and decays. The accounting principles at issue here will be considered in more detail in the case of the Durham bursar, the business methods of whose office were different in degree rather than in kind from those of the other obedientiaries. The bulk of the income of the sacrist, almoner, chamberlain and the others consisted of assized rents from landed property in the north of England together with tithes from appropriated churches long ago assigned to their use. By modern standards, there were many unnecessary complications in the system, including a series of cross-payments (often fictitious) from one obedientiary to another. Each office tended to run into debt on occasion, but the amount of money handled was in no case exceptionally large and it does not appear to have been too difficult for a reasonably conscientious Durham monk to keep his obedience in a fairly competent state.[1] Overhead charges were, however, always considerable, and approximately a third of the expenses of all obedientiaries consisted of payments to their rent-collectors and servants, repairs to property and other management costs. Not much more than half of any obedientiary's net income was devoted specifically to those activities for which the office had been created, whether the upkeep of the church in the case of the sacrist or the provision of clothing in the case of the chamberlain.[2]

---

[1] This was expressly declared to have been the case in one of Bishop Walter Skirlaw's visitations (Loc. XXI, no. 20, ii).

[2] These conclusions are based on a study of surviving obedientiary rolls from the first half of the fifteenth century. It need hardly be said that the monks themselves

To these generalisations there was one important exception, the monastic terrar or *terrarius*, in the unique position of having virtually no financial commitments within the monastery at all. As the special position of the terrar within the monastic administration has caused much confusion in the past, it may be as well to point out immediately that this was an office which changed its character radically on several occasions during its history. Although perhaps not one of the oldest Durham obediences, like those of the sacrist, hostillar, chamberlain, almoner and cellarer (all of which were in existence by the end of the twelfth century), the office of terrar had emerged by at least the 1230s, when its holder was clearly an important and influential land-agent on behalf of the prior.[1] The creation a generation later of a systematised central receiving office or bursary imposed upon the terrar the more specific role of being the bursar's roving emissary, responsible for the collection of revenues which appeared not on his own but the bursar's accounts. Throughout the later middle ages these two officers were therefore colleagues and not rivals. In the words of a Durham chapter diffinition of the early 1320s, '*unus sit Terrarius qui ... equitat sine superfluis expensis: et sit alius Bursarius residens ad Scaccarium*'. In itself this division of functions between itinerant terrar and resident bursar was quite logical and finds close parallels elsewhere, notably in the relationship between the foreign monk-seneschal and treasurer at the cathedral priory of Ely.[2] However by the mid-fourteenth century, the bursar too was in the habit of leaving the monastery for long periods to preside over meetings of the halmote courts with the terrar and to supervise manorial and agricultural policy on the convent's estates: at this period it becomes almost impossible to make an intelligible distinction between the administrative spheres of the

never attempted to distinguish between administrative costs and other expenses: the sections of the rolls entitled *Expense Varie* and *Expense Necessarie* include items of an extraordinarily miscellaneous kind. For an excellent general survey of the financial problems raised by the late medieval obedientiary system, much of it completely applicable to Durham, see Professor C. N. L. Brooke's introduction to *The Book of William Morton, Almoner of Peterborough Monastery, 1448–1467* (Northants. Record Soc. XVI, 1954).

[1] *Scrip. Tres*, p. xl; cf. *Durham Annals*, pp. 35, 107, 195; Scammell, *Hugh du Puiset*, p. 94.

[2] Loc. XXVII, no. 16; *Ely Chapter Ordinances and Visitation Records, 1241–1515*, ed. Evans, pp. xii–xiii, 24–8.

two officials.[1] Yet another change in the terrar's duties was to be brought about by the almost universal leasing of the convent's manorial demesnes at the beginning of the fifteenth century, a development which relieved him of many of his previous responsibilities in the field of estate management. Although the terrar continued to work closely with bursar and prior's lay steward on the business of assigning and collecting rents, there is no doubt that his office had now been deprived of much of its original *raison d'être*. It was for this reason, and also because the small income he now enjoyed in his own right had been assigned merely to enable him to perform administrative duties on behalf of the bursar, that it became common practice for the fifteenth-century terrar to hold the office of hostillar as well.

There remains for much more detailed consideration the convent's central and most important financial department, the Durham bursary or *officium bursariatus*. Although the author of the *Rites of Durham* misled later historians by his belief that the bursar's duty 'was to Receave all the Rentes that was perteyning to the house', his error was not unnatural in view of the prominence of this officer.[2] The Durham bursar received well over two-thirds of the total money income of the monastery. His financial position did not change essentially between 1300 and the Dissolution; and the continued importance of the bursar's office for 250 years is a tribute to the success of the thirteenth-century monastic reformers in centralising at least the greater part of the receipt of revenues in the hands of one obedientiary. The institution of the Durham bursar is, of course, to be placed within the context of similar developments in almost all large English Benedictine houses during the late thirteenth century. In the south of England the reform was most strongly sponsored by Archbishop Pecham (1279–92), whose ideal of complete centralisation of monastic revenues was, however, often to be modified in practice as a result of the reluctance of prelates and

---

[1] *Halmota Prioratus Dunelmensis, 1296–1384* (Surtees Soc. LXXXII, 1889), pp. 36, 70, 78, 80, etc.; Halmote Court Roll, 1420; Halmote Court Book, 1400–39, fo. 105v; Terrar, 1401/02; Halcrow, 'The Administration and Agrarian Policy of the Manors of Durham Cathedral Priory', pp. 3–12.

[2] *Rites*, p. 99. The error was followed by James Raine who described the Durham bursar's rolls as 'embodying the whole proceedings of the monastery in a summary way': *The Durham Household Book* (Surtees Soc. XVIII, 1844), p. ix.

obedientiaries to relinquish all their separate endowments.[1] At Durham the strongest pressure towards financial centralisation seems to have emanated less from a reforming bishop than from the northern General Chapters of the Black Monks. By the 1280s the Benedictines of the province of York had officially come round to the view that the provisioning of their monasteries should be the work of a triumvirate of bursar, cellarer and granator; at a meeting in Durham in 1276, they had already specifically decreed that 'a bursar should be appointed at Selby to account for the receipts of that house'.[2] Durham Priory had apparently established its own bursar's office only a few years earlier. This officer had not been mentioned among the major obedientiaries of the house (the sacrist, chamberlain, hostillar, almoner and terrar) in chapter ordinances of 1235 and 1252, and seems to have made his first recorded appearance in 1265 when Prior Hugh of Darlington required him to deliver money to the *custodes communae*.[3] During the following years references to the bursar in the Durham chronicles are sufficiently frequent to make it clear that he had taken up a crucial role in the monastic administration. The first surviving bursar's account roll (1278–9) shows that the main outlines of the system to be followed for the next two and a half centuries were already in being.

Of all the many ways in which English monasteries of the late thirteenth century reacted to the legal obligation and economic need for a more centralised financial system, the method adopted at Durham was in some ways the least logical. As we have seen, the concentration of funds in the hands of a principal treasurer or bursar stopped well short of the complete centralisation adopted at Christ Church, Canterbury. On the other hand, the decision to entrust the Durham bursar with the sustenance of the prior as well as the general provisioning of the entire community inevitably placed him in an ambiguous position. To a modern accountant the practice adopted at Norwich Cathedral Priory whereby the two offices of the prior's *camera* and the monastic cellarer were quite distinct – both handling approximately £700 per annum in the late fourteenth

---

[1] R. A. L. Smith, 'The *Regimen Scaccarii* in the English Monasteries', *T.R.H.S.*, Fourth Series, XXIV (1942), 73–94; Snape, *English Monastic Finances*, p. 42.

[2] Pantin, *Chapters* I, 226, 238, 251.

[3] *Scrip. Tres*, pp. xl, xlvii–xlix, 70, 72; *Durham Annals*, p. 66; Bursar, 1278/79; *Dur. Acct. Rolls* II, 484–9.

century – would seem much less likely to cause confusion.[1] However, the financial organisation developed at Durham Priory was apparently common enough in other late medieval English monasteries. Despite the valuable work by R. H. Snape, R. A. L. Smith and many others, this whole subject cries out for thorough reassessment. The important factor was less, as is too often assumed, the introduction of a central bursar, receiver or treasurer into a particular house than the exact proportion of the total monastic revenues which was assigned to him. Not surprisingly, the closest analogies to the Durham bursar seem to be found in other northern English Black Monk houses. The almost complete destruction of the financial records of Saint Mary's, York, and Whitby makes it difficult to generalise with any confidence in these two cases; but at Selby Abbey the bursar held a very similar position to his counterpart at Durham, receiving £547 out of a total monastic income of £730 at the time of the Dissolution.[2] At Selby, and even more at Durham, it can be readily imagined that one of the greatest practical disadvantages of such a system was that it threw a quite extraordinary degree of financial responsibility on the shoulders of one monk, the bursar himself. When Prior Wessington asked various members of his community to take up the office in 1438, they replied that they would rather be imprisoned or leave Durham completely for a more rigorous religious order.[3]

The vast range of the bursar's financial obligations is indeed the first impression to be gained from his great account rolls, without any doubt the source by which the economic fortunes of the convent in the later middle ages can be best assessed. This was certainly the opinion of the Durham monks themselves: despite the fact that the bursar's rolls did not provide a complete record of the monastery's income, the prior and chapter habitually disregarded the revenues of the separately endowed obedientiaries when attempting to estimate the *status monasterii*. It was the usual, if somewhat misleading, prac-

---

[1] W. Hudson, 'The Camera Roll of the Prior of Norwich in 1283', *Norfolk and Norwich Archaeological Society* XIX, 272–3.

[2] Archbishop's House, Westminster, Se/Ac/9 (Selby Bursar's Account, 1416/17); East Riding of Yorkshire Record Office, Beverley, DDLO/20, nos. 1, 4 (Selby Bursar's Accounts, 1431/32, 1479/80); *Valor Ecclesiasticus* v, 12–14; cf. *Cartularium Abbathiae de Whiteby* II (Surtees Soc. LXXII, 1881), pp. 553–85, 600–25.

[3] Loc. XXI, no. 20 (vi).

tice of the priors of Durham to respond to the Benedictine statutes requiring the presentation of an annual *status* or *ratiocinatio* of their convent by the delivery of the bursar's roll alone.[1] Similarly, the long inventories 'of the movable and immovable goods of the Durham priorate' produced on the succession of a new prior were based completely on the bursar's annual account rolls, of which they are essentially only a more formal and simplified version. The great inventories of 1446 and 1464, which provide a much more adequate guide to the monastic economy at Durham than any other documents in print, omit mention of the goods and revenues of all obedientiaries except the bursar.[2]

The bursar's annual account rolls themselves, highly stereotyped in form, are among the longest non-governmental accounts ever produced in medieval England. Although an example of a paper roll survives from as early as 1435/6, they were usually written on both sides of five or six membranes of parchment, stitched together head to tail in Chancery fashion. Despite their length, large sections of the rolls were severely condensed versions of an elaborate substructure of subsidiary accounts (*doggeta*), surveys, rentals, tallies and indentures. The accounting year normally ran from one Whitsuntide to the next, so that shortly after its completion each *compotus* could be examined by specially appointed monks who reported their findings to the convent's annual chapter in June. Although it is unusual for more than one to survive, three copies of the roll were made, one for retention by the prior, one by the sub-prior and one by the bursar himself. The evidence of later additions, emendations and interlineations to these rolls leaves no doubt that they were subjected to much more detailed scrutiny than the accounts of other obedientiaries.[3] Little can be known of the number and names of the monastic auditors, but the chancellor, not unnaturally, often seems to have been one of their number: in 1442 Robert Westmorland was described as '*super visu et auditu compotorum magis ceteris est circumspectus*'.[4] Although the Durham monks never evolved a formalised permanent committee of financial experts like the

---

[1] Pantin, *Chapters* II, 111, 117, 122, 127, 230.

[2] The 1446 inventory (Loc. XIII, no. 22) is printed in full in *Scrip. Tres*, pp. cclxxxv–cccviii, and that of 1464 (Loc. XVIII, no. 110) in *Feodarium Dunelm.*, pp. 98–211.

[3] The detailed queries arising from the examination of Bursar, 1445/46, survive as Loc. XXI, no. 20 (i).   [4] Loc. XXI, no. 20 (v).

seniores ad scaccarium at Christ Church, Canterbury, there is no doubt that they followed the activities of the bursar's office with intense and critical interest. And as annual bursar's accounts survive for all but two (1417/18 and either 1429/30 or 1430/31) of the years of Wessington's priorate, it need hardly be said that the financial operations of the convent during this period may be studied in enormous and often bewildering detail. The following can only be a highly simplified account of a very complex economic system.

The main features of the monastic economy at Durham emerge most rapidly and intelligibly from an analysis, first of the bursar's expenditure, and secondly of the sources of his income. Between 1416 and the autumn of 1438 (when the bursar's office was divided between three monks), the *summa omnium expensarum* recorded in the bursar's annual accounts averaged £1,400, the highest total being that for 1433–4 (£1,694) and the lowest that for 1423–4 (£1,333). However, the first item of expenditure on the accounts was always the *superplusagia*, that is the surplus of expenses over receipts carried over from the previous year's roll. This was a considerable sum, which might be as high as £199 (as in 1427–8) and averaged only a little less than £100 throughout the period. Far from forming 'a mass of floating capital', as has sometimes been suggested,[1] this surplus must be deducted from the total to arrive at an accurate estimate of the bursar's real expenditure, an average of about £1,300 per annum. Besides the *superplusagia*, there were normally twenty-two other headings of expenditure, the contents of which may be briefly summarised by reference to the typical account for 1422–3. Expenses in the category of *Garderoba* amounted to £52 13s. 9d. and consisted largely of payments for purchases of cloth in bulk from York merchants; some of this cloth was transferred to the chamberlain for conversion into monastic dress, but most went to provide liveries for the prior's and the convent's *generosi*, valets and grooms.[2] In 1422–3 the bursar spent almost £56 on buying red and white wine from merchants of Newcastle-upon-Tyne. Newcastle merchants were also the chief suppliers of *ferrum Hispanicum*, the most expensive item in the *Marescalcia* section of the

---

[1] E.g., Knowles, *Rel. Orders* II, 317.
[2] Individual obedientiaries were expected to provide liveries for their own servants except at times of a '*liberatura specialis*' (cf. *Rites*, pp. 144–7).

account, which also included horse-shoeing costs and totalled nearly £45. Fodder for the convent's horses cost the bursar almost £50 in 1422–3, and repairs to the prior's and bursar's property both within and without the abbey precincts came to slightly over £60. Payments to servants, counsellors, chantry chaplains, and legal proctors at Rome, London and York were divided into the three categories of soulsilver, pensions, and stipends: these amounted to not far short of £100 in all. The *Expense Necessarie*, a very lengthy and miscellaneous collection of items, totalled over £34 and included expenses incurred by the prior on his journeys through the country. Almost completely devoted to the prior's expenditure were the *Expense Prioris* (£11 9s. 11d.), *Elemosina Consueta* (£7 9s. 8d.) and *Dona et Exennia* (£8 5s. 3½d.), the items of which were usually paid on the superior's express order ('*per preceptum prioris*') either directly by the bursar or through the agency of the prior's chaplains. Over £25 was consumed in either the repayment of rents or in fixed allowances set against specific sources of receipt. In 1422–3 the bursar also paid almost £23 in '*Contribuciones*', levied in that year by the Benedictine Provincial Chapter and the Convocation of York.

The total of all these miscellaneous expenses, not including the previous year's 'surplus' of £150, came to slightly over £482 in 1422–3. Large as the sum is, it was greatly surpassed by the remaining items of expenditure recorded on the bursar's roll, namely the money delivered to the cellarer by indenture and that spent on the purchase of wheat, barley and malt, almost all of which was delivered to the granator. This financial dependence of the cellarer and granator on the bursar's office was almost complete, and is the central key to the operation of the Durham financial system throughout the later middle ages. Cellarer and granator were receiving heavy subsidies from the bursar as early as 1292,[1] and it will be seen that their financial subordination to this obedientiary was only removed for seven years in the history of the house, by Prior Wessington between 1438 and 1445. Except for this short period, the Durham cellarer had no independent income apart from negligible sums like the 11s. 1d. which he derived from assized rents in 1429–30.[2] The money

---

[1] Bursar, 1292/93; *Dur. Acct. Rolls* II, 493.
[2] Cellarer, 1429.

delivered from bursar to cellarer averaged £390 per annum between 1416 and 1443, although there was considerable variation from year to year depending on the current price of meat as well as the extent of the hospitality offered by the prior and chapter. The bursar normally made one large cash delivery each year, but was prepared to advance the cellarer a supplementary £100 in times of need.[1] Several of the indentures between cellarer and bursar survive to show that almost all this money was spent on '*Expense infra Coquinam*', that is the purchase of cattle, sheep and pigs (all bought at short notice and apparently slaughtered in the monastic precincts) as well as fish, poultry, eggs, spices, cheeses and butter. Animals received by the cellarer from the convent's own stock-farms were included as purchases in his indentures with the bursar. The cellarer's own accounts, on the other hand, were drawn up by weeks and months and give a very detailed impression of monastic consumption. Thus in a typical week (19 to 25 July 1432) there were eaten at Durham the carcases of 5 cattle, 22 sheep, 2 calves and 13 piglets as well as a cart-load of fish, 22 hens and 400 eggs.

Although equally dependent on the bursar, the granator differed from the cellarer in that he received not money but produce in kind. Examination of the bursar's accounts, the granator's accounts and the indentures between the two officers makes it clear that the granator never handled cash. In Wessington's priorate (except between 1438 and 1445), as at the Dissolution, the granator's office was purely 'to Receyve all the whet that came and all the malte corne, and to make accoumpte what malt was spente in the weeke, and whate malt corne was delyuered to the kilne and what was Receyved from the kylne and howe moch was spente in the house'.[2] Between 1416 and 1438 the granator normally accounted for about 370 quarters of wheat or rye each year as well as for up to 1,200 quarters of barley and other malt-corn. Now that the convent had adopted a policy of farming both their manorial demesnes and many of their tithes, the bursar was compelled to buy about four-fifths of the granator's grain supplies on the cash market, from a multitude of local villagers rather than from a few entrepreneurs.[3] Thus it was

---

[1] See, e.g., Cellarer, 1416/17, 1430/31.   [2] *Rites*, p. 100.
[3] Bursar and Granator's indentures, 1416/17, 1417/18, 1423-9, 1433/4. Throughout Wessington's priorate the bailiff of Pittington, still '*in manu domini*' when other

the Durham bursar, whose agents or 'cators' bought the grain, rather than the granator, who had to face the problem of fluctuating wheat and barley prices in County Durham. Between 1416 and 1438, the bursar's bill for grain delivered to the granator averaged a little less than £400 per annum. But in those periods, like the late 1430s, when the prices of wheat and barley rose above their usual levels, the monastic grain costs might rise to £450 or more a year.[1] Almost all the granator's supply of barley was malted, occasionally with an admixture of oats, at the convent's malt-kiln, apparently situated in the south-west corner of the monastic precinct. Similarly it was in the monastic granary, of which substantial remains survive on the south side of the abbey garth, that the wheat ground at the 'abbey mill' on the Wear was stored for baking into loaves at the convent's kitchen. As much as a quarter of the granator's annual stock of wheat might be delivered to servants of the monastery living outside the convent, at a normal rate of 2 bushels for every three weeks. On the generally accepted assumption that monastic corn liveries of this type (approximately 35 bushels of wheat a year) were expected to sustain a family of three or four, the priory clearly received enough corn to feed at least three hundred individuals throughout the year. Whereas the community's consumption of bread seems to have risen a little above its normal average of nine or ten quarters of wheat a week during the winter months of January and February, the monks and their servants evidently drank ale heavily and consistently throughout the year: few months passed without at least 100 quarters of grain being converted into malt.[2]

It can therefore be concluded that of the £1,300 or so annually spent by the bursar in the period between 1416 and 1438, rather more than a third was paid for grain delivered to the granator, rather less than a third transferred to the cellarer for the purchase of meat and other victuals, and the remaining forty per cent or so devoted to the bursar's other responsibilities. Needless to say, this

Durham manors had been put to farm, continued to dispatch grain to the granator (see, e.g., Pittington, 1427/8, for a delivery of 57 quarters of wheat to the granator by tally).

[1] Bursar, 1416–38, Empcio Frumenti, Empcio Ordei et Brasei.
[2] Granator, 1415–32; see *Rites*, pp. 100, 159, 281–2; cf. J. Z. Titow, *English Rural Society, 1200–1350* (London, 1969), pp. 82–3; H. S. Bennett, *Life on the English Manor, 1150–1400* (Cambridge, 1937), p. 95.

brief survey of the bursar's expenses has done less than full justice to the exceptionally valuable light thrown by the buying policy of the greatest bulk purchaser in northern England on the great variety of economic activity in the area. Here we can see in vivid detail such important features of the late medieval northern economy as the dominance of the Newcastle merchant in the importation of French wines or the frequent need to resort to London dealers for more luxurious items like *rumney* wine, cloves and ginger. The *Garderoba* sections of the Durham bursar's accounts are indeed among the best evidence we have for the startling rise in the late fifteenth century of the new West Riding woollen industry at the expense of the city of York's cloth merchants and drapers, the convent's main suppliers of clothing material during Wessington's priorate.[1]

From the standpoint of the monks of Durham, however, the main conclusion to be derived from a study of the bursar's expenditure is obvious enough. As buyers in cash of the whole range of consumer products available to the more prosperous members of late medieval English society, they were inevitably extremely sensitive to movements in prices. Here again the lack of any satisfactory collection of price data for northern England in the later middle ages, a collection which would need to draw heavily on Durham's own records, makes generalisation hazardous. However, although annual and indeed seasonal variations can easily confuse the picture, the copious information provided by Durham's obedientiary and manorial accounts leaves no reasonable doubt that the first half of the fifteenth century was a period of price stability rather than inflation. A few commodities did tend to increase in value during Wessington's priorate, but never to a very considerable extent. Much more significant is the way in which so many items, like French red wine (at approximately £3 a pipe), Spanish iron (at 8d. a stone), wax (at 6d. a pound), tallow (at 1s. a stone) and even boots (at 3s. 4d. a pair) and socks (at 2d. a pair), kept their price from year to year.[2] Although the monks of Durham may have occasionally profited from the advantages usually enjoyed by a bulk

---

[1] Bursar, 1404–79, Garderoba; *Dur. Acct. Rolls* III, 649–56; cf. *V.C.H. Yorkshire, City of York* (1961), p. 90.

[2] Figures derived from various series of Durham obedientiary accounts, especially those of the bursar, sacrist and hostillar.

purchaser and bought their goods at a slightly lower price than that offered to individual buyers, there is no evidence whatsoever that they regularly bought at an artificially low or high rate. Indeed a comparison of the prices recorded in the bursar's accounts with those paid in very different parts of the county by the heads of Durham cells or the reeves of the convent's manors makes it abundantly clear that the prior and chapter were absolutely at the mercy of general market factors in north-eastern England.

But it was, of course and for reasons already stated, to a rise in corn prices that the Durham bursar and the entire monastic community were most vulnerable. During the fifteenth century, when the Durham monks spent much more on the purchase of grain than they received by its sale at the manorial and village level, they had a vested interest in low cereal prices. On the whole it is hard to resist the conclusion that they were generally fortunate. Corn prices in County Durham fluctuated widely from year to year in a manner only too familiar in all areas of late medieval England. There is no need to urge the point that any bad harvest could produce a crisis in the monastery of more or less serious dimensions. In their attempts to come to terms with this bewildering situation, especially when leasing arable land within the county, the Durham bursars conventionally estimated the price of wheat at 6s. 8d., barley at 4s. 0d., and oats at 1s. 8d. a quarter.[1] In actual fact throughout the early and mid-fifteenth century the prices of these grains (which significantly tended to rise and fall together to a quite remarkable degree) were generally below these estimates. In only fifteen of the fifty years between 1406 and 1456 can the price of wheat be proved to have risen above the level of 6s. 8d. a quarter. Throughout most of this period the Durham bursar could often buy wheat at less than 5s. 0d., and even on occasion (as in 1427/8) at 3s. 4d. a quarter.

This is not to deny that a sudden and unforeseeable jump in grain prices would sometimes plunge the monastery into acute economic difficulties. The cost of cereals rose above its usual variable level in 1410–11, 1421–2, 1432–3 and, above all, in 1437–9. The national phenomenon of heavy rain throughout the summer of 1438 and the consequent failure of the harvest created near famine conditions

---

[1] *Scrip. Tres*, pp. ccxcv, ccxcix. The estimates of grain prices in this paragraph are derived from Bursar, 1406–47; Cellarer, 1438–45; Granator, 1438–45.

in that year and pushed the price of the convent's wheat up to 13s. 4d., its barley to 6s. 0d. or 7s. 0d., and even its peas and beans (usually bought at 2s. 0d.) to 6s. 0d. a quarter respectively. In many ways the late 1430s presented the most serious of all fifteenth-century challenges to Durham's economy: it was the dreaded experience of excessive '*caristia granorum*' that helped to persuade Prior Wessington, as he himself acknowledged, to sponsor the division of the Durham bursary at exactly this time.[1] Within a few years, however, Durham corn prices had retreated to their more stagnant level; and it is only in the last two decades of the fifteenth century that we have evidence, as yet completely unassessed, for the beginning of sustained and long-term inflation.[2] Nothing in the experience of the fifteenth-century monks of Durham seems to have remotely paralleled the alarming experience of the great famine of 1315–17 when 'a quarter of wheat was sold for twenty shillings, and even a quarter of peas and beans as well as barley cost twenty-four shillings'.[3] Like most large corporations with fixed incomes at such times, the Durham monks of the early fifteenth century were for-tunate to live in an age of stagnant cereal and other prices, just as they seem to have been fortunate to enjoy the advantages of the stable wages which succeeded the rise of labour costs in the half-century immediately after the Black Death.[4] Such features of Durham's economy were of course common to many areas of England at the time. Despite the many unsolved technical problems involved (whether, for instance, the '*mensura prioris Dunelmensis*' varied significantly from grain measures used elsewhere), it seems

---

[1] Loc. XXI, no. 20 (vii); Loc. XXVII, no. 1 (a). On the national harvest failure of 1438 see J. E. Thorold Rogers, *A History of Agriculture and Prices in England*, III, *1401–1582* (Oxford, 1882), pp. 36–8; Jacob, *The Fifteenth Century*, p. 383.

[2] Bursar, 1484–7, Empcio Frumenti, Ordei, Avenae, Pis. et Fabarum; and see the table of grain prices in *Finchale Priory*, p. cccclvi. Further research among the volu-minous price material available for the early Tudor period at Durham seems likely to throw doubt on the general applicability of such grain price indices as those in *The Agrarian History of England and Wales*, ed. H. P. R. Finberg, IV (1967), 815–17.

[3] *Scrip. Tres*, p. 96; cf. *Finchale Priory*, pp. viii–xii.

[4] Thus the weekly wages of masons tended to rise from 2s. 0d. or 2s. 6d. to 2s. 6d. or 3s. 0d. between the building of the monastic kitchen in the late 1360s and that of the cloister forty years later (*Dur. Acct. Rolls* II, 569–73; Loc. II, no. 19). There-after wages and stipends of all sorts tended to remain remarkably stable: the cost of threshing and winnowing a quarter of wheat at Elvet Hall was exactly the same (4d.) in 1528–9 as it had been in 1447–8 (Elvet Hall accounts).

certain that in many ways the priory's fortunes were as dependent on national as local economic trends. To the Durham monks, their economic problems were their own; to the historian it is their representative rather than unique qualities which make them most significant.

The cost of provisioning and administering the fifteenth-century priory of Durham may well have been relatively stable, but there remains for investigation the even more fundamental problem of the extent of the decline in its sources of income. It was certainly the fall of their revenues rather than any rise in their expenditure that naturally obsessed the Durham monks themselves. To this obsession the most impartial guide is once again the bursar's annual account rolls. The receipts sections of these accounts reveal immediately that almost all of the bursar's revenues fell into two main and familiar categories: money derived from *bona temporalia*, that is income from manors, vills, pastures, tenements and mills, and from *bona spiritualia* consisting almost exclusively of garbal tithes sold (with a few exceptions) to local tenants and landowners. The bursar also derived some income from the sale of wool, hides and tallow as well as surplus live-stock and fodder, the profits of the prior's secular and spiritual courts, and a few church pensions; but these were of comparatively little financial significance and rarely amounted to more than £70 per annum in all . The bursar's income from his extensive spiritualities in the north of England deserves much closer attention, especially in view of the monks' own belief that its gradual diminution was the major cause of their financial difficulties.

According to the monastic valuation made during Wessington's priorate, the bursar's spiritual possessions were then worth a round £500, a somewhat cursory and optimistic assessment for in the early fifteenth century the bursar's rolls themselves show a real income of about £400 from the '*Recepta de Ecclesiis*'.[1] Even so, the fact that about a third of the receipts of the bursar (and indeed of most other Durham obedientiaries) derived from churches appropriated to the convent's use makes it evident that without that much maligned method of supporting late medieval corporations Durham Priory could hardly have survived. Income from the sale of corn tithes was received by the bursar from ten of the monastery's

---

[1] Bursar, 1416–38, Recepta de Ecclesiis; cf. *Scrip. Tres*, p. ccli.

appropriated churches, eight vicarages in County Durham (Jarrow, Monk Wearmouth, Monk Hesleden, Pittington, Billingham, Aycliffe, Heighington and East or Kirk Merrington) and two in Yorkshire (Northallerton and Eastrington). In a special category were the issues from the churches of Norhamshire and Elandshire, which were collected by the proctor of Norham and then delivered to the bursar at the mother house.[1] Although some tithes, notably those of Pittington near Durham, were retained *in manu domini prioris* and delivered in kind to the monastic granator, the great majority were sold on the spot or leased for a term of years to local tenants. Thus in 1445 the prior and chapter had leased their Eastrington tithes to John Portington for twenty years at £24 per annum: less than twenty years later these same tithes were being farmed for only £18 a year.[2] The bursar's accounts and rentals leave no doubt that by the mid-fifteenth century the Durham chapter positively preferred to lease nearly all the tithes from its appropriated churches for cash; but a scarcity of tenants willing to farm such tithes could on occasion confront the bursar with the problem of marketing tithe corn himself.

In 1436–7, one of the few years in which the Durham monks showed themselves prepared or able to generalise about the reasons for their economic *malaise*, it was argued that the long-term decline in the convent's income from these spiritualities lay at the heart of its problems. A table was then constructed, on the basis of surviving bursar's rolls, to show that the bursar's '*Recepta de Ecclesiis*' had fallen from a total of £1,467 in 1293 to £616 in 1348, and £411 in 1350 ('*post Pestilenciam Magnam*'). Despite some recovery in later years this figure had fallen to £397 in 1420, and was as low as £353 in 1436. Although, for various reasons, these crude totals undoubtedly exaggerate the severity of the decline in income from appropriated churches, such calculations were by no means completely tendentious. These figures can be checked against the surviving bursar's rolls, which may also be used to extend the estimates to the eve of the Dissolution. The accompanying table, despite its

---

[1] Selections from the proctor of Norham's accounts have been printed by James Raine in translation in *North Durham*, pp. 266–82. It ought to be added that this proctor's income was largely, but not exclusively, derived from Northumbrian *spiritualia*, part of which helped to sustain the priory of Holy Island.

[2] Bursar, 1445/46, Decime; *Scrip. Tres*, p. cccv; *Feodarium Dunelm.*, p. 209.

many inevitable technical inadequacies, probably does give – as the Durham monks themselves believed – a fairer impression of the overall decline in the monastery's revenues than any other single source. Although the conversion of grain tithes into cash totals was subject to a variety of artificial and non-economic factors, it is the great geographical range of these sources of income – deriving as they do from parishes in Yorkshire and Northumberland as well as very different areas of County Durham – which makes them provide a really significant index to the convent's income. The conclusions which emerge are obvious and important enough. It was the fourteenth century which saw a really catastrophic collapse of Durham Priory's income from spiritualities, most conspicuous in the districts immediately north and south of the Tweed but very pronounced elsewhere in the north of England. A degree of stability was, however, achieved again in the early fifteenth century, although at a much lower level than that before the Black Death. This stability was seriously threatened by a severe if short-term economic crisis in the 1430s and 1440s, from which the Durham monks were nevertheless able to emerge in the later fifteenth century with their sources of spiritual income relatively intact – as indeed they were to remain until the Dissolution.

It seems equally clear, although more difficult to demonstrate in detail, that the bursar's massive and highly variegated income from his *temporalia* was subject to the same sort of economic chronology. Estimated, again somewhat optimistically, at a net £1,000 per annum during Wessington's priorate, these receipts from '*bona temporalia*' were of course far and away the most important source of the convent's revenues. It followed that the entries dealing with such receipts formed by far the longest and most prominent section of the bursar's annual account rolls. From 1419 until the Dissolution they were invariably divided into ninety or so separate sub-sections, each arranged under the name of a locality where the prior and chapter held a manor, vill, group of tenements, cluster of rents, or rights to a money pension. Such a geographical arrangement makes it less than easy to produce a meaningful categorisation of these sources of income; but an analysis of the bursar's rolls between 1408 and 1418 in conjunction with the bursar's rental of 1411 produces the following result. At that period, a quite representative one,

Recepta de ecclesiis

	1293			1348			1350			1392			1420			1430			1436			1446			1464			1537		
	£	s.	d.	£	s.	d.	£	s.	d.	£	s.	d.	£	s.	d.	£	s.	d.	£	s.	d.	£	s.	d.	£	s.	d.	£	s.	d.
Scottish churches	149	5	8	—			—			—			—			—			—			—			—			—		
Norham	260	0	0	139	3	0	111	2	0	23	1	10	28	4	0	99	3	1	39	8	10	[80	11	6]	[£20]			[c. £63]		
Holy Island	158	0	8	}			—			—			—			—			—			—			—			—		
Ellingham	58	3	4	—			—			—			—			—			—			—			—			—		
Jarrow	60	0	0	80	0	0	44	0	0	46	19	0	35	6	8	29	6	4	31	6	8	29	2	0	32	5	4	35	19	7
Monk Wearmouth	—			—			—			20	0	0	13	13	4	12	0	0	7	13	4	6	0	0	4	13	4	4	10	6
Monk Hesleden	60	0	0	46	0	0	30	0	0	36	13	4	31	10	0	27	13	4	27	7	0	18	17	9	24	13	4	25	16	8
Pittington	80	0	0	60	18	4	36	3	4	34	13	4	35	1	8	32	13	4	28	3	4	22	0	0	24	10	0	25	0	11
Billingham	120	0	0	—			—			69	11	6	56	6	4	57	18	8	54	14	4	46	0	0	76	6	2¼	52	4	10
Aycliffe	111	6	8	70	0	0	1	0	0	31	5	0	30	13	4	24	10	0	24	8	4	19	0	0	21	0	4	23	8	3½
Heighington	128	0	0	49	13	4	17	11	0	39	6	8	41	3	4	47	6	8	48	3	4	40	13	4	37	8	2	37	3	4
Merrington	63	0	0	50	13	4	22	0	0	25	2	6	31	6	8	27	13	4	26	7	4	26	2	2	20	0	0	33	11	0½
Northallerton	88	0	0	66	13	4	71	1	2	59	6	8	51	0	0	47	16	8	41	13	4	38	13	4	37	13	4	36	6	8
Eastrington	125	0	0	53	6	8	57	18	11	41	6	10	37	6	8	26	13	4	23	14	8	24	0	0	18	0	0	22	0	0
Complete totals	1,466	16	4	616	8	0	410	16	8½	452	0	8½	396	12	0	432	14	9	353	0	6	351	0	1	316	10	0½	c. 359	1	10
Total: Durham and Yorks	841	6	8	477	5	0	299	14	5	404	4	5	368	8	0	333	11	8	313	11	8	270	8	7	296	10	0½	296	1	10

Sources. Reg. II, fos. 356v–357; *Scrip. Tres*, pp. ccciv–cccv; *Feodarium Dunelm.*, pp. 98, 208–9, 302–3; *Dur. Acct. Rolls* III, 687–90.

58% of all 'temporal income' was derived from the assized rents of a variegated mixture of tenements and messuages in the north-east of England; 18% from manors at farm; 10% from bondage tenements; 8% from the leasing of 14 corn mills; and 4% only from commuted labour services or '*opera*'.[1]

The most significant and revolutionary development in estates policy at Durham in the early fifteenth century was undoubtedly the decision to lease almost all the convent's manorial demesnes. In 1442 the monks of Durham reckoned that there were twenty manors attached to the bursar's office, of which ten were *maneria maiores* and the others *maneria minores*, alternatively known as granges.[2] In an important and influential study Miss E. M. Halcrow was the first to reveal that the leasing of these manors marked the critical stage in the decline of demesne farming on the convent's medieval estates. However, her reliance on the often erratic series of extant Durham manorial rolls left this conclusion in a state of some chronological vagueness which the receipts sections of the bursar's accounts can immediately rectify. A few manorial demesnes had been leased almost in their entirety during the late fourteenth century, like the manor of Belasis east of Billingham which was farmed to a local landowner for 15 years as early as 1373. However, and as we have already seen, seven of the bursar's ten *maneria maiores* were still unleased in 1407–8, and it was the years between that date and 1416 (when only Pittington and Beaurepaire were still *in manu*) which mark the crucial turning-point.[3] It is worth noticing that Prior Hemingburgh of Durham (1391–1416) was an almost exact contemporary of Prior Thomas Chillenden (1391–1411), who had established a thoroughgoing leasehold system on the Christ Church, Canterbury, estates by 1396. Only by a few years therefore does Durham Priory fail to conform to the established generalisation that 'by the last decade of the (fourteenth) century, landlords nearly everywhere had ceased to farm their own land'.[4]

---

[1] Bursar, 1409–18; Bursar's Rental, 1411; cf. Loc. XXI, no. 20 (ii).

[2] Loc. XXI, no. 20 (ii). For the most important of these manors, see Figure 4, p. 280.

[3] Bursar, 1407/8, 1409/10, 1416/17, Redditus Assise; *Halmota Prioratus Dunelmensis, 1296–1384* (Surtees Soc. LXXXII, 1889), p. 120. See above, p. 94, and Halcrow, 'Decline of Demesne Farming', pp. 355–6.

[4] McKisack, *The Fourteenth Century*, p. 340; cf. Smith, *Canterbury Cathedral Priory*, p. 192; *Cambridge Economic History* I (1966), 587–90.

Quite apart from the impact of this policy of manorial leasing on the social as well as economic patterns of monastic life at Durham, income derived from such leases is of particular interest as a more revealing guide to variations in the convent's revenues than can be provided by the heterogeneous collection of other rents received by the bursar. On the whole, the chronological pattern revealed by the sums for which the bursar's manors could be farmed during the long period between 1416 and the Dissolution is strikingly and significantly similar to that displayed by income from grain tithes in the north of England. Thus the manor of Ketton north of Darlington was leased for £24 a year in 1444, a figure which fell to £22 in 1446 and 1464 but thereafter recovered to its former level of £24 by the 1530s. Similarly, the manorial demesnes of Belasis seem to have been farmed at the steady rate of £6 13s. 4d. throughout the century and a half before the Dissolution.[1] Long-term stability rather than serious and universal decline is indeed the lesson to be learnt from a study of the fluctuations in the bursar's receipts from his farmed manors during the late medieval period. This is not, of course, to deny the possibility of short-term falls in the convent's income from manorial farms and other rents due to a conjuncture of particularly adverse economic circumstances. Here again the evidence points to the late 1430s and 1440s as a period in which the prior and chapter found it especially difficult to farm their manors at reasonable terms. In nearly every case the money received from the farm of each of the prior's manors at that time was a good deal less than forty or eighty years later. Sometimes a manor could not be farmed at all, and in 1446 Ferryhill and Bewley were in the prior's hands '*propter defectum tenencium*'.[2] That a scarcity of tenants was not a permanent difficulty is, however, sufficiently proved by the fact that in the latter half of the fifteenth century the prior and bursar went on to lease the previously unfarmed manorial demesnes of Pittington and Beaurepaire, thus putting a complete stop – for all practical purposes – to demesne farming on their own estates.[3]

---

[1] Bursar, 1422/23, 1443/44; *Scrip. Tres*, pp. ccxcvii–ccxcviii; *Feodarium Dunelm.*, pp. 143, 158; *Dur. Acct. Rolls* III, 676, 679.

[2] *Scrip. Tres*, pp. ccxcvi, ccxcix.

[3] Miss Halcrow ('Decline of Demesne Farming', p. 356) suggests that the leasing of Pittington after 1451 marked the final abandonment of demesne farming; but Pittington was still in the prior's hands in 1453/54 (Granator), and Beaurepaire was

At Durham, as elsewhere in late medieval Europe, it would not be difficult to interpret this contraction of demesne farming as a recognition of defeat on the part of the large corporate landlord. There is no doubt whatsoever that the manorial and agricultural revenues of the monks of Durham were much less substantial in the early fifteenth than they had been in the late thirteenth century. Nor is it hard to speculate on some of the reasons for this decline, impossible though these are to quantify. Natural disaster certainly played an important part, and the monks of Durham were themselves quick enough to point out the ruinous effects of such calamities as an outbreak of plague among their tenants or murrain among their cattle. Similarly, the great rain-storms and '*tempestates aquarum*' of early September 1401 were long remembered for the havoc they caused to the convent's mills and other property.[1] Much more emphasis, however, was placed by prior and chapter on acts of war than acts of God. The disastrous effects of the Anglo-Scottish wars during the later middle ages on the economy of monasteries both north and south of the Tweed is still perhaps insufficiently appreciated: even as far south of the border as Tynemouth fear of armed assault might be so acute as to prevent the sowing of corn for four consecutive years.[2] The fact that so large a proportion of Durham Priory's original endowments of land lay in the extreme north of the old Northumbria made the convent particularly vulnerable to border warfare. The almost complete loss of all its spiritual income north of the Tweed as a result of the Scottish wars of Edward I and Edward III was unquestionably the greatest single economic disaster in the history of the monastery. In the first years of the fifteenth century the area immediately south of the Tweed was allegedly almost completely evacuated and 'deserted by its inhabitants'. Even

the last important manor to be put to farm (without its domestic buildings) except for the hostillar's manor of Elvet Hall. The sacrist's manor of Sacristonheugh was regularly, although not always, leased from 1412 onwards (3.3. Sac., no. 29a; Sacrist, 1438–46).

[1] 4.6. Ebor., no. 2.

[2] B.M. Cotton MS., Nero D. vii, fo. 51v. Scottish petitions to the papacy in the fifteenth century tell a frightening and no doubt largely genuine story of ruin and corruption at border monasteries like Kelso and Dryburgh Abbeys: see Vatican Archives, Register of Supplications (Mrs A. I. Dunlop's calendar in the Department of Scottish History and Literature, University of Glasgow), 279, fo. 52; 542, fos. 159, 255; 614, fo. 106v.

in 1446, a year of comparative tranquillity, it had to be admitted that the profits and issues of the churches of Norham, Ellingham and Holy Island were '*casualia*': only if the truces between the two kingdoms were observed could the proctor of Norham dispatch his debts of £80 to the Durham bursar.[1]

However, it would undoubtedly be a mistake to regard the Anglo-Scottish hostilities of the fourteenth and fifteenth centuries, intermittent in their intensity, as the only or even the most important explanation for the diminution of Durham Priory's landed income in the later middle ages. So much of the available evidence, however much it may await detailed assessment, reveals the classic symptoms of falling population – low cereal prices, stagnant land values, contraction in the acreage of arable farming, scarcity of tenants – that it is hard not to interpret the convent's economic difficulties in terms of the now conventional thesis of general demographic decline. The omission of County Durham from so many governmental taxation records, from Domesday Book to the 1377 and 1381 Poll Tax returns and beyond, makes it exceptionally difficult to place developments there in a national context. Nevertheless, there can be no doubt that the county underwent a massive colonising movement during the twelfth and thirteenth centuries, a movement in which the prior and chapter of Durham probably played a leading role. The repetitious regularity of the plans of the convent's 'green villages' at places like Kirk Merrington, Ferryhill and Hett still testifies to the monks' ability to sponsor important centres of grain production during the course of the twelfth century.[2] As late as the 1290s Prior Richard of Hoton '*Spendingmor redegit in culturam*', although it may be significant that by this date the extension of arable was met with serious resistance on the part of the tenants of the neighbouring villages of Tudhoe and Hett who feared the loss of their rights to common pasture.[3] By the early fourteenth century evidence for further agrarian colonisation seems almost completely lacking, and the counties of Durham and (especially) Northumberland began to display signs of a contraction in the amount of their

---

[1] 4.6. Ebor., no. 2; *Scrip. Tres*, p. ccxc, and cf. p. 103.

[2] H. Thorpe, 'The green villages of County Durham', *Transactions of the Institute of British Geographers* 15 (1949), 155–80; *Durham History from the Air*, ed. N. McCord (Durham County Local History Society, 1971), p. 20.

[3] *Scrip. Tres*, p. 74.

cultivated land. The convent's surveys of the mortality among their tenants-at-will in 1349–50 thoroughly document the disastrous effects of the first outbreak of bubonic plague, especially in Billing-ham, Wolviston, Bewley and other villages in the south-east of Durham county. Nor was Durham immune from the phenomenon of the 'deserted village': fifteen or so villages in the county, none of them admittedly ever of major importance, are now known to have become depopulated in the late medieval or early Tudor periods.[1]

One of the most familiar consequences of both sustained war and population decline is the reduction of previously cultivated land to pasture. According to the monks of Durham, as well as other land-lords like the canons of Bolton Priory who similarly held a large proportion of their estates on marginal land, such a process was reducing their revenues seriously by the middle of the fifteenth century.[2] The conversion of arable land to pasture was bound to have an immediately adverse effect on the economy of a house like Durham which was, as we have seen, so heavily dependent on its possession of garbal tithes. Here again, however, the transformation of large numbers of Northumberland villages into predominantly pastoral communities had more severe consequences for the Durham chapter than any comparable development in their own county. John Leland's failure to find 'resonable good corne' when he travelled through the central and western parts of Durham in the early sixteenth century is well known; but it must not be allowed to disguise the fact that these districts, including those immediately west of Durham city itself, had never been capable of sustaining much cereal production at any time in the middle ages.[3] Certainly the familiar hypothesis that landlords in the later middle ages might positively compensate for the decline in their arable husbandry by increased stock and especially sheep farming finds little support among the Durham records.

[1] Loc. IV, nos. 4–6; *V.C.H. Durham* II, 258–9; M. Beresford, *The Lost Villages of England* (London, 1954), 239–40, 349–50; *Durham History from the Air*, p. 24.

[2] Misc. Chrs., no. 5727; *History...of Priory of St Mary, Bolton-in-Wharfedale* (Thoresby Soc. XXX, 1928), p. 107; Thompson, *The English Clergy*, p. 112.

[3] Leland's *Itinerary* I, 69–74; H. C. Darby (ed.), *Historical Geography of England before A.D. 1800* (Cambridge, 1936), p. 347. The climatic and other difficulties which inhibit the growing of corn in the middle and upper Wear valley are summarised in Smailes, *North England*, pp. 50–71.

The prior and chapter had indeed been alive to the possibility of the profits to be derived from pasture farming well before 1300. From that date onwards they can be proved to have operated a sophisticated and apparently efficient system of stock raising on an inter-manorial basis. By the fifteenth century, however, such activity was increasingly concentrated on the convent's two great stock farms of Muggleswick and Le Holme, situated in the upper Derwent valley and at the mouth of the Tees respectively. Both were served by a staff of professional herdsmen and shepherds and supervised by a monk *instaurator* or *supervisor stauri*. Valuable as the cattle breeding station at Muggleswick and the sheep ranch of Le Holme were in furnishing the convent with large consignments of meat, it would be idle to pretend that they brought the monks an enormous income in the fifteenth century. Indeed the bursar's annual profits in selling wool from these and other sources fell from their fourteenth-century level of £100 to little more than £20 or so in the mid-fifteenth century. The extremely interesting stock accounts of Muggleswick and Le Holme reveal either a deliberate contraction of pastoral farming or an inability to stabilise the situation. The number of cattle at Muggleswick was in a state of constant flux, dropping from over 600 (of which the majority were oxen) in 1435–6 to 433 in 1446 and 159 in 1464.[1] On the extensive flats of Le Holme – where salt pans provided the convent with much of its salt – grazed what was probably the single largest flock of sheep in the late medieval county. Nevertheless, in a situation where at least 10 per cent of all newly-born lambs often died of murrain, there was little prospect of regular stability. The totals of 1,200 or 1,500 sheep recorded at Le Holme in 1416–17 and 1446–7 fell to less than 400 in 1464. Impressive though some of these figures may appear, one has only to compare them with the thousands of sheep farmed by the East Anglian abbeys of the later middle ages to appreciate that animal husbandry can never have been an important means of economic salvation to the Durham monks.[2]

---

[1] Muggleswick Account, 1435/36; *Scrip. Tres*, p. ccciv; *Feodarium Dunelm.*, pp. 207–8.

[2] *Dur. Acct. Rolls* II, 309–22; *Scrip. Tres*, p. ccciv; *Feodarium Dunelm.*, p. 208; cf. E. Power, *The Wool Trade in English Medieval History* (Oxford, 1941), pp. 34–5, and the reservations on this issue expressed by Professor Postan in *Cambridge Economic History* I (1966), 591.

The same argument inevitably applies – and much more strongly – to the prior and chapter's participation in the early coal-mining industry. Although the convent held coal-bearing land throughout the county, they could never hope to become important coal exporters for the reason that few of the mines they opened up lay on a navigable river or near the coast. The monastery's important sources of coal were all concentrated within a ten-mile radius from Durham itself, the actual points of exploitation being determined by the 'pit and adit' system whose drainage requirements necessitated the digging of pits in hilly country. It was accordingly on the slopes of Ferryhill, West Rainton and in the area around Beaurepaire that the convent had established its most successful mines, administered by local supervisors under the control of the monk (usually the terrar) appointed by the prior as *receptor denariorum proveniencium de mineris carbonum*.[1] Although wooden faggots continued to be cut for use in the conventual kitchen and elsewhere, there is no doubt that by the early fifteenth century coal had replaced timber as the most important fuel in the monastery. Some of the monastic pits were sunk deep enough to require the use of candles, but most of the mines were inevitably very small-scale enterprises worked by the labour of a team of only two or three hewers.

However, it was undoubtedly a lack of adequate marketing facilities rather than technological immaturity in mining operations themselves which kept the level of production so comparatively low. Coal was normally sold to local lords and tenants at the pithead itself; and the monks were apparently helpless in the face of a situation like that at Aldin Grange in 1445, where 67 chauldrons lay in two heaps at the top of the pits because they could not be sold.[2] Limited local demand constantly raised the threat of overproduction, a danger met by a system of careful regulation and restriction which foreshadows the cartels and monopolies associated

---

[1] Account rolls for various of the convent's mines survive for the period between 1409 and 1445 (see Misc. Chrs., nos. 5443, 5517, 5876), but tend to throw more light on the monk receiver's general expenditure than on mining operations as such. Also informative are the bursar's accounts and (especially) the relevant sections of his rentals, e.g. Bursar's Rental, 1432, fos. 20v–37v.

[2] Mines Accts., 1444/45; and see (more generally) J. B. Simpson, 'Coal Mining by the Monks', *Transactions of the Institute of Mining Engineers* XXXIX (1909–10), 572–600; J. U. Nef, *The Rise of the British Coal Industry* (1932), I, 136–9; *V.C.H. Durham* II, 320–5.

with the Newcastle hostmen in the sixteenth century. In 1398 the Durham bursar had spent over £14 on sinking a new pit at Aldin Grange; but in the following year the prior entered into a restrictive lease with John Fossor and Richard Cowhird, by which these two lessees undertook to supply the monastery and Beaurepaire with coal for seven years on condition that the prior himself mined no coal in that area.[1] Similarly, in 1418–19 the prior of Finchale was paid £10 per annum not to work his mines at Broom; meanwhile the prior and bursar let their own pits at Broom go out of production and relied on supplies from Richard Cowhird.[2] Even when the monks resumed direct mining of the Broom and Aldin Grange pits in the 1440s, their net annual profits from the sale of coal there were rarely more than £10. The comparative abundance of timber and, above all, the high cost of transport (which doubled the price of a chauldron after a journey of only a dozen miles) gave Durham Priory no real opportunity to engage in large-scale capitalistic exploitation of coal-mining in the fifteenth century.

The later fame of north-eastern England as a pastoral and mining region must not therefore be allowed to disguise the essential realities of the situation – that in the late middle ages the welfare of Durham Priory depended absolutely on the prosperity of arable agriculture. As is well established, although not always sufficiently well known, the southern and eastern parts of Durham county fell squarely within the area of the open-field 'system' and three-course crop rotation. Any doubts on this score are soon dispelled by a reading of the priory's halmote records or the terms of its leases of manorial demesnes. The indenture by which the prior and chapter farmed their estate at Nun Stainton, south of Ferryhill, to the Yorkshire nunnery of Nun Monkton in 1392 conveys an exceptionally detailed impression of the extraordinarily variegated and dispersed ploughed strips or selions which made up so much of the convent's landed property. Similarly, the presence on so many of the prior's manors of several plough-teams, usually of six oxen, is eloquent testimony to the primacy and ubiquity of arable farming

---

[1] *Dur. Acct. Rolls* III, 601; *Calendar of the Greenwell Deeds*, ed. J. Walton (Newcastle upon Tyne, 1927), pp. 119–20; cf. Blake, 'Medieval Coal Trade of the North East', p. 22.

[2] Mines Accts., 1409/19; Bursar, 1416–41, Focale; cf. Commoner, 1430/31, for the lack of income from the coal-mines at Hett that year.

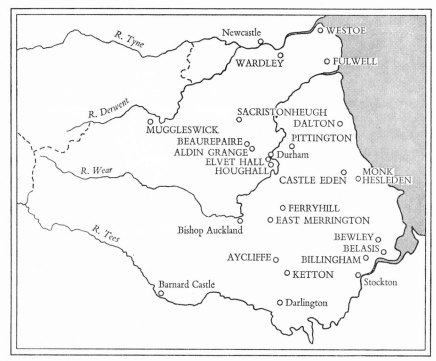

Fig. 4. The manors of the priory of Durham in the fifteenth century

on their estates.[1] In this connection the geographical distribution of
the bursar's landholdings is of particular significance, for they
coincide to a quite remarkable extent with what are still the richest
arable areas in the county of Durham. The bursar held no estates of
much consequence in the Durham dales or in the north-west of the
county. Apart from a group of manors and tenements around the
city of Durham itself, his properties were largely concentrated in
four main clusters within the county. In the north-east of the
palatinate lay an almost continuous series of manors and tenements
along the south bank of the Tyne, from Felling and Wardley in the
west to Westoe and South Shields in the east. Located several

[1] Cart. II, fos. 203–4; *Feodarium Dunelm.*, pp. 164–5, 172. For evidence of three-
course rotation (10 acres sown with wheat; 12 with oats; 10 fallow and manured,
later to be sown with wheat) as far north as Sacristonheugh in 1427, see S. L.
Greenslade, 'Sacristonheugh', *Transactions of Architectural and Archaeological Society
of Durham and Northumberland* x, Part 3 (1950), 257.

miles to the south was a much more widely dispersed group of manors, including Fulwell, Dalton, Monk Hesleden and Castle Eden, scattered throughout the eastern portion of the county. The third concentration of bursar's estates, the most dense of all, was situated in the extreme south-east and included Billingham, Belasis, Le Holme and Bewley. Finally the convent held extensive and valuable estates in the central and southern half of the county, most of which lay between Darlington and Ferryhill.

Although the prior and chapter lived in constant fear of the dreaded and to them largely inexplicable phenomenon of '*sterilitas terre*', all these regions of the county were still capable of producing large quantities of corn in the fifteenth century. Admittedly the paucity of manorial accounts for this period makes it impossible to generalise with confidence about grain yields. But the unique collection of Elvet Hall accounts (of which no less than 51 survive for the period between 1383 and 1529) is of particular interest in showing that, despite considerable vicissitudes, the reeve there could often count on the eminently respectable yields of 1:4 from seed in the case of wheat, slightly more in the case of rye, and much more in the case of barley.[1] The copious evidence of the Elvet Hall and other accounts, as well as the terms of leases, also disposes of the legend that, on the convent's manors at least, the production of grain for human consumption was sacrificed in favour of corn fodder for livestock. All allowances made for great chronological and regional variation, the case of the convent's manorial demesnes at Ferryhill in 1446 seems thoroughly representative: 40 acres were sown with wheat, 27 with barley, 45 with oats, 13 with peas or beans, and 7 with blandcorn.[2] Of course, as is often and sometimes platitudinously said, lowland Durham was a region of mixed farm-

[1] A conclusion based (somewhat problematically) on a comparison between the corn recorded as having been kept for seed at the end of one year and the amount received '*de exitibus grangie*' in the next consecutive reeve's account (e.g. Elvet Hall, 1447/48, 1448/49). These Elvet Hall yields certainly appear to be more favourable than most of the seed yield ratios – of often very dubious validity – tabulated in B. H. Slicher Van Bath, *The Agrarian History of Western Europe, A.D. 500–1850* (London, 1963), pp. 328–9.

[2] *Scrip. Tres*, p. ccxcix. For analogous information about crop distribution, see ibid., pp. ccxciii, ccxcv, ccc, and especially the manorial accounts of Elvet Hall (which tended to specialise in barley production during the first half of the fifteenth century) and Pittington.

ing; but it would be difficult to prove that husbandry on most of the bursar's manors was more 'mixed' and more devoted to stock-raising than was common in much of Yorkshire and midland England. When Thomas Page, one of the prior's tenants at Harton near Westoe, died in 1378 he left behind him 3 oxen, 1 horse, 4 cows, 4 sheep and 5 pigs; but the cash value of these animals was surpassed by the £6 13s. 4d. at which his crops of wheat, barley, peas and oats – then standing in the fields – were valued after his death.[1]

However, the monks' ability to profit from these very real possibilities of successful arable farming on their Durham estates depended absolutely on their success in securing suitable tenants. The question of 'Who were farming the English demesnes at the end of the middle ages?' is as important and as unanswered in County Durham as anywhere in the country. At this early stage of research satisfactory generalisation is virtually impossible. For most of the late medieval period Durham Priory clearly did find tenants for all its manorial demesnes as well as the great majority of its village tenements. On the whole it would seem that the farmers of the prior's manors fell into three main categories – groups of three to ten villagers who combined together to lease arable land and then held it severally in equal fractions; prosperous local landowners, usually of 'valet' or yeoman status rather than knights or esquires; and men of higher rank, sometimes merchants of Newcastle-upon-Tyne, who leased manorial demesnes on a speculative basis. The second group tended to be the most numerous, although the third category was nearly always able to secure more favourable conditions, and in particular a longer term of years, when leasing the demesnes in question. Thus Robert Rodes, the prior's lay steward, took out a farm on the manor of Wardley for a period of forty years in the 1440s, and the Thornton family seem to have held the vill of Ludworth (not one of the prior's manors) for as long a time in the mid-fifteenth century.[2] Long leases of this type were however

---

[1] *Halmota Prioratus Dunelmensis*, p. 151; *English Historical Documents* IV, ed. Myers, p. 1000.

[2] Bursar, 1445/46; *Scrip. Tres*, pp. ccxcii, ccxcv; *Feodarium Dunelm.*, p. 130. Similar variations in the social status of the lessees of the estates of the archbishop of Canterbury are well brought out by F. R. H. Du Boulay, 'Who were Farming the English Demesnes at the End of the Middle Ages?', *Econ. H.R.*, Second Series, XVII (1965),

quite exceptional, the usual term during most of the fifteenth century being a period of anything between five and fifteen years. This system of leasing monastic land for a relatively short period of years at a specified money rent, the lease likely to be renewed just before the expiry of the term, had been widely applied to small parcels of tenant land within a particular village from the late fourteenth century onwards. In the early years of the fifteenth century it was systematically extended to the convent's manorial demesnes, and a generation later even to those groups of tenements so concentrated in one locality that they could be described (if not satisfactorily defined) as the convent's 'vills'. The first recorded example of this last type of lease appears to date from 1435 when seven villagers began to farm the entire vill of Wallsend for six years at an annual rent of £12 7s. 3½d.[1]

Durham Priory's thoroughgoing adoption of a policy of short-term renewable leaseholds was by no means typical of all late medieval monasteries, and was undoubtedly different from the system usually practised by the bishop of Durham, most of whose tenants apparently held from him for life.[2] By depriving the great majority of their tenants, whether intentionally or not, of legal copyhold right and converting them *de facto* into 'onelie theire tennaunts at will', the prior and chapter left a complicated and often baneful legacy to the future. When, in 1577, the Dean and Chapter of Durham made a general refusal to acknowledge a descendible customary estate on the part of their tenants, they could do so because 'an aunciént booke and register of the leases made by the predecessors of the saide Deane and Chapiter, shewed to the Lord president and councell in the north parts, that the lands in contention belongeinge to that house, had manie tymes bene letten for yeres

---

450–5; cf. B. Harvey, 'The Leasing of the Abbot of Westminster's Demesnes in the Later Middle Ages', ibid. XXII (1969), 20–1.

[1] Halmote Court Book I, 1400–39, fo. 133.

[2] *V.C.H. Durham* II, 227; cf. J. Youings, 'The Church', *Agrarian History of England and Wales* IV, ed. Finberg, p. 319, who demonstrates the general difficulty of distinguishing in practice between 'long' and 'short' term monastic leases. Nevertheless, the more flexible system adopted by the Durham chapter may help to explain why their rents fell less drastically in the early fifteenth century than those of the bishop of Durham or – especially – the Percy family (Storey, *Thomas Langley*, pp. 69–70; J. M. W. Bean, *The Estates of the Percy Family, 1416–1537* [Oxford, 1958], pp. 22–42).

by lease'.[1] Indeed they had; but it is much more difficult to estimate the financial advantages of a short-term leasehold system to the Durham monks of the fifteenth century than to the Durham canons a hundred years later. On the whole, and provided the bursar, terrar and lay steward supervised the critical business of assigning leases efficiently and scrupulously, it appears to have been a relatively satisfactory and economical method of stabilising rents at a period of stagnant prices and a comparative scarcity of tenants. On the other hand, the fact that so many leaseholds – of isolated tenements as well as manorial demesnes – were liable to fall vacant so often undoubtedly did create an atmosphere of considerable insecurity; the leasing methods employed by the Durham bursar made him acutely vulnerable to short-term economic crises. It seems sufficiently clear that the convent's administrative and financial misfortunes in the late 1430s and early 1440s were due to exactly this sort of crisis, experienced (significantly enough) at approximately the same period that the archbishops of Canterbury too were finding it 'rather harder to make satisfactory leases'.[2]

Under close scrutiny one therefore doubts whether the Durham evidence accords with the optimistic belief that 'as the landlords withdrew altogether from farming, the peasants, fortified by ample tenancies and long leases, entered into their own', or even that 'The emphasis changed to large-scale tenant farming'.[3] The fifteenth-century rural scene in the north-east was clearly too complex to be so easily summarised; and it would be a great mistake to assume that a tenant's ability to lease part or all of one of the prior of Durham's manors was always a passport to material prosperity and enhanced social status. Several farmers of the convent's manors in the mid-fifteenth century found the experience rendered them '*impotentes*' rather than the reverse; and the great inventory of 1446 leaves no doubt whatsoever of the then reluctance on the part of villagers all over the county to take up available leases on terms acceptable to the convent. In South Shields the situation was so

---

[1] *Halmota Prioratus Dunelmensis*, p. xxxviii. For discussion of the issues here, see E. Kerridge, *Agrarian Problems in the Sixteenth Century and After* (London, 1969), pp. 86–9.

[2] F. R. H. Du Boulay, *The Lordship of Canterbury* (London, 1966), p. 225.

[3] A. R. Bridbury, *Economic Growth: England in the Later Middle Ages* (London, 1962), p. 92; Halcrow, 'Decline of Demesne Farming', p. 356.

severe that most of the vill lay waste and completely depopulated.[1]
It is known from chronicle sources that the mortality rate in
northern England was notoriously severe in 1438–9; and there can
be no reasonable doubt that a serious epidemic, probably of bubonic
plague in combination with typhus, was responsible for most of
the difficulties which threatened the monastic economy at Durham in
the following years.[2]

The extent to which a period of economic adversity is transformed into one of complete financial disarray does, however,
depend on a complex of variable human factors. It is time to return
from the convent's estates to the monastery itself, and to examine
Prior Wessington's own allegation that the economic 'collapse' of
the last years of his priorate was the result of personal and administrative weakness – and in particular the fecklessness and improvidence of Thomas Lawson, monastic bursar from 1432 until 1438.
In the exceptionally interesting dossier the prior prepared a few
years later to justify his decision to divide the bursar's office between
three monks in response to this crisis, he repeatedly made the point
that by their very nature the duties of the Durham bursar were
bound to exceed '*vires unius viri*'.[3] From the beginning of the
century successive bursars had constantly asked to be allowed to
resign, 'alleging that the labour of the said office was unbearable for
one man'. During twenty-one years in John Hemingburgh's
priorate, and despite a short-lived attempt to secure greater continuity by associating two monks in the office, there had been no
fewer than thirteen different bursars. Between 1419 and 1432 Prior
Wessington and his monks had been served by three successive
bursars, none of whom had been particularly successful in keeping
arrears, wastes and decays to a tolerable minimum. Finally, during
the autumn of 1432 and in the absence of a more suitable candidate,
the prior appointed as bursar Thomas Lawson, a comparatively
junior monk who had just spent four years as the convent's cellarer.

[1] Bursar, 1437–46; *Scrip. Tres*, p. ccxciii; *Feodarium Dunelm.*, p. 172.
[2] *Historical Collections of a London Citizen in the Fifteenth Century*, ed. J. Gairdner
(Camden Soc., New Series, XVII, 1876), p. 181; J. M. W. Bean, 'Plague, Population and Economic Decline in England in the Later Middle Ages', *Econ. H.R.*,
Second Series, XV (1963), 429.
[3] Loc. XXI, no. 20, a file of seven documents, whose account of the division of the
bursar's office in 1438–45 is followed here.

Although Lawson had been chosen on the advice of the brethren, this appointment soon revealed itself as one of the most unfortunate ever made at the priory. When asked, a year later, to present his first annual account, the new bursar complained that he had not the time to do so and showed instead an inventory or '*statum dicti officii in scriptis modo grosso*'. After Prior Wessington continued to press for a proper account, Lawson became acutely distressed and was alleged to have been on the point of committing suicide. In the end Lawson did produce his five annual account rolls, all of which still survive at Durham. As always, the real index to the economic position of the bursar lay not in the stereotyped receipts sections of his accounts but in the allowances for arrears, decays of rent, and wastes (where tenements had fallen in value because repairs had been neglected and buildings had collapsed), all recorded at the foot of the roll. Lawson's accounts reveal less than the usual allowances of approximately £100 for *Decasus* and £60 for *Vastum*, but a rise in the level of current yearly arrears from £115 to £265 between 1433 and 1436.[1] Much more seriously, a study of these bursar's rolls makes it absolutely clear that Lawson systematically suppressed mention of many of the very heavy debts he was incurring in these years: it was later alleged that the bursar had left debts of over £1,210 'concealed from the prior and convent'. Rumours of this extraordinary improvidence soon began to spread through the convent and the exposure of Lawson's inadequacies could not be long delayed. A report produced by the Durham terrar, Henry Helay, and the clerk of the bursary confirmed the monks' worst fears. At the time when the news of his concealed debts was made public at Durham, Lawson was touring the convent's estates. Rather than return home to meet the justifiable anger of his fellows, he fled from his lodgings in the middle of the night and disappeared into hiding. Lawson's attendants reported their inability to say whether he was living or dead. 'In which situation', as Wessington later declared to Bishop Neville, 'the prior took the advice of his brethren, who thought it best to appoint someone else to the bursar's office; he

---

[1] Bursar, 1433/34, 1435/36, Exoneraciones. It is essential to make a distinction here, as always, between arrears carried over from previous years (many of them *illevabilia* and therefore amounting to a very considerable sum indeed) and the current year's arrears: the latter averaged only £40 or so in the bursar's accounts of the 1420s.

accordingly offered it to various monks, as insistently as he could. But they all refused absolutely, believing that the labour would be too much for them... In which perplexity, the prior remembered the proverb "*Levius portatur quod a pluribus portatur*", and he talked to his brethren about the possibility of dividing the bursary, to which division they all agreed and no one objected.'

The division of the Durham bursary between 1438 and 1445 was the most interesting and radical administrative experiment at the monastery between the institution of the bursar's office in the mid-thirteenth century and the Dissolution. Although an experiment which failed, it deserves to be remembered for the way in which it compelled the Durham monks to articulate – in a way they rarely did – their attitude to financial and economic problems. There can be little doubt that the reform was very much Wessington's own plan, and it was he who first proposed the division 'in the presence of the sub-prior and the majority of the chapter'. On the other hand, the prior was probably justified in his later claim that his suggestions had met with the general approval of his monks. Four years afterwards, fifteen of the more senior members of the chapter had not changed their opinion that 'it would be more expedient and useful for the said office to remain divided rather than be united'. The division itself revolutionised the roles of three obedientiaries – the bursar himself, the cellarer and the granator. In the summer of 1438 a new system came into operation whereby the bursar's sources of income were divided into three sections of approximately equal value, the first of which was retained by the bursar, the second entrusted to the cellarer, and the third to the granator. In this way, the bursar's financial responsibilities were reduced by two-thirds, and the cellarer and granator escaped from their previous dependence on the bursar's office to become obedientiaries with independent revenues, for which they accounted quite separately to Wessington and the annual chapter. The complicated task of dividing the bursar's traditional items of receipt and expenditure among the three officers had been delegated by the prior to his future chancellor, Robert Westmorland, and to John Oll, '*in officio Bursarie magis expertus*'. Westmorland and Oll made their division remarkably quickly and the new regime began on 24 August 1438. From that date until Martinmas 1445, a period of slightly more than seven years, the solitary financial supremacy of the Durham bursar was replaced by a system in which bursar, cellarer and granator had independent and equal responsibility for the convent's welfare.[1] Naturally the cellarer's main duty continued to be the purchase of meat and other provisions, while the granator now bought his own wheat and barley; the bursar, with a greatly reduced income, still found most of the convent's cloth and wine, and provided the prior with the money for his necessary expenses as well as the pensions and stipends of his servants and counsellors. But between 1438 and 1445 each of the three obedientiaries was made responsible for the repair of his own property and the payment and liveries of his own servants. So far had the bursar lost his traditional ascendancy that his total receipts during this period averaged only £440, while those of the cellarer were in the region of £460 and the granator, now the wealthiest of all Durham obedientiaries, received over £500 per annum.[2]

Whether the new system was an improvement on the old soon became an issue hotly debated in the Durham cloister. It is as obvious now as it was then that there were advantages and disadvantages to both arrangements. Perhaps the experiment of a divided bursary was never given an altogether fair trial; as we have seen, the period between 1438 and 1445 was one in which the convent's economic problems were unusually severe. At the very time that he introduced the new administrative changes Wessington was compelled to take various unpopular measures, including the imposition of contributions on cells and obediences in order to repay the debts left by Thomas Lawson. Nevertheless, the majority of these were inevitably inherited by the new bursar, cellarer and granator, who thus began their terms of office in unfortunate circumstances. Rents continued to decline after 1438, the price of grain was exceptionally high, and Wessington himself acknowledged that the three obedientiaries were unable to maintain their buildings in a fit state of

---

[1] The operation of this new system is fully revealed in the surviving bursar's, granator's and cellarer's accounts of 1438–45. When editing selections from these *compoti* for the Surtees Society, Canon Fowler realised that they failed to conform to the normal pattern, but his complete failure to show that the bursar's office had become divided (*Dur. Acct. Rolls* I, 62; III, 625, xxxiv, lv–lvi) has naturally puzzled later historians (Knowles, *Rel. Orders* II, 316).

[2] Bursar, Cellarer, Granator, 1438–45, Recepta praeter Arreragiis.

repair.[1] The monastery's expenses on the Coldingham and Lytham causes during the last years of Wessington's priorate weakened its financial position still further. One of the prior's motives in dividing the bursary had been the hope that he and his monks would be spared the losses incurred by a constant succession of new bursars; but between 1438 and 1445 there were three different cellarers and two granators, although only one bursar. Despite the division of the bursary, Wessington still found it difficult to appoint suitable administrators.[2] But the strongest economic argument against a divided bursary was that it led to an unnecessary duplication of labour and administrative expenses. By 1440, as the prior later admitted to Bishop Neville, 'certain members of the convent argued that this division cost more in horses and servants, as well as causing the absence of more persons from divine services'. The prior could find no convincing answer to this objection and merely restated the familiar proposition that in the last few years the bursar's responsibilities had become too onerous for one monk to support.

The party of Durham monks who '*inter se laborabant dictum officium ad statum pristinum revocare*' seized the opportunity of Bishop Neville's visitation of the convent in July 1442 to bring the issue into the open.[3] Neville, however, refused to take any action on the matter until it had been fully debated among the Durham monks, and it was at this stage (in late 1442) that Wessington produced a lengthy defence of his reform. Although the prior wrote somewhat bitterly about that group of monks who wished to proceed '*in lesionem libertatis sue*', he was temporarily successful in securing general support for his views. On receiving the unlikely news that '*unanimes estis et concordes*', Bishop Neville informed the prior and chapter, '*nos super disposicionem dicti officii vos totaliter dimittimus per presentes*'.[4] But the experiment of a divided bursary had obtained only a short reprieve. In November 1445, presumably because of renewed

[1] Loc. XXI, no. 20 (vii).

[2] It remains surprising that after his return to Durham the improvident Thomas Lawson became cellarer again, from March 1440 until his death three years later. In this capacity he ran up new debts of over £200, all concealed from the prior and chapter (Loc. XXI, no. 20 (vii); Bursar, 1442/43, Elemos. Consueta).

[3] See above, p. 235.

[4] Loc. XXI, no. 20 (iii) is a copy of Neville's letter. It can be dated on internal evidence to the spring of 1443.

hostility by Durham monks, Wessington was compelled to restore the old system. From that date until the Dissolution, the bursar continued to enjoy his financial supremacy, and the cellarer and granator were once again completely dependent on him for their revenues.[1]

It cannot be denied that Wessington's one major attempt at reform of the convent's financial machinery had ended in failure. Such a failure is not altogether surprising in the case of a prior who seems to have showed no great interest in the details of financial management. Wessington had no objection to a central receiving office as such; and he only introduced his alternative system because he could find no Durham monk prepared to shoulder the responsibilities of the bursary. In marked contrast to many late medieval English religious superiors who took important obediences into their own hands and established a financial autocracy,[2] Wessington's solution to his financial problems was decentralisation. It can certainly be said that in this sphere, as in so many others, the prior showed himself a traditionalist and conservative. A paradoxical effect of the experiment of 1438–45 was to take the monastic administration at Durham back to the period before 'the fully articulated obedientiary system had been seriously breached in the thirteenth century by the widespread introduction of a central treasury or receiving office'.[3] In any case no purely administrative reform, whether conservative or radical, could have more than an indirect effect on the mainsprings of Durham's finances, the harsh economic realities which caused its rent-roll to fluctuate from year to year. Several lay landlords of the fifteenth century were able to maintain and even enhance their material position by acquiring new property through inheritance, marriage or royal patronage. It is precisely because such a solution to its financial problems was denied to Durham, as to nearly all the great English monasteries, that its economic problems are of such great interest. As the Durham monks once complained to Bishop Neville, 'except for the manor of Houghall, which is hardly worth twenty marks when put to farm

---

[1] The complete restoration of the undivided bursary is proved by the surviving bursar's and cellarer's accounts of 1445/6; but there is no evidence to explain why Wessington should have reintroduced the old system at Martinmas 1445 rather than earlier or later.

[2] See the examples collected in Knowles, *Rel. Orders* II, 328–30.

[3] Ibid. II, 328.

these days, we have not acquired any lordship, land or military fee for 160 years'.[1]

Seen in this light, the apparently melancholy story of monastic finances in later medieval England does, of course, take on quite a different complexion. Few modern corporations, whether industrial, ecclesiastical or educational, could conceivably contemplate with equanimity the prospect of a permanently fixed income. Yet this was essentially the situation of late medieval English monasteries over a period as long and sometimes longer than 200 years. At a period when there were few parish churches left in England which were worth the labour and expense of appropriation, when it was notoriously difficult to persuade the more prosperous laymen in the country to bequeath really large endowments to the established religious houses, and when bishops and other ecclesiastics might provide financial assistance for building enterprises but not a regular subvention to the regular operations of the religious life, the struggles of so many monastic chapters to maintain their economic strength deserve our sympathy and respect. Against this background the constant ability of Durham, like other great houses, to recover from the threat of serious financial disaster is remarkable and even 'astonishing'.[2] Needless to say the Durham monks owed their very real degree of financial success to their skill in coming to terms with the general economic situation of their day. In the north-east at least, and despite various recent arguments to the contrary, the evidence points unmistakably to general and widespread economic recession, but to a recession that could nevertheless be made to serve the purposes of a monastic landlord on a fixed income. As we have seen, heavy mortality, intermittent warfare, and the exorbitant cost of litigation might produce a crisis like that of the late 1430s and 1440s; but from such situations the monks of Durham always managed to emerge with their revenues relatively intact and without the need to reduce their recruitment or standard of living at all drastically. The total net receipts of the bursar's office over the later medieval period tell, in short, a story of success rather than failure.

[1] Loc. XXI, no. 29.
[2] C. N. L. Brooke, introduction to *The Book of William Morton*, p. xvii; cf. Dobson, 'Richard Bell, Prior of Durham (1464–78) and Bishop of Carlisle (1478–95)', pp. 200–2.

Although the bursar's annual income in the first half of the fourteenth century had often exceeded £2,000 (e.g. £2,200 in 1330-1),
it was already as low as £1,470 in 1347-8. At £1,496 in 1353-4
and £1,463 as late as 1536-7, it remained at much the same level
until the Dissolution.[1] The implications of such financial stability
for the social and economic history of late medieval England need
no particular urging. It has sometimes been too readily assumed
that a rentier economy is *ipso facto* an inefficient economy. Despite
occasional lapses, this is not a view supported by the evidence at
Durham.[2] There it would be positively difficult to conclude that the
fifteenth-century convent enjoyed a smaller proportionate share of
the total wealth in the county than it had done 200 years earlier.
It is tempting to suppose, what might be of some comfort to the
economic historian, that the spiritual ascendancy of the late medieval
community of Saint Cuthbert continued to be based on an equivalent economic dominance in the north.

There is, however, a final and more enduring testimony to the
ability of the last generations of Durham monks to do more than
just make both ends meet. It was in the century after the first outbreak of the Black Death that the prior and chapter rebuilt or remodelled almost the whole of their own accommodation on the
peninsula at Durham. For whatever reason, and to our own relief,
the Durham monks never rebuilt their cathedral church in the
thirteenth century when it was fashionable – as the examples of
York Minster and Saint Mary's, York, will always remind us – to
do so. Nevertheless, the new and often imposing Perpendicular
windows inserted into the church during the priorates of John
Fossor (1341-74) and John Wessington should not be forgotten as
the last major medieval contributions to the fabric of Europe's

---

[1] Bursar, 1330/31, 1347/48, 1353/54, Recepta praeter Arreragiis; *Dur. Acct. Rolls* III,
690. For reasons already mentioned these figures must be regarded as estimates –
reasonably accurate – of the potential income of the bursar, i.e. without allowances
for current arrears, wastes and decays.

[2] Nor apparently by that of the archbishop of Canterbury: see F. R. H. Du Boulay,
'A Rentier Economy in the later Middle Ages: the Archbishopric of Canterbury',
Econ. H.R., Second Series, XVI (1964), 427-38. For another case of a northern
monastery where 'The *rentier* existence was a reasonably secure, even if fairly
stagnant one', see *Bolton Priory Rentals and Ministers' Accounts, 1473-1539*, ed.
I. Kershaw, Yorkshire Archaeological Society, Record Series, CXXXII (1970),
p. xxiv.

greatest Romanesque building.[1] Perhaps the most cogent reason for the decision not to rebuild the Anglo-Norman church in the later medieval period was that the precocious work of its original masons remained structurally sound. To this generalisation there was one notorious and typical exception – the central tower, rebuilt piecemeal at various periods in the fifteenth century after several catastrophes, of which the most serious were lightning storms in 1429 and 1459.[2] Despite extensive re-modelling by Gilbert Scott in 1859, the central tower still stands, perhaps accidentally 'noble in proportion', as 'a fitting and harmonious summit' to an incomparable cathedral. It is a fitting tribute too not only to the efforts but to the finances of the fifteenth-century community of Saint Cuthbert. Letters written by Prior Richard Bell in the 1470s leave no doubt that it was the monks of Durham themselves who had to bear the onerous costs of the 'reddification of our steple'.[3]

Besides bringing the architectural development of their cathedral to its final stages, the late medieval monks of Durham completely transformed the monastic buildings to its south. The extensive reconstruction of the Durham cloister and the buildings around it during the century after the Black Death ought to be seen, which it rarely is, as one of the most sustained and impressive feats in the history of medieval English architecture. By the late 1360s work is known to have started on the new monastic and prior's kitchen, built – under the inspired supervision of John Lewyn – as a detached unit to the south of the conventual refectory.[4] The monks' equally impressive, if more conventional, new dormitory was apparently constructed very rapidly indeed at the turn of the century, between 1398 and 1404.[5] Hardly had the monks moved their beds into this

---

[1] Loc. XXVII, no. 1; *Scrip. Tres*, pp. 131–2, cxli–cxlii, cclxxii–cclxxiii; cf. W. Greenwell, *Durham Cathedral* (sixth edition, Durham, 1904), pp. 72–3, 91–2.

[2] Reg. Parv. II, fo. 39; Loc. XXVII, no. 1; and see the valuable article by M. G. Snape, 'Durham Cathedral: an "Unknown" Fire', *Trans. of the Architectural and Archaeological Society of Durham and Northumberland*, New Series (forthcoming).

[3] Reg. Parv. III, fos. 158, 160; cf. J. E. Bygate, *The Cathedral Church of Durham* (Bell's Cathedral Series; London, 1899), pp. 21–2; Boyle, *Comprehensive Guide to the County of Durham*, pp. 328–30.

[4] Some of the relevant kitchen building accounts have been printed, less than adequately, in *Scrip. Tres*, pp. 132–3, and *Dur. Acct. Rolls* II, 569–73; cf. J. Harvey, *English Mediaeval Architects* (London, 1954), p. 169.

[5] Misc. Chrs., no. 6073; Loc. II, no. 13; Reg. II, fo. 215; *Scrip. Tres*, pp. clxxx–

great timber-roofed hall, than they made preparations for an even more expensive piece of reconstruction, that of the cloister itself. And as this great enterprise of the *opus claustri* came to a close in the years immediately after 1416, the new cloister alleys were furnished and decorated, together with the monastic carrells therein.[1] Thanks to a disastrous 'restoration' in the late eighteenth century, the late medieval Durham cloister has withstood the ravages of time much less successfully than the new library built over the slype in the same period (1414–18). Wessington's library and the later reconstruction of the prior's apartments to the south-east of the cloister are discussed in detail elsewhere; and no attempt can be made here to recapitulate the architectural history of early fifteenth-century Durham in all its complexity. However, it ought to be mentioned that no sooner had the new cloister and library been completed than work began on the monastic infirmary immediately south of the dormitory. Durham office-holders regularly contributed to the expenses of this building between 1419 and 1430; and a solitary surviving account of the *supervisor operis Infirmarie* in 1420 shows that activity was then in full progress under the control of John Bell, a mason who had already supervised work on the cloister.[2] Also rebuilt during Wessington's priorate was the southernmost room in the convent's guest-house, that 'King's Chamber' which survived to the Dissolution as the most sumptuous of many guest apartments at the monastery, 'deservinge that name, in that the king him selfe myghte verie well haue lyne in yt for the princelynes thereof'.[3]

Indeed the only major conventual building at Durham not rebuilt or thoroughly refurbished in the period between the 1360s and 1430s seems to have been the monastic refectory or frater, later wainscoted by Prior Thomas Castell (1494–1519) and converted

clxxxii, clxxxvii–cxc; contributions made to the '*dormitorio*' in contemporary obedientiary accounts; Sacrist, 1406/7.

[1] Loc. II, no. 19 (a long although not complete series of the cloister building accounts); Almoner, 1419–21; *Scrip. Tres*, pp. 146, cciv–ccv, cclxxiii–cclxxiv. On the exceptionally interesting early history of the Durham cloister, see W. H. St John Hope's communication in the *Proceedings of the Society of Antiquaries of London*, Second Series, XXII (1909), 416–24, the conclusions of which are confirmed by E. Gee, 'Discoveries in the Frater at Durham', *Archaeological Journal* CXXIII (1966), 73.

[2] The account is printed, with many very serious errors, in *Dur. Acct. Rolls* I, 269–71.

[3] *Rites*, p. 90; Loc. XXVII, no. 1; cf. *Dur. Acct. Rolls* I, 147–8, 150, 160–1.

into a library by Dean Sudbury in the 1680s. This fact is itself no doubt indicative of the late medieval community's partial withdrawal from the rigours of a refectory regime to alternative and more informal eating-places. The best known of these was 'a place called the lofte' at the west end of the frater which can perhaps be more or less safely identified with the *solarium caritatis* of the convent's records. Although this room dated from at least the early fourteenth century, in 1430 it was re-vaulted and two new windows inserted into its northern wall under the supervision of Thomas Ayre, monastic refectorer.[1] Two years later Ayre began accounting for the construction of a new monastic laver or lavatory, built from marble quarried at Egglestone Abbey in Teesdale, and situated near the door from cloister into refectory.[2] It is literally true that at early fifteenth-century Durham there can have been no monk 'free from the necessity of avoiding masons' scaffolding in the cloister or watching the sailing cloud through gaps in the unfinished vaulting'.[3]

After John Wessington's resignation in 1446 the pace of building operations at Durham noticeably slackened. Of the last priors of Durham, only Thomas Castell was remembered as a great builder; and even his structural alterations to the monastic precincts were largely confined to the rebuilding of the abbey gatehouse and its chapel as well as the repair of the Four Doctors' window in the north transept of the cathedral. The obvious explanation is no doubt the correct one. The massive building enterprises of the first half of the fifteenth century had been so extensive and successful that relatively little alteration was required in the subsequent and final period of the convent's history. By late medieval standards as well as ours, the living conditions of the twelfth and thirteenth-century Durham monks must have been crude and insanitary; but by 1440

---

[1] *Scrip. Tres*, pp. ccccxlii–ccccxliii. Despite a recent suggestion that the 'loft' was a gallery over the west end of the frater, its exact location and relationship with the *solarium caritatis* still remains a partly open question: see M. Johnson, 'Recent Work on the Refectory of Durham Cathedral', *Trans. of Architectural and Archaeological Society of Durham and Northumberland*, New Series, I (1968), 90.

[2] *Scrip. Tres*, pp. ccccxliii–ccccxlv; the octagonal laver basin still survives, but the foundations of the laver house itself have been returfed since their excavation at the beginning of this century: W. H. St John Hope, 'Recent Discoveries in the Cloister of Durham Abbey', *Archaeologia* LVIII (1903), 437–60.

[3] D. Knowles, *The Historian and Character* (Cambridge, 1963), p. 210.

or so the prior and chapter had largely achieved their aims of greater magnificence, material comfort, structural sub-division, and privacy. Needless to say, the Durham monks would have been unable to finance the whole of this formidable building programme exclusively from their own resources. Thus the complete recon-struction of the monastic cloister, the most expensive building project of all, was made possible only by gifts and bequests of £600 from Bishop Skirlaw and a further contribution from Bishop Langley, who paid at least £239 so that the fourth walk of the cloister might be completed in 1419.[1] Similarly, the thorough renovation of the Galilee chapel between 1428 and 1435, costing about £500, was financed by Bishop Langley in preparation for his burial there.[2] The bishops of Durham, for obvious reasons, stood alone as regular providers of really substantial financial assistance to the building enterprises of the Durham monks. Only occasional monetary contributions were to be expected by this period from the charity of local nobles, county gentry, and pilgrims to Saint Cuth-bert's shrine. It remains astonishing how much capital the monks of early fifteenth-century Durham were able to devote to building expenses from their own fixed and limited resources at a time of apparent stringency. The total cost of internal *structurae et reparaciones* during Wessington's priorate (including the sacrist's building ex-penses but neither the new cloister nor the Galilee chapel) were estimated at £2,354 2s. 9d., an average of almost £80 a year.[3] If a modern visitor to the Durham peninsula wishes to gain some impression of the late medieval prior and chapter's financial success, he has only to follow a hackneyed but invaluable piece of advice and look around him.

[1] Loc. II, no. 19; *Scrip. Tres*, pp. 145–6, cciv–ccv. But the bishop's contributions to new dormitory and cloister did not relieve the monks themselves of '*graves et immense expense*' on these projects (4.6. Ebor., no. 2).

[2] *Scrip. Tres*, p. 146; Storey, *Thomas Langley*, p. 197.

[3] Misc. Chrs., nos. 5727, 7131; Loc. XXVII, no. 1; *Scrip. Tres*, p. cclxxiv.

Chapter 9

THE DURHAM CELLS

Let an enquiry be made concerning those monks who reside in cells, to discover whether they live honestly and according to the Rule.[1]

In their mother house of Durham the monks of Saint Cuthbert were able to maintain the level of religious life at a standard which was rarely scandalous, sometimes edifying and nearly always respectable. The position of the monastery's dependencies in the later middle ages was usually much more depressing. All of the cells, except Durham College, Oxford, had been founded or re-founded in the eleventh and twelfth centuries during a period of private benefaction and general good-will, 'when the old orders were still lords of the ascendant'.[2] This early optimism proved not to be entirely warranted and the later history of most of these small houses, like small monasteries everywhere in England, is one of financial decline and occasional crisis as well as of a somewhat chequered spiritual life. In retrospect it might well seem that the priory of Durham would have lost little, either in the worldly or the spiritual spheres, if it had been deprived of five or six of its nine dependencies. Yet the Durham monks, with their obsessive interest in the traditional liberties and possessions of Saint Cuthbert's church, were naturally devoted to the preservation and not the liquidation of their cells; in particular, they were prepared to fight a century-long and almost ruinously expensive campaign to retain their control over Coldingham in Scotland. The prior and chapter's attitude to the dependencies can indeed only be understood in terms of their own rather than more modern values. The inherent weaknesses of the system were inherited from the past. It was the fifteenth-century prior of Durham's duty to maintain as much stability as possible in the none too favourable conditions of his day. In this he was by no means

---

[1] Articles of enquiry for a late fourteenth-century monastic visitation, probably composed by Uthred of Boldon (Pantin, *Chapters* II, p. 88).

[2] Knowles, *Rel. Orders* I, 308. Nevertheless Gerald of Wales launched a savage attack on Benedictine cells at a very early date in their history: *Giraldi Cambrensis Opera* (Rolls Series, 1861–91), IV, 31–7.

unsuccessful as may appear from the following account of the methods by which the mother church controlled the inmates of its cells.

Quieta, non movere is then a phrase which not unfairly summarises the history of most of Durham's cells in the later middle ages. Their spiritual and economic condition showed few signs of either marked degeneration or advancement during the fifty years between 1400 and 1450. Although each of the dependencies enjoyed its own individual and sometimes idiosyncratic peculiarities, all were alike in being subjected to the strong central authority of the prior and chapter at Durham. Two of the daughter houses do however demand individual attention as they provoked crises which shattered the somewhat monotonous and even tenor of the routines which bound Durham and its cells together. The anomalous situation by which a group of English monks still served the Scottish priory of Coldingham had long been Durham's obvious Achilles' heel, and during the priorate of John Wessington, the convent only just succeeded in preserving the *status quo* against the aggression of Scotland's monks and magnates. More unexpected was the attempt made by William Partrike, prior of Lytham in the 1440s, to secure his independence from Durham. Partrike launched one of the most dangerous attacks ever made on any prior of Durham's authority and occasioned the most dramatic crisis of Wessington's own career. Yet a third Durham dependency deserves separate discussion – but for a very different reason.[1] Alone among the Durham cells of the fifteenth century, the history of Durham College, Oxford, gave cause for congratulation rather than despondency. Although the constitutional status and administrative organisation of this college was assimilated to that of the other daughters of Durham, it possessed its own distinctive and academic *raison d'être*. Durham College trained monks for the future at a time when the other cells only too often offered little but a nostalgic memorial to the misplaced idealism of the past. So, at least, it may appear to us; but one must never deny the possibility – rarely capable of proof – that several Durham monks found service in the cells more personally and spiritually rewarding than the following melancholy survey suggests.

[1] See below, Chapter 10.

'HANDMAIDS TO DURHAM'

Until the loss of Coldingham in 1462, the monastery of Durham
had nine cells dependent upon it. These were the small houses of
Jarrow and Monk Wearmouth in the north-east of Durham
county; the priory of Holy Island; the priory of Coldingham, north
of Berwick; the priory of Saint Leonard's near Stamford in the
diocese of Lincoln; the priory of Lytham on the Lancashire coast;
the priory of Finchale, three miles north of Durham, and the small
cell of Farne, both of which owed their initial reputation to solitary
hermits rather than regular monks; and finally, Durham College,
Oxford, whose history begins in the last quarter of the thirteenth
century although it only achieved regular collegiate status after its
re-foundation by Bishop Hatfield in 1381.[1] All these dependencies
were served by professed monks from the central monastery and
all, including the priories and Durham College, were regularly
described as 'celles' by the Durham community. So large a number
of dependencies is a tribute to the pioneering activities of the early
Durham monks as well as to the reputation of Saint Cuthbert
himself. Of all English Benedictine houses, only St Albans rivalled
Durham in this respect.[2] Few other Black Monk monasteries had
more than two or three cells and even Christ Church, Canterbury,
held only the priory of Dover and Canterbury College, Oxford.[3]
It is not, therefore, particularly easy to find parallels for Durham's
numerous progeny. An especially unfortunate feature of the
Durham situation was that not one of her cells (with the possible

---

[1] Most of these cells had experienced some form of monastic life in the Anglo-
Saxon period but, despite Durham's desire to prove the contrary, continuity had
been broken in all cases. The dates at which they were permanently occupied by
Durham monks on a residentiary basis often remain very obscure, and may (for
example) be as late as the mid-thirteenth century in the case of Jarrow (*Scrip. Tres*,
pp. xl, lviii). I am grateful to Mr Alan Piper for his advice on these issues.

[2] In 1400 the abbot of St Albans also controlled nine cells but in the course of the
following fifty years he lost Beadlow (Beaulieu) and Wymondham and gained only
the alien priory of Pembroke: see *Annales J. Amundesham* (Rolls Series, 1870–71),
II, 105–12; *Reg. John Whethamstede* (Rolls Series, 1872–73), I, 48–54, 147–52, 416–17;
II, 26, 178.

[3] A few of the larger Benedictine monasteries held four to six cells but no more,
e.g. Norwich, Gloucester, Tewkesbury and Saint Mary's, York (D. Knowles and
R. N. Hadcock, *Medieval Religious Houses: England and Wales* [Cambridge, 1953],
pp. 58–82).

exception of Durham College) was large enough to enjoy a flourishing community life of the sort found at the dependent priories of Dover and Tynemouth. At the end of the thirteenth century both Coldingham and, to a lesser extent, Finchale had evolved a genuine *esprit de corps*, but this was long extinct at the time of Wessington's election.

The prior's first responsibility towards the Durham cells was to see that they were adequately served by Durham monks.[1] It was possible for him to hold an individual cell in his own hands for a short time; but such a course of action was to be contemplated only at times of crisis and even then it was unsafe to leave any cell without a superior for even a few months. In April 1441 Richard Barton, prior of Stamford, wrote to Wessington asking him to leave his office unfilled while he moved to Oxford and lectured on the Sentences in preparation for his doctorate in theology. Wessington replied that he dared not leave the cell empty of a governing monk in case the royal escheators took it into the king's hands; that Wessington's anxieties were justified is shown by the litigation from which Abbot Whethamstede suffered after the claim that the cell of Beadlow had escheated to the king was put forward in 1435.[2] The prior was therefore careful to replace a deceased or resigned superior of a cell immediately. Appointments to these positions were made formally by the prior of Durham's letters patent under his large seal ('*sub oblongo sigillo domini prioris*').[3] Full powers of administration over the spiritualities and temporalities of the cell were delegated to

---

[1] During the first half of the fifteenth century the number of Durham monks resident in any given cell varied within fairly narrow limits. There were usually nine monks at Finchale, three at Holy Island and two each at Lytham, Stamford, Jarrow and Wearmouth. Farne was sometimes unoccupied, sometimes served by a solitary master but usually attended by two monks. By the terms of Bishop Hatfield's foundation statutes, the convent was required to maintain eight student monks, including the warden, at Durham College; in fact, between 1417 and 1431, seven was the average number of monks receiving commons at the college (Durham College, 1417–31; cf. 4.6. Ebor., no. 1). Coldingham was subject to greater vicissitudes in number; the prior there had only one monk-fellow in January 1438 but three in June 1446 (Reg. III, fo. 217; Loc. XVI, no. 6). It can therefore be claimed with some confidence that there were normally about thirty members of the Durham community away from the mother house at any one time as opposed to forty or more under Wessington's immediate control (cf. *Scrip. Tres*, p. cclxxxv).

[2] *Annales J. Amundesham* (Rolls Series, 1870–71), II, 109; Reg. Parv. II, fo. 136.

[3] Reg. Parv. II, fo. 96.

the new prior or master and the terms of his appointment, otherwise not specific, required him to render an annual account of the receipts and expenses of his dependency.[1] In addition, the warden of Durham College was expressly given the right to chastise and even to expel any secular student under his care who proved an unworthy member of the Oxford community.[2] One of the traditional liberties of the cathedral church of Durham, expressed in *Le Convenit* of 1229, was that the lord prior (as the priors of Durham were usually called to distinguish them from the priors of the cells) should be completely free to appoint and remove all '*monachi officiales*' at his pleasure.[3] The Durham prior did not therefore need to obtain episcopal consent or confirmation when appointing priors and masters to the five Durham cells of Finchale, Jarrow, Wearmouth, Holy Island and Farne. The warden of Durham College, who had no spiritual responsibilities outside his own community, could also take office without reference to any ecclesiastical or university authority.[4] But the three priories of Stamford, Lytham and Coldingham, the last two of which incidentally involved a cure of souls normally delegated to a parochial chaplain, were subject to the normal canonical practice of presentation to and admission by the local ordinary.[5]

As well as appointing the superiors of the cells, the prior of Durham also had full power to choose obedientiaries in those few dependencies where they still existed. In the thirteenth century Coldingham had needed the services of a terrar, almoner and sacrist; but although the two latter offices still survived in 1405, there is no sign that Wessington made regular appointments to them after 1416. But he selected the sub-prior and cellarer of Finchale as well as the two Oxford bursars, who accounted to their local superior

[1] For a printed example, see *Finchale Priory*, p. 34.

[2] Reg. III, fo. 279.

[3] *Feodarium Dunelm*, p. 213. According to Durham custom, however, the priors of Coldingham and Stamford were appointed by the lord prior after consultation with his chapter: Loc. XXI, no. 20 (ii).

[4] The college was, however, subject to visitation by the bishop of Lincoln (Durham College, 1422/23).

[5] Instruments of resignation and letters of presentation were sent to the bishop of Lincoln, in the case of Stamford; to the archdeacon of Richmond, in the case of Lytham; and to the bishop of St Andrews in the case of Coldingham (Reg. III, fos. 68v, 111, 115, 199, 254; Reg. Parv. II, fos. 48–50).

and not to Durham.[1] The prior also regularly commissioned two Durham College monks to hear the confessions of their fellows, a duty normally delegated to the sub-prior at Finchale.[2] More significantly, all monks, and not only superiors and obedientiaries, were transferred to or removed from the Durham cells at the prior's sole discretion. In October 1442 the prior of Stamford reported to Durham that his companion, Thomas Hexham, wished to leave the cell and suggested that he should be replaced by William Birden from the mother house: Wessington refused on the grounds that Hexham was well liked in Lincolnshire and that Birden was still too young, 'and it would be expedient for him to wait a little longer in the cloister'.[3] When the prior did decide to move a monk from one dependency to another, he sent him a letter, for presentation first to his existing superior, who gave him his travelling expenses, and secondly to the head of his new community who had no alternative but to admit him. Such letters of removal were issued under the prior's small or signet seal and were recorded in his personal register.[4]

For obvious reasons the power to dispatch an unruly subject to a distant daughter house is perhaps the most formidable weapon at the disposal of a religious superior. The prior of Durham's complete control over the mobility of his own monks made it easy for him to succumb to the temptation of sending his more rebellious and unpopular subjects into what might be described as unofficial exile. At Durham, as elsewhere, this practice had once given rise to frequent complaints; in 1354 Prior Fossor was charged at Hatfield's visitation with sending monks to the cells for no good cause or because they opposed him in chapter.[5] In the fifteenth century too,

[1] Reg. Parv. II, fos. 43, 46, 79, 86, 123; cf. *Durham Annals*, p. 107.
[2] Reg. Parv. II, fos. 20, 85.
[3] Ibid., fo. 169.
[4] Ibid., passim. Although numerous, the entries do not amount to anything like a complete register of removals.
[5] B. Harbottle, 'Bishop Hatfield's Visitation of Durham Priory in 1354', *Arch. Ael.*, Fourth Series, XXXVI (1958), 95. Compare the injunction made by Bishop William Bateman in 1347 that disobedient monks should not be sent to the cells but rather be reformed at Norwich itself: Cheney, 'Norwich Cathedral Priory in the Fourteenth Century', p. 106. This type of complaint was extremely common, for only the most obdurate monk in an extremely ill-disciplined house would dare to defy his abbot's sentence of exile (Pantin, *Chapters* II, 51–2; III, 292).

removal from the central monastery was often regarded as a punish-
ment; and in August 1433 the prior transferred George Cyther from
Lytham to Finchale with the special instruction not to call at the
mother house on the journey.[1] However, there is no evidence to
suggest that Wessington wantonly persecuted his monks by sending
them arbitrarily to the cells and this particular grievance does not
emerge among the *comperta* of late medieval Durham visitations. In
May 1443 Wessington wrote that he would send no monk to the
cell of Stamford who was likely to bring shame on the reputation
of Saint Cuthbert and his monks.[2]

The prior was faced with the major difficulty that service in the
dependencies was generally extremely unpopular among his monks.
During the early 1430s the master of Farne, Thomas Moreby,
petitioned repeatedly to be allowed to resign before Wessington at
last found a replacement for him.[3] Wessington did not value
mobility for its own sake, and when monks were recalled to Durham
it was usually at their own request. Even the superiors of the cells,
whose status was much higher than it would have been at Durham,
willingly exchanged a priorate for an obedience at Durham. The
length of tenure of any prior, master or warden was rarely more
than seven years. In the thirty years between 1416 and 1446, there
were six masters of Jarrow, five priors of Stamford, and at least
twelve masters of Farne. There was, admittedly, never any scarcity
of monks who wished to enjoy the amenities of Durham College
and Finchale. The convent also occasionally recruited a monk who
genuinely preferred to spend most of his religious life outside
Durham itself. Such a man was Richard Barton who went to
Durham College immediately after ordination in 1412 and three
years later moved to Stamford as the prior's companion. At Oxford
again in the 1420s, he received his baccalaureate in theology and
served as warden of Durham College from 1428 to 1431. After a
few years as third prior, feretrar and chamberlain at Durham, he
became prior of Stamford in May 1440, a position which he resigned
only in July 1462 when 'broken by age'.[4] Of the forty years of his

---

[1] Reg. Parv. II, fo. 172.   [2] Ibid., fo. 172r.

[3] Ibid., fo. 91. For earlier protests against exile in the cells, see Loc. XXVII, no. 12;
Durham Annals, pp. 104–6.

[4] Durham College, 1413–16, 1428–31; Feretrar, 1434–9; Reg. III, fo. 254. Cf.
Emden I, 122.

active religious life, Barton had spent at least thirty away from Durham. His long headship of a cell was exceeded only occasionally in the history of the monastery, for instance by John Aclyff who was prior of Coldingham, often *in absentia*, between 1391 and 1418.[1] Barton and Aclyff led unusual careers but no Durham monk was likely to escape completely from some years' service in the cells. A total of 132 monks entered the monastery between 1383 and 1441 and, except for half-a-dozen who died young, they can all be shown to have passed at least a year away from the mother house. Despite its unpopularity, occasional residence in the dependencies may be one of the reasons why Durham apparently suffered less from internal dissension and intrigue than many other fifteenth-century English religious houses.

The effects of such a high rate of mobility were no doubt more beneficial to the central monastery than to the dependencies themselves. In James Raine's words, 'they were all stocked from Durham, and, what struck still more deeply at the root of attachment, their inmates, including even their respective priors themselves, were almost yearly migrating from Cell to Cell at the command of the Mother Church'.[2] Raine's other comment, that in none of the cells 'could an aged monk glory as the scene of his youth' does, however, need qualification. All Durham monks certainly passed their novitiate at the mother house, for the prior there, unlike the abbot of St Albans,[3] never allowed the heads of the subordinate houses to receive the professions of entrants into the monastic life. But when a Durham monk did have a regional connection with a particular cell, his prior was always ready to make use of it. Robert Scremerston, presumably if not certainly a native of the Northumbrian village of that name, spent the whole of the twelve years between 1438 and 1450 at either Coldingham, Holy Island or Farne.[4] As was made clear on various occasions, a monk's ability to secure the good-will of local landowners was often an overriding consideration when placing him in a cell. Much more than the mother house herself, the fifteenth-century dependencies were extremely vulnerable to the

[1] Reg. III, fo. 59; cf. Emden I, 10–11.   [2] Raine, *North Durham*, p. 132.

[3] The prior of Tynemouth, for example, enjoyed privileges much more extensive than those of any superior of a Durham cell; *Reg. John Whethamstede* (Rolls Series, 1872–73), II, 44–6.

[4] Loc. XXVII, no. 8; Reg. Parv. II, fos. 98, 123, 185.

claims of any local families who considered themselves the rightful patrons of a cell. Without the benevolence of the Homes at Colding-ham, the Stanleys at Lytham, the Hiltons at Wearmouth and the Ogles at Holy Island and Farne, all these houses found it extremely difficult to collect their revenues and protect themselves from ex-ternal aggression. On hearing of Lord Stanley's good offices at Lytham in 1474, Prior Bell was 'right gladde in my hert that I and my brethir have getyn so worthi a protectour in that Cuntry'.[1] The interference of the local patron often proved embarrassing, as in 1441 when the Lord of Hailes and Sir David Home pressed their own candidate for the priorate of Coldingham on Wessington only to meet with his refusal: 'this L yheere, in the whilke the prior hase been in that religion, was never monke of Doresme promote to priore or office be request of seculer men'.[2] Such a claim could not have been put forward in many other English monasteries of the fifteenth century.[3]

Apart from his power to assign those monks he wished to each cell, Wessington had a variety of methods at his disposal by which he could supervise the fortunes of each dependency. It is somewhat surprising that the prior of Durham did not follow the example of the abbot of St Albans and make occasional visitations of his dependencies. Except for some periods of relaxation at Jarrow, Wessington does not appear to have visited his cells at all. He did, however, issue legislation, either in his own right or after consul-tation with the Durham chapter, which was to be observed through-out the subordinate houses. Wessington's greatest achievement in this direction appears to have been an ordinance of 1430, of which no copy now survives, 'to reform the errors and irregularities of our brethren who now live in the cells'.[4] The most commonly reported of these 'irregularities' were not criminal or sexual offences but the frequenting of taverns and the discarding of woollen for linen clothing. Individual monks known to be leading particularly ill-

---

[1] Reg. Parv. III, fos. 153v–154.

[2] Ibid., II, fo. 143.

[3] Compare the Duke of Gloucester's success in procuring the priory of Tynemouth for Nicholas Boston in 1478; *Reg. John Whethamstede* (Rolls Series, 1872–73), II, xxxvi–xliii, 182–5.

[4] Reg. Parv. II, fo. 46. For thirteenth-century injunctions to the Durham cells, see *Durham Annals*, pp. 99–103.

disciplined or scandalous lives received letters from Wessington warning them to mend their ways; examples are the Durham College fellow, Thomas Brogham, who preferred archery and drink to lectures and divine service, and John Harom who was eventually removed from the mastership of Farne for conversing with ribalds and wandering about the mainland with clothes torn and covered in mud.[1] Wessington's ability to correct these errant monks depended on his having regular news from the outlying cells. Hence the central importance to the Durham cell-system of the annual chapter at the mother house which the superiors of all cells were expected to attend.

Of all English Benedictine houses, the monastery of Durham appears to have been the most faithful in its observance of the third chapter of Benedict XII's constitutions of 1336 which called for general or annual chapters where priors and masters of cells should account for their expenses *'extra monasterium'*.[2] The annual chapter had become a regular feature of the Durham year as early as 1345[3] and by immemorial custom was invariably held on the first Monday after Ascension Day. At these meetings, not only were administrative reforms proposed by a select group of diffinitors, but monk officials, whether at Durham or in the cells, were required to render their accounts to auditors deputed by the chapter. Wessington and his colleagues, in their replies to Bishop Neville's 1442 *comperta*, categorically affirmed that this had been Durham practice for over fifty years. The traces of somewhat rudimentary audit which can still be detected on monastic account rolls confirm their statement, as does the fact that yearly accounts at Durham and the cells normally ended at Ascension Day or Whitsunday, a few days later. The survival of these accounts at Durham is proof in itself of annual intercourse between the cells and the mother house.[4] The priors

---

[1] Reg. Parv. II, fos. 133, 174.

[2] Pantin, *Chapters* II, 230.

[3] *Reg. Richard of Bury*, p. 262. But as early as 1235 a Durham statute had required ' *Quod Priores et Procuratores Cellarum debeant certificare Priorem Dunelmensem de redditibus Domorum suarum semel in anno*' (*Scrip. Tres*, p. xl). Cf. Reg. Parv. IV, fo. 28v.

[4] During the thirty years of Wessington's priorate, accounts remain for all but four years at Durham College, for all but three years at Finchale, and for never less than twelve years at any cell except Coldingham. James Raine printed many of the Finchale, Coldingham, Holy Island, Jarrow, Wearmouth and Farne account rolls

and masters of the dependencies were supposed to be present in person and only received a special summons if they had proved reluctant to attend in the past.[1] Wessington's own reliance on the annual chapter emerges from a letter to Sir David Home in March 1441: 'thar for at our annuall chapetre befor Whyttsonday, at the whilk will be the priour of Coldyngham, as I suppose, and other priours that langes till us I sall common with them and other of my brether: and son eftre send yowe ane answere'.[2] If any prior was unable to attend the annual chapter, he sent official letters of proxy, appointing as his representative one of his own monks who presumably carried the year's account roll to Durham.[3] The chance survival of the memorandum which Richard Barton, prior of Stamford, gave his proctor to the 1443 annual chapter illustrates the connection between local and central superior. Barton asked his representative to urge Prior Wessington to send him two new monks from Durham as well as the chapter's letters of confraternity to a Nottingham burgess and his wife who had given financial aid to the priory of Stamford. The rumour had reached Barton that he was being maligned by Henry Helay, a senior Durham monk, but he had no intention of resigning and wished to hear news of the previous year's annual chapter and episcopal visitation.[4]

It was also at the Durham annual chapter that Wessington imposed money contributions on the obediences and cells, to be paid within the coming financial year. The central monastery's right to collect pensions from its dependencies was well-established on the principle that 'the limbs ought naturally to support the head'; but it naturally led to occasional resentment on the part of the priors of the cells.[5] From the mid-fourteenth century until 1412 the major

(either in full, selection or translation) in various volumes of the Surtees Society and *North Durham*; unfortunately Raine's treatment of Roman numerals was far from satisfactory and his transcriptions of these cannot be used with much confidence.

[1] Reg. Parv. III, fo. 12. At St Albans the priors of the cells apparently only came before the abbot when formally summoned to do so: *Reg. John Whethamstede* (Rolls Series, 1872–73), II, 123.

[2] Reg. Parv. II, fo. 122.

[3] Misc. Chrs., nos. 5472, 6843–6847; Loc. XVI, nos. 7, 11; Reg. III, fo. 116.

[4] Loc. XXV, no. 152.

[5] Compare the complaint of the priors of the St Albans cells in 1422: *Annales J. Amundesham* (Rolls Series, 1870–71), I, 83–5.

office-holders at Durham and its subordinate houses had contributed regularly towards the expenses of their brethren at Oxford.[1] In 1412–13, by which date the new collegiate foundation had emerged from its early years of financial embarrassment and was able to live of its own, the '*pensiones officiorum et cellarum*' were diverted to help pay for Thomas Rome's inception as doctor of theology.[2] Throughout his priorate Wessington imposed contributions as he saw fit and primarily in the interests of his building programme at Durham. The construction of the monastic library (1414–18), the remodelling of the Durham infirmary (1419–30), of the prior's apartments (1424–36), and the repair of the central tower after its destruction by lightning (1432–6), were all largely financed out of contributions made by the obediences and cells. During his last six years as prior, Wessington levied particularly heavy pensions from his cells in order to relieve the Durham bursary from the serious debts contracted by the inefficient Thomas Lawson. This type of income was not assigned to a Durham obedientiary but held in a special '*Compotus Pensionum*', providing an emergency fund on which the prior could draw to meet the costs of building or extraordinary litigation.[3] Not all nine Durham cells contributed to this fund, for Durham College and Farne were usually exempted, while Stamford paid only at rare intervals. The other dependencies were assessed in view of their financial position as it fluctuated from year to year; so, in September 1443, Wessington wrote to inform William Partrike at Lytham that he had imposed a pension of £5 on his cell, 'because it is said that your priory is rich enough in cattle, sheep and horses as well as other income and rents'.[4] During the earlier years of Wessington's priorate, however, Lytham usually forwarded only £1 to the central monastery, Finchale and Holy Island £2 each, while Jarrow and Wearmouth could rarely afford more than a few shillings.[5] But although the cells made only a small contribution to the economic welfare of the mother house, it is only right to emphasize that they did not usually receive financial assistance from

---

[1] Durham College, 1396–1412; Jarrow, 1400–12.

[2] Durham College, 1412/13.

[3] The '*compoti pensionum*' for the years 1441/4 survive as Misc. Chrs., nos. 5649–51, 7138.

[4] Reg. Parv. II, fo. 174.

[5] Finchale, Holy Island, Lytham, Jarrow, Wearmouth, 1416–36.

Durham themselves. In general, all ten religious houses served by Durham monks were expected to be self-supporting.

It is therefore not surprising that the annual income of each cell largely determined not only its material prosperity but sometimes its spiritual welfare. None of the Durham dependencies was very wealthy and at the Dissolution the total clear value of all eight cells was estimated at only £433 as compared with £1,366 for the mother house itself.[1] A hundred years earlier the average annual receipts of each cell between 1416 and 1446 can be calculated from its account rolls. The following figures consist of the average *recepte de claro* of each cell (they do not include the *remanentia*, *arreragia* and *mutuaciones* regularly included as items of receipt in the account) and are reckoned only to the nearest pound: Finchale, £190; Durham College, £185; Coldingham, £100 (?); Holy Island, £88; Lytham, £75; Stamford, £68; Jarrow, £38; Wearmouth, £32; and Farne, £15.[2] These totals may be accepted only as an approximate guide to the financial situation of each cell. The account rolls cannot be expected to give a proper impression of the importance of a demesne farm to the economy of a particular cell. When William Partrike succeeded Richard Haswell at Lytham in 1431, he inherited a stock of 30 'avers', 31 ploughing oxen, 31 pigs, 112 cattle and 260 sheep.[3] Apart from the profits made by the sale of animals and animal produce on the cash market, Partrike and his fellow monks received deliveries of food in kind which never appeared in the cell's accounts. At the other extreme was Durham College, Oxford, which had no home-farm and was so dependent on money income that its accounts appear to be a much

---

[1] B.M. Additional MS. 37,021 n, fo. 4 ('Valor Possessionum . . . Dunelmensis'); *Valor Ecclesiasticus* v (1825), 299–306. Finchale was valued at over £122; Durham College at £115; Holy Island at £48; Lytham at £48; Jarrow at £38; Stamford at £25; Wearmouth at £25; and Farne at £12. The *valet de claro* totals of the *Valor Ecclesiasticus* were, of course, subject to various deductions not made in the *recepte de claro* of the cells' accounts.

[2] The original account rolls of all the cells have been consulted in the calculation of these averages except in the case of Finchale, where use has been made of *Finchale Priory*, pp. clxx–ccxlvi. As no prior's accounts for Coldingham survive between 1416 and 1446, it has been necessary to use the receipts '*de claro*' of 1405–6 (£100 8s. 6d.); Coldingham was heavily in debt this year and there is every reason to suppose that its income continued to decline in the next fifty years.

[3] Lytham Miscellanea, no. 16.

more accurate guide to its real economic position. But it was sometimes possible for a superior to suppress details of his real income
and return a fraudulent statement of his financial position to the
annual chapter.[1] The malpractice of a particular prior may be partly
discounted when considering a period as long as thirty years; but
there is another reason why the receipts recorded in the account roll
must not be equated with the true income of the cell. The appearance
of receipts in the first half of the account does not necessarily imply
that the sums recorded were actually collected for they were liable
to wastes, decays and arrears (either *levabilia* or *illevabilia*), sometimes,
but not always, allowed for at the end of the *compotus*. It is by a close
study of this last section of the account roll, and not of the receipts
themselves – where many items, such as the *redditus assisae* remained
frozen at a fixed amount for many years – that the business abilities
of individual masters and priors can best be judged.

Despite the limitations of their annual account rolls as a reliable
index to the wealth of the cells, it is obvious that (except for Durham
College, Oxford) Finchale was by far the richest of the nine Durham
dependencies. By the time of Wessington's priorate, Finchale had
long been converted into a regular 'holiday villa' or *villegiatura* for
monks from the mother house an hour's ride away. In this capacity
it enjoyed a prosperity and a way of life which would have startled
and probably scandalised its twelfth-century hermit and patron,
Saint Godric. It is not easy to recapture the rhythms and routines
of monastic life at Finchale from the stereotyped formulae of its
numerous account rolls. But the remarkable consistency of the sum
(normally varying only between £16 and £19) expended year
after year on the oblations of the prior and his fellows proves that
there were nearly always eight or nine monks in residence. Of these,
perhaps a half were temporary inmates sent from Durham *ad
spaciandum*, usually for a three-weekly period.[2] The other Finchale
monks included several elderly or sick brethren who retired and
often died there.[3] The superiors of the cell often fell into this
category themselves. The priorate at Finchale was an attractive and

[1] William Partrike was charged with this offence in 1444 (Misc. Chrs., no. 5637).
[2] *Finchale Priory*, pp. 30–1; but it should be stressed that this unusually informative
ordinance of 25 Sep. 1408 was only a temporary measure.
[3] Reg. Parv. II, fos. 35, 47; *Finchale Priory*, pp. clxxxiii, clxxxvii, ccxix.

prestigious office, usually reserved for the most distinguished or venerable members of the community, like Uthred of Boldon, Robert Rypon, William Barry and that future bishop, Richard Bell, who ruled the cell between his abortive (1456) and successful (1464) attempts to secure election as prior of Durham. By the close of the fourteenth century there was no longer any danger, as there had been a century earlier, that a large body of Finchale monks might form a dissident lobby at odds with official policy in Durham itself.[1] As early as 1364–5 the south aisle of the nave of the priory church had been incorporated into the cloister in apparent recognition of the fact that the number of monks there had fallen for ever. Throughout the fifteenth century, the monastic buildings, and especially the prior's apartments, were subjected to drastic modification and reconstruction in order to provide comfortable accommodation for Durham monks on vacation. The extent to which life at Finchale was transformed during the later middle ages emerges even more clearly from a study of its present ruins and their ground-plan than a reading of its records.[2] The site is deservedly famous as a *locus classicus* of the partial conversion of a medieval monastery into a quasi-domestic building complex.

The community's other two cells in Durham county, Jarrow and Monk Wearmouth, did remarkably little to enlarge the reputation they still enjoyed as the monasteries of Bede and Benedict Biscop. The original homes of reformed Benedictinism in the north of England, it is hardly unfair to claim that they never recovered from Bishop William of Saint Calais' transfer of their twenty-three inmates to Durham in the summer of 1083. At that time Pope Gregory VII had argued that the diocese of Durham lacked the resources to sustain Jarrow and Wearmouth as well as Durham.[3] His comment is more apposite to the later middle ages than to his own era. Certainly the two cells were never well endowed after 1083; and there is no indication that the Durham chapter ever intended to provide either house with more than a handful of

---

[1] J. Scammell, 'The Case of Geoffrey Burdon, Prior of Durham (1313–1321)', *Rev. Bénédictine*, LXVIII (1958), 227.

[2] D. Knowles and J. K. St Joseph, *Monastic Sites from the Air* (Cambridge, 1952), plate 20; C. Peers, 'Finchale Priory', *Arch. Ael.*, Fourth Series, IV (1927), 193–220; *V.C.H. Durham* III, 148–54.

[3] Symeon, *Hist. Ecc. Dun.*, I, 121; cf. *Feodarium Dunelm.*, p. liv.

resident monks. Exactly when the two cells began their history as regular monastic communities after 1083 is very uncertain. Recent excavations of the sites have so far raised more problems than they have solved, but suggest that neither dependency ever underwent a really extensive building programme in the course of its history as a Durham cell – with the welcome result that both still preserve substantial sections of their Anglo-Saxon fabric.[1] During the fifteenth century both Jarrow and Wearmouth were apparently often on the brink of outright insolvency. The masters there regularly failed to balance their income and their expenditure. In 1427–8, for example, the master of Wearmouth recorded an excess expenditure of £14 over an annual income of £52; five years later, in 1432–3, the master of Jarrow had an income of over £46 but spent £30 more than that amount.[2] The financial losses at Jarrow gave particularly serious grounds for alarm. Between 1416 and 1421 the master there had to be subsidised by several Durham obedientiaries in order to pay his debts; the cell was apparently '*in manu domini prioris*' in 1427–9; and fifty years later the deterioration was still so pronounced that Prior Bell of Durham again thought it advisable to take the cell into his own hands.[3] In such circumstances, it is scarcely surprising that the masters of Jarrow and Wearmouth, however worthy, were obscure and transitory figures. There were eight different masters of Jarrow between 1408 and 1424. The Durham chapter managed to preserve the continuity of Benedictine monastic observance at both cells; but in practice no individual Durham monk wished to stay in either for long.

In no Durham daughter house was the contrast between the glorious past and the difficult present more striking than at the priory of Holy Island. It was almost inevitable that the first generation of Benedictine monks at Durham should regard the reestablishment of monastic life on the island of Saints Aidan and Cuthbert as one of its primary objectives. But even in the twelfth century it is possible to detect a serious discrepancy between the grandeur of the new Romanesque conventual church and the rel-

---

[1] H. M. and Joan Taylor, *Anglo-Saxon Architecture* (Cambridge, 1965), I, 338–49, 432–46; R. Cramp, 'Excavations at the Saxon Monastic Sites of Wearmouth and Jarrow: an interim report', *Medieval Archaeology* XIII (1969), 21–66.

[2] Wearmouth, 1427/28; Jarrow, 1432/33; cf. Reg. III, fo. 62.

[3] *Jarrow and Wearmouth*, pp. xiii–xiv; Bursar, 1427–29.

ative meagreness of its endowments. The Durham chapter had diverted only a small proportion of their patrimony in Northumberland to the sustenance of the Holy Island cell; and the monks there had few reserves on which to call when the outbreak of Anglo-Scottish hostilities in the 1290s inaugurated a period of prolonged crisis. The monks of Lindisfarne were particularly vulnerable because so large a proportion of their income (more than was the case in any other Durham cell except Wearmouth) derived from the sale of garbal tithes. Border warfare along the Northumbrian coast encouraged the conversion of large tracts of tenant land from arable to pastoral husbandry during a period of ceaseless fluctuations in the price of corn. The revenues of Holy Island were therefore subject to great and unpredictable vicissitudes. Henry Helay, prior of the cell, accounted for an income of over £34 from garbal tithes in 1440–1; but in the following year this figure dropped to £9 16s. 8d. 'because the tithes of Buckton, Fenwick, Haggerston, Fenham, Beal and Holy Island could not be sold'.[1] To these and similar economic problems the Durham chapter had only one solution at its disposal: by the early fifteenth century the number of resident monks on Lindisfarne had been reduced from five or six to two or three. An inventory of the priory's goods made in 1416 testifies to the paucity of its collection of service-books as well as to the need to keep supplies of armour in store.[2] As numbers fell, so the original dorter and frater were abandoned and the prior's quarters were converted to accommodate members of the now small community.[3] The transformation of Holy Island into a miniature monastery supervised by a skeleton staff of monastic caretakers had particularly damaging results in a region where the irrelevance of this debased monastic ideal to the harsh realities of Northumbrian life forced itself upon the minds of local inhabitants. The fifteenth-century prior of Holy Island was faced with the indifference and sometimes hostility of his secular neighbours and parishioners, many of whom refused to contribute towards the upkeep of their parish church. In a characteristic letter to Durham, Thomas Ward, prior of Holy Island from 1448 to 1457, reported

---

[1] Holy Island, 1440–42. [2] Raine, *North Durham*, pp. 117–18.
[3] A. Hamilton Thompson, *Lindisfarne Priory* (H.M.S.O. Guide, 1949); Knowles and St Joseph, *Monastic Sites*, Plate 19.

that 'I am vexit by two fals lordans, Ric' Ogill and John of Hall, for thai wald haf the gudds of Sanct Cuthbert, and in fayth of me thai sall haf non, for the qwilk thai ar wonder worth (*sic*)'.[1] Nor was Holy Island as immune from war itself as James Raine believed. The advantages of its geographical position were as obvious to the English government as to the monks themselves. Despite the inadequacy of its harbour, Holy Island provided English commanders with a valuable off-shore base from which to defend the Border against marauding Scots. Edward Balliol spent the winter of 1335–6 at Holy Island after the battle of Culblean, and long before the construction of a royal fort there by Henry VIII the strategic importance of the site was fully recognised. In the early fourteenth century, the prior of the cell was reluctantly compelled to crenellate his monastery and Lindisfarne became, as the ruins of its barbicans and gatehouse still testify, a fortified monastery. Holy Island deserves, perhaps more than any other English monastery and certainly much more than Durham itself, Scott's famous but misleading line, 'Half church of God: half castle 'gainst the Scot'.[2]

Six miles south-east of Holy Island lay the Inner Farne, the seat of the poorest but most exotic of the jewels in Durham's crown. In this case it is doubtful whether memories of Saint Cuthbert's miracles and death on the island would alone have sufficed to persuade the Durham monks to found a cell on so isolated and uncongenial a site. But the revival of the eremitical tradition at Farne in the twelfth century and the arrival there after 1150 of two Durham solitaries, Bartholomew of Farne and Thomas, the ex-prior of Durham, presented the chapter with a spiritual opportunity as well as an economic problem. They grasped the opportunity but never satisfactorily solved the problem. Shortly after the ascetic Bartholomew's death, probably in 1193, Farne was developed, no doubt erratically, into a regular Durham daughter house. But little attempt was then made to provide the new cell with independent resources and it emerged too late to gain any share of Saint Cuthbert's great patrimony in the north. The beneficence and charity of thirteenth-century Northumbrian barons, particularly the De Vescis of Alnwick, was insufficient to ensure the cell's future:

[1] Loc. xxv, no. 43; cf. Reg. Parv. II, fos. 3, 55, 112; Holy Island, 1410–21.
[2] *Harold the Dauntless*, Third Canto, I.

monasticism on Farne would certainly never have survived until the Dissolution had it not been for the helpful intervention of English monarchs. Early in his reign, Edward III took steps to preserve the cell from complete financial collapse; and by means of a complicated and controversial arrangement, the crown hence-forward charged the mayor and burgesses of Newcastle-upon-Tyne with an annual fee farm of £9 3s. 4d. payable to the master of Farne.[1] Although it is unlikely that there was a continuous tradition of ascetic spirituality on the island, during the late fourteenth century one Durham monk at Farne proved himself to be an articulate and impressive practitioner of the contemplative life.[2] Whether the now celebrated 'monk-solitary of Farne' had any fifteenth-century heirs is very much open to doubt. It is true that the cell was only aban-doned for short periods and at times of acute military crisis. But the conventual library on the island was almost pathetically small and the regular practices of monastic observance lapsed on several occasions. It was all too easy for the monks of Farne to escape the supposedly vigilant eye of the prior of near-by Holy Island. Of several monks in both cells it seems to have been true that 'many tymes you tak' a boote and roith unto the land at thin own liberty'.[3] During the mid-fifteenth century the behaviour of several masters and fellow monks at Farne caused minor scandals; and some would certainly have endorsed, though not in its original sense, a twelfth-century description of the island as 'a kind of purgatory upon earth'.[4]

The priory of Saint Leonard's, Stamford, was a rarity among the Durham cells in that its origins did not spring from the presence there of a noted saint or ascetic. Prior Wessington's identification of its site with the monastery founded at 'Stanford' by Saint Wilfrid in 658 has received little support from more recent historians.[5]

---

[1] 1.5. Regal., no. 1; 1.1. Spec., no. 39; *C.Cl.R.*, *1343–46*, p. 523; *1399–1402*, p. 248. For Prior Wessington's lengthy collection of evidences on this topic, see Misc. Chrs., no. 5631; Loc. xx, no. 26; cf. Farne, 1427–31.

[2] W. A. Pantin, 'The Monk-Solitary of Farne: a Fourteenth-Century English Mystic', *E.H.R.* LIX (1944), 162–86; H. Farmer, 'The Meditations of the Monk of Farne', *Studia Anselmiana*, Fourth Series, XLI (1957), 141–245.

[3] Reg. Parv. III, fo. 136.   [4] Symeon, *Hist. Ecc. Dun.* I, 312.

[5] D.C.D., MS. B. III. 30, fo. 38; *Rites*, p. 139. Cf. *Venerabilis Baedae Opera Historica*, ed. Plummer, I, 325. Perhaps the most learned discussion of this problem is to be found in a private letter of March 1723 written by the Stamford historian, Francis Peck (B.M. Lansdowne MS. 991, fos. 251v–261).

The nature and geographical grouping of the endowments of the Stamford cell make it reasonably clear that the house owed its existence less to the piety of a single founder than to the desire of the Durham monks to establish a colony where their revenues from sources south of the Trent could be diverted. This process must have been in train by 1146 when Pope Eugenius III confirmed Durham's possession of the monastery of St Leonard outside the borough of Stamford together with fourteen acres of land and seven manses.[1] The surviving twelfth-century remains of the Romanesque conventual church were obviously designed for more than the two or three monks resident in the later middle ages. Unfortunately the 55 extant account rolls of the cell all date from the period after 1364, years during which the cell had declined into comparative insignificance. Until the middle years of the fourteenth century, Stamford had retained some distinction as a house which preserved a tradition of private scholarship and study. Thereafter the fortunes of the cell apparently declined in the face of academic competition from Durham College, Oxford. The Durham chapter retained its control of Stamford throughout the fifteenth century without serious scandal or challenge to its authority, and Bishop William Alnwick's visitation of the priory on 21 October 1440 throws a little light on the conduct of religious life there.[2] Of the two monks then in residence, Thomas Hexham declared that 'they do not rise for matins at night because of the smallness of their numbers'. At the same time, the prior, Richard Barton, called attention to the basic weakness of other Durham cells besides his own when he complained of the inadequacy of his financial resources: 'and that is the reason why the priors of this place are changed so often and have no desire to remain here'.

THE COLDINGHAM CAUSE

When Wessington became their prior in 1416, the monks of Durham had held Coldingham, near the Berwickshire coast and nine miles north of Berwick itself, for more than 300 years. The

---

[1] *Papsturkunden in England*, ed. W. Holtzmann (Berlin, 1932–52), II, no. 51. For a preliminary report of recent excavations at the site, see *Medieval Archaeology* XII (1968), 167–8. [2] *Lincoln Visitations* II, 346–7.

cell owed its origins to the enthusiastic zeal of the early Benedictine monks at Durham, to the patronage of the Scottish monarchs, and to the memory of one of the most famous Celtic double monasteries on a near-by site. Prior Wessington's own brief account of the foundation is acceptable enough: 'Edgar, king of the Scots, gave this place – out of reverence to God and Saint Cuthbert – to the monastery of Durham; but as time passed the prior and brethren at Durham preferred to erect a church and place their own monks there'.[1] By the middle of the twelfth century Coldingham was being gradually converted into a regular conventual priory served by Durham monks; for the next hundred years and more it was much the most prosperous of all Durham's cells as well as being one of the richest monasteries in Scotland. Even during these golden years, there is evidence that the presence of an English monastery on Scottish soil caused legal difficulties and emotional prejudice. During the thirteenth century the greatest danger was the possibility that the English monks of Coldingham might secure their independence from Durham. The outbreak of Anglo-Scottish hostilities in the 1290s put an abrupt end to this prospect but at the terrible price of shattering the political harmony on which the security and welfare of the priory rested. The Durham monks now had to learn the bitter lesson that it had been unwise of their predecessors to allow the memory of past history (the unified Anglo-Saxon kingdom of Northumbria) to triumph over current political reality.

The '*causa de Coldingham*' can therefore be said to have begun its long and tortuous progress at the very beginning of the fourteenth century. It was marked by a dramatic decline in the revenues and consequently of the numbers of monks attached to the cell. In the 1230s it had been thought proper that thirty resident monks should serve Coldingham as opposed to seventy at Durham itself. A century later, only a handful of Durham monks still lived in the Scottish priory. What made their position precarious and often untenable for years at a time was the chauvinistic nationalism of the late medieval kingdom of Scotland. The relationship of the Coldingham monks with their tenants and immediate neighbours appears to have been relatively tranquil. But the survival of this small nest of

[1] MS. B. III. 30, fo. 38. For a fuller discussion of statements in this and the next paragraph, see Dobson, 'Last English Monks on Scottish Soil', pp. 1–6.

English monks aroused the insecurity and jealousy of more formidable vested interests. The Scottish government could be persuaded, with little apparent justification, that the prior of Coldingham was a traitor and spy. When in July 1378 Robert II decided to expel the Durham monks for ever and replace them by Benedictines from Dunfermline, it must have seemed that all was lost. Yet in fact Durham's control of Coldingham survived for almost another century. Against all the odds and all the analogies (for no other English dependency on Scottish territory survived the first phase of the wars of independence), the community of Saint Cuthbert launched a temporarily successful counter-attack. For this tactical victory, the major credit must go to Prior Wessington, whose greatest achievement it was. Only a detailed survey of the complex history of the Coldingham cause between 1416 and 1446 can serve to demonstrate the skill, energy and persistence with which the Durham monks perpetuated an almost intolerable situation.

Although Wessington was never entirely free from anxiety as to the future of Coldingham, the periods of most acute tension came at the beginning and at the end of his priorate. In 1416 the titular prior of Coldingham was still John Aclyff, appointed as long ago as 1391. Aclyff's term of office had been extremely unhappy as he had been excluded from Coldingham for several years at a time by the Dunfermline monks. In 1401–2 Aclyff and his two fellow-monks were living on Holy Island; and he was again formally expelled from Scotland by the Duke of Albany in 1409.[1] A strongly-worded letter to the Scottish governor from Henry IV secured Aclyff's reinstatement, but whatever the prior's abilities as a theologian,[2] he does not appear to have been a capable administrator. In 1410 Prior Hemingburgh was forced to remind him that 'it is said the waste, isolation and remiss rule (of Coldingham) are the reasons why the Scots attack our rights'.[3] In November 1416, when he attended Wessington's election, Aclyff was the second senior monk in the convent, soon to be receiving medical treatment for his eyes.[4] A successor as prior of Coldingham was obviously needed, and

[1] Holy Island, 1401/2; Reg. Parv. II, fo. 12.
[2] W. A. Pantin, 'A Benedictine Opponent of John Wyclif', *E.H.R.* XLIII (1928), 73–7.
[3] Reg. Parv. II, fo. 13.
[4] Reg. III, fo. 51; Terrar, 1417/18, 1418/19.

Wessington chose the Durham bursar, William Drax, who had already served at Coldingham as sacrist.[1] The succession of one superior of Coldingham by another was always a traumatic process because of the very real danger that either the bishop of St Andrews would refuse admission or the king of Scotland the restoration of the temporalities. It was also certain that the monastery of Dunfermline, some of whose monks had actually been able to install themselves at Coldingham for long periods during the previous thirty years,[2] would present a candidate to the bishop of St Andrews when they heard of the vacancy. Fortunately for Wessington, his Scottish opponents failed to agree among themselves. Andrew Raeburn, the seventh in the consecutive line of Dunfermline priors of Coldingham, was promoted to the priory of Urquhart (a Dunfermline dependency), and his claim to the Durham dependency was contested at Rome and elsewhere between Robert Boumaker, an Arbroath monk, and William Broun from Dunfermline.[3]

In the meantime, Wessington was able to secure Drax's position as rightful prior of Coldingham. Drax had been presented to Bishop Henry Wardlaw on 31 January 1418, was admitted by him eighteen months later at St Andrews and inducted at Coldingham on 27 July 1419.[4] The new prior had already sworn fealty to Albany and received the temporalities of the cell from him.[5] Wessington, largely through the intercession of two powerful Scottish lords, the Earls of Douglas and March,[6] had scored a notable victory, but one which was to be almost immediately sacrificed. Shortly after Drax took up residence at Coldingham, a serious fire broke out there which, according to the Scots, was a deliberate act of arson and sacrilege on the part of 'a serpent nourished in the bosom of the

---

[1] Misc. Chrs., nos. 1433, 1434, 1436.

[2] *Coldingham Corr.*, p. 254.

[3] C.P.L. VII (1417–31), pp. 125–6; *Calendar of Scottish Supplications to Rome, 1418–22*, ed. E. R. Lindsay and A. I. Cameron (Scottish History Society, Third Series, XXIII, 1934), pp. 44, 65, 123–4, 146, 165.

[4] Reg. II, fo. xi; Reg. III, fo. 59.   [5] Reg. II, fo. xi.

[6] Archibald, fourth Earl of Douglas, was appointed chief bailie of Coldingham by the prior and chapter of Durham in May 1414 (Reg. III, fo. 41); George Dunbar, Earl of March, was received into the monastic confraternity in January 1418 and claimed in a letter of about this time to Joan Beaufort that he had always supported the Durham monks at Coldingham (Loc. xxv, no. 137; Reg. III, fo. 59).

kingdom'.[1] The scandal was such that Drax was forced to return to Durham, probably as early as August 1419, and did not return to Coldingham for five years.[2] Moreover, the Dunfermline monk, William Broun, was still actively appealing to Rome, and in June 1422 Wessington and his convent appointed proctors at the Curia to defend their right to Coldingham.[3] In the spring of 1424 the return of James I to Scotland after his long captivity in England gave Wessington an unexpected opportunity to retrieve what must have seemed a hopeless situation. The negotiations which accompanied the king's release were conducted in the Durham chapter-house during March and Wessington was able to approach him personally on the question of Coldingham.[4] In the first parliament of the reign, which opened at Perth on 26 May 1424, the claims of Durham and Dunfermline were considered and Drax declared to be the rightful prior; he was restored to Coldingham under royal orders to maintain divine services there and to repair the damage caused by the fire.[5] Although Walter Bower claimed that James I later regretted his generosity to Drax, the period between 1424 and 1440 was one of comparative stability at Coldingham. Unfortunately neither prior's nor sacrist's account rolls survive after 1413, but it is clear from Wessington's correspondence and leases of property that the cell was normally occupied by Durham monks at this time and that some form of religious life survived there. In November 1436 Henry VI took the Coldingham prior and monks into his special protection, and in March 1438 warned his English subjects not to abuse the hospitality offered them by the cell.[6]

During the middle years of Wessington's priorate, the Coldingham affair continued to be a matter for appeal and counter-appeal at Rome. William Broun succeeded in reopening the case in 1427 but soon secured the priory of Urquhart and his claims were inherited by yet another Dunfermline monk, Stephen Bryge.[7]

---

[1] *Scotichronicon Joannis de Fordun*, ed. W. Goodall (Edinburgh, 1759) II, 163–5.

[2] Drax was in Durham county on 23 August 1419 (Reg. III, fo. 68) and was almoner at the mother house from 1420 until 1424 (Almoner, 1420–4).

[3] Reg. III, fo. 96.

[4] Reg. III, fo. 105; Misc. Chrs., no. 1064; Bursar, 1423/24, Expense Necessarie.

[5] *Acts of the Parliaments of Scotland* (Record Commission, 1814–75), II, 25.

[6] *Rot. Scot.* II, 298; Raine, *North Durham*, Appendix, pp. 80–1.

[7] *C.P.L.* VII (1417–31), p. 492; *The Apostolic Camera and Scottish Benefices, 1418–88*, ed. A. I. Cameron (Oxford, 1934), p. 107.

Bryge's activities at the Curia continued to cause Wessington anxiety, and it was with almost undisguised relief that he passed on to one of his representatives at Rome in January 1440 the rumour that the Dunfermline monk had died.[1] But the most prominent feature of the history of Coldingham in the years between 1424 and 1440 was the establishment of the Home family as the real arbiters of the destinies of the priory. Even by fifteenth-century Scottish standards, the rise of the border house of Home from its humble origins to magnate status was remarkably rapid, and was always closely linked with those designs on Coldingham which eventually led to the battle of 'Sauchieburn' and the murder of James III.

The traditional Scottish lay protectors of Coldingham had been the Earls of Douglas and it was in 1406 that Archibald, fourth Earl of Douglas, appointed Sir Alexander Home his sub-keeper of the lands and rents of the priory.[2] In 1414 Douglas was bailie and Sir Alexander Home sub-bailie of Coldingham and both men enjoyed 'gret fees' in respect of their offices before their deaths as companions-in-arms at Verneuil in August 1424.[3] Although Wessington made William Douglas, Earl of Angus, 'special protector and defender' of Coldingham in January 1428,[4] he henceforward looked for real protection to David Home of Wedderburn, younger brother of Sir Alexander. In May 1428, he was appointed bailie of Coldingham for four years and the same office was conferred on him for a further four years in May 1432, and yet another five years in May 1437.[5] David Home and his wife were given letters of confraternity by the Durham monks on 12 March 1433; and throughout the period he enjoyed a pension of over five English marks together with the very substantial perquisites and powers deriving from his supervision of the priory's estates.[6] In early 1439 however, David Home, now a knight, decided to raise his demands and asked Wessington to increase his annual pension to a hundred shillings and grant him the bailiary of Coldingham for life. Wessington offered no objections to the first of Sir David Home's requests but refused to

---

[1] Reg. Parv. II, fo. 114.
[2] Raine, *North Durham*, Appendix, pp. 34–5.
[3] Reg. III, fo. 41; *Coldingham Corr.*, pp. 86–8.
[4] Raine, *North Durham*, Appendix, p. 98; *Coldingham Corr.*, pp. 101–2, 106–7.
[5] Reg. III, fo. 129; Reg. Parv. II, fos. 69, 96; *Coldingham Corr.*, pp. 102, 105, 108.
[6] *Coldingham Corr.*, pp. 102–9.

consider the second. Home was ill-advised enough to ignore Wessington's letter of 15 March in which the prior reported that 'ryght grett instance has been made to me of notabill persons to prefer certayn persons to the said office, whilke I haff put by, and sa fully purpase to do in tym commyng'.[1] The allusion can only be to David Home's nephew, Sir Alexander Home (son of the Sir Alexander who was killed at Verneuil) and his overlord, Lord Adam Hepburn of Hailes, who attempted during the following years to remove Sir David from the bailiary in their own interests. The bitter rivalry which developed between the two Homes was most embarrassing for Wessington whose letters to both parties reveal an understandable desire not to be involved in the contest. Sir David Home paid a surprise visit to Durham in September 1441 and carried back to Scotland indentures to the effect that he should remain bailie of Coldingham for forty years.[2] But the younger Home received stronger support from the Scottish magnates and his kinsman, Bishop Kennedy of St Andrews; on 14 May 1442 the uncle's indentures were invalidated by a grant of the bailiary of Coldingham for life to Sir Alexander.[3]

The office of bailie of Coldingham was Sir Alexander's reward for his services in helping Wessington to replace William Drax by a new prior, John Oll, in 1441 and 1442. Drax had long petitioned for release from his priorate and Wessington finally gave Oll letters of presentation and sent him to Scotland. Through the help of Sir Alexander, and not of Sir David Home, Oll arrived in St Andrews on 6 December 1441 and there held a long conversation with Bishop Kennedy. In the written report of the interview which he sent to Wessington, Oll was unable to be very reassuring. Kennedy had used the nationalist argument that the kingdom's enemies should 'kepe right wele in the realme of ingland' and shown Oll a letter he had received from James II and his barons forbidding him to admit an Englishman to the priory of Coldingham. The Act of the Scottish Parliament in May 1424, on which Wessington and Oll had placed great store, was declared invalid because James I had promised to restore the Durham monks to

[1] Reg. Parv. II, fo. 101; Misc. Chrs., no. 1074.
[2] *Coldingham Corr.*, pp. 120–1. Misc. Chrs., no. 1070 is the draft of this agreement.
[3] Raine, *North Durham*, Appendix, p. 105; Reg. III, fo. 275.

Coldingham only when in danger of his life. There then appeared before Bishop Kennedy the latest of the Dunfermline claimants, William de Boys, who carried with him letters of presentation from his abbot and was accompanied by various doctors 'and the hale universite with mony baronis assistand'. Kennedy asked Oll to return to his presence a month later (7 January 1442) with a full collection of documentary evidence as to the justice of the Durham case and therefore 'as yit all is stopped'.[1] Oll returned to Coldingham through what he described as a hostile countryside to find that Drax had died in his absence. As one of Bishop Kennedy's objections to Oll's promotion was that his predecessor was still alive and he had received no certificate of his voluntary resignation, Drax's death simplified one problem and Wessington sent Oll new letters of presentation, dated after the death of the old prior. In his accompanying letter of 20 December 1441, Wessington gave Oll much concrete advice as to the conduct of his case before the bishop, told him to spare neither labour nor expense and said that he had persuaded both the Homes to co-operate in pressing for Oll's admission.[2] But it was once more Sir Alexander, rather than Sir David, who risked the hostility of his fellow countrymen and spoke on Oll's behalf before Bishop Kennedy and his council at St Andrews on 10 January 1442. A comparatively full record of the proceedings survives and Bishop Kennedy was apparently convinced by the weight of evidence sent from Durham as well as by two excellent speeches from Sir Alexander Home and John Oll who ended by declaring that 'it lettis noght at thai (William de Boys and the four Dunfermline monks present) say I am ane Inglishman, for so war ever monkis of Durham to quham the said Priory of Coldingham was granntid'.[3] On 18 January Bishop Kennedy, after much consultation with his lawyers, formally invested Oll with his priorate and confirmed the Durham 'evidences' under a public instrument. Four days later, in the presence of both Homes and three other

---

[1] Oll's interesting letter was only discovered a few years ago at Durham and was not printed by James Raine in his somewhat erratic collection of Coldingham material for the Surtees Society. The present reference is Misc. Chrs., no. 7193.

[2] Reg. Parv. II, fo. 149. On 1 January Wessington wrote to Sir Alexander Home sending him a memorandum of seven articles '*pro admissione prioris de Coldingham*' (Misc. Chrs., no. 1098; Reg. Parv. II, fo. 150; printed twice in *Coldingham Corr.*, pp. 95–6, 130–2). [3] *Coldingham Corr.*, pp. 246–58.

Durham monks, Oll was inducted into the priory of Coldingham.[1] In the following spring, at Stirling, James II received Oll's fealty, restored his temporalities and took Coldingham under his special protection.[2] '*Cum maxima difficultate*', as Wessington put it, the Durham cause had triumphed, largely because of Sir Alexander Home's influential support as well as Wessington's shrewd manipulation of the Scottish fear of war with England. The prior had written to Bishop Kennedy on Christmas Eve 1441 reminding him that if the church of Durham was deprived of its ancient possessions and rights, 'it would be the cause and occasion of starting war between the kingdoms'.[3]

As in 1419, Wessington's success in maintaining a line of Durham priors at Coldingham was not followed by the tranquillity for which he must have hoped. Like Drax, John Oll secured the priorate only to find himself plunged immediately into the maelstrom of Border violence and feud.[4] The quarrel between Sir David and Sir Alexander Home over the bailiary of Coldingham and the lands of Aldcambus broke out once more, and the former bitterly resented the loss of his office and lands to his nephew. In May 1442, even before Oll had received his temporalities from the king, Sir David Home believed that 'to forthir the said Sir Alexandre the said Prior has put the hows in perall, as is weill kend to the cuntre'. As a result of Sir David's anger Oll retired precipitately to Berwick taking all the Durham monks with him.[5] According to Wessington, at long last disillusioned with his old bailie of Coldingham, Sir David Home's action in forcibly entering and occupying the priory had been sacrilegious and an act of war.[6] John Oll and his monks were soon able to return to Coldingham, however, and Sir David Home gradually disappeared from the scene leaving his nephew in control of the landed possessions of the priory. On 4 January 1443, Wessington and the convent again conferred the bailiary of Cold-

---

[1] Reg. III, fos. 274–5.

[2] Raine, *North Durham*, Appendix, p. 21; Reg. Parv. II, fo. 152; Reg. III, fo. 275.

[3] Reg. Parv. II, fo. 147; *Coldingham Corr.*, pp. 126, 129.

[4] No attempt is made here to deal in detail with the complexities of local Scottish politics as they affected Coldingham. The best study is by A. I. Dunlop, *The Life and Times of James Kennedy, Bishop of St Andrews* (Edinburgh, 1950), pp. 48–54, 76–81, 120–3, 232–3. In this book Kennedy's handling of the Coldingham affair is looked on more favourably than the evidence seems to warrant.

[5] Loc. xxv, no. 6.   [6] Reg. III, fo. 276.

ingham on Sir Alexander, and his son of the same name, this time for a term of sixty years.[1] Sir David Home was compensated for his losses and, after sending Wessington a vivid account of all his grievances, discharged his nephew of his debts in January 1444.[2] John Oll was subjected to violence once again, on this occasion at the hands of Sir Patrick Hepburn, son of the Lord of Hailes, who ambushed the prior and his companions as they were travelling home from Edinburgh to Coldingham. They were carried off to the castle of Dunbar and only released on promise to pay ransoms which, in his own case, Oll reported to be insupportable. On 28 April 1446 James II ordered Hepburn to restore the prior's property and, at the same time, instructed Oll not to pay his ransom.[3] Wessington's final year as prior of Durham had ended with yet one more outrage towards the prior of Coldingham and it is not surprising that Oll laid down his office in January 1447.[4]

Even more ominous for the future than the violence displayed towards Oll in Scotland was the course of events at the Curia during Wessington's last years. The prior fought a long legal battle with Bishop Kennedy over the convent's spiritual patronage in Scotland; but neither he nor Oll could 'goo throgh with hym to have his goode lordshipp and will' and they were forced to pay the bishop £150 in cash before he would release his claims.[5] Nor had William de Boys, the Dunfermline monk, accepted Oll's admission to the priory in January 1442; as early as October of that year Boys was at the Curia and had reported to his abbot that he was carrying all before him there.[6] However, Wessington managed to prevent the Dunfermline monks from having the judgement of 18 January 1442 reversed. A more sinister omen for the future was the appearance before 1446 of Master Patrick Home, a kinsman of Sir Alexander, as a powerful and turbulent personal force in the Scottish church. In the 1440s Patrick Home's designs and gifts for litigation were still aimed at the archdeaconry of Teviotdale but

---

[1] Ibid., fo. 287.
[2] Misc. Chrs., no. 1087; *Report on the Manuscripts of Colonel David Milne Home* (Historical Manuscripts Commission, 1902), p. 21.
[3] Raine, *North Durham*, Appendix, p. 22. Cf. *Coldingham Corr.*, pp. 156–7.
[4] Oll was described as sub-prior at Durham in 1446/47 (Bursar, Reparaciones Domorum).   [5] *Coldingham Corr.*, p. 160.
[6] Reg. Parv. II, fo. 170; *C.P.L.* IX (1431–47), p. 298; *Coldingham Corr.*, pp. 144–5.

it was this clerk who was to succeed, where the Dunfermline monks had failed, in separating Coldingham from Durham.[1] However unstable the life of Durham monks at Coldingham in the years of Wessington's priorate it compares favourably with that of the thirty years either before 1416 or after 1446. Despite all his difficulties and adversaries, Wessington maintained the continuity of the Durham cause at Coldingham during a period when a less conscientious or more realistic prior might have abandoned hope.

It remains surprising that the priors of Durham retained their control of Coldingham for so long. It is true that Wessington was at pains to make the most of his convent's very impressive legal and historical rights to the priory, but the real reasons for his ability to preserve the connection with Coldingham lay elsewhere. By appealing to the English government and magnates he secured some form of protection against the alienation of the cell. As long as the Scottish king and nobles feared English reprisal, they were extremely cautious in their handling of the Coldingham affair. Wessington quite deliberately exploited Scottish reluctance to risk war for Coldingham's sake alone; in a pointed letter of August 1441 to the Lord of Hailes he wrote that 'if seynt Cuthbert and the house of Doresme suld be spoylid of thayre possession, continued sa mony yheres, hitt is likly to turn bath the reawmes and dyverse places of both the marches to diseese: for in thatt case, the whilke Gode sheld suld fall, the prior of Doresme must of need sewe to the kyng and lordes of Ingland, and alsa to the kyng and lordes of Scotland for remedy to be hadd: and he supposes att that suld be sun brekyng of treues'.[2] Wessington did not find it difficult to secure the support of the greatest English lords and when, for instance, John Oll came before James II at Stirling on 11 June 1442 to obtain restitution of the Coldingham temporalities, he carried with him letters of recommendation from Cardinal Beaufort and the Earls of Salisbury and Northumberland.[3] But more necessary than the protection afforded by the English lords was that which only a Scottish magnate could provide. If Wessington continued

---

[1] Dobson, 'Last English Monks on Scottish Soil', pp. 1–25, considers the last phase of the struggle from 1461 to 1478.

[2] Reg. Parv. II, fo. 143.   [3] Ibid., fo. 152; Reg. III, fo. 277.

to be able to send Durham monks to Coldingham, even in periods of open warfare between English and Scots, this was because the priory was supported by formidable Scottish Border families. If it had not been for his own efforts, David Home informed Wessington in 1443, 'the sayde place had bene pesable in Scotts mennis possession, suppose I say it'.[1] But the Homes did not render their services without demanding a high price; and it was to be the irony of the Coldingham case that the family used by Wessington to protect the cell from the machinations of Dunfermline monks and other adversaries was, after his own death, to be responsible for the final expulsion of the last English and Durham monks from the Scottish kingdom.

THE LYTHAM CASE

'Sen the first fundation of the kirke of Durham was ther neuer sich a thing so preiudiciall attempt agayns the priuileges and the libertes therof.'[2] So wrote the chancellor of the monastery, Robert Westmorland, when the alarming news first reached Durham that William Partrike, prior of Lytham, had secured a bull of perpetuity. The extravagance of Westmorland's language might seem barely warranted by the occasion, the renunciation of obedience by the prior of a small and distant cell. But Partrike's rebellion led to the *cause célèbre* of Wessington's priorate for its implications were rapidly appreciated at Durham.[3] If successful, Partrike would have established a precedent which might have led to the complete disintegration of the ties which bound Durham's daughter houses to the central monastery. Partrike's revolt was itself essentially a personal act and he might have been pacified at any time by the convent's grant of the priorate of Lytham for the term of his life.[4] But Wessington never contemplated such an offer for fear that Lytham would escape completely from Durham's control. The alternative was a

---

[1] Misc. Chrs., no. 1087. [2] Loc. IX, no. 8.

[3] Over a hundred documents connected with the case of William Partrike are preserved at Durham, mostly in Loc. IX, Lytham Miscellanea (a varied set of documents including Lytham inventories) and Misc. Chrs., no. 5637 (a set of 16 rolls). No other medieval Durham law case, with the possible exception of the dispute with Bishop Bek at the end of the thirteenth century, seems better recorded.

[4] Compare the grant of perpetuity made by St Albans to the prior of Bynham in 1472: *Reg. John Whethamstede* (Rolls Series, 1872–73), II, 111.

long and bitter struggle, pursued throughout 1444 and 1445, to deprive a most determined and unscrupulous adversary of the cell.

The priory of Lytham, founded in the late twelfth century and situated so near the Ribble estuary that it often suffered from sea storms and drifting sand, was one of the most isolated as well as one of the more prosperous Durham cells. An unusually complete sequence of account rolls between 1412 and 1443 reveals that the priors there enjoyed a high standard of living and owned such luxuries as a 'blewe bedd of State wyth a liberte and a grete tre of tapestry worke'.[1] But the characteristic feature of the history of this priory was the hostility displayed towards the Durham monks by their neighbours. Of Partrike's five predecessors as prior, Richard of Birtley (1373-9) and William Aslakby (1379-85) found the cell uncongenial and asked to be returned to Durham. Thomas of Corbridge (1389-1405) and Robert Masham (1405-12) both found it necessary to purge themselves of incontinence with local women, while Masham and Richard Haswell (1412-31) were engaged for many years in serious litigation 'because of the malice of their neighbours'.[2] In 1425 some of Haswell's tenants had been excommunicated for destroying Lytham property and refusing to pay tithes and mortuaries.[3] Three years later Haswell was involved in a particularly bitter tithes dispute with the vicar of Kirkham who stood up openly in public and told all that the 'Prior was cussyt and stode cussyt ... and wit his fynger pontyt a lad standyng by him, and said that he had as myche powere to syng a mas as the sayde prior'.[4] In the late fifteenth and early sixteenth centuries, the Butler family carried on a lengthy feud with the Durham monks at Lytham, whom they disliked as foreigners, and whose prior alleged that he only narrowly escaped the indignity of 'dowking in the see'.[5]

---

[1] Lytham, Miscellanea, Inventory of 8 March 1446. This inventory and some other Durham records were consulted by Lt.-Col. H. Fishwick and utilised in his *History of the Parish of Lytham in the County of Lancaster* (Chetham Society, New Series, LX, 1907). See also J. Tait in *V.C.H. Lancashire* II, 107–11, and (for the storms there) *The Fabric Rolls of York Minster* (Surtees Soc. XXXV, 1859), p. 240.

[2] Loc. IX, no. 14.   [3] Ibid., no. 15.

[4] Ibid., no. 39. See, for a collection of evidence on this case, York, Borthwick Institute, CP. F. (Cause Papers: Fifteenth Century), no. 167.

[5] Loc. IX, nos. 35, 36, 55–61. Saint Cuthbert's crosses, used for demarcating the boundaries of the priory's estates, were frequently torn down by the Butlers throughout this period.

William Partrike may conceivably have been a Lancastrian himself for in later years he wrote of his 'cosyns' in the area.[1] More certainly, he entered the Durham community in 1414, rapidly received minor orders and was priest by 1419.[2] Wessington appears to have considered him a promising administrator, for he was granator from 1421 to 1427 and then bursar for two years until 1429.[3] Although he left a long list of arrears in this last office, the prior appointed Partrike the steward of his household for two years and then presented him on 17 June 1431 to the priory of Lytham, vacant on the resignation of Richard Haswell who had requested to be moved home.[4] During his first ten years at Lytham Partrike contented himself with the large measure of independence enjoyed automatically by the head of a distant cell. He paid the annual contributions imposed on him by Wessington and the chapter and accounted regularly to them every Ascension Day. Although he returned to Durham only a few times in the whole of his priorate, he was careful to send proctors to represent him at annual chapters, Bishop Neville's election and the visitations of 1438 and 1442.[5] More ominous for the future were a series of ugly incidents in the late 1430s involving two of Partrike's fellow monks at Lytham. Robert Erghowe was charged with stealing some of Partrike's personal property and George Cyther of 'heghtyng and strykyng of seculares' in general and an assault by knife and stone on the chaplain of the priory church in particular. Both monks escaped public indictment only because Thomas Urswike, receiver-general of the Duchy of Lancaster, referred their crimes to Wessington who rapidly moved the culprits to other cells in order to 'hush up the slander'.[6]

At the least, this scandal throws doubts on the prior of Lytham's ability to discipline his subjects; but it was also accompanied by a variety of accusations made against Partrike himself. Among the 'various grievous points' with which Erghowe and Cyther charged their old superior, the most serious, because the most easily substantiated, was that of excessive *peculum* and *proprietas*. One of the stories which reached Durham was that Partrike, suffering from so severe

[1] Misc. Chrs., no. 5622.
[2] *Liber Vitae*, fo. 70v; Reg. Langley, fo. 261v; Bursar, 1418/19, Elemos. Consueta.
[3] Granator, 1421–5; Bursar, 1427–9; Reg. III, fo. 113.
[4] Reg. III, fo. 140.   [5] Misc. Chrs., nos. 5637 (xi), 5472.
[6] Loc. xxv, no. 39; Reg. Parv. II, fos. 115–16.

an illness that he believed himself to be on the point of death, bequeathed large quantities of jewels and money to his secular friends. He left Wessington, to whom the disposition of the goods of deceased monks properly belonged, only twenty marks and that at the instance of his fellow-monks standing round his death bed.[1] It was probably at this point that the prior of Lytham should have been removed from his office; but when, in January 1440, Partrike came to Durham to rebut the charges made by Erghowe and Cyther, Wessington allowed himself to be convinced and wrote to Thomas Urswike on 11 January that the accused had been more sinned against than sinning.[2] However, at Bishop Neville's visitation of the mother house in July 1442, Partrike was one of the only two Durham monks personally detected of *proprietas*. The prior of Lytham had not attended the visitation and was so infuriated by these charges that he wrote an angry letter to Wessington on 4 October 1442 attributing the accusations to malice. He alleged, in a revealing admission, that recent expenses on litigation had reduced his personal fortune to its level in 1420, before he occupied his first obedience.[3] In this letter to his superior Partrike let slip the curious remark, 'for I thynke to be a monke as lang as I leefe', which must suggest that the possibility of doing otherwise had already crossed his mind. The visitation of July 1442 was the turning-point in the career of William Partrike. Henceforward he complained incessantly of persecution by his Durham brethren if not, at first, by Wessington himself.

By 1442 Partrike was already engaged in private negotiations at Rome and in October of that year he received a papal dispensation to have a portable altar. Four months later, on 23 February 1443, Partrike's representative at the Curia, relying no doubt on Italian ignorance of the nature of the relationship between Durham and its cell, that is on *tacita veritas* quite as much as on the *suggesta falsitas* of which he was later accused, procured a bull permitting the prior to remain at Lytham until his death.[4] For the time being the Durham chapter remained completely oblivious of the bull. Partrike continued to account, sent a proctor to the annual chapter and even made a visit to Durham where Robert Westmorland tried unsuccessfully

[1] Misc. Chrs., no. 5637 (xi).   [2] Reg. Parv. II, fo. 116.
[3] Loc. IX, no. 18; Lytham, Miscellanea, no. 5.
[4] *C.P.L.* IX (1431–47), p. 318; Loc. IX, no. 14; Misc. Chrs., no. 5637 (v).

to cure him of his obsession with the malice displayed towards him by his brethren.[1] However, throughout 1443 Partrike was still engaged in securing his position. His successes at Rome were crowned on 4 December by a papal dispensation to hold an ecclesiastical benefice in addition to his priorate.[2] The previous day at Westminster Partrike had received royal licence to use the bull of perpetuity and a pardon for its contravention of the Statutes of Provisors.[3] Although Wessington remained completely unaware of the fact, the slightest pressure from Durham would now suffice to cause Partrike to renounce his allegiance.

Such pressure was already forthcoming. On 8 September 1443 Wessington had written to Partrike informing him that the monastery's annual chapter had imposed on Lytham a contribution of £5 to help meet the enormous new debts resultant from Thomas Lawson's disastrous term of office as cellarer.[4] It was unfortunate for Wessington that his attempt to extricate the convent from the most serious financial crisis of his priorate led directly to the most dangerous rebellion against his authority. For Partrike was no exception to the rule that loyalty lies weakest at the pocket; irked by the unusually heavy contributions raised from him in the past few years to help the monastery in its difficulties,[5] he had no intention of sending this further levy. On 13 January 1444 Wessington was compelled to write again, more curtly, demanding payment within the next month.[6] On 10 February Partrike replied, not to Wessington, from whose jurisdiction he now regarded himself as completely free, but to the monastic chancellor, Robert Westmorland, informing him that he was now prior of Lytham for life.[7] To the news of his bull of perpetuity, and the royal 'perdun for prouysion', Partrike added his own radical interpretation; he now regarded himself as comparable to any beneficed rector or vicar, responsible only to his ordinary, the archdeacon of Richmond, and 'exemptt utterly fro' the prior'.

Reaction was immediate; Westmorland informed Wessington, who naturally asked to see the bull and royal pardon. But before the com-

---

[1] Loc. IX, nos. 8, 32, 70.
[2] Loc. IX, no. 24; *C.P.L.* IX (1431–47), p. 355. This was the 'bull of capacity' which Partrike could never be persuaded to surrender.
[3] *C.P.R.*, *1441–46*, p. 237.
[4] Reg. Parv. II, fos. 173–4.   [5] Misc. Chrs., nos. 5649–51, 7138; Lytham, 1440–3.
[6] Reg. Parv. II, fo. 181.   [7] Misc. Chrs., no. 5622.

munity at large was officially notified of Partrike's rebellion, West-morland wrote on 16 February to Lytham mixing appeals to loyalty with threats of 'future heaviness' and suggesting a personal meeting at Barnard Castle.[1] It was not yet certain that Partrike was absolutely committed to his schemes; the possibilities of a peaceful settlement were further explored in a series of letters between the Lytham prior and Westmorland, in which the correspondents were not so fully absorbed in public animosity as to neglect the customary politenesses and exchanges of information about their respective illnesses.[2] Not-withstanding Westmorland's assertion that he might 'full euyll labore for the sciatica' and Partrike's counter that he had been 'right sick and like to die', the two monks eventually met at the Augus-tinian priory of Bolton in Craven for what proved to be an abortive attempt at reconciliation.[3]

Meanwhile the convent had already approached Bishop Neville, who professed that he was willing to revive the charges against Partrike made at his visitation two years earlier. Secure in this know-ledge, Wessington and his chapter met on 5 March 1444 and formally cited Partrike to appear before them.[4] The only result of this citation was to widen the division between the two parties, for when Thomas Clough, Wessington's messenger, arrived at Lytham five days later, he was met in the priory orchard by Partrike himself who refused, '*animo irato*', to receive the letters and unnerved Clough by vague threats of physical violence. These were almost made good when early on the following morning Clough was attacked by three armed men who advanced on him with drawn weapons and threatened to make him eat his citations with the box in which he carried them. Completely thwarted, the envoy withdrew and brought back his alarming report to Durham on 15 March.[5]

So Wessington, in March 1444, had no alternative but to take legal action against his disobedient monk. The convent's muniments were combed in search for evidence to prove that the priors of Lytham were removable at the will of the priors of Durham. The

[1] Loc. IX, nos. 8, 33.   [2] Ibid., nos. 32, 52.

[3] In the annual chapter at Durham in June 1444 Westmorland received three pounds '*versus Bolton in Craven ad loquendum cum Willelmo Partrike per unam septimanam integram cum sex equis*' (Misc. Chrs., no. 7138).

[4] Loc. IX, no. 20; Misc. Chrs., no. 5622 (iv); Reg. III, fo. 301.

[5] Loc. IX, no. 20; Reg. IV, fos. 15–16.

appropriate transcripts were then dispatched to York where a tuitorial appeal had been lodged soon after 9 March.[1] The prior made one more attempt to settle the issue out of court. At the instance of one of his Yorkshire counsellors, John Portington, Justice of the Common Pleas, Wessington sent Robert Westmorland and John Gateshead, the convent's bursar, to York where on 3 August a vague but amicable agreement was apparently reached.[2] This success was short-lived. Partrike left York for Lancaster, where he found no difficulty in discovering new legal arguments sympathetic to his cause. In a letter written at Laxton on 17 August he omitted mention of the guarantees he had made at York and suggested yet a further conference, this time at London.[3] This *prima facie* evidence of bad faith was confirmed a month later when Partrike further consolidated his position by securing institution and induction to the parish church of Saint Olaf in Chester.[4] Partrike's bull of perpetuity remained the greatest obstacle to action by the Durham monks and Wessington waited anxiously for news from his proctor at the Curia. At last, on 16 December 1444, a papal mandate ordered the archbishop of York and others to enquire into the circumstances of the Lytham case.[5]

The new year opened with a formidable assault on Partrike's position, against which his only defence was a refusal to answer citations and a reliance on local Lancastrian support. After a chapter meeting on 2 January 1445 at which Wessington and thirty-four monks made a formal protestation against Partrike's acquisition and use of his papal and royal privileges, the convent proceeded nine days later to revoke the prior's appointment and present Henry Helay in his stead.[6] Accordingly, on 17 April, Master Robert Dobbes, as vicar-general of the archdeacon of Richmond, cited Partrike to appear before him at York to explain why Helay should not be instituted and inducted into the priory. The apparitor entrusted with the delivery of this citation was informed that Partrike held the cell '*manu forti et laicali*', and fearing death or mutilation if he visited Lytham itself he attached the vicar-general's mandate to the church

---

[1] Reg. III, fos. 301–3, 305; Loc. IX, no. 66.   [2] Loc. IX, nos. 7, 34.

[3] Ibid., no. 12; Lytham, Miscellanea, no. 6.   [4] Loc. IX, nos. 48, 49.

[5] Misc. Chrs., nos. 5622, 5637 (iii); Reg. IV, fo. 24; *C.P.L.* IX (1431–47), p. 458.

[6] Loc. IX, nos. 63–4; Reg. IV, fos. 15v–17.

door at Preston. Partrike was as unresponsive to the demands of his ordinary as to those of his religious superior. Dobbes's successive citations and mandates were torn down from various Lancashire churches by the prior's partisans; and his contumacious failure to appear at York led to the sequestration of the goods of the cell on 4 October 1445 and a sentence of excommunication by the arch-deacon's vicar-general exactly a month later. When, on 12 January 1446, Partrike 'damnably refused to appear' for the fifth time since the previous May, Dobbes decided to appeal to the Crown for a writ of *significavit* and the prior's imprisonment.[1] In the meantime, Wessington and the convent had approached the royal government directly and raised doubts as to the validity of Partrike's dispensation from the operation of the Statutes of Provisors. As early as 14 February 1445 writs of *praemunire facias* had been sent to various English sheriffs asking them to summon Partrike before the king to answer for his alleged offences against the statutes.[2] Wessington and the monks then contemplated even more extreme measures and drafted a petition for presentation to parliament by which Partrike was to be compelled to return to Durham and to be prevented at all costs from leaving for Rome. At the end of 1445, a letter was sent to Henry VI asking him to annul Partrike's letters patent of December 1443, 'and they shall pray to god for youre hignes'.[3]

Partrike's temerity in withstanding pressure from so many and such exalted quarters throughout 1444 and 1445 deserves some explanation. Wessington and the Durham monks never had any doubt that he was being supported by influential Lancastrians and could point to the Lytham case as an illustration of the evils of main-tenance. 'I trust wele', wrote Robert Westmorland on 5 March 1444, 'yhe haaf greit supportacion of your neghbures and frenndes in the countre bod tak no boldnesse thar by.'[4] The warning was in vain for throughout the next two years it was to 'certen maystyrs, cosyns and frendes of myn' that the prior of Lytham looked for support.[5] Of all Partrike's allies, his two monk-fellows at the cell,

---

[1] *Register of Archdeacons of Richmond*, 1442–74, I, ed. A. H. Thompson (Yorkshire Archaeological Journal xxx, 1930), pp. 85–91.

[2] Loc. IX, nos. 4, 45.

[3] Loc. IX, no. 54; Lytham, Miscellanea, nos. 13–15. There seems, however, to be no evidence that the Lytham case ever came before parliament.

[4] Loc. IX, no. 32.   [5] Misc. Chrs., no. 5622.

John Rihall and Thomas Wheill, were the least important. Although they continued to obey him as their superior during the course of the dispute, their position was unenviable. For some time Wheill was very unpopular at Durham because Partrike, never a fluent scribe and suffering from arthritis at the time, employed him to write his cantankerous letters to the mother house. Wheill later claimed that he had tried to persuade Partrike to drop his attempt at securing independence from Durham and that he had never been 'privy to the Prior of Litham's working'; Partrike's real abettors, he continued, were the gentlemen of Lancashire who had designs against the house of Durham and its senior monks, although not against Wessington and his sub-prior.[1]

The Lancastrian gentry were traditionally hostile to the cell of Lytham; and the main characteristic of Partrike's priorate, as compared with those of his predecessors and successors, was his willingness to come to terms with this hostility and conciliate his neighbours at the expense of his Durham brethren. Of all his early patrons, by far the most influential was Sir Thomas Stanley, controller of the royal household and receiver-general of the Duchy of Lancaster in November 1443.[2] Stanley regarded Partrike as his protégé and wrote to Wessington on 31 August 1444 that he was 'a gude preste and haseben' of my dole and felawship' who had 'shewed me kyndnesse sith tyme he com to lethom'.[3] Partrike secured Stanley's support by promising him the stewardship of the cell and in later years asked his chaplain to 'laber to my Maister Stanley and ye best whyse that yhe can to mak him wrath wit ye house of Durham, for be God me thynke he haf causis'; this was after the convent had deprived Stanley of the stewardship and before his anger was finally assuaged by a financial *placebo* of over £5 in 1450.[4] Even more deeply committed to Partrike's cause was Stanley's cousin, Thomas Haryngton, who was steward of the Amundesham hundred in which Lytham

---

[1] Loc. IX, nos. 13, 20; cf. Reg. III, fos. 306v–307.

[2] R. Somerville, *History of the Duchy of Lancaster* I (London, 1953), 494; J. S. Roskell, *Knights of the Shire for the County Palatine of Lancaster, 1377–1460* (Chetham Society, New Series, XCVI, 1937), pp. 162–72.

[3] Loc. IX, no. 7.

[4] Ibid., no. 67; cf. Lytham, 1449–51. It may be noted that Edward Stanley, Earl of Derby, was steward of Lytham Priory at the Dissolution: *Valor Ecclesiasticus* V (1825), 305.

lay and many times member of parliament for Lancashire.[1] Haryngton was one of the beneficiaries of a will made by William Partrike
on 3 May 1445,[2] and wrote letters to Durham on the prior's behalf.
According to Westmorland, only the convent's reverence for
Haryngton had prevented them from taking much stronger measures
against Partrike in the summer of 1444.[3] Other supporters of
Partrike's cause were Sir William Assheton, Christopher Boyne
(with whom the prior deposited his charters for safe-keeping), and
many lesser men like Oliver Butler and Roger Tinkler who provided him with armed protection.[4] Partrike's chaplain, Thomas
Harper, was perhaps more intimate with the prior than anyone;
described by Prior Ebchester as a base enemy of the monastery,
Harper was eventually persuaded by his master to go to the Curia,
'what to do God knows', and the convent was relieved to hear of
his death on the journey there.[5]

Throughout 1444 and 1445 Wessington attempted to build up a
party of supporters strong enough to oppose the Partrike faction. He
sent John Gateshead several times to London in an attempt to win
over lawyers and members of the royal household. Gateshead also
visited Archbishop Kemp no less than nine times about the Lytham
case between Michaelmas of 1443 and 1444, and another four times
in the winter of 1444–5.[6] Wessington's counsellors, Masters John
Marshall and John Norton as well as John Portington, contributed
memoranda and briefs in the interests of the convent.[7] In Lancashire,
Thomas Urswike began to denounce Partrike and in December 1445
wrote to Henry Helay of the 'fowle untristy gouernance that he
ussis'.[8] Wessington also enlisted the aid of the Earl of Northumberland who wrote on the monastery's behalf to an unnamed Lancashire
lord, probably Stanley, in February 1445.[9] The prior of Durham

---

[1] Somerville, *History of the Duchy of Lancaster*, pp. 499–500; Roskell, *Knights of the Shire*, pp. 179–86.

[2] Loc. IX, no. 43; this document is one more proof that Partrike now regarded himself as a secular clerk.   [3] Loc. IX, nos. 12, 34; Lytham, Miscellanea, nos. 4, 6.

[4] Loc. IX, nos. 20*, 30, 43; Lytham, 1448–50.

[5] Harper's mission to Rome occurred after Partrike's return to Durham (Loc. IX,
nos. 11, 30, 37, 67; Reg. Parv. III, fos. 27–8, 46).

[6] Bursar, 1443/44, 1444/45, Expense Necessarie.

[7] Loc. IX, nos. 7, 19, 22, 34; Lytham, Miscellanea, no. 10; Reg. Parv. II, fo. 183.

[8] Loc. IX, no. 6. Cf. Roskell, *Knights of the Shire*, pp. 147–51.

[9] Loc. IX, no. 62; Bursar, 1444/45 Expense Necessarie.

made the claim that Partrike's 'deed may turn a bad example to all patrons of benefices spirituall and temporall';[1] but he seems to have been unable to induce any English magnate to take very positive action against his rebellious monk. Stanley's influence at the royal court was probably the biggest single reason why Partrike continued to occupy the priory of Lytham for almost two years after his withdrawal of allegiance from Durham.

But by the end of 1445 Partrike had been excommunicated and it was unlikely that he could assert his independence for much longer. On 2 December Wessington and a small group of thirteen senior monks met and decided that, if he renounced his bull of perpetuity, he would be received at Durham as a wayward child rather than an obdurate sinner. It was out of the question that he should remain at Lytham among the convent's enemies but the mastership of Wearmouth was suggested as a possible compensation.[2] More grudgingly, the convent agreed to Partrike's demand that the case should be settled before arbitrators. John Gateshead was appointed the convent's representative and travelled to London where he and Partrike came before Sir Thomas Stanley and Master Richard Andrew, canon of York and king's secretary, who completed their award on 24 February 1446.[3] Partrike was treated remarkably leniently although required to surrender his bull of perpetuity and resign the priory of Lytham before a notary of St Paul's. Partrike was then to return to Durham and be admitted 'in gentill and easy wyse'; he was to be excused for life 'of rysing at matyns and all other maner of obseruances at any tym to be doon in the Queer, intablyng, kepyng of the Fratour and comyng to the Chapitour and all other observaunces of religion bot as any Doctor of Divinite doth, or at any time doon in the monasterie aforesaid'. The prior and convent were also required to give Partrike an annual pension of £2, his own chamber in the infirmary, a servant and a place at the prior's table. The greatest and most surprising concession allowed him to retain the papal bull permitting him to hold an ecclesiastical benefice. Stanley and Andrew appear to have expected that Partrike's return to Durham would be only temporary.

---

[1] Loc. IX, no. 7.   [2] Ibid., no. 19.
[3] Ibid., nos. 5, 22; Lytham, Miscellanea, nos. 2, 7: cf. Bursar, 1445/46, Expense Necessarie.

When the award reached Durham, Wessington was dismayed at the generosity of the arbitrators towards Partrike. Insufficient care had been taken to ensure that he left his priory in a fitting state; during his turbulent years at Lytham, he had involved the house in heavy debt and also alienated many of its lands. Wessington agreed to allow Partrike the general status of a graduate doctor resident in the monastery but refused to seat him at his table and was extremely anxious that he should give up all his bulls. Many of the articles of the decree made by Stanley and Andrew have the word *proprietas* written against them in the monastic copy, and the convent's general opinion was that the terms of the award were 'hard to bear'. However, to have rejected the agreement would have been to prolong the Lytham case even further; Wessington, now seriously ill himself, accepted the advice of his counsellor, John Portington, and accepted the award as far as it was compatible with the rules of monastic observance and canon law.[1] Accordingly the terms of the decree were put rapidly into effect. Although Partrike left outstanding debts of over £70 he was allowed to deliver his final inventory of the cell on 8 March 1446.[2] Four days later Henry Helay was presented to the priory of Lytham once again and this time canonically instituted on 21 March and later inducted by the Dean of Amounderness.[3] On 19 March Partrike returned to Durham where he was received with ceremony if not enthusiasm and a fortnight later was officially pardoned for all his past transgressions.[4] The prodigal had returned, Lytham once more acknowledged its dependence on Durham, and a satisfactory solution to the problem appeared to have been achieved. It is probably no coincidence that Wessington resigned his priorate within a few weeks of Partrike's return.

The case of William Partrike was, however, the subject of an unfortunate and distressing epilogue. Wessington's successor as prior, William Ebchester, was a man whom Partrike had long regarded as his 'deedly enemy'.[5] After March 1446 Partrike seems to have been surprised at the quite understandable coldness displayed

---

[1] Loc. IX, no. 29.
[2] Loc. IX, no. 26d; Lytham, Miscellanea, Inventory of 8 March 1446.
[3] Rev. IV, fo. 27; *Register of the Archdeacons of Richmond*, ed. Thompson, p. 95.
[4] Reg. IV, fos. 27–8.   [5] Misc. Chrs., no. 5622 (iv).

towards him in the Durham cloister. It seems that Robert Westmorland's hope 'that vexation will give you sense' was never fulfilled.[1] Partrike's miseries and intrigues at Durham are revealed in
four letters written by him to his old chaplain, Thomas Harper,
between 1446 and 1449.[2] Written *de profundis*, the letters compel
some sympathy for his plight; but their contents certainly justify the
other monks' endorsements of *malicia contumacia* and their use of
them as evidence against the author.[3] Partrike's lament that Ebchester
'luffyd me never and Robert Westmorland and John Gatished and
Richard Bell ar cheff wit hym, an none of them luffis me', was
followed, in the earliest of his letters, by the plaintive 'for in gode
fayth I wote noght wat me is best to do'. Although Partrike had
surrendered most of his privileges in a vain attempt to mollify his
prior, he now placed all his hopes on Harper's projected visit to the
Curia.

Complaining that he was 'more stric' bon than any whyfe is to
hyr husband', Partrike's dearest and most secret desire was that the
monastery of Durham should be excommunicated by the pope, 'and
that wald I be fulfayn of'.[4] In June 1447 and again in February 1448
Prior Ebchester wrote to Master William Gray, the king's proctor
at the papal court, asking him to look out for signs of anyone still
working in Partrike's interests.[5] Two years later, on receiving news
from Rome that there was a Franciscan from Bristol still active at the
Curia on Partrike's behalf, Ebchester decided to expose this still
rebellious monk before his fellows. On 7 November 1450 the prior
and eighteen of his senior monks summoned Partrike before them
and showed him the evidence they had collected of his intrigues at
Rome. Although Ebchester appealed to him to give up all thoughts
of using his bull of capacity to hold a benefice, he remained obdurate
and a few days later displayed, to the great consternation of the monks,
Bishop Walter Lyhert's letters of 22 August 1450 instituting him to

---

[1] Loc. IX, no. 34.

[2] Ibid., nos. 11, 30, 37, 67. The first and last of these are badly mutilated.

[3] It is impossible to know whether Partrike's letters were intercepted before they
left Durham or returned to the monks after Harper's death. The latter explanation
for their survival among the monastic archives seems most likely, and it was unfortunate for Partrike that his old chaplain disobeyed his instructions to burn the
letters.

[4] Loc. IX, no. 67.   [5] Reg. Parv. III, fos. 16v–17v, 27v–28.

a rectory in the diocese of Norwich. The prior and convent wished to prevent Partrike's departure because of the scandal to their church and religion, and they threatened him with excommunication if he had alienated any of the monastery's possessions. When Ebchester and the senior monks went to inspect Partrike's private chamber on 18 November they discovered a straw-covered bed in an otherwise empty room, showing that their fellow had fulfilled his early promise to Harper, 'I will sell my beddynge and get some money'.[1] At this stage, the community of Durham finally abandoned their attempt to keep Partrike in the cloister; he seems to have left the convent shortly after this denouement for he disappears completely from the monastic records after 1450.

William Partrike's recalcitrance must be placed in the context of similar acts of rebellion, reflected in petitions for bulls of perpetuity, made by English monks in the period before and after 1400.[2] Other priors of Durham cells had sometimes been tempted by their institution and induction into what they argued was an ecclesiastical benefice to describe themselves as 'perpetual priors'. Such arguments presented a real danger to the authority of the mother house. Only a few years after the Lytham case of 1444–6 the priory of Wymondham in Norfolk was permanently detached from St Albans by its superior, Stephen London, who, like Partrike, secured the support of local knights against the central monastery.[3] Wessington and his chapter were fully aware of the possibilities of such a development at Lytham and it has been seen that they spared neither their labours nor their money[4] in the attempt to bring Partrike home to Durham. On the other hand, it seems likely that Wessington might have spared himself and his monks much anxiety if he had recalled Partrike from Lytham before he had become so firmly entrenched in the cell; in a letter of October 1444 to Sir Thomas Stanley, Wessington himself admitted that he had been blamed by many of his brethren for being 'too slow in pursuing' Partrike.[5] Exactly how far he can be criticised for his failure to control this most insubordinate of fifteenth-century Durham monks remains an open

---

[1] Loc. IX, nos. 37, 38.

[2] See Knowles, *Rel. Orders* II, Chapter XII, 'The Loosening of Discipline', pp. 167–74.

[3] *Annales J. Amundesham* (Rolls Series, 1870–71), II, 366–9.

[4] Wessington and his monks reckoned in 1446 that the 'causa de Lethom' had cost them over £100: Loc. XXI, no. 20 (vii). [5] Loc. IX, no. 7.

question. Other members of the community of Saint Cuthbert may often have been discontented with their lot; but Partrike alone was prepared to risk the consequences of open rebellion. As the Durham monks long remembered, he came uncomfortably close to a success which would have undermined the mother church's relationship towards all its daughters and prejudiced Saint Cuthbert's reputation as the most vigilant of all the English saints.

Chapter 10

THE INTELLECTUAL ACTIVITIES
OF THE DURHAM MONKS

At no time have the general mass of Benedictines been learned. But they have tended to produce at all times individuals reincarnating the type of Ven. Bede.[1]

The importance of the role played by the university-educated monk in late medieval religious life is now a familiar theme. The concept of '*le moine universitaire*', a phrase apparently first coined by Dom Ursmer Berlière, has been applied to England for over forty years and to great effect by Dr W. A. Pantin in a series of studies of monk scholars and monastic colleges.[2] More recently, the results of Dr Pantin's researches have been absorbed and developed by Professor Knowles in his three volumes on the *Religious Orders in England*. The significance of the university monk is not, moreover, merely that of an academic backwater. In an age when visitation records so often speak of monasteries '*tam in spiritualibus quam in temporalibus multipliciter collapsi*', it has proved rewarding and refreshing to consider monks who were scholars if not saints. Professor Knowles once compared English monasticism in 1300 to a tree that had ceased to blossom.[3] Pleasure at finding later bloom has sometimes led to some exaggeration of the beauty of the flower, some failure to consider on how few branches it occurred at all. But of these branches Durham was probably the most important. 'Perhaps more than any other monastery Durham came to be governed and administered by university monks.'[4] It seems possible to go even further: the exposure of large numbers of Durham monks to Oxford learning,

---

[1] C. Butler, *Benedictine Monachism* (London, 1924), p. 337.
[2] Among the most important are 'Abbot Kidderminster and Monastic Studies', *Downside Review* XLVII (1929), 198–211; 'Gloucester College', *Oxoniensa* XI–XII (1945–7), 65–74; *Canterbury College, Oxford* (Oxford Historical Society, New Series, VI–VIII, 1947–50); 'Some Medieval English Treatises on the Origins of Monasticism', *Medieval Studies presented to Rose Graham* (Oxford, 1950), pp. 189–215; *The Letter Book of Robert Joseph* (Oxford Historical Society, New Series, XIX, 1967).
[3] Knowles, *Rel. Orders* I, 319.　　　　[4] Ibid., II, 20.

Oxford scholastic techniques, and Oxford academic society was the greatest single cultural influence on the convent during the last 250 years of its existence. Durham's debt to its monastic colony at Oxford, Durham College, can hardly be exaggerated; and a study of this college is an essential preliminary to any survey of the intellectual interests and preoccupations of the fifteenth-century community of Saint Cuthbert.

DURHAM COLLEGE, OXFORD

Early in the fourteenth century the Durham chronicler, Robert Graystanes, compared Prior Hugh of Darlington's decision to send Durham monks to study at Oxford in the late 1280s to Adam's sin '*unde fuit occasio redempcionis nostre*'.[1] Graystanes's sentiment might not have appealed to Saint Benedict but was undoubtedly shared by the great majority of his fellows at Durham. Throughout the later middle ages, large numbers of Durham monks actively desired to spend long periods of their lives working and studying in Oxford: it was they who put substance into the pious hopes and regulations of successive popes and Benedictine Chapters. More remarkably, the Durham chapter established its separate monastic colony in Oxford at a very early date. Christ Church, Canterbury, was the only other English monastery which also succeeded in founding a regular university collegiate establishment of its own. Durham's achievement is all the more impressive when one remembers that almost all the other Black Monk scholars at Oxford during the later middle ages were confined to the extremely limited accommodation provided by their joint community at Gloucester College.

The history of the Durham cell at Oxford falls into two quite distinct periods, those before and after the foundation of a regular college on the existing site by Bishop Thomas Hatfield in 1381. The contrast between the original small manse or *hospitium* and the later well-endowed and prosperous college is reflected in the surviving records at Durham, few of which throw light on the obscure history of the early settlement at Oxford. According to Graystanes's well-

---

[1] *Scrip. Tres*, p. 73. Graystanes, an Oxford graduate himself, was probably referring in particular to the role played by these first university monks in the subsequent struggle against Bishop Antony Bek.

known but misleading narrative, the latter was the by-product not of abstract reforming principles but of a bitter personal feud between two senior Durham monks, Hugh of Darlington and Richard of Hoton. When Darlington was elected prior of Durham for the second time in January 1286 he exiled Hoton to the Lytham cell and 'sent monks to study at Oxford', apparently in an attempt to convince Hoton's partisans within the convent of his own benevolence. '*Malo occasionem administrante bono*', Graystanes went on to record the foundation and building of the '*locum Oxonie*' by Hoton when he succeeded Darlington as prior in March 1290.[1] In fact Durham monk scholars had already begun to find their way to Oxford by 1278;[2] and as early as 1286 the Durham chapter's plan to build a manse north of Canditch or Broad Street had led to a grant of arable land '*in bello monte*' from the abbess of Godstow.[3] The small colony of Durham monks quickly struck roots on Oxford soil and the first buildings were soon ready for occupation. Geoffrey of Burdon, later prior of Durham (1313–21) and one of the first residents in the Durham cell, was accused of admitting a woman to the common dormitory there.[4] More happily, in 1311 Geoffrey of Haxby became the first Durham monk to incept in theology. Bishop Kellaw's letter to the prior and chapter made the appropriate comment: 'it has hitherto been unknown for any member of the church of Durham to become sufficiently proficient in Holy Scripture to deserve the degree of Doctor of Divinity'.[5]

The early Durham cell at Oxford was undoubtedly small and impoverished, depending for its survival on heavy financial subsidies from the obedientiaries of the mother house. However, a superior of the manse, with the title '*Prior Oxonie*', had emerged by 1316 and not long afterwards several Durham monks began to demonstrate their academic prowess. In October 1333 the community could count three doctors and one bachelor of theology among its members.[6] John of Beverley, prior of the Oxford manse at that date, was a monk of some intellectual distinction, and his dialogue on Saint

---

[1] *Scrip. Tres*, p. 73. [2] *Dur. Acct. Rolls* II, 486, 492.

[3] 1.5. Ebor., no. 9; cf. Blakiston, *Trinity College*, p. 3; H. E. Salter, *Survey of Oxford* II (Oxford Historical Society, New Series, XX, 1969), pp. 187–8.

[4] *Records of Antony Bek* (Surtees Soc. CLXII, 1953), p. 145.

[5] *Reg. Palatinum Dunelmense* (Rolls Series, 1873–8), I, 45–6; cf. *Reg. of William Greenfield* (Surtees Soc., 1931–40), IV, 366. [6] *Scrip. Tres*, p. 120.

Benedict's Rule was still being cited as an important authority by Black Monk prelates in 1421.[1] John of Beverley's scholastic reputation was, however, soon overshadowed by that of a younger Durham monk, the celebrated Uthred of Boldon. For most of the long period of fifty-six years between his adoption of the habit at Durham in 1341 and his death at Finchale in 1397 Uthred dominated the intellectual life of his convent in an unprecedented way. But Uthred was by no means typical of the Durham university monk. Except for two brief periods as subprior towards the end of his career, he was something of a stranger to the Durham cloister. During the twenty years after 1347, Uthred was apparently permanently resident in Oxford as a practising teacher and controversialist; but from August 1367 onwards most of his life was spent in relative but interrupted tranquillity as prior of Finchale.[2]

Uthred of Boldon's theological and philosophical abilities were fully recognised within his own life-time, not only by his fellow monks but at Oxford and within the kingdom at large. Interest in Uthred's numerous treatises has recently been intense, leading to several detailed analyses which have confirmed John Leland's belief that 'never was there a monk of Durham College more learned than he'. Uthred was no doubt fortunate in his time. His remarkably original and unorthodox view that salvation depended on the individual's response to the '*clara visio*' of God experienced at the point of death led to censure by Archbishop Langham in 1368 yet not to complete disgrace.[3] But the subsequent appearance and condemnation of Wycliffe's heresies at Oxford precluded the possibility,

---

[1] Pantin, *Chapters* II, 118–19; cf. Emden I, 183.

[2] The details of Uthred's career (to which Emden I, 212–13 is the best short guide) present many problems. As Professor Knowles has pointed out (*Rel. Orders* II, 48), the *vita compendiosa* written at Durham some years after his death (printed from B.M. Additional MS. 6162, fo. 31v. in *Bulletin of Institute of Historical Research* III [1925–6], 46) is difficult to reconcile with other documentary evidence for his life. Although professed at Durham as '*Vthredus de Bolton*' in 1342 (*Liber Vitae*, fo. 69v), he was styled '*Uthredus de Bamburgh*' in the following January (*Reg. Richard of Bury*, p. 155). This fact, together with his Northumbrian Christian name and Friar Trevytlam's malicious charge that he was '*Scottus genere*' (*Tryvytlam de Laude Universitatis Oxoniae*, ed. H. Furneaux [Oxford Historical Society XXXII, 1896], p. 208), suggests a birth-place near the Anglo-Scottish border rather than Boldon village in County Durham as is usually supposed.

[3] D. Knowles, 'The Censured Opinions of Uthred of Boldon', *Proceedings of the British Academy* XXXVII (1952), 305–42.

perhaps remote in any case, that Uthred's ability to fish in the dangerous waters of speculative theology would be inherited by later Durham monks. In this context it is significant that John Aclyff, Uthred's junior colleague and prior of the Oxford cell in the 1370s, was chosen by the Presidents of the English Benedictine organisation to defend orthodox opinions against the heresies of Wycliffe himself.[1] Neither Aclyff nor any of his successors were able to rival Uthred's skill and profundity as a theologian. In the strict sense, Uthred founded no school. Nevertheless there is no doubt that Uthred's influence on the Durham community was considerable, and continued to be so long after his death. Many of his treatises were preserved and read at Durham, where Prior Wessington quoted with respect Uthred's adaptation of the scholastic dictum '*quod non est bonum perdere substanciam propter accidens*'.[2] Several of the themes discussed by Uthred, and particularly the antiquity and historical basis of the monastic ideal, continued to attract the eager attention of a number of Durham monks until the Dissolution. Nor was the Durham chapter insensitive to the prestige it gained from the presence of so distinguished an intellectual among its members. This must have been one of the many factors which encouraged fourteenth-century Durham priors to continue their long and difficult struggle to establish the Oxford cell on a more prosperously regular basis. Uthred's own last recorded visits to London and Oxford in the early 1380s were devoted to the promotion of the new Durham College – not the least of his many services to his brethren.[3]

Throughout the middle of the fourteenth century the Durham monks had projected a series of abortive schemes for the establishment of an Oxford college which would enjoy complete economic independence and render the connection between university and monastery more permanent and certain. Finally, in the late 1370s, Prior Robert Walworth succeeded in engaging the interest of his sick and elderly bishop, Thomas Hatfield. Unfortunately for the convent, Hatfield died in May 1381 before the detailed arrangements of the new foundation had been completely settled. However,

[1] Pantin, 'A Benedictine Opponent of John Wyclif', pp. 73–7; cf. Emden I, 10.
[2] Reg. Parv. II, fo. 133, printed in *Scrip. Tres*, p. cclxiii.
[3] *Dur. Acct. Rolls* III, 591–3.

Hatfield's own intentions had already been clearly expressed in a quinquepartite covenant of 1 March 1381, and it was this 'ordinance' which formed the basis of the new college's 'statutes'.[1] As this 1381 agreement was observed quite scrupulously by Durham monks until the dissolution of the college, its principal provisions must be summarised, however briefly. The new foundation was dedicated to the honour of the Holy Trinity, the Blessed Virgin Mary and Saint Cuthbert, the first part of which dedication Sir Thomas Pope preserved – as he preserved the existing buildings – when he founded the present Trinity College on the site in 1555. Hatfield intended his bequest to be invested in such a manner that the college would be certain of an annual income of 200 marks. This sum was to support eight student monks, all nominated by the Durham chapter according to the principles laid down by Pope Benedict XII's bull, *Summi magistri* of 1336. The monks were to concentrate their studies within the fields of philosophy and theology; the 1381 covenant is otherwise uninformative as to the details of their academic curriculum, but it can certainly not be accidental that no mention was made of the study of canon law. Full provision was, however, made for regular monastic observance at the college, together with an elaborate series of masses and obits to be said for the souls of Edward III, Queen Philippa, Hatfield's relatives and others. The prior of Durham was to appoint, with the advice of his senior monks, one of the eight college fellows as prior or warden. The latter enjoyed full disciplinary authority over his colleagues and was instructed to hold a weekly chapter in which to correct their religious and academic failings. The financial management of the college was entrusted to two other fellows, appointed as 'receivers' not by the warden but by the prior and chapter of Durham. These *receptores* were to present a quarterly account of their income and expenditure to the warden, who in turn was required to account annually to the prior and chapter of his mother house. But the most interesting feature of Hatfield's foundation, and no doubt the reason for the bishop's promotion of

---

[1] The original Durham copy of this indenture survives as 2.5. Ebor., no. 15. This document was not seen by President Blakiston who relied on the inferior versions printed in *Concilia* II, pp. 614–17 and *Scrip. Tres*, pp. 140–1. It is no reflection on Blakiston's extremely valuable introduction to *Some Durham College Rolls* (Oxford Historical Society XXXII, 1896, pp. 1–76) to suggest that the history of Durham College now deserves thorough re-investigation.

the enterprise, was the inclusion on the foundation of eight secular students in grammar and theology. Conceivably influenced by the collapse a few years earlier of Archbishop Islip's plan for a combination of monks and secular fellows at Canterbury College,[1] Hatfield expected the eight scholars at Durham College to be undergraduates pursuing their studies there for seven years. Four boys were to be selected from the city and diocese of Durham, and two each from the bishop of Durham's lordships of Allerton and Howden. Hatfield reserved for himself the choice of all secular scholars until his death, after which nomination was to revert to a committee of four or five senior monks at Durham. It has already been seen that monastic control of these scholarships was soon under heavy pressure from members of the northern nobility and gentry.[2]

Few university foundations can have had a more difficult and litigious infancy than Durham College, Oxford.[3] During the twenty-five years that followed Bishop Hatfield's death it seemed improbable that the new college would ever prove a viable economic concern. Admittedly, Hatfield's legacy of £3,000 was handsomely large: at an early stage Prior Robert Walworth proposed to invest this money in the purchase of annuities within the city of London. His friends in the city, who apparently included his namesake William Walworth, mayor of London, had advised him that an outlay of 1,000 marks in capital would then produce an annual return of 100 marks. This scheme, like another to divert the revenues of the alien priory of Burstall, proved impracticable and the Durham chapter was forced to adopt the more conventional method of appropriating churches to the college's use. In a letter to Bishop Hatfield, Prior Walworth had already noted a serious objection to this means of endowing the college. Because of the Great Schism, appropriations were only secure if confirmed by several and successive popes. There were other and more intricate problems. By 1381 Durham had already appropriated most of its more obviously wealthy churches to its own use, and so Hatfield's bequest had to be applied to the purchase of new ones

[1] Pantin, *Canterbury College, Oxford*, III, 184–206.

[2] See above, pp. 170–1.

[3] See (besides the documents cited by Blakiston in *Some Durham College Rolls*, pp. 12–14, 56–60) 3.2. Pap., nos. 14, 18; 2.5. Regal., no. 7; Reg. II, fos. 254–5; *C.P.L.* V (1396–1404), pp. 21, 600–1; *C.P.R.*, *1381–85*, pp. 239, 371–2; *1385–89*, pp. 233, 243; *1405–08*, p. 179.

from Lord John Neville of Raby. After a complex period of negotiation, the convent finally emerged with a total of four churches (Bossall, Ruddington, Fishlake and Frampton) which they then applied, after paying the archbishop of York and bishop of Lincoln for licence to do so, to the purposes of the new college. As was usual, appropriations showed little profit during the first years because of the need to pension the dispossessed incumbents. Because of these pensions (averaging no less than £70 per annum for almost a generation), expensive litigation on patronage issues, and a series of exceptional fees for lawyers at London, York and Lincoln, the college was heavily in debt at the turn of the century.[1] In 1404 when the financial condition of the college was still extremely feeble, the chancellor and masters of the university of Oxford unexpectedly began proceedings against the prior of Durham for his failure to maintain the statutory complement of eight monks and eight secular scholars. This accusation came before the Official of the then bishop of Durham, Walter Skirlaw. On this favourable territory the tide was turned in favour of the defendants by means of an eloquent but not unjustified plea on the well-worn theme of monastic poverty. As the Durham monks themselves acknowledged, it was Bishop Skirlaw who had preserved Durham College from 'annihilation and destruction'.[2]

The year 1405 therefore marks a genuine turning-point in the history of Durham College. From this time onwards the financial position of the new foundation rapidly improved and the monks were able to maintain seven or eight fellows there without undue difficulty.[3] The strains and stresses of the early years were forgotten in an extensive building programme at the college during the twenty years after 1405. A gatehouse had been constructed as early as 1397; but only in 1405 did work begin on the new and sumptuous chapel.

---

[1] Durham College, 1394–1403; 4.5. Ebor., no. 6; *Dur. Coll. Rolls*, pp. 56–60. As Mayor Walworth had property interests in Walworth, Surrey, and not Walworth, Durham (S. Thrupp, *The Merchant Class of Medieval London* [University of Michigan, 1948], p. 372), Blakiston's suggestion that he was related to Prior Walworth seems unlikely.

[2] The large Durham file of evidence pertaining to this case survives as 4.6. Ebor., no. 2; cf. Reg. II, fo. 184. Dr Pantin informs me that such university intervention in the affairs of a college is unparalleled at this period.

[3] The payments of commons and oblations entered in the Durham College accounts usually record the exact number of monks and secular scholars in residence; cf. 4.6. Ebor., no. 1.

Measuring 60 by 26 feet and costing over £135, it contained altars to Saints Oswald, Aidan, Nicholas and Catherine as well as much armorial glass which survived until the construction of the present Trinity College chapel in 1691.[1] Immediately after the dedication of Durham College chapel in 1409, the building of the '*novum opus Oxonie*' (a college quadrangle to the north of the chapel) was undertaken. A few years later financial contributions were raised from the mother house and other Durham cells towards the expense of a new college library. This building, situated on the eastern side of the quadrangle, was largely completed in 1417–18 at an approximate cost of £42.[2] Trinity College still preserves much of the original fabric of this early fifteenth-century college library as well as several panels of its original armorial glass, including that of the Wessington family.[3] With dimensions of 27 by 18 feet, the library at Durham College must have been one of the most attractive in late medieval Oxford. Its amenities were presumably not the least of the factors which encouraged close relations between Durham monks and Oxford secular scholars. The contents of this library were certainly well-known to that famous fifteenth-century Oxford figure, Thomas Gascoigne.[4]

After 1427, when the heavy expenditure on the initial building programme began to slacken, Durham College seems to have become one of the most materially prepossessing as well as spacious in the university: its exceptionally large grove was said to include no less than 3,000 trees when surveyed in 1546.[5] The warden was often asked to let rooms to Oxford secular students and graduates as well as to Benedictine monks from Whitby or York, whose northern loyalties may have prejudiced them against joining the majority of Black

---

[1] *C.P.L.* VI (1404–15), pp. 245, 278; Wood's *City of Oxford* II (Oxford Historical Society XVII, 1890), 269–71.

[2] Durham College, 1417–19; Lytham, 1414/15. The library was fitted with new desks and tables in the early 1430s (Durham College, 1431/32).

[3] M. Maclagan, *Trinity College, 1555–1955* (Oxford, 1955), pp. 9–11, plate 7 (c). See the plan in B. H. Streeter, *The Chained Library* (London, 1931), p. 223.

[4] Gascoigne, *Loci e Libro Veritatum*, ed. J. E. T. Rogers (Oxford, 1881), pp. 157, 164–5. Mr N. R. Ker has suggested that Gascoigne gave to Durham College a copy of Bede's life of Saint Cuthbert (now B.M. Harleian MS. 1924 with missing folios in Bodleian Library, Oxford, Digby MS. 41): see Emden II, 747.

[5] *The Early History of St John's College, Oxford* (Oxford Historical Society, New Series, I, 1939), pp. 88–91.

Monk students at Gloucester College.[1] By the middle years of John Wessington's priorate at Durham the four churches appropriated to the college were providing a fairly stable net annual income of £175, somewhat more than Bishop Hatfield had originally predicted. There was undoubtedly a slow and long-term decline in revenue as the college found it progressively more difficult to secure tenants who would farm tithes at the original rates; but handsome compensation was provided for this in 1458 when a fifth church, Brantingham in Yorkshire, was appropriated to the college.[2] The financial background to the activities of the college in the fifteenth century was therefore apparently a happy one of prosperity within fairly wide limits. In many years the surplus was large enough to permit a small piece of building or the purchase of a few additions to the library. After the early years of the century, the college was completely self-sufficient and had realised Hatfield's aim of being no longer dependent on the charity of the central monastery. Full details of the financial, but not the academic, organisation of the college are supplied by the accounts and inventories of the warden and two bursars or 'receivers' sent yearly to Durham for audit. Warden William Ebchester's '*Status Collegii*' of Michaelmas 1428 is incidentally of particular interest as apparently the earliest inventory of Oxford college-rooms to survive. But no attempt can be made here to discuss the detailed practicalities of life at Oxford as led by warden, fellows and secular scholars. On the other hand, no study of monastic life at fifteenth-century Durham would be complete without some reference to a much more difficult question – the general significance to Saint Cuthbert's community of the Oxford university education enjoyed by so many of its members.

Durham College provided university training if not for all at least for a very great number of fifteenth-century Durham monks. Of the 132 recruits received into the mother house between 1383 and 1441, no fewer than 51 can be shown to have spent some part of their careers at Durham College.[3] This is, of course, a minimum figure;

---

[1] Durham College, 1414–25; cf. Reg. Parv. III, fo. 135; A. B. Emden, 'Northerners and Southerners in the organisation of the University to 1509', *Oxford Studies presented to Daniel Callus* (Oxford Historical Society, New Series, XVI, 1964), 1–30.

[2] 3.5. Regal., no. 4; *C.P.R., 1452–61*, p. 425. The net annual income of the college was still as high as £115 at the Dissolution (see above, p. 309, n. 1).

[3] To the Durham university monks of this period listed in Emden's *Biographical*

the Durham College accounts rarely specify the names of the monk-fellows except when they received travelling expenses. The survival of a few more visitation or election certificates would presumably have added several more names to the total. It is probably no exaggeration to claim that almost half of all Durham monks received some form of university education. Only a small proportion of these remained at Durham College for more than five or six years – the average period of university residence of Westminster monks at this period. In general, the Durham College fellows appear to fall into a few distinct categories. There were several monks who were allowed to establish themselves permanently at the college and who eventually died there; although examples of this type of career are less common than at Canterbury College, such a man was Thomas Forster who first went to Oxford in 1422 before ordination as priest, became a bursar of Durham College in 1424, and apparently held this office continuously until his death in 1436–7.[1] Another group of Durham monks who specialised in legal form and procedure are all known to have spent three or four years at Oxford before returning to become proctors and representatives of the monastery in its constant stream of litigation; Wessington's three successive chancellors, John Fishburn, William Dalton and Robert Westmorland, all conformed to this pattern.[2] There was a larger group of monks who seem to have lived at Oxford for only a year or two, and for whom Durham College was a sort of finishing-school before they returned to an administrative career among the Durham obediences; the case of Henry Helay, a fellow of Durham College only from 1405 to 1407 but bursar of Durham later, illustrates this alternative *cursus honorum*.[3] Whatever their subsequent careers, there can be little doubt that most Durham monks who went to study at Oxford were in their very early twenties when they first arrived. Monks tended to make their first appearance among the college records within

Register of the University of Oxford (a most valuable guide) may be added five new names as well as several corrections. These figures may be compared with those of Westminster monks (*c.* 70 between the 1330s and the Dissolution) who attended Oxford University: B. F. Harvey, 'The Monks of Westminster and the University of Oxford', *The Reign of Richard II*, ed. F. R. H. Du Boulay and C. M. Barron (London, 1971), p. 113.

[1] Bursar, 1422/3, Dona et Exennia; Durham College, 1424–37.
[2] Durham College, 1405–11, 1429–31.
[3] Durham College, 1405–7; Almoner, 1405/6; Bursar, 1417–19.

four or five years of the date of their profession; and it is possible to estimate the exact age of those fellows who had received dispensations to be promoted to priest's orders when they attained their twenty-second year of age.[1] Several monks left for Oxford before their ordination as priests at the hands of the bishop of Durham or his suffragan; William Dalton, for instance, received minor orders in the northern diocese, but went to Durham College in late 1422 and was priested by Archbishop Chichele's suffragan at Salisbury on 18 September 1423.[2]

Little information survives as to the course of study pursued by the Durham university monks. They had all received some instruction in grammar and probably other liberal arts as novices at the mother house.[3] When they took up residence at Durham College, most fellows presumably continued their study of the Arts but, as members of a monastic Order, were exempted from the need to graduate in this Faculty.[4] No Durham monk in the later middle ages is known to have graduated in canon law,[5] and it has been seen that Bishop Hatfield had intended the members of the college to concentrate on philosophy and theology.[6] The study of these two subjects was probably the staple occupation of Durham monks at Oxford for such time as they were free from their administrative responsibilities and their heavy commitments in choir and at the celebration of masses. Relatively few monks actually graduated in theology, for the simple reason that the course of study was a long one and the prior of Durham needed his more able monks to fill the obediences at home.

In the circumstances, it is surprising that as many as eleven of the 132 monks who entered religion at Durham between 1383 and 1441

---

[1] E.g. Richard Bell and William Seton were both at Oxford in their twenty-second year (Emden I, 161–2; III, 1671–2).

[2] Almoner, 1422/23; Reg. Langley, fos. 255, 264; *Register of Henry Chichele* (Canterbury and York Society, 1937–47), IV, 357.

[3] See the list of books in the novices' cupboard at Durham (above, pp. 63–4).

[4] *Statuta Antiqua Universitatis Oxoniensis*, ed. Strickland Gibson (Oxford, 1931), pp. cxv–cxvii. Cf. the other important concession that monks need only spend one year in the study of theology at the Oxford schools before admission to their opponency.

[5] A minority of monks from other Benedictine houses did graduate in canon law, e.g. Wessington's contemporaries, Richard Godmersham of Christ Church, Canterbury, and William Morton of Peterborough (Emden II, 779, 1322). *Concilia* II, 614.

became bachelors of theology, an average of approximately two graduations a decade. Thomas Rome obtained his baccalaureate shortly before 1400; William Ebchester in 1421; Robert Moreby shortly before 1425; Richard Barton, John Mody and John Burnby in the 1430s; Robert Emyldon, junior, in 1443–4; William Seton in 1447–8; Richard Bell in 1452; William Elwike in 1456; and Thomas Caly in 1458.[1] This steady stream of university degrees continued at an accelerated rate until the Dissolution and was, in itself, a tribute to the effectiveness of Bishop Hatfield's re-endowment of the college.[2] In 1380 the Durham monk-graduate had been a relatively rare phenomenon, of whom the only living examples were Uthred of Boldon and John Aclyff.[3] But it is noticeable that all wardens of Durham College from Uthred de Boldon onwards felt it incumbent upon themselves to obtain a university degree. The usual procedure during Wessington's priorate was for the new warden to supplicate for his baccalaureate a few years after his appointment; so William Ebchester, warden in 1419, obtained his bachelor's degree in 1421, while Richard Barton and John Mody, wardens in 1428 and 1431, graduated respectively in 1430–1 and 1435–6.[4]

The wardens of Durham College inevitably held a position of much prestige within the university. Their precedence in scholastic processions was a matter for continuous controversy which seems to have been finally settled only in 1522, when Archbishop Warham ruled that the Benedictine '*prior studentium*' was to be followed by either the warden of Durham or of Canterbury College according to the relative seniority of their baccalaureates.[5] In the early 1420s William Ebchester defended his independence against a '*prior studentium*' who wished to subject the warden of Durham College to his authority.[6] Some wardens penetrated into the realm of uni-

---

[1] The degrees of all these eleven monks are noticed in Emden's *Biographical Register*, except for that of Robert Moreby who is credited with the baccalaureate in a list of 31 June 1425 (Reg. III, fo. 113).

[2] There were five doctors and nine bachelors of divinity among the Durham monks at the Dissolution: see *Letters and Papers of Henry VIII*, XVI (1540–1), 712.

[3] Emden I, 10, 212.

[4] Feretrar, 1420/21; Durham College, 1430/31, 1435/36. Barton and Mody were each assigned ten marks by Wessington to meet their expenses in reading the Sentences.

[5] *Canterbury College, Oxford*, ed. Pantin, III, 144–5.

[6] *Dur. Coll. Rolls*, p. 76. For Prior Wessington's memorandum on this issue, see ibid., pp. 27–33.

versity officialdom. John Burnby, *cancellarius natus* in 1445, acted as Gilbert Kymer's commissary between 1447 and 1450: the chancellor's court often met in Durham College during these years.[1] The warden was also often chosen by the priors of Durham to act as an agent in the south of England. John Mody was commissioned to secure the *congé d'élire* from Henry VI on the death of Bishop Langley in 1437; and when in 1424 Wessington found difficulty in maintaining any monks at Stamford, he gave Warden Ebchester custody of the cell for eighteen months.[2] No warden, however, was allowed to establish himself permanently at Durham College. Most of them were in their early forties when appointed, and in their late forties when recalled to Durham either to fill a major obedience there or to be transferred to an important priorate. Of the five wardens of Durham College during Wessington's priorate, William Ebchester and John Burnby became priors of Durham, John Mody sub-prior, Thomas Rome sacrist and Richard Barton prior of Stamford.

Although thirteen of the last eighteen wardens of Durham College proceeded from the baccalaureate to the doctorate in theology, only four monks obtained this second degree during Wessington's priorate. In these cases, considerations of individual ambition, monastic pride and scholastic attainments were partly overshadowed by the question of the cost of the doctorate. Only nine doctors of divinity may have been resident in Oxford University on 4 March 1414; and, of these, only one was a Benedictine monk, Thomas Rome, then warden of Durham College.[3] William Ebchester, who incepted in 1426, was subsidised by his monastery to the extent of £20 but was forced to find as much again from other sources.[4] Even more instructive were the negotiations which preceded the simultaneous inception of three Durham monks, Richard Barton, John Burnby and John Mody, in the summer of 1441. The matter was first raised by Warden Mody in a letter of February 1440 in

---

[1] *Registrum Cancellarii Oxoniensis, 1434–1469*, ed. H. E. Salter (Oxford Historical Society, 1932), I, 108, 145, 176, 179; *Munimenta Academica Oxoniensis* (Rolls Series, 1868), II, 586, 588. [2] Reg. III, fos. 216–18; Stamford, 1424–6.

[3] *Snappe's Formulary and Other Records* (Oxford Historical Society LXXX, 1924), p. 183.

[4] Reg. Parv. II, fo. 137. For a fourteenth-century example of a Durham monk at Oxford whose prior could not afford to pay his inception expenses, see Pantin, 'Letters from Durham Registers, c. 1360–1390', in *Oxford Formularies* (Oxford Historical Society, 1942), I, 225; cf. Knowles, *Rel. Orders* II, 24.

which he asked for permission to receive a doctorate. The prior immediately responded with the comment that Mody's two brothers, Barton and Burnby (both of whom had received their baccalaureates earlier than Mody himself) were senior to the warden and it would cause much scandal in the monastery if a senior doctor in the university should yet be a minor in the convent. Wessington remembered, however, that in his Oxford days he had seen three Glastonbury monks incept at the same time and wondered whether the university authorities would be prepared to follow this precedent.[1] In this way the church of Saint Cuthbert would not only gain prestige but save money by having the expense of only one feast for three graduations. In the previous autumn, at the instance of Master John Norton, ex-chancellor of Oxford, Wessington had promised the university the nomination to the rectory of Appleby when it next fell vacant, and the prior hoped that this action would now stand him and his three monks in good stead.[2] The Durham chapter was prepared to contribute £20 to the total inception expenses of Barton, Burnby and Mody, but they were expected to find the remainder for themselves.[3]

By the autumn of 1440 Wassington had developed considerable enthusiasm for the project but was then confronted with the unexpected resistance of one of the monks concerned. Richard Barton, prior of Durham's cell at Stamford, was not at all eager to pay anything whatsoever towards the costs of his inception feast. During the winter of 1440–1, Wessington urged Barton to change his mind and warned him not to prejudice the inceptions of his two colleagues by his own idleness. On 7 February 1441, Wessington summoned Warden Burnby to Durham and asked him to call at Stamford on the way to collect Barton's reply to his letter.[4] As late as 25 April, Wessington was still worried about Barton's negligence and reminded him either to go to Oxford to complete his form or to obtain a grace '*de non regendo*'.[5] The proctors of the university intro-

---

[1] Reg. Parv. II, fo. 117.   [2] Reg. III, fo. 241.

[3] It was anticipated that the university would demand £30 *loco convivii*, in lieu of the feast supposed to be given by the three inceptors to the regent masters (Reg. Parv. II, fo. 131). The normal rate of this composition fee was £20 for *one* endowed religious.   [4] Reg. Parv. II, fo. 134.

[5] Ibid., fos. 136–7. The grace mentioned would have dispensed Barton from the obligation incumbent upon incepting doctors of lecturing at Oxford for two years.

duced another complication for they had doubts as to Barton's eligibility for this concession in that as prior of Stamford he was an 'instituted monk'. On 27 May Wessington solemnly testified that Barton was a regular Durham monk and wrote to Master John Killingworth, junior and northern proctor of the university; he pointed out that although he and his brethren had long hoped for a simultaneous inception, to the glory of God and the honour of the church and diocese of Durham, he did not wish Barton's inadequacies to stand in the way of the speedy graduation of his two fellows.[1] In the event, Barton obtained his grace and all three monks were doctors of theology by 5 July 1441 when they were commended to the Presidents and Provincial Chapter of the Black Monks by the university of Oxford.[2] So successful a conclusion to so tortuous a process is some tribute not only to Wessington's powers of persuasion but also to the value he set upon the doctorate as the final academic distinction available to a Durham university monk.

The most obvious conclusion to emerge from a study of the role played by Durham College in the fifteenth century is therefore the immense importance attached by the monks themselves to university education in general and a university degree in particular. By a common late medieval paradox, high administrative authority was largely entrusted to monks who had gained their reputation less as administrators than as scholars. During and after John Wessington's priorate, a bachelor or doctor's degree in theology became a *sine qua non* for those monks who aspired to the very highest office at the central monastery. Nor was the prestige consequent on a successful academic career confined within the walls of Durham itself. Graduates in canon law or theology, and Durham monks among them, were in great demand at meetings of Convocation and other national assemblies. But perhaps no clerical group in late medieval England was more conscious of the value of a university degree than the Black Monks themselves. Their Provincial Chapters at Northampton, bodies largely controlled in practice by a small number of university monks, consistently stressed the need for a large quota of Benedictine graduates. Even the intellectually undistinguished abbey of Selby in Yorkshire was compelled by the Presidents of the

---

[1] Reg. III, fo. 266; Reg. Parv. II, fo. 138.
[2] *Epistolae Academicae Oxon.* (Oxford Historical Society, 1898), I, 199–200.

Benedictine Chapter in 1426 to contribute the not inconsiderable sum of £9 5s. 3d. towards the inception expenses of a Durham monk and future prior, William Ebchester.[1] Whether the leaders of late medieval monastic opinion were justified in placing such emphasis on university education is a more difficult and open question. Contemporaries were undoubtedly impressed by the success of Bishop Hatfield's foundation for Durham monks at Oxford, a college which prospered at a time when many other academic institutions notoriously (like the ill-fated Cistercian house of Saint Bernard at the same university) did not.[2] As late as 1513 no less a person than Bishop Richard Fox, founder of Corpus Christi College, Oxford, 'the first Renaissance college in England', seriously contemplated the establishment of an Oxford college for eight Winchester monks on the pattern he must have already encountered when bishop of Durham.[3]

Bishop Fox, whose genuine zeal for the better education of the English clergy can hardly be questioned, clearly did not share Hastings Rashdall's characteristically nineteenth-century view that monastic colleges at Oxford and elsewhere 'possess very little importance in the history either of learning or of education'.[4] Rashdall, conditioned to a view of late medieval monks sinking into a 'deeper quagmire of moral degeneration', was obviously less than fair; and in general the contribution of monks and monastic colleges to the life and work of the late medieval university stands in urgent need of thorough and detailed reassessment. For obvious reasons the historians and antiquarians who held fellowships in post-Reformation Oxford and Cambridge were usually at no particular pains to emphasise the debt their universities owed to medieval monks. But it now seems increasingly clear that this debt was

---

[1] East Riding Record Office, Beverley: DDLO/20, no. 1; Selby Bursar's Account, 1431–2, memb. 2v.

[2] For the way in which this Cistercian studium at Oxford became 'a subject of reproach and obloquy' see *Letters from the English Abbots to the Chapter at Cîteaux, 1442–1521*, ed. C. H. Talbot (Camden Fourth Series IV, 1967), p. 13 and passim.

[3] J. G. Milne, *The Early History of Corpus Christi College, Oxford* (Oxford, 1946), p. 2; *V.C.H. University of Oxford*, p. 219.

[4] H. Rashdall, *Universities in Europe in the Middle Ages*, ed. F. M. Powicke and A. B. Emden (Oxford, 1936), III, 190. According to Archdeacon Thorp, its most forceful promoter, the University of Durham was – when founded in 1832 – 'the legitimate successor of Durham College': C. E. Whiting, *The University of Durham, 1832–1932* (London, 1932), p. 37.

indirectly manifest at almost every level – from the architectural influence of the college cloister or quadrangle to the concept of 'fellowship' within a self-contained institution. Nor does it seem without some symbolic significance that the most revolutionary instrument of the late medieval 'New Learning', Erasmus's Greek edition of the New Testament, should have apparently first got seriously under way when the author was residing at Oxford, not in a secular college but a monastic one, the Augustinian canons' college of Saint Mary off New Inn Hall Street. More generally, the role of members of the religious orders in fifteenth-century Oxford appears to have been of increasing numerical significance at a time when the number of monastic colleges expanded contemporaneously with a probable decline of the total university population to a thousand or so: of the nine doctors of theology cited to Congregation by the chancellor of the university in 1414, three were seculars, three friars and three monks.[1] But of all the many criticisms raised against the 'university monks', perhaps the most common yet most problematic is the allegation that 'When they at last returned (to their mother houses), they found little scope for their academic talents'.[2] Where else in late medieval England, one wonders, could academic talents have found fuller scope outside a university than within a religious community? No one should underestimate the pressures which threatened, for good or ill, to transform the fifteenth-century monastic cloister itself into what Abbot Kidderminster of Winchcombe was to call a 'little university';[3] and those who reject the abbot's view that 'theology may be as fruitfully studied in the cloister as the university' are criticising not late medieval monasticism but monasticism in general. Exactly how far Durham Priory itself was able to put such an ideal into practice will never be an easy question to answer; but at least a few clues may be afforded by a survey, however rapid and inadequate, of the books kept, read and written in or near the cloister there.

[1] *Snappe's Formulary and Other Records* (Oxford Historical Society, 1924), pp. 114–15, 181–6; Rashdall, *Universities* III, 135–6, 332.
[2] A. G. Dickens, *The English Reformation*, p. 54.
[3] Knowles, *Rel. Orders* III, 92. The role of the university-trained senior monk in lecturing to the younger members of his community within the mother house has, by its very nature, left little record.

LEARNING IN THE CLOISTER

The monastic library at Durham is deservedly one of the most celebrated collections of books ever formed in medieval England. It owes most of its present fame to the survival of almost 600 of its volumes and to the fact that well over half of these still remain within one of their original homes – the treasury or *Spendement* by the western walk of the Durham cloister. Despite Robert Hegge's suspiciously picturesque description of the early seventeenth-century Durham library as one infested by jackdaws and pigeons, 'a place of a Sepulchre rather than a place to conserve books',[1] no other medieval English library has been able to resist the inexorable processes of change and decay with such remarkable success. This is a fact which in itself makes it difficult to set the achievements of the Durham monks within their own medieval context. A library which is now unique was certainly not so in the later middle ages. But there can, of course, be no doubt that Durham's conventual library had no rivals north of York and was famous long before the period of destruction and dispersion of books inaugurated by the Dissolution. During the fifteenth century individual Durham manuscripts were borrowed from the library, usually by means of a written indenture, by a variety of prelates, clerks and laymen throughout the north of England.[2] By the time of Wessington's priorate, many of the convent's older books were already highly valued and regarded as among the greatest treasures of the monastery. Such, for example, were the eighth-century Lindisfarne Gospels, the *Liber Vitae* which lay on the high altar of the cathedral church, and the twelfth-century illuminated copy of Bede's prose life of Saint Cuthbert, now British Museum Additional Manuscript, no. 39943. Not surprisingly, these exceptionally precious manuscripts and several of the other outstanding prizes in Durham's library found their way into the hands of private collectors in the period after the Dissolution. As Humfrey Wanley wrote in 1723, 'I understand that they have Books, Charters and other things there which will be more useful to the World in

---

[1] R. Hegge, *The Legend of Saint Cuthbert*, ed. George Smith (Darlington, 1777), pp. 13–14.

[2] Misc. Chrs., nos. 2352, 2477, 4297, 7146, and 7170 are interesting examples of such indentures.

my Lords Library (the Harleian Library) than in that remote corner of the Kingdom'.[1] Although this type of argument has in practice more often led to the loss rather than the preservation of Durham's medieval books, a sufficiently astonishing number (perhaps over half of the original total) survive to guarantee the employment of bibliographers and bibliophiles for many generations to come. Despite the dedicated work of many recent scholars, and in particular of Sir Roger Mynors and Dr N. R. Ker,[2] there can be no doubt that the monastic library at Durham still has many important secrets to disclose, especially in the field of book production.

No attempt will be made here to assess the value of the collection of books kept at late medieval Durham in its own right, but rather to make a preliminary exploration of the extent to which those books may reflect the intellectual tastes and reading habits of the fifteenth-century monks themselves. Needless to say, such an exploration is bound to be impressionistic. Nothing is more difficult than to prove that the user of a library, unless he happens to write himself, actually reads the books available to him. Nor does an institutional library always cater for the personal predilections of its readers: it seems highly probable that, like Oxford and Cambridge college libraries in the sixteenth century, those of fifteenth-century English monasteries were often 'conservative buyers'.[3] Many Durham monks may well have had in their possession a variety of books regarded as insufficiently 'serious' to find their way into the conventual library. Paradoxically, it was the cheapest, most elementary and most frequently read books which have left the least trace among the surviving Durham manuscripts. In particular, of the many simple grammar and service books which must have filled church and cloister on the eve of the Dissolution, hardly one survives. Nevertheless, it would be premature to retire completely defeated from this important field. As will be seen, the inscriptions, additions

---

[1] *Diary of Humfrey Wanley, 1715–26*, ed. C. E. and R. C. Wright (The Bibliographical Society, London, 1966), II, 227.

[2] R. A. B. Mynors, *Durham Cathedral Manuscripts to the end of the Twelfth Century* (Oxford, 1939); N. R. Ker, *Medieval Libraries of Great Britain* (Royal Historical Society, Second Edition, 1964) – the indispensable guide to the present location of all Durham Priory's manuscripts and printed books to survive.

[3] J. K. McConica, *English Humanists and Reformation Politics under Henry VIII and Edward VI* (Oxford, 1965), p. 88.

and scrawled annotations to many Durham manuscripts often throw more light on the purchasing and reading patterns of Durham monks than do the texts themselves. So also do the three large and detailed book-catalogues produced within the monastery towards the end of the fourteenth century. These catalogues or inventories, printed very inadequately from the original Durham manuscript B. IV. 46 by Botfield and Raine as *Catalogi Veteres* in 1838, are deservedly famous for the way in which they reveal the contents of a great monastic library in its prime. But they are of almost equal importance for the information they provide as to the problems of library organisation and management within the monastery.

The first half of the fifteenth century was in many ways a critical period in the history of the acquisition and collection of books by Durham monks. In particular, it marked a decisive turning-point in the development of more sophisticated methods whereby the existing collection was listed, housed and administered to meet the specific needs of the late medieval community. The central figure in this transformation was undoubtedly John Wessington, in his capacity as chancellor of the convent from 1407 until his election as prior in 1416.[1] At Durham, as Dr Pantin has rightly stressed, 'both the muniments and the library seem to have been in the charge of the same monastic official, who is called "Librarius" down to about 1395, and "Cancellarius" after that date'.[2] Durham was therefore an important exception to the usual monastic custom by which the precentor of a religious house was also its librarian.[3] The Durham monks laid this additional responsibility on the shoulders of their chancellor, whose registry or *Spendement* was at the same time his office as well as the convent's most secure book store. Because they were under no obligation to render annual accounts, the Durham

---

[1] See above, p. 90. Thomas Rome was recorded as chancellor in May 1406; and although Wessington cannot be proved to have held the office until March 1409, gifts made to him by various obedientiaries in the previous two years make clear his close association with the convent's library and muniments (4.5. Ebor., no. 3; Reg. III, fos. 22–5; Loc. XVIII, no. 72; *Catalogi Vet.*, p. 40).

[2] W. A. Pantin, *Report on the Muniments of the Dean and Chapter of Durham*, p. 2. The title of *Cancellarius* was occasionally used earlier, e.g. in 1371 (1.1. Archid. Dunelm., no. 13; Misc. Chrs., no. 2420); but I have discovered no example of the use of *Librarius* after 1400.

[3] *The English Library before 1700*, ed. F. Wormald and C. E. Wright (London, 1958), p. 20.

chancellors' duties have to be inferred, often with considerable difficulty, from a miscellaneous variety of records. It is, however, abundantly clear that the chancellor was not only one of the most influential of all Durham's obedientiaries but also – from the historian's standpoint – perhaps the most important.

Wessington was himself only one in a long line of remarkably energetic and apparently extremely able late medieval chancellors. The activities, and often the handwriting, of Robert Langchester, William Appleby, Thomas Rome, John Fishburn, William Dalton, Robert Westmorland, William Seton, Richard Billingham and Thomas Swalwell, successively chancellors of the convent, are inescapably familiar to modern students of the monastery's manuscripts and archives. No doubt the nature of the chancellor's office induced the monk who held it to become more articulate than his fellows; and it is certainly due to the personal zeal of a long succession of indefatigable monastic chancellors that both the muniments and manuscripts of Durham were so scrupulously arranged and preserved. John Wessington was himself unusually active in this field during the years immediately before 1416. As we have already seen, his tenure of the chancellor's office coincided with the final stages of a complete reorganisation of the convent's archives. Given the fact that he was also responsible for the custody of the monastic library, it is not perhaps surprising that he should wish to carry through an analogous rearrangement of the community's collection of books. Great though Wessington's services were to the cause of more efficient record-keeping at Durham, his contribution to the welfare of the convent's manuscripts was even greater: no other librarian or chancellor in the monastery's history seems to have made a greater personal impact on its library. As his motives were to make the convent's books more accessible to individual members of the community and to provide a library service designed to meet the needs of fifteenth-century monks, his work deserves attention not only in its own right but for its reflection of a new approach to the concept of learning in the Durham cloister.

At the very beginning of the fifteenth century the chancellor of Durham was apparently responsible for approximately a thousand separate volumes, the '*Libri Sancti Cuthberti*', many of which comprised – it is important to stress – several quite distinct works. Of these volumes the great majority were kept either in the *Spendement* (495 in 1391) or in cupboards in the cloister (386 in 1395); but there were additional and much smaller collections of books reserved for the use of the novices and for reading in the refectory and infirmary.[1] The source of this information is, of course, the three library catalogues compiled at Durham in the late fourteenth century, all well known and available to John Wessington when he became chancellor of the monastery in 1407. The most elaborate of these catalogues was a list of books preserved in the *Spendement*, written in a late fourteenth-century book-hand and arranged under a subject and author classification, with the addition of a simple letter-mark for the easier identification of each manuscript within a particular class.[2] A close counterpart of this catalogue was in use in early 1392 when William Appleby succeeded Robert Langchester as librarian;[3] but after this had been used for several years, Wessington reverted in about 1409 to the cognate book-hand catalogue, which served both himself and his successor as chancellor, John Fishburn, as a check-list and register of withdrawals until at least 1422.[4] The third

[1] *Catalogi Vet.*, pp. 10–39, 46–79, 80–4. Even after making allowances for the smaller collections, for books on loan to cells or individual monks, and for the many uncatalogued grammar and service books, it seems unlikely that there were ever as many as 3,000 volumes in monastic possession at Durham (Knowles, *Rel. Orders* II, 344). A total of 1,200 books would appear to be a more likely estimate, an impressive collection but one easily surpassed by the monastic libraries of Saint Augustine's and Christ Church, Canterbury. The (probably exceptional) library of the house of Austin Friars at York held at least 646 volumes at the close of the fourteenth century: M. R. James, 'The Catalogue of the Library of the Austin Friars at York', *Fasciculus Joanni Willis Clark dicatus* (London, 1909), p. 16.

[2] MS. B. IV. 46, fo. 34r; *Catalogi Vet.*, pp. 85–116. This catalogue was almost certainly written after 1377 for an indenture of that year records the borrowing of a *Scholastica Historia* without recording the letter-mark (B) assigned to it in *Catalogi Vet.*, p. 94 (Misc. Chrs., no. 2477). As Robert Langchester became librarian of the monastery by 1379 (Reg. II, fo. 218), it is tempting to believe that he must have been responsible for the systematic re-cataloguing of the books in the *Spendement*.

[3] *Catalogi Vet.*, pp. 10–39, probably (on internal evidence) the text from which ibid., pp. 85–116 was copied.

[4] Later annotations to the original book-hand *Spendement* catalogue record the delivery of books to Durham College in October 1409 and to the novices' book-cupboard in October 1422. It ought to be mentioned in passing that the most serious defect of Raine's edition of MS. B. IV. 46 was his failure to distinguish between the original lists of books and the new items and marginalia added during subsequent years. Only a new edition (urgently needed) could provide an adequate impression of the extent to which these catalogues were used by Wessington, Fishburn and other chancellors.

and very different catalogue, a list made by William Appleby in
1395 of books kept in the *communi armariolo* and other places in the
cloister, also remained in constant use until the same date.[1] Yet a
fourth catalogue, now lost (no doubt like several others), was
apparently produced under Wessington's own direction: the '*tabula
super libros claustri et librarie*' attributed to the prior in the list of his
writings can hardly be identified with the earlier inventories of
Langchester and Appleby. Moreover, after 1418 the monks of
Durham normally reserved the word '*libraria*' for the separate room
built by Wessington, and this new catalogue must presumably have
been made necessary by the transfer of volumes to the new library
from the *Spendement* and cloister.[2]

The construction of a separate building for the housing and reading of books was indeed Wessington's greatest achievement as
custodian of the Durham manuscripts. Wessington's new library,
the only one in the history of the monastery, cannot have failed to
draw its inspiration from the prior's experience of Oxford college
libraries at the turn of the century. The new library of Durham
College was in fact being built almost contemporaneously. In the
early fifteenth century 'the great age of library-building began' and,
thanks to Wessington, Durham was one of the first religious houses
(earlier even than Christ Church, Canterbury)[3] to be provided with
a room reserved exclusively for the preservation of books. In 1414
the reconstruction of the Durham cloister was nearing completion
and Wessington seized the opportunity of suggesting the insertion
of a small library over the parlour or slype and between the chapter-
house and the south transept of the cathedral. No detailed building
accounts of the operation survive but it seems clear that the new
library took four years to build and was completed by 1418, at a
total cost of over £90.[4] As was usual at Durham in such cases of

---

[1] *Catalogi Vet.*, pp. 46–79. R. A. B. Mynors has identified a draft of this catalogue
among the fly-leaves of D.C.D., MS. B. II. 1 in his *Durham Cathedral Manuscripts
to the end of the Twelfth Century*, p. 3.

[2] The fifteenth-century inscription on D.C.D., MS. B. I. 11 reads (fo. 2r) '*de communi
libraria et non de claustro*'. See Rud, *Codicum Manuscriptorum Ecclesiae Cathedralis Dunelmensis Catalogus*, p. 83. The inscription may be by Thomas Swalwell, i.e. of *c.* 1500.

[3] *Literae Cantuarienses* (Rolls Series, 1887–9), III, 171; cf. Knowles, *Rel. Orders* II,
352–3. The new library at the secular cathedral of Saint Peter's, York, was also
built a little later (1418–19) than that at Durham: *York Fabric Rolls* (Surtees Soc.
XXXV, 1859), p. 38.   [4] Loc. XXVII, no. I (a); *Scrip. Tres*, p. cclxxiii.

extraordinary building expenditure, most of the cost was met by the imposition of annual pensions on the richer cells and obediences.[1]

Wessington's library, for many years used by the registrar of the Dean and Chapter, has been the cathedral song-school since 1900.[2] Only the partly original timber roof is of much interest to the modern visitor for the two large Perpendicular windows inserted by Wessington in the east and west walls of the room were drastically restored in the early nineteenth century. More regrettably still, no trace of the original library fittings survives: as early as 1628 the Dean and Chapter of Durham had reformed 'the rudnes of the old Stalles by making a faire frame of Shelves and other conveniences'.[3] However, the dimensions of the room (60 ft × 16½ ft) leave little doubt that the books were, as at Lincoln or Canterbury, kept in presses or lecterns standing at right-angles to the two windows. A contemporary reference to '*reparacio descorum*' in Wessington's library makes it virtually certain, despite the well-known ambiguity of such phrases, that the room was intended to be used for private reading by the monks as well as serving as a book-store. There is, of course, no doubt that nevertheless many Durham monks continued to read in their carrells in the cloister until the Dissolution. Nor did Wessington's library bring the history of the organisation of Durham's book-collections to an end. As appears from a familiar inscription added to several surviving Durham manuscripts ('*Iste liber assignatur Nouo Armariolo in Claustro Ecclesie Dunelmensis per venerabilem patrem Magistrum Johannem Auklande priorem eiusdem ecclesie*'), an important new book-cupboard was built in the cloister within forty years of Wessington's death. Such evidence makes it abundantly clear, as do the large purchases of printed books by Durham monks at a slightly later date, that the conventual library continued to expand at a steady rate throughout the last century of its existence.[4]

However, the most important reorganisation of the monastery's

[1] E.g. Finchale, 1415–18; Jarrow, 1415–17; Wearmouth, 1415/16; Feretrar, 1414–18.

[2] H. D. Hughes, *A History of Durham Cathedral Library* (Durham, 1925), p. 6.

[3] Transcript of Dean and Chapter of Durham's Act Book, Vol. I, p. 114; cf. pp. 86, 99, 118, 142. John Cosin was a prebendary of Durham at this period.

[4] See, e.g., York Minster Library, MS. XVI. D. 9, fo. 1r; Jesus College, Cambridge, MSS. 45, 54; Bodleian Library, Oxford, MS. Laud Misc. 368, fo. 7v. The last three paragraphs owe much to the expert advice of Mr Ian Doyle and Mr Alan Piper.

collections of manuscripts necessarily took place soon after 1418 as a direct consequence of the building of Wessington's new library. This reorganisation, quite capable of reconstruction despite several technical difficulties, still awaits thorough analysis. But only a brief description of the arrangements and contents of the new library will be attempted here, purely with a view to the valuable insight these provide into the attitudes of the early fifteenth-century monks themselves. When John Fishburn began to stock this library with books, he must have been guided by the wishes of his fellow monks as well as those of his prior and predecessor as chancellor. It is immediately clear that the Durham chapter had no intention of removing all the convent's manuscripts to the new room off the east cloister. Rather they decided to add a third repository to their existing collections in the *Spendement* and the cupboards in the cloister. Accordingly, notes added by Fishburn to the book-hand *Spendement* catalogue after 1416 show that of the 507 manuscripts previously kept in the treasury, 35 were moved to their new location '*in libraria*'. Similar annotations to the 1395 catalogue of books in the cloister reveal the transfer of many more books (127 out of 386) from the cupboards there to Wessington's library.[1] But these were only the first volumes removed to the new room, which eventually came to hold far more than these 162 manuscripts. The most valuable and indeed indispensable guide to the contents of the new library is provided by the systematised press-marks added to the books installed there, most of which remain perfectly visible on the manuscripts once in that library which still survive.

These press-marks were formed, on the precedent set by the classification of the convent's muniments as found in the *Repertorium Parvum*, by two Arabic numerals followed by a capital letter; so, for example, the inscription $2^a\ 3^i$ A indicates that the manuscript in question was the first book on the second side of the third press or desk in Wessington's library.[2] As over 150 of the more than 500 Durham manuscripts still in existence bear this type of press-mark it seems possible to establish the main outlines of the new library's arrangement. There were apparently ten presses or desks in the room,

---

[1] *Catalogi Vet.*, pp. 85–116, 46–79.
[2] Examples of such press-marks are illustrated in Mynors, *Durham Cathedral Manuscripts*, Plates 19, 21, 34.

all of them double-sided except for numbers I and IV which conceivably stood in the two west corners. Each side of a desk held from twenty to twenty-five volumes (there is no example of a press-mark with a doubled alphabetical letter) and therefore the library, in its final form, presumably contained a total of about 450 volumes. Desks I to III were devoted to glossed copies of the Bible and to patristic works, while Desks IV to VI (comprising perhaps another 125 manuscripts) contained a collection of later, and predominantly scholastic, religious texts. On one side of Desk VII was kept a series of histories and saints' lives; on the other was placed a set of Latin classics and medical treatises. Books on canon and civil law were to be found in Desks VIII and IX, leaving the tenth desk reserved almost exclusively for an impressively large set of Aristotelian works.[1] The general layout of Wessington's library, as well as the amount of space assigned to particular subjects and authors, holds no great surprise for the student of medieval book-collections. The arrangement of the early fifteenth-century library at Durham was thoroughly representative of monastic practice elsewhere.[2] On the other hand, it would appear from those manuscripts which do survive that a definite attempt was made to avoid unnecessary duplication and to see that all the volumes transferred to the new room were in good condition. By the 1420s the Durham community had acquired, for the first time, what is perhaps best described as a specially designed reference library. All the available evidence suggests that the latter was closely analogous to, although probably rather better stocked than, Oxford college libraries of the same period. As the author of the *Rites of Durham* remembered with his usual affectionate nostalgia, the last generations of Durham monks had 'the librarie at all tymes to goe studie in besydes there Carrells'.[3]

The construction of this new 'Lybrarie in the south angle of the

---

[1] This brief description of the contents and arrangement of Wessington's library is based completely on the surviving press-marks of the manuscripts, to which the best (although still not absolutely complete) printed guide is Ker, *Medieval Libraries*, pp. 61–76. The survival-rate of particular sections of the library naturally varies considerably: thus 15 MSS. still bear the mark $1^a\ 3^i$, but only 6 MSS. preserve the mark $2^a\ 3^i$.

[2] See, e.g., R. M. Wilson, 'The Contents of the Mediaeval Library', *The English Library before 1700*, ed. F. Wormald and C. E. Wright (London, 1958), pp. 85–111.

[3] *Rites*, p. 83. Compare the distinction in Oxford colleges between the chained reference and a separate 'lending' library.

Lantren . . . betwixt the Chapter house and the Te Deum wyndowe' is therefore itself clear evidence of the desire of early fifteenth-century Durham monks to provide themselves with a more 'professional' working library than ever before. The same conclusion seems to emerge from a study of the new books acquired by the community at this period. Thanks to the survival of the three great catalogues and various supplementary lists of about the same period, it is quite possible to form a detailed impression of titles of the great majority of books *in situ* at Durham on the eve of the building of Wessington's library. Allowances have inevitably to be made for the usual medieval practice of binding several separate works into a single volume, to which one entry in a catalogue can rarely be expected to provide an adequate guide. Much more unfortunate is the fact that no catalogue of Durham manuscripts survives for the period after 1420; our knowledge of book acquisition by the monks during the last century of their existence has to depend on the much more occasional, although often very illuminating, evidence of the extant manuscripts and their inscriptions. Despite these difficulties, it seems clear that the Durham monks made no radical departures in the sphere of acquiring new books until at least the time when the printing press provided them with opportunities hitherto absolutely unparalleled. No attempt can be made here to describe the extent and range of the Durham libraries at the beginning of the fifteenth century.[1] Nor would such a description necessarily throw direct light on the intellectual interests of the monks of Wessington's priorate: great institutional libraries are often and inevitably fossilised memorials to the reading habits of previous generations.

However, it is certainly significant that in the early fifteenth century the Durham library was characterised by the range and comprehensiveness of its collections rather than by any easily identifiable distinctive features of its own. Two hundred years earlier the collection of manuscripts at Durham had been almost precociously distinguished. At the end of Hugh du Puiset's pontificate, the community of Saint Cuthbert owned not only the recent works of contemporary canonists but a rich series of classical texts which could

[1] Professor S. L. Greenslade provides a useful summary in 'The Contents of the Library of Durham Cathedral Priory', *Transactions of the Architectural and Archaeological Society of Durham and Northumberland* XI (1965), 347–69.

stand comparison with those in the greatest cathedral libraries (Bec, Corby, Cluny, Lorsch) of the age.[1] By 1400 the scene had undoubtedly changed, and Durham's still impressive library now seems of interest primarily because it had become so representative of monastic book-collections elsewhere. Although of a respectable size, the convent's stock of scientific and medical works betrays no obvious sign of the enlivening personal interest brought to the contemporary book-catalogue of the Austin Friars at York by Master John Erghome. Similarly the Durham library's collections of romances, and especially non-biblical French romances, was perfunctory by the standards of Saint Mary's Abbey, Leicester, in the later middle ages.[2] Of the 900 and more books recorded in the catalogues used by the Durham chancellors during the first years of the fifteenth century, only two are said to have been in English ('*in Anglico*'); and by the late fifteenth century an Anglo-Saxon version of the Rule of Saint Benedict might be misinterpreted as a text '*in gallico*'.[3] As Professor Greenslade has noted, the most obvious characteristic of the Durham library in the years before and after 1400 was an 'increase in manuals, *compendia* and other quick aids to learning'.[4] But is this development too not likely to be an indirect result of the application of university methods and techniques within the monastic cloister? It would be unfair, as we have already seen, to use the evidence of the surviving catalogues as incontrovertible proof that the mental horizons of Durham monks had contracted between the twelfth and fifteenth centuries. However, these catalogues do make it abundantly clear that by the late medieval period the convent's official book-collections were displaying all the features, good

[1] Mynors, *Durham Cathedral Manuscripts*, passim; *Catalogi Vet.*, pp. 1–10; Scammell, *Hugh du Puiset*, pp. 102–4.

[2] *Catalogi Vet.*, pp. 56, 77–9, 107; cf. James, 'Catalogue of the Library of the Austin Friars at York', pp. 74–7, 82–3; M. R. James and A. H. Thompson, 'Catalogue of the Library of Leicester Abbey', *Transactions of the Leicestershire Archaeological Society* xx and xxi (1938–40); Thompson, *Abbey of St Mary of the Meadows, Leicester* (1949), pp. 204–30.

[3] *Catalogi Vet.*, pp. 30, 33, 107, 111; R. M. Wilson, *The Lost Literature of Medieval England* (2nd edn, London, 1970), pp. 77, 153, 157; Mynors, *Durham Cathedral Manuscripts*, pp. 44–5.

[4] Greenslade, 'Contents of Library of Durham Cathedral Priory', p. 367. For some representative examples of these *tabulae* or *compendiae*, see the books acquired for the convent by its librarian in the 1390s, William Appleby (MSS. B. iii. 14, 31; *Catalogi Vet.*, pp. 42, 50, 83, 84).

and bad, of an academic library. Once again the influence of Oxford University on Durham Priory seems almost blatantly evident.

It is for this reason that one may be well advised to doubt the conventional view that the monks of late medieval Durham, like their counterparts in other large English religious houses, were living in 'an intellectual backwater'.[1] From this point of view, it seems particularly unfortunate that receptivity to Italian scholarship, 'humanist' learning and the Greek language have long been regarded as the main criteria for intellectual vigour in fifteenth-century England. Such criteria are *a priori* unlikely to have been much in evidence within a northern monastery during a century when the university of Oxford itself was notoriously slow to respond to the 'New Learning'. Knowledge of the interesting but thoroughly exceptional classical tastes of Prior William Selling of Christ Church, Canterbury (which appear to have left no permanent legacy to his fellow monks), or of the humanism of early sixteenth-century Winchcombe and Evesham must not lead us to expect similar manifestations at Durham. If so, we should certainly be disappointed. Many years have passed since P. S. Allen demonstrated the qualitative difference between the collection of books formed by the 'Italianate' Bishop John Shirwood of Durham (1484–94) and those associated with the exactly contemporary prior of his cathedral church, John Auckland. The latter, with a few exceptions (of which the most interesting is the present Durham Cathedral MS. C. III. 18, a late eleventh-century copy of Suetonius), tend to consist of the traditional patristic and scholastic texts of the medieval period.[2] A very similar pattern is betrayed by an examination of the titles of the very large number of printed books – almost all produced at continental presses, and especially those of Basle, Strasbourg and Paris – bought by Durham monks between the 1480s and the Dissolution. Over eighty printed books acquired by the conventual library of Durham still survive; several of these – like a copy of John Major's commentaries on the *Sentences*, printed at Paris in 1529,

---

[1] Greenslade, 'Contents of Library of Durham Cathedral Priory', p. 368.

[2] P. S. Allen, 'Bishop Shirwood of Durham and his Library', *E.H.R.* xxv (1910), 445–56. The best guide to the books either acquired by Prior Auckland or assigned by him to the new cupboard in the Durham cloister is, once again, Ker, *Medieval Libraries*, p. 252. MS. C. III. 18, not to be found in the catalogues of *c.* 1400, offers no evidence as to how and when it was acquired by the Durham library.

or Trithemius's *Sermons to the Monks* bought by the Durham monk, William Wylom, for 12*d.*, probably at Oxford – were by contemporary authors.[1] Not one of these printed books appears, however, to have been a Greek text; and it would be unwise to make much of the fact that three of the famous eleven Greek manuscripts written by Emmanuel of Constantinople *circa* 1468 eventually found their way into the chapter library at Durham. As is well known, Emmanuel's most important patron was Archbishop George Neville of York rather than a Benedictine community; and the manuscripts in question, which incidentally betray very little textual evidence of ever having been read at all, seem to have reached the Durham library after rather than before the Dissolution. Similarly, the recent suggestion that the passage of Greek which occurs in one Durham book (now MS. McLean 169 in the Fitzwilliam Museum, Cambridge) was written by the monk Robert Emyldon in 1439 is unlikely to prove that he could read Greek with ease.[2]

Inability to read Greek does not, however, in the fifteenth century as at any other period, necessarily imply insensitivity to new currents of thought and a mood of sustained intellectual torpor. The most important conclusion to emerge from a short study of the printed books acquired by the Durham monks before and after the close of the fifteenth century is the enthusiasm with which they seized the opportunity of the much greater and cheaper availability of the standard authorities in the fields of medieval theology and canon law. The members of the chapter were clearly eager to possess at Durham all the major works of such already familiar figures as Origen, Jerome, Ambrose, Augustine, Bonaventure and Aquinas, including new printed editions of texts they already held in less satisfactory manuscript copies. But many of the books, both printed and in manuscript form, acquired by the Durham monks during the last sixty years of their existence clearly provide evidence of a somewhat more adventurous spirit. Significantly enough, the earliest dated copy of any Durham printed book to survive appears to be an

---

[1] Ushaw College Library, xviii, B. 6. 7; York Minster Library, x. G. 13 (see inscription on last page); cf. Ker, *Medieval Libraries*, pp. 60–76.

[2] MSS. C. i. 15 (Aristotle), C. iv. 1 (Plato); Harleian MS. 3100 (Suidas acquired by Harley from the Durham chapter). See R. Weiss, *Humanism in England during the Fifteenth Century* (3rd edn, Oxford, 1967), pp. 145, 185; and M. R. James, *A Descriptive Catalogue of the McLean Collection of Manuscripts* (Cambridge, 1912), p. 325.

edition of Duns Scotus printed in 1473; it was to be followed by such diverse and fashionable works as those of Giuniano Maggio, the Neapolitan philologist, John Major and many others.[1] For obvious reasons the intellectual tastes of the Durham monks during Wessington's priorate are likely to strike the twentieth-century historian as considerably more conventional and staid; but there is at least some evidence that in the early fifteenth century too the community of Saint Cuthbert was less 'astoundingly conservative and narrow in its tastes' than has often been alleged. More important still, this evidence reveals the existence of an important minority of Durham monks who not only collected books themselves but were sometimes genuinely 'occupied in most godly writing and other exercissis in auncient tyme'.[2]

In the first place, the names of individual monks during the first two decades of the fifteenth century often occur in the library catalogues either when they borrowed a book from the convent's central collections or when they had been the agents through whom new volumes were added to the collections; in this latter case, the standard phrases used by the chancellors were '*ex procuracione domini A.B.*' or '*per A.B.*'. More illuminating still are the inscriptions of ownership and the casual jottings to be read in many of the monastic manuscripts which still survive. The name of a Durham monk may occur in a book from the common monastic library which he was allowed to keep for his personal use over a number of years; an example is a fourteenth-century collection of ten devotional works which carries the inscription '*Liber Sancti Cuthberti Dunelm' cuius usus conceditur Domino Roberto Ebchester Monacho Dunelm' per Venerabilem Patrem Magistrum Willelmum Ebchester quondam Cathedralis Dunelm' Priorem*'.[3] Many other books were acquired by individual Durham monks and held by them as their personal property until death, when they either reverted to the common library or were distributed among the younger friends and colleagues of their owner.

It is a commonplace of English monastic library study that most books entered the religious house by means of individual benefaction rather than as the result of a systematic acquisition policy on the part

[1] Ker, *Medieval Libraries*, pp. 71–6; Hughes, *Durham Cathedral Library*, pp. 44–5; cf. A. Hobson, *Great Libraries* (London, 1970), pp. 58–9.

[2] *Rites*, p. 88.   [3] MS. B. IV. 30, fo. ii v.

of the convent.[1] This rule holds good for early fifteenth-century Durham with the qualification that at this period it was the monks themselves rather than the lay or ecclesiastical patron who brought the majority of new books into the monastic library.[2] Some manuscripts were passed on from one monk to another for several years before they were eventually absorbed into the common library. Thus Stephen Howden acquired a glossed psalter written at the beginning of the fifteenth century and gave it to William Dalton, Wessington's chancellor.[3] A more extreme example of a book which was held successively by various Durham monks for perhaps a century before finding its way into the monastic library is MS. B. IV. 41, a collection of treatises and statutes primarily concerned with the Benedictine Order. Three Durham monks, Robert Masham, John Fishburn and William Dalton, were instrumental in either the writing or the collection of this manuscript's constituent quires; in the middle of the century it came into the hands of the future prior, Richard Bell, who gave it to Richard Billingham in 1461; the manuscript later went to William Elwike, sub-prior in the 1480s, who in his turn gave it to John Manby, a monk who did not die until after 1494.[4] All seven monks had been students at Durham College and the fortunes of this single volume suggest that a clearer light is often thrown on the reading habits of individual monks by knowledge of the books they held in their own right rather than of those preserved in the common library of the monastery.

The conclusions that emerge from this type of study of the early fifteenth-century library catalogues and the extant Durham manuscripts are themselves of some interest. Twenty-nine of the Durham monks who entered religion between 1383 and 1446, almost a quarter of the total, can be shown either to have owned books, pro-

---

[1] 'The library catalogue therefore very often presented the form of a shelf-list which continued as a list of benefactions': F. Wormald, 'The Monastic Library', *The English Library before 1700*, p. 25. Cf. M. R. James, *The Ancient Libraries of Canterbury and Dover* (Cambridge, 1903), p. xxxix, for the arrangement of the books at the priory of Christ Church by donors.

[2] Bishop Langley and Master William Doncaster seem to have been the only notable benefactors of the Durham library during Wessington's priorate (*Catalogi Vet.*, pp. 48–9, 119–21).

[3] MS. A. IV. 5, fo. iii v.

[4] MS. B. IV. 41, fo. 290v; the first of the two inscriptions has been erased but is clearly visible under ultra-violet light.

cured them for the monastic library, or borrowed them for relatively lengthy periods. Incomplete as this estimate inevitably is, it presumably includes all Durham monks of the period whose intellectual and literary interests were at all pronounced. Almost all members of this group were fellows or ex-fellows of Durham College; and it seems clear that most of the new books which found their way into the monastic library during the course of the fifteenth century were originally acquired by individual monks at Oxford. According to the terms of Bishop Hatfield's foundation of Durham College in 1381, its resident fellows were indeed entitled to a regular book allowance from the two college bursars. This may explain why a colophon to a Durham volume containing the second part of Vincent of Beauvais's *Speculum Historiale*, records that this book was written to the requirements of the vicar of Banbury in 1448; about forty years later it was assigned to the new cupboard in the Durham cloister by Prior John Auckland, a former bursar and warden of Durham College.[1] Inscriptions on a late fourteenth-century copy of Robert Holcot's lectures on the Sapiential Books show another way by which a book might find a place on the shelves of the Durham monastic library. This volume was pledged in an Oxford University loan chest ('*in cista Regine*') for 17s. od. in 1412 and was later bought by William Ebchester for four marks; Ebchester wrote his own name in the book, but long after he had left Oxford he assigned it, as prior of Durham, to the monastic library.[2] Three of the only four fifteenth-century bindings which survive in the Dean and Chapter's library at Durham were the work of Oxford binders, possibly Theodore Rood and Thomas Hunte, in 1481.[3] The volumes concerned are all printed books and there is no doubt that when the Durham monks began to buy such works at the end of the century Oxford was the usual source. Similarly, when, on 7 February 1441, Prior Wessington wanted a good psalter, of the secular use, to give '*cuidam nobili quem de sacro fonte suscepi*' it was to Master John Burnby, warden of Durham College, that he wrote.[4]

During Wessington's life-time, as later, the most assiduous acquirers of manuscripts were the wardens of Durham College. The collection made by Thomas Rome, warden between 1409 and 1418,

---

[1] MS. B. I. 32, fos. 1v, 336v.   [2] MS. A. III. 27, fos. 1r, 227r.
[3] Hughes, *Durham Cathedral Library*, p. 51.   [4] Reg. Parv. II, fo. 134.

may be considered as one of many possible examples. Rome procured for the monastic library a set of extracts from the *Pera Peregrini* (Bodleian Library, Oxford, MS. Laud Misc. 389); a composite volume including Bonaventure's meditations (MS. B. III. 22); a collection of 266 alleged sermons by Saint Augustine (MS. B. III. 6); more sermons by James de Voragine; an unidentifiable *Exposicio sive Postilla super Psalterum*; and finally, the most modern work, Philip Repington's lectures on the Gospels.[1] It is likely that most, if not all, of these books came from Oxford. A more specialised interest in canon law was shown by the chancellors of the monastery. Robert Westmorland owned Innocent IV's *Apparatus super decretalibus* and the *Summa* of Bartholomew de Sancta Concordia, the latter bought from the executors of Bishop Langley's spiritual chancellor, Master Thomas Hebden.[2] But perhaps the most interesting collection of books known to have been held by any of Wessington's monks is that of Henry Helay in 1422. Helay's monastic career was that of an administrator rather than a scholar; and it is all the more surprising to find him in possession of nine books, all apparently for his own use as they were described as '*Libri Henrici Helaugh Missi Stamfordiam*' and their second folios cannot be identified with those of any books in the common library. Helay's small library was remarkably well-balanced and included some devotional works, two books of the *Sentences* and a glossed *Decreta*, as well as accounts of the life and origins of Saint Cuthbert and the letters (*Epistola*) of Ailred of Rievaulx.[3]

Although many of his monks owned, procured, borrowed and presumably read such texts, Wessington's priorate is not a period in which one might expect much evidence of written work on the part of the Durham brethren themselves. Service-books for use in the choir may have continued to be written and sometimes bound by the monks; but as few of these survive it is impossible to be certain as to the normal manner of their production. The convent no doubt entrusted the writing and embellishment of their most precious books to skilled professional scribes; perhaps the best feats

---

[1] *Catalogi Vet.*, pp. 51, 52, 63, 71, 76; Ker, *Medieval Libraries*, p. 257. The inscription, '*Ex procuracione fratris T. Rome*', was inserted in the 1395 'cloister' catalogue and on the first folios of the manuscripts themselves by the same hand.

[2] MS. C. III. 9, fo. 13r; MS. C. III. 11, fo. 4r.   [3] *Catalogi Vet.*, p. 116.

of penmanship performed at the monastery in the later middle ages were the volumes written in the 1380s by a Breton, William de Stiphol, working at Finchale and Durham under the direction of Uthred of Boldon and the sub-prior Robert Blacklaw.[1] Nevertheless, the years before and after 1400 coincided with an unusually active period in the intellectual life of the convent. Uthred of Boldon did not die until 1397 and was succeeded as sub-prior first by John Aclyff, a noted theologian who died in 1420–1, and then by Robert Rypon who died a year later and left to posterity manuscripts of his sermons as well as a reputation as a celebrated preacher.[2] Prior Wessington's own largest work, his history of the church of Durham, seems to belong to the period immediately preceding 1416, as do the collections of '*tabulae*' and concordances compiled by Robert Masham who died *circa* 1418.[3] Richard Segbroke, the compiler of a series of devotional works, including extracts from Richard Rolle, had died in 1396.[4] By comparison, the thirty years between 1416 and 1446 would appear much less productive were it not for the writings and collections made by the prior himself and his three chancellors, John Fishburn, William Dalton and Robert Westmorland. The hands of these three men can be identified both in finished manuscripts and in numerous drafts and memoranda they wrote in the course of their official duties. Hardly surprisingly, none of the chancellors has left evidence of an active interest in philosophy or theology; but Fishburn and Dalton wrote detailed accounts of the acts of Benedictine Provincial Chapters, and it was Westmorland who compiled the list of Wessington's literary works.[5] The most prolific writer among the monks of Wessington's period was, however, Robert Emyldon, junior, who entered the convent in 1423, graduated as a bachelor in theology in 1443–4 and died about 1450. Emyldon's name occurs on many surviving Durham manuscripts and he is known to have transcribed in his highly idiosyncratic hand several lengthy classical and patristic texts, all of which apparently

---

[1] MSS. A. I. 3 and A. I. 4; B.M., Burney MS. 310. Thomas Rud in his description of the first of these manuscripts (*Codicum Manuscriptorum Ecclesiae Cathedralis Dunelmensis Catalogus*, pp. 3–4) wrote of '*membranae pulcherrimae*'.

[2] See the references in Emden I, 10, 212–13; III, 1,618.

[3] MSS. B. IV. 41 and B. IV. 43; B.M., Harleian MS. 3858 (see fo. 154v). Cf. Pantin, *Chapters* II, p. xii for a note on Robert Masham.

[4] See B.M., Arundel MS. 507, especially fos. 92–3. [5] See above, p. 237.

came to the monastic library after his death.[1] Emyldon's transcriptions are of traditional authorities, and there is little trace in Wessington's priorate of interest in rhetoric or *eloquentia* for its own sake, the '*florida verborum venustas*' so obvious in the works of Abbot John Whethamstede of St Albans.

But it is, of course, the surviving written work of Prior Wessington himself which appears to reflect most faithfully both the achievements and the limitations of learning in the Durham cloister during the first half of the fifteenth century. 'He had no pretension to that scholarship which tempts men to write history merely to exhibit their own style of composition or to illustrate their political or poetical views of life.'[2] Bishop Stubbs's comment upon an earlier northern chronicler, Roger of Howden, can be applied with even less hesitation to the historical work of John Wessington of Durham written more than two centuries later. When one considers the quantity and variety of Wessington's literary production, it is remarkable what little information, even by the standards of the late medieval English monastic chronicle, it provides as to the personality, prejudices and predilections of their author. In none of his many works does Wessington use the first person singular, and on only one occasion did he consider it relevant to refer to an incident of his personal life.[3] Whether in his large history of the church of Durham or in his smallest tract, the prior was not an original or creative historian; he never used his own words where those of Bede, Symeon, or the 'foundation charters' of his monastery would serve the purpose equally well. Indeed it is but little exaggeration to suggest that Wessington's personal contribution to the historical literature of Durham is confined to linking clauses between extracts from older authorities. An uncharitable commentator might see in Wessington's work the *reductio ad absurdum* of the medieval author's well-known desire for anonymity, and his disinclination to abandon the safety of his established sources for the dangers of a private judgement. As a historian, Wessington wrote – and this is, of course, his real significance – less as a private individual than as the incarnation and

---

[1] York Minster Library, MS. XVI. I. 1; Mynors, *Durham Cathedral Manuscripts*, p. 43; Emden I, 642.

[2] *Chronica Rogeri de Houedene* (Rolls Series, 1868–71), I, p. xxvi.

[3] Loc. II, no. 6, where Wessington recalled crossing the Wear as a young monk in 1394.

embodiment of the Durham historiographical tradition as it had survived into the fifteenth century. Identifying himself with the proud position of the church of Saint Cuthbert, he gloried in the past and showed much less interest, as an author, in the present or the future.

All Prior Wessington's compilations can indeed be said to have been concerned with either the historical rights and customs of the church of Durham or the special status of the Benedictine Order in the Christian Church. No attempt can be made here to discuss in the detail it deserves Wessington's remarkably large and diverse literary output.[1] Thanks to the survival of no less than three different copies of a list '*in quo recitantur compilaciones facte per Johannem Wessyngton Priorem pro defensione ecclesiae Dunelmensis*', the great majority of his productions can still be identified in items now dispersed among the muniments of his monastery.[2] But the thirty-seven titles of the latest version of this list, compiled by Robert Westmorland, the monastic chancellor, in 1446, do not in themselves provide a complete index to Wessington's writings. At least fifty separate compilations must have been either composed by the prior or written under his close personal supervision. Needless to say, these writings differ greatly in size, content and purpose; but they almost all fall into one of three categories. An important group of treatises concerned itself with the general history of Benedictine monasticism, especially in England. A second and much larger group consisted of those collections of evidence with which Wessington defended the rights, liberties and possessions of the church of Durham '*adversus malicias et machinaciones ipsam molencium impugnare*'.[3] In a class of its own and unquestionably the prior's most laborious achievement was a large-scale account of the early history of the see of Durham.

Wessington's history of the church of Durham was first identified by Sir Edmund Craster almost fifty years ago in his deservedly famous article on 'The Red Book of Durham'.[4] Surviving in three

---

[1] An attempt to provide a detailed description and identification of Wessington's writings can be found in my 'The Priory of Durham in the time of John Wessington, Prior 1416–46' (Oxford, Faculty of History, D.Phil. thesis, 1962), pp. 480–541, 580–6, which provides the evidence for the following paragraphs.

[2] Reg. II, fos. ix v–x v, to be compared with the earlier drafts, Misc. Chrs., nos. 5727 (c) and 5727 (a) – the last printed in *Scrip. Tres*, pp. cclxviii–cclxxi.

[3] Misc. Chrs., no. 5727; cf. B.M., Cotton MS., Vitellius A. IX, fo. 74r.

[4] H. H. E. Craster, 'The Red Book of Durham', *E.H.R.* XL (1925), 504–32.

different manuscript versions (Bodleian Library, Oxford, MS. Laud Misc. 748; Lincoln's Inn Library, London, Hale MS. 114; and British Museum, Cotton MS. Claudius D. iv), in its original draft and unrevised form this chronicle was designed to relate the famous story of the church of Lindisfarne, Chester-le-Street and Durham to at least the year 1356. Although the relationship between these three manuscripts raises various difficult technical problems, not all of them yet completely resolved, by far the most interesting feature of Wessington's history is undoubtedly his use of the so-called '*Liber summi altaris ecclesie Dunelmensis*', skilfully reconstituted and printed by Sir Edmund Craster. Wessington's use of Bede, Symeon and the earlier domestic Durham chroniclers is predictable enough; and for information on more general history he could rely on the '*Libri historiarum*' preserved in the monastic cloister at the beginning of the fifteenth century. But only the most partial witness could regard Wessington's ambitious venture, despite its incidental interest, as an unqualified success. In attempting to broaden the basis of the traditional narrative history of Durham, as it had crystallised in the late fourteenth century, by the insertion of documents and extracts from other chronicles, the prior tended to destroy the internal balance of that history. It could never be said of Wessington, as it has been written of Robert Graystanes, that 'he assimilates the documents, and creates an almost continuous narrative . . . generally there is great compression and the wearisome prolixity, which comes from quoting legal materials, is to a large extent avoided'.[1] Apart from the question of literary form, Wessington's history is not quite comprehensive or systematic enough to fulfil what was probably its author's main intention – the production of a comprehensive and reliable source-book for practical use against the convent's legal adversaries. The obvious comparisons with those other massive works of monastic historical compilation produced at the end of the middle ages, the chronicles of William Thorne, Thomas of Elmham and John Flete, are rarely in Wessington's favour. As Professor Offler noticed, Wessington's 'attempt to lift history writing at Durham out of the rut on to a new level of competence was not in the long run successful': it was the manuscripts of the fourteenth-century version of the Durham history, the *Gesta Episcoporum*, which found con-

[1] Professor Barlow's introduction to *Durham Annals*, p. xxxiii.

tinuators between Wessington's own life-time and the reign of Elizabeth.[1] Wessington's major chronicle, apparently composed in the years immediately before he became prior in 1416, therefore marks an isolated if significant attempt to recall rather than genuinely to revive one of the proudest monastic historical traditions in the country.

Prior Wessington's enthusiasm for the history of his own monastery was readily consonant with his interest in the more general history of Benedictine monasticism. As a historian of his house Wessington was unable to achieve the distinction of his predecessors; but in his capacity as a student of monastic origins and theory, the prior was a central figure in a field of scholarship well cultivated by late medieval English Black Monks. Dr Pantin's investigation of this *genre* of monastic literature has already revealed that although the priory of Durham was only one of several religious houses concerned with such issues, the northern monastery played an unexpectedly prominent part in their dissemination.[2] Of ten surviving manuscripts produced at Durham in the late middle ages which contain important treatises relating to monastic origins and ideals, eight appear to have been compiled in the period of Wessington's own priorate. Thus a work on monastic law entitled *Abbas vel Prior*, usually ascribed to Uthred of Boldon, survives in five Durham manuscripts and can be proved to have been used by Wessington himself.[3] But perhaps the most interesting, and certainly the most neglected, of the prior's own ventures into the field of Benedictine history is his '*De fundacione monasteriorum nigrorum monachorum in regno Angliae*': of this work, four copies survive, the earliest and fullest within the Durham manuscript B. III. 30, a volume known to have been compiled by Wessington on the evidence of a fifteenth-century inscription to that effect.[4] Wessington's treatise on this

---

[1] Offler, *Medieval Historians of Durham*, p. 17; The Lincoln's Inn Hale MS. 114 was, however, read and annotated by Thomas Swalwell, chancellor of the monastery at the beginning of the sixteenth century (fo. 1r).

[2] W. A. Pantin, 'Some Medieval English Treatises on the Origins of Monasticism', *Medieval Studies presented to Rose Graham*, ed. V. Ruffer and A. Taylor (Oxford, 1950), pp. 189–215.

[3] Loc. XXI, no. 6. The five MSS. are now D.C.D., B. IV. 26, 41, 45 and Jesus College, Cambridge, 41, 61.

[4] '*Volumen de Johanne Wessyngton pro parte laborata infrascripta sunt contenta*' (MS. B. III. 30, fo. 208v).

subject consists of a series of notes on the foundation of forty of the most famous English Benedictine houses. Although completely derivative, the production of this concise guide to the establishment of the major Black Monk houses from a wide variety of sources was a considerable achievement on Wessington's part. Closely analogous was a guide to famous monks which Wessington appended to the well-known treatise on the origins of monachism which began with the words '*Quia de ortu sacrosanctae religionis monachorum*'. The starting-point of this enterprise was a series of pictures, apparently painted on wood and long since destroyed, which were to be seen at the altar of Saint Benedict and Saint James in the cathedral church. Wessington's intention was to provide a guide to these pictures in the form of short biographies of each monk (148 in all), written on parchment and attached to two or more 'tables' or wooden boards placed in the vicinity of the altar for ease of consultation.[1] The prior provided a separate list of authorities for his biographies, ranging from Cassian's *Collationes* to the *Historia Aurea*, which provides convincing evidence of his ability and that of his monks to extract information from the patristic Christian texts as well as Durham's own historical works.[2] The motive of this laborious compilation, and several smaller ones of the same type, is characteristic of the mentality of the Durham monks in the early fifteenth century. In Wessington's own words, this information has been collected 'so that monks of our own day may appreciate how glorious God made their fathers and founders (*institutores*)'.[3]

The third and final category of Wessington's writings consists of a series of works where the prior's desire to edify and instruct was related to concrete and practical objectives. For a period of over thirty years, Wessington defended the rights, liberties and possessions of the church of Durham by the production of collections of evidence. Although Wessington usually compiled such quasi-legal dossiers only when confronted with a specific piece of litigation, the finished compilations were carefully preserved among the convent's muniments in the hope that they might be pressed into further service

---

[1] MS. B. III. 30, fo. 6r.   [2] Ibid., fo. 5.

[3] Ibid., fo. 47r; cf. B.M., Harleian MS. 4843, fo. 216. This was exactly the advice offered to the prelates of the English Benedictine houses as a whole by Henry V in his speech to the extraordinary Benedictine assembly of 1421 (Pantin, *Chapters* II, 99).

in the event of a future revival of the same dispute. The survival of so many of Wessington's collections of evidence among the Durham archives is itself perhaps the greatest single tribute to the value of the prior's work in the eyes of his fellow monks. At least thirty of Wessington's compilations have been identified at Durham as well as another ten documents of the same type which can be assigned to the prior with a high degree of probability.[1] In the circumstances, it is obviously impossible to describe these works in any detail. Three were written by Wessington on behalf of his bishop; the first, '*De origine libertatis regie ecclesie et episcopatus Dunelmensis*' for Bishop Langley in 1433, and the other two, demonstrating the bishop's right to lordship in Barnard Castle and the manor of Trillesden, for Robert Neville in the early 1440s. But the majority of Wessington's dossiers (twenty-four out of the listed total of thirty-seven) were written to aid his monastery in legal proceedings. Two of the compilations related to Durham cells. Early in his priorate, Wessington defended the warden of Durham College, Oxford, from the intervention of the Benedictine '*prior studentium*'; and at the end of his life he wrote '*pro jure et interesse prioris et conventus Dunelmensis super ecclesia, terris et prioratu de Lethom*'. The remaining twenty-two compilations can be divided, very approximately and only for the sake of convenience, into two groups: a set of seven works involving spiritual jurisdiction, almost all designed for presentation before the bishop of Durham or his officers; and finally, fifteen compilations on purely temporal matters, where the usual adversary was a group of unruly tenants or a turbulent local knight.

Some of Wessington's compilations were designed to be read aloud, often before the sessions of the bishop's justices at Durham, while others were meant to be studied more carefully and in private by the lay or ecclesiastical authority to whom they were directed. In either case, most of the works in question were quite lengthy documents, usually written in a small hand on both sides of a roll. The usual length of a typical Wessington compilation was perhaps 1,500 or 2,000 words, but there were several works which, like the '*rotulum satis longum*' on the question of '*dimidiaciones*' from the

---

[1] See, for example, Loc. XXI, no. 12, endorsed '*De libertatibus episcopi et prioris Dunelmensibus, permixtis ut patet*', which was certainly a Wessington compilation but consists of nothing but transcripts of charters from the convent's registers.

courts of the bishop of Durham, were at least three times as large. The length of a Wessington compilation is not, however, in itself a very significant index to its value. Many of the prior's apparently major writings are extremely repetitive and include long transcriptions from papal, royal and episcopal privileges which all serve to substantiate one another but only rarely make an independent contribution to the problem at issue. The more general the topic on which the prior was engaged, the more likely he was to set out a long series of extracts from Durham chronicles and charters and leave them to speak for themselves. Fortunately much of the litigation facing the convent during Wessington's priorate involved specific and concrete issues which compelled him to elaborate on the implications of his sources. There is no doubt that the more precise and particular the occasion the more interesting and more relevant was Wessington's choice of '*evidenciae*'.[1]

Wessington can have spared neither himself nor his associates in the accumulation of such evidence. The prior's conscientiousness and his knowledge of a wide variety of historical and literary source material is not in doubt. On the other hand, all Wessington's compilations cannot be regarded as equally successful. From the modern standpoint, much of the evidence adduced by the prior seems, as has been noted, of doubtful relevance. President Blakiston criticised the way in which Wessington paraded inapposite citations from the Digest and Decretals in his *Responsiones contra Priorem Studentium*.[2] It is equally difficult to see what one of Saint Cuthbert's lesser miracles should have had to do with a quarrel about shipping rights on the Tyne in Lancastrian England.[3] One sometimes suspects that Wessington's determination to pursue all problems to their historical origins was partly calculated. By converting an issue from a purely legal into a largely historical problem he forced his opponents into a sphere where they could not hope to rival his own expert knowledge. Many, if not all, of Wessington's compilations were successful in practical terms and it seems certain that contemporaries were

---

[1] Compare, for instance, Wessington's very general treatment of the theme, '*de origine libertatis regie ecclesie et episcopatus Dunelmensis*' (Reg. III, fos. 164–7) and his precise and relevant proof '*quod iniusta sit subtraccio unius marce per maiorem et ballivos ville Novicastri de elemosina regis concessa monachis apud Farneland commorantibus*' (Misc. Chrs., no. 5631; Loc. XX, no. 26).

[2] *Dur. Coll. Rolls*, p. 27.   [3] Loc. II, no. 3.

impressed by the results of the prior's labours. There is an un-expected glimpse of Wessington at Bishop Auckland on 21 July 1426 expounding before Langley's counsellors the reasons for the abbatial status of the prior of Durham.[1] Both Bishop Langley and Bishop Neville asked Wessington for his help in their own suits, and one of the prior's compilations was designed for presentation at an English parliament. The prior's own words to Bishop Neville in January 1440 may be applied to his whole literary career: 'I haff doon my diligence and shewid in yees maters such euidence and wrytyng as I haff.'[2]

In his conservatism and his preoccupation with the history of his own house, Wessington appears to stand in sharp and unflattering contrast to his great contemporary among the English Black Monk prelates, John Whethamstede. Although in the context of a Poggio or Aeneas Sylvius, the abbot of St Albans may appear to be 'one of the last of the English medieval polymaths rather than one of the early English humanists',[3] the more appropriate comparison with the prior of Durham leaves little doubt as to the novelty and originality of Whethamstede's intellectual interests. Yet one of the more paradoxical results of modern scholarship has been the rise of Wessington's reputation as a monk-scholar at the same time that Whethamstede's voluminous writings have received increasingly adverse criticism. This process is reflected in Professor Knowles's short but well-balanced portraits of the two monks. To Wessington is attributed 'a masculine, accurate, trained mind' while Whetham-stede appears as a possible neurotic who cannot be said to have been a man 'of powerful and direct intelligence'.[4] Whatever the truth in that comparison, it would be idle to deny that Wessington is a much more significant figure in the history of English thought and learn-ing than Whethamstede just because the former was so much more representative of the common literary interests of the monks of Durham and other large English Benedictine houses. The intrinsic interest of Wessington's writings lies less in their subject-matter than in the extremely detailed and systematic way in which the prior

[1] B.M., Cotton MS. Vitellius A. IX, fo. 75.
[2] Reg. Parv. II, fo. 112.
[3] Weiss, *Humanism in England during the Fifteenth Century*, p. 38.
[4] Knowles, *Rel. Orders* II, 192, 197.

approached his often familiar themes. Wessington's knowledge of the Durham monastic archives is particularly impressive and although he relied throughout his life on only a dozen or so earlier English chronicles he was closely acquainted with them all and able to extract those passages which served his purpose. The modernity of Wessington's scholarship must not be exaggerated; and it is difficult, for instance, to agree with the view that a set of somewhat bald, factual notes composed in 1437–8 on the action taken during previous vacancies of the see of Durham is really 'a finished synthesis' succeeding 'in doing exactly that at which much fine modern historical scholarship aims'.[1] Undoubtedly Wessington's major chronicle and the best of his other compilations do reveal a skilful and not completely uncritical handling of historical evidence, qualities still relatively rare in early fifteenth-century England. But any attempt to emphasise the novelty of Wessington's historical techniques would be misleading if it disguised the central fact that in his attitude to learning as in his attitude to office, the prior was primarily a defender of the *status quo*. It is indeed his very conservatism that makes Prior Wessington a suitable representative of the main currents of intellectual interest that passed through the Durham cloister during his life-time. What he wrote is rarely dramatic for the simple reason that it preserves the common-places of his milieu and his monastery. In his literary work can be recaptured more intensely than in any other source the intense corporate pride of the Durham monks in themselves and their community.

[1] R. Brentano, 'The *Jurisdictio Spiritualis*: an example of fifteenth-century English historiography', *Speculum* XXXII (1957), 329.

CONCLUSION

Despite the fact that it is notoriously 'a weighty and responsible task for a historian to sit in judgment upon monastic worth',[1] few historians have been able to resist exactly that temptation. During the many centuries since the dissolution of the English monasteries, successive generations of antiquaries and scholars have generalised with surprising confidence about a way of life for which they have rarely felt much personal sympathy. As is well known, their verdict has normally been a highly critical one: and it remains axiomatic among the great majority of modern historians of the late medieval church as of the Reformation that the religious life practised in fifteenth-century England was vitiated by fundamental flaws and inadequacies. At worst, we are presented with a veritable desert interspersed by only the occasional fountain of living water; at best, the relaxation of rigorous monastic observance had allegedly led to 'an indefinable spiritual rusticity'.[2] Such considered judgements cannot be easily cast aside. Yet it is often hard to resist the conclusion that the posthumous reputation of late medieval English religious houses has suffered the worst of all possible fates. To be judged by the ideal standards of their own religious order and to be found wanting is, after all, the natural outcome for most monks at most times. Much more seriously, fifteenth-century monasticism has continuously been assessed by twelfth-century standards, the latter a product of a very different age as reflected in a very different type of historical source. Perhaps the greatest danger confronting all monastic historians is their almost inevitable, because largely unconscious, entanglement in the still pervasive myth of general moral decline in late medieval England.

To such large problems of historical interpretation there can of course be no final solution. As Professor Knowles pointed out towards the close of his monumental survey of medieval English monastic history, grey walls and broken cloisters will continue to

---

[1] H. O. Evennett, 'The Last Stages of Medieval Monasticism in England', *Studia Monastica* II (1960), 418.

[2] Dickens, *The English Reformation*, pp. 16–17; Knowles, *Rel. Orders* III, 460.

'pose for every beholder questions that words cannot answer'.[1] Remote though the world of the late medieval monk may increasingly seem, there can be no doubt of its perennial fascination, nor that it will be subject to continuous reassessment by future generations in the light of their own experience of the religious life. This book has been completed at a time when – to an extent inconceivable and unpredictable a few years ago – the very survival of traditional Christian monasticism seems to be at issue.[2] Whatever the outcome of the present debate, for many well-informed observers the most serious monastic 'crisis' since the Reformation, its relevance to the medieval historian is unmistakably direct. In the twentieth century, as in the fifteenth, it proves pointless to trace the course of monastic development purely in terms of its own traditional ideals: the religious house is always in part a product of the society from which it is trying to escape. In the famous words with which Erasmus brought the argument of *Enchiridion Militis Christiani* to a close, '*Monachatus non est pietas, sed vitae genus pro suo cuique corporis ingeniique habitu, vel utile, vel inutile*'. As 'a way of life', however unusual and distinctive, rather than an absolute, the historian need not be too diffident in relating monasticism to the social pressures and needs which give it concrete shape.

This study has accordingly been an analysis of monastic life at early fifteenth-century Durham in practice rather than in theory. Indeed the most obvious general conclusion to emerge from this investigation of the monks of Saint Cuthbert is the extent to which a group of men passionately devoted to the preservation of past traditions were nevertheless controlled by the dominant forces of their own age. As we have seen, many of these forces have left a permanent imprint upon the surviving archives – throwing into prominent relief such themes as Durham Priory's dependence upon favourable economic conditions and skilful financial management, its close involvement in a complex pattern of contemporary patronage and 'lordship', and its sensitivity to the national intellectual climate through the agency of Durham College, Oxford. By a not altogether unwelcome paradox, the convent's muniments often

[1] Knowles, *Rel. Orders* III, p. 468.
[2] G. Moorhouse, *Against All Reason* (London, 1969); D. Knowles, *Christian Monasticism*, p. 224.

provide information more indispensable for an understanding of the world outside the monastic walls than of the conduct of the religious life within. As the largest English corporation north of York, the cathedral church and monastery of Durham has a major historical significance which often transcends its religious objectives.

In the last resort, therefore, the voluminous records left to posterity by the monks of fifteenth-century Durham are of importance because of the unique opportunity they provide to appreciate an exceptionally wide range of human activity. It may indeed be this very variety which offers the central clue to the undoubted transformation of the large English religious house in the later middle ages. The priory of Durham had been founded in 1083 to fulfil the then universally-held belief that a large and monolithic religious community engaged in a ceaseless round of formal liturgy was the highest expression of Christian aspiration; but in the fifteenth century this ideal was itself being eroded by a new emphasis on the individual conscience and a more informal personal devotion. All in all, the most significant feature of monastic life at late medieval Durham was probably its ability to respond to these developments rather than to ignore them. The increasingly complex specialisation of human labour and function within the community no doubt afforded the individual monk a greater opportunity to display his own particular talents. Similarly the almost complete reconstruction of the monastic buildings at Durham during the century after the first outbreak of the Black Death has left a permanent memorial to the prevailing desire to sub-divide many of the architectural manifestations of the common religious life in the interests of individual members of the community. The conversion of the unitary religious institution into a metaphoric as well as literal 'house of many mansions' was not without its dangers and has naturally evoked criticism. Any qualitative assessment of the value of the life led by the monks of Saint Cuthbert during this period must in any case depend on the allowances we make for ways of thought and social influences very different from our own. Nevertheless, fifteenth-century Durham's relatively high public reputation and freedom from internal dissension may suggest that it did not absolutely fail to reconcile the contradictory claims of individual and community, of this world and the next.

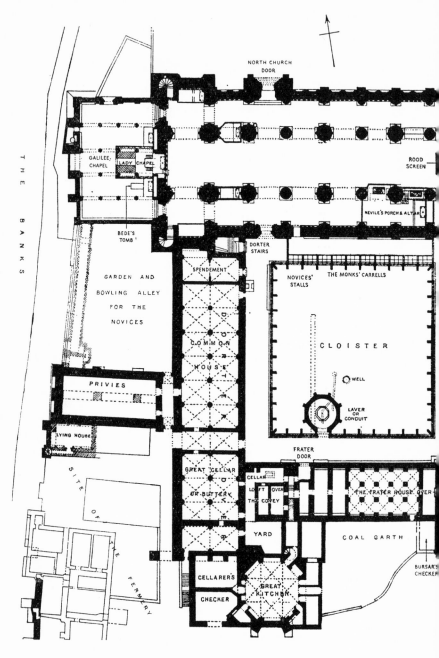

Fig. 5. Plan of the priory of Durham in the later middle ages, based upon the plan drawn by W. H. St John Hope in 1903 and first published in *The Rites of Durham*, ed. J. T. Fowler (Surtees Soc. CVII, 1903). Medieval walls existing or of which the

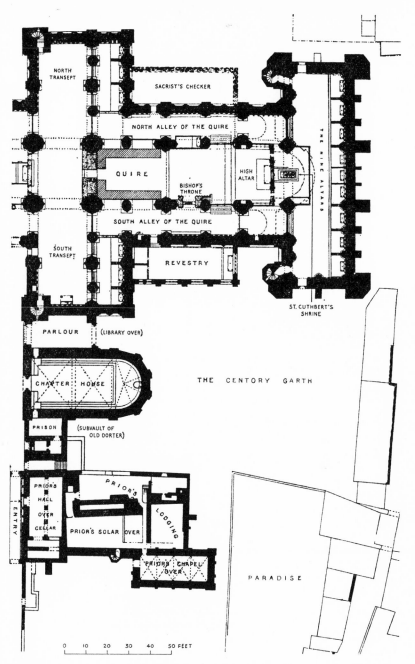

NORTH
TRANSEPT

SACRIST'S CHECKER

NORTH ALLEY OF THE QUIRE

THE NINE ALTARS

QUIRE

BISHOP'S
THRONE

HIGH
ALTAR

SOUTH ALLEY OF THE QUIRE

SOUTH
TRANSEPT

REVESTRY

ST. CUTHBERT'S
SHRINE

PARLOUR   (LIBRARY OVER)

CHAPTER HOUSE

THE   CENTORY   GARTH

PRISON   (SUBVAULT OF
OLD DORTER)

PRIOR'S

PRIOR'S
HALL
OVER
CELLAR

ENTRY

LODGING

PRIOR'S SOLAR OVER

PRIOR'S CHAPEL
OVER

PARADISE

0   10   20   30   40   50 FEET

sites are known are shown in black. The total internal length of the cathedral
church is 470 feet and it covers an area of 44,400 square feet.

BIBLIOGRAPHY

UNPRINTED SOURCES

Muniments of the Dean and Chapter of Durham: records in book form

The best general account of the history and arrangement of the Durham muniments is W. A. Pantin's *Report on the Muniments of the Dean and Chapter of Durham* (privately printed, 1939).

Registrum I	'*de dimissionibus terrarum*', etc., to *c.* 1400.
Registrum II	Prior and chapter's letter-book, 1312–1401.
Registrum III	Prior and chapter's letter-book, 1401–44.
Registrum IV	Prior and chapter's letter-book, 1444–86.
Registrum V	Prior and chapter's letter-book, 1486–1538.
Registrum Parvum I	See B.M., Cotton MS. Faustina A. VI.
Registrum Parvum II	Prior's letter-book, 1407–45.
Registrum Parvum III	Prior's letter-book, 1446–81.
Registrum Parvum IV	Prior's letter-book, 1484–1519.
Cartuarium I	'*de generalibus munimentis per Angliam*', written *c.* 1407–10.
Cartuarium II	'*de specialibus munimentis infra Dioc. Dunelmensem*', written *c.* 1407–10.
Cartuarium III	(a) Part I, fos. 1–48: largely '*Eboracensia*': written *c.* 1500.
	(b) Part II, fos. 1–152: '*de munimentis specialibus et generalibus in diocesibus Ebor. et Lincoln.*': written *c.* 1407–10.
	(c) Part II, fos. 153–353: '*Generalia*': written *c.* 1500.
Cartuarium IV	'*Specialia*': written *c.* 1500.
Cartuarium Vetus	Written *c.* 1230.
Rentale et Cartuarium Elemosinarie	The rentals are of 1424–40 and the cartulary written *c.* 1500.
Cartuarium Evidenciarum Communarii	Written in the late XV and early XVI cents.
Tabula Evidenciarum Sacristarie Dunelm.	Bound with rental of 1500.
Repertorium Parvum	Inventory of muniments, written *c.* 1401.
Repertorium Magnum	Inventory of muniments, written *c.* 1461.
Feodarium Melsanby	Written in 1430 and printed as *Feodarium Prioratus Dunelmensis* in Surtees Soc. LVIII, 1872.
Rentals of Bursar	1396, 1411: bound together. 1432.
Halmote Court Books	3 vols. (1400–1528).
Capitula Generalia Prioris Dunelm.	Acts of the prior's spiritual court, 1435–56.
Registrum Papireum Diversarum Literarum Cancellarie Dunelm.	Durham formulary, written *c.* 1395.

Transcript (xix cent.) of Dean and Chapter Act Book	Vol. I (1578–83; 1621–1726).

Muniments of the Dean and Chapter of Durham: charters, rolls and other documents

Documents catalogued in the 'Repertorium Magnum'

Papalia	Papal bulls, usually listed in chronological order of popes. Very few of these survive for the period of Wessington's priorate.
Regalia	Royal charters, letters patent, etc., but do not include the more informal royal correspondence with the priors of Durham.
Pontificalia	Charters, confirmations, compositions, etc., of the bishops of Durham, generally arranged in chronological order. Especially valuable are those sections (7, 8 and 9. Pont.) relating to episcopal visitations and the elections of bishops and priors.
Archidiaconalia Dunelmensia	Documents relating to the prior's archidiaconal jurisdiction over the convent's appropriated churches in the archdeaconry of Durham. Especially numerous are the records of disputes between the prior and the archdeacon of Durham.
Archidiaconalia Northumbrensia	Documents of a similar nature to those in Archid. Dunelm., but relating to the prior's jurisdiction in the archdeaconry of Northumberland. Archid. North. contains more valuable material for the early fifteenth century than Archid. Dunelm.
Specialia	Title deeds, legal evidence, etc., of monastic property in the diocese of Durham. These documents are all arranged under place names.
Eboracensia	Similar deeds, etc., of monastic property held in the diocese of York and (despite the title) elsewhere in England. They include, for instance, a valuable collection of documents relating to Durham College, Oxford (5. and 6. Ebor.).

Locelli

A most important collection of over 1,600 documents, first formed at the end of the fifteenth century. Several of the original documents are now missing and many more have strayed into Miscellaneous Charters, but 23 of the original 40 Locelli still survive. Of these the following are of especial value:

Locellus I	Mortuary rolls, letters of confraternity, etc.
Locellus II	Miscellaneous legal and financial documents, including several of Wessington's compositions.
Locellus V	Records relating to pleas, assizes and inquisitions, including documents connected with the Heron case of 1428–31.

Locellus IX	Records relating to the priory of Lytham in the later middle ages.
Locelli XIII and XVI	Citations, certificates, letters of proxy, etc., of elections of priors of Durham.
Locelli XVIII and XIX	Records of the payment and collection of royal and papal taxation.
Locellus XXI	Appeals and evidence relevant to lawsuits, containing the largest single group of Wessington's compositions.
Locellus XXV	Original correspondence of kings, magnates, bishops and others to the prior of Durham, largely dating from 1400 to 1460.
Locellus XXVII	Records of episcopal visitations of the convent as well as a few fifteenth-century chapter ordinances and diffinitions.

Miscellaneous charters

A very large supplementary class of documents (almost all of medieval date), numbering almost 7,200. This collection was formed and catalogued, very unsystematically, by Joseph Stevenson and Canon Greenwell in the mid-nineteenth century. Its contents are genuinely miscellaneous and include many documents from the Locelli as well as others which are little more than scraps of paper. Very few were ever registered in the monastic registers or cartularies.

Account rolls ('compoti') of Durham obedientiaries

The majority of the annual *compoti* rendered by Durham obedientiaries in the first half of the fifteenth century still survive and are kept in separate boxes among the muniments there, viz:

Almoner	Feretrar
Bursar	Granator
Cellarer (weekly and monthly as well as annual accounts)	Hostillar
	Master of the Infirmary
Chamberlain	Sacrist
Commoner	Terrar

Occasional copies of the inventory (*status* or *ratiocinatio*) made by an obedientiary at the time of his retirement from the office also survive and are normally preserved in the same box as his *compoti*. Kept in separate boxes are the indentures (*indenture*) between one obedientiary and another; most numerous and most valuable are the indentures between the bursar and cellarer, and the bursar and granator. (Selections from all these accounts, inventories and indentures, except those of the granator, were printed by Canon Fowler in *Durham Account Rolls*.)

Account rolls ('compoti') of the Durham cells

The majority of the annual *compoti* rendered by the superiors of Durham cells in the first half of the fifteenth century still survive and are kept in separate boxes among the muniments there, viz:

Bibliography

Prior of Coldingham (no *compotus* survives after 1405/6. The sacrist of Coldingham's accounts were also returned to Durham, but none survive after 1412/13). The Coldingham cell accounts are an exception to the general rule in no longer forming a separate collection but being incorporated into Miscellaneous Charters.

Prior of Finchale
Prior of Holy Island
Prior of Lytham
Prior of St Leonard's, Stamford
Warden of Durham College (the *compoti* of the two bursars of the college, rendered quarterly and not annually, were also returned to Durham)
Master of Jarrow
Master of Monk Wearmouth
Master of Farne

As in the case of the Durham obedientiaries, inventories of the goods of each cell were normally called for when one superior was replaced by another: several of these survive in the same boxes as the account rolls. In the case of both Durham College and Lytham, the boxes containing inventories also include many documents of a more general, non-financial interest. In particular, the collection kept in *Lytham, Miscellanea*, furnishes evidence of crucial importance to the understanding of the Lytham case of 1444–6; as the documents in this box were unlisted, they have been numbered by me.

Manorial, stock-farm and other account rolls

Few manorial and stock-farm accounts survive at Durham after 1416. However, the following *compoti* provide much information relevant to the monastic economy between 1416 and 1446:

| Elvet Hall | Muggleswick |
| Le Holme | Pittington |

Of particular interest are the collection of *Mines Accounts* from 1409 to 1453 (presented by the monk-receiver) of payments and issues from the convent's coal-pits. Three of these accounts (1427–30) have strayed to Miscellaneous Charters, no. 5443.

For five accounts, rendered by the prior's chaplain, of '*ludi*' at Beaurepaire in the 1390s, see Miscellaneous Charters, nos. 210–14.

For accounts of the *Pensions imposed on obedientiaries and cells* at annual chapters from 1441 to 1444, see Miscellaneous Charters, nos. 5649–51, 7138.

Halmote court rolls

A long series of these rolls survives for the early fifteenth century, but they are of only incidental value to the internal history of the monastery.

Special collections

Elemosinaria	Almoner's Deeds
Sacristaria	Sacrist's Deeds
Additional Rolls	A class of miscellaneous rolls created by Dr J. Conway Davies in 1956. It consists of over 50 documents, most of which seem to have strayed from other sections of the muniments.

Bibliography

Manuscripts of the Dean and Chapter Library, Durham

The following list does not include those Durham manuscripts examined merely for the information to be gathered from press-marks and inscriptions of ownership. All the volumes are described in T. Rud, *Codicum Manuscriptorum Ecclesiae Cathedralis Dunelmensis Catalogus Classicus Descriptus* (Durham, 1825).

A. III. 27.	(Holcot on the *Liber Sapientiae*; xiv cent.)
A. IV. 5.	(Glossed psalter; early xv cent.)
B. I. 32.	(Vincent of Beauvais; xv cent.)
B. II. 35.	(Bede's *Ecclesiastical History*, etc.; xii–xv cents.)
B. III. 6.	(Sermons of Saint Augustine; xiv cent.)
B. III. 22.	(Bonaventure, etc.; xiv cent.)
B. III. 30.	(Wessington's *collectanea*; xv cent.)
B. IV. 26.	(Benedictine statutes, etc.; xiii–xv cents.)
B. IV. 30.	(Alexander Neckham, etc.; xiv cent.)
B. IV. 41.	(Benedictine statutes, etc.; xiii–xv cents.)
B. IV. 42.	(Misc. devotional treatises; xiv–xv cents.)
B. IV. 43.	(Book of 'tables' or indices; *c.* 1400)
B. IV. 45.	(Benedictine statutes, etc.; xiv–xv cents.)
B. IV. 46.	(Monastic Library catalogues; xiv–xv cents.)
C. III. 9.	(*Apparatus super Decretalibus*; xiii cent.)
C. III. 11.	(Bartholomew de Sancta Concordia; *c.* 1400)
C. IV. 25.	(Durham formulary; *c.* 1390)

Manuscripts of the British Museum, London

Additional MSS. 6162	(Lawrence of Durham, etc.; xv cent.)
24059	(Durham chronicles, etc.; late xiv cent.)
39943	(Bede; xii cent.)
Arundel MS. 507	(Devotional treatises; late xiv cent.)
Burney MS. 310	(Eusebius, etc.; 1381)
Cotton MSS. Julius D. IV	(Latin 'Brut', etc.; xiv cent.)
Julius D. VI	(English chronicle; xiii cent.)
Claudius D. IV	(Wessington's history of church of Durham; xv cent.)
Vitellius A. IX	(Wessington's *collectanea*; xv cent.)
Vitellius C. IX	(Christopher Watson's history of Durham; xvi cent.)
Vitellius E. XII	(Benedictine statutes, etc.; xv cent.)
Vespasian A. VI	(Durham chronicles; xiv cent.)
Titus A. II	(Symeon, etc.; xiv cent.)
Domitian VII	(Durham *Liber Vitae*; xi–xvi cents.)
Faustina A. VI	(Prior of Durham's small register, *c.* 1322–1406)
Harleian MSS. 1804	('Horae', Kalendar, etc., of Durham; late xv cent.)
1924	(Bede; xii cent.)
3858	(*Opus vii Custodiarum*; early xv cent.)
4688	(Bede's commentaries, etc.; xii cent.)
4843	(William Todd's *collectanea*; early xvi cent.)
5234	(Isidorus, Uthred of Boldon, etc.; xiii–xiv cents.)
Lansdowne MS. 397	(Devotional works owned by Wessington; xiv cent.)

Bibliography

Stowe MS. 930   (Durham annals, register; xii–xiv cents.)

Other manuscripts and records

Beverley, East Riding County Record Office
DDLO/20   (Obedientiary and other accounts of Selby Abbey;
                                  xv–xvi cents.)

Cambridge, Jesus College Library
MS. 41 (Q.B.25)   (Benedictine statutes, etc.; xiii–xv cents.)
MS. 61 (Q.G.13)   (Benedictine statutes, etc.; xiv–xv cents.)

Durham, Department of Palaeography and Diplomatic, Durham Bishopric Records
Register of Bishop Thomas Hatfield (1345–81) ⎫ (both registers are in the possession
Register of Bishop Thomas Langley (1406–37) ⎭ of the Dean and Chapter of Durham)
Receiver-General's Accounts
    No. 190237 (Howden)
    Nos. 188686, 189782, 189809–11, 190184 (Receiver of Durham 1416–39)
    Nos. 189600–5 (Sheriff and Escheator)

Durham, Bishop Cosin's Library, University Library
MS. V.ii.6.   (Symeon of Durham; early xii cent.)

Durham, County Record Office, County Hall
The Salvin Papers (deposited 1964)

London, Lambeth Palace Library
MSS. 10, 11 and 12   (Historia Aurea, 3 vols.; xiv cent.)
MS. 483   (Pseudo-Grosseteste; xiv cent.)

London, Lincoln's Inn Library
Hale MS. 114   (Wessington's history, or '*Liber Ruber Dunelmensis*';
                                  xv cent.)

London, Public Record Office
Exchequer: *King's Remembrancer:* Subsidy Rolls, Clerical Series (E. 179); 62/11–
                                  62/40.
        Exchequer of Receipt: Receipt Rolls, nos. 680–90, 885.
Palatinate of Durham
    Chancery Records: Enrolments of Bishops Langley and Neville (3/34–3/47).
    Chancery Records: Warrants and Grants (3/206, nos. 1–11).
    Chancery Records: Abstracts of Inquisitions *post mortem* (Register II).

Oxford, Bodleian Library
Carte MS. 177   (Inventory of Durham muniments, etc.; xiv cent.)
Fairfax MS. 6   (Durham chronicles; late xiv cent.)
Laud Misc. 262   (Sermons; xiv cent.)
           389   (*Pera Peregrini*; xiv cent.)
           392   (Hugh of St Victor, etc.; xii cent.)
           700   (Durham chronicles; late xiv cent.)
           748   (Wessington's history of church of Durham; early
                                xv cent.)

Oxford, St John's College Library
MS. 77   (Transcript of a xv cent. St Albans Register)

Bibliography

Ushaw College Library, Co. Durham

MS. xviii.F.5.11   ('*Liber Sacriste*' of *c.* 1500)

Vatican City, Archivio Segreto Vaticano

Reg. Lat., no. 370   (Contains on fos. 32v–33r the copy of a bull dispensing the monks of Durham from full observance of the more stringent Benedictine statutes: 27 February 1440)

Westminster, Records of the Roman Catholic Archbishop

Se/Ac   (Obedientiary and other accounts of Selby abbey, xv–xvi cents.)

York, Borthwick Institute of Historical Research

York Archiepiscopal Registers: Richard Scrope (1398–1405)
                                 Henry Bowet (2 vols.; 1407–23)
                                 John Kemp (1425–52)
                                 Sede Vacante Register (*c.* 1300–1556)

Cause Papers: Fifteenth Century (CP. F)
    No. 167:   Appeal of prior of Lytham against abbot of Vale Royal, 1428.
    No. 188:   Appeal concerning prior of Durham's spiritual jurisdiction over the church of Fishlake, 1452–3.

York, Minster library

MS. xvi. I. 12. (Durham histories; xiii–xv cents.)
MS. xvi. D.9. (W. de Alvernia; xv cent.)
Various printed books once in the library of Durham Priory.

PRINTED SOURCES

Records of the priory and bishopric of Durham

Account rolls of the abbey of Durham. Extracts from the, ed. J. T. Fowler (3 vols.; Surtees Society, Vols. xcix, c, ciii; 1898–1901).

Bek, Antony, Bishop and Patriarch, 1283–1311. Records of, ed. C. M. Fraser (Surtees Society, Vol. clxii, 1953).

Calendars of Chancery Enrolments of the Bishops of Durham, 1333–1457 (printed in the appendices of the Reports of the Deputy Keepers of the Public Records, nos. xxxi–xxxiv, 1870–3).

Calendar of Inquisitions Post Mortem, etc., of the Palatinate of Durham (printed in the appendices of the Reports of the Deputy Keeper of the Public Records, nos. xliv, xlv, 1883–4).

Catalogi Veteres librorum ecclesiae cathedralis Dunelm., ed. B. Botfield (Surtees Society, Vol. vii, 1838).

Coldingham, The Priory of. The correspondence, inventories, account rolls and law proceedings, ed. J. Raine (Surtees Society, Vol. xii, 1841).

Depositions and other ecclesiastical proceedings from the courts of Durham, ed. J. Raine (Surtees Society, Vol. xxi, 1845).

Dunelmensis, Historiae, Scriptores Tres, ed. J. Raine (Surtees Society, Vol. ix, 1839). See Appendix of illustrative documents.

Durham Annals and Documents of the Thirteenth Century, ed. F. Barlow (Surtees Society, Vol. clv, 1945). See Appendix of illustrative documents.

Bibliography

Durham College Rolls, Some, ed. H. E. D. Blakiston (Oxford Historical Society, Vol. XXXII, 1896: *Collectanea, Third Series,* pp. 1–76).

Durham Episcopal Charters, 1071–1152, ed. H. S. Offler (Surtees Society, Vol. CLXXIX, 1968).

Durham household book, The: or the accounts of the bursar of the monastery of Durham from Pentecost 1530 to Pentecost 1534, ed. J. Raine (Surtees Society, Vol. XVIII, 1844).

Feodarium Prioratus Dunelmensis, ed. W. Greenwell (Surtees Society, Vol. LVIII, 1872).

Finchale, The Priory of. The charters of endowment, inventories and account rolls, ed. J. Raine (Surtees Society, Vol. VI, 1837).

Fox, Richard, Lord Bishop of Durham, 1494–1501. The Register of, ed. M. P. Howden (Surtees Society, Vol. CXLVII, 1932).

Halmota Prioratus Dunelmensis, A.D. 1296–A.D. 1384, ed. W. H. Longstaffe and J. Booth (Surtees Society, Vol. LXXXII, 1889).

Hatfield's, Bishop, Survey, ed. W. Greenwell (Surtees Society, Vol. XXXII, 1857).

Jarrow and Monk-Wearmouth. The inventories and account rolls of the Benedictine houses or cells of, ed. J. Raine (Surtees Society, Vol. XXIX, 1854).

Langley, Thomas, Bishop of Durham, 1406–1437. The Register of, Vols. I–VI, ed. R. L. Storey (Surtees Society, Vols. CLXIV, CLXVI, CLXIX, CLXX, CLXXVII, CLXXXII, 1956–67).

Liber Vitae Ecclesiae Dunelmensis, ed. J. Stevenson (Surtees Society, Vol. XIII, 1841).

Liber Vitae Ecclesiae Dunelmensis. A collotype facsimile of the original manuscript, etc., Vol. I, ed. A. H. Thompson (Surtees Society, Vol. CXXXVI, 1923).

Obituary Roll of William Ebchester and John Burnby, Priors of Durham. The, ed. J. Raine (Surtees Society, Vol. XXXI, 1856).

Registrum Palatinum Dunelmense. The Register of Richard de Kellawe, lord palatine and bishop of Durham, 1314–1316, ed. T. D. Hardy (4 vols.; Rolls Series, 62, 1873–8).

Richard d'Aungerville, of Bury. Fragments of his register and other documents, ed. G. W. Kitchin (Surtees Society, Vol. CXIX, 1910).

Rites of Durham . . . written 1593, ed. J. T. Fowler (Surtees Society, Vol. CVII, 1903). An augmented edition of *A Description or breife declaration of all the ancient monuments, rites and customes . . . within the church of Durham before the suppression,* ed. J. Raine (Surtees Society, Vol. XV, 1842).

Sanctuarium Dunelmense et Sanctuarium Beverlacense, ed. J. Raine (Surtees Society, Vol. V, 1837).

Statutes of the Cathedral Church of Durham, The, ed. A. H. Thompson (Surtees Society, Vol. CXLIII, 1929).

Tunstall, Cuthbert, Bishop of Durham, 1530–59, and James Pilkington, Bishop of Durham, 1561–76, The Registers of, ed. G. Hinde (Surtees Society, Vol. CLXI, 1952).

Uthredi monachi Dunelm., Vita Compendiosa, printed from B.M., Additional MS. 6162, fo. 31v, in *Bulletin of the Institute of Historical Research,* Vol. III (1925–6), p. 46.

Wills and Inventories illustrative of the history . . . of the northern counties of England, Part I, ed. J. Raine (Surtees Society, Vol. II, 1835).

Other ecclesiastical records and sources

Abingdon Abbey, Accounts of the Obedientiars, ed. R. E. G. Kirk (Camden Society, New Series, Vol. LI, 1892).

Apostolic Camera and Scottish Benefices 1418–88, The, ed. A. I. Cameron (London, 1933).

Benedict, Saint, The Rule of, ed. J. McCann (London, 1952).

Benedicti, Sancti, Regula Monasteriorum, ed. C. Butler (Herder & Co.; Freiburg, 1927).

Bibliography

Benedictine Kalendars, English, after A.D. 1100, ed. F. Wormald (2 vols.; Henry Bradshaw Society, Vols. LXXVII, LXXXI; 1939, 1946).

Bury St. Edmund's Abbey, Memorials of, ed. T. Arnold (3 vols.; Rolls Series, 96, 1890–6).

Calendar of entries in the Papal Registers . . . Papal Letters, 1198–1484 (13 vols.; London, 1893–1955).

Calendar of entries in the Papal Registers . . . Petitions to the Pope, Vol. I, 1342–1419 (London, 1896).

Calendar of Scottish Supplications to Rome, 1418–22, ed. E. R. Lindsay and A. I. Cameron (Scottish History Society, Third Series, Vol. XXIII; 1934).

Canterbury College, Oxford, ed. W. A. Pantin (3 vols.; Oxford Historical Society, New Series, Vols. VI–VIII; 1947–50).

Cantuarienses, Literae, ed. J. B. Sheppard (3 vols.; Rolls Series, 85, 1887–9).

Chapters of the English Black Monks, Documents illustrating the activities of the General and Provincial, ed. W. A. Pantin (3 vols.; Camden Third Series, Vols. XLV, XLVII, LIV; 1931–7).

Chichele, Henry, Archbishop of Canterbury, 1414–43. The Register of, ed. E. F. Jacob (4 vols.; Canterbury and York Society, Vols. XLII, XLV, XLVI, XLVII; 1937–47).

Christ Church Letters, ed. J. B. Sheppard (Camden Society, New Series, Vol. XIX, 1877).

Corpus Juris Canonici, ed. E. Friedberg (2 vols.; Leipzig, 1879–81).

Ely Chapter Ordinances and Visitation Records, 1241–1515, ed. S. J. A. Evans (Camden Third Series, Vol. LXIV, 1940: *Camden Miscellany XVII*, Part I).

Gloucestriae, Historia et Cartularium Monasterii Sancti Petri, ed. W. H. Hart (3 vols.; Rolls Series, 33, 1863–7).

Hexham, The Priory of, Vol. II: Its Title Deeds, Black Book, etc., ed. J. Raine (Surtees Society, Vol. XLVI, 1865).

Hyde abbey, Winchester, The Monastic Breviary of, ed. J. B. Tolhurst (6 vols.; Henry Bradshaw Society, Vols. LXIX–LXXI, LXXVI, LXXVIII, LXXX; 1932–42).

James, M. R., *The Ancient Libraries of Canterbury and Dover* (Cambridge, 1903).

Lyndwood, W., *Provinciale . . . cui adjiciuntur constitutiones legatinae D. Othonis et D. Othoboni, etc.* (Oxford, 1679).

Monasticon Anglicanum, ed. W. Dugdale (re-ed. J. Caley, H. Ellis and B. Bandinel, 6 vols. in 8; London, 1817–30).

More, Prior William, Journal of, ed. E. S. Fagan (Worcestershire Historical Society, 1914).

Morton, The Book of William, Almoner of Peterborough Monastery, 1448–1467, ed. P. I. King (Northants. Record Society, XVI, 1954).

Northern Convocation, The Records of the, ed. G. W. Kitchin (Surtees Society, Vol. CXIII, 1907).

Northern Registers, Historical Papers and Letters from the, ed. J. Raine (Rolls Series, 61, 1873).

Osmund, Saint, The Canonization of, ed. A. R. Malden (Wilts. Record Society, 1901).

Papsturkunden in England, ed. W. Holtzmann (3 vols.; Berlin, 1932–52).

Reyner, C., *Apostolatus Benedictinorum in Anglia* (Douai, 1626).

Richmond, The Register of the Archdeacons of, 1442–74, ed. A. H. Thompson (2 vols.; Yorkshire Archaeological Journal, Vols. XXX, XXXII; 1930, 1935).

Selby Abbey. Two obedientiary rolls of, ed. B. Holt (Yorkshire Archaeological Society, Vol. CXVIII, 1953. Part II of *Miscellanea, Vol. VI*, ed. C. E. Whiting).

Testamenta Eboracensia: A Selection of Wills from the Registry at York, Vols. I–III, ed. J. Raine and J. Raine, jun. (Surtees Society, Vols. IV, XXX, XLV; 1836, 1855, 1865).

Bibliography

Visitations of religious houses in the diocese of Lincoln, 1420–49, ed. A. H. Thompson (3 vols.; Lincoln Record Society, Vols. VII, XIV, XXI; 1914–29; or Canterbury and York Society, Vols. XVII, XXIV, XXXIII; 1915–27).

Visitations in the diocese of Lincoln, 1517–31, ed. A. H. Thompson (3 vols.; Lincoln Record Society, Vols. XXXIII, XXXV, XXXVII, 1940–7).

Visitations of the diocese and province of York, 1407, 1423. Documents relating to, ed. A. H. Thompson (Surtees Society, Vol. CXXVII, 1916. Part III of *Miscellanea, Vol. II*).

Wilkins, D., *Concilia Magnae Britanniae et Hiberniae* (4 vols.; London, 1737).

Winchester, St Swithun's Priory, Compotus rolls of the Obedientiaries of, ed. G. W. Kitchin (Hampshire Record Society, 1892).

Worcester, Early Compotus rolls of the Priory of, ed. J. M. Wilson and C. Gordon (Worcestershire Historical Society, 1908).

Worcester of the fourteenth and fifteenth centuries. Compotus rolls of the Priory of, ed. S. G. Hamilton (Worcestershire Historical Society, 1910).

Worcester, The 'Liber Albus' of the Priory of, Parts 1 and 2, ed. J. M. Wilson (Worcestershire Historical Society, 1919).

York, the Abbey of St Mary. The Ordinal and Customary of, ed. Abbess of Stanbrook and J. B. L. Tolhurst (3 vols.; Henry Bradshaw Society, Vols. LXXIII, LXXV, LXXXIV; 1936–51).

Chronicles and annals

Amundesham, Annales monasterii S. Albani, a Johanne . . . , ed. H. T. Riley (2 vols.; Rolls Series, 28, 1870–1).

Baedae, Venerabilis, Opera Historica, ed. C. Plummer (2 vols.; Oxford, 1896).

Bede, *Historiae Ecclesiasticae Gentis Anglorum*, ed. J. Smith (Cambridge, 1722).

Christ Church, Monastic Chronicle of, 1331–1415 (anonymous), ed. C. E. Woodruff (Archaeologia Cantiana, Vol. XXIX, 1911).

Christ Church Priory, Chronicle of William Glastynbury, monk of, 1418–48, ed. C. E. Woodruff (Archaeologia Cantiana, Vol. XXXVII, 1925).

Cuthbert, St., The Life of, in English Verse, c. A.D. 1450, ed. J. T. Fowler (Surtees Society, Vol. LXXXVII, 1891).

Cuthbert, St., Two Lives of, ed. B. Colgrave (Cambridge, 1940).

Dunelmensia, Gesta, A.D. 1300, ed. R. K. Richardson (Camden Society, Third Series, Vol. XXXIV, 1924: *Camden Miscellany XIII*, Part I).

Dunelmensis, Historiae, Scriptores Tres, ed. J. Raine (Surtees Society, Vol. IX, 1839).

Durham Annals and Documents of the Thirteenth Century, ed. F. Barlow (Surtees Society, Vol. CLV, 1945).

Elmham, Thomas of, Historia Monasterii Sancti Augustini Cantuariensis, ed. C. Hardwick (Rolls Series, 8, 1858).

Flete, John, *The History of Westminster Abbey*, ed. J. A. Robinson (Notes and Documents relating to Westminster Abbey, No. 2; Cambridge, 1909).

Hardyng, The Chronicle of John, ed. H. Ellis (London, 1812).

Hexham, The Priory of. Vol. I: Its Chroniclers, Endowments and Annals, ed. J. Raine (Surtees Society, Vol. XLIV, 1864).

Houedene, Chronica Rogeri de, ed. W. Stubbs (4 vols., Rolls Series, 51, 1868–71).

Jocelin of Brakelond. The Chronicle of, ed. H. E. Butler (Nelson's Medieval Classics, 1949).

Polychronicon Ranulphi Higden monachi Cestrensis, ed. C. Babington and J. R. (9 vols., Rolls Series, 41, 1865–6).

Bibliography

St. Albans Chronicle, 1406–1420, The, ed. V. H. Galbraith (Oxford, 1937).

Scotichronicon of J. Fordun with Continuation of W. Bower, ed. W. Goodall (2 vols., Edinburgh, 1759).

Stone, John. Chronicle of Christ Church, Canterbury (1415–71), ed. W. G. Searle (Cambridge Antiquarian Society's Publications, Vol. XXXIV, 1902).

Symeonis Dunelmensis Opera et Collectanea, Vol. I, ed. J. Hodgson Hinde (Surtees Society, Vol. LI, 1868).

Symeonis Monachi Opera Omnia, ed. T. Arnold (2 vols., Rolls Series, 75, 1882–5).

Thorn's, William, Chronicle of St. Augustine's, Canterbury, trans. A. H. Davis (London, 1934).

Twysden, R., Scriptores Decem (Oxford, 1652).

Walsingham, Thomas, Historia Anglicana, ed. H. T. Riley (2 vols.; Rolls Series, 28, 1863–4).

Wharton, H., Anglia Sacra (2 vols.; London, 1691).

Whethamstede, J., Registra quorundam abbatum monasterii S. Albani, qui saeculo XVmo. floruere (2 vols.; Rolls Series, 28, 1872–3).

York, The Historians of the Church of, and its Archbishops, ed. J. Raine (3 vols.; Rolls Series, 71, 1879–94).

Public Records

Calendar of Charter Rolls, Vols. I–VI, 1226–1516 (Public Record Office, 1903–27).

Calendar of Close Rolls, 1307–1485 (Public Record Office, 1892–1954).

Calendar of Documents relating to Scotland, 1108–1509, ed. J. Bain (4 vols.; Scottish Record Office, 1881–8).

Calendar of Fine Rolls, 1272–1471 (Public Record Office, 1911–49).

Calendar of Letters and Papers, foreign and domestic, of the reign of Henry VIII, Vol. XVI, 1540–1 (Public Record Office, 1898).

Calendar of Patent Rolls, 1307–1494 (Public Record Office, 1894–1914).

Calendarium Inquisitionum Post Mortem sive Escaetarum, ed. J. Caley and J. Bayley (4 vols.; Record Commission, 1806–28).

Foedera, conventiones, litterae . . . , ed. T. Rymer (20 vols.; London, 1704–35).

Proceedings and Ordinances of the Privy Council of England, ed. N. H. Nicolas (7 vols.; Record Commission, 1834–7).

Rotuli Parliamentorum: Edward I–Henry VII (6 vols.; London, 1783).

Rotuli Scotiae in turri Londinensi . . . asservati, ed. D. Macpherson et al. (2 vols.; Record Commission, 1814–19).

Scotland. The Acts of the Parliaments of, ed. T. Thomson and C. Innes (12 vols.; Record Commission, 1814–75).

Select Cases before the King's Council, 1243–1482, ed. I. S. Leadam and J. F. Baldwin (Selden Society, Vol. XXXV, 1918).

Taxatio ecclesiastica Angliae et Walliae auctoritate P. Nicholai IV, c. A.D. 1291 (Record Commission, 1802).

Valor Ecclesiasticus temp. Henr. VIII . . . institutus, ed. J. Caley and J. Hunter (6 vols.; Record Commission, 1810–34).

Other printed sources

Bekynton, Thomas, Secretary to King Henry VI, and Bishop of Bath and Wells, Official correspondence of: Memorials of the Reign of King Henry VI, ed. G. Williams (2 vols.; Rolls Series, 56, 1872).

Bentley, Samuel, Excerpta Historica, or Illustrations of English History (London, 1831).

Ellis, H., *Original Letters illustrative of English History* (three series, 11 vols.; London, 1824–46).

Gascoigne, T., *Loci e Libro Veritatum*, ed. J. E. T. Rogers (Oxford, 1881).

Greenwell Deeds. A Calendar of the, ed. J. Walton (*Archaeologia Aeliana*, Fourth Series, Vol. III, 1926).

Historical Manuscripts, Ninth Report of the Royal Commission on (3 vols.; 1883–4). Vol. I, Appendix: Report by J. B. Sheppard on MSS. of Christ Church, Canterbury.

Home, Colonel David Milne, Report on the manuscripts of (Historical Manuscripts Commission, 57, 1902).

Leach, A. F., *Early Yorkshire Schools* (2 vols.; Yorkshire Archaeological Society, Record Series, Vols. XXVII, XXXIII; 1899–1903).

Oxford, Formularies which bear on the history of, c. 1204–1420, ed. H. E. Salter, W. A. Pantin, H. G. Richardson (2 vols.; Oxford Historical Society, New Series, Vols. IV, V; 1942).

Oxon., Epistolae Academicae, ed. H. Anstey (2 vols.; Oxford Historical Society, Vols. XXXV, XXXVI; 1898).

Oxoniensia, Munimenta Academica, ed. H. Anstey (2 vols.; Rolls Series, 50, 1868).

Oxoniensis, Statuta Antiqua Universitatis, ed. Strickland Gibson (Oxford, 1931).

Oxoniensis, Registrum Cancellarii, 1434–1469, ed. H. E. Salter (2 vols.; Oxford Historical Society, Vols. XCIII, XCIV; 1932).

Paston Letters. The, ed. J. Gairdner (4 vols.; Westminster, 1900; the fourth volume – Introduction and Supplement – 1907).

Pii Secundi Pont. Max. Commentarii, Aeneas Sylvius Piccolomini (Frankfurt, 1614).

Pius II. The Commentaries of, trans. F. A. Gragg, ed. L. C. Gabel (Smith College Studies in History, Vol. XXII, Nos. 1–2; 1936–7).

Plumpton Correspondence, ed. T. Stapleton (Camden Society, Old Series, Vol. IV, 1839).

Repressor of over much blaming of the clergy, by Reginald Pecock, The, ed. C. Babington (2 vols.; Rolls Series, 19, 1860).

Snappe's Formulary and Other Records, ed. H. E. Salter (Oxford Historical Society, Vol. LXXX, 1924).

Ventris, The Reports of Sir Peyton (2 vols.; London, 1696).

SECONDARY AUTHORITIES

(RESTRICTED TO DURHAM, ITS CHURCH AND ITS CELLS)

Allan, R. H.	*Historical and Descriptive View of the City of Durham* (Durham, 1824).
Allen, P. S.	'Bishop Shirwood of Durham and his Library'. *English Historical Review* XXV (1910), 445–56.
Barlow, F.	*Durham Jurisdictional Peculiars* (Oxford, 1950).
Battiscombe, C. F. (ed.)	*The Relics of Saint Cuthbert* (Oxford, 1956).
Billings, R. W.	*Architectural Illustrations and Description of the Cathedral Church of Durham* (London, 1843).
Bilson, J.	'Durham Cathedral: the Chronology of its Vaults'. *Archaeological Journal* LXXIX (1922), 101–60.
Blair, C. H. Hunter.	*Catalogue of the Seals in the Treasury of the Dean and Chapter of Durham, from a Manuscript made by*

Bibliography

	the Rev. *William Greenwell* (collected from *Archaeologia Aeliana*; Newcastle-upon-Tyne, 1911–21).
Blakiston, H. E. D.	*Trinity College* (University of Oxford, College Histories: London, 1898).
Boyle, J. R.	*A Comprehensive Guide to the County of Durham* (London, 1892).
Brentano, R.	*York Metropolitan Jurisdiction and Papal Judges Delegate (1279–1296)* (University of California Publications in History, LVIII; Berkeley and Los Angeles, 1959).
	'The *Jurisdictio Spiritualis*: an Example of Fifteenth-Century English Historiography'. *Speculum* XXXII (1957), 326–32.
Carr, A. A.	*A History of Coldingham Priory* (Edinburgh, 1836).
Carter, J.	*Plans, Elevations, etc., with some Account of the Cathedral Church of Durham* (London, 1801).
Colgrave, B.	'The History of British Museum Additional MS. 39943'. *English Historical Review* LIV (1939), 673–7.
	'Note on a Stained Glass Window formerly in Durham Cathedral'. *Durham University Journal* XXXVII (1944–5), 12–14.
Cramp, R.	'Excavations at the Saxon Monastic Sites of Wearmouth and Jarrow: an interim report'. *Medieval Archaeology* XIII (1969), 21–66.
Craster, H. H. E.	'The Red Book of Durham'. *English Historical Review* XL (1925), 504–32.
	'Some Anglo-Saxon Records of the See of Durham'. *Archaeologia Aeliana*, Fourth Series, I (1925), 189–98.
	'A Contemporary Record of the Pontificate of Ranulf Flambard'. *Archaeologia Aeliana*, Fourth Series, VII (1930), 33–56.
	'The Patrimony of Saint Cuthbert'. *English Historical Review* LXIX (1954), 177–99.
Davies, J. Conway.	'A Recovered Manuscript of Symeon of Durham'. *Durham University Journal* XLIV (1951–2), 22–8.
	'The Muniments of the Dean and Chapter of Durham'. *Durham University Journal* XLIV (1951–2), 77–87.
Denholm-Young, N.	'The Birth of A Chronicle'. *Bodleian Quarterly Record* VII (1932–4), 325–8.
	'Richard de Bury (1287–1345)'. *Transactions of the Royal Historical Society*, Fourth Series, XX (1937), 135–68.
Dobson, R. B.	'Richard Bell, Prior of Durham (1464–78) and Bishop of Carlisle (1478–95)'. *Transactions of the Cumberland and Westmorland Antiquarian*

	and Archaeological Society, New Series, LXV (1965), 182–221.
	'The Last English Monks on Scottish Soil: the Severance of Coldingham Priory from the Monastery of Durham, 1461–78'. *Scottish Historical Review*, XLVI (1967), 1–25.
Donaldson, R.	'Sponsors, Patrons and Presentations to Benefices in the gift of the Priors of Durham during the later Middle Ages'. *Archaeologia Aeliana*, Fourth Series, XXXVIII (1960), 169–77.
Eyre, C.	*The History of St Cuthbert* (London, 1858).
Farmer, H.	'The Meditations of the Monk of Farne'. *Studia Anselmiana*, Fourth Series, XLI (1957), 141–245.
Fasti Dunelmenses.	*A Record of the Beneficed Clergy of the Diocese of Durham down to the Dissolution*, ed. D. S. Boutflower (Surtees Society, Vol. CXXXIX, 1926).
Fishwick, H.	*The History of the Parish of Lytham in the County of Lancaster* (Chetham Society, New Series, Vol. LX, 1907).
Fowler, J. T.	'An account of the excavations made on the site of the Chapter-house of Durham Cathedral in 1874'. *Archaeologia* XLV (1880), 387–9.
Fraser, C. M.	*A History of Antony Bek, Bishop of Durham, 1283–1311* (Oxford, 1957).
	'Gilly-corn and the Customary of the Convent of Durham'. *Archaeologia Aeliana*, Fourth Series, XXXIII (1955), 35–60.
	'Some Durham Documents relating to the Hilary Parliament of 1404'. *Bulletin of the Institute of Historical Research* XXXIV (1961), 192–9.
	'Law and Society in Northumberland and Durham, 1290–1350'. *Archaeologia Aeliana*, Fourth Series, XLVII (1969), 47–70.
Gee, E.	'Discoveries in the Frater at Durham'. *Archaeological Journal* CXXIII (1966), 69–78.
Greenslade, S. L.	'John Washington, Prior of Durham (1416–1446)'. *Historical Magazine of the Protestant Episcopal Church* XVI, no. 3 (1947), 233–45.
	'The Last Monks of Durham Cathedral Priory'. *Durham University Journal* XLI (1948–9), 107–13.
	'Sacristonheugh'. *Transactions of the Architectural and Archaeological Society of Durham and Northumberland* X, Part 3 (1950), 251–7.
	'The Contents of the Library of Durham Cathedral Priory'. *Ibid.* XI (1965), 347–69.
Greenwell, W.	*Durham Cathedral* (Sixth ed., Durham, 1904).
Halcrow, E. M.	'The Decline of Demesne Farming on the Estates of Durham Cathedral Priory'. *Economic History Review*, Second Series, VII (1955), 345–56.

'The Social Position and Influence of the Priors of Durham as illustrated by their Correspondence'. *Archaeologia Aeliana*, Fourth Series, XXXIII (1955), 70–86.

'Obedientiaries and Counsellors in Monastic Administration at Durham'. *Archaeologia Aeliana*, Fourth Series, XXXV (1957), 7–21.

Harbottle, B.   'Bishop Hatfield's Visitation of Durham Priory in 1354'. *Archaeologia Aeliana*, Fourth Series, XXXVI (1958), 81–100.

Hay, D.   'The Dissolution of the Monasteries in the Diocese of Durham'. *Archaeologia Aeliana*, Fourth Series, XV (1938), 69–114.

Hegge, Robert.   *The Legend of Saint Cuthbert* (1626): ed. George Smith (Darlington, 1777); ed. J. B. Taylor (Sunderland, 1816).

Hepple, R. B.   'Uthred of Boldon'. *Archaeologia Aeliana*, Third Series, XVII (1920), 153–68.

Hughes, H. D.   *A History of Durham Cathedral Library* (Durham, 1925).

Hunter, C.   *Durham Cathedral as it was before the Dissolution of the Monastery* (Durham, 1733).

Hutchinson, W.   *The History and Antiquities of the County Palatine of Durham* (3 vols.; Newcastle-upon-Tyne, 1785–94).

Johnson, M.   'The North-East Altar in the Galilee of Durham Cathedral'. *Transactions of Architectural and Archaeological Society of Durham and Northumberland* XI (1965), 371–90.

'Recent Work on the Refectory of Durham Cathedral'. Ibid., New Series, I (1968), 85–91.

Kitchin, G. W.   *The Story of the Deanery, Durham, 1070–1912* (Durham, 1912).

Knowles, M. D.   'The Censured Opinions of Uthred of Boldon'. *Proceedings of the British Academy* XXXVII (1952), 305–42.

Lapsley, G. T.   *The County Palatine of Durham* (Harvard Historical Studies, vol. 8; New York, 1900).

Le Neve, J.   *Fasti Ecclesiae Anglicanae, 1300–1541*, VI (Northern Province), ed. B. Jones (University of London, 1963).

McCord, N. (ed.)   *Durham History from the Air* (Durham County Local History Society, 1971).

Maclagan, M.   *Trinity College, 1555–1955* (Oxford, 1955).

Mynors, R. A. B.   *Durham Cathedral Manuscripts to the end of the Twelfth Century* (Oxford, 1939).

Offler, H. S.   'The Tractate *De Iniusta Vexacione Willelmi Episcopi Primi*'. *English Historical Review* LXVI (1951), 321–41.

'William of St. Calais, First Norman Bishop of Durham'. *Transactions of Architectural and Archaeological Society of Durham and Northumberland* x (1950), 258–79.

Medieval Historians of Durham (Inaugural lecture as Professor of Medieval History; University of Durham 1958).

'The early archdeacons in the diocese of Durham'. *Transactions of Architectural and Archaeological Society of Durham and Northumberland* xi (1962), 193–202.

'The Date of Durham (*Carmen de Situ Dunelmi*)'. *Journal of English and Germanic Philology* LXI (1962), 591–4.

Rannulf Flambard as Bishop of Durham (1099–1128) (Durham Cathedral Lecture, 1971).

Pantin, W. A.   *Report on the Muniments of the Dean and Chapter of Durham* (originally part of a report presented by F. M. Powicke and W. A. Pantin to the Pilgrim Trustees; privately printed, 1939).

'A Benedictine Opponent of John Wyclif'. *English Historical Review* XLIII (1928), 73–7.

'The Monk-Solitary of Farne: a Fourteenth-Century English Mystic'. *English Historical Review* LIX (1944), 162–86.

'Two Treatises by Uthred of Boldon on the Monastic Life'. *Studies in Medieval History presented to F. M. Powicke*, ed. R. W. Hunt, W. A. Pantin and R. W. Southern (Oxford, 1948), 363–85.

Peers, C.   'Finchale Priory'. *Archaeologia Aeliana*, Fourth Series, IV (1927), 193–220.

Raine, J.   *Saint Cuthbert* (Durham, 1828).

A Brief Account of Durham Cathedral (Newcastle-upon-Tyne, 1833).

The History and Antiquities of North Durham (London, 1852).

Richardson, R. K.   'The Bishopric of Durham under Antony Bek, 1283–1311'. *Archaeologia Aeliana*, Third Series, IX (1913), 89–229.

Rud, T.   *Codicum Manuscriptorum Ecclesiae Cathedralis Dunelmensis Catalogus Classicus Descriptus* (Durham, 1825).

St John Hope, W. H.   'Recent Discoveries in the Cloister of Durham Abbey'. *Archaeologia* LVIII (1903), 437–60.

An untitled communication on the Durham cloister excavations, *Proceedings of Society of Antiquaries of London*, Second Series, XXII (1909), 416–24.

Scammell, G. V.   *Hugh du Puiset, Bishop of Durham* (Cambridge, 1956).

Scammell, J.   'Some Aspects of Medieval English Monastic Government: The Case of Geoffrey Burdon, Prior of Durham (1313–1321)'. *Revue Bénédictine* LXVIII (1958), 226–50.

'The Origin and Limitations of the Liberty of Durham'. *English Historical Review* LXXXI (1966), 449–73.

Storey, R. L.   *Thomas Langley and the Bishopric of Durham, 1406–1437* (London, 1961).

Surtees, R.   *The History and Antiquities of the County Palatine of Durham* (4 vols.; London, 1816–40).

Thompson, A. Hamilton.   'Archbishop Savage's Visitation of the Diocese of Durham, *sede vacante*, 1501'. *Archaeologia Aeliana*, Third Series, XVIII (1921), 43–52.

'The Manuscript List of Churches dedicated to St Cuthbert, attributed to Prior Wessyngton'. *Transactions of the Architectural and Archaeological Society of Durham and Northumberland* VII (1935), 151–77.

'The Collegiate Churches in the Bishoprick of Durham'. *Durham University Journal* XXXVI (1944), 33–42.

'Thomas Langley, Bishop of Durham, 1406–37'. *Durham University Journal* XXXVIII (1945), 1–16.

Lindisfarne Priory (H.M.S.O. Guide, 1949).

Victoria County History, Durham (3 vols., 1905–28).

Whiting, C. E.   *The University of Durham, 1832–1932* (London, 1932).

'The Durham Trade Gilds'. *Transactions of Architectural and Archaeological Society of Durham and Northumberland* IX (1941–43), 143–416.

Whitworth, T.   'Deposits beneath the North Bailey, Durham'. *Durham University Journal* LXI (1968), 18–31.

UNPUBLISHED DISSERTATIONS

Cooper, J.   'Some aspects of Eleventh-century Northumbrian History with special reference to the last four Anglo-Saxon Archbishops of York'. Ph.D., Cambridge, 1968.

Donaldson, R.   'Patronage and the Church: a Study in the Social Structure of the Secular Clergy in the Diocese of Durham (1311–1540).' Ph.D., Edinburgh, 1955.

Halcrow, E. M.   'The Administration and Agrarian Policy of the Manors of Durham Cathedral Priory'. B.Litt., Oxford, 1949.

Storey, R. L.   'Thomas Langley, Statesman and Bishop, *c.* 1360–1437'. Ph.D., Durham, 1954.

INDEX

The names of Durham monks (distinguished by the use of capitals) are followed by the dates within which they appear in surviving records as members of Saint Cuthbert's Community.

Index

Kidderminster, Richard, abbot of Winchcombe, 79, 359

Killerby, John, *generosus*, 121-2

Killingworth, John, university proctor, 357

Kimblesworth (Co. Durham), rectory, 149

Kirk Merrington (Co. Durham)
manor, 93, 275
vicarage, 269, 271

Kirkby on Bain (Lincs.), 151 *and* n.4

Kirkcudbright, Galloway, 19

Kirkham (Lancs.), vicar of, 328

Kirton, Edmund, abbot of Westminster, 112

KYBLESWORTH, William (1390-1417), 59

Kymer, Gilbert, university chancellor, 355

Kyngton, John, monk of Christ Church, Canterbury, 61

Lamberton (Berwicks.), vicarage, 146 n.2

Lampton, Robert, lawyer, 131-2

Lancaster, 333

Lancaster, Humphrey of, Duke of Gloucester, 162

Lancaster, John of, Duke of Bedford, 161, 174, 188, 215
petitioner for benefices, 158, 160, 164
writes to Wessington, 75, 174

LANGCHESTER, Robert (1357-1407), as chancellor, 363-5

Langham, Simon, abp of Canterbury, 345

Langley, Thomas, bp of Durham, 9, 186, 192 n.1, 201, 218, 225, 355 *and passim*
books, 374 n.2
election and enthronement, 52, 215, 227 n.2, 228
foundations, 60 n.1, 72, 160, 296
loans to king, 175-6
officials, 29 n.2, 106-7, 138, 376
relations with monks, 63-5, 83-5, 88-9, 223-4
relations with Wessington, 69, 74, 94-5, 106-7, 109, 166, 179, 189-90, 198, 223-4, 383, 385
see also Durham, bishops, visitations

Langton, Thomas, prior's steward, 128-9, 175
Sybil, wife of, 128

Latimer, Lord, *see* Neville, George

LATON (LAYTON), John of (1306-25), 4 n.1

LAWSON, Thomas (1418-43), 59 n.1
as bursar, 67, 285-8, 308
as cellarer, 59 n.1, 285, 289 n.2, 331

Lax, John, proctor at Curia, 213-14

Laxton (? Notts.), 333

Le Convenit (1229), 62, 222, 231-2, 235, 301

Le Holme (Salt Holme, Co. Durham), 277, 281

Leicester, Saint Mary's Abbey, 112 n.2, 370

Leland, John, 38, 43, 46 n.3, 276, 345

Levesham, of exchequer, 180

Lewyn, John, master mason, 293

Liber Vitae Dunelmensis, 56, 79 n.3, 360

Lichfield Cathedral, 229

Lincoln, diocese, 150, 177 n.5
bishops, 232, 349; *see also* Gray, Alnwick
dean and chapter, 233; library, 366

Lindisfarne, *see* Holy Island

Litlington, Nicholas, abbot of Westminster, 100

London, 10, 74, 262, 333, 336, 346, 348-9
diocese, 75
purchases at, 104, 127-8, 265
Wessington's visits, 92-3, 241
see also exchequer, Westminster Abbey

London, Stephen, pr of Wymondham, 340

Lounde, John, vicar-general, 138-9

Loury, John, clerk, 148

Ludi, 97-8, 104, 118; *see also* Beaurepaire

Ludworth (Co. Durham), 282

Lumley (Co. Durham), lords of, 195

LUMLEY, John (1414-23), 63

Lumley, Marmaduke, bp of Carlisle, 156, 158, 163 n.1, 217

Lyes, Thomas, vicar-general, 88-9

LYHAM, William (1412-62), 196 *and* n.1

Lyhert, Walter, bp of Norwich, 339

Lytham Priory (Lancs.), 125, 232, 253, 299, 303, 305, 327-41, 344